# The Companion to Said Nursi Studies

# The Companion to Said Nursi Studies

Edited by
IAN S. MARKHAM
& ZEYNEB SAYILGAN

☙PICKWICK *Publications* • Eugene, Oregon

THE COMPANION TO SAID NURSI STUDIES

Copyright © 2017 Wipf and Stock Publishers. All rights reserved. Except for brief quotations in critical publications or reviews, no part of this book may be reproduced in any manner without prior written permission from the publisher. Write: Permissions, Wipf and Stock Publishers, 199 W. 8th Ave., Suite 3, Eugene, OR 97401.

Pickwick Publications
An Imprint of Wipf and Stock Publishers
199 W. 8th Ave., Suite 3
Eugene, OR 97401

www.wipfandstock.com

PAPERBACK ISBN: 978-1-4982-9222-1
HARDCOVER ISBN: 978-2-4982-9224-5
EBOOK ISBN: 978-1-4982-9223-8

*Cataloguing-in-Publication data:*

Names: Markham, Ian S. | Sayılgan, Zeyneb

Title: The companion to Said Nursi studies / edited by Ian S. Markham and Zeyneb Sayılgan.

Description: Eugene, OR: Pickwick Publications, 2017 | **Includes bibliographical references and index.**

Identifiers: ISBN 978-1-4982-9222-1 (paperback) | ISBN 978-2-4982-9224-5 (hardcover) | ISBN 978-1-4982-9223-8 (ebook)

Subjects: LCSH: Nursi, Said, 1873–1960 | Nurculuk | Islam—20th century | Islam—Turkey | Islam—doctrines | Islamic sociology | Islam and politics | Islam and science | Islam—Relations—Christianity

Classification: BP253.Z8 M36 2017 (paperback) | BP253.Z8 (ebook)

Manufactured in the U.S.A. 08/16/17

To Ibrahim Abu-Rabi' (1956–2011)

—the initial inspiration behind this book

# Contents

*Acknowledgements* | ix
*Introduction* | xi
*Contributors* | xiii

## Section One: History and Biography

1 Late Ottoman Intellectual History and Nursi | 3
 —M. Sait Özervarli

2 Said Nursi from the Ottoman to the Republican Periods: A Short Biography | 23
 —Şükran Vahide

3 My Meeting with Said Nursi | 41
 —Fred A. Reed

## Section Two: Theology

4 Said Nursi's Qur'anic Hermeneutics | 51
 —Yamina Mermer & İsra Yazicioğlu

5 Concept of God in the *Risale-i-Nur:* God through His Creative Activity | 69
 —Yamina Mermer

6 The Significance of Resurrection and the Afterlife in the Writings of Bediüzzaman Said Nursi | 87
 —Cüneyt Şimşek

7 The Problem of Evil in the Writings of Bediüzzaman Said Nursi | 105
 —Cüneyt Şimşek

8 A Graceful Reconciliation: Said Nursi on Free Will and Destiny | 129
 —Ümeyye İsra Yazicioğlu

9 Supplication as Agent and Fruit of Transformation for Bediüzzaman Said Nursi | 146
 —Lucinda Allen Mosher

10 The Moral World of Said Nursi | 161
 —M. Salih Sayilgan

**11** Morality and Ethics in the Risale-i Nur | 178
—Suendam Birinci Pirim, Harun Pirim

**12** The Importance of the Sunna in Islamic Spirituality: Said Nursi's Approach | 192
—M. Salih Sayilgan

**13** The Prophetic Virtue of Compassion as a Core Principle of the Risale-i Nur | 205
—Zeyneb Sayilgan

## Section Three: Nursi and Society

**14** An Outline of the Social Theology of Said Nursi | 223
—Syed Farid Alatas

**15** The Risale-i Nur as an Epistemological Ground for the Framework of a Sociology of Science | 243
—Alparslan Açikgenç

**16** Said Nursi's View on Materialism, Positivism, and Sciences | 264
—Yunus Çengel

**17** The *Medresetü'z-Zehrâ*—Explorations into Its Nature and Significance | 286
—Zeyneb Sayilgan

**18** Spiritual and Moral Reform of Muslim Inmates: The Model of Said Nursi | 305
—Benaouda Bensaid

**19** The Dissemination of the Risale-i Nur in Europe and the United States | 322
—Zeyneb Sayilgan

**20** Christian–Muslim Engagement | 340
—Thomas Michel

**21** Roman Catholic Theological Engagement with Said Nursi | 356
—Leo D. Lefebure

## Section Four: Nursi and Politics

**22** Said Nursi's Positive Action as a Method of Serving Belief and Peace | 379
—Ahmet Yildiz

**23** Religious Struggle in Modern Turkey: Said Nursi's Interpretation of *Jihad* | 392
—Şükran Vahide

**24** The Nation State and Nationalism in the Thought of Said Nursi | 412
—Elmira Akhmetova

**25** The Future of Nursi Studies | 426
—Ian S. Markham

*Index* | 431

# Acknowledgements

The Editors are grateful to Robin Parry, Brian Palmer, and Ian Creeger at Pickwick Publications for their dedication and hard work in enabling these volumes to appear. We are grateful to Faris Kaya for his continuing support for Nursi Studies.

*Ian S. Markham*
Working on a project like this is a great honor. I am grateful to the warmth of the Nur community and their support for research in this area. Finding time for research needs a supportive home environment. So as always, I am deeply grateful to my companion in the journey, my wife Lesley, and my energetic conversation partner and son, Luke.

*Zeyneb Sayılgan*
I would not be where I am in my life today without the sacrifices and support made by my dear parents, Sürethan and Ümran Salim. They dedicated themselves to raise their six children as devout and educated individuals. To them I will be forever thankful. May God grant them eternal happiness. My ultimate gratitude rests with God who has enabled the completion of this project.

# Introduction

SOMETIMES THERE IS A very remote connection between perception and reality. For much of the Western world, you say the word "Islam" and people think of the bombings in Paris, ISIS, blasphemy laws in Pakistan, anti-Semitism, women unable to drive in Saudi Arabia, and Malala shot in the head for wanting to go to school.

Both historically and today, these associations are unfair. Historically, Islam is the religion that preserved the wisdom of the Greek classical age through the so-called "Dark Ages." It created the House of Wisdom in the 800s, where a library combined with an academy to create a preeminent place of learning long before the West. In the ninth century, it gave us Al-Razi, the chemist, philosopher, and physician; in the twelfth century, it gave us Al-Idrisi, the brilliant cartographer. And today, this is the religion that has over a billion adherents, the overwhelming majority of whom simply want to love God, raise their children, participate fully in a community, and make a difference in countless small ways to improve the lives of those around them.

Part of the contemporary scene is the Nur movement. It is probably one of the largest Islamic movements in the world. This volume is the most substantial overview in English of the inspiration behind that movement—the remarkable life and work of Bediüzzaman Said Nursi (1877–60). Said Nursi was born as the Ottoman Empire was in steady and permanent decline. As Mustafa Kemal Atatürk came to prominence in the new secular Turkish Republic, it was Said Nursi who set out to demonstrate that pluralism, democracy, and Islam can co-exist. In addition, he argued that any faithful Muslim reading the Qur'an and Hadith with care should see that fidelity to Islam involves a commitment to peace and dialogue. Using metaphor, story, parable, and classical arguments, he set forth his apologetic for Islam in his masterpiece, the *Risale-i Nur*. The authenticity of his life, coupled with the richness of his theology, has made Nursi an inspiration to literally millions of people.

Over the last twenty years, more and more comparative religion specialists in the West are becoming acquainted with Said Nursi. And this volume is a celebration of that reality. Nursi studies is now an established discipline. As this volume testifies, Christians and Muslims are grappling with the wisdom of this remarkable, rich thinker.

This book bears witness to the reality of Islam. As you read the articles, the perceptions that dominate the media in the West are just that. Here is an Islamic perspective that unequivocally condemns terrorist activities (and says so often, even if their voices

*Introduction*

are never reported). But this is more; here is a rich theological mind, whose writings are helping Christians and Muslims think afresh about apologetics, about hope, and faith.

Ian S. Markham and Zeyneb Sayılgan

# Contributors

**Alparslan Açıkgenç**, currently Chairman of the Department of Philosophy at Yıldız Technical University, Istanbul, has extensive teaching and administrative experience in different world universities. His main interest is research in the history of the scientific traditions of diverse civilizations, primarily Islamic and Western.

**Elmira Akhmetova** is Assistant Professor in History and Civilization at International Islamic University Malaysia (IIUM). She is the author of *Islam in Russia: Historical Facts and Current Developments* (Kuala Lumpur: IAIS Malaysia, 2013) and of various papers about Islam in Russia, the ideas of Said Nursi, and Islamic history.

**Syed Farid Alatas** is Associate Professor of Sociology at the National University of Singapore. He lectured at the University of Malaya in the Department of Southeast Asian Studies prior to joining NUS. His areas of interest are historical sociology, the sociology of social science, the sociology of religion, and inter-religious dialogue.

**Benaouda Bensaid** earned his Bachelor Degree (Hons.) in Islamic Studies from Algeria, Masters Degree from International Islamic University Malaysia, and PhD from the Institute of Islamic Studies, McGill University, Canada. Bensaid is currently associated with the College of Art and Science, Effat University Jeddah, Saudi Arabia.

**Suendam Birinci Pirim** is a PhD candidate through Hartford Seminary's joint doctoral program with the University of Exeter in England. Her area of study is comparative theologies with a focus on Christianity and Islam. She is the book-review editor of the *Muslim World* and has published in *Reviews in Religion and Theology*. She has co-authored *An Introduction to Said Nursi: Life, Thought, and Writings*.

**Yunus A Çengel** is the Dean of Engineering at Adnan Menderes University in Turkey and Professor Emeritus at the University of Nevada, Reno, USA. He received his degrees from Istanbul Technical University and North Carolina State University. He has written several books on Engineering and has presented many papers on Said Nursi.

**Bilal Kuşpınar** is Chair of the Department of Philosophy and Director of the International Rumi Centre for the Study of Civilization at the Necmettin Erbakan University.

He was previously Professor at the Ahlia University in Bahrain. He has degrees from Selçuk University, Konya, Turkey, the Middle East Technical University, Ankara, Turkey and McGill University, Montreal, Canada. He has presented and written several essays on Nursi.

**Leo D. Lefebure** is the Matteo Ricci, S.J., Professor of Theology at Georgetown University in Washington, DC. He has degrees from the Divinity School of the University of Chicago and the University of Saint Mary of the Lake. He is the author of the award-winning *True and Holy: Christian Scripture and Other Religions,* and several essays on Nursi and Christianity.

**Ian S Markham** is the Dean and President of Virginia Theological Seminary and Professor of Theology and Ethics. He has degrees from King's College London, the University of Cambridge, and the University of Exeter. He has written and edited three books on Said Nursi.

**Yamina Mermer** is director of Always Receiving Nur, a spiritual retreat center. Previously, she was Associate Professor of Islamic Studies at Carthage College (Wisconsin, US). She has degrees from Durham University in England and Indiana University at Bloomington. Her areas of expertise are Quranic Studies, Islamic theology, as well as religion and science. She has published extensively on Islamic philosophy of science.

**Thomas Michel** teaches in the Theology Department of Georgetown University's School of Foreign Service in Doha, Qatar. He holds a PhD in Islamic Thought from University of Chicago and has written extensively on Said Nursi's *Risale-i Nur.*

**Lucinda Allen Mosher** is the Assistant Academic Director of the *Building Bridges Seminar* (an international Christian-Muslim dialogue). Concurrently, she teaches at Hartford Seminary and Séminaire de Théologie d'Église Épiscopale d'Haïti. She holds degrees from Boston University, University of Massachusetts-Lowell, Hartford Seminary, and General Theological Seminary (NYC). She has contributed essays about Bediüzzaman Said Nursi's thought to several books and journals.

**Harun Pirim** is Assistant Professor in the Systems Engineering Department at King Fahd University of Petroleum and Minerals. He has degrees from Mississippi State University and from Dokuz Eylül University in Izmir, Turkey.

**Fred A. Reed** is an international journalist and award-winning literary translator. After several years as a librarian and trade union activist at the *Montreal Gazette,* Reed began reporting from Islamic Iran in 1984, visiting the Islamic Republic thirty times since then. He has also reported extensively on Middle Eastern affairs for *La Presse,* CBC Radio-Canada and *Le Devoir.*

*Contributors*

**Salih Sayılgan** is a PhD candidate in Religion and Culture at the Catholic University of America in Washington, DC. He has degrees from the University of Alberta and Marmara University in Istanbul, Turkey. His Master thesis was concerned with Said Nursi's understanding of non-violence.

**Zeyneb Sayılgan** is Visiting Assistant Professor of Islamic Theology and Religious Pluralism at Virginia Theological Seminary. She has degrees from Georgetown University, Hartford Seminary, and the Johannes Gutenberg University of Mainz, Germany. Her Master thesis focused on Said Nursi's and Paul Tillich's understanding of human impotence.

**Cüneyt Şimşek** teaches Arabic at Northern Virginia Community College. He earned his doctorate in Arabic and Islamic Studies from Uludağ University, Turkey. He worked as a visiting scholar for six months between 2004 and 2005 at Hartford Seminary; for two years between 2008 and 2010 in the Alwaleed Center of Georgetown University; and between 2010 and 2011 in the Ali Vural Ak Center of George Mason University.

**M. Sait Özervarlı** is Professor and Chair of the Department of Humanities and Social Sciences at Yıldız Technical University, Istanbul. He has degrees from Marmara University and did his Post-doctoral research at Harvard University. He wrote books and articles mainly on Ottoman and Islamic thought.

**Şükran Vahide** is a freelance writer and researcher who has written extensively on Said Nursi and has translated a large part of his works into English. Among her published works are *Islam in Modern Turkey: An Intellectual Biography* (2005), and chapters in collective works on different aspects of his thought.

**Ümeyye İsra Yazıcıoğlu** is Assistant Professor of Theology and Religious Studies at St. Joseph's University, PA. She has degrees from the University of Virginia and Marmara University in Istanbul Turkey. Her latest book is *Understanding the Qur'anic Miracle Stories in the Modern Age* in which she dedicates a chapter on Nursi's perspective on miracles.

**Ahmet Yıldız** is the Head of the Department of the Research Center in the Grand National Assembly of Turkey. He holds degrees from Boğaziçi University, Istanbul and Bilkent University, Ankara. He has written several scholarly articles on Said Nursi, of which one is awarded best academic article of the year by the journal *Muhafazakar Düşünce* (Conservative Thought) in 2014.

# Section One

# History and Biography

# 1

# Late Ottoman Intellectual History and Nursi

## M. Saİt Özervarlı

Most cultural traditions and the major world religions, including Judaism and Christianity, faced various challenges in the nineteenth century while confronting European modernity and introducing their praxis and faith to the younger generations who grew up with new ideas. The Muslim world, too, in order to overcome this problem and adapt to new conditions underwent significant changes with major educational reforms and the establishment of modern schools. One impact that modern education, the growing interest in modern science and thought, and cultural interactions, had on the Ottoman intellectual milieu is that it gave rise to a group of radical modernists, who argued that faith and reason, religious beliefs and modern life were incompatible. The alternative approach, however, suggested that within the Ottoman context, Islamic religious tradition could be understood and explained in a new style in accordance with the need of modern times.

The complex relation between religious/cultural tradition and modernization makes the case of late Ottoman intellectual history interesting, not least because of various reactions by thinkers in its last century. Nursi is one of these figures who sought to demonstrate a way for transforming society through a modern religious discourse. In fact, the overall neglect regarding the contribution of religious scholars to the question of modernization is mostly caused by the hitherto exclusive focus on the radical *secularist* perception of modernization and the failure to see its dynamic interaction with the existing cultural factors of society. Ottoman society, which was traditionally deeply religious and brought together cultural elements from the East and the West, is a good example to illustrate the existence and availability of multiple pathways within modernization efforts. Focusing on Nursi helps to draw a more nuanced understanding of the relationship between the "old" and the "new" for a better comprehension of late Ottoman history in general. In order to place the various aspects of Nursi's thought as presented in this *Companion* volume in its larger Ottoman context, I will briefly introduce in this chapter the major intellectual trends that emerged before and during his lifetime as a preliminary to the following sections.

## THE IMPACT OF MODERNIZATION ON OTTOMANS AND THE EMERGENCE OF NEW INTELLECTUAL MOVEMENTS

Late Ottoman society began its modernization program by the end of the eighteenth century, which was accelerated by the state's "Reorganization" program (*tanzimat*) beginning in 1839. Even with these wide scale changes and reforms the end of the Empire was unavoidable. Its collapse was final with the declaration of the new Turkish republic. The pressures for modernization came out of the increasing number of travelers to Western European countries, the establishment of new institutions and schools, and the growing interest in modern science and thought, among other cultural factors. State officials increasingly felt the need to make urgent changes in the Ottoman educational system and other administrative institutions.[1] The willingness of the officials to allow changes opened the way for the foundation of new schools and major educational reforms, including the establishment of new elementary, middle, and high schools, especially during the last quarter of the nineteenth century, the early part of Nursi's life.[2] At the same time, the Ottoman state also engaged in efforts to establish new higher educational institutions, beginning with the formation of professional engineering, medical, and military schools in the late eighteenth and early nineteenth centuries.[3] This rapid educational movement culminated with a modern university (*darülfünun*) in Istanbul, which was opened in 1900 after previously failed attempts.[4] Modern-educated Ottomans soon began to emphasize in their writings the importance of European sciences. Translations from European languages, mainly French, into Turkish and Arabic accelerated during this period. Modern sciences had already

---

1. See Ortaylı, *Studies*, 99–108. For an examination of Ottoman transformation through the formations of new classes and the rise of elite groups see Göçek, *Rise of the Bourgeoisie*.

2. On the education reforms and the new elementary middle, and high schools (*ibtidaiye*, *rüşdiye*, and *idadiye*) during this period see Kodaman, *Abdülhamid Devri*. For a broader look at the changes in the nineteenth-century Ottoman Empire, see Ortaylı, *İmparatorluğun En Uzun Yüzyılı*.

3. Similar *mühendishane*, *tıbbiyye*, and *harbiye* schools were established in the humanities after the *tanzimat*, following the French model of grandes écoles, such as The School of Political Science (*mekteb-i mülkiye*, 1859), Lycee de Galatasaray (*mekteb-i sultani*, 1868), The Law School (*mekteb-i hukuk*, 1880). Even in Paris an Ottoman school, the *mekteb-i osmani*, was founded in 1857 to prepare students sent there by the state for French education. For information on these early professional schools by some Western authors, who either taught there or saw them in their visit, see Toderini, *Letteratura Turchesca*; MacFarlane, *Turkey and Its Destiny*.

4. For more analytical investigations into the changes of the post-Tanzimat era schooling system see Findley, *Ottoman Civil Officialdom*, 131–73; İhsanoğlu, "The Genesis of 'Darulfünun,'" 827–42; Alkan, "Modernization from Empire to Republic," 47–132; Somel, *The Modernization of Public Education*; Fortna, *Imperial Classroom*; Akiba, "A New School for Qadis," 125–63.

gained popularity among Ottomans when an encyclopedia of physical science was published for the first time in Ottoman Turkish and became a pioneer in the modernization of scientific terminology.[5] Later other scientific periodicals followed it to promote modern science among the Ottomans.[6] Science was seen by many officials and learned figures the only tool to solve the problems of the Empire.[7]

Meanwhile a hardly predicted development took place, which was the emergence of popular materialism and positivism among a group of modern-educated Ottomans. An elite group of Westernist intellectuals such as Beşir Fuad, Abdullah Cevdet, and Baha Tevfik, adopted the nineteenth-century scientific theories of German *Vulgarmaterialismus* from mostly the post-Feuerbach period of works.[8] This group of radical elites believed in the supremacy of science in all aspects of life and proposed to take its foundations by adopting a complete European worldview, "with both its roses and thorns," since there was no future without it.[9] Nevertheless, in order to reach their goals some of them did not hesitate to use Islamic language and terminology, as they realized that "without an Islamic guise, scientism would never take root among the masses."[10] They thought that if they had used Christian sources directly, Muslim minds would not allow them to enter their sphere. Therefore, the materialists named their leading journal *içtihad*, a central term of Islamic law, in order to emphasize their connection to their Islamic roots.[11] Since their emphasis in Ottoman public space was mostly on science, and because they tried to hide their materialistic worldview behind an Islamic camouflage, their movement was more like a "materialist scientism" rather than a "scientific materialism," the more common description of their sources in Western literature.

European sources of Ottoman materialism were mainly the French translations of the works of German materialists Ludwig Büchner and Ernst Haeckel, along with other French authors, such as Claude Bernard and Gustave Le Bon, known for their anti-religious views and opposition to metaphysical discussions.[12]

---

5. İshak Efendi, the Chief-instructor of the Engineering School, published by the mid-nineteenth century his four-volume encyclopedia entitled *Mecmua-yi Ulum-i Riyaziye*. On İshak Efendi see İhsanoğlu, "Başhoca Ishak Efendi," 157–68.

6. *Mecmua-yi Fünun* (1863–67), a monthly periodical of Münif Paşa's *Cemiyet-i İlmiye-i Osmaniye* (Ottoman Scientific Society), and *Mecmua-yi Ulum* (1879–80) of Hoca Tahsin Efendi's *Cemiyet-i İlmiye* (Scientific Society) are among other similar publications to be named.

7. For the perception and admiration of modern European science by the late Ottomans see Yalçınkaya, *Learned Patriots*; and Burçak, "A Remedy for All Ills."

8. For a detailed study on Ottoman materialists see Hanioğlu, "Blueprints for a Future Society," 29–116. For further readings on the history of materialism in Ottoman-Turkish thought see Ülken, *Türkiye'de Çağdaş Düşünce Tarihi*, 233–56; Akgün, *Materyalizmin Türkiye'ye Girişi*; Doğan, *Osmanlı Aydınları*.

9. Cevdet, "Şime-i Muhabbet," 1979–84. Cf. also Lewis, *The Emergence of Modern Turkey*, 231.

10. Hanioğlu, "Blueprints for a Future Society," 28. Other radical modernists, like Celal Nuri (İleri), who combined naturalistic/deistic views with Islamic political goals, were also accused by his contemporaries of "trying to introduce materialistic conceptions under the guise of a defense of Islam." See Mardin, *Religion and Social Change in Modern Turkey*, 142.

11. *İçtihad* was published by Abdullah Cevdet in Istanbul between 1904–28 with some interruptions and title changes.

12. Büchner, *Madde ve Kuvvet* and Haeckel,

Büchner and Haeckel were a part of the nineteenth-century movement of naturalist and biological materialism in Germany, which also affected other parts of Europe as the new scientific philosophy and the ideology of future. The movement also included scientists, such as Carl Vogt and Jacob Moleschott, and its ideas spread mostly through popular scientific journals.[13] The preoccupation of radical modernist thinkers with mostly European materialist literature became a visible fact "to the utter amazement of visiting foreign scholars."[14] Charles MacFarlane, a British traveler, gives a striking account of this astonishing influence during his visit of Istanbul and the newly established Medical School of Galatasaray (*mekteb-i tıbbiye*) earlier in 1847–48.[15]

Positivism was also influential among radical modernist Ottomans. The origins of the history of Ottoman contact with positivism extend back to the early nineteenth century, when Ottoman administration willingly entered a process of modernization. It was within this period that Auguste Comte, the founding father of positivism, wrote a letter on February 4, 1853 to Mustafa Reşid Paşa, the former Grand Vizier and the political force behind the modernization process, inviting him to embrace the principles of positivism. Earlier, Comte had also sent a similar letter to the Russian Tsar Nicola I. Both letters were later published in the preface of his *Systeme de la politique positive*.[16] In his letter to Reşid Paşa, Comte presents to him the religion of humanity, the superiority of positivistic approaches towards history, society, and politics, and expresses, more specifically, the rationalist and progressive character of Islam which, having purportedly saved Muslim societies from tumult and chaos in the past, was destined to help them in modern times by shifting them directly from the theological stage to the positivistic, auspiciously enabling them to bypass the otherwise indispensable metaphysical bridge.[17] Pierre Laffitte, the disciple of

---

*Vahdet-i Mevcud.*

13. For more details on the history and views of those so-called scientific materialists see Gregory, *Scientific Materialism*; Freuler, *La Crise*, 55–86.

14. Hanioğlu, *The Young Turks*, 12–13. The admiration of modern science and overlooking of its Islamic past was not limited to the materialists. Even a non-materialist, such as Şemseddin Sami Fraşeri, in one of his articles writes: "For just as we cannot cure even malaria with the medicine of Ibn Sina, so we can neither operate a railroad engine or steamship, nor use the telegraph, with the chemistry of Jahiz and the wisdom of Ibn Sina. For this reason, if we wish to become civilized, we must do so by borrowing science and technology from the contemporary civilization of Europe, and leave the study of the works of Islamic scholars to the students of history and antiquity." See Fraşeri, "Medeniyet-i cedidenin ümem-i İslamiyye'ye nakli," 179–84. For its English translation see Kurzman (ed.), *Modernist Islam*, 150.

15. He wrote in his account: "It was long since I had seen such a collection of downright materialism. A young Turk, seemingly about twenty years of age, was sitting cross-legged in a corner of the room, reading that manual of atheism, the 'Système de la Nature!' Another of the students showed his proficiency in French and philosophy, by quoting passages from Diderot's 'Jaques le Fataliste. . . . Cabanés's Rapport de Physique et du Morale de l'Homme occupied a conspicuous place on the shelves. I no longer wondered it should be commonly said that every student who came out of Galata Serai, after keeping the full term, came out always a materialist . . .'" See MacFarlane, *Turkey and Its Destiny*, 270–71.

16. See Comte, *Système de la politique positive*, XLVII–L. The book is translated into English by J. H. Bridges, F. Harrison et all.

17. For the Turkish translation of Comte's letter to Reşid Paşa see Meriç, "Mustafa Paşa ve Mithat Paşalarla A. Comte ve Pozitivistler,"

Comte, continued paying close attention to contact with Ottomans, even visiting Midhat Pasha, an influential figure considered as the successor of Reşid Paşa, accompanied by a group of positivists in the year of 1877. While explaining Comtean philosophy to Midhat during his visit of Paris, Laffitte and his colleagues assured him, in a written proposal, that they had utterly freed themselves from Christian and racial biases, and were aiming to establish a new system for the joint benefit of both Eastern and Western societies. They also expressed their admiration of Ottoman policy for protecting the languages and cultures of minorities and supporting the existence and integrity of the Ottoman Empire, aspects that keep its political and legal system intact. In his response, Midhat Paşa expressed "his joy to be in the company of those who are far from all kinds of religious and ethnic racism," and emphasized his pleasure about their avoiding "Christian stereotypes," which he saw in the discourse of other Europeans, not to mention their acknowledgement of Muslim contribution to world civilization.[18]

A few others like Rıza Tevfik, influenced by British philosophers, adopted an Anglo-Saxon version of ethico-political and evolutionary positivism with a frequent reference to Herbert Spencer and John-Stuart Mill.[19] However, they were not able to create a strong impact on Turkish intellectual history during their lifetime and the early Republican period. On the other hand, Ziya Gökalp (1876-1924), a very significant figure in modern Ottoman/Turkish thought, combined positivism with Durkheimian sociology with a hope of constructing ideological bases for Turkish nationalism.[20] This fact was observable in the issues of the *İctimaiyat Mecmuası* (Sociological Journal), published by Ziya Gökalp and his circle, which covered numerous translations from Durkheim's writings.[21] Initially expressed as a general scientific insight, the Durkheimian doctrine of national solidarity and public morality was subsequently regarded as a source of inspiration by Gökalp for a secular ideology within the Turkish nation-building context.[22]

Under the impact of these multi-level interactions, various tendencies began to appear in scientific publications in the Ottoman capital during the 1870s and 80s. By then, modern sciences had already gained popularity through encyclopedias and journals in Ottoman Turkish. Science came to be seen by many officials and learned figures as the only tool to solve the problems of the Empire. One such figure is Beşir Fuad, renowned for having translated many popular scientific books from Western languages. Among

---

31–32.

18. See Robinet, *Adresse des positivists a Midhat-Pasha*. The Turkish translations are published in the article cited in the previous footnote.

19. Tevfik, "Spencer'in Felsefesi," 233–45; and Ibid, "Hürriyet," Ulum-i İktisadiyye ve İctimaiyye Mecmuası, 19–39. Also see Wasti, "Feylesof Rıza," 83–100.

20. See Ülken, "Durkheim et l'enseignement," 13–14; and Parla, *The Social and Political Thought*.

21. The journal issues (1–6) have recently been transliterated into modern Turkish by Mehmet Kanar. The earliest sociological journals are considered to be *American Journal of Sociology* (1895) and *L'Année sociologique* (1896).

22. Collins, "The Durkheimian Movement," in *The Cambridge Companion to Durkheim*, 119. See also Parla and Davison, *Corporatist Ideology*, 26–27.

other references to modern nineteenth-century thinkers and scientists, Fuad also cites Auguste Comte and his disciple Emile Littre, and encourages his disciple Fazlı Necib, through letters, to examine and study their books.[23] Therefore, this connection of ideas shows that modernization of thought among the Ottomans cannot be analyzed independently from the developments in modern European history. Werner Heisenberg in his *Physics and Philosophy* states, "The nineteenth century developed an extremely rigid frame for natural science, which created an open hostility towards religion." The rigid framework, he points out, "is beginning to dissolve in the twentieth century as a result of the relativity theory and quantum mechanics."[24] The openness of modern physics, Heisenberg suggests, may help to some extent to reconcile the older traditions with the new trends of thought.[25] Heisenberg's observation is also valid for Ottoman intellectual history. Following radical suggestions by some elites, moderate approaches by a number of Muslim scholars appeared on the scene. Nursi is one of those Muslim figures and this chapter will present how he as an Ottoman scholar tried to present a solution from a religious point of view.

Nineteenth-century materialist and positivist thought was particularly influential in the Ottoman Empire, partly due to the elitist approach among some intellectuals to save society through a new design, by changing its cultural dimensions from above and reconstructing a new social entity in order for it to be a part of the new civilization of Europe.[26] Therefore, the exclusive, imposing, and future-designing understanding of materialistic or positivistic science was ideal for them. It also quite fitted the ambitions of the revolutionary "Young Turks," the rising political group of that period, who, unlike the previous "Young Ottoman" movement,[27] turned into a radical Westernist organization, and began to distance themselves from religious culture. In fact, there was a close relation between Young Turks and the radicalist elite, who were often politically affiliated with the group. This explains why "the Young Turk *Weltanschauung*, as it developed between 1889 and 1902, was vehemently anti-religious, viewing religion as the greatest obstacle to human progress."[28]

On the other hand, the radicals were not the only group who focused on modern European thought. The growing interest in the developments of European science also pushed some other moderate intellectuals and bureaucrats of various tendencies to discuss the need for modernization, though they disagreed with the materialists on its content and extent

23. Fuad, *Mektuplar*, 34–35, 43.

24. Heisenberg, *Physics and Philosophy*, 197–99.

25. Heisenberg, *Physics and Philosophy*, 202. See also Voll, "Renewal and Reformation in the Mid-Twentieth Century," 249.

26. Kılıçzade İ. Hakkı proposes this design project in a dream form, in which "The present *medrese*s will be abolished and a perfect *medrese* of Literary Sciences on the model of the College de France will be established instead of Süleymaniye *Medrese*si, and another exalted *medrese* on the model of the Ecole Polytechnique will replace Fatih *Medrese*si." See Hakkı, "Pek Uyanık Bir Uyku," 1226–28. The text of Kılıçzade, which shows many parallels with the Republican reforms, is translated into English by Hanioğlu as an appendix to his "Garbcılar," 176–58.

27. Mardin, *The Genesis of the Young Ottoman Thought*, 404; and his *Religion and Social Change*, 122.

28. Hanioğlu, *Preparation for Revolution*, 305.

as well as its measures and methods.[29] It is not surprising, therefore, that European criticisms of materialist scientism, such as Henri Poincaré's critical relativism, Emile Boutroux's scientific indeterminism, and Henri Bergson's creationist and progressive evolutionism attracted the attention of certain Ottoman academicians, who translated these authors into Turkish as a response to the transmission of popular scientism into Ottoman language and culture.[30] *Darülfünun* professors such as İsmail Hakkı (Baltacıoğlu), Mehmed Emin (Erişirgil), Mustafa Şekib (Tunç), and Rıza Tevfik (Bölükbaşı) began to take interest in the intuitionist nature of Bergsonianism, and few thinkers outside of the academy were inclined to examine the revolutionary character of dialectical materialism as a reaction to studies on positivist evolutionism. *Dergah* journal was the main voice of the Turkish Bergsonians and continued to be published for a long time. Mustafa Şekib, while criticizing the Turkish version of the Comtean-Durkheimian positivism, emphasized the importance of intuitionist philosophy in providing a convenient atmosphere for creative thinking and dashing efforts.[31] The debates continued after the war. Hilmi Ziya Ülken, a well-known historian of Turkish thought, points out that during the armistice (*mütareke*) with European powers in the depressive atmosphere of the postwar period (1918–20), Turkish thinkers were depending on more ground-breaking and innovative movements in hope of bringing urgent solutions to their conditions. Bergsonianism offered a spiritual command of intuition, and the other one a material power of change.[32]

Influenced by these further translations, the new generation of modern religious scholars had a chance to contact other sources of European thought and felt more confident to emphasize an alternative approach towards modernization.[33] Extreme materialistic views may have sparked opposition, especially among the religious circles, but they also kindled a general curiosity towards modern science and thought among readers. Thus, just as the radical intellectuals had

29. For instance, members of the newly established translation offices, such as *Te'lif ve Tercüme Dairesi*, began to translate certain classics of European modernism, such as the work of Descartes: See Descartes, *Usul Hakkında Nutuk*; Barbe, *Tarih-i Felsefe*; Bertrand, *Mebadi-i Felsefe-i Ilmiyye*.

30. Poincaré, *İlim ve Faraziye*; Boutroux, *İlim ve Din*; Bergson, *Şuurun Bila Vasıta Mutaları Hakkında*. Mustafa Şekip (Tunç, 1886–1958), a professor of philosophy and psychology at *darülfünun*, was the main Ottoman Turkish disciple of Bergsonian philosophy, and influenced many of his students during this period. Among his many translations from Henri Bergson, see *Yaratıcı Tekamül'den Hayatin Tekamülü*. For a short description of Turkish Bergsonian thought see Fındıkoğlu, "Türkiye'de Bergsonizm I–II." On the thought and impact of Mustafa Şekip see Altıntaş, *Mustafa Şekip Tunç*.

31. See Tunç, "Memleketimizde Felsefenin İnkişafı," 25–34.

32. Ülken, *Türkiye'de Çağdaş Düşünce Tarihi*, 375. Also see İrem, "Bergson and Politics," 873–82.

33. Unlike early Orientalistic theses some scholars emphasize no direct connection between modernization and westernization. Cf. Voll, "The Mistaken Identification of 'The West' with 'Modernity,'" 1–12. Jacques Waardenburg points out that although modernity has often been linked to Western liberalism and democracy, there is no reason that modernity should only refer to the West. In fact, modernity can occur in different societies and cultures. As it is observed, many societies reformulate their cultural-religious traditions in order to function within their new conditions, and each has their own characteristics. See Waardenburg, "Some Thoughts on Modernity," 318–9.

done, they translated some other books from European thinkers, showing the rational and spiritual aspects of modern thought, and the criticism of popular materialism by them.[34] One should note that "religious scholars" in the Sunni Ottoman context would not refer to an institutional body of clerics, but rather to a group of lay scholars who studied religious disciplines either in old *madrasa*s or modern institutions and they were in favor of change in methods of learning. They replaced the old "*ulama*" (traditional scholars) and began to use a new discourse in presenting issues of religion.[35] Nursi belonged to this group, although he did not have a formal education in modern schools. He was not the first Ottoman scholar to present traditional Islamic thought in light of the challenges of modernization; however, he influenced the society more than any other fellow scholar. He and other moderate religious thinkers emerged as an alternative voice against the defenders of radical scientism in the process of the modernization of Ottoman thought. He rejected the notion of conflict both between Islamic tradition and modernization and between true religion and pure science. The modernization process had its origins in earlier centuries of Islamic and Ottoman intellectual history, but it accelerated in the nineteenth century.[36] The earliest modern-minded religious scholar was Ahmed Cevdet Paşa (1822–95), who headed a committee to codify Islamic civil law through the project of *Mecelle* in order to transform Ottoman society within a framework connected to its cultural roots. By simplifying religious language, addressing new questions, and referring to Western civilization he opened the way of a new understanding in late Ottoman religious thought. In his *Tezakir*, he expressed that his method and language of scholarship gained widespread popularity.[37]

Moreover, following the first confrontation, the failure of the First Constitution and the strict state control on all intellectuals—including the *ulama*—during the Hamidian era pushed religious scholars to get more interested in modern discussions, and to seek alliances with the radical modernist thinkers, who were mostly affiliated with the Young Turks, then in opposition. Consequently, during the Second Constitutional period and the rule of the Young Turks through the Committee of Union and Progress (*İttihad ve Terakki Fırkası*), the difference between the two understandings of modernization surfaced and dominated the debates.[38] In keeping with an openness towards the modernization of thought, the new generation of religious intellectuals began to call for reform (*ıslah*) in the traditional

---

34. See for example Bourdel, *İlim ve Felsefe*; Fonsegrive, *Mebadi-yi Felsefeden*; Seailles, *Tahlili Tarih-i Felsefe*. On the history of resistance to the materialist philosophy by late Ottoman religious scholars, see Bolay, *Türkiye'de Ruhçu ve Maddeci Görüşün Mücadelesi*, and Toku, *Türkiye'de Anti-Materyalist Felsefe*.

35. For a good survey of this group of scholars see Bein, *Ottoman Ulema*. For the context and transformation of these *ulama* also see Özervarlı, "Intellectual Foundations," 518–34.

36. Waardenburg, "Some Thoughts on Modernity," 317.

37. Paşa, *Tezakir*, 72.

38. After a very short period of good relations with the CUP, religious thinkers began to declare their opposition to them and wrote critical articles in their journals, like *Beyanülhak* and *Sırat-ı Müstakim*. This was followed by the policies of the CUP to diminish the role of religion in many aspect of social life. See Hanioğlu, *Preparation for Revolution*, 306–8.

*madrasa* school system.³⁹ They also called for methodological changes within the traditional Islamic disciplines of Qur'anic exegesis, Islamic law, and especially Muslim philosophical theology in order to meet the challenges of modern Western thought. One should remember that the issue of renovation (*tajdīd*) and revival (*iḥyā'*) in Islamic disciplines of learning is not exclusively modern but has deep historical roots.⁴⁰ This familiarity offered precedents for nineteenth-century scholars of Islamic thought as they sought to meet the challenges of materialism.

It should also be noted that although the individuals in this group shared a view of Islamic thought as one of the indispensable forces in modernizing Ottoman culture, they did not represent a single voice; they debated the relationship of Islam to various modern realities among themselves and indeed disagreed on many issues. These religious oriented thinkers, including Nursi, though different in their priorities and emphases, were united in reviving Islamic thought, rejecting materialistic theories, and considering the role of religious culture.⁴¹

And even though they differed on many levels, they had frequent interactions with those of other "lines," and there were even co-authors of same journals. Said Nursi as one of these modern religious scholars who deeply engaged in the revitalization of Islamic thought in modern Ottoman/Turkish society, among others may be more acquainted to social theology.⁴² He devoted his life to a restoration of religious expression in the public sphere, aiming to re-establish Islam as a live and practiced religion in an age of criticism, positivistic scientism, and radical secularism. This was done in two major efforts, which makes him different from other Ottoman religious thinkers: first, strengthening Islamic beliefs and thought, primarily against the challenges of materialistic thought; and second, addressing common people in order to create a social public resistance against the marginalization of religion in Ottoman Turkish society. Therefore, his intellectual efforts had two dimensions: first, the reconstruction of theoretical Islamic thinking; and the second, providing answers to modern social questions faced by the members of his society, who were jeopardized by the apparent clash between new challenges and their traditional culture.

## NURSI IN OTTOMAN INTELLECTUAL AND RELIGIOUS CONTEXT

As has already been pointed out, Nursi was a part of the resistance to challenges posed by neo-materialist and positivist

---

39. On reform attempts to revitalize madrasa programs see Ergun, "II. Meşrutiyet Döneminde *Medrese*lerin Durumu," 59–89; Jacob, "L'enseignement religieux en Turquie," 112–42; and Sarıkaya, *Medreseler ve Modernleşme*.

40. For example, the renowned eleventh-century scholar al-Ghazali titled one of his last books *Iḥyā' 'ulūm al-dīn* (The Revival of Islamic Disciplines), written when he returned from a period of seclusion due to his dissatisfaction with the educational system and intellectual establishment of his age. Similar attempts took place in late medieval and pre-modern times with a variety of objectives.

41. For example, comparing the views of Mehmed Şemseddin (Günaltay) and Şeyhülislam Mustafa Sabri could be a good case to know about the differences in their approach. For an anthology of selective writings of various members of this group see Kara, *Türkiye'de İslamcılık Düşüncesi I-II*.

42. Özervarlı, "The Reconstruction of Islamic Social Thought," 532–53.

ideas on religion in late Ottoman and modern Turkish society. He devoted his life to defend religion against the attacks, which were largely in the name of science and progress. He grew up in an age when science and modernization was placed as the main rival of religion. The well-known historian of religion Max Müller was complaining in 1878, when Nursi was a newborn, as following: "Every day, every week, every month, every quarter, the most widely read journals seem just now to vie with each other in telling us that the time for religion is past, the faith is a hallucination or an infantile disease, that the gods have at last been found out and exploded."[43] Nursi lived in a time, when some influential figures of Europe, such as Charles Darwin, Sigmund Freud, Emile Durkheim, and so on, were claiming that the extinction of religion was only a matter of time. Ottoman society was heavily under the influences of these thinkers through translations and newly established medical or engineering schools. There is no need to add the above-mentioned local physicians and scientists like Beşir Fuad, Abdullah Cevdet, Ahmed Rıza, who were openly promoting materialistic and positivistic ideas. Thus, growing up in these circumstances, it is not surprising that a pious and devout man such as Nursi would make anti-religious thoughts, what he called materialism (*maddecilik*) or naturalism (*tabiatçılık*), his main target.[44]

Nursi highlighted that in "this age, many are losing the case [of belief] because of the plague of materialism,"[45] and repeated the idea in many of his writings. According to Nursi "in this century, materialism is widespread, and materiality is thought to be the source of everything."[46] In his view, despite a strong religious tradition from the past, the reason for a sharp increase in recent materialistic movements was assuming connections between modern sciences and unbelief. This is because contemporary materialistic movements reflect modern science according to their atheistic views. Historians of modern thought are aware that under the impacts of the Newtonian mechanic worldview, and the deistic approaches of the Enlightenment towards religion, in the nineteenth century science reached "an extremely rigid frame" in its history,[47] through the emergence of some materialistic and positivistic theories in the natural and social sciences. According to the materialistic theories, which explain all phenomena in terms of matter, science is sufficient for solving *all* kinds of problems and for imposing universal laws for every society.[48] "Science alone is objective, open-minded, universal, cumulative, and progressive. Religious traditions by contrast, are said to be subjective, closed-minded, parochial, uncritical, and resistant to change."[49] This open hostility toward religion in the West then penetrated into other parts of the world, and pushed them into a period of cultural and intellectual unrest.[50] Therefore, Nursi analyzed modern Western civilization from two aspects. One of them derives

43. Müller, *Lectures*, 218.
44. Özervarlı, "The Reconstruction of Islamic Social Thought," 536–37.
45. Nursi, *The Rays*, 224.
46. Nursi, *The Letters*, 525.
47. See Heisenberg, *Physics and Philosophy*, 197.
48. Chadwick, *The Secularization of the European Mind*, 233.
49. Barbour, *Religion in an Age of Science*, 5.
50. Özervarlı, "Said Nursi's Project," 320–21.

from Christian roots, and developed some cultural and social activities, as well as technological developments, and the other focuses on the source of the darkness of materialistic thought.[51] To him, materialism is based on a philosophy that does not depend on revelation and that gives priority to power, benefit, conflict, and racism. Therefore, it was causing an increase in human need. He warned that any civilization that based itself on these principles couldn't create happiness for all of society, and it will most probably push the masses into economic and social difficulties.[52]

Noticeable from his writing, Nursi's mission and self-responsibility was protecting Muslim people's faith from the attacks of Western materialistic and positivistic movements, which were spreading through the Islamic world during his time.[53] In the opening passage of his *Tabiat Risalesi*, which was written as a polemic against naturalist and materialist theories of modern science, he describes the influence of atheism even among conservative intellectuals and bureaucrats as "trying to subvert, poison, and destroy their mind."[54] In his collection of works, the *Risale-i Nur*, in order to set a barrier against the spreading Western materialism, he concentrated on explaining the fundamentals of belief in a way that addresses modern man's understanding, instead of issues of worship and other daily practices of religion. However, he did not do that in the same language and methods of classical Islamic disciplines. He used a new language of rational spirituality, with a pioneering focus and priority in his stance and prospects, and formulated the necessity and urgency of change in his words as "*the old condition is impossible (to revive); either new condition or total annihilation.*"[55] Nevertheless, the essence of this harmonious relationship between non-materialistic science and religion in Said Nursi's thought can be easily found in Islamic thought, and also due to the fact that in Islamic intellectual history there was no such rigid controversy or debate between the two sides, in contrast to their competing opposition in modern Western thought.

For his aim of explaining and defending Islamic faith Said Nursi considered the Qur'an as his first source, both in content and in style. He usually opened the chapters of his writings with a Qur'anic verse related to the subject. The themes, words, and emphases of the Qur'an seems to be a source of inspiration for him. So, he is an Islamic scholar "who has drawn from the Qur'an principles of Muslim behaviour appropriate to our times."[56] Nursi's collection can be regarded to some extent as a commentary on the Qur'an. He himself divided traditional exegesis (*tefsîr*) of the Qur'an into two groups. The most common are those which comment on the literal text of the Qur'an chapter by chapter, from beginning to the end. The other sort of exegesis, among which Nursi esteemed his own writings as a most suitable example, proves the truths of the Qur'anic verses.[57] Actually, he tried to write an exegesis of the first category during the early years

---

51. Nursi, *The Flashes*, 160.
52. Nursi, *The Words*, 146.
53. Cf. Mardin, *Religion and Social Change*, 8.
54. Nursi, *The Flashes*, 232.
55. Nursi, *Risale-i Nur Külliyatı*, 1940.
56. Mardin, *Religion and Social Change*, 18.
57. Nursi, *Risale-i Nur Külliyatı*, 1057.

of the First World War, entitled *İşaratü'l-İ'caz*, a commentary on the Fatiha and the beginning of al-Baqara, but he left it unfinished. In its introduction, he says that he never had the intention of producing an exegesis, but he felt it necessary to demonstrate to other scholars an example of a new *tefsîr*, which people need and expect to be written.[58] But even in *İşaratü'l-İ'caz*, Said Nursi mostly focused on the principles of faith rather than historical facts and other subjects.[59]

It is quite clear that Said Nursi insisted on the adequacy of dealing with the essentials of faith in modern times, which characterize the majority of the subjects in the Qur'an, and not the legal disagreements between scholars.[60] Therefore, what he was really interested in were issues of faith and the Qur'anic approach to them. Although he benefited from Sufi ideas, and respected all moderate Sufi movements, which followed the Qur'an and the *Sunna*, and rejected a total dismissal of mystical legacy, he did not identify himself with any spiritual order (*tarīqa*).[61] What he did was revive a theology based on the Qur'an and the methods of contemporary education. Through this Qur'anic theology Nursi could make a serious attempt to protect the Islamic faith from materialistic challenges of the age, using an experimental approximation rather than any philosophical and/or theoretical methods. He explains that in his early years, he had suffered spiritual damage since his mind was occupied with philosophical opinions taken from theological texts. On the other hand, the mystical approach left him dissatisfied, as he felt that the Qur'an was the best guide, rather than another human intermediary. Therefore, he turned towards the Qur'anic guidance, which appealed to his reason as well as to his heart.[62]

Being aware of changes that took place in the modern period, Nursi characterized the new age with three new concepts: property, freedom, and science.[63] However, as it is comparable to some other Muslim thinkers of his time, he cannot be understood through a sharp,

58. Nursi, *Risale-i Nur Külliyatı*, 1155. In the introductory chapter of *İşârâtü'l-İ'câz*, which is entitled *İfadetü'l-merâm*, he gave a lengthier analysis on the necessary requirements for creating a contemporary *tafsīr*. In his arguments, Nursi states that the Qur'an, as a revealed book, includes many different subjects, each of which necessitates a special kind of learning. Therefore, a certain scholar whose knowledge is limited by time, place, and a specific type of expertise, cannot handle writing a *tafsīr* alone without the cooperation of specialists of various branches. A single scholar would not be able to consider all the characteristics of human beings who are subjected to the Qur'anic message, as they have different capacities and levels of understanding. Besides, he may not be able to distance himself from sectarian attitudes. A commission of a joint *tafsīr* project is expected to read previous *tafsīrs*, select useful comments in them, and then ruminate on new interpretations by investigating all related sciences, while nevertheless respecting each other's freedom of thought throughout the process. According to Nursi, only via this method can a *tafsīr* gain the respect and confidence of a broad range of Muslims (see Nursi, *Risale-i Nur Külliyatı*, 1157). Cf also "Muhakemat," in Nursi, *Risale-i Nur Külliyatı*, 1989–90.

59. In a work entitled *İşârâtü'l-İ'câz*, Said Nursi used quotations from classical-period *ulama*, such as the Mu'tazilite and Sunni commentators al-Zamakhshari and Fakhr al-Din al-Razi, as well as linguistics experts like al-Jahiz and al-Sakkaki. He is also influenced by Abd al-Qahir al-Jurjani, especially in his explanations on the superiority (*i'jaz*) of the Qur'anic text.

60. "Sunuhat," in Nursi, *Risale-i Nur Külliyatı*, 2046.

61. Nursi, *The Letters*, 518–35.

62. "Mesnevi-i Nûriye," in Nursi, *Risale-i Nur Külliyatı*, 1277.

63. Mardin, *Religion and Social Change*, 173.

dichotomist division between tradition and modernization. He regarded a balance between tradition and modernization that brought about an alternative approach compared to the discourse of radical modernist thinkers. The balance can be described as protecting the unchangeables/essentials while clearing obstacles for changeables/details. This is the reason why Nursi criticized Musa Bekuf (Bigiyef), a modernist thinker from Kazan, for being excessively in favor of renewal and making false concessions to modernity in respect of his ideas.[64]

Although being a disciple of the Islamic scholarly and spiritual tradition, Nursi was not a blind follower of the historical methodology of classical Islamic disciplines. In addition, though he belonged to the tradition of renewal (*tecdid*) and revivalism (*ihya'*) in Islamic thought,[65] he was not a modernizer in the Western sense. Being aware of modern conditions and representing a position between total rejection (of old *ulama*) and revolutionist line (of positivist Young Turks), he played an important role in the transformation of concepts of and solutions to social issues. In accordance to his moderate approach, Nursi should be seen as a man of mission who felt the responsibility of protecting the religious beliefs of his people. However, his emphasis on the middle-way approach, between too much and too little (*ifrat* and *tefrit*),[66] does not suggest similarities between him and early representatives of postmodernism. Therefore, John O. Voll's insistence in locating Nursi closer to postmodern thinking is to analyze him in a Western context, which would not be consistent with his own.[67]

The other late-period Ottoman scholars, too, as it was discussed above, highlighted the necessity of methodological changes in order to strengthen faith in Islam among the modernizing Ottomans, and to bring their disciplines up-to-date and renew their appeal. Some of them had various official positions, either as professors in the theology department of the newly established Western-style university (*dârülfünûn*) or at the office of the Grand Mufti. However, Nursi unlike his immediate contemporaries, continued his awakening and revitalizing efforts without taking any position at the university or a religious institution. He indeed had some affiliations for a period, such as being a member of *daru'l-hikmeti'l-islamiye*, the higher council of Islamic thought, which sought "to find solutions for problems confronting the Islamic world," and getting involved in the Teachers' Association (*cemiyet-i müderrisîn*), the main aims of which was "to produce students of the *'ulama* profession who would be thoroughly informed of the Islamic sciences and have knowledge of the modern sciences sufficient for the needs of the times."[68] However, he did not engage in this kind of organization for his professional career, but rather for solving the current problems and deep crises of his changing society. Therefore, he had more influence on traditional Ottoman society than other fellow religious scholars, for he was a trusted personality, who was not potentially tainted by personal

64. Nursi, *The Flashes*, 371.

65. See Leaman, "Nursi's Place in the Ihya Tradition," 314–24.

66. See Nursi, *The Flashes*, 43.

67. Voll, "Renewal and Reformation in the Mid–Twentieth Century," 252, 256, 259.

68. Vahide, *Islam in Modern Turkey*, 136, 142.

gains or political obligations. This is the reason that Nursi, unlike other scholars of his age, became a founder of a socio-religious movement, which still exists in Turkish society.

Nursi's achievement in being so influential in society mostly came from his usage of a more convincing, popular style in his writings, addressing people of a middling intellectual standard without the elaboration of a theoretical system of thought, though sometimes he gave details of a deeper knowledge to satisfy his more intellectual readers as well. For example, he used a dialectical method in controversial dialogues with Satan, in rejecting Satanic claims that the Qur'anic text is actually coming from a human origin.[69] While his contemporaries—such as İzmirli İsmail Hakkı,[70] Mehmed Serafeddin,[71] and Elmalılı Hamdi[72]—distanced themselves from popular beliefs and rhetorical styles, he used fable and metaphor in order to facilitate understanding of his message by a greater majority of his readers.[73] In such cases, he gave some concrete examples from everyday life by using fables and interesting comparisons. For example, when Nursi discussed questions about praying (duâ) to God, he simplified the problem through a classification of it. Following his description of it as an innate need, and dividing it into oral and actual, he offered some explanations for a potential variety of results after praying, despite God's call to the believers for praying any time and his promise to respond to them (Q 40/60). Comparing a praying person with a patient's demands from his doctor, he argued that God replies to people's prayers sometimes by giving what was wanted, sometimes by postponing it in order to give a better reward in the Hereafter, or by rejecting it outright for some reason. Praying and prayers, according to Nursi, should not be performed for their results, but based on the proper time for them. The negative results of praying do not mean that they were not heard or not accepted; rather, it means that the time for praying has not yet ended.[74] Moreover, in order to protect the religious loyalty of the majority of people to their faith, Nursi did not reject any Islamic knowledge, which gained a common acceptance in society, even if it were to lack a reliable source. He even tried to explain some inadequate prophetic sayings (hadith) so that common people would not have doubts about their religion.[75]

The main characteristic of Said Nursi's revitalization project in his "Old Said" period was the combination of Islamic disciplines (ulûm-i diniyye) with contemporary sciences (funûn-i medeniyye) and learning. The truth, according to Nursi's early writings, could only be reached through this combination that is between religious sciences, which are light for illuminating the inner conscience, and modern sciences, which are light for illuminating reason. Otherwise if they are separated, the former alone will give rise to fanaticism, and

69. See Nursi, *The Words*, 365–76.

70. See Özervarlı, "Alternative Approaches to Modernization in the Late Ottoman Period," 77–102.

71. Özervarlı, "Transferring Traditional Islamic Disciplines into Modern Social Sciences in Late Ottoman Thought," 317–30.

72. Özervarlı, "Modification or Renewal?" 43–60.

73. Cf. Eickelman, "Qur'anic Commentary," 265.

74. Nursi, *The Words*, 325–27.

75. Nursi, *The Flashes*, 127–32.

the latter will bring about doubtfulness and uncertainty.[76] This approach was a combination of religious tradition with a non-materialistic modern learning, which could provide both continuity and change. Through use of this method, the Islamic religious culture would ensure its identity, and also be able to respond to the new questions raised by the modern age. Nursi's lifelong dream of creating an eclectic university, which he planned to call the *Medresetüzzehrâ*, also would have the advantages of both the classical *madrasas* and the modern schools. During his stay in the district of Van in the year of 1895–96, Said Nursi had a chance to stay with people who had acquired a modern educational background in the Governor's residence, and the opportunity of gaining information about mathematics and logic. His interest in sciences led him to write short treatises on algebraic equations and mathematical problems. From his discussions on modern questions with the Governor of Van and his employees at the end of his teenage years, Said Nursi might have formed his initial ideas about the actual situation of the Islamic disciplines in his day, and the difficulties of Muslim scholars in answering contemporary problems. The reason for his first trip to Istanbul in the years of his "Old Said" period during the reign of Sultan Abulhamid II, was also to publicize his opinions about the establishment of a new school in which both religious and scientific courses could be taught side by side.[77]

In his later writings, however, Nursi made a clear distinction between natural scientific philosophy and Qur'anic philosophy, as the former examines the universe by its nominal meaning (*mânâ-yi ismî*), while the latter does so through its indicative meaning (*mânâ-yi harfî*). The ordinary philosopher, in his examination of the universe, will attribute the qualities of the existent beings to themselves; however, a philosopher who believes in God will remember their Creator and praise the perfection of His creation in all parts of the universe. In the second view, each object and each event is directly connected to its Creator. Thus, according to Nursi, "a philosophy without religion is an untruthful sophistry and an insult to the universe."[78] The combination of science with religion in Nursi's thought is connected to the perfect design in the universe, which he compares to a beautifully organized garden in the springtime and which is a starting point for his experimental theology. He follows al-Ghazali concerning the design argument by referring to his famous "best of all possible worlds" idea.[79] He is aware of the existence of "apparent" evils, but he dismisses that they can be used as a counter-argument against design. The creation of evil is not intended in an absolute way, but as a close relation to the better understanding of good. Therefore, one cannot use the existence of a relative imperfection, negativity, or evil as an argument against the design of the universe and therefore against the wisdom of God.[80] Through a complete observation and reflection on the natural world, it will

---

76. "Münazarat," in Nursi, *Risale-i Nur Külliyatı*, 1956.

77. Özervarlı, "Said Nursi's Project of Revitalizing Contemporary Islamic Thought," 323–24.

78. Nursi, *The Words*, 145. For a detailed and comparative study on Nursi's *ismî* and *harfî* distinction as an alternative scientific paradigm, see Yamina B. Mermer, "The Hermeneutical Dimension of Science," 270–96.

79. See, for instance, Nursi, *The Rays*, 39.

80. Nursi, *The Letters*, 62–63.

be accepted that goodness is essential and general, while evil and imperfections are relative and limited.[81]

Despite his efforts to make a harmony between science and religion, Nursi did not have a mechanistic worldview, since he did not accept a necessary relation of cause and effect in the universe. He did not regard natural laws as having their own existence separate from God, but saw them rather as a relational order set in place by God himself. Although he emphasized the relation between cause and effect, he did not regard it as an unconscious chain in and of itself by means only of a successive appearance. The order of the universe, which is sustained by God's laws (*sünnetullah*), is totally in his control and it is his will to ensure its continuity. All natural causes are only veils for God's will and acts, which cannot be performed independently.[82] Therefore, Şerif Mardin's selections of some phrases of Said Nursi which imply his "mechanistic view of nature"[83] does not reflect Nursi's general thought on the causation and the natural laws. It is true that Nursi used words like "machine," "factory," etc., for nature, in order to emphasize its perfect order, but *not* in a Newtonian deistic sense.[84] One of the main reasons for Nursi's use of these modern words may well be to attract the attention of educated readers in his time, who were under the influence of scientific terminology.

In Nursi's thought, the Qur'an is in fact a translation of the great book of the universe and its speaking language. It reads the book of the universe in its mosque, and it is the light (*nûr*) of the life of the universe and the intellect of its conscience. On the other hand, the universe is the proof of the Qur'an and its expounder. The passage of time is the best interpreter throughout the ages, and many other meanings of the Qur'an will be discovered by new scientific inventions in successive centuries.[85] One can see Nursi's strong relation with the Qur'an in his following statement: "While there is a perpetual miracle like the Qur'an, searching for further proof appears to my mind as superfluous; while there is a proof of reality like the Qur'an, would silencing those who deny it weigh heavily on my heart?"[86] It is obvious from this and many other passages that there is an interdependent relationship between the Qur'an and the universe in Nursi's thought. The universe is dependent on the Qur'an for its meaning to be understood, as the Qur'an interprets, expounds, or even translates the book of the universe. Nursi's methodology on Qur'anic interpretation is mainly a reflection on the universe, which is symbolized by the metaphor of the book. It was a new approach to understanding the Qur'an in his age, which attempts to expose an

81. "Muhakemat," in *Risale-i Nur Külliyatı*, 1995–96. Cf.Özervarlı, "Said Nursi's Project of Revitalizing Contemporary Islamic Thought," 325.

82. Nursi, *The Words*, 300–301. For example, one cannot see earthquakes, according to Said Nursi, as natural events without any purpose. Cf. Nursi, *The Words*, 187–88.

83. See Mardin, *Religion and Social Change*, 213–14.

84. In a Newtonian physical system, God has established a set of clearly-defined rules and mechanisms that determine the workings of the universe, and therefore has no need to interfere directly in its functioning.

85. "Muhakemat," in Nursi, *Risale-i Nur Külliyatı*, 1989.

86. Nursi, *The Words*, 375.

important aspect of the Qur'an in relation to the modern age in particular.[87]

## CONCLUSION

Unlike the radical members of the materialist and positivist circles, the religious-minded intellectual group, which Nursi belonged to, had an alternative approach towards modernization and reconciliation between religion and modern science. They suggested that the true modernizers would not deny the cultural heritage, but rather work positively to both appraise the past and to look into the requirements of the future. To them, it was the duty of learned members of society to support the required changes. More interestingly, they did not see any conflict in re-appropriating old norms for the new challenges and demands of modernity. The Islamic tradition was flexible and rich enough to accommodate to modern times. Indeed, it can embrace them and thereby avoid stagnation by re-appropriating old norms for new challenges. Development is not restricted to the Western context, as it already existed in the tradition of Islamic thought, though it was to a certain extent neglected in the latest phase of the premodern period.

It should be emphasized that Said Nursi's aim among the reformers was not to set up a theoretical system, but to reinforce the faith and beliefs of his people. His voluminous writings and their influence on the religious generations of Turkish society is the real outcome of his efforts. He was addressing a general public that was under the influence of the impact of modernity since the late Ottoman times, and had questions regarding the understanding of religion. Nursi in response to that need proposed to examine the physical universe, which is the subject of science, under the guidance of revelation as an evidence for its truthfulness. Surely, by stressing the need for Qur'anic theology, which employed both one's heart and one's reason in searching for the way to God in everything, he can easily be regarded among the late Ottoman scholars who attempted to revitalize Islamic religious thought. In his project of revitalization, he did not disconnect himself from Islamic intellectual traditions and historical roots when answering questions by his contemporaries, but used a new discourse to resolve newly emerged difficulties in their mind concerning issues of religion.

## BIBLIOGRAPHY

Akgün, Mehmet. *Materyalizmin Türkiye'ye Girişi ve İlk Etkileri*. Ankara: Kültür ve Turizm Bakanlığı Yayınları, 1988.

Akiba, Jun. "A New School for Qadis: Education of the Sharia Judges in the Late Ottoman Empire." *Turcica* 35 (2003) 125–63.

Altıntaş, Hayrani. *Mustafa Şekip Tunç*. Ankara: Kültür Bakanlığı Yayınları, 1989.

Alkan, Mehmet O. "Modernization from Empire to Republic and Education in the Process of Nationalism." In *Ottoman Past and Today's Turkey*, edited by Kemal H. Karpat, 47–132. Leiden: Brill, 2000.

Barbe, Abbe E. *Tarih-i Felsefe*. Translated by Bohor Israil. Istanbul: Matbaa-i Amire, 1914.

Barbour, Ian G. *Religion in an Age of Science*. London: SCM, 1990.

Bein, Amit. *Ottoman Ulema, Turkish Republic: Agents of Change and Guardians of*

---

87. See Vahide, "The Book of the Universe," 474, and 483.

*Tradition*. Stanford: Stanford University Press, 2011.

Bertrand, Alexis. *Mebadi-i Felsefe-i Ilmiyye ve Felsefe-i Ahlakiyye*. Translated by Salih Zeki. Istanbul: Matbaa-i Amire, 1915.

Büchner, Ludwig. *Madde ve Kuvvet*. Translated by Baha Tevfik and Ahmed Nebil from French edition. Istanbul: Dersaadet Kütüphanesi, 1911.

Burçak, Berrak. "A Remedy for All Ills, Healing the 'Sick Man of Europe': A Case for Ottoman Scientism (Seyyid Mustafa)." PhD diss., Princeton University, 2005.

Cevdet, Abdullah. "Şime-i Muhabbet." *İctihad* 89 (January 29, 1914) 1979–84.

Cevdet Paşa, Ahmed. *Tezakir*, edited by Cavid Baysun. Ankara: Türk Tarih Kurumu, 1986.

Chadwick, Owen. *The Secularization of the European Mind in the Nineteenth Century*. Cambridge: Cambridge University Press, 1975.

Collins, Randall. "The Durkheimian Movement in France and World Sociology." In *The Cambridge Companion to Durkheim*, edited by Jeffrey C. Alexander and Philip Smith, 101–35. Cambridge: Cambridge University Press, 2005.

Comte, Auguste. *Système de la politique positive*. Paris: L. Mathias, 1854.

Descartes, Rene. *Usul Hakkında Nutuk*. Translated by İbrahim Edhem. Istanbul: Mahmud Bey Matbaasi, 1894.

Doğan, Atila. *Osmanlı Aydınları ve Sosyal Darvinizm*. Istanbul: Istanbul Bilgi Üniversitesi Yayınları, 2006.

Eickelman, Dale. "Qur'anic Commentary, Public Space and Religious Intellectuals in the Writings of Said Nursi." *The Muslim World* 89.3–4 (July–October 1999) 260–69.

Ergun, Mustafa. "II. Meşrutiyet Döneminde *Medrese*lerin Durumu ve Islah Çalışmaları." *Dil ve Tarih–Coğrafya Fakültesi Dergisi* 30.1–2 (1979–82) 59–89.

Fındıkoğlu, Ziyaeddin Fahri. "Türkiye'de Bergsonizm I–II." *Cumhuriyet Gazetesi*, January 13 and 15, 1941.

Findley, Carter Vaughn. *Ottoman Civil Officialdom: A Social History*. Princeton: Princeton University Press, 1989.

Fortna, Benjamin C. *Imperial Classroom: Islam, the State, and Education in the Late Ottoman Empire*. Oxford: Oxford University Press, 2002.

Fraşeri, Şemseddin Sami. "Medeniyet-i cedidenin ümem-i İslamiyye'ye nakli." *Güneş* 1.4 (1883) 179–84.

Freuler, Léo. *La crise de la philosophie au XIXe siecle*. Paris: J. Vrin, 1997.

Fuad, Beşir. *Mektuplar*, edited by C. Parkan Özturan. Istanbul: Arba, nd.

Göçek, Fatma Müge. *Rise of the Bourgeoisie, Demise of Empire: Ottoman Westernization and Social Change*: New York: Oxford University Press, 1996.

Grandin, Nicole, and Marc Gaborieau, eds. *Madrasa: La transmission du savoir dans le monde musulman*. Paris: Arguments, 1979.

Gregory, Frederick. *Scientific Materialism in Ninenteenth-Century Germany*. Dordrecht, Boston: Riddel, 1977.

Hanioğlu, M. Şükrü. "Blueprints for a Future Society: Late Ottoman Materialists on Science, Religion and Art." In *Late Ottoman Society: The Intellectual Legacy*, edited by Elisabeth Özdalga, 29–116. London: Routledge–Curzon, 2005.

———. "Garbcılar: Their Attitudes toward Religion and their Impact on the Official Ideology of the Turkish Republic." *Studia Islamica* 86 (1997) 133–58

———. *Preparation for Revolution: The Young Turks, 1902–1908*. Oxford: Oxford University Press, 2001.

———. *The Young Turks in Opposition*. New York: Oxford University Press, 1995.

Haeckel, Ernst, *Vahdet-i Mevcud: Bir Tabiat Aliminin Dini (Monisme)*. Translated by Baha Tevfik. Istanbul: Dersaadet Kütüphanesi, 1911.

Heisenberg, Werner. *Physics and Philosophy: The Revolution in Modern Science*. New York: Harper and Row, 1958.

İhsanoğlu, Ekmeleddin. "Bashoca Ishak Efendi: Pioneer of Modern Science in Turkey." In *Decision Making and Change* in the Ottoman Empire, edited by Caeser E. Farah, 157–68. Kirksville: The Thomas Jefferson University Press, 1993.

———. "The Genesis of 'Darulfünun': An Overview of Attempts to Establish the First Ottoman University." In *Histoire économique et sociale de l'Empire ottoman et de la Turquie (1326-1960)*, edited by Daniel Panzac, 827–42. Paris: Peeters, 1995.

İrem, Nazım. "Bergson and Politics: Ottoman Turkish Encounters with Innovations." *The European Legacy* 16.7 (2011) 873–82.

İshak Efendi, Başhoca, ed. *Mecmua-yi Ulum-i Riyaziye*, 4 vols. Cairo: Bulak Matbaası, 1841–45.

İsmail Hakkı, Kılıçzade. "Pek Uyanık Bir Uyku." *İctihad* 55 (1913) 1226–28.

Jacob, Xavier. "L'enseignement religieux en Turquie de la fin de l'Empire Ottoman a nos jours." In *Madrasa: La transmission du savoir dans le monde musulman*, edited by Nicole Grandin and Marc Gaborieau, 112–42. Paris: Arguments, 1999.

Kodaman, Bayram. *Abdülhamid Devri Eğitim Sistemi*. Ankara: Türk Tarih Kurumu, 1988.

Kurzman, Charles, ed. *Modernist Islam: 1840-1940*. Oxford: Oxford University Press, 2002.

Leaman, Oliver. "Nursi's Place in the Ihya Tradition." *The Muslim World* 89.3–4 (1999) 314–24.

Lewis, Bernard. *The Emergence of Modern Turkey*. Oxford: Oxford University Press, 1961.

MacFarlane, Charles. *Turkey and Its Destiny: The Result of Journeys Made in 1847 and 1848 to Examine into the State of That Country*. London: Murray, 1850.

Mardin, Şerif. *Religion and Social Change in Modern Turkey: The Case of Bediüzzaman Said Nursi*. Albany, NY: State University of New York Press, 1989.

Mardin, Şerif. *The Genesis of the Young Ottoman Thought*. Princeton: Princeton University Press, 1962.

Meriç, Ümit. "Mustafa Paşa ve Mithat Paşalarla A. Comte ve Pozitivistler." *Tarih ve Toplum* 14 (February 1985) 31–32.

Mermer, Yamina B. "The Hermeneutical Dimension of Science: A Critical Analysis Based on Said Nursi's *Risale-i Nur*." *The Muslim World* 89.3–4 (1999) 270–96.

Müller, Max. *Lectures on the Origin and Growth of Religion*. London: Longmans, 1878.

Ortaylı, İlber. *İmparatorluğun En Uzun Yüzyılı*. Istanbul: Hil Yayın, 1995.

———. *Studies on Ottoman Transformation*. Istanbul: ISIS, 1994.

Özervarlı, M. Sait. "Alternative Approaches to Modernization in the Late Ottoman Period: Izmirli Ismail Hakkı's Religious Thought against Materialist Scientism." *International Journal of Middle East Studies* 39.1 (2007) 77–102.

———. "Intellectual Foundations and Transformations in an Imperial City: Istanbul from the Late Ottoman to the Early Republican Periods." *The Muslim World* 103.4 (2013) 518–34.

———. "Modification or Renewal? Elmalılı Hamdi's Alternative Modernization Project in Late Ottoman Thought." In *Modernism and Modernity in the Mediterranean World*, edited by Luca Somigli and Domenico Pietropaolo, 43–60. New York: Legas, 2006.

———. "The Reconstruction of Islamic Social Thought in the Modern Period: Nursi's Approach to Religious Discourse in a Changing Society." *Asian Journal of Social Science* 38 (2010) 532–53.

———. "Said Nursi's Project of Revitalizing Contemporary Islamic Thought." In *Islam at the Crossroads: On the Life and Thought of Bediüzzaman Said Nursi*, edited by İbrahim Abu-Rabi', 317–33. New York: State University of New York Press, 2003.

———. "Transferring Traditional Islamic Disciplines into Modern Social Sciences in Late Ottoman Thought: The Attempts of Ziya Gökalp and Mehmed Şerafeddin." *The Muslim World* 97.2 (2007) 317–30.

Parla, Taha. *The Social and Political Thought of Ziya Gökalp 1876–1924*. Leiden: Brill 1985.

Parla, Taha, and Andrew Davison. *Corporatist Ideology in Kemalist Turkey*. Syracuse, NY: Syracuse University Press, 2004.

Robinet, Jean-François. *Adresse des positivists a Midhat-Pasha, ancient Grand-Vizir de l'Empire ottomane*. Paris: Ritti, 26 Auguste 1877.

Sarıkaya, Yaşar. *Medreseler ve Modernleşme*. Istanbul: İz Yayıncılık, 1997.

Somel, Selçuk Akşin. *The Modernization of Public Education in the Ottoman Empire, 1839–1908: Islamization, Autocracy, and Discipline*. Leiden: Brill, 2001.

Tevfik, Rıza. "Hürriyet: İngiliz Hakim-i Meşhuru John-Stuart Mill Hürriyeti Nasıl Anlıyor?" *Ulum-i İktisadiyye ve İctimaiyye Mecmuası* 2.5 (1325 A.H.) 19–39.

———. "Spencer'in Felsefesi." *Ulum-i İktisadiyye ve İctimaiyye Mecmuası* 1.2 (1324 A.H.) 233–45.

Toderini, Giambattista. *Letteratura Turchesca*. Venezia: Presso G. Storti, 1787.

Tunç, Mustafa Şekib. "Memleketimizde Felsefenin İnkişafı." *İş* 3.10 (1937) 25–34.

Ülken, Hilmi Ziya. "Durkheim et l'enseignement des sciences sociales en Turquie." *Sosyoloji Dergisi* 15 (1960) 7–27.

———. *Türkiye'de Çağdaş Düşünce Tarihi*. İstanbul: Ülken Yayınları, 1992.

Vahide, Şükran. "The Book of the Universe: Its Place and Development in Bediüzzaman's Thought." In *A Contemporary Approach to Understanding The Qur'an: The Example of the Risale-i Nur*, edited by the Publisher, 466–83. Istanbul: Sözler Neşriyat, 2000.

———. *Islam in Modern Turkey: An Intellectual Biography of Bediüzzaman Said Nursi*. Edited by İbrahim Abu-Rabiʻ. New York: State University of New York Press, 2005.

Voll, John O. "The Mistaken Identification of 'The West' with 'Modernity.'" *American Journal of Islamic Social Sciences* 13.1 (1996) 1–12.

———. "Renewal and Reformation in the Mid-Twentieth Century: Bediüzzaman Said Nursi and Religion in the 1950s." *The Muslim World* 89.3–4 (1999) 245–59.

Waardenburg, Jacques. "Some Thoughts on Modernity and Modern Muslim Thinking about Islam." In *Islam and the Challenge of Modernity*, edited by Sharifah Shifa al-Attas, 317–50. Kuala Lumpur: ISTAC, 1996.

Wasti, Syed Tanvir. "Feylesof Rıza." *Middle Eastern Studies* 38.2 (2002) 83–100.

Yalçınkaya, M. Alper. *Learned Patriots: Debating Science, State, and Society in the Nineteenth-Century Ottoman Empire*. Chicago: Chicago University Press, 2015.

# 2

# Said Nursi from the Ottoman to the Republican Periods

## A Short Biography

ŞÜKRAN VAHİDE

### INTRODUCTION

BEDİÜZZAMAN SAİD NURSİ (?1877–1960) divided his life into two main periods. He was dismissive of his earlier life insofar as it was in the second period, that of the "New Said," that he founded the movement for the revitalization of religious belief and moral renewal based on his writings, known collectively as the *Risale-i Nur* (hereafter, *Risale*). This movement, with its various offshoots, has continued to grow since his death, and is now active in many countries worldwide. The New Said emerged following the Ottoman defeat in the First World War and saw the first thirty-eight years of the Turkish Republic. Nursi's early life, the "Old Said" era, coincided with the final decades of the Ottoman Empire, and was spent in active pursuit of solutions for the backwardness of his native Kurdistan, with a view to aiding the unity and progress of the empire as a whole. Nursi's dismissal of his many useful ventures in this period was most probably due to his seeking solutions in the fields of politics and public life rather than religious renewal, and in philosophy and science rather than in divine revelation; he later considered these pursuits counterproductive to his constant objectives of renewal and revitalization. This chapter will trace Nursi's life and describe his endeavors in both periods, briefly placing them in historical context.

## EARLY YOUTH AND EDUCATION, ?1877–1891

Said Nursi[1] was born in the village of Nurs south of Lake Van in the east of the Ottoman Empire, in either 1873 or 1877.[2] The fourth of seven children, his father was a smallholder whose family belonged to the settled Kurdish population of the area. Nursi's exceptional learning abilities soon became apparent. He began to learn the Qur'an at the age of nine, then for the following five years moved from *medrese* (religious school) to *medrese* in the region, impatient with the lengthy curricula and insisting on following his own course. Most of the *medreses* in the region were owned and run by members of the Naqshbandī/Khālidiyya order.[3] By 1891 he had mastered the basics of Arabic grammar, the first stage of *medrese* education. That year he travelled up to Bayezid (now, Doğubeyazıt), where he entirely immersed himself in his studies and again skipped many works in the syllabus. In three months he acquired sufficient knowledge to be awarded a diploma certifying that he had completed the course.[4] From this point on Nursi was almost entirely self-taught. Setting out on foot alone, he travelled back south to the area of Bitlis and Siirt. He had disdained to submit to any of the Khālidī shaykhs[5] and had rejected the educational methods followed in their *medreses*. From an early age, he clearly felt that fresh methods were needed to meet the challenges of the times.

## MOLLA SAID EMBARKS ON THE CAREER OF RELIGIOUS SCHOLAR AND TEACHER, 1892

Said Nursi had now earned the right to the title Molla. Measuring up successfully with the local *ulema* (religious scholars) in the places he visited led him to give up the dervish life he was inclined to in order to establish himself as a religious scholar and teacher. Presenting himself to be questioned concerning his knowledge in the *medreses*, as was the custom, he invariably replied correctly to all the questions put to him, and also won the debates and contests of knowledge held to test him. He gained a reputation for having prodigious knowledge and began to attract students and a following.

---

1. The earliest biographies are: Abdurrahman (Nursi's nephew), *Bediüzzaman'ın Tarihçe-i Hayatı*, published in 1919 (hereafter, Abdurrahman), and a brief variant version: Hamza. *Bediüzzaman Said-i Kürdî'nin Tercüme-i Hâlinden bir Hülâsadır* (hereafter, Hamza), appended to: Badī'uzzamān, *Ishārāt al-iʿjāz*. In 1957–58, Nursi directed several of his unnamed students in the writing of his "official" biography: Collective, *Risale-i Nur Müellifi Bediüzzaman Said Nursî* (hereafter, *Tarihçe*). See also Mardin, *Religion and Social Change*; Şahiner, *Bilinmeyen Taraflarıyla Bediüzzaman Said Nursî*; Badıllı, *Bediüzzaman Said Nursî'nin Mufassal Tarihçe-i Hayatı*; Vahide, *Islam in Modern Turkey*.

2. The date for Nursi's birth in his "official" biography is 1873: *Tarihçe*, 31, whereas the most frequently cited date, 1293 according to the Rumi calendar, that is, 1877, is recorded in two official documents dated 1921; see Albayrak, *Son Devrin İslam Akademisi*, unpaged appendix; Eng. tr., Vahide, *Islam in Modern Turkey*, 144–45.

3. Bruinessen, *The Kurds and Islam*, 17; Bruinessen, *Agha, Shaikh, and State*, 222–34.

4. Abdurrahman, 8–10. Due to the antiquated teaching and learning methods, cumbersome texts, and copious commentaries and glosses, the course generally took up to fifteen or twenty years.

5. Nursi nevertheless had great affection and respect for several of the Khālidī shaykhs, and had benefited from them in various ways. See, Abdurrahman, 28; Algar, "Sufism and *Tarikat*," 200–204; Nursi, *Barla Lahikası*, 276, 285; Nursi, *Emirdağ Lahikası* (hereafter, *Emirdağ*), 1:53.

Nursi's decision to pursue scholarship should be seen against the backdrop of the political problems of the region: the presence of foreign missionaries and the Armenian question,[6] both of which were exploited by the European powers to the detriment of the Ottomans, as well as the widespread lawlessness and disorder. These matters must have been a constant reminder of Ottoman weakness vis-à-vis Europe, which reflected on Islam itself, and acted as a spur and goad to an ambitious young Muslim scholar like Nursi.

When continuing his debates with the *ulema*, Nursi made a visit to the town of Mardin in 1892. There, he became acquainted both with the struggle for constitutional government—of which he was later to become an energetic supporter—and with the wider issues facing the Islamic world.[7] Nevertheless, it was not politics, but education where Nursi had decided to direct his energies—and specifically the revitalization of *medrese* education[8]—since it formed the first step towards securing the unity and progress of his fellow Kurds within the Ottoman Empire.[9] It was also around this time that he further established himself by mediating in tribal disputes, a function undertaken by influential shaykhs.[10]

## BITLIS 1896–98, VAN 1898–1907

Throughout this period Said was continuing to amass knowledge, memorizing standard works on the Islamic sciences. His two-year stay in Bitlis 1896–98 at the invitation of the governor, Ömer Sabri Bey,[11] provided further opportunity for study: he memorized around forty basic texts on both such "instrumental" sciences as Arabic grammar and logic, and the "high" sciences of Qur'anic exegesis (*tafsīr*) and theology (*kalām*). His intention was to preserve his position among the *ulema*.[12] It was after he moved to Van that he is recorded as mixing with government officials, teachers, and other secular intelligentsia, although in Bitlis he had stayed in the governor's residence.

In Van, too, he found favor with the governor, Tahir Pasha,[13] who offered him valuable support and patronage, although one of Molla Said's most salient characteristics was his independence. Most importantly, Tahir Pasha encouraged Nursi in his studies, allowing him the use of his library and giving him the opportunity to meet with the officials. For it was Nursi's acquaintance with the official classes, who had been the recipients of the European-inspired educational reforms of the Tanzimat and were skeptical of the ability of Islam to secure the empire's future, that led him to realize that as they stood, the Islamic sciences,

---

6. See, Mardin, *Religion and Social Change*, 42–65.

7. Bediüzzaman, *Münâzarat*, 145.

8. Molla Said-i Kürdî, ". . . Mebusana Hitabı," 196.

9. Bediüzzaman, "Fihriste-i Makâsıdı," 3; "Kürdler Neye Muhtaçtır?," 2.

10. Abdurrahman, 18–22. For the shaykhs, see Bruinessen, *Agha, Shaikh, and State*, 233–34.

11. Ömer Sabri Pasha was governor of Bitlis from 1312 Rumi/1896 to 1314/1898. See, Kırmızı, *Abdülhamid'in Valileri*, 210. For Nursi's reference to his stay, see, *Emirdağ*, 1:263.

12. Abdurrahman, 26.

13. İşkodralı Tahir Paşa (1849–1913) was governor of Van from 1898 to 1906, when he was appointed governor of Bitlis. See, Kırmızı, *Abdülhamid'in Valileri*, 12.

particularly *kalām*, could not answer such doubts. He therefore himself took up the study of the modern sciences, mastering them sufficiently to defeat in argument the teachers in the government schools. It was by virtue of these achievements that he became widely known as Bediüzzaman (the Wonder of the Age). Modern science was unknown to the *ulema* of the region and even denounced by them. Molla Said, however, formulated plans for *medrese* reform based on the joint teaching of the modern and religious sciences, which he applied in his *medrese* in Van. His goal was to found a university-level *medrese* in Kurdistan where his ideas would be put into practice. A large part of his time in Van was spent travelling around the tribes of the area, working as a teacher, guide, and mediator in disputes.[14] He thus established himself in the region as an independent, respected, and influential religious scholar.

Tahir Pasha was also instrumental in setting Nursi on his future course both by informing him of intended threats to the Qur'an, so that Nursi made the understanding and proof of it his ultimate goal;[15] and by encouraging him to visit Istanbul. In Istanbul, however, Nursi got caught up in the constitutional movement and with his educational projects, so turned to expounding the Qur'an only just before the First World War.

## ISTANBUL 1907-10

Molla Said arrived in Istanbul towards the end of November 1907, armed with a letter of introduction to Sultan Abdülhamid from Tahir Pasha;[16] his intention was to obtain official support for his educational projects. He was eventually successful, probably the following May, in presenting a petition to the palace. In the intervening period, he endeavoured to establish himself among the *ulema* and intellectuals of Istanbul, not for self-promotion, but to draw attention to the problems of his underdeveloped home region.[17]

Nursi's enterprise in seeking government support for his educational projects was not well received at the palace, and landed him in custody. However, this did give him the opportunity to explain his ideas on the subject,[18] and led to those ideas being discussed by the cabinet, though without favorable result. It is not known when Nursi regained his freedom, but within three days of the constitution being reinstated on July 23, 1908 he was joining in the universal rejoicing, and gave a public address entitled "An Ode to Freedom" (*Hürriyet'e Hitab*),[19] extolling constitutionalism and freedom from despotism, and urging that they be based on the shari'a.

Nursi's initial support of the Committee of Union and Progress (hereafter, CUP), which had forced the reinstatement of the constitution, turned into opposition—a position shared by the majority of leading *ulema* and intellectuals—as within months it resorted to illegal methods and violence in order to retain power. Nevertheless, his belief in

---

14. Abdurrahman, 29–31.
15. Nursi, *Sikke*, 76.
16. BOA.Y.PRK.UM, 80/74. 10/L/1325. The text was later published in the press: Molla Said-i Meşhur, "Kürdler Neye Muhtaçtır?" *Şark ve Kürdistan*, 2; Eng. tr., Vahide, *Islam in Modern Turkey*, 37–38.
17. See, Ibid., 38–41.
18. Ibid., 42–49.
19. Bediüzzaman, "Hürriyete Hitab," 4–17.

the principles of constitutionalism as the sole solution for the empire's ills was undamaged, and he continued to propagate them among the students and teachers of the Istanbul *medreses* and his many fellow countrymen resident there. During these months he was very active, also publishing his ideas in the now free and flourishing press.

## VAN—DAMASCUS—ISTANBUL—RUMELIA—VAN, 1910-14

Nursi returned to Van in the spring of 1910, where he made a tour of the tribes of the area accompanied by some of his students, in order to explain to them the benefits of constitutionalism. He later published his exchanges with them in the work *Münâzarat*, together with a work addressing the *ulema*, *Muhâkemat*.[20] He then made his way south to Damascus, where the following spring he gave his celebrated sermon in the Umayyad Mosque at the invitation of the local *ulema*. In the face of growing Arab nationalism, it was a call to unity, again of a non-political nature, and to moral renewal and cooperation in progress and development.[21]

Nursi returned to Istanbul via Beirut in order to renew his efforts to win official support for his proposed university/*medrese*, the *Medresetü'z-Zehrâ*. He found the opportunity to present his case when invited to join the Sultan's Rumelia journey in June 1911[22] as a representative of the eastern provinces. His case was accepted in principle, and he later received an advance of a thousand gold liras.[23]

Nursi made his way back to Van, where he continued to teach his students and compose works based on his teaching. One was on logic, *Ta'liqāt*,[24] another was his Qur'anic commentary *Ishārāt al-i'jāz*, which he continued on the front after the outbreak of the First World War.[25] The foundations of the *Medresetü'z-Zehrâ* were finally laid on the shores of Lake Van, but its construction ceased in the disturbed conditions running up to the War.

## THE GREAT WAR, 1914-18

Said Nursi enlisted in the army as a regimental *mufti* on the declaration of war, August 3, 1914, and was sent to the Caucasian Front at Erzurum, where he fought until his division fell back to Van in April 1915. After the fall of the city, he was detailed by Enver Pasha, the commander-in-chief of the army, to raise a militia force, which he led in many valiant actions for which he was later awarded a war medal. Among his recorded services are such humanitarian acts as saving women and children from certain slaughter in the midst of the fighting and sending them back to their people.[26] He fell prisoner to the Russians after the fall of Bitlis (March 3, 1916), and was sent eventually to a prisoner-of-war camp in Kosturma on

---

20. Bediüzzaman, *Azametli Bahtsiz bir Kıta'nın ... Münâzaratı*; Bediüzzaman, *Mariz bir Asrın ... Muhâkematı*.

21. Badī'uzzamān, *al-Khuṭba al-Shāmiyya* [1329/1911]; Eng. tr., *The Damascus Sermon*.

22. Zürcher, "Sultan Mehmed V's Visit to Kosovo," 84–94.

23. Badıllı, *Mufassal Tarihçe*, 1:345–53.

24. Badī'uzzamān, *Ta'liqāt*.

25. Badī'uzzamān, *Ishārāt al-I'jāz*; Eng. tr., *Signs of Miraculousness*.

26. BOA.HR.SYS.HU, kr.110, dos.12-2, nr. 19–33.

the Volga in northwestern Russia. He escaped in the spring of 1918 and made his way to Istanbul, arriving around June 20, 1918.

## ISTANBUL, 1918-22

Nursi returned to a city that was to be occupied by allied forces soon after the signing of the Mudros Armistice (October 30, 1918), signaling the start of a bitter period of defeat,[27] and one of inner turmoil for himself. He was worn out by his experience of war and captivity and the death and destruction he had witnessed, but was given no chance to rest and recuperate. Within weeks of his return, he was appointed on the recommendation of Enver Pasha to the newly founded *Darü'l-Hikmeti'l-İslâmiye*, a learned body attached to the *Şeyhülislâm*'s Office.[28] For two years after his return, Nursi was active combating the occupying forces with his pen, and publishing other works on topical and religious subjects.[29] He was a founder-member of the Green Crescent Society (*Hilâl-i Ahdar Cemiyeti*), established on March 5, 1920 to combat the spread of alcohol and other addictions,[30] and of the *Medrese* Teachers' Association (*Cemiyet-i Müderrisîn*), founded February 19, 1919, to promote the interests of the *ulema* and Muslims generally.[31] He opposed the setting-up of an autonomous Kurdistan in the vacuum left by the collapse of the empire. He also supported the independence movement in Anatolia, holding out in the *Darü'l-Hikmet* against the pressure brought to bear on it to openly oppose and condemn the national forces in Anatolia.

Since his return, Nursi had requested leaves of absence from his post and had retreated into solitude, overcome by distress at events. Then, sometime after the reoccupation of Istanbul by the British in March 1920, he experienced a "spiritual awakening" that resulted in the birth of the New Said. He himself explained how, overwhelmed by his realization that all his acquired knowledge provided no answers concerning death and the ephemerality of things, he eventually found enlightenment in the Qur'an and its teaching of divine unity.[32] The Arabic works[33] he wrote in the course of this quest contain descriptions of his momentous inner struggle and how the way of the New Said finally became clear to him.[34] In contrast to the ways of the *ulema* on the one hand and the Sufis on the other, this path was traversed through an alliance of reason and heart. This resulted in the pieces he wrote being in the form of "reasoned proofs," and since they replied to doubts arising from science and philosophy, these proofs answered his questions and healed his wounds. They also led him to "the way of reflec-

27. See, Criss, *Istanbul Under Allied Occupation*.

28. Berkes, *Development*, 416; Albayrak, *Son Devrin*, 7–9.

29. Vahide, *Islam in Modern Turkey*, 153. See chapters 7 and 8 for this period.

30. Şahiner, *Bilinmeyen*, 185–86.

31. Tunaya, *Türkiye'de Siyasal Partiler*, 2:382–85. Nursi was a founder-member of this society: ibid., 2:383 fn 6.

32. See, Nursi, *Letters*, 409–10.

33. In Turkish transcription: *Katre, Habbe, Şemme, Zerre, Hubab, Zuhre, Şule*, and their addenda; see Nursi, *Emirdağ*, 1:42. They were subsequently (in 1955) collected together in *al-Mathnawī al-'Arabī al-Nūrī*.

34. See Nursi, *al-Mathnawī al-'Arabī*, 35, 170, 206, 318; Nursi, *Mesnevî-i Nûriye*, 7–8; Nursi, *Flashes*, 303–5.

tive thought," and thus formed the basis of the New Said's thought, which within a few years would find expression in the *Risale*.³⁵

Throughout this period the War of Independence was continuing in Anatolia. In April 1920 the nationalists formed a national assembly in Ankara. In recognition of his services to the cause, Nursi received repeated invitations to join them, which he responded favorably to only after the final victory in September 1922. He arrived in Ankara in November.

## ANKARA, 1922-23

Nursi met with both success and disappointment in Ankara. On November 1, the Grand National Assembly voted to abolish the sultanate and assigned itself the right to appoint the caliph. In the midst of these events, he was given an official welcome in the assembly and asked to offer prayers for its success.³⁶ Differences that had been submerged during the independence struggle surfaced after the elation at the final victory subsided. Although one of Nursi's aims in coming to Ankara had been to support those wanting to strengthen the Islamic component of government and rebuild Islamic civilization, he found to his dismay that some influential deputies in the assembly were in favor of further Westernization and secularization. He saw too that atheistic currents were active, so published a work to rebuff them,³⁷ and also a ten-point "manifesto," dated January 19, 1923, calling on the deputies to perform their religious obligations, especially the prayers. Reputedly, its effectiveness caused Mustafa Kemal Pasha, President of the Assembly, to berate Nursi in public,³⁸ to which he received an angry response.³⁹ Nursi's main purpose in coming to Ankara, however, was once again to seek support for his university, the *Medresetü'z-Zehrâ*. Although some Westernist deputies opposed the idea, he convinced the majority that an institution offering religiously based modern education was necessary in the ethnically mixed eastern provinces, for a bill proposing its building⁴⁰ was signed by 167 deputies out of 200 and sent before the necessary committees. But once again, the project came to nothing; in March 1924, the *medreses* were closed down, and by the time it was finally rejected by the assembly the following year, Nursi had been sent into exile.

In April 1923, Nursi left Ankara, having turned down Mustafa Kemal's offers to join the new government as a deputy, with posts in the administration of religious affairs and as chief preacher in the eastern provinces. He had seen the way things were going and understood

---

35. Nursi, *Flashes*, 377-78.

36. *TBMM Zabit Ceridesi*, I/24 (9 Teşrin-i Sâni 1338 [9 November 1922]), 457.

37. Nursi, *Flashes*, 233. The short Arabic work was included in *al-Mathnawī al-'Arabī*, when that collection was compiled by Nursi in 1955, in the section entitled *Dhayl al-dhayl li'l-ḥabba*. See, Nursi, *al-Mathnawī al-'Arabī*, 252-55; *Mesnevi-i Nûriye*, 130-33. An expanded version was included in *Lem'alar* (*The Flashes Collection*) as the 23rd *Lem'a*, "Tabiat Risalesi" (Treatise on Nature); Eng. tr. *Flashes*, 232-53.

38. Mustafa Kemal had in fact dismissed the GNA's resident Imam (prayer-leader) soon after the victory in the War of Independence. See Hanioğlu, *Atatürk*, 145-46, quoted from Bozkurt, *Atatürk İhtilali*, 139.

39. *Tarihçe*, 125-28. For partial translation of the manifesto, see Vahide, *Islam in Modern Turkey*, 169-71.

40. *TBMM Zabit Ceridesi*, I/27 (21.2.1339 [1923]), 419.

that he could not work along with the new leaders. He returned to Van by way of Istanbul, where he retired into seclusion.[41]

## VAN, 1923–25 OR 1924–26

It is not known how long Nursi remained in Istanbul on his way to Van. He may have stayed for some time, because four of his works were published that year (1923), with one possibly the next year.[42] These were the continuation of the first works of the New Said, and were all in Arabic. At some point, he made the journey to Van, where he stayed firstly with his brother Abdülmecid, and then retreated to a mosque. It was a grievous experience for him to see at first hand the destruction wrought on the city during the war, with his *medrese* razed to the ground, and only the memory of his students and friends remaining; most had been killed or had died in the migrations.[43] The survivors noted the change in him—his sober clothes and his speaking of matters to do with belief, emphasizing their importance. In the summer months he retired with a small group to a mountain cave, where he spent his time in prayer and contemplation.

No political solutions had been found for the area. The conflicting ambitions of those seeking independence or autonomy for Kurdistan and others led to unrest, which was exacerbated by the government's radical secularizing reforms. In February 1925 a revolt[44] broke out that was to have far-reaching consequences, not least for Nursi, who was approached in the run-up to the revolt, but had refused to give it his support.[45] He was sent into exile as a result.

There are conflicting reports as to when Nursi was arrested and attached to one of the caravans of deportees being sent into exile in western Anatolia. Evidence now shows that it was in 1926.[46] Having made the overland trek to Erzurum and Trabzon, the group of several hundred exiles was boarded on a ship for Istanbul. An event occurred here on April 29, 1926 that was mentioned both in the daily press and in Nursi's writings: the burning down of the former Şeyhülislâm's Office, which had been made into a girls' high school on the abolition of the institution in March 1924.[47]

Nursi was sent first of all to the town of Burdur. Early the next year, he was removed to the provincial center of Isparta, from where, on March 1, 1927,[48] he was taken alone by rowboat to the remote village of Barla, up the western side of Lake Eğirdir, since there was no road.

---

41. *Tarihçe*, 131.

42. *Zuhra*, AH 1341 [1922–23]; *Dhayl al-Zuhra*, AH 1341 [1922–23]; *Dhayl al-Ḥubāb*, AH 1341 [1922–23]; *Shuʻla*, AH 1342 [1923–24].

43. Nursi wrote a moving piece describing this. See *Flashes*, 313–14.

44. The Shaykh Said Revolt. See, Olson, *Emergence*, esp. 91–127; Bruinessen, *Agha, Shaikh, and State*, 265–305; Zürcher, *Turkey*, 178–79.

45. For anecdotes describing this, see, Vahide, *Islam in Modern Turkey*, 180–82.

46. It was previously thought to have been March 1925. See, Ibid., 182–85.

47. *Cumhuriyet* 2/710 (17 Şevval 1344/30 Nisan [April] 1926), 2; 2/711 (18 Şevval 1344/1 May 1926), 1; Nursi, *Sikke*, 130.

48. T. C. Dahiliye Vekâleti. Emniyet İşleri Umum Müdürlüğü. İ. B., Hususî: 4883. 27/5/1935, including an official report, headed: "Isparta Vilâyetinin 125 sayılı ve 16/5/935 tarihli yazısı," (Isparta Province Memo No: 125, dated 16 May 1935), which gives this date.

# BARLA, MARCH 1, 1927–JULY 24, 1934

Said Nursi had not been convicted of any crime that he should have been sent into exile. He was one of the at least twenty thousand people[49] of all sorts, including tribal and religious leaders, who had been deported from Eastern to Western Anatolia under the emergency powers accorded the government by the Law on the Maintenance of Order, rushed through the assembly on the eruption of the Shaykh Said Revolt in 1925 and another the following year. He was an influential religious leader who in Ankara in 1922–23 had not concealed his opposition to the evident intention of Mustafa Kemal to pursue the path of Westernization, and had refused to be co-opted into the regime. As Mustafa Kemal consolidated his power, all opposition was silenced and opponents were eliminated, even heroes of the War of Independence.[50]

The 1920s saw the string of secularizing reforms that abolished the remaining Islamic institutions, and outlawed such symbols of Islamic identity as the fez and Arabic alphabet and replaced them with Western-inspired models. During these years, Nursi was relatively free. He attracted "students" by degrees from among the local people, who acted as scribes and helpers. He began to compose pieces proving questions of belief, worship, and morals according to the Qur'an-inspired method of the New Said. And he was very much alone, spending much of his time in the mountains and countryside in thought, prayer, and contemplation. It was after 1931, when the sole political party, the People's Party, adopted a policy of actively propagating Kemalism among the population at large and the regime took on a totalitarian character,[51] that the authorities stepped up their pressure on him by posting two of their agents to Barla—the district officer and a teacher. They made it their business to keep Nursi under surveillance, harass him, and restrict his movements.[52] How these developments impacted on Nursi can be seen from his letters, many of which form the answers to questions put to him by his students. Nursi found his solitude conducive to writing, for in the less than seven-and-a-half years he was in Barla he completed the collections that were to be designated *Sözler* (The Words) and *Mektûbat* (Letters), and the first eighteen parts of *Lem'alar* (Flashes). The greater part of the pieces consists of proofs and explanations of the main "truths of belief" and of a whole range of questions related to religion. The first was a substantial treatise proving the resurrection of the dead and life of the hereafter,[53] which he was able to have printed in Istanbul and sent to Ankara to be given to deputies in the national assembly. But this was an exception, for the composition, writing out by hand, and dissemination of the treatises were all of necessity car-

49. Zürcher, *Turkey*, 179.

50. Koçak, "Siyasal Tarih (1923–1950)," 101–4.

51. In 1931, Atatürk's party, the People's Party, virtually merged with the state and gained control over all aspects of political life. It founded the cultural and educational institutions called People's Houses and People's Rooms the aim of which was to propagate the six principles of Kemalism among the population. See, Zürcher, *Young Turk Legacy*, 253–57; Tunçay, *Türkiye Cumhuriyeti'nde*, 317–31; Koçak, "Siyasal Tarih," 113–16.

52. Nursi, *Letters*, 415–18; Badıllı, *Mufassal Tarihçe*, 813–21.

53. The Tenth Word. See, Nursi, *Words*, 59–132.

ried out away from the prying eyes of the authorities, especially after the banning of the Arabic alphabet in 1928.

Nursi was asked repeatedly about his situation, and also about his attitude to politics.[54] As far as his relations with the government were concerned, his legal position seems unclear. He believed he had been exiled unjustly, since he had neither been involved in the Shaykh Said Revolt, nor had committed any misdemeanor. In consequence, he refused to recognize the government in the matter, declining to report every day to the police while in Burdur, and in Barla declining to make petition to the authorities on the announcement of the two general amnesties of 1928 and 1933,[55] which was the condition for their application. He argued that the treatment he received was arbitrary and outside the law, and that it was only his serving religious belief that drove the authorities to isolate and mistreat him "on account of atheism," making false accusations of political involvement. But further to this, he appears to have himself chosen to remain in Barla because he saw the advantages of his situation for his service to religion, which he continued to pursue in a low-key, unobtrusive manner in disregard of the ongoing secularizing and Westernizing reforms.

In regard to secularism, Nursi did not overtly oppose it, but faced with the Kemalist version,[56] he on occasion cited a more liberal interpretation based on the principles of the separation of worldly and religious matters and freedom of conscience, according to which his service of the faith was perfectly licit.[57] As time progressed, however, and his writings spread and his students increased in number, the measures taken against them became increasingly severe, leading to three terms of imprisonment in the period until 1950. The reasons given in the report cited above for his removal from Barla to the provincial center of Isparta (July 24, 1934) were his spreading "negative propaganda" and receiving visitors and communicating with people in various other places; in other words, he was suspected of having founded a new *tarikat* or Sufi order,[58] which had been outlawed in 1925. Inquiries of all involved were launched. In Isparta, Nursi was held under close surveillance, with police posted permanently on his door. Nevertheless, during the nine months he was there, a small number of his students continued to serve his needs, and he composed from the Nineteenth to the Twenty-Sixth Flashes.[59] On the orders of the interior ministry, on March 30, 1935, his house was searched and some handwritten books and papers seized. Following further searches in various places, on April 25, the arrests of Nursi and his students began. They were put in Isparta Prison.

## ESKİŞEHIR PRISON, MAY 1935–MARCH 1936

That the episode of Eskişehir Prison was a storm in a teacup is shown among

---

54. Nursi, *Letters*, 63–67, 82–96.

55. *TBMM Zâbit Ceridesi*, III/4 (7.5.1928), 61–62; IV/17 (26.10.1933), 51–57.

56. See, Zürcher, *Turkey*, 243–44; Hanioğlu, *Atatürk*, 159, 230, 231.

57. See, Nursi, *Rays*, 289–91, 305, 386; Nursi, *Letters*, 493; *Tarihçe*, 195, 205.

58. "Isparta Vilâyetinin 125 sayılı ve 16/5/935 tarihli yazısı," (1–2).

59. Badıllı, *Mufassal Tarihçe*, ii, 934–35.

other things[60] by the complaint lodged in the above-mentioned report[61] about the public prosecutor's having blown up the case—in reality "a minor police incident"—out of all proportions, with alarmist "false reports." These reports caused the minister of the interior himself, together with the commander-in-chief of the gendarmerie, fifty-two gendarmes, twenty police and three inspectors, plus two more inspectors from the ministry of justice and two from the civil service, to all descend on Isparta as though to quell some major disturbance threatening the state. And what might have been an unimportant case was imbued with considerable seriousness. Around May 12, Nursi and thirty-one of his students were bundled into trucks and taken eventually to Eskişehir Prison, some 330 kilometers to the north, to be joined by others from elsewhere, some of whom had not even a tenuous connection with Nursi. Despite the appalling conditions, for Nursi, who was put into solitary confinement, and for his students, who were in wards, the prison became a "*Medrese*-i Yûsufiye," a school recalling the trials of the Prophet Joseph, the patron of prisoners. As far as they could, the students continued to write out Nursi's writings; here he composed the Twenty-Eighth to the Thirtieth Flashes and the First and Second Rays, and when the trial commenced, his defense speeches.[62]

According to Nursi himself, witnesses in the prison, and the way the trials were conducted, the court was under pressure from Ankara to convict and even to condemn him. Certainly he was frequently denied his rights when it came to his defense, which he conducted himself. He nevertheless succeeded in refuting all but one of the charges against him, which were made under article 163 of the criminal code and involved the exploitation of religious sentiments in such a way as to disturb public order. He refuted "exploiting religion with the idea of political reaction," founding a new *tarikat* or Sufi order, and setting up an organization for political ends, at the base of all of which was the infringement of the principle of secularism. But he was eventually convicted due to a short piece expounding verses of the Qur'an about the veiling of women and women's inheritance, although it had been written before the foundation of the republic and acceptance of the new codes. Arbitrarily he was sentenced on August 19, 1935 to one year and fifteen days imprisonment with hard labor, which was reduced to eleven months, to be followed by one year's compulsory residence in Kastamonu; fifteen of his students were sentenced to six months, and the rest were acquitted. He was released in March, 1936.

## KASTAMONU, MARCH 1936– SEPTEMBER 27, 1943

For his first three months in this provincial center in the Ilgaz mountains to the south of the Black Sea, Nursi stayed "as a guest" in a police station, until he was assigned a small house immediately opposite and in full view of it. With his thus

---

60. See Vahide, *Islam in Modern Turkey*, 215–25 for the whole episode of Eskişehir Prison.

61. "Isparta Vilâyetinin 125 sayılı ve 16/5/935 tarihli yazısı," (5–6).

62. Nursi, *Müdâfâlar*, 33–93. The pieces here comprise only one of three parts of Nursi's defense, and were designated the Twenty-Seventh Flash.

being under constant scrutiny, his seven-and-a-half years in Kastamonu were extremely constraining. He nevertheless attracted loyal helpers and students who, despite the dangers, assisted him personally and with the writing out and distribution of the *Risale*. A constant stream of letters and parts of the *Risale* passed between him and his students in Isparta and elsewhere, carried by what became known as Nur postmen, since it was unsafe to use the state postal service.

Nursi carried on writing, completing the Third to the Ninth Rays inclusive. The Seventh Ray, *The Supreme Sign* (*Âyetü'l-Kübra*), marked the high point or final form of the reflective thought on "the book of the universe" that forms the basis of his method of qur'anic interpretation. It consists of the observations of a traveler through the cosmos who learns of the testimony of each of its realms to its Maker's existence and unity. Addressing the reason by utilizing logic, reasoned argument, and scientific facts, and addressing the heart by uncovering the Divine Names and acts behind the apparent face of beings, Nursi aimed to induce in his readers what he called "certain, affirmative belief" (*iman-ı tahkiki*), belief that would remain unshaken by the assaults and skepticism of science. He also aimed to demonstrate the logical absurdity of nature and causation, the concepts underlying the scientism that was one of the mainstays of Kemalism. Many of his letters to his students now explained this method, offering comparisons between it and the ways of Sufism on the one hand, and formal Islamic *kalām* (theology) on the other.[63]

There were now ever-increasing numbers of Nur students writing out the *Risale*. Although previous to this Nursi had begun to urge them to develop a collective consciousness and sense of unity as a step towards building a community, he now sought to explain to them that community's objectives and mode of service, and to encourage them to cultivate the moral qualities necessary for its formation.[64] A defining characteristic of the Nur community was non-involvement in politics and disregard for all "worldly" matters.[65] Nursi's insistence on this should be seen against the backdrop of the repression and economic difficulties of the war years.[66] Sporadic arrests of Nur students in various places and seizure of the *Risale* led finally in early September, 1943, to the arrest of Nursi and twenty-two others, to be followed by their transferral to Denizli in south-western Turkey.

## DENIZLI PRISON, OCTOBER 1943–JUNE 1944

In all, 126 Nur students from all over Turkey were taken to Denizli of whom seventy-three were put in the prison. It seemed a fatal blow had been dealt to the movement, but contrarily to all expectations the imprisonment yielded numerous beneficial results, not least the bringing together of the students, and the countrywide publicizing of the *Risale* due to the court case and the sympathy it aroused. Nursi's sojourn in Denizli Prison was noteworthy for the pieces[67] he wrote

63. For example, Nursi, *Letters*, 38–39, 381–82, 383–86; Nursi, *Kastamonu Lahikası* (henceforth, *Kastamonu*), 10, 25, 171–72, 174–75.

64. Ibid., 102, 106–7, 135, 186, 190, 200.
65. Ibid., 69–71, 73–77, 80–81, 84, 104, 108.
66. Zürcher, *Turkey*, 207–9.
67. The Eleventh Ray, *The Fruits of Belief*; Eng. tr., Nursi, *Rays*, 213–91.

for the prisoners despite his solitary confinement in a tiny dank cell. A network of sympathizers and students distributed those writings both inside and outside the prison and the area around it. The prison truly became a "School of Joseph," and many of the other prisoners reformed, a fact that counted in their favor during their trials. The charges brought against the students in Denizli Court were virtually the same as in Eskişehir. As on that occasion, Nursi exposed the plans that had been laid against them by "atheists" because of their "belief and . . . services to belief and to public order." Building his defense on a defense of the *Risale*, he reused his previous speeches, to a large extent. On the strength of a positive report from the committee of experts in Ankara, on June 16, 1944, the court finally ruled for their acquittal and immediate release, as well as the return of any confiscated books.

## EMIRDAĞ, AUGUST 1944–JANUARY 1948

Despite the process of democratization that was instituted after the Second World War, marked by the founding of the Democrat Party (DP) in January 1946 and softening of some of the strict secularist measures,[68] the RPP government was unrelenting in its treatment of Nursi and the Nur movement. This progressively worsened over the 1940s. Nursi was found a small house, actually two rooms over a shop, in the center of the provincial town of Emirdağ. Again, he was isolated and watched, but he continued to attract students who, with considerable self-sacrifice, devoted themselves to assisting him. He was now around seventy years of age and suffered from various chronic ailments. He nevertheless tirelessly persisted not only in his own daily worship and contemplation, but also in his work on the *Risale*. The composition of it was now mostly complete; Nursi's most time-consuming task was the correction of handwritten parts, which were now put into collections for distribution. Its dissemination was greatly facilitated when a Nur student bought one of the first duplicating machines to come to Turkey in 1946 or 1947; it could duplicate a hundred pages a minute.[69] With some collections, such as *A Guide For Youth*, being printed in the Latin alphabet for the first time, the *Risale* was immediately accessible to the younger generation, who no longer knew the Ottoman/Arabic alphabet; this attracted young students, who were to become the backbone of the Nur movement after 1960.

As the Nur movement took form, Nursi explained the mode of struggle he foresaw it pursuing within society, which he perceived was threatened by a general moral decline due to the loosening of traditional Islamic constraints on the one hand, and by the rise of communism and its moral depredations on the other. This objective he called the "jihad of the word" or moral jihad (*cihad-ı mânevî*) and positive action.[70] It was the struggle of the *Risale* first and foremost to develop certain, conscious belief, with the ability to withstand and combat the assaults of materialistic science, and also to strengthen traditional Islamic values, which would

---

68. Koçak, "Siyasal Tarih (1923–1950)," 138–39, 141–43.

69. Badıllı, *Mufassal Tarihçe*, 2:1373, 1407–9.

70. See, Nursi, *Rays*, 289–90; *Emirdağ*, 2:241–47.

have the effect of strengthening society to stand firm against the stratagems of the forces of irreligion to destabilize it and cause anarchy; this was a moral and intellectual jihad against the moral and spiritual destruction wrought by materialistic and atheistic currents.

Towards the end of 1947, the authorities stepped up their harassment of both Nursi and Nur students in other provinces. In January the arrests started. Nursi and a total of fifty-four students were rounded up for questioning and a smaller number were sent to the prison in Afyon.

## AFYON PRISON, JANUARY 23, 1948–SEPTEMBER 20, 1949

Although Nursi laid the blame on a small minority of 5 percent within the RPP and exonerated the rest,[71] it was clear that both the imprisonment of himself and his students and their trial[72] were part of an official conspiracy by the ruling party aimed at dealing a final blow at them now it was approaching the end of its more than quarter-century in power. It was only Nursi's indomitable spirit, and the students' devotion to him and to the *Risale*, that allowed them to survive the inhuman treatment, and to conduct their defenses despite being deprived of many rights. The outcome of the trial was a foregone conclusion, for the charges against them were the same as previously, although Denizli Court had acquitted them. The case dragged on for six-and-a-half months, the court finally announcing its verdict on December 6, 1948. It sentenced Nursi to two years' imprisonment for "exploiting religious feelings and inciting the people against the government," which was reduced to twenty months because of his age. His students received varying sentences, mostly six months.[73] They applied to the court of appeal, which on June 4, 1949, quashed Afyon Court's decision. They then should have been released, but having recourse to illegal delaying tactics, Afyon Court made Nursi serve the full term it had sentenced him to. He was finally released in the early hours of September 20, 1949.[74]

## THE THIRD SAID, SEPTEMBER 1949–MARCH 23, 1960

The victory of the Democrat Party in the general elections of May 1950 marked the start of a new era for Nursi and the Nur movement, as it did for the country. Turkey now had a government that had wide popular support and intended to reflect the people's will. It was sympathetic towards religion, with its first piece of legislation being the repeal of the ban on the Arabic call to prayer (June 16, 1950). Moreover, following the pro-Western policy adopted by the RPP after the Second World War,[75] it took a firm stand against communism; Nursi said that it was assisting the Nur students in their struggles to prevent the moral corruption of atheism. He persisted in supporting the DP throughout the 1950s, even as its popularity waned.

It was partly because of the greater interest Nursi evinced in current affairs during this period that it became known

---

71. Nursi, *Emirdağ*, 2:245.
72. See, Vahide, *Islam in Modern Turkey*, chapter 15.
73. Badıllı, *Mufassal Tarihçe*, 3:1696, 1698
74. Ibid., 1712–14, 1718.
75. Tunçay, "Siyasal Tarih," 178–79.

as the Third Said era, but it has also been associated with the great expansion in the activities of the Nur students, the spread of the *Risale*, and the growth of the movement.[76] This was greatly enhanced after 1956, when all the legal restrictions on the *Risale* were finally lifted, and students in Ankara began to have it printed on modern presses in the Latin alphabet. It also continued to be copied out by hand in thousands of homes throughout Anatolia.

The general amnesty of July 14, 1950 brought Nursi his freedom and finally he settled in Isparta, where he kept with him a small number of young students to train and to assist him. Although the DP went some way to answering popular demand for greater religious freedom, it remained bound to the Kemalist principle of secularism,[77] which was reflected in continuing pressures on Nursi and the Nur students and legal procedures being brought against them. Court cases brought him twice to Istanbul, in 1952 and 1953, which once again served to publicize his work and increase the numbers of his sympathizers and followers.

Nursi's seeing at close quarters the results of Westernization and secularization led him to expound a number of basic moral principles taken from the Qur'an and hadith that he called "fundamental laws," the application of which he believed would rectify such social ills as wastefulness, idleness, pleasure-seeking, and economic inequality. As principles that can be practiced personally in daily life, they reflect his desire to effect moral-social renewal from the bottom up. He sought to inculcate them in his students, and to draw the attention of Prime Minister Menderes and religious deputies towards them by letter.[78] He also looked on them as a salve for the wounds afflicting humanity generally in the post-war world. He believed the universal practice of these principles would bring justice and happiness, and contribute to the building of "true" civilization. General reconciliation was a goal he both worked for and urged in this period, on the level of science and learning, and politically, as is seen from his letter to the president and prime minister congratulating them on the signing of the Baghdad Pact in 1955.[79] Related to this were his efforts to strengthen "the brotherhood of belief" between Muslims worldwide by having the *Risale* translated into Arabic and copies sent to many different countries.

Despite his advancing years, Nursi devoted much time to tasks related to the *Risale*. He instituted the communal readings (*ders*) of the *Risale* that were to become the central activity of the Nur community, and each day would hold readings with the students who stayed with him. All over Turkey, Nur centers (*medrese* or *dershane*) where the students would gather opened. Nursi made a series of visits to Ankara and Istanbul at the end of 1959 to visit some of these, but by early 1960, his health was failing. On March 20, 1960 he set off with three of his students for Urfa in south-east Turkey, where on March 23 he died peacefully in his sleep.[80]

76. *Tarihçe*, 537–39.
77. Zürcher, *Turkey*, 243–45.
78. Nursi, *Emirdağ*, 2:81–84, 98–101, 162–64, 172–75. Also, Vahide, *Islam in Modern Turkey*, 317–18, 327–29.
79. Nursi, *Emirdağ*, 2:222–25.
80. Şahiner, *Bilinmeyen*, 446–63; Badıllı, *Mufassal Tarihçe*, 3:2128–30, 2140–52.

## CONCLUSION

With the didactic writings of his maturity, the *Risale-i Nur*, Said Nursi sought to impart a conscious living faith to all classes of people so as to rebuild the Muslim self and revitalize Turkish society, which, in his view, was being threatened by the penetration of materialistic science and philosophy. For he believed that both worldly and otherworldly salvation were to be found in divine revelation and the application of its principles, whereas materialism was destructive of humanity and detrimental to its progress. Faced with a powerful Westernizing regime, he had the percipience to abandon politics and despite his disadvantageous position, turn his attention to the renewal of religious belief. In time, this resulted in the formation of the Nur community, which adhering to his principles of the jihad of the word and positive action, spearheaded a wide movement for religious and moral revitalization.

## BIBLIOGRAPHY

Abdurrahman. *Bediüzzaman'ın Tarihçe-i Hayatı*. Istanbul: Necm-i İstikbal Matbaası, 1335 [1919].

Albayrak, Sadık. *Son Devrin İslam Akademisi: Dar-ül Hikmet-il İslamiye*. Istanbul: Yeni Asya, 1973.

Hamid Algar. "Sufism and *Tarikat* in the Life and Works of Bediüzzaman Said Nursi." *Journal of the History of Sufism* 3 (2001) 199-221.

Badıllı, Abdülkadir. *Bediüzzaman Said-i Nursî'nin Mufassal Tarihçe-i Hayatı*. 3 vols. 2nd ed. Istanbul: n.p., 1998.

Berkes, Niyazi. *The Development of Secularism in Turkey*. New York: Routledge, 1998.

BOA.HR.SYS.HU, kr.110, dos.12-2, nr. 19-33. In *Arşiv Belgelerine Göre Kafkaslar'da ve Anadolu'da Ermeni Mezâlimi. I. 1906–1918*, edited by İsmet Binark, 191-92. Ankara: Devlet Arşivleri Genel Müdürlüğü, 1995.

BOA.Y.PRK.UM, 80/74. 10/L/1325. In Cemalettin Canlı and Yusuf Kenan Beysülen, *Zaman İçinde Bediüzzaman*, 104. Istanbul: İletişim, 2010.

Bozarslan, M. Emîn, ed. *Kürd Teavün ve Terakki Gazetesi* 1908–1909. Uppsala: Deng, 1998.

Bozkurt, Mahmut. *Atatürk İhtilali*. Istanbul: Istanbul Üniversitesi Yayınları, 1940.

Bruinessen, Martin van. *Agha, Shaikh, and State. The Social and Political Structures of Kurdistan*. London: Zed, 1992.

———. *The Kurds and Islam*. Tokyo: University of Tokyo, 1999.

Canlı, Cemalettin and Yusuf Kenan Beysülen. *Zaman İçinde Bediüzzaman*. Istanbul: İletişim, 2010.

Collective, *Risale-i Nur Müellifi Bediüzzaman Said Nursî. Hayatı, Mesleki, Tercüme-i Hâli*. Istanbul: Sözler, 1976.

Criss, Nur Bilge. *Istanbul Under Allied Occupation 1918–1923*. Leiden: Brill, 1999.

*Cumhuriyet* [*Gazetesi*] 2/710 (17 Şevval 1344/30 Nisan [April] 1926).

———. 2/711 (18 Şevval 1344/1 May 1926).

Hamza. *Bediüzzaman Said-i Kürdî'nin Tercüme-i Hâlinden bir Hülâsadır*. Addendum to: Badî'uzzamān. *Ishārāt al-i'jāz fī maẓānn al-ījāz*. Istanbul: Evkâf al-Islāmiye Matbaası, 1334 [1918].

Hanioğlu, M. Şükrü. *Atatürk: An Intellectual Biography*. Princeton: Princeton University Press, 2011.

Isparta Vilâyetinin 125 sayılı ve 16/5/935 tarihli yazısı," (Isparta Province Memo No. 125, dated May 16,1935). In T. C. Dahiliye Vekâleti. Emniyet İşleri Umum Müdürlüğü (Interior Ministry of the Turkish Republic. General Directorate of Police). İ. B., Hususî: 4883. 27/5/1935.

Kırmızı, Abdulhamit. *Abdülhamid'in Valileri. Osmanlı Vilayet İdaresi 1895–1908*. Istanbul: Klasik, 2008.

Koçak, Cemil. "Siyasal Tarih 1923–1950." In *Türkiye Tarihi 4: Çağdaş Türkiye 1908–*

1980, edited by Sina Akşin, 85–173. Istanbul: Cem, 1989.

Mardin, Şerif. *Religion and Social Change in Modern Turkey: The Case of Bediüzzaman Said Nursi*. Albany, NY: State University of New York Press, 1985.

Nursî, Bediüzzaman Said. Ottoman Turkish and Arabic texts published under various names. The names are alphabetized according to transcription, then the works:

———. Badīʻuzzamān. *Dhayl al-Dhayl*. In Nursi, *al-Mathnawī al-ʻArabī al-Nūrī*, edited by Iḥsān Qāsim al-Ṣāliḥī, 252–55. Istanbul: Sözler, 1994.

———. Badīʻuzzamān. *Dhayl al-Ḥubāb*. Istanbul: Necm-i Istikbal Matbaası, AH 1341 [1922–23].

———. Badīʻuzzamān. *Dhayl al-Zuhra*. n.p., AH 1341 [1922–23].

———. Badīʻuzzamān. *Ishārāt al-Iʻjāz fī Maẓānn al-ījāz*. Istanbul: Evkāf al-Islāmiye Matbaası, 1334 [1918].

———. Badīʻuzzamān. *al-Khuṭba al-Shāmiyya* [1329/1911], bound in *Sunûhat*. Istanbul: Evkāf al-Islāmiye Matbaası, 1338/1336 [1920].

———. Badīʻuzzamān. *al-Mathnawī al-ʻArabī al-Nūrī*, edited by Iḥsān Qāsim al-Ṣāliḥī. Istanbul: Sözler, 1994.

———. Badīʻuzzamān. *Shuʻla*. Istanbul: Necm-i Istikbal Matbaası, AH 1342 [1923–24].

———. Badīʻuzzamān. *Taʻlīqāt ʻalā Burhān al-Galanbawī fī'l-Manṭiq*. Facsimile edn. Istanbul: Sözler, 1993.

———. Badīʻuzzamān. *Zuhra*. Istanbul: Necm-i Istikbal Matbaası, AH 1341 [1922–23].

———. Bediüzzaman. *Azametli Bahtsız bir Kıta'nın, Şanlı Tali'siz bir Devletin, Değerli Sahibsiz bir Kavmin Reçetesi veyâhud Bediüzzaman'ın Münâzaratı*. Kostantıniye: Matbaa-yı Ebuzziyâ, 1329 [1913].

———. Bediüzzaman. *Mariz bir Asrın, Hasta bir Unsurun, Alil bir Uzvun Reçetesi veyâhud Saykalu'l-İslâmiyet veyâhud Bediüzzaman'ın Muhâkematı*. Kostantıniye: Matbaa-yı Ebuzziyâ, 1327 [1911].

———. Bediüzzaman-ı Kürdî. "Hürriyete Hitab." In *Nutuk*. Dersaadet [Istanbul]: İkbal-ı Millet Matbaası, 1326 [1910].

———. Bediüzzaman-ı Kürdî Saîd. "Bediüzzaman-ı Kürdî'nin Fihriste-i Makâsıdı ve Efkârının Programıdır." *Volkan* 84 (3 Rebiülevvel 1327/ 12 Mart 1325/ 25 March 1909).

———. Molla Said-i Kürdî. "Bediüzzaman Molla Said-i Kürdî'nin Mebusana Hitabı." *Kürd Teâvün ve Terakkî Gazetesi* 4 (3 Zilhicce 1326/13 Kânunıevvel 1324/[26 December 1908]), 16. In *Kürd Teâvün ve Terakkî Gazetesi*, edited by M. Emin Bozarslan, 196. Uppsala: Deng, 1998.

———. Molla Said-i Meşhur. "Kürdler Neye Muhtaçtır?" *Şark ve Kürdistan* 1 (25 Şevval 1326/[11] Teşrin-i Sâni 1324/ 19 Teşrin-i Sâni-i Efrenci [November] 1908).

Nursî, Bediüzzaman Said. Turkish texts published in Latin script:

———. *Barla Lahikası*. Istanbul: Envar, 1994.

———. *Emirdağ Lahikası*. 2 vols. in 1. Istanbul: Envâr, 1992.

———. *Kastamonu Lahikası*. Istanbul: Sinan Matbaası, 1960.

———. *Mesnevî-i Nûriye*. Translated by Abdülmecid Nursî. Istanbul: Sözler, 1980.

———. *Müdâfâlar*. Istanbul: Tenvir, 1988.

———. *Sikke-i Tasdik-i Gaybî*. Istanbul: Sinan Matbaası, 1960.

Nursi, Bediüzzaman Said. English translations of Nursi texts:

———. *The Damascus Sermon*. Translated by Şükran Vahide. Istanbul: Sözler, 2004.

———. *The Flashes Collection*. Translated by Şükran Vahide et al. New ed. Istanbul: Sözler, 2011.

———. *Letters 1928–1932*. Translated by Şükran Vahide et al. New ed. Istanbul: Sözler, 2010.

———. *The Rays Collection*. Translated by Şükran Vahide et al. Istanbul: Sözler, 2013.

———. *Signs of Miraculousness: The Inimitability of the Qur'an's Conciseness.*

Translated by Şükran Vahide. New ed. Istanbul: Sözler, 2013.

———. *The Words*. Translated by Şükran Vahide et al. Istanbul: Sözler, 2008.

Olson, Robert. *The Emergence of Kurdish Nationalism and the Sheikh Said Rebellion, 1880–1925*. Austin: University of Texas Press, 1989.

Şahiner, Necmeddin. *Bilinmeyen Taraflarıyla Bediüzzaman Said Nursî*. 61st printing. Istanbul: Nesil, 2011.

*TBMM Zabit Ceridesi* (Proceedings of Grand National Assembly), I/24 (9 Teşrin-i Sâni 1338 [9 November 1922]), 457.

———. I/27 (21.2.1339 [1923]), 419.

———. III/4 (7.5.1928), 61–62.

———. IV/17 (26.10.1933), 51–57.

T. C. Dahiliye Vekâleti. Emniyet İşleri Umum Müdürlüğü (Interior Ministry of the Turkish Republic. General Directorate of Police). İ. B., Hususî: 4883. 27/5/1935.

Tunaya, Tarık Zafer. *Türkiye'de Siyasal Partiler*. Vol. 2. *Mütareke Dönemi 1918–1922*. 2nd ed. Istanbul: Hürriyet Vakfı, 1986.

Tunçay, Mete. "Siyasal Tarih (1950–1960)." In *Türkiye Tarihi 4: Çağdaş Türkiye 1908–1980*, edited by Sina Akşin, 177–87. Istanbul: Cem, 1989.

———. *Türkiye Cumhuriyeti'nde Tek Parti Yönetimi'nin Kurulması 1923–1931*. Istanbul: Tarih Vakfı, 2005.

Vahide, Şükran. *Islam in Modern Turkey: An Intellectual Biography of Bediüzzaman Said Nursi*. Albany, NY: State University of New York Press, 2005.

Zürcher, Erik J. "Sultan Mehmed V's Visit to Kosovo in June 1911." In *The Young Turk Legacy and Nation Building. From the Ottoman Empire to Atatürk's Turkey*, 84–94. London: I. B. Tauris, 2010.

———. *Turkey: A Modern History*. London: I. B. Tauris, 1998.

———. *The Young Turk Legacy and Nation Building: From the Ottoman Empire to Atatürk's Turkey*. London: I. B. Tauris, 2010.

# 3

# My Meeting with Said Nursi

## Fred A. Reed[1]

1. Excerpted from my *Then We Were One: Fragments of Two Lives*. Vancouver, Talonbooks, 2011.1

When we first met in Urfa, in southeastern Turkey, Bediüzzaman ("Wonder of the Age") Said Nursi had been dead nearly forty years. Yet for me he lived and breathed with vitality: bright of eye, broad of vision, stern yet compassionate of manner, indomitable of character, impatient and demanding of himself, generous and forgiving of others. In the person of Nursi, I encountered a man who had known great suffering, had ample reason to hate, and yet did not. Because he had known deprivation and hunger, I reasoned, he had ample reason to crave wealth and provision, and yet he did not.

In him, I found a challenge to my deeply ingrained, long-standing belief in retributive social justice through violence if necessary, a belief that he gradually and inexorably, as though in the course of a low-key and intimate conversation, broke down and reconstituted.

From my mother, I inherited an inclination to stubbornness and a certain sharpness of tongue; from my father, shyness and a reverence for the beauty of the world. In Said Nursi, I located many of those same qualities in proportions that varied, and that ebbed and flowed like the tides, the hours, or the seasons. His stubbornness and sharpness of tongue well suited him to challenge the last of the Ottoman sultans, and later, the founder of the Turkish Republic, Mustafa Kemal Atatürk. The wild mountains in which he grew up had nourished a love for the beauty of the world he would locate in the Second Revealed Book, that of the Universe.

Under the hammer blows of World War I, the Ottoman Empire that had spanned three continents and represented, through the office of the caliph, the transnational Pan-Islamic ideal, disintegrated. Nursi, who had fought in the freezing trenches of Eastern Anatolia against invading Russian and Armenian forces, was captured and imprisoned in

Kostroma, northeast of Moscow on a bend of the Volga. In his two-year confinement, and in the ensuing years of upheaval, the hot-blooded combatant for the Islamic state saw his own ideals brought low.

Renouncing militant action, Nursi threw his support behind Atatürk and the newly founded republic. But, he insisted, the new state must respect the religious beliefs of the immense majority of its citizens.

Atatürk had other ideas, and men like Nursi were given no choice except to comply. Swept up on the flimsy pretext of Kurdish separatist rebellion (though he had warned precisely and explicitly against such action and called for unity of Turks and Kurds), Said was dispatched into a cycle of exile, house arrest, trial, and imprisonment that would last thirty years.

How could I not be drawn to such a man? In him action coexisted with spiritual depth and fierce pride. He was a contrarian and a political activist with an enlightened vision for the future of his society, a religious scholar of prescience and presence whose world had come tumbling down around him, putting his beliefs to the severest test. He had rubbed elbows with the mighty and, in exile and deprivation, kept the company of shepherds and fishermen, and communed with the birds. Almost single-handedly, he kept faith—his own and that of a nation—alive in its darkest hour.

In the sharpness and intransigence of his character, Said Nursi reminded me of Nikos Kazantzakis, the Cretan author whose books had set my mind ablaze and in my youth carried me away with him to Greece. Like Kazantzakis, who revealed his artistic destiny in his failure as a philosopher, Nursi, too, had failed in his attempts at worldly action. The wreckage around him he transmuted into undiluted spiritual essence. No need, after all, for me to abandon Kazantzakis; he had become part of the substrate of idea and principle, like the sediment of deep geological time, adopted, set aside or transcended, forever integrated into the finely textured composite of what we call experience. The more I heard about Bediüzzaman Said Nursi, the more I wanted to know. I set out to find him.

In the late fall of 1997, I traveled to Istanbul to begin research for the book that would become Anatolia Junction.[2] Since I'd first heard Nursi's name six months before in what I naively saw as a chance encounter in an office in the industrial suburb of Yenibosna, and learned more about his life and times, it had become clear that he held the key to the story I wanted to tell: that of the hidden history of the country itself as seen through one man's attempt to recover the spiritual heritage Atatürk had attempted—but failed—to sweep away.

My research would necessarily follow two simultaneously converging and diverging trajectories: one through time and the other through space. In my effort to understand the present, I would plunge into the past in an attempt to grasp the elusive figure of Nursi. And at the same time, I would travel to the farthest geographical limits of his homeland in eastern Turkey, to trace his path and follow in his footsteps.

Immediately on arrival, I queried Professor Faris Kaya, who had befriended

2. Fred A. Reed, *Anatolia Junction: A Journey into Hidden Turkey.* Vancouver, Talonbooks, 1999

me at the meeting in Yenibosna and, more importantly, helped me define my project. Would he be able to facilitate what must have seemed like an unconventional undertaking? Not only could he do so, he responded; he would place at my disposal all the resources of what I would come to identify as the loosely structured movement dedicated to preserving and studying Nursi's works.

"They are expecting you," Professor Kaya concluded. "You will get all the assistance you need from the students of Said Nursi, wherever you go. But you must make haste," he added. "Winter is coming and heavy snow will block the roads and cut off the villages you wish to visit."

I set out, on a waveringly secularist wing and a prayer.

In the late 1990s, private airlines had not yet begun to challenge the monopoly of Turkish Airlines, the national carrier. Seats were scarce to all destinations, but Professor Kaya's office found me a one-way ticket for Erzurum, the quintessentially Turkish city in High Anatolia. From there, I would continue my way eastward by bus, the preferred mode of transport in the hinterland. The transportation costs would be mine to assume; in the cities and towns I visited, I would be a guest of Nursi's students, as his followers styled themselves. A two-man delegation of local leaders, academics who could speak a bit of English, met me at the airport when I arrived on the first leg of my journey to the East, just as later others like them would await me at bus stations at subsequent stops. Guest status in cities like Erzurum, Van, Diyarbakır, and Urfa conferred no privilege and less luxury.

Accommodation consisted of a bed in the movement's dormitories, called *dershane* (houses of recitation); my food was the residents' meager rations, washed down with unlimited amounts of tea. Often I craved fresh fruit. As my hosts hurried me past public markets on the way to the day's destination, I would cast longing glances over the displays of oranges and apples and bananas, pomegranates and quinces; salivate over tubs of thick golden comb honey, catch the whiff of freshly ground coffee wafting on the breeze, pick up the yeasty tang of fresh-baked bread. It could wait.

For evening entertainment, the young men who had come to live in the *dershane* while they attended high school or university would gather by the dozens in the central reading room, where they sat cross-legged on the floor while an elder read, then analyzed a passage from Nursi's *Risale-i-Nur*, the "Treatise of Light." Though television and newspapers were nowhere to be seen, the young men I encountered possessed an acute awareness of injustice in the world, particularly as it impacted their coreligionists, whether in Turkey or Palestine. Nursi's elegant, lofty, incantatory language gave both shape and substance to their piety. Among them I encountered little doctrinal rigidity, and much enthusiasm and curiosity. Most of these young men, of late high school and early college age and of modest background, had never met a foreigner before, least of all at such close range. Their gentleness, the sweetness of their smiles and their determination to try out their English and share their beliefs—and have me pronounce those beliefs acceptable, even though I was singularly unqualified to do so—never failed to move me. Though they could not have known it, and though I ill understood it myself at the time, these young men, in their sincerity, slowly rekindled in me hope for a common future, breathed new life into the ties of fraternity that my younger brother's death by his own hand had severed nearly twenty years before.

As I made my way across the parched landscape of Far Anatolia during those vivid late autumn days, everything conspired to reaffirm the spirit of resistance I'd detected in Said Nursi. In Van, the ancient city at the eastern extremity of the lake of the same name, my hosts escorted me through the ruins of the old town, which had been bombarded into rubble by invading Russian forces during the bitter fighting of 1916. Where violent combat once raged, now weeds reigned luxuriant in the remains of the prosperous houses and commercial buildings that a century ago had made the city, with its Armenian majority, seem like a tiny outpost of Europe.

Here Nursi had petitioned Sultan Abdülhamid for permission and support to establish an educational institution that would combine the religious curriculum of the Islamic *madrasa* tradition with the European outlook of scientific rationalism that had penetrated the empire in the late nineteenth century. The salvation of the nation, and of the worldwide Muslim community, would depend on the cooperation and coexistence of traditional religious knowledge with the Western curriculum.

At the far western extremity of the lake lay Tatvan, my point of departure for the uplands of the Taurus Range. The Kurdish insurgency, which was then at its peak, made nighttime travel unsafe; military checkpoints lined the main highways, and village guards armed and paid by the government patrolled the interior. "More dangerous than the Kurdish rebels of the PKK," said some, in a whisper, referring to the Kurdistan Workers' Party. As for the army, it swaggered about like an occupying power during daylight hours, but withdrew to the safety of its fortified encampments as soon as the sun sank low in the sky.

After a journey of three hours by car over dusty and potholed roads, we reached Nurs, the village where Nursi was born and that gave him his last name, nestled in a gentle fold of the canyon wall overlooking a swift stream. Electricity had only recently arrived; nothing else had changed. Visitors were infrequent, his distant relatives assured us, as we feasted on a simple and hearty meal of stewed chickpeas and fermented wheat and yogurt soup, fresh-baked bread, and cheese. Better that way, they said. An influx of devotees, no matter how well meaning, would only upset the delicate human and natural ecology of this place. That natural ecology had lavished upon the young Said the proximity of the nighttime firmament that inspired awe and reverence; the wild mountain gorges in which the Kurds had learned to cherish their independence and their sense of self-reliance.

The materialist that still lingered in me wanted to explain Nursi's character by the physical and social surroundings in which he'd grown to manhood. Yet all of what is today eastern Turkey had contrived to produce but a single Said. His roots were indeed here, in this tiny village of stone houses quarried from the cliffs that towered high above us, but he had transcended his native soil to emerge first upon a national, then an international stage.

The arid and apparently barren landscape through which I traveled, as I drew ever closer to the elusive object of my quest, concealed a secret garden of the spirit that only my pursuit of Said Nursi could have allowed me to discover. Dream tracks crisscrossed a land once peopled by a complex mosaic of populations, of linguistic and religious groups. Some of them were rigidly orthodox, others heterodox in the extreme. Sunni Muslim legal scholars intersected, though perhaps never personally met, the stargazing, planet-worshipping Sabians of Harran through the esoteric doctrines that had survived the centuries; itinerant Sufis carried their message of self-effacement in coarse-cloth beggar's bags slung over their shoulders.

To them all, and particularly to the Sufis, Nursi had lent a voracious ear. He sat at their feet, drew nourishment from their teachings, debated them with all the self-assurance of a prodigy, absorbing as he did the core curriculum of Islam's traditional intellectual discipline. The pupil's role grated on his hypersensitive and prideful nature; not for him the discipline of sitting for months, perhaps years, at a master's feet; not for him the lengthy apprenticeship that, among the Sufis, represented both a way of life and a spiritual path. Nursi had already begun to formulate the dictum that his legatees in Istanbul had repeated to me: "Ours is not a time for Sufi orders—*tarīqa*; it is a time for the truth of the higher Reality—*haqīqa*."

Anxious to measure himself against this truth, Nursi had set out from his native village to Van and, then, in an arching path through the ancient cities of Far Anatolia. A feeling of urgency likewise spurred me on. If I hastened my pace, perhaps I could overtake him, catch sight of him or, failing that, a glimpse of his shadow, for now I found myself crossing the same landscape he had crossed and, perhaps, traveling the same roads. On a golden afternoon in the hillside city of Mardin, I rested in the courtyard of the Ulu Camii, the great mosque, and looked upwards at the minaret. There, on a visit to the town, Nursi had circumambulated the cornice as a crowd of the astonished faithful looked on from twenty-five yards below.

The boldness of his gesture surely matched his mood. In Mardin, he had met an emissary of the mercurial crypto-Shiite Pan-Islamic reformer Jamal al-din al-Afghani. The arrival of Western colonialism in the Muslim heartland had thrown the world of Islam into a turmoil from which it is still struggling to extricate itself. Al-Afghani and his fellow reformers argued that Muslims must return to the founding tenets of their faith, purify it of the dross of superstition. But, more vitally, they must take full account of the dynamic evolution of scientific knowledge that had reduced Muslims to powerless observers of their own backwardness. Al-Afghani's message seduced—if that is the appropriate term—Said Nursi, particularly in its appeal to constitutionalism as a sovereign remedy for the despotism that had come to be identified with Islamic rule . . . and still is to this day.

Mardin, by virtue of its dramatic geographical setting overlooking the north Syrian plain, played the role of an advanced—though symbolic—observation post. The day was warm and hazy when I traveled there by minibus from Diyarbakır with two Nur students. From the esplanade of the mosque, as I gazed toward the far horizon, I imagined that I could make out the four minarets of the great Umayyad Mosque in Damascus, nearly six hundred miles to the southwest across the barren desert.

In that mosque in early 1911, Nursi delivered a sermon to an estimated ten thousand worshippers packed into its spacious prayer hall and courtyard. He addressed those present, and those "in the great mosque of the world," as he would later put it,[3] on the backwardness that afflicted Islamic civilization, and identified high among the contributing factors the love of enmity and despotism, which he likened to an acutely contagious disease.

More than a century later, Nursi's diagnosis rings as true as it did then, perhaps more so. His hearers may have paid him heed, but the high and mighty, the despots at whose golden-slippered feet he laid the cause of Islam's decline, have learned precious little, and—with the possible exceptions of Imam Khomeini's overthrow of the Shah and the first years of the AK (Justice and Development) Party in Turkey—achieved even less. Nursi's suggested remedy, a return to the guiding principles of the Qur'an, may no longer be equal to the task. The decay has become pervasive; the putative center of the Muslim world has been captured by a toxic variant of literalist extremism that would exclude any but self-proclaimed and self-defined "true believers" from the circle of divine intimacy, though such intimacy cannot be circumscribed by the salaried exegetes of the Saudi religious establishment, and as surely excludes them as it lies within reach of all who seek it.

Such gloomy thoughts had not even entered my mind thirteen years before, as the express bus from Diyarbakır sped southwestward toward Urfa, the last stop on my December journey into Nursi's past. Of the many places to which my spiritual travels have brought me, none except Damascus could rival, in its timeless feel, this millennia-old city on the edge of Upper Mesopotamia that claims to be the birthplace of the Prophet Abraham, he who is revered as the forefather of Jews, Christians, and Muslims, and who subsequently returned to join the combat against idols.

The atmosphere when I arrived in mid-afternoon sparkled with an effervescence that might well have been the projection of my emotional state. Old Urfa nestles in a shallow depression surrounded by ochre hills, an oasis in the shale-strewn high desert at the center of which lies a large rectangular ceremonial pool surrounded by tree-shaded tea gardens and religious dependencies known as the Halillürahman Dergah. The pool, part of an intricate system fed by underground springs, teems with hundreds of thousands of plump and glossy carp.

The low, sand-colored dwellings and narrow lanes of the old quarter, sparsely planted with palm trees, could plausibly have witnessed the arrival of the venerable patriarch Abraham on his way to Canaan. The archetypal agriculturalist, Abraham had come to warn the ruler, Nimrod the Hunter King, against idol worship, and in so doing had humiliated the monarch. For that offense, he must die:

---

3. Bediüzzaman Said Nursi, *The Damascus Sermon*, www.saidnur.com/foreign/en/risaleler/sermon1.htm

*They said: Burn him and help your gods
If you have been ones who do so!*
(Qur'an, 21:68)[4]

The king's men lashed the prophet and patriarch to the stake and kindled the blaze. God saw this and commanded:

*O fire!
Be coolness and peace for Abraham!*
(Qur'an, 21:69)[5]

As the flames licked at Abraham's flesh, they were miraculously transmuted into cooling water, and the logs into fishes. From the escarpment where Nimrod's throne stood, the water poured down the steep slope and into the basin below to form a pool, constantly replenished and teeming in perpetuity with plump and glossy carp, into whose mouths visiting pilgrims throw handfuls of food specially prepared for them.

To this place, where caravans have for millennia passed, came Bediüzzaman Said Nursi, in late March 1960, on his last earthly voyage, with a high fever and with certain knowledge of his death, as his metallic-gold Chevrolet, a gift of his devoted followers, made its way across the barrens of Anatolia toward the fatal rendezvous in Urfa.

Room 27 of the Hotel İpek Palas, which in 1960 had been Urfa's finest, had not been touched by any of the subsequent cut-rate renovations that had reduced it to the mean, dingy, and foul-smelling place I visited nearly forty years after Said Nursi's death. The wall clock still shows ten minutes to three, the hour at which the ailing Said departed this world on March 23, as the friends that who had been keeping deathwatch murmured over his lifeless body: "We are from God and to Him is our return."

On the afternoon of the following day, for we had not hurried, and had even tarried, moving hesitantly toward it in a kind of tacitly agreed, spiraling circumambulation, my guides from the local Nur movement dormitory led me to a small rotunda enclosed by wrought-iron grillwork. Through the metal filigree I looked down upon a rectangle of polished marble aligned on the southeast axis, in the direction of Mecca. They had brought me at last, by a circuitous and felicitous roundabout route that curiously replicated my long march across eastern Turkey, to Nursi's empty grave, the monument that encapsulated the paradox I had set out to unravel, and that ended by unraveling me. Here, on the day after his death, Said had been buried. The town's shopkeepers closed their doors; thousands of mourners joined the burial procession under a light spring rain.

Two months later, on May 27, 1960, a military coup overthrew the government of Turkey's first elected Prime Minister Adnan Menderes and martial law was proclaimed. A decision taken at the highest level was implemented. Two weeks more had elapsed after the coup d'état when, in early July, the military authorities declared an overnight curfew in Urfa and deployed troops and tanks around the Dergah. Then commandos armed with sledgehammers in addition to their guns forced their way into the rotunda that overlooks the sacred pool, smashed the marble sarcophagus, and from it extracted the shrouded corpse it contained. They deposited the remains in a lead coffin and then inserted it into a

---

4. *The Sublime Qur'an*, trans. Laleh Bakhtiar. www.sublimeQur'an.org, 2009.

5. Ibid.

larger wooden casket, which they loaded aboard an army aircraft at a nearby military aerodrome. From there it was flown to a smaller airfield in the interior where it was placed in a truck and driven over winding mountain roads to a location then unknown, but known today as a hillside graveyard on the outskirts of Isparta.

So ended the last days of the man they called the "wonder of the age." So, too, had ended my quest for his elusive presence.

Soon afterward I visited Isparta, where his body rested for a time before being removed once again, this time by his followers. Two hours north lay the mountain village of Barla, where Nursi spent the first years of his exile, in conversation with the birds, while he dictated what would become his Risale-i-Nur to the semi-literate peasants who became his scribes and, in delivering them to nearby towns and villages and then to the extremities of Turkey, his postmen. Nursi had warned his followers against transforming his gravesite into a place of veneration or, worse, of pilgrimage. The danger would have been real enough considering the esteem in which millions of Turks held, and still hold him, today. His followers respected the injunction to the letter: only two people, they told me, know where he was finally buried. I have some reason to believe that the number is somewhat larger, and that I may have been shown the place. Out of respect for his memory, I would never reveal it.

Instead of a shrine to which the devout would flock, his name has been perpetuated in his voluminous writings. Now, in hundreds of humble dormitories and study halls scattered across Turkey and in university classrooms and seminar rooms in many countries, Nursi's spiritual legacy is studied, quoted, weighed, and measured by the equally exacting standards of academic study and deep piety.

Said Nursi radiated qualities that drew me to him, qualities similar to those I'd found in the Iranian friends I'd come most to admire, but in him, were magnified multifold: forbearance, courage, lucidity, indomitableness, compassion for the downtrodden, and a notable lack of same for the purveyors of injustice. Those were the qualities I'd strived toward as a draft resister, a trade unionist, and a man of the political Left, qualities my wife and I hoped to transmit to our children, an intention upon which they will judge us; qualities that my brother's brief life had deeply embraced.

In Nursi I came to know the most eloquent, most vital and yet frailest and most fully human embodiment of those principles. Even though, when we met, he had been dead for forty years, I felt as though he were looking me in the eye; seeing through me, in fact. His penetrating gaze had touched my heart.

# Section Two

# THEOLOGY

# 4

# Said Nursi's Qur'anic Hermeneutics

## Yamina Mermer & İsra Yazıcıoğlu

### APPROACHING THE QUR'AN

"The Qur'an surpasses all other speech. . . . Indeed, four things enhance the power, beauty and greatness of an utterance: *speaker, audience, purpose and context*. In other words, it is not just the context that matters, unlike what the literati suppose."
—B. Said Nursi, *Mesnevî-i Nûriye*

In the above quote, Said Nursi highlights the importance of the factors that determine the meaning of an utterance, in addition to its content. Hence the very same sentence can have completely different meanings depending on who is saying it. For instance, if it is my boss who tells me, "You are fired," it will have a grave consequence, whereas if it is my friend, it might be a tease.[1] Thus, "who" is speaking in a text is as crucial in establishing its meaning as its semantic content (i.e., the words uttered). The same applies to all the other elements of speech, such as context, audience, and purpose; each is essential to interpretation and is as important

---

1. Nursi himself gives an example from a Qur'anic verse. As part of the story of Noah's ark, the Qur'an states, "And the word was spoken: 'O earth, swallow up thy waters! And, O sky, cease [thy rain]!' And the waters sank into the earth, and the will [of God] was done." (Q 11:44) According to Nursi, since the speaker here is God (i.e., the One who has genuine power over the earth and the heavens), this very command to earth and the sky is eloquent. In contrast, if it were a human being who was uttering the same command, it would not be eloquent, it would convey mere wishful thinking and delusional talk. Nursi, *Risale-i Nur Külliyatı, Mesnevî-i Nûriye*, 2:1363. *Risale-i Nur Külliyatı*, henceforth *RNK*, refers to a comprehensive compilation of Nursi's books in two volumes, totaling over two thousand pages. Whenever I refer to this source, I specify the particular book under discussion as well as the volume number. Please note that this text is also available online at <www.risaleinur.com.tr>. Unless otherwise noted, all the English translation of Qur'anic verses is from *The Message of the Qur'an*, trans. Muhammad Asad (Gibraltar: Dar al-Andalus, 1984).

as the content of the speech. In his approach to the Qur'an, in addition to the *content* of a text, Nursi takes the following four factors into account: (1) speaker (*mutakallim*), (2) audience (*mukhātab*), (3) purpose (*maqṣad*), and (4) context (*maqām*).[2]

In regards to the purpose of the Qur'an, Nursi identifies the *maqāṣid*, or overall aims, of the Qur'an. The idea is that a faithful reading of the Qur'an is only possible by reading its parts in view of these overarching purposes. Traditionally, there have been slightly different views of what these main aims of the Qur'an are. In general, however, it has been agreed upon that the Qur'an is about faith in one God and the establishment of human life in connection to and in response to this God, who is known through his different attributes, such as mercy, power, and wisdom. Similarly, according to Nursi, the Qur'an's very purpose is to guide us in answering core human questions about the meaning of existence and to solve the "riddle" of the universe. More specifically, the purpose of the Qur'an is to establish four major points: (1) *tawḥīd*, or the oneness of God—that is, the oneness of the source of all the power, beauty, and perfection reflected in the world—and *'ubudiyya*, the worshipful response to the One; (2) prophethood (*al-risālah*); (3) resurrection (*hashr*); and (4) justice (*'adāla*).[3]

According to Nursi, any particular issue mentioned in the Qur'an is discussed not for its own sake but only as a *means* to convey and teach these major aims. Indeed, the Qur'an never talks about things for their own sake but rather for the sake of their signification of God's attributes (i.e., things as signs of God). In other words, for Nursi, the Qur'anic purpose is never about giving technical information about history, social norms, or nature, or about providing literary entertainment (hence the Qur'an's insistence that it is not "poetry" or "the fables of the ancients").[4] Rather, whatever the Qur'an talks about—from a prophetic narrative, to a description of end of times, to a bee making honey, to financial contracts—the aim is to make the transcendent known to its audience.

Before we further delve into Nursi's hermeneutics of the Qur'an, it may be helpful to note some of the recent trends in hermeneutics in order to better appreciate Nursi's emphasis on the factors influencing the meaning of an utterance. Over the last several decades, "performance theory," also referred to as pragmatic or semiotic analysis, has acknowledged the importance of factors beyond the content of a text or utterance that determine interpretation. Performative hermeneutics emphasizes that each utterance or performance is a convergence of the content of what is, the fact that it is said, the particular way it is said, and the performer or particular speaker who says it to a certain audience.[5] The semantic meaning

---

2. Nursi, *Sözler*, RNK 1:195–96; Nursi, *Mesnevî-i Nûriye*, RNK 2:1363; Nursi, *Words*, trans. Şükran Vahide, 443–44.

3. For a helpful survey of *maqāsid* of Qur'an in classical scholars, as well as Nursi's, see Ziyad Khalil Muhammad al-Daghamin, "The Aims of the Qur'an in Bediüzzaman Said Nursi's Thought," in *A Contemporary Approach to Understanding the Qur'an*, 356–58.

4. Nursi, *Sözler*, RNK 1:167; *Muhâkemat*, RNK 2:1986.

5. For instance, the important philosopher of language, Herbert Paul Grice, perceptively notes that what a speaker implicates in saying what he says is carried not only by what he says but also

is not sufficient in conveying the meaning of the speech because utterances are not always used to make simple true or false statements only. In other words, they are not purely constative—rather they may comprise various kinds of speech acts. Consider a simple statement such as, "It is cold today," for instance. Depending on the "performative context," this statement could imply that "The weather is cold and hence I am not going out"; or "It is cold in here—would you please put the heater on?"; or "It is cold; let us have some hot tea." The utterance can make full sense only within its pragmatic or semiotic context. Similarly, semioticians such as Charles S. Peirce and Umberto Eco also emphasized that the words signify meaning through the implicit background of not only linguistic conventions but also the meta-linguistic contexts.[6]

Unfortunately, it is easy to overlook these other crucial aspects that effect meaning, and assume that only the verbal content matters in understanding an utterance, as Nursi points out in the opening epigraph.[7] Marco De Marinis attributes this bias towards the content of the text at the expense of its performative context to the fact that the semantic content is "generally the only component of the performance that is *present* and *persistent*." In other words, the text is the only element that is lasting and thus readily available to the interpreter whereas the rest of the performance parts are regarded as "*ephemeral* and *non-persistent*" and hence easy to overlook.[8]

At the risk of oversimplifying, we might note that in the mainstream *tafsīr* or line-by-line commentary genre, with its strong focus on linguistics, such semiotic features of the Qur'anic text have been frequently overlooked. In the *tafsīr* genre, the purely semantic approach to the text has often been privileged over semiotic reading. In contrast, Nursi insists on reading the Qur'an with an explicit emphasis on its author, purpose, and audience. Approaching the Qur'an as a believer, Nursi understands it as the highest level of revelation of the Transcendent intended for the spiritual edification of the audience. And, most strikingly, Nursi emphasizes the cosmos as the "performative context" of the Qur'an, to which we shall now turn.

---

by the fact that he says it and by his saying it in a certain way. Grice, *Studies in the Way of Words*, 39.

6. For instance, Eco emphasizes, "Without doubt verbal language is the most powerful semiotic device that man has invented, but ... nevertheless other devices exist, covering portions of a general semantic space that verbal language does not." Eco, *Trattato di semiotica generale*, 234–35, quoted in Marco de Marinis, *The Semiotics of Performance*,17. Similarly, Peirce departs from Ferdinand de Sausseure (who is considered the founder of semiotics, along with Peirce) who put forth a dyadic vision of signification. In Sausseurian semiotics, there is the sign, such as a word or an utterance, and there is the object that it represents, such as a thing or a situation. In the same way, the word "apple" represents the object apple, and the utterance "I am surprised" represents my state of mind. Peirce adds a third element, the "interpretant," to the dualistic (sign-object) account of Saussurean semiotics, and emphasized the contextual and consequential aspect of signification. See for instance, Hartshorne and Weiss, eds., *The Collected Papers of Charles Sanders Peirce*, 5:484.

7. Nursi, *Mesnevî-i Nûriye*, *RNK* 2:1363 (italics added).

8. De Marinis, *The Semiotics of Performance*, 16

## PUTTING THE QUR'AN IN ITS COSMIC CONTEXT

According to Nursi, the Qur'an is "an eternal commentary on the great book of the universe."[9] This short description encapsulates a rich (re)conceptualization of the Qur'an: the Qur'an is not just a text to comment on, rather it is itself a commentary: it is a commentary on the cosmos. In other words, the Qur'an uncovers the meaning of the universe we exist in, like a truthful commentary that explains the meaning of an utterance. Nursi's identification of the cosmos as the meta-text of the Qur'an reflects an attentive reading of the Qur'anic discourse. After all, the Qur'an employs the very same term *aya* (pl. *ayāt*, lit. "sign") to denote both the Qur'anic text and cosmic phenomena. Both the Qur'anic text and its metatext, the cosmos, are "signs" of God. In other words, both the Qur'an and the cosmos "speak of" God and "announce" his Beautiful Names, *asmā al-ḥusnā*.[10] There are, therefore, two types of divine speech: one speech through creation and the other verbal speech. Both speeches are essential for human beings to understand the meaning of their existence and the world they live in. The universe is a dynamic "discourse" constantly revealing and pointing to the transcendent, and this discourse is only intelligible through the Qur'an's interpretation.

Not only are the Qur'an and the cosmos both discourses pointing to God, but they also complement each other in their signification of the transcendent. The Qur'an complements the cosmos in that only through the Qur'an (and earlier scriptures revealed by God), can one decipher what the universe is "saying" (i.e., how the cosmos is speaking of the One). The cosmos complements the Qur'an, in that without the cosmos, the Qur'an would not make sense. To attend to the Qur'an while failing to note its cosmic context would be like listening to an incredible artist describe her artistic activity, without looking at the artistic activity itself.[11] Nursi describes how these two discourses revealed by God (*kalām al-takwinī* and *kalām al-tadwinī*) complements each other as follows: "In order *to describe His act to both eye and ear,* the Maker describes His act while performing it: as a true Artist, He unravels His art as He works it, and as a true Bestower of bounties He displays His blessings in the very act of bestowing."[12]

Furthermore, Nursi suggests that the cosmos can speak even more loudly than the verbal divine speech through the Qur'an. After all, the Qur'anic description of God as merciful would not

---

9. In a similar vein, he defines the Qur'an as "the pre-eternal translator of the mighty Book of the Universe; the post-eternal interpreter of the various tongues reciting the verses of creation; the commentator of the book of the Worlds of the Seen and the Unseen; the revealer of the treasuries of the Divine Names hidden in the heavens and on the earth; the key to the truths concealed beneath the lines of events; the tongue of the Unseen World in the Manifest World; the treasury of the post-eternal favours of the Most Merciful and of the pre-eternal addresses of the Most Holy, which come from the World of the Unseen beyond the veil of this Manifest World . . ." Nursi, *Words*, 376–77.

10. A verse that Nursi refers to often is, "The seven heavens extol His limitless glory, and the earth, and all that they contain; and there is not a single thing but extols His limitless glory and praise" (Q 17:44).

11. Nursi, *Words*, 444. See also Yamina Mermer and Redha Ameur, "Beyond the Modern: Sa'id al-Nursi's View of Science," 126–27.

12. Nursi, *Words*, trans. Ş. Vahide, 444 (italics added).

be intelligible to us if we did not actually witness any mercy in action in the world. Similarly, how could one understand the Qur'anic references to God's wisdom, without observing divine wisdom instantiated in the world?[13]

For Nursi, then, the Qur'an is like a treasure map, disclosing treasures of meaning embedded in—or expressed through—the world around and within us.[14] References to the "treasures of *asmā al-ḥusnā*" embedded in the dynamic flow of the cosmos is a common theme in the *Risale*. Without Qur'anic guidance, one experiences life like a deaf person watching a movie; he can guess part of what is going on but not quite fully understand what it is about. Through the help of the Qur'an, one can understand that while things pass away and come and go, the meanings that they signify and tantalizingly point to—such as wisdom, power, beauty, majesty, and life giving—are stable; they reveal an eternal source. In Nursi's words, "The activity of [divine] power in the cosmos and the flow of beings is so meaningful in that the All-Wise Maker is making all the beings in the universe speak through such activity.... Thus, the dynamism and transience in the cosmos ... is a *speech* glorifying God. The constant activity in the universe is a *silent speech* ...."[15] Through the guidance of the Qur'an, one learns to hear the silent speech of the universe. Thereby, the continuous flux of the world, instead of becoming painful in its apparently endless reenactments of separation and death, becomes an enjoyable show, continuously renewing the reflections of the various Beautiful Names of God.

In sum, in Nursi's hermeneutics, the cosmos is the performance of the Qur'anic text. In fact, Nursi also intriguingly, and perhaps even provocatively, describes the cosmos as "*Qurʾan al-kabīr*" or the macro-Qur'an. With a subtle use of the literal meaning of the Qur'an ("recitation"), Nursi says that the Qur'an is "reciting" the "Qur'an of the universe."[16] At this point, we may note that Nursi's reference to the universe as the meta-text of the Qur'an and his focus on the cosmic phenomena as signs of the Beautiful Names of God has precedents in classical scholars such as Abu Talib al-Makkī (d. 998), Abu Hamid Muhammad al-Ghazālī (d. 1111), and Muhyiddin Ibn ʿArabi (d.1240), as well as Jalal al-din al-Rumī (d.1273).[17]

Such emphasis on the cosmic context of the Qur'an achieves several significant results at once. First, it emphasizes the indispensability of the Qur'an in interpreting existence. Hence, unlike classical Muslim philosophers, such as Ibn Rushd (d. 1198), Nursi does not consider even the sharpest human intellect capable

---

13. Of course, for Nursi, in order to "read" the signs of mercy and wisdom in the universe, one needs to be trained by the Qur'an in understanding its "sign language."

14. Nursi, *Words*, 376–77.

15. Nursi, *Mektûbât*, *RNK*, 481. (Our translation, italics are added). See also Nursi, *Letters*, trans. Ş. Vahide, 340.

16. "In the great mosque of the universe, the Qur'an is reciting the universe. Let us listen." (Tk.: "Kâinat mescid-i kebirinde Kur'ân kâinatı okuyor, onu dinleyelim.") Nursi, *Sözler*, *RNK* 1:12; Nursi, *Words*, 44.

17. In the classical literature one finds various references to the universe as the "book of creation" (e.g., *kitab al-kawn kitab al-sunʿ*, and *kitab al-khalq wa al-tadbīr*.) Ibn ʿArabi, for instance, regarded the Qur'an as a *kawn masṭūr* or "logo-cosmos" that manifests the macro-cosmos, which is itself a manifestation of the divine Reality (*al-Haqq*). See Akkach, *Cosmology and Architecture in Premodern Islam*, 96.

of deciphering the meaning of existence on its own without cues from its Maker through verbal speech (i.e., through the Qur'an or an earlier divine revelation).[18] Likewise, Nursi recognizes the need for Qur'anic guidance, even in an age of unprecedented scientific and technological progress, because as the Qur'an interprets the *meaning* of existence, it remains indispensable, even as we become more skilled at observing and making use of the cosmos through science and technology.[19] Second, Nursi's emphasis on the "cosmic context" of the Qur'an highlights the necessity of engaging with the world we live in so far as to understand the message of the Qur'an. Any truthful commentary of the Qur'an must pay attention to reality, which includes both our experience of the world "out there," so to speak, and also the "inner world" of the human soul.

Another crucial corollary to Nursi's recognition of the cosmic context of the Qur'an is the "confirming" of the Qur'anic message.[20] In fact, Nursi suggests that there are two types of Qur'anic commentaries: one that mainly focuses on explaining the semantics of the Qur'an, and the other that gives "evidences" for the "truths" of the Qur'an. He considers the traditional line-by-line commentary genre to mainly fall into the first category, though not without occasional brief excursions into the second category. Nursi places the *Risale-i Nur* in the second category in that it focuses on "demonstrating the truths of the Qur'an." The Qur'anic invitation to reflect and meditate upon the cosmos calls its readers not to simply accept but to discover the Qur'anic truths in the world. To put it metaphorically, the best reading of a treasure map is to utilize it to discover the treasure, and as one finds the treasure one confirms the truthfulness of the treasure map. That is, genuine openness to Qur'anic guidance will lead us to experience it in our life—both in the cosmos, and inside within our souls, or as the Qur'an says, *fi al-āfāq wa fi al-anfus* (Q 41:53).

In order to further appreciate how Nursi reads the Qur'an in its cosmic context, let us look at his interpretation of the following Qur'anic passage and compare it with some of the predominant trends in traditional *tafsīr*.[21]

> *Let human being, then, consider* [the sources of] his food: [how it is] that We pour down water, pouring it down abundantly; and then We cleave the earth [with new growth], cleaving it asunder, and thereupon We cause grain to grow out of it, and vines and edible plants, and olive trees and date-palms, and gardens dense with foliage, and fruits and herbage, for you and for your animals to enjoy. (Q 80:24–32, italics added).

In the well-known traditional line-by-line commentaries like Abu Ja'far Muhammad al-Tabari's (d. ca. 923) or Ibn Kathir's, the passage is interpreted by simply paraphrasing its semantic content. In other words, the text is read simply as a statement, and the Qur'anic invitation to actually consider the cosmic phenomena is glossed over. Instead, Ibn

---

18. Nursi, *Sözler*, RNK 1:141.

19. For a discussion of how Nursi sees the relation between the Qur'an and modern science, see Yazıcıoğlu, "Perhaps their Harmony is not that simple."

20. Nursi, *Şualar*, RNK 1:1089.

21. Of course, the traditional line-by-line commentaries we shall refer to do not represent the entire genre of *tafsīr*. Our aim is to simply highlight some of the widely known and popularly read medieval exegetes as a foil to discuss Nursi's hermeneutics.

Kathīr (d. 1373) mainly interprets the passage as saying that the believer should be thankful to God for food, while al-Tabarī spends the bulk of his exegesis on the etymology of the words. In contrast with these readings that miss the semiotic function of the Qur'anic verses, the classical theologian-exegete Fakhr al-din al-Razi (d. 1209) notes that the above Qur'anic passage discloses signs in the universe. He suggests that if one were to look at natural phenomena, such as the growth of plants, closely, one would discover deep meanings in them, revealing God's agency and qualities. Though al-Razi does not offer an explanation of how these meanings would be discovered, he does go beyond mere semantic analysis and connects the verse to its meta-text.[22] Nursi takes al-Razi's approach further, explaining more clearly *how* the natural phenomena or cosmos function as signs, revealing the treasures of God's attributes, *al-asmā al-ḥusnā*. Let us look at his exegesis more closely to see how he reads the Qur'an within its cosmic context.

Nursi first highlights the last part of the Qur'anic passage: "for you and for your animals to enjoy." He suggests that by highlighting the "purposeful sequence" in the growth of vegetation, the Qur'anic passage teaches how to perceive the "hidden" agency of God implied in natural processes. The Qur'an invites its audience to pay attention to the beneficial results of these natural processes as they indicate purpose and care. And since the natural causes involved in this process of growth of grains and fruits lack the capacity to consciously plan out things or have mercy, these purposeful events reveal the agency of a wise and merciful One. In Nursi's words:

[The Qur'an] is in effect saying: "Rain comes from the sky in order to produce food for you and your animals." Since water does not possess the ability to have mercy for you and your animals and thus produce food accordingly, it means that *the rain does not come [on its own], it is sent*. And the earth cleaves up and yields forth food for you. But lacking feelings and intelligence, it is far beyond the ability of the earth to think of your sustenance and feel compassion for you, so it does not produce the food on its own.[23]

Thus, the Qur'an explains how this natural process is a sign. Or to use Nursi's metaphor, the Qur'an enables its audience to hear the "silent speech" of phenomena praising God. The flourishing of fruits and grains are means through which mercy and generosity of the Unseen Creator are manifested.

In light of this Qur'anic passage, as well as others that speak explicitly about cosmic phenomena, Nursi suggests that one of the main aims of the Qur'anic discourse is to change our superficial understanding of the world. More specifically, Nursi perceptively suggests, like his predecessors such as Jalal al-dīnal-Rumi (d. 1273), that correcting our misunderstanding of natural causality is a main purpose of the Qur'an. According to Nursi, the Qur'an teaches the reader to notice the surprising "gap" between what we habitually call the cause and its effect. Many tend to think that natural causes are responsible for cosmic phenomena,

---

22. We accessed Tabarī's, Ibn Kathīr's and Razi's commentaries on this passage through the comprehensive database maintained by Jordanian Ministry of Religious Affairs at www.altafsir.org.

23. Nursi, *Words*, 435 (modified translation and italics added). For original text, see: *Sözler*, *RNK* 1:192.

while in reality they are simply "apparent" causes, being employed by the Causer of causes, the Creator. The Qur'an discloses that between an apparent cause and what seems to be its effect there exists a transcendental gap. For these apparent causes lack the appropriate qualities, such as wisdom, power, mercy, and so on, to create the results attributed to them. Hence, contrary to our usual assumption, unconscious clouds cannot create rain, lifeless rain cannot create life, and parents are not the makers of their children. Nursi offers a metaphor here: it may at first seem that mountains are joined to the sky at the horizon. But when one pays attention and get closer, he sees that there is a huge distance between the two, and it is within this vast distance that "the stars rise and other things are situated." So too, says Nursi, "The distance between [apparent] causes and effects is such that it may be seen *only with the light of the Qur'an* through the telescope of belief." And "it is within this long distance between apparent cause and its effect that the Divine Names [*al-asmā al-ḥusnā*, i.e., attributes of God] each rise like stars. The place of their rising [*maṭla'*] is this distance."[24] In Nursi's hermeneutics, therefore, both the cosmic *ayāt* and the Qur'anic *ayāt* are places where flashes of *al-asmā al ḥusnā* "rise up" and emerge.[25]

For instance, Nursi suggests in the above passage, by calling the audience to look at the growth of grains, fruits and other vegetation, that the Qur'an teaches how "numerous Divine Names ... like All-Compassionate, Provider, Bestower, and All-Generous" are disclosed or articulated through cosmic phenomena.[26] Nursi's interpretation of this passage shows how the Qur'anic message explains or deciphers the meanings of the creational/cosmic *ayāt*. It also exemplifies how a believer can see the unfolding of the meaning of the Qur'anic message in the world and confirm its truth.

Nursi's hermeneutics, then, takes the cosmic context of the Qur'an seriously. It is not surprising, then, that he shares his reflections on the Qur'anic verse, "Behold, then, these signs of God's mercy—how He gives life to the earth after it had been lifeless!" (Q 30:50) only after making extended retreats by himself in the countryside, meditating on nature. His reflective activity resulted in *Treatise on Resurrection*, which explains in the light of the Qur'an the ways in which the universe gives news of a life after death.[27] Likewise, it is noteworthy that Nursi starts his treatise devoted to interpreting Qur'anic verses on gratitude by saying, "Just as the Wise Qur'an shows gratitude to be the purpose of creation, similarly this macro-Qur'an of the universe [Ar. *Qur'an al-kāinat al-kabīr*] demonstrates that gratitude is the most important result of creation."[28] Once again, the signs of the verbal Qur'an enlighten the signs of the "macro-Qur'an" cosmos and in turn the cosmic signs embody and corroborate the message of the Qur'an.

Another striking example of Nursi's reading of the Qur'an in its cosmic context is his interpretation of the Qur'anic phrase *bismillah* or "In the name of God." *Bismillah* is not simply an invocation that

---

24. Nursi, *Words*, 435 (modified translation and italics added).

25. Ibid., and see also Nursi, *Sözler*, *RNK* 1:192.

26. Nursi, *Words*, 436.

27. Nursi, *Sözler*, *RNK* 1: 19–43; *Words*, 59–132.

28. Nursi, *Mektûbât*, *RNK* 1:520–22.

a believer is called to utter. Rather, it is a key expression that the entire universe expresses. In other words, cosmic phenomena unfold in God's name, *bismillah*, disclosing the hidden divine agency through which everything happens.[29]

Nursi's awareness of the cosmic context of the Qur'an is relevant not only for the passages explicitly mentioning cosmic phenomena, which make up a large part of the Qur'an, but also for the passages that are often thought to be unrelated to the interpretation of the universe. For instance, as Yamina Mermer notes, the verse saying, "There shall be no coercion in matters of faith" (2:256) would mean not only that one should not force faith upon others, but that faith and coercion "cannot *ontologically* co-exist... because faith is a free choice and a state of being willingly open to the divine speech; it is a state of grateful surrendering to the grace of God. The use of force would negate all these qualities and the result would not be 'faith' but hypocrisy."[30] In a similar fashion, Nursi interprets the Qur'anic descriptions of *shirk* or attributing partners with God as "an awesome injustice" as reflecting a cosmic reality. Nursi argues that the *shirk* perspective disconnects the cosmos from its prestigious connection to the Eternal One, and thus constitutes an extremely unfair insult against all beings.[31] Nursi also interprets the Qur'anic passage about belief marking the distinction between the highest and lowest form of human existence (Q 95:4–6) by directly referring to the way in which belief makes a difference in the actual unfolding of human nature and in its way of being in the world.[32]

Nursi's approach of reading the Qur'an in its cosmic context is also reflected in his engagement with Qur'anic stories of the prophets. According to him, prophetic stories represent universal principles. Thus Qur'anic narratives are again commentaries on existence, helping human beings to discern the "signification" process embedded in the way history and human nature manifest and unfold in the world. For instance, Nursi interprets Adam being taught "all the names" (Q 2:31) as representing key truths about the purpose of human beings and their unique mission and potential as humans. All humanity is gifted with the potential of discovering the world around them and through that engagement they get to know the Creator with all his Beautiful Names.[33] Such an approach explicitly takes into consideration the Qur'anic author, audience and purpose in appreciating the content. Nursi is clear that these stories are not being told for the sake of narrating a historical account; the Wise Creator speaking in the Qur'an would not simply give information that would have no implication for human beings' here-and-now. So if the divine voice in the Qur'an is referring to an interaction between Adam and the angels, it is for the purpose of edifying the audience. If the angels prostrate before Adam while

---

29. For an analysis of Nursi's interpretation of *bismillah* see Yazıcıoğlu, "Redefining the Miraculous."

30. Mermer, "Islam: A Dissenting Prophetic Voice," 83.

31. *The Rays: From the Risale-i Nur Collection*, trans. Ş. Vahide, 19–20.

32. Nursi, *Words*, 319–27. Similarly, Nursi interprets the verse about not bragging (Q 3:188) in light of reflection on nature, and the verse about hearts being only satisfied with remembrance of God (Q 13:28) in cosmic context. See, respectively: *Words*, 139–40 and *Words*, 692.

33. Nursi, *Words*, 253–54.

Satan challenges him in the Qur'anic narrative (Q 2:34), then it must be alerting the reader of the human potential, his helpers as well as his foes in his human journey on earth.[34] Whether it is the Zulqarnayn's story, the golden calf incident, Mary's virgin birth, Abraham's search for God, or Jonah's prayer in the whale, for Nursi every Qur'anic story is told with the aim of revealing a truth that enlightens the reader's way of being in the world and hence connects him to his Sustainer (*rabb*).[35]

As he defines the Qur'an as a truthful commentary on the cosmos, Nursi is also aware that there are competing interpretations of the world—for instance, the materialist interpretation or the various "imbalanced" spiritual approaches. Nursi contrasts their understanding of the cosmos with the Qur'anic one. What he calls "materialist philosophy" that contrasts with Qur'anic wisdom is actually an umbrella term that includes various approaches to the world that either reject or ignore divine guidance revealed in the Qur'an and earlier divine revelations. He outlines a number of key problems with such approaches to the universe. First, unlike the Qur'anic approach, materialist philosophy completely misses the truth about the cosmos. It acts like a clueless chemist looking at calligraphy in a language foreign to him. The chemist may give a superb analysis of the quality of the ink and paper, but he misses the meaning inscribed through the calligraphy, not even realizing that it is a piece of writing that signifies meaning! Similarly, materialist philosophy fails to note that the world is full of signs pointing to the transcendent.[36] Also, the materialist approach places the ego at the center of everything and defines everyone's mission as advancing himself, rejecting the fact that the self is "indicative," revealing and reflecting the beautiful qualities of One *other than itself*.[37] Furthermore, Nursi contrasts social implications of materialist philosophy with that of Qur'anic wisdom. While the former sees power as the arbiter of truth and at the heart of social dynamics, Qur'anic wisdom places truth in place of power: it is not that the powerful have truth, rather, the truthful have power (i.e., "right is might, rather than might is right.")[38]

Another interesting contrast between Qur'anic wisdom and materialist philosophy that Nursi offers is about the way each of them approaches regularities in the world. For Nursi, one of the main aims of the Qur'an is to cut through the veil of familiarity (Ar. *ulfa*), and show that what we usually overlook as normal is actually extraordinary, revealing the wonderful maker behind the scenes. In contrast, materialist philosophy fails to perceive how extraordinary the incredible regular occurrences in the world are and identifies them as "normal," and instead finds exceptions to the norm and "freaks" as interesting and worthy of attention.[39]

---

34. Ibid., 254.

35. See Nursi, *The Flashes: From the Risale-i Nur Collection*, trans. Ş. Vahide, 17–20; 147–50; Nursi, *Words*, 254.

36. Nursi, *Words*, 143–45.

37. Ibid. 144. The Qur'anic view reveals that our life, for instance, is not truly ours but a gift of the Bestower of life, given to us, to reveal his beauty and then taken away according to divine will. For a detailed discussion of such contrasts between Qur'anic wisdom and materialist philosophy, see Nursi, *Flashes*, 159–66.

38. Nursi, *Words*, 146.

39. Nursi, *Words*, 150.

Nursi also distinguishes Qur'anic wisdom from spiritual approaches that are imbalanced, so to speak. He argues that coming from the comprehensive perspective of the Creator, the Qur'an reveals the truths of cosmos appropriately, unlike various spiritual explorers whose limited visions lead them to focus on one aspect of reality at the expense of others. Hence, the Qur'anic vision appropriately notes in a balanced manner the manifestations of both divine majesty and beauty, and of both divine immanence and transcendence in the cosmos. The Qur'an reveals the truths of *al-asmā al-ḥusnā* manifesting in the universe in a balanced way and offers guidance through teachings that reflect such a vision.[40] In this regard, it is also interesting how Nursi understands the Qur'an not being poetry (Q 36:69). By rejecting its identification as poetry, the Qur'an dissociates itself from a sentimentalist approach to the universe that imposes one's wishful thinking onto the cosmos.[41]

It is also noteworthy that Nursi's emphasis on the cosmic context of the Qur'an makes it more accessible to a non-specialized audience. Any general reader who is willing can learn to read the "signs" of God in the cosmos in light of the Qur'anic guidance. In contrast, with its privileging of semantics over semiotics, the traditional exegesis often favors the linguistic expert over the general reader. To be sure, himself being an expert in Arabic and Qur'anic eloquence [*balagha*], Nursi appreciated and made use of the benefits of such an expertise.[42]

Nevertheless, by focusing on the semiotic reading of the Qur'an and using the semantics in its service, Nursi's approach enables the general readers to access the Qur'anic meanings, despite their lack of expertise in Arabic linguistics.

Another frequent motif in traditional exegetical literature is the genre of *asbāb al-nuzūl* or occasions of revelation. It does not come as a surprise that Nursi's hermeneutics, attentive to universal lessons communicated through specific stories, de-emphasizes this genre. This must be not only because they are often unreliable in terms of their historical authenticity, but also because their use often narrows down the Qur'anic guidance to a particular historical circumstance and detracts the reader from its cosmic context and implications for the audience's edification here and now. An interesting example would be Nursi's reading of the Qur'anic verse, "God has purchased the lives and possessions of the believers in return for Paradise" (Q 9:111). *Asbāb al-nuzūl* literature reads the verse in the context of the oath of Aqaba in the late Meccan Period. This oath was taken by a small group of men and women from Medina, who accepted Muhammad's message and invited him to migrate to Medina. They promised to both worship only One God and to defend the Prophet from physical attacks as they would defend their own selves and families. While clearly aware of such reports, Nursi places the above verse in its "cosmic context," as pointing to a universal bargain available to everyone. The selling of one's self to God in return for Paradise means using one's body and faculties, such as reasoning, heart, and senses, in God's name, *bismillah*. Nursi argues that such a "transaction"

---

40. Ibid., 453–57.

41. Nursi, *Sözler*, RNK 1:53, *Words*, 151.

42. To get a sense of Nursi's fine command of Arabic *balagha*, see his *Ishārat al-iʿjāz*.

perfectly matches human nature and the cosmic reality in that it enables human beings to interact meaningfully with the world and transcend transience.[43]

In sum, while Nursi is aware that the Qur'an has been revealed over a period exceeding two decades under a variety of different circumstances, he does not wish to allow that fact to overshadow the overall purposes of the Qur'an that unfold within its universal cosmic context. Indeed, for Nursi it is a remarkable feature of the Qur'an that it is an overall unified text with relevance for all types of readers across the ages, despite being revealed over a period of two decades under many different circumstances of revelation.[44]

Nursi also de-emphasizes the *israiliyyat*, or the haggadic stories, borrowed mainly from Jewish and Christian oral sources used in some traditional commentaries to "fill in" the assumed "missing" details in Qur'anic stories. As is well known, aversion to *israiliyyāt* is a common tendency in the modern Muslim approaches to the Qur'an. In the contemporary age, the perceived "lack of detail" in the Qur'anic narratives in comparison with the biblical and haggadic stories has increasingly been noted as worthy of appreciation. For instance, if the Qur'an does not hold Eve responsible for Adam's eating of the forbidden fruit, it is not to be "complemented" with extra-Qur'anic stories about how she is to be blamed. Rather the absence of such detail in the Qur'an is meaningful in itself.[45] In a way similar to these contemporary trends, Nursi regards silence of the Qur'an in narrative details as meaningful in itself and worthy of note. He criticizes the use of extra-Qur'anic stories that overlooks the Qur'an's cosmic context and purpose of connecting human beings to their Creator. Such uncritical use of *israiliyyāt*, even when found in classical tafsīr, is not a genuine exegesis of the Qur'anic meanings, but a distortion.[46]

At this point, we may also note that Nursi affirms the classical Islamic understanding that the Qur'an, being a discourse from the Eternal, contains endless meanings that are accessible to various audiences all at once, and across the ages till the end of time. In the next and final section, let us take a closer look at how the Qur'an speaks to a contemporary audience in Nursi's perspective.

---

43. Such a connection to a universal bargain also has precedents in the tradition in that in the tafsīr literature one encounters the saying attributed to Imam Jafar al-Sadiq or Hasan al-Basri that this transaction includes every believer in the world. Similarly, Razi also suggests that the *jihad* reference in the following part of the verse includes forms of struggle in God's path that are other than defense in battlefield. Nursi's exegesis takes such references further and explains *how* the bargain can indeed be universally applicable to all audiences of the Qur'an.

44. Nursi, *Sözler, RNK* 1:187. Here, Nursi refers to classical scholars such as al-Zamakhshari (d. 1143), Sakkaki (d. 1229), and Abd al-Qahir al-Jurjani (d. 1078) as having demonstrated the connections across the verses and the overall coherence of the Qur'an. He adds that while the various circumstances of revelation do not at all disturb the internal unity and harmony of the Qur'an, they have some effect on the flow of the text. Their effect is enriching, like the "bumps and excrescences appear on a tree, not to spoil the harmony of the tree, but to produce fruit which will be the means for the tree reaching its adorned perfection and beauty." In other words, "These factors stick out their knobbly heads in order to express meanings which will enhance the Qur'an's fluent [order]." (Nursi, *Words*, 426–27).

45. See Mattson, *The Story of the Qur'an*, 192–94.

46. Nursi, *Muhâkemat, RNK* 2:1985–88.

# READING THE QUR'AN IN THE MODERN AGE

"As time grows older, the Qur'an grows younger."
—B. Said Nursi, *Mektûbât*

According to Nursi, the Qur'an speaks to all periods of history and to all classes of people. Since it is coming from the Eternal One, unlike other writings, it does not become outdated or "old" as time progresses. Rather, Nursi claims that the Qur'an is an unending, inexhaustible treasury of guidance, whose treasures are revealed even more as time goes on. Indeed, Nursi claims, each age has a special share of the word of God, in addition to the universal message of the Qur'an of making God known with his Beautiful Names that is pertinent across all ages.[47]

A fascinating aspect of the modern age is the advance in exploration of the universe. Nursi notes how in the contemporary age, scientific disciplines have undergone exponential growth, giving rise to the creation of disciplines within disciplines in order to study natural phenomena in various detailed ways. For Nursi, these developments in the study of nature relate anew to a crucial aspect of the Qur'anic discourse: its constant reference to the universe as *ayāt* or "signs." When considered in light of the Qur'an, each scientific discipline serves to confirm and elucidate the Qur'anic interpretation of the cosmos as pointing to the wisdom and other beautiful attributes (*asmā al-ḥusnā*) of the Divine. After all, sciences could not exist at all had there been no order or consistency in the world.[48] Interestingly, referring to the verse, "We have adorned the lowest heaven with lamps and made them [missiles] for stoning devils . . ." (Q 67:5), Nursi also suggests that when interpreted in the light of the Qur'anic teachings on *ayāt*, each scientific discipline can enlighten different aspects of the order in the universe, each becoming like a star piercing through the darkness of disbelief, a *najm al-thaqib*, defeating the suspicions about God cast by the devils.[49]

Nursi of course was not naïve; he was aware that the unprecedented exploration of nature in the modern age has often been combined with turning away from God. It is a popular notion that belief in God is not relevant in an age of science. It is often suggested, for instance, that rain was associated with God in the past because people did not know enough about the formation of rain. It is surmised that since today we have a scientific description of the water cycle, we do not need to believe in God anymore. Nursi challenges such understanding of God as a "gap-filler" and cogently argues for both the relevance and significance of Qur'anic "commentary" on the universe in the modern age. To put it simply, Nursi suggests that the *fact* that we can describe, for instance, the water cycle in the world and predict rain does not obviate the *interpretive* question: is this purposeful, useful, and life-giving process a work of blind natural causes, or do they signify a merciful and purposeful Life-Giver behind this process? Indeed, the fact that we know how to describe natural phenomena better does not decrease, but in fact *enhances*, the need to decipher their meaning as signs: what does this regular and beneficial process "say" to us? The

---

47. Nursi, *Letters*, 456.
48. *Muhâkemat*, RNK 2:1986.
49. Nursi, *Isharat al-i'jāz*, RNK 2:1216.

water process is not a veil to divine creativity; on the contrary, it is like a mirror reflecting it. Hence, in the modern age, the Qur'anic interpretation of the cosmos remains ever essential.

The Qur'an teaches the reader how to decipher the script of the eternal divine qualities, such as mercy, power, and wisdom, dynamically inscribed through the constant flow of creativity in the cosmos. In this regard, it is significant that Nursi reads the Qur'anic call to people of the book (*ahl al-kitāb*) to come to a common word, "Say: O people of the book! Come unto a word [that is] equitable between you and us" (Q 3:64), as including a call to people of learning (*ahl al-maktab*). Just as the people of the book receive a special invitation in the Qur'an because they are familiar with other addresses of God to humanity through scriptures, people of the modern age receive a special call from the Qur'an as well because they are familiar with divine addresses to humanity through creativity manifest in the cosmos. They are aware of many facts about the universe that were not available to people in previous centuries. And just as the people of the book are invited to go through a transformation in the light of the Qur'an, this modern scientific study of nature needs enlightenment from the Qur'an. It is also noteworthy that while Nursi emphasizes the harmony between the Qur'an and science, he insightfully criticizes pseudo-scientific claims that science inherently clashes with religion, including the Qur'an.[50]

Living at a time of great social and political change, Nursi also saw the Qur'an as relevant in contemporary sociopolitical contexts.[51] In interpreting various Qur'anic commandments, Nursi notes a crucial principle: in the Qur'an, the divine author speaks not with a limited human vision but with a comprehensive view of human life and cosmic realities. Hence, Qur'anic injunctions address both ideal and non-ideal conditions, as in the case of polygamy, and may come in general principles (*'āmm*) that need to be interpreted when applied to a particular situation (*takhsīs*), as in the case of relations with "people of the book."[52] Although he occasionally offered insightful interpretations of implications for sacred law or *sharī'a* in the Qur'an, Nursi was not preoccupied with Islamic Law in interpreting the Qur'an, unlike many of his contemporaries. Instead, Nursi focused on the commonly underappreciated cosmic and existential context of the Qur'an. In his treatise on *ijtihād,* or legal interpretation, interestingly written as an interpretation of "if they referred it to the Messenger and those in authority among them, those seeking its meaning would have found it out from them" (Q 4:83),[53] Nursi stresses the importance of a holistic approach to *sharī'a* that is based on the Qur'anic spirit of justice and compassion instead of a piece-meal approach motivated by trumping lasting spiritual priorities with a misunderstanding of what is perceived as the "needs of the times."[54]

---

50. See Yazıcıoğlu, "Perhaps Their Harmony Is Not That Simple," 346–52.

51. For a brief discussion of Nursi on contemporary politics, see Yazıcıoğlu, "Sa'id Nursi."

52. See Nursi, *Münazarat, RNK* 2:1944, 1955. Similarly, Nursi suggests *jihad* or struggle against evil is to be conducted through non-violent means, since the evil now has taken a different form.

53. English translation is from M. A. S. Abdel Haleem's *Qur'an: A New Translation*, 58.

54. Nursi, *Sözler, RNK* 1:212–16; *Words*, 495–502.

As a contemporary interpreter of the Qur'an, Nursi also engaged with some of the contemporary criticisms of the Qur'an. One criticism was about the repetitiveness of the Qur'an; it was claimed that the Qur'an repeats itself over and over again. Nursi responds by highlighting not only the basis of the Qur'anic content but also the basis of the interaction between the Qur'an and the reader's life. He suggests that the Qur'an is "nourishment" for the human heart and the mind, and like "light and water" for the human spirit. Repetition is boring and problematic only when it does not meet a need. In contrast, if the need keeps occurring, repeating the meeting of that need is not boring; on the contrary, it is pleasurable. For instance, we eat every day and breathe every moment. Nobody finds it boring to eat when they are hungry or to breathe every moment. Similarly, the Qur'anic statements enlighten and nourish the spirit and the heart and that nourishment is needed each day over and over again, and it is fulfilling to the reader aware of his spiritual needs.[55]

Another criticism directed at the Qur'an was its supposed lack of organization. As is well known, the Qur'an does not follow a particular linear organization: it does not follow a timeline or a narrative plot, nor is it organized in the order it was received by Prophet Muhammad. According to Nursi, the wisdom behind such lack of a rigid order is that it frees each verse to interconnect with many other verses at once. In his dense book on Qur'anic hermeneutics, *Muhakemât*, composed in Arabic and translated by his brother Abdulmecid Nursi into Ottoman Turkish, Nursi offers the metaphor of concentric figures in a painting where "one and the same dot becomes the eye of a character, the silhouette of another's face, the mouth of another and the nasal opening of yet another figure.... [Similarly] there are such intersecting relations across the words of the Divine speech."[56] In a similar vein, Nursi gives the metaphor of stars in the sky so as to describe the relationship between Qur'anic verses. When one looks at the sky at night, it seems at first that the stars are scattered "randomly" without any organization, whereas, they are of course organized, otherwise there would be havoc in space. But they are organized in a way that does not marginalize any particular star. For if there is no definite center, there is no periphery; one could take any star as a center and see the other stars from its angle. Similarly, the verses of the Qur'an are like stars and their loose organization constitutes the Qur'an's intra-textual richness, strength and flexibility rather any lack.[57]

Nursi's response to contemporary criticisms of the Qur'anic style is quite original. Viewed at the background of some of the recent trends in Qur'anic studies, we may understand his approach better. Recently, several scholars noted the need to question our expectations of a linear organization from the Qur'an. A typical linear text inevitably narrows down the interrelationship across its parts, by requiring a beginning, climax, end and particular flow of its chapters. In contrast, as Michael Sells highlights, the Qur'an (lit. "recitation") is a primarily oral text, which allows for dynamic relationship across its passages.[58] Similarly, Wil-

55. Nursi, *Words*, 251, 767.

56. Nursi, *Muhâkemat*, RNK 2:2017.

57. Nursi, *Words*, 151.

58. See Sells, *Approaching the Qur'an* and

liam Graham and others have analyzed the dynamic aspect of the *kitāb* or book in the Qur'an, suggesting that the Qur'anic discourse flows like a dynamic conversation that any reader could enter at any point, without feeling left out for not having heard or read the "beginning" of the text. In this connection, we may also note Nursi's presentation of the Qur'an being arranged like a hologram. Nursi suggests the vital themes of the Qur'an, which are repeated in various forms to fulfill recurring human need for meaning and for connection to the transcendent, are contained in all parts of the Qur'an. In other words, like a hologram, the major themes of the Qur'an are found everywhere in the text, in every *sura*, every *aya* and even in every word. Nursi suggests that there is a profound wisdom and compassion in this style: since not everyone can read the entire Qur'an at short intervals, each chapter, including the short ones, are packed with the essential nutrients that represent the gist of the entire Qur'an, so to speak.[59]

Another criticism of the Qur'an that Nursi addresses is that the Qur'an frequently talks about seemingly petty things, even though it claims to be from God and full of wisdom. For instance, various stories about ancient people are narrated in the Qur'an: why would a sacred text care to narrate such an event of the past? As noted earlier, for Nursi, the answer is that these stories are not at all minor. Rather each of these stories is the "tip" of an iceberg of meaning, the tip of a universal law of creation manifest in the cosmos. These particular narratives represent and communicate profound and widely applicable principles. For Nursi,

since the Qur'an speaks to all classes, and all ages, and the majority of people are common people, these stories are narrated so as to convey universal lessons in a form accessible to all. Thus, for instance, Moses' insistence that his people sacrifice a cow in response to the divine command is a crucial lesson about confronting idols. Nursi notes that the Children of Israel had spent a long time in Egypt, where cows had become an object of veneration because of their indispensability for agriculture, and therefore survival. The Children of Israel must have internalized the tendency to think that this animal is not just a *means* but a *source* of their survival. The episode of sacrificing the cow is thus a story about a people confronting their idol in tangible terms.[60] Therefore, this particular episode narrated in the Qur'an conveys a valuable lesson in *tawḥīd* that can be applied to our own moments of idolizing a created thing. The story then cautions us against our turning a finite blessing into an idol, worthy of adoration in itself, and thus depriving ourselves of the eternal source of that blessing.[61]

Finally, another important critical question that Nursi both acknowledges and insightfully responds to is, "Is the Qur'an really the word of God?" Among other things, Nursi suggests that the fact that the Qur'an is in a human language might be used as a pretext for rejecting its divine authorship.[62] Such a treatise is

---

Madigan, *The Qur'an's Self-Image.*

59. Nursi, *Words*, 250.

60. Ibid., 254–55.

61. Similarly, for Nursi, miracle stories in the Qur'an also convey crucial principles, interrupting our *ulfa* or familiarity with the cosmos that leads to a superficial attitude. For a detailed analysis of Nursi's interpretation of Qur'anic miracle stories, see Yazıcıoğlu, *Understanding the Qur'anic Miracle Stories in the Modern Age*, 123–63.

62. Nursi, "Discussion with the Satan,"

especially interesting, given W. Cantwell Smith's remark in the late 1960s that he did not know of any scholar in the Muslim world who explicitly raised and discussed such a question about the Qur'an's authorship.[63]

In conclusion, Nursi approaches the Qur'an with an emphasis on its author, audience, purpose, and its semiotic context: the cosmos. For Nursi, the Qur'an is the treasure map for existence filled with treasures of meaning pointing to the majesty and beauty of the transcendent. Indeed, the Qur'an is a dynamic "recitation" or commentary on the cosmic show unfolding in each moment. Nursi's striking attitude to the Qur'an reflects a deep grasp of the Qur'an's main themes and overall spirit and also enables the audience to relate to the Qur'an in the here-and-now. With such an understanding, Nursi interprets various Qur'anic passages, whether they are referring to nature, prophetic stories, or Qur'anic injunctions, in a way that allows the reader to both relate to and confirm the meanings of the Qur'an. Building on some of the most insightful approaches within the classical Islamic tradition, and displaying profound awareness of the challenges and opportunities of a modern era, Nursi is a crucial Qur'anic interpreter who is worth studying further.

## BIBLIOGRAPHY

Abdel Haleem, M. A. S. *The Qur'an: A New Translation.* New York: Oxford University Press, 2004.

Akkach, Samer. *Cosmology and Architecture in Premodern Islam: An Architectural Reading of Mystical Ideas.* New York: State University of New York Press, 2006.

al-Daghamin, Ziyad Khalil Muhammad. "The Aims of the Qur'an in Bediüzzaman Said Nursi's Thought." In *A Contemporary Approach to Understanding the Qur'an: The Example of the Risale-i Nur,* 20th–22nd September, 1998, 353–79. Istanbul: Sözler *Yayınevi,* 2000.

Grice, Herbert P. *Studies in the Way of Words.* Cambridge: Harvard University Press, 1989.

Jordanian Ministry of Religious Affairs. www.altafsir.org. Tabarī's, Ibn Kathīr's and Razi's commentaries are in this comprehensive database.

Madigan, Daniel *The Qur'an's Self-Image: Writing and Authority in Islam's Scripture.* New York: Princeton University Press, 2001.

Marinis, Marco de. *The Semiotics of Performance.* Bloomington, IN: Indiana University Press, 1996.

---

*Letters,* 365–76. While we do not have room to discuss this treatise by Nursi, Mermer's observation of methodological assumptions in approaching a text that claims to be God's word is helpful in understanding Nursi's main claim in the treatise: "Methodologically, we are supposed to consider a document as it claims to be unless proved otherwise and read it accordingly. Now the messenger who brought the Qur'an never claimed to be its author; he asserted that it was revealed to him by God. The Qur'an itself professes to be an address of the Creator of the heavens and the Earth. Consequently, we will regard each verse of the Qur'an as the word of God. But if after that [assumption] it does not make sense; if it is inconsistent in itself or in relation to the universe to which it often refers, then we will have the right to suspect its claim. If however from the beginning we reject the claim that the Qur'an is God's word, then what we will read will not be the Qur'an anymore, but some text allegedly written by Muhammad. And Muhammad would no longer be the messenger of God but an impostor who lied in the name of God." See Mermer, "Principles of Qur'anic Hermeneutics,.

63. "In the Muslim World, you will not find, or would not have found for centuries gone by, a lecture announced for theologians carrying as its title the question . . . ['Is the Qur'an Word of God?'] Nor do I know of any book in the Muslim word with this title, Muslims do not publicly ask, Is the Qur'an the word of God." W. C. Smith, *The Questions of Religious Truth,* 47.

Mattson, Ingrid. *The Story of the Qur'an Its History and Place in Muslim Life*. New York: Wiley-Blackwell, 2008.

Mermer, Yamina. "Islam: A Dissenting Prophetic Voice." In *Scripture, Reason, and the Contemporary Islam-West Encounter*, edited by Basit B. Koshul and Steven Kepnes, 67–104. New York: Palgrave Macmillan, 2007.

———. "Principles of Qur'anic Hermeneutics." *The Journal of Scriptural Reasoning* 5:1 (2005). Online at <http://jsr.lib.virginia.edu/vol-5-no-1-april-2005-islam-and-scriptural-reasoning/principles-of-Qur'anic-hermeneutics/>.

Mermer, Yamina, and Redha Ameur. "Beyond the Modern: Sa'id al-Nursi's View of Science." *Islam and Science* 2 (2004) 119–60.

*The Message of the Qur'an*. Translated by Muhammad Asad. Gibraltar: Dar al-Andalus, 1984.

Nursi, Bediüzzaman Said. *The Flashes: From the Risale-i Nur Collection*. Translated by Şükran Vahide. Istanbul: Sözler Yayınevi, 1995.

———. *Ishārat al-i'jāz*. Edited by Ihsan Qasim al-Salihi. Istanbul: Sözler Yayınevi, 1994.

———. *The Letters*. Translated by Şükran Vahide. Istanbul: Sözler, 1994.

———. *The Rays: From the Risale-i Nur Collection*. Translated by Şükran Vahide. Istanbul: Sözler Yayınevi, 2002.

———. *Risale-i Nur Külliyatı*. Vols. 1 & 2, Istanbul: Yeni Nesil Yayınları, 1996. Includes *Mektûbât, Mesnevî-i Nûriye, Muhâkemat, Münazerat,* and *Sözler*.

———. *The Words: From the Risale-i Nur Collection*. Rev. ed. Translated by Şükran Vahide. Istanbul: Sözler, 2004.

Peirce, Charles S. *The Collected Papers of Charles Sanders Peirce*. Edited by Charles Hartshorne and Paul Weiss. Cambridge: Harvard University Press, 1931–35.

Sells, Michael. *Approaching the Qur'an: The Early Revelations*. 2nd ed. Ashland, OR: White Cloud, 2007.

Smith, William Cantwell. *The Questions of Religious Truth*. New York: Schribner's, 1967.

Yazıcıoğlu, Isra. "Perhaps Their Harmony Is Not That Simple: Said Nursi on the Qur'an and Modern Science." *Theology and Science* 11.4 (2013) 339–55.

———. "Redefining the Miraculous: Al-Ghazālī, Ibn Rushd, and Said Nursi on Qur'anic Miracle Stories." *Journal of Qur'anic Studies* 13.2 (2011) 86–108.

———. "Sa'id Nursi." In *The Princeton Encyclopedia of Islamic Political Thought*, edited by G. Böwering et al., 481–82. Princeton: Princeton University Press, 2011.

———. *Understanding the Qur'anic Miracle Stories in the Modern Age*. University Park, PA: Penn State University Press, 2013.

# 5

# Concept of God in the *Risale-i-Nur*
## God through His Creative Activity

### YAMINA MERMER

## INTRODUCTION

THERE IS NO SPECIFIC passage in the *Risale-i-Nur* that deals with the concept of God. Rather, following the Qur'anic text closely, the entire corpus is devoted to getting to know God through his signs (*ayāt*) in the creation, to unlock the "treasuries" of the Divine Names in the universe, to witness the oneness of God and to connect to him in surrender and love. Nursi is very conscious that God cannot be grasped without reference to his creative activity, and without the seeker engaging with life. For the Beautiful Attributes (*asmā' al-ḥusnā*) of God are displayed through the unfolding of the universe. And these names point to the existence of the One, the source of these attributes. It would be impossible to do justice to the entire corpus of the *Risale* in this short paper, therefore I shall focus on Nursi's understanding of the ways in which the creation reveals the divine.

Since Nursi draws extensively and creatively from the rich Islamic legacy, it would be best to discuss his approach in relation to noteworthy accounts of creation that have emerged in classical Islam, more specifically, Islamic theology (*kalām*) and philosophy. While these two streams of Islamic thought both engaged with the Qur'an and the universe, they articulated the process of creation differently and arrived at diverging notions of the divine. Whereas the mainstream theology described the relationship between the universe and the Creator as direct, the philosophical approach conceived it as indirect and mediated. The former was crystallized in the notion of creation out of nothing, and the latter emphasized creation out of matter. Both of these views referred to empirical observation and the

Qur'anic discourse to support their views, and also deeply disagreed with each other. Nursi's approach interestingly offers an interpretation of the world in the light of the Qur'an that reconciles these two views; for him, creation out of nothing happens within creation out of matter. As I shall demonstrate, his approach shows a careful engagement with the Qur'anic text as well as the "book of creation," and yields a rich conception of the divine as revealed through the universe.

In what follows, therefore I first give a general background on Nursi's Qur'anic hermeneutics. Next, I analyze the Ashari School's theory of creation ex nihilo, as represented by al-Ghazali, and how their reading of the Qur'an influenced their conception of God and the world. Then, I consider Ibn Rushd's understanding of causation and how it led him to read the doctrine of creation out of matter from the Qur'an. Finally, I turn to Nursi's account of creation, which claims that creation out of nothing occurs within creation out of matter, and I will discuss how such an approach informs his understanding of the divine. I will also analyze how Nursi's conception of creation and therefore of the Creator is a result of his hermeneutical approach to the Qur'an.

## THE QUR'AN ON THE RELATION BETWEEN THE WORLD AND THE DIVINE

The Qur'an often appeals to God's creative activity to indicate his wisdom as well as his power to bring about resurrection. It also frequently refers to creation to refute *shirk* (ascribing partners with God). The Qur'anic formula, in which God describes himself as "the Creator of every thing" is reiterated many times (Q 6:102; 13:16; 39:62; 40:62). It is also clear from the Qur'an that God is the omnipotent agent of creation; he knows all its details (Q 5:97; 57:41; 7:185) and regulates it (Q 17:12). Everything takes place by reason of his foreknowledge (Q 11:6; 23:62). Indeed, "He it is who holds the heavens so that they do not fall on the earth" (Q 22:65) and "He it is who preserves heaven and earth from destruction" (Q 35:65).[1]

It is clear that the Qur'an's depiction of God is very different from the Aristotelian notion of prime mover. The latter acts through and with other things and agents, and hence is far from being a completely independent agent. It is for this reason that al-Ghazali in his *Tahāfut al-falāsifa* accused the Muslim Aristotelian philosophers of not giving a real scope of action to God. The latter held a philosophical model of beings coming about necessarily through the causal efficacy of their originators (causes), and ending with the first cause. In contrast, Muslim theologians understood from the Qur'an that God is the sole cause of every single thing; creatures arise from nothing at God's creative command, "Be." For, "when He wills a thing, He merely says to it 'Be' and it is" (Q 36:82). The commentators and theologians have interpreted this verse in a way favorable to the doctrine of creation from nothing.[2]

---

1. Unless otherwise noted, English translation of Qur'anic verses is from Muhammad Asad, *The Message of the Qur'an*.

2. Ibn Sina, who was a philosopher, also held to creation ex nihilo, but not in time as the theologians believed. In his *Tis' rasā'il fi al-ḥikm*, Ibn Sina contended that the Qur'an implied a creation from eternity, out of nothing, and not in time. See al-Alousi, "The Problem of Creation in Islamic Thought," 12.

On the other hand, there are other verses in the Qur'an that could well be understood as creation out of matter. For instance, the Qur'an says, "We made out of water every living thing" (Q 21:30). Muslim philosophers, like al-Farabi in his *al-Jam' bayna ra'yay al-hākimayn*, and Ibn Rushd in his *Faṣl al-maqāl* and *al-Kashf 'an manāhij al-adillah*, contended that these verses clearly implied creation out of matter. They also claimed that time and matter existed before creation. It is interesting to notice that both parties—those who advocate creation out of nothing and those committed to the view that God created out of matter—pointed to verses from the Qur'an to support their apparently divergent views.

## NURSI'S QUR'ANIC HERMENEUTICS[3]

In his exposition of *usūl al-tafsīr* (methodology of Qur'anic exegesis), Nursi notes that speech derives its power[4] from four sources: the speaker, the person addressed, the purpose, and the form of speech.[5] In other words, in order to understand a speech it is necessary to consider the following points: Who is speaking? Whom does the speech address? What is the purpose of such speech? In what form is it said?

For instance, if speech is in the form of command or prohibition, it looks to the speaker's will and power in accordance with his position. Think of the phrase "Forward, march!" It is an effective command if a commander utters it. The same words have no effect if a soldier utters them because he has no authority. Although the two phrases are the same in form, they are very different in meaning. Hence, it is crucial to know who is speaking in order to understand speech. So when the Qur'an says, "Be and it is." (36:82), the meaning of this command depends on who the speaker is. If it is the Creator of all things—an omnipotent and omniscient being—then it is reasonable. However, if it is the word of Muhammad, then it is nonsense and derisory. In this sense, to treat the Qur'an as a historical text written in a certain time, by a certain person, namely Muhammad, is to strip it of its properties. As W. C. Smith acknowledges, "The Qur'an therefore was seen by the West as not truly scripture; and in effect, as not scripture at all. It was studied and treated not as scripture but as any other book."[6]

---

3. Mermer, "Principles of Qur'anic Hermeneutics."

4. As is well known, rhetorical art (*balagha*) is very important in the Arabic language. It was especially important at the time the Qur'an was revealed. According to *balagha*, speech is considered powerful if it expresses a meaning in a concise form and in a way that addresses not only reason, but all the senses, including imagination. The tools used to achieve this aim are the meaning of the words employed, their order, the style and manner of exposition (*bayān*), fluency and so on. In Arabic literature, the power, beauty, and fineness of speech stemmed from its form.

5. Nursi, "Sözler," in *Risale-i Nur Külliyatı*, 298. (*Risale-i Nur Külliyatı* will henceforth be shortened as *RNK*.) From my knowledge, Muslim scholars have not raised this issue as overtly as Nursi has. It is expected however, that the commentators were aware of this grave hermeneutical issue. I believe that it is possible to peruse their work and deduce it from there, perhaps by interpreting it and looking for evidences here and there. Abu Harith al-Muhasibi's '*Al-Aql wa fahm al-Qur'an* may be a good starting point. However, it exceeds the scope of this paper.

6. W. C. Smith, "The True Meaning of Scripture: An Empirical Historian's Non-reductionist Interpretation of the Qur'an," 489.

Since the Qur'an claims to be an address in the name of the Creator of the heavens and the earth, no matter what the reality is, Nursi suggests it should be read accordingly. Here, Nursi's approach is reminiscent of Toshihiko Izutsu's comment that the Qur'an should be allowed to "interpret its own concepts and speak for itself."[7] After that, if it still does not make sense and lacks consistency, only then may one have the right to dismiss that claim. In speaking for itself, the Qur'an rejects the assumption that Muhammad composed it: "Or do they say, 'He fabricated the (Message)'? Nay, they have no faith! Let them then, produce a recital like unto it, if (it be) they speak the truth!" (Q 52:33–34)

Nursi also stresses the importance of the audience of the Qur'an. For example, if a professor speaks to a child, wisdom requires that he speaks according to the child's capacity if he wants to make himself understood, which is the aim of speech. The form of his speech is limited by the child's limitations, and this fact does not indicate the limitation of the speaker. In the same way, the Qur'an has been revealed in accordance with human understanding, in order to avoid alienation. It uses allegories and metaphors to make it easy for ordinary people to grasp deep truths that otherwise would be very difficult to communicate.

This brings us to the issue of purpose as a crucial matter in interpretation. Scholars of exegesis held various views on the Qur'an's aim, but they agreed on three main aims (*maqāsid al Qur'an*)[8]:

unity of God, prophethood, and resurrection. Nursi emphasizes that these aims constitute the main themes of the Qur'an.[9] They are interrelated and all-pervasive. Every chapter, every verse, points to these aims. So when the Qur'an mentions creation, its purpose is to expound and explain the main aims and more specifically *tawḥīd*, in different contexts. The Qur'an speaks of beings not for themselves but for their Creator. Its goal is not to give detailed explanation of things themselves, but to show how they make their Creator known, i.e. they function as signs. That is why the Qur'an cannot be regarded as a book supplying information about the universe. It is neither a scientific report nor a theological account. Hence, it is not surprising that there is no passage in the Qur'an that deals specifically with the process of the creation; that is just not its aim.[10]

In relation to the purpose of the Qur'an, Nursi points to another crucial hermeneutical feature of the Qur'an: its recurrent reference to the universe in order to combine the word of God (revelation) and his act (creation). In the Qur'an, God describes his acts of creation to "both eye and ear." He describes his act while performing it, he explains his art as he works it, and describes his gifts of mercy as he bestows them.[11] That is, just as God makes his existence and presence perceptible through deed, he also communicates his presence and existence through speech.[12] He speaks as he creates.

---

7. Izutsu, *Ethico-Religious Concepts in the Qur'an*, 3.

8. al-Razi, *Mafātih al-ghayb*, xx, 226; Abu Ishaq İbrahim Ibn Musa al-Shatibi, *Al-Muwafaqāt* (ta'liq: 'Abdullah Diraz), iii, 280; Nursi, *Isharat-ul- i'jaz fi madani al- ijaz*, 10.

9. See for instance, RNK, *Isharat al-i'jaz*, 1159.

10. Ibid.

11. Nursi, *Words, From the Risale-i Nur Collection*, 444.

12. Nursi, *The Supreme Sign*, 49–50.

Or it could be said he makes creation speak through the Qur'an. In the words of Nursi, "the Qur'an is the eternal interpreter of the various tongues reciting the verses (signs) of creation."[13] According to this view, revelation and creation expound and interpret each other and thus they confirm each other. Therefore, it is not possible to understand one without referring to the other. Nursi's conclusion is that a successful reading of the Qur'an requires a parallel reading of creation, and vice-versa: a successful reading of the creation requires paying attention to the Qur'an. The distinctiveness of Nursi's approach to the Qur'an and the universe will emerge more clearly as we now turn to looking at the classical Islamic theological and philosophical views on creation.

## CREATION OUT OF NOTHING

In two passages, the Qur'an uses the term "nothing" explicitly to describe the previous condition of the creation. In both contexts, it emphasizes God's absolute power. He who can create what was once "nothing" can also produce a child in a barren woman and raise the dead at the Day of Judgment. Such an emphasis suggests creation out of nothing in its strict sense because producing from nothing requires the application of infinite power.

> [Zachariah] exclaimed: "O my Sustainer! How can I have a son when my wife has always been barren and I have become utterly infirm through old age?" Answered [the angel]: "Thus, it is; [but] thy Sustainer says, 'This is easy for Me—even as *I have created thee aforetime out of nothing.*'" (Q 19:8–9, emphasis added)

> But does man not bear in mind that *We have created him aforetime out of nothing?* And so, by thy Sustainer, [on Judgment Day] We shall most certainly bring them forth . . . (Q 19:67–68, emphasis added)

The first verse implies a refutation of natural causation: It seems that the woman cannot give birth to a child because she is barren, but in fact she is barren because so far God has not willed her to bear a child. When (or if) God wills her to bear a child, then she is not barren anymore. Bearing a child and "being barren" are both contingent attributes; they are not essential to the woman. So when a woman bears a child, she does so only by God's leave.

The Ash'arites understood these verses as meaning that causes have no power whatsoever to produce the effect attributed to them. Their reasoning is simple: Since God says in the Qur'an that he is the creator of everything, then nothing other than God can have the power to create anything. Moreover, given the repeated Qur'anic statement that "God is Powerful over all things," the theologians concluded that God has the power to act unrestrained. He acts directly without any intermediary; secondary causes have no real agency. In fact, they concluded, to attribute to natural causes the power to create amounts to attributing partners to God (*shirk*), for it is said in the Qur'an:

> Say, "Who is the Sustainer of the heavens and the earth?" Say: "It is God." Say: "Why, then, do you take for your protectors, instead of Him, such as have it not within their power to bring benefit to, or avert harm from, themselves?" . . . Or do they assign to God partners that have created the like of what He creates, so that this

---

13 Nursi, "Sözler" in *RNK*, 290.

act of creation appears to them to be similar to His? Say: "God is the Creator of all things; and He is the One who holds absolute sway over all that exists." (Q 13:16)[14]

To be sure, Ash'arite theologians did not deny that there is causality in the world.[15] They accepted that every act has an agent; no event can happen without being caused. However, they rejected that causes play an efficient role in the creation of effects that follow them in time. They endorsed what could be termed as "vertical causation," according to which everything is directly linked to an effective agent, who creates both the cause and the effect in an orderly manner.[16]

In order to ground their idea of creation and justify it, the Ash'arite theologians formulated the theory of the indivisibility of matter, also known as atomism. They developed it in such a way that their conception of God's omnipotence and their idea of creation could readily be deduced from it. Their argument was that if matter were inherently divisible, it would possess in itself the possibility of its determination, and the idea of transcendent cause would be superfluous. But if matter (the atom) is indivisible, it follows that the intervention of a transcendent cause that bestows on matter and composite beings their determination and specification is necessary. The concept of a creative God becomes apparent.[17] Obviously, this doctrine of atomism agrees with the Qur'anic vision of the creation, precisely because that is what it was designed for in the first place. What is lacking in this Ash'arite approach is that it does not engage with the empirical data per se, or meditate on nature so as to affirm the Qur'anic view of creation. Instead, it is speculative theology, in the sense that it projects a particular view of the universe by starting from a number of Qur'anic passages.

Indeed, as M. Fakhry rightly noted, except in their contention that the natural efficacy of causes is incompatible with the fundamental Qur'anic concept of an omnipotent God and his sovereignty, the Ash'arite scholars did not offer much justification for their rejection of "secondary causation."[18] It was al-Ghazali (d. 1111), however, who proceeded beyond mere theological affirmation and undertook a systematic refutation of the concept of necessity of the causal nexus.[19] To be sure, he also started with the Qur'an and concluded with affirming the Qur'anic view. However, throughout his analysis he also engaged empirical data and logical analysis.

According to al-Ghazali, to attribute powers of creativity to causes was incompatible with the unity of God as expounded in the Qur'an. So he started by questioning the very nature of the correlation between the so-called cause and effect. After close empirical observation of natural causality and a rigorous logical analysis, al-Ghazali contended that

---

14. "To ascribe partners to God" has been understood as meaning "to ascribe to things a share in God's creative power." See Gimaret, *Theories de l'acte humain en theologie musulmane*, 375.

15. Frank, "The Structure of Created Causality According to Al-Ash'ari," 14.

16. Fakhry, *A History of Islamic Philosophy*, 234.

17. Corbin, *History of Islamic Philosophy*, 121–22.

18. Fakhry, *Islamic Occasionalism and Its Critique by Averroes and Aquinas*, 56–57.

19. Fakhry, *A History of Islamic Philosophy*, 257.

necessity belongs to the sphere of logical relations. Necessity has no scope beyond that sphere. No necessary correlation can be asserted between two distinct conditions or events, such as fire and burning.[20] The observed correlation between concomitant events represents an order established by God's will.

For example, the philosophers claimed that it is in nature of fire to ignite and it cannot but do so. Especially inspired by the Qur'anic miracle passages, (such as Abraham's miraculous survival in fire, Q. 21:69), al-Ghazali denied this necessity and maintained that it is God who creates that action of fire.[21] He asserted that the natural relationships between events are the outcome of a psychological habit, which the philosophers mistook for logical necessity. Their only evidence for this presumed necessity is an empirical proof. But all that experience attests is that the cause is conjoint to the effect—the effect "occurs *together with* the cause and not *through* it."[22] The only thing that can be affirmed through experiential observation is, for example, that the combustion of cotton occurs when it comes in contact with fire. But this does not prove that it is fire that produces the combustion, or that there may not be another reason. For al-Ghazali, the notion of natural causes generating or producing effects is unintelligible. His conclusion is that all activity must be referred to God because fire is inanimate and has no will, and cannot therefore produce anything whatsoever.[23]

The significance of al-Ghazali's argument about the unfounded necessity of the causal nexus can be appreciated against the Western post-Humean debate on causation. The importance of al-Ghazali's groundwork lies more in his willingness to expound his theological affirmation through logical and experiential evidences, unlike many of his Ash'arite predecessors. In other words, al-Ghazali attempted to confirm his reading of the text through a reading of creation, that is to say, the world. His approach displays a more interactive reading between the Qur'an and the "book of the creation." Nevertheless, his argument is still one-directional, as it starts from the Qur'an and looks at nature from that perspective. It still needs an incorporation of the move from the other direction, namely, a reflection on nature as it informs the understanding of the Qur'an.

Daniel Gimaret observes that however mediocre the Ash'arites' arguments against natural causation may be, their having recourse to *khāliq kulli shay* (the creator of all things) makes their position incontestably stronger than that of their opponents. The objections of their opponents could easily be refuted because "it is not imaginable to put a limit to God's power."[24] This is probably one of the main reasons Ash'arism "not only survived all criticism leveled at it, but succeeded in attaining a key position in Sunni Islam."[25] In other words, Ash'arism was successful because it based its doctrines primarily

---

20. For a deeper analysis of natural causality in the light of the Qur'an, see Mermer, "Induction, Science and Causation," 243–82.

21. For a brief analysis of al-Ghazali's approach, see: Yazıcıoğlu, "Redefining the Miraculous," 89–92.

22. al-Ghazali, *Tahafut al-falasifah*, 279.

23. Fakhry, *Islamic Occasionalism*, 60–64.

24. Gimaret, *Theories de l'acte*, 394–95.

25. Corbin, *History of Islamic Philosophy*, 120.

on the reading of scriptural verses. The problem was that they did not engage in a parallel reading of the "creational" verses (the world), as the Qur'an itself suggested. They just projected the Qur'anic conclusions onto the world. Nevertheless, their position was more consistent with the Qur'anic view than that of their opponents, who did the opposite: As we shall see below, the philosophers "read" the world from a mindset that took the Aristotelian perspective as a given, and interpreted experience according to their preconceptions of it, and then they tried to interpret the scriptural text according to such understanding of the world. That is, they attempted to project their reading of the world onto the Qur'anic verses despite the resulting discrepancy. Both used reason, but the second group gave precedence to reason over revelation, rather than using reason to verify the truth of revelation.

## CREATION OUT OF MATTER

The Muslim philosophers showed verses from the Qur'an to support their view of creation out of matter. They claimed for instance, that this verse indicates a creation out of matter: "Are, then, they who are bent on denying the truth not aware that . . . We made out of water every living thing? Will they not, then, believe?" (Q 21:30). The commentators on the Qur'an and the theologians[26] agreed that God created all beings out of water, but they insisted that water itself was also created from nothing since God is the Creator of all things (see, for example, 40:62); since water is obviously lifeless, it cannot sustain itself, let alone create anything. The philosophers, however, advocated creation out of matter as an alternative to creation out of nothing, which they rejected. Ibn Rushd believed in the eternity of the world and of "prime" matter, which was the substratum of becoming and change in the universe. According to this thesis, creation in time does not make sense and God is reduced to the role of a prime mover. It is this thesis that Ibn Rushd defended against the theologians's doctrine of creation ex nihilo, "in the name of genuine Aristotelianism."

Ibn Rushd interpreted "creation out of matter" as meaning that matter had natures or active powers inherent within it that allowed it to act as it does. The verse mentioned above (Q 21:30), however, contains no information about the nature of matter. There is no hint that water is actually active, not passive. As a matter of fact, the agent according to the verse is *God* and not water since the subject refers to God himself: "*We* made out of water every living thing." The Ash'arites perceived the determinism in the idea of natural causation and they were not satisfied with it, because for them it was incompatible with the fundamental idea of the Qur'an, which affirms the coexistence of absolute divine freedom of choice and will with absolute power.[27] Majid Fakhry observes that the determinism of Ibn Rushd's view of the universe "can hardly leave any scope for belief in an effective

---

26. The Mutazila agreed unanimously on the idea of creation ex nihilo. But they also held that God acts in two ways, directly and indirectly by the natures or forces that he put in things. The Mutazila believed in natural causation just as the philosophers and consequently their view of creation out of nothing was substantially different from that of the Ash'arites. See al-Alousi, 278.

27. Corbin, *History of Islamic Philosophy*, 121.

providence of God. Averroes (Ibn Rushd), it is true, concedes that God plays the role of Author and Preserver of the universe; but it is difficult to see how this role can be interpreted in any but deistic terms."[28]

According to Ibn Rushd, "it is self-evident that things have essences and attributes which determine the special functions of each thing."[29] This claim is not as simple as Ibn Rushd's statement seems to suggest: What is a "thing" apart from its essence and attributes? Is it possible to separate a thing from its properties? Is there a part of the thing that is more "persistent" than its properties or what happens to it? Are not the so-called functions of a thing the modes of being of that thing? With what power, knowledge, or will do they achieve these functions?

Ibn Rushd claimed, for example, that what makes a certain thing "fire" is its burning power. Fire burns under all conditions unless an obstacle, such as talc, hinders its action. In other words, Ibn Rushd used experience to vindicate his claim, but as we will see, it is agreed among contemporary philosophers that experience is in fact a dogma because it does not speak for itself; it is made to speak through interpretation.[30] F. Schuon is reported to have remarked that the Qur'anic verse, "We said, 'O fire be cool, and a means of safety for Abraham!'" (Q 21:69), can be used as an argument against al-Ghazali in favor of the causal approach. Schuon thought that if fire were not necessarily a burning agent, then God would not have commanded it to cool.[31] According to Nursi, however, the verse indicates that fire, just like other causes, does not act according to its wishes and nature; it does not act blindly, but performs a duty under a command. Nursi reasons that if it ceases to burn at the command of God, then the burning itself is tied to the divine command. Hence, it burns because it is commanded to do so, and therefore, it did not burn Abraham because it was commanded not to burn him. In other words, fire is the recipient of divine command and not an independent agent. It acts accordingly.[32]

Actually, the action of "burning" is not that simple: it is a reaction which involves not only the burned material before and after the burning—for example: cotton and ashes—but also oxygen and the laws according to which the cotton and other materials burn. That is, "burning," like any other event, cannot be isolated from the rest of the universe, which is an inseparable whole. Nursi likes to emphasize that all events are interrelated; therefore, for one event to occur, the whole universe has to be there in the first place. Hence, in order for a cause to produce an effect, however small it is, it has to be able to produce the whole universe in which that effect takes place and from which it cannot be separated. Similarly, the occurrence of "burning" is incumbent on innumerable conditions. In order for a thing (fire) to have the power to burn, it has to have the power and knowledge to control all the conditions involved in burning, and that is far from being evident. In Nursi's view, it is either acting under the command of one who possesses a comprehensive power

---

28. Fakhry, *Islamic Occasionalism*, 123–24.

29. Ibn Rushd, (Averroes), *Tahafut al-tahafut*, 318.

30. Gadamer, *Truth and Method*, 430.

31. Bakar, *Tawhid and Science*, 99.

32. Nursi, "The Words: The Second Station of The Twentieth Word," 269.

and knowledge, or it itself possesses such power and knowledge.

Throughout his *Tahafut al-tahafut*, Ibn Rushd reiterated the charge of skepticism against the Ash'arites, on account of their rejection of necessity of natural causation. He undertook a thorough exposition of the nature of the necessary concomitance of knowledge and causation, in the course of his refutation of al-Ghazali's arguments. Ibn Rushd wrote "it is self-evident that all events have four causes, agent, form, matter, and end, and that they are necessary for the existence of the effects."[33] This summarizes Aristotle's theory of causation. The "agent" is the motor cause or the principle of motion. This type of cause is usually identified as "efficient cause" or "what acts in order to make something exist," such as fire makes the burn exist when coming in contact with cotton, or "what produces a thing by acting on another thing."[34] This efficient cause progressively became the model of the modern concept of causation. To be a "cause" means to act on another thing to produce an effect. Now the nature of this relation is not evident at all, as the long debate on causation in the history of Western philosophy of science can witness.

Like Ibn Rushd, Cartesian philosophy and that of the scholastics supposed the relation between cause and effect to be necessary, as logical relations are necessary. In the West, the modern philosophy of causation began with David Hume's challenge to the necessity of the causal nexus. Hume, just like al-Ghazali, contended that the statement "A causes B" does not have intuitive certainty, like the statements of logic. His argument was that we could discover nothing in A itself that should lead to produce B. Only the experience of the constant conjunction of events of the kind A with events of the kind B can give us knowledge about cause and effect. It is an empirical matter that has no *a priori* certainty. Hume argued that,

> Were any object presented to us, and were we required to pronounce concerning the effect, which will result from it, without consulting past observation: After what manner, I beseech you, must the mind proceed in this operation? It must invent or imagine some event, which it ascribes to the object as its effect: And it is plain that this invention must be entirely arbitrary. The mind can never find the effect in the supposed cause, by the most accurate scrutiny and examination. For the effect is totally different from the cause and consequently can never be discovered in it.[35]

In analyzing Hume's view on causation, Bertrand Russell asserts that when we judge that A causes B, it actually means that we frequently observed their conjunction; "we have no right to say that A must be followed by B, or will be followed by B on future occasions."[36]

Hume's skepticism is based on his rejection of the principle of induction, which in this case could be stated as follows: The greater the number of cases of a law in which A has been found associated with B (A and B being classes of events), the more probable it is that A is always

---

33. Ibn Rushd, Averroes,'*Tahafut al-tahafut*, 319

34. Frank, ed., *Faut-Il chercher aux causes une raison?* 201

35. Hume, *An Enquiry Concerning Human Understanding*, 29.

36. Russell, *History of Western Philosophy*, 640.

associated with B. A sufficient number of cases of association of A with B make this law approach certainty. Russell demonstrates that if this principle is true, causal inferences, which the Ash'arites and later Hume in the West rejected, are perfectly valid. But if this principle is not true, then "every attempt to arrive at general scientific laws from particular observations is fallacious. The principle itself cannot of course, without circularity, be inferred from observed uniformities, since it is required to justify any such inference."[37]

The general principles of science, such as causal laws, and the scientific method itself all depend upon the inductive principle. Induction is used to justify inferences from what has been examined to what has not been examined. All arguments that argue as to the future or the inexperienced parts of the past or the present on the basis of experience assume the validity of the inductive principle. The logic of induction first conjectures that induction is valid, and then it concludes that causation is true; whereas, from the point of view of logic, it should be the other way around: induction can be justified only by proving that causation is true, or that the relation between cause and effect is necessary. That is, this principle cannot be proved by appeal to experience without begging the question. In other words, logically universal statements cannot be inferred from particular ones, no matter how numerous they are.

Inductive inferences can only be justified if the relationships between causes and effects are necessary, a priori truths. However, these relations are empirical and can only be established a posteriori; therefore, induction is not logically grounded. It is also, as Russell claims, "incapable of being proved by an appeal to experience,"[38] because it calls for the experience of the future, which is, as a matter of fact, impossible. That is, like any other type of rationalism, Averroist rationalism can also be refuted by Humean arguments. As Russell admits, "the problem of the justification of induction is one of the most difficult and most debated problems of Western philosophy."[39] Indeed, if induction cannot be justified, science cannot claim to yield knowledge, because the scientific method of knowledge is inductive. Hume's searching analysis has shown that the scientific theories and laws are never verifiable, and that the problem of knowledge is extremely difficult; so difficult that even to the present there is no accepted solution.

Karl Popper attempted to circumvent the difficulties raised by Hume and formulated for this purpose the principle of falsification, according to which a scientific theory holds until it is disproved. In order words, falsification, not verification, is the appropriate object of the observational and experimental procedures of science.[40] However, it has been noted that the appeal to falsification implicitly accepts the basic idea that there are clear criteria for determining under what conditions a conjecture or hypothesis is to be rejected. But the contemporary philosophers of science have argued that the proper standards of criticism are not as clear as Popper suggested. In Thomas Kuhn's words, "if any and every failure to fit were ground for theory re-

---

37. Ibid., 647.

38. Russell, *The Problems of Philosophy*, 38.
39. Russell, *The Problems of Philosophy*, 38
40. Popper, *The Logic of Scientific Discovery*, 32–42.

jection, all theories ought to be rejected at all times."[41] In Paul Feyerabend's view, Popper's apologetic stand leads to a further closure and to a new, masked form of dogmatism.[42]

Against the background of the contemporary debate on causation and the theory of knowledge, it appears that Ibn Rushd's solutions represent a rather naive reading of the causal problem, in its relation to the more general problem of knowledge. In fact, Ibn Rushd perceived the significance of the knowledge of causes and effects for any genuine metaphysical or theological worldview, but he confused causation and causality because he took causation for granted. Causality is the principle that nothing comes into being without being caused; every act has an agent. Causation means that the existence of every thing is necessitated by the cause—the cause is efficient in producing the effect. It is true that knowledge is bound to causality, but it is not obvious how it is related to causation. Causality is observed, but not causation; causation is an interpretation. According to philosophers of modern science, causation is a metaphysical or dogmatic interpretation of causality. As a matter of fact, causation has been recognized as the source of the problem of knowledge in modern philosophy.

Going back to the Ibn Rushd doctrine of creation, which he claimed was contained in the Qur'anic text, Husam Muhi el-Din al-Alousi states that the reason for Ibn-Rushd holding such a doctrine might be his philosophical commitment to the view. He asserts that the Qur'an is not the source of the philosophers' doctrine of creation, "but merely a source by which they attempted to justify their view in order to gain respectability for it in orthodox circles."[43] Indeed, it appears that Ibn Rushd understood the world according to Aristotelian philosophy, and then he projected the outcome onto the Qur'an, but without much success.

I mentioned previously the parallel reading of the Qur'an and the universe that Nursi suggests. This reading is really a hermeneutical circle, but the starting point is the scriptural text and not reason. For how would it be possible for contingent and limited reason to understand and interpret the world as it is, without distortion? According to Gadamer, understanding is achieved through the "play" of one's prejudices and the "things-themselves." He summarizes his elucidation of the happening of understanding, as "understanding understands itself."[44] He actually describes an essentially closed circle of understanding because there is no criterion outside reason to refer to and against which one can check one's understanding. This has been the general trend in contemporary philosophical hermeneutics: we can only hope to get closer to understanding things but we can never be sure that our interpretations conform to the "things-themselves."[45] This is where revelation plays a crucial role: the text provides a means of understanding, or in Nursi's language, the Qur'anic signs read or reveal the creational signs (ayāt). The

---

41. Kuhn, *The Structure of Scientific Revolutions*, 146

42. Feyerabend, *Science in a Free Society*, 142.

43. al-Alousi, *The Problem of Creation*, 88–89.

44. Gadamer, *Truth and Method*, 236.

45. Dummet, *Truth and Other Enigmas*, 458.

latter witness to the truth of the text and confirm its truth.

Whenever a philosopher came up with what he took for a firm foundation, another philosopher challenged his claims and argued that what was supposed to be necessary, or indubitable was open to doubt and questioning. Michael Dummet, a leading objectivist philosopher wrote:

> Just because the scandal caused by the philosophy's lack of a systematic methodology has persisted for so long, it has been a constant preoccupation of philosophers to remedy that lack, and a repeated illusion that they had succeeded in doing so. Husserl believed passionately that he at last held the key, which would unlock every philosophical door; the disciples of Kant ascribed to him the achievements of devising a correct philosophical methodology; Spinoza believed that he was doing for philosophy what Euclid had done for geometry, and before him, Descartes supposed that he had uncovered the one and proper philosophical method. I have mentioned only a few of many examples of this illusion.[46]

There is no reason one cannot add Ibn Rushd to this list.

## ORIGINATION WITHIN COMPOSITION

In Nursi's view, both creation out of nothing or origination and creation out of matter (in the form of composition) can be observed in the universe.[47] How are they related to each other? What is their meaning? How can the activity observed in the universe be interpreted and what view of God does that yield? Nursi believes that the answers can be found in the Qur'anic call to observe the universe. As to the Qur'an, it refers the reader to the creative activity in the universe and invites her/him to think about the way things have been made in the form of signs that carry meaning about something beyond themselves.[48] Nursi asserts that he extracts his method of reading the universe from the Qur'anic verses. How he achieved this is beyond the scope of this paper. I am only concerned with reviewing some of his basic arguments in order to give an idea of what constitutes Nursi's reading of the creational signs under the guidance of the Qur'anic signs. In fact, he repeatedly calls the universe "embodied Qur'an."[49]

Throughout his whole works, Nursi reiterates the inseparability and interconnectedness of all things and beings in the universe. All things are so interrelated, he writes, that in order to produce the least effect one has to produce and control the whole cosmos. For that single effect, however tiny or insignificant it may appear to us, can only take place within the cosmos; it cannot exist on its own. The effect and the cosmos are inseparable. Thus, in order to produce a single effect, or to manage a single particle, it is necessary to subjugate the whole cosmos and control it. That means that the creator of one thing can only be the creator and sustainer of all causes and all effects. No effect, nothing, exists on its own independently of the whole universe. Nursi often starts his arguments by referring to the universe because this is what the Qur'an bids the

---

46. Dummet, *Truth and Other Enigmas*, 458.
47. Nursi, "Lem'alar," in *RNK*, 685.
48. See, Qur'an, 3:190; 10: 6; 13:2; 13:3; 13:4; 14:5; 14:5; etc.
49. Nursi, " Sözler," in *RNK*, 49–50.

reader do. "We observe in the universe" is a phrase that he often uses.

Nursi observes that there are in the universe countless events occurring in countless places all at the same time, without any intermediary—for example, the blooming of multitudes of trees and plants in spring and the hatching of innumerable kinds of birds and other animals. He notes that when each particular event is considered from the point of view of the affirmation of divine unity, it is perceived in connection with all related events, and it is understood that all these events, these creative acts, proceed from a law of creativity. Thus, whoever performs one creative act must be the author of all the creative acts that are tied to the universal law of creativity. Hence, whoever gives life to a fly, for instance, must be the one who creates all insects and animals. For those motions proceed all according to the same universal laws of attributes of perfection such as life, mercy, power, and knowledge.[50] If, however, an event is not looked at from the point of view of the affirmation of divine unity (*tawḥīd*), it will be perceived in isolation from the other events of the same kind, and eventually, it will be ascribed to causes, chance, and unconscious nature.[51]

All particles comply with that law of creativity as though knowingly, without deviating from their aim until they reach their appointed position. This way, they proclaim that they are proceeding at the command of an infinitely wise, powerful, merciful One.[52] That is, they are signs glorifying their Maker, as the Qur'anic text that Nursi often quotes states, "The seven heavens extol His limitless glory, and the earth, and all that they contain; and there is not a single thing but extols His limitless glory and praise: but you fail to grasp the manner of their glorifying Him!" (Q 17:44). Thus Nursi explains that things and beings function as signs because of the way they are related to each other, that is, because of the way causes are tied to effects. So the purpose in creation out of matter, or rather creation in the form of composition, as Nursi calls it, is to tie the effects to causes in such a way that they reflect their Maker's attributes of perfection. For Nursi, beings are signs in the sense that they have been made in such a way that it is impossible to ascribe them to anyone other than the Maker of all things.

Nursi understands that creation by command means creation through laws. The earth for instance, is made to spin as easily as particles are caused to move and spin. This demonstrates a comprehensive law of power that is in force in the universe. Through that law, the omnipotent Creator causes the solar system to travel in space. These laws are a universal manifestation of divine command and will. Through these laws, "God himself directs everything personally and listens to the plaints of all things."[53] A single insect is brought to life with the same ease and the same law as the whole species of insects. Through that law of bestowing life, every spring the Creator restores life to a tree and raises the whole earth to life. Through the same law, he will raise beings to life at resurrection. The Qur'an alludes to this law with the verse, "your creation

---

50. Nursi, "Mektubat," in *RNK*, 504.
51. Nursi, "Şuâlar," in *RNK*, 848–54.
52. Nursi, "Sözler," in *RNK*, 234–35.

53. Nursi, "Şuâlar," in *RNK*, 850

and your resurrection is but as a single soul" (31:28).⁵⁴

The God of the philosophers cannot do this. He is in partnership with other principles and things in his causal power. For Ibn Rushd, as al-Ghazali pointed out, God is coexistent with the universe itself, and thus far from being an independent agent. Nursi thinks that, from a theological point of view, this "allots the rest of His sovereignty to causes and intermediaries, and thus opens the way to associating partners with God in a most comprehensive manner."⁵⁵ Nursi warns his readers that the laws of the attributes of perfection should not be confused with the causal, horizontal relations between cause and effect. For Nursi, natural laws, if they exist, could still not be identified with God's commands. They refer to constructional relations between things and events themselves, and not to their relation with their Maker. Those laws are theoretical constructs and thus cannot sustain external reality.⁵⁶

Nursi holds that the utmost speed and facility apparent in the creation of beings are decisive evidences for the perfection of the Maker's power. Everything is so easy in relation to him that it is understood that he creates with a mere command. The Qur'anic decree, "Indeed, His command when He wills a thing is 'Be and it is'" (36:82), expresses the absolute ease in his creating.⁵⁷ "Unto Him belongs every being that is in the heavens and on earth: all things devoutly obey His will" (30:26), also expresses that all things are submissive to the command of the divine power. The greatest is as easy as the smallest in relation to the essential and infinite power that is the source of the creative activity observed in the universe. In Nursi's view, there is no indication in the universe, and no logical or rational reason suggesting that causes are efficient and produce the effect. Like the effect, the apparent causes are also contingent; they are all created, as the Qur'anic verse teaches: "Now those things some people invoke beside God cannot create anything, since they themselves are but created" (Q 16:20). This is what he means by creation from nothing, or origination. Causes are not executives of divine power, but its heralds. They are not partners to God in his creation, but signs pointing to his existence and proclaiming his attributes of perfection. He alone brings beings into existence out of nothing, and creates everything necessary for them, also out of nothing.⁵⁸ In spring for example, divine power gives existence, out of nothing, to the forms and attributes of beings as well as their components and all their conditions and states.⁵⁹.

54. Nursi, " Mektubat," in *RNK*, 483.
55. Nursi, " Sözler," in *RNK*, 242.
56. Nursi, " Sözler," in *RNK*, 227–28.
57. Nursi, " Sözler," in *RNK*, 260.

58. Nursi makes it clear that "out of nothing" does not mean absolute nonexistence, which does not exist anyway. For nothing exists outside the sphere of divine knowledge, so that something can be cast there. Relative nonexistence, he explains, is external; it is a sort of title for something concealed but existent in divine knowledge. Some scholars called these beings existent in divine knowledge "latent realities." To go to extinction, they said, is to be temporarily divested of external dress and to enter upon existence in divine knowledge (i.e., existence in meaning). In other words, ephemeral beings leave external existence, and their essences are clothed in what has the meaning of existence. They pass from the sphere of divine power to that of divine knowledge. See Nursi, "Mektubat," in RNK, 373.

59. Nursi, "Lem'alar," in *RNK*, 686.

The Qur'an mentions creation out of matter. At the same time, creation from the elements and other things in the form of composition can be observed in the universe. Nursi holds that if it is referred to causes and nature, then innumerable difficulties arise: causes do not possess comprehensive knowledge and power and therefore cannot create from nothing and nonexistence. They would have to create things in the form of composition only. However, to create one being they would have to collect its parts from all over the globe. Even if they did, they would need to preserve them in orderly form without dispersing. It would also be necessary for them to make the gathered particles into a living body that constantly changes. This is so difficult as to be impossible and therefore precluded.

On the other hand, if the creation is attributed to one single being, that being is bound to have infinite knowledge and power that prevails over all things. Hence, it is extremely easy for him to give external existence to things, which are present in his knowledge, and bring them out of apparent nonexistence. Nursi says it is "as simple as striking a match" or like "transposing an image from photographic film to paper"; he just says "Be" and it is.[60] Creation in the form of composition also becomes very easy when attributed to one omniscient and omnipotent being. All the necessary particles are gathered according to the law of his power. They assume by divine knowledge, a specified measure and proportion in order to form a living being. And through the law of providing, he sends particles, which act at his command, to that being and employs them in it.[61] Nursi concludes that ascribing all things to one single being is so easy as to be necessary.[62] However, if the creation of everything is not directly ascribed to him, if it is referred to causes instead, it becomes necessary to accept that each cause has inherent in it infinite power and knowledge. That is to say, if the effect is not attributed to an omnipotent Maker but to causes instead, it becomes necessary to accept that each cause is omnipotent and omniscient. Nursi deduces this logic from the following Qur'anic verses:

> God puts forth a Parable: a man belonging to many partners at variance with each other, and a man belonging entirely to one master: are those two equal in comparison? Praise be to God, but most of them have no knowledge (Q 39:29).

> O my two companions of the prison! (I ask you): are many lords differing among themselves better, or the One God, Supreme and Irresistible? If not Him, you worship nothing but names which you have names—you and your fathers—for which God has sent down no authority: the command is for none but God. He has commanded that you worship none but Him: that is the right religion, but most men understand not (Q 12:39–40).

According to Nursi, these verses teach that it is easier for all things to proceed from one center than for one thing to issue out of many causes. For example, a commander orders a thousand soldiers to advance with one command, the same, as he would order one soldier. However, if the command of one soldier is to be

---

60. Nursi, " Şuâlar," in *RNK*, 856–58.

61. Nursi, "Lem'alar," in *RNK*, 686.

62. Nursi, " Mektubat," in *RNK*, 460–64.

assigned to a thousand officers, the result will be chaos.[63]

In conclusion, according to Nursi, both kinds of creation converge at one point: God both originates and composes. There is origination within composition. Why is it so? God wants to make himself known and loved. So he forms beings out of the elements of the universe in order to demonstrate his many attributes of perfection, like wisdom, mercy, power, and knowledge.

## CONCLUSION

As we have seen, understanding of the Qur'an and the universe directly influences the conception of God. The Ash'arite theologians based their theology on their reading of the Qur'an. Accordingly, they rejected the idea of creation out of matter, because as it was understood it was in apparent conflict with the Qur'anic concept of deity. They argued that the model of creation through the causal efficacy of their originating causes, ending with the prime mover, could not be reconciled with the God of the Qur'an, who possessed absolute power and will. Their reasoning was that, since God is an omnipotent agent, he must be responsible for the creation of everything in the world, as the Qur'an states. This method is intelligible only if one accepts the translation of causation into language referring to God's actions. It does not supply a method to justify such translation.

The philosopher Ibn Rushd perceived the significance of causality in connection with the issue of knowledge. However, he read the world and interpreted experience according to his preconceptions of it, and then he tried to interpret the scriptural text accordingly. He attempted to read his own understanding in the Qur'an despite the resulting discrepancy. That is, rather than using reason to verify the truth of revelation, he gave precedence to reason over revelation. He therefore understood creation out of matter in a way that was clearly incompatible with the basic aim of the Qur'an, which is *tawḥīd*.

Nursi believed that a proper reading of the Qur'an is incumbent on a parallel reading of the universe. He also contended that the Qur'anic verses supply the method required for a correct reading of the world. In his works, he practiced a reading of the world in harmony with the scriptural text. He showed how causality can be used to establish that everything, every cause and every effect, is a sign pointing to the knowledge of God—not the knowledge of the causes or the effects, but the knowledge of the divine attributes and the laws of their manifestation in this world. Thus, Nursi demonstrated that things are not signs because the Qur'an says so, rather the Qur'an says so because they do function as signs; and that the Qur'an instructs its audience to witness the signs of God in the universe. Within this hermeneutical context, it appears that creation takes place in two forms: through origination and through composition out of the elements. These two types of creation are not incompatible, but complementary. God both originates and composes; there is origination within composition. It is on this profound understanding of God as the Creator that Nursi then builds his discussion of the Beautiful Names of God, which further clarifies the concept of God. The topic of

---

63. Nursi, "Mektubat," in *RNK*, 467.

*asmā' al-ḥusnā* or the Beautiful Names and Attributes of God is treated with so much detail in the *Risale* that it would be the topic for another paper, or a book, rather.

## BIBLIOGRAPHY

al-Alousi, Husam Muhi Eldin. "The Problem of Creation in Islamic Thought," PhD diss., University of Cambridge, 1965.

al-Ghazali. *Tahafut al-falasifah*. Edited by M. Bouyges. Beirut, 1927

al-Razi, Fakhr al-Din Muhammad ibn 'Umar. *Mafātiḥ al-ghayb*. Beirut: Dar al-Fikr, 1981.

al-Shatibi, Abu Ishaq İbrahim Ibn Musa. *Al-Muwafaqāt*. Beirut: Dar al-Ma'rifa, n.d.

Bakar, Osman. *Tawhid and Science*. Kuala Lampur: S.I.P.S, 1991.

Corbin, Henry. *History of Islamic Philosophy*. London: Islamic Publications, 1993.

Dummet, Michael. *Truth and Other Enigmas*. London: Duckworth, 1978.

Feyerabend, Paul. *Science in a Free Society*. London: NLB, 1978.

Frank, Richard M., ed. *Faut-Il chercher aux causes une raison? L'Explication causale dans les sciences humaines*. Paris: Librairie Philosophique J. Vrin, 1994.

———. "The Structure of Created Causality According to Al-Ash'ari: An Analysis of the Kitab al-Luma' # 82–164." *Studia Islamica* XXV (1969) 13–75.

Gadamer, H. G. "The Problem of Historical Consciousness." In *Interpretative Social Science: A Reader*, edited by P. Rainbow and W. M. Sullivan, 103–60. Berkley: University of California Press, 1979.

———. *Truth and Method*. London: Sheed and Ward, 1981.

Gimaret, Daniel. *Theories de l'acte humain en theologie musulmane*. Paris: Librairie Philosophique J. Vrin, 1980.

Hume, David. *An Enquiry Concerning Human Understanding*. Oxford: Oxford University Press, 1978.

Izutsu, Toshihiko. *Ethico-Religious Concepts in the Qur'an*. Montreal: McGill University Press, 1966.

Kuhn, Thomas S. *The Structure of Scientific Revolutions*. Chicago: University of Chicago, 1970.

Mermer, Yamina B. "Induction, Science and Causation: Some Critical Reflections," *Islamic Studies* 35.3 (1996) 243–82.

———. "Principles of Qur'anic Hermeneutics." *The Journal of Scriptural Reasoning*, 5.1 (2005). Online: https://jsr.shanti.virginia.edu/back-issues/vol-5-no-1-april-2005-islam-and-scriptural-reasoning/principles-of-Qur'anic-hermeneutics/

*The Message of the Qur'an*. Translated by Muhammad Asad. Gibraltar: Dar al-Andalus, 1984.

Nursi, Bediüzzaman Said. *The Flashes: From the Risale-i Nur Collection*. Translated by Şükran Vahide. Istanbul: Sözler, 1996.

———. *Isharat-ul- i'jaz fi madani al-ijaz*. Istanbul: Yayınları, 1987.

———. *Letters*. Translated by Şükran Vahide. Istanbul: Sözler, 2001.

———. *Sözler Risale-i Nur Külliyatı*. Vols. 1 & 2. Istanbul: Nesil Yayınları, 1996.

———. *The Supreme Sign: Observations of a Traveler Questioning Creation Concerning His Maker*. Translated by Hamid Algar. Berkley: Risale-i Nur Institute of America, 1979.

———. *The Words: From the Risale-i Nur Collection*. New and rev. ed. Translated by Şükran Vahide. Istanbul: Sözler, 1998.

Popper, Karl. *The Logic of Scientific Discovery*. London: Routledge, 1992.

Rushd, Ibn (Averroes). *Tahafut al-tahafut*. Translated by S. Van Den Bergh. London: Oxford University Press, 1954.

Russell, Bertrand. *History of Western Philosophy*. London: Allen & Unwin, 1961.

———. *The Problems of Philosophy*. Oxford: Oxford University Press, 1980.

Smith, Wilfred Cantwell. "The True Meaning of Scripture: An Empirical Historian's Non-reductionist Interpretation of the Qur'an," *International Journal of Middle East Studies*, II (1980), 487–505.

# 6

# The Significance of Resurrection and the Afterlife in the Writings of Bediüzzaman Said Nursi

## CÜNEYT ŞİMŞEK

### INTRODUCTION

Throughout the history of Islamic thought, the concepts of resurrection (*ḥashr*) and the afterlife (*akhirah*) have generally not been analyzed by Muslim scholars according to rational evidence. *Mutakallimūn*, the doctors of *'ilm al-kalām*,[1] have primarily dealt with this topic under the title of *al-sam'iyyāt*,[2] merely referring to its references in the Qur'an and *hadīth* rather than studying it independently. Furthermore, while books have been written by Islamic scholars concerning the stages after death, including the circumstances in the grave, paradise, and hell, no model has been developed to prove these concepts rationally. In fact, Bediüzzaman Said Nursi himself notes that, for Muslim scholars, "resurrection rests entirely on traditional proofs; it cannot be rationally examined."[3]

---

1 'Ilm al-kalām is the discipline that brings discursive arguments to the service of religious beliefs (*'aqa'id*) in Islam. It, thus, provides a place for reflexion and meditation and, hence, for reason in the elucidation and defence of the content of the faith." Gardet, "llm al-Kalam."

2 According to the *mutakallimūn* there are three fundamental Islamic doctrines: "the unity and uniqueness of God (*tawḥīd*), prophecy (*nubūwwa*) and the ultimate return (*ma'ād*)." "Typically in late *kalām* manuals, eschatological teachings are subsumed under the category of *sam'iyyāt*, 'matters heard/received in faith,' since unlike the other two great categories of theological concern, metaphysics and prophecy, they are considered to lie outside the reach of rational proof. The theologian's task here is simply to defend scriptural predictions from denial or misinterpretation rooted either in false scriptural exegesis or in an inappropriate extension of ratiocination into this uniquely revelatory area." Hermansen, "Eschatology," 309.

3. Nursi, *The Words*, 106.

This article consists of four parts. In the first part, I will touch upon the importance of the Qur'anic concepts of resurrection and the afterlife in the ideas of Said Nursi. The second part will deal with Nursi's methodology for proving the existence of a bodily resurrection and the afterlife. As such, this part will not be about the proofs concerning resurrection and the afterlife that Nursi puts forward in his treatises. Instead, it will simply give a general idea about what methodology he uses in putting forth those proofs. The third part will focus on some of the arguments supporting bodily resurrection and the afterlife. The fourth and final part will talk about the general possibility of their existence.

## THE IMPORTANCE OF RESURRECTION AND THE AFTERLIFE IN THE QUR'AN

Nursi notes that one-quarter of the Qur'an explicitly refers to resurrection and the afterlife, while one-third refers to these subjects implicitly.[4] The Qur'an not only contains over one thousand verses that mention resurrection[5] and the afterlife but also speaks with a style that bases all other subjects on these concepts.[6] According to Nursi, it is because of this emphasis that belief in the afterlife is accepted, along with the belief in God, as one of the two greatest pillars of faith in Islam.[7]

Proofs for the coming of resurrection and the afterlife can be based on rational comparisons made between the acts of God that we witness in this world and those that are expected to take place during resurrection and the afterlife. The verses of the Qur'an that talk about

---

4. Nursi, *The Rays*, 578. See also, Abdel Haleem, "Qur'an and Hadith," 29.

5. Nursi claims that "resurrection has many degrees. It is obligatory to believe in some of them; they must be acknowledged. Whereas others become apparent according to levels in spiritual and intellectual development, and for these, knowledge pertaining to both are necessary. In order to present cogent and strong proofs for the simplest and easiest level, the All-Wise Qur'an points out a power capable of opening up a truly vast realm of resurrection. The degree of resurrection in which it is necessary for all to believe is this:

"After human beings die, their spirits depart for another realm. And their bodies rot except for a minute cell from the base of the spine which will act as a seed. It remains intact, and on the Day of Resurrection God Almighty will create the human body out of it and return its spirit to it. This degree is so simple, then, it may be seen every spring through millions of examples. Sometimes in order to prove this degree, the verses of the Qur'an point out the unlimited activity of a power capable of raising to life all particles, and sometimes the traces of a power and wisdom capable of sending all creatures to extinction and then recalling them. Then they point to the activity and traces of a power and wisdom able to scatter the stars and shatter the heavens, and sometimes to the activity and manifestations of a power and wisdom capable of causing all animate creatures to die and then raising them to life again all at once at a single trumpet-blast. Sometimes the verses demonstrate the manifestations of a power and wisdom that will raise to life the face of the earth and animate creatures all separately. And sometimes they demonstrate the traces of a power and wisdom that, lopping off its mountains, will cause the globe of the earth to disintegrate completely, and then restoring it will transform it into an even more excellent form. That is to say, apart from the Day of Resurrection, in which it is obligatory for everyone to believe and to acknowledge, with that power and wisdom, God Almighty can create numerous other degrees and resurrections." Nursi, *The Words*, 642–43. Nursi also says, "At the resurrection there will be the return of spirits to their bodies, the revivification of the bodies, and the remaking of the bodies." Ibid., 125.

6. Nursi, *The Rays*, 24, 212, 241.

7. Nursi, *Kastamonu Lahikası*, 211.

resurrection call attention to the works of God in this world that are observed by all of humanity, like trees, flowers, rain, storms, animals, seasons, and stars, and to the particular and universal well-ordered acts continuously taking place within these works.[8] In other words, they refer to "worldly resurrections" at the micro and macro levels and connect them to the relevant Divine Names of God.[9]

8. Qur'anic verses providing proof of resurrection include the following: "God who created you first will raise you up again." Qur'an 17:49–52. "Raising up the dead is similar to giving life to the earth after rain." Qur'an 7:57. See also Qur'an 22:5, 30:19, 30:50, 35:9. For belief in resurrection in general, see Qur'an 2:281, 17:71, 22:7, 30:25, 36:69, 50:20.

9. The concept of Divine Names and Attributes of God has more than one classification in Muslim books and has been one of the most controversial matters in ʿilm al-kalām. Since it is beyond this paper to explore all the details of this subject, I will base my paper on one description that Nursi gives in many places in the *Risale-i Nur Collection*. Nursi, rather than simply referring to the Qur'an and the hadith of Prophet Muhammad, uses an intellectual approach when discussing the Names and Attributes of God. According to him, the classification of all the divine qualities to which the whole ordering of the cosmos testifies can be stated as follows:

> A beautiful and profound book necessarily presupposes the act of writing and a well-built house presupposes the act of building; and the acts of writing beautifully and building well presuppose the names of writer and builder; and the titles of writer and builder obviously imply the arts and attributes of writing and building; and these arts and attributes self-evidently necessitate one who will be qualified by the names and attributes, and be the artist and craftsman. For just as it is impossible for there to be a deed without a doer, or a name without one designated by the name, so too it is not possible for there to be an attribute without one qualified by the attribute, and for there to be a craft without a craftsman.
>
> On the basis, then, of this truth and principle, the universe with all the beings it contains resembles a collection of profound books and letters written by the pen of Divine Determining, and countless buildings and palaces constructed with the hammer of Divine Power. Each of these singly in thousands of ways and together in uncountable ways utters the following testimony:
>
> These innumerable *dominical and merciful deeds*, and the endless manifestations of *the thousand and one Divine Names* which are the source of the deeds, and the infinite manifestations of *the seven transcendent attributes* which are the source of the Beautiful Names, in endless and infinite ways point to and testify to *the necessary existence and unity of an All-Glorious Essence* Which is the source of those all-embracing, sacred seven attributes and is qualified by them. And so too all the instances of beauty, loveliness, perfection, and exquisiteness found in those beings self-evidently testify all together to the sacred beauties and perfections of the dominical deeds, and the Divine Names, and attributes, and qualities, which are fitting and worthy of them, and to the sacred beauty of the Most Pure and Holy Essence.
>
> So the truth of dominicality that manifests itself within the truth of activity reveals and makes itself known in qualities and acts such as creating, originating, fashioning and bringing into being, with knowledge and wisdom; determining, forming, administering and changing with regularity and balance; transforming, causing to descend and perfecting, with purpose and will; and feeding, nurturing, and bestowing generosity and bounty, with tenderness and mercy. And within the truth of the manifestation of dominicality, the truth of the immediately perceived revelation of

## RESURRECTION AND AFTERLIFE IN NURSI'S WRITINGS

The concept of the resurrection of all living beings plays an important role in Nursi's works. The author has written multiple treatises in which he attempts to prove the existence of an afterlife; and in nearly every one of these treatises in which he explains the pillars of Islamic faith, he consistently connects these pillars to the subject of the afterlife. It is through this connection, Nursi argues in the *Risale-i Nur*, that "the belief in the afterlife has been given equal weight[10] to the belief in God."[11]

He argues that being able to provide rational proof of resurrection and the afterlife is particularly necessary in modern times. According to him, it has become mandatory in our time to provide proof for each of the pillars of faith in a way that satisfies both the human mind and heart, as respect for religious authorities and submission to religion have decreased and naturalist science and materialistic philosophy have come to dominate our way of thinking.[12] It is for this reason he places an emphasis on providing rational proof for the afterlife just as he does for the other pillars of faith.

## TWO DIFFERENT METHODOLOGIES IN OLD SAID AND NEW SAID[13]

The books written by Nursi on the concept of resurrection[14] in the periods of

---

Divinity makes itself known and recognized through the compassionate and munificent manifestations of *the Beautiful Names* and through the Glorious and Beauteous manifestations of *the seven affirmative* attributes: *Life, Knowledge, Power, Will, Hearing, Sight,* and *Speech.*

Nursi, *The Rays*, 168-69. See also, Nursi, *The Words*, 648-49.

10. In his uncompleted *tafsīr*, *The Signs of Miraculousness* [*Ishārāt al-i'jāz*], Nursi says that "the fundamental aims of the Qur'an and its essential elements are fourfold: divine unity [*al-tawḥīd*], prophethood [*al-nubūwwa*], the resurrection of the dead [*al-ḥashr*], and justice [*al-'adāla*]." Nursi, *Signs of Miraculousness*, 19, 37, 59, 181, 194. Nursi, *Ishārāt al-i'jāz*, 23-24, 40, 177. Although most of his treatises and books are devoted to the above-mentioned aims of the Qur'an, they place much more emphasis on two aims in particular, namely, divine unity and the resurrection of the dead. Thus, "equal weight" most probably refers to the equal amount of emphasis Nursi places on these subjects in his works.

11. Nursi, *Kastamonu Lahikası*, 21.

12. Nursi, *The Letters*, 39.

13. Historically, the first period of Nursi's life, the "Old Said" period, roughly covers the time between 1878 and 1922; the transition period is from 1922 to 1925; and the "New Said" period is from 1926 to his death in 1960.

14. These treatises can be divided into four groups: 1) The treatises that aim to prove the existence of resurrection and afterlife by addressing mostly reason/intellect, including a) *Muḥākamāt*, 167-70; b) *Ishārāt al-i'jāz*, 61-67; *Signs of Miraculousness*, 59-66; and c) "The Twenty-ninth Word" (in *The Words*), 533-56; 2) The treatises that aim to prove their existence using a universal/comprehensive methodology that addresses both intellect and heart together, such as a) "Lāsiyyamā" (in *al-Mathnawī al-'arabī al-nūrī*, 83-101); b) "The Tenth Word" (in *The Words*, 59-107); and c) "The Seventh Topic" (in *The Rays*, 230-41); 3) The treatises that deal with the individual and social fruits and benefits of belief in the afterlife along with the rational proofs of it, including a) "The Eighth Topic" (in *The Rays*, 242-55); b) "The Ninth Ray" (in *The Rays*, 201-12); 4) The treatises addressing some controversial subjects concerning hell and heaven as mentioned in the Qur'an and hadīth, such as a) "The Twenty-eighth Word" (in *The Words*, 513-20); b) *Ishārāt al-i'jāz*, 191-201; and

Old Said and New Said, as well as the period of transition between the two, are different in terms of the author's methodology and style. The stylistic differences include an increase during the New Said period in his emphasis on the relationship between the Divine Names and resurrection and the afterlife through his detailed comparisons by means of stories. It is also during this period that he makes an attempt to reach out to a wider audience.[15] On the other hand, the books written during the Old Said period are dominated by a methodology where the connection between the Divine Names and the concepts of resurrection and the afterlife remains relatively weaker and there are concise references to the concept of resurrection. As for the books of the transition period, they demonstrate some traces of the styles and methodologies used during the other two periods.

In both *Nokta Risalesi'* (*The Point*), an Old Said-period book, and "The Twenty-ninth Word" of *Sözler* (*The Words*), written in the New Said period, Nursi provides rational proofs of the existence of angels and the resurrection of humankind. Both treatises, according to Nursi, combine the outlook of the mind with the intuition of the heart.[16] However, in his most important work on the subject of resurrection, "The Tenth Word" of *Sözler*, written in 1928, he speaks strongly about the "arguments set forth which raise the heart to the level of perfect belief."[17] It should be noted that Nursi's emphasis on "the heart" in "The Tenth Word," rather than detracting from the role of the mind, actually refers to a combination of the concepts of heart and mind. This usage begins during his transition period and continues through his New Said period. For the New Said, the heart never leaves the mind and the balance between the two is very important.[18]

In *Muhākamāt* (*The Judgments*),[19] a work of the Old Said period, the subjects of resurrection and the afterlife are explained in a very brief manner with a clear emphasis on bodily resurrection. This section of the work, which is presented in the form of introductory remarks, discusses some of the issues covered in Nursi's later treatises about resurrection and the afterlife.[20] Nursi also wrote, in Arabic, "Ten Proofs" of resurrection in *Signs of Miraculousness* (*Ishārāt al-i'jāz*) while on the battlefront during World War I, and "Four Sources" about the same issue in the short Turkish treatise, *The Point* (*Nokta Risalesi*, 1918).[21] Even though both of these treatises are more detailed than the section in *Muhākamāt*, they generally use the same logic and concise style. "The Twenty-ninth Word" (1928–30) in *The Words*, one of the first

---

c) *Signs of Miraculousness*, 211–23.

15. Nursi, *The Words*, 59.

16. Bediüzzaman Said Nursi, *al-Mathnawī al-'arabī al-nūrī* (Istanbul: Sözler Publications, 1994), 245; Nursi, *The Words*, 538.

17. Nursi, *The Words*, 538.

18. When describing the methodology followed in his works, Nursi claims that it is a journey carried out through reason under the auspices of heart and through heart under the supervision of reason (Nursi, *al-Mathnawī al-'arabī al-nūrī*, 35). To Nursi, what paves the way for the understanding of resurrection and afterlife, which is "so profound, and at the same time, so exalted a path," is nothing but an "effulgence" coming from the wisdom of the Qur'an and "compassion" from God (Nursi, *The Words*, 107).

19. *Muhākamāt*, written as a general methodology for Islamic sciences and published in 1911, is one of the most important works of the Old Said period.

20. Nursi, *Muhākamāt*, 167–70.

21. Nursi, *Asār-ı badi'iyya*, 66–82.

works of the New Said period, can be regarded as a very detailed description of the subject of the afterlife as described in *Nokta Risalesi*.

## TWO TREATISES: "LASIYYAMA" AND "THE TENTH WORD"

"Lasiyyama," another Arabic treatise of Nursi's transitional period in *al-Mathnawī al-ʿarabī al-nūrī*,[22] is very reminiscent of "the Tenth Word" from *Sözler* with regard to its style and content. This treatise bases belief in resurrection and the afterlife on the Divine Names. When we come to "The Tenth Word," the author gives information about his writing process as follows:

It was about thirty years ago and just this season. I was walking through these orchards with the almond trees all in blossom when suddenly the verse, "So think on the signs of God's mercy, how He gives life to the earth after its death; indeed, He it is who will give life to the dead, and He is powerful over all things" (Qur'an, 30:50) came to mind. Its meaning became clear to me that day. I was both walking and repeating it over and over again at the top of my voice. I recited it forty times. In the evening I returned and together with Şamlı Hafız Tevfik wrote the "Tenth Word." That is, I dictated and Hafız Tevfik wrote it down.[23]

Nursi divides "The Tenth Word" into two parts: "Twelve Aspects" and "Twelve Truths." When explaining why he wrote his treatises "in the form of metaphors, comparisons and stories," he states that his intention was "to facilitate comprehension and to show how rational, appropriate, well-founded and coherent are the truths of Islam."[24] The meaning of the stories are explained in the twelve Truths of the second part of "The Tenth Word."[25]

Although it is in "The Tenth Word" that Nursi focuses on the proof of resurrection and the afterlife, he also touches upon almost every major issue that he discusses in his books and treatises. Therefore, despite being unique in its style and methodology, "The Tenth Word" is actually a very comprehensive summary of the rest of the *Risale-i Nur Collection*.

In a letter to a friend, Nursi gives some information regarding the

---

22. Nursi, *al-Mathnawī al-ʿarabī al-nūrī*, 83–101.

23. Vahide, *Islam in Modern Turkey*, 194.

24. Nursi, *The Words*, 59.

25. In all of his treatises, especially the ones on resurrection and the afterlife, the examples Nursi gives all share some striking properties: 1) These examples are recurring examples for everyone; 2) Their equivalents are abundant; 3) They are usually easy to grasp; 4) Those that pertain to human life can be experienced by everyone; 5) They are rational but not scientific. Nursi, *The Words*, 438.

Concerning this last property, it is important to remember that according to Nursi, complicated scientific information only addresses the experts and, as such, cannot easily provide evidence for non-experts. This is due to the fact that every individual can be classified as a layman in areas other than his own field of expertise, and, thus, he has no options other than to show blank awe and blind imitation in those other areas. Whereas in matters of faith, the evidence must be more obvious than what it is pointing at and must help explain the issue in its breadth, confusing scientific information serves to do the exact opposite. Those who are not experts are obliged to follow blindly, which is contrary to the purpose behind providing the evidence. In the Qur'an, the evidence pertaining to the knowledge of God, resurrection, and the afterlife generally does not require any expertise, and so it addresses everyone. This, in turn, is a reflection of divine justice. Nursi, *The Words*, 251–52.

methodology behind his discussion of the subject of resurrection in "The Tenth Word."

Each [of the twelve "Truths" of which the main part of the work is composed] proves three things at the same time. Each proves both the existence of the Necessarily Existent One, and His names and attributes, and then it constructs the resurrection of the dead on these and proves it.[26]

In fact, when "The Tenth Word" is read thoroughly, it can be seen that Nursi follows this methodology throughout the entire treatise. Nursi announces that "everyone from the most obdurate unbeliever to the most sincere believer can take his share [of knowledge] from the Truths."[27] "Because," he continues, "in each, the gaze is turned towards beings, works [creation]."[28] Addressing the reader of "The Tenth Word," he goes on to explain,

> (The Tenth Word says:) is this in the text? There are well-ordered acts in these [creations], and a well-ordered act cannot be without an author. In which case it has an author. And since the act has been carried out with order and balance, its author must be wise and just. Since he is wise, he does nothing in vain. And since he acts with justice, he does not permit rights to be violated. There will therefore be a great gathering, a supreme tribunal. The Truths have been tackled in this way. They are succinct, and thus prove the three things [the existence of the Necessarily Existent One, His names and attributes, and the resurrection of the dead] at once.[29]

The "beings" (*mawjūdāt*) and "works" (*āsār*) referred to above are important concepts of the *Risale-i Nur* used to prove the existence of God and help people comprehend His names and attributes. This is due to the fact that all individuals confront, with all of their material and spiritual faculties, the beings and works created by God. By virtue of this common ground, "The Tenth Word" is, according to Nursi, a work that addresses everyone.[30]

Nursi believes that the source of the truth and perfection in his writings, in other words, their method and content, is the Qur'an. Accordingly, he describes his treatise on resurrection as consisting "of a few droplets filtered from hundreds of verses."[31] Through this description, the author alludes to the proof of existence of the Necessarily Existent One, the manifestations of the Divine Names, and how the Divine Names require the resurrection of humankind and the existence and eternity of the afterlife.

---

26. Nursi, *Barla Lahikası*, 320. Vahide, *Islam in Modern Turkey*, 195.

27 Nursi, *Barla Lahikası*, 320 (first quotation); Vahide, *Islam in Modern Turkey*, 195 (second quotation).

28 Nursi, *Barla Lahikası*, 160.

29. Ibid.

30. In another letter, Nursi complains that the value of "The Tenth Word" is not sufficiently appreciated—perhaps by some of his disciples at the time. He says that he himself read this treatise more than fifty times and every time he read it he enjoyed it and felt the need to read it again. This joy and need, he feels, comes from his desire to understand "the sciences of belief" (*ulūm-u imāniye*). Nursi, *The Letters*, 422, 499. According to him, people always need this kind of knowledge, just as they need daily nutrition. Nursi, *Barla Lahikası*, 310.

31. Nursi, *The Letters*, 434.

## SECTION TWO: THEOLOGY

### THE CONCEPT OF RESURRECTION AND THE DIVINE NAMES

It can be claimed that one of the most prominent aspects of Nursi's works is that they establish the relationship between the Divine Names of God and the pillars of Islamic belief. The Divine Names occupy the central position in virtually all of his treatises. The reason behind this emphasis is Nursi's belief that everything depends on the Divine Names, in general, and the name of Truth (*al-Haqq*), in particular. Nursi describes *al-Haqq* as "the source, sun, and protector of all realities."[32]

Although the relationship between the Divine Names and the afterlife was essentially established during the Old Said period, Nursi's first full-fledged effort to bring these concepts together took place in "Lasiyyema" during his transition period.[33] In this treatise, Nursi first points to the acts (*afʿāl*) of the Divine Names, such as administration, ordering, regulation, nurturing, protection, and adornment of beings. Then he describes the Divine Names that are the sources of these acts. Next, building on the relationship between the Divine Names and the resulting qualities, he proceeds to provide proof for the end of time, the resurrection of humankind, the afterlife, and eternal heaven or hell. However, the relation between the Names and the afterlife is applicable only to those names that are related to "the ordering of the cosmos," such as The Bestower of Bounties, The Creator, The Giver of life, The Generous Provider, The Just, The Compassionate, and The Sustainer.[34]

As previously mentioned, Nursi discusses how the twelve truths of "The Tenth Word" point first and foremost towards the existence of The Necessarily-Existent Being and His names and attributes. He then uses these concepts to develop the argument behind the resurrection of humankind. For the first two matters, i.e., the existence of the Necessarily-Existent Being and his Divine Names, the methodology Nursi follows is not different from that which is used in the rest of his treatises on the existence and unity of God. This methodology, which has various applications throughout the *Risale-i Nur Collection*, can be briefly described as reaching knowledge of God through the examples of continuous creation in this world.[35] By seeing the art, proportion, beauty, and wisdom of this life, humans can find the Divine Names and reach the knowledge of God.[36] Likewise, the depictions of the universe in the Qur'an reveal the existence of the Divine Names and attributes that are reflected on beings in this world.[37]

Now, let's have a look at how this relationship between the existence of the Necessarily-Existent Being and his names and attributes and the resurrection of the dead is pursued in "The Tenth Word":

1) Nursi first draws one's attention to the art, wisdom, conservation, and

---

32. Nursi, *The Words*, 68.

33. Nursi, *al-Mathnawī al-ʿarabī al-nūrī*, 83–101.

34. Nursi, *The Words*, 102.

35. Ghazali points to contemplating on creation as the agent by which faith takes root. Ghazzalī, *al-Hikmah fī makhluqat Illah*, 14, 111–12.

36. Nursi, *The Letters*, 384–86, 527.

37. For an example of a verse ending with the Divine names and their relationship to the content of the verse, see Nursi, *The Words*, 428–443.

purposefulness in God's creation, establishing them from particular to universal. These works are the result of creation, that is, his creating existence from nonexistence. The examples are from things that are available to everybody, are continuously created, and are continuously replaced by the same or similar things. In this respect, the universe is like an exhibition that is full of and continuously replenished with countless artworks, a palace with perfect management, and an army cared for flawlessly.

2) Secondly, Nursi proposes that the equipping of creation with wisdom, benefit, purpose, and beauty and its continuous change are the result of the acts of the Divine Names. Thus, it is not enough that something is simply created from nothing; it still needs the continuous manifestation of the relevant Divine Names—especially if it is a living being—in order to exist and be changed according to wisdom and purpose.[38] In this context, Nursi says:

> Furthermore, life comprises sustenance, mercy, grace, and wisdom, which are dominant in the planning and administration of the universe. It is as if life fastens them on behind it and draws them into the place it enters. For example, when life enters a body, the Name of All-Wise is also manifest; it makes its home well and orders it with wisdom. In the same way, the Name of All-Generous is manifest, and it organizes and decorates its dwelling according to its needs. At the same time, the manifestation of the Name of All-Compassionate is apparent; it bestows all sorts of bounties for the continuance and perfection of life. And again at the same time, the manifestation of the Name of Provider appears; it produces the sustenance, material and immaterial, necessary for the perpetuation and unfolding of the life, and in part stores them up within its body.[39]

Nursi thus proposes that one can logically reason that nothing can come to existence from nonexistence on its own. He then claims, similarly, that nothing can subsist on its own or control its ever-changing existence.[40] For example, a flower's shape, color, smell, seed, growth, the proportionality of the materials in its body, and its change according to certain rules are creations that take place in front of our eyes. This is the case because when the flower did not exist, none of these aspects existed either, and they will cease to exist when the flower dies.[41] All of these changes are meant to take place in a way that reveals wisdom, knowledge, justice, and purpose, and, thus, the acts causing them must also have those traits. If it is assumed that the lifeless, unconscious materials that make up a flower are the real causes behind all of these properties, then they must act with a comprehensive knowledge, perfect coordination, and immediate attention to each other and in exact proportionality so that a flower, from its seed to its full-grown state, will result. This requires that those materials possess knowledge, will, and power like a deity.[42] Therefore, according to Nursi, if all of these perfect works of art are not attributed to one God, then the creation of each and every thing becomes as difficult as the creation of the universe.

38. Nursi, *The Words*, 91, 537.

39. Ibid., 707.
40. Ibid., 60, 85.
41. Ibid., 313.
42. Nursi, *The Words*, 90, fn/24; Nursi, *The Letters*, 284.

What is more, every atom in the universe must possess these god-like properties. This is due to the fact that every being, especially the living ones, is a miniature of the whole, and therefore, its creator must be one that is capable of creating the whole. If the creation of beings is attributed to a single Creator, the creation of the whole becomes as easy as the creation of a single being.[43] For example, in order to create an apple, one must be able to create the entire apple species. Furthermore, one must be able to create spring, the season that serves as the workshop where apples are created. This is due to the fact that an apple is a miniature plan of a tree, a garden, and, ultimately, the universe.[44]

3) Next, Nursi proposes that there must be a necessarily-existent Creator, an agent who has the attributes of a Wise, Generous, Merciful, Just, Preserver and Provider who has his own willpower. In other words, he suggests that there must be a being who has the attributes that are reflected in the actions that take place within creation. Thus, it is concluded that knowledge can only come from a knowledgeable one, conscious power can only come from a powerful one, wise compassion can only come from a compassionate one, and so forth.[45]

4) At this stage, Nursi, after providing proof for the existence of God, his unity, and his names and attributes, talks about the relationship between God's Divine Names and the afterlife. Following are a few examples about how Nursi demonstrates this relationship between the Names and the afterlife.

Nursi claims that all of the Divine Names manifested in the ordering of the cosmos require the existence of an afterlife.[46] He first describes how these Names manifest in beings and deeds in the universe and gives various examples. Then he explains why the manifestation of each name is that name's requirement, and he establishes the existence of the afterlife as a logical conclusion to the requirement of the Divine Names. The following are some examples of this relationship between the Divine Names and the afterlife.

## THE RELATIONSHIP BETWEEN GENEROSITY AND THE AFTERLIFE

Nursi shows the relationship between generosity and the afterlife by using examples we witness in ourselves and in our surroundings. As he notes, all the things we need to survive, such as sustenance, water, oxygen, are given to us. All of these bounties point to the existence of a Generous Being. They must be carefully chosen to fulfill all of our needs and desires as lifeless, unconscious, uncompassionate things that can neither know our needs or desires nor fulfill them. Thus, the presence of these bounties reveals several things:

- These bounties show the existence of a being who has the attribute of Generosity.
- They are given to all living beings at the times when they are most vulnerable and in need, like when babies are first born.

---

43. Nursi, *The Words*, 70–72; Nursi, *al-Mathnawī al-ʿarabī al-nūrī*, 87.

44. For Nursi's proposition "He who can create one thing can create everything," see Nursi, *The Words*, 301–6, 311–12.

45 Ibid., 79–80.

46 Ibid., 102.

- These bounties, which are given in a timely manner and in accordance with one's special needs, show that the Creator of these bounties has infinite compassion, knowledge, power, and will and knows us and treats us accordingly.

- They are being given to us in an unceasing manner. There is no evidence that suggests that the source of these bounties will come to an end. On the contrary, there are many strong signs that point to the infiniteness of these bounties, such as their abundance, their continuity without cessation, and their continuous renewal on earth.[47]

- These bounties show that the act of giving is the requirement of the Divine Name of Generous, that is, this name wishes to always provide us with bounties. Since God continuously creates the universe out of nothing, shows his infinite knowledge, will, power, wisdom, and sovereignty, and is free of all kinds of needs and necessities, it cannot be said that he provides us with these bounties because of an obligation or a need on his part. Therefore, it makes sense that it is his attribute of Generosity that results in the bestowal of infinite bounty and kindness upon his creation.

- Considering that the attribute of Generosity wishes to give bounties continuously and there is no evidence that this generosity will ever end, we can conclude that it will manifest itself forever just like all the other everlasting names of God.

- For the attribute of Generosity to manifest forever, the locus of its manifestation, this world and its inhabitants, needs to be perpetual.

- The bestowal of infinite bounty requires infinite gratitude in return. Infinite gratitude, by definition, requires the perpetual existence of those who receive the infinite bounty so that they can demonstrate their gratitude infinitely.

- However, those who receive the infinite bounty are mortal and temporary, and the bounties cannot be manifested in this world continually. Furthermore, the limited pleasures of this life are incompatible with the requirements of an infinite generosity.[48] "Only a millionth part of all this, like one drop from the ocean," actually manifests itself in our transitory world.[49]

- If our existence was based on nothing more than these worldly pleasures, we would have to deny the existence of the infinite generosity that we continuously experience.

- Instead, the existence of permanent death would "transform compassion into disaster, love into affliction, blessing into vengeance, intellect into a tool of misery, and pleasure into pain," and "the very essence of God's mercy would vanish."[50]

---

47. Nursi says, "The absoluteness, the comprehensiveness, and appearance in infinite form of the dominical deeds (are) seen at work in the cosmos. It is only God's wisdom and will that limits and restricts those deeds, as well as the inherent capacities of the objects and places in which they manifest themselves." Nursi, *The Rays*, 177.

48. Ibid., 79.
49. Ibid., 76.
50. Ibid.

- Therefore, there must be another realm where compassion, love, blessing, intellect, and pleasure can be manifested forever that is appropriate to the infinite generosity. This place is the hereafter.

It is in this way that direct relation between the Divine Names of God and the existence of the hereafter is established. Other examples of this relationship include the following.

## THE RELATIONSHIP BETWEEN WISDOM AND THE AFTERLIFE

- Wisdom in creation indicates the existence of a Wise Creator. God has absolute wisdom that manifests in the universe.
- The nature of divine wisdom rejects useless things and works.
- If an everlasting realm is not created, everything will fall into futility.
- Therefore, in order to save everything from futility and meaninglessness, divine wisdom requires an everlasting realm. Nursi describes this realm as "the greatest of all instances of his wisdom, the most significant of all sources of benefit, the most necessary of all results, that which makes His wisdom into wisdom, His blessings into blessings, his mercy into mercy, the source and aim of all of His wisdom, bounty, mercy and beneficence."[51]

## THE RELATIONSHIP BETWEEN JUSTICE AND THE AFTERLIFE

- Justice in everything in the universe shows the existence of a Just Creator.
- The real nature of justice is incompatible with cruelty.
- If "the oppressor retains his power, and the oppressed, his humiliation, as they both depart and migrate from this realm," this situation cannot be reconciled with the real nature of justice.[52]
- Therefore, divine justice requires the existence of both reward and punishment.

## THE RELATIONSHIP BETWEEN BEAUTY AND PERFECTION AND THE AFTERLIFE

- All Divine Names have infinite beauty and perfection.
- Beauty and perfection desire to see and be seen in the mirror of beings.
- Perpetual beauty and perfection require perpetual manifestation of the Divine Names.
- Perpetual manifestation requires that people understand and appraise the beauty and perfection of his Names to be perpetual.
- Thus, the infinite beauty and perfection of God require the existence of a perpetual place in which those people who are appreciative of his beauty and perfection will reside forever.[53]

---

51. Ibid., 96–97.

52. Ibid., 61.

53. Ibid., 79–80, 97.

In summary, by looking at the beings and actions in the universe, Nursi establishes that there must be a necessarily-existent Creator who has the attributes necessary to create such beings and actions. He then ascertains that the concepts of resurrection and the afterlife are the requirement of those names.

> All the Divine Names manifest in the ordering of the cosmos logically require the existence of resurrection, indeed make it imperative. . . . Just as this world, with all its creatures, decisively demonstrates the existence of the Glorious Maker, so too do His sacred attributes and Names indicate, show and logically require the existence of the hereafter.[54]

## THE NECESSITY OF BODILY RESURRECTION

According to the majority of Muslims, resurrection is merely a bodily process. According to some Muslim philosophers, the verses of the Qur'an that talk about the afterlife cannot be understood literally, as they are expressed through similitudes in order for the public to better comprehend their meaning.[55] Ghazzalī and many other scholars, however, view the return after death as both a spiritual and a bodily experience.[56] Nursi, like these scholars, claims that the Qur'anic verses addressing the physical aspects of the afterlife cannot be interpreted solely in favor of spirituality, as the explicit meanings of these verses do not allow such implicit interpretations.[57]

The concept of bodily resurrection has a prominent position in the Islamic creed. The resurrection of all of humanity after death and the beginning of an eternal life is the matter that gives the most meaning to existence in this world.[58] Nursi, when explaining the afterlife, emphasizes the material aspects of the resurrection of humankind. When handling this issue, he first discusses the evidences for the importance of the material world. Then, he builds the evidences for the physical aspects of the afterlife. As in other matters, Nursi handles this issue in light of the Divine Names. According to him, the reasons behind the material aspects of this world are the same reasons behind the material aspects of the afterlife. Some of these reasons can be listed as follows:

- Most instruments and capabilities that can measure and feel material and spiritual pleasures are material. For example, much of the sustenance coming from the Divine Name Sustainer (*Razzaq*) cannot be appreciated without the tasting ability of the tongue.[59]

- Permanent manifestation of the Divine Names in a way befitting their grandeur and magnificence only happens within the material beings.

---

54. Ibid., 102.

55. al-Ghazzalī, *Tahafut al-falasifah*, 229; Ibn Sina, *Kitāb al-najat*, 326; Nursi, *The Words*, 107; Hermansen, "Eschatology," 319.

56. al-Taftazānī, *Sharḥ al-maqāsid*, 5:93; al-Razī, *Muhassal*, 223.

57. al-Taftazānī, *Sharḥ al-maqāsid*, 5:93; Al-Ghazzalī, *The Incoherence of the Philosophers*, 213–14, 219; Ziai, "Islamic Philosophy," 67; Ziai, "Islamic Philosophy (*falsafa*)," 77; Al-Mahdaly, *Dirāsa fi al-samʿiyāt*, 77.

58. Nursi, *The Words*, 82, 96.

59. Ibid., 514.

Spirituality alone is not able to reflect this magnificence and glory.[60]

- In this world, many aspects of both obedience to and rebellion against God are committed using parts of the physical body. Accordingly, wisdom and justice require that the afterlife, where all acts are guaranteed to be rewarded or punished, must possess material aspects to contain the rewards and punishments of the physical members of the body.[61]

- Most bounties that lead humans to pray, thank, glorify, or appreciate are material. Therefore, the human being, who is the most conscious and contemplative reader of the book of the universe, will be resurrected after death and will continue his journey to eternity in the company of both his spirit and body.[62]

## THE POSSIBILITY OF BODILY RESURRECTION

According to Nursi, this realm shows the pillars of belief in two different ways, *explicitly* and *implicitly*. Although all of existence points to God's existence explicitly, it points to resurrection and the afterlife both explicitly and implicitly.[63]

For the *mutakallimūn*, resurrection is possible and there are many traditional proofs from the Qur'an and *Sunna*h that support its occurrence. According to the *mutakallimūn*, the proof of resurrection is the initial creation of existence (*ibtidā*). The Power that created existence from nothing the first time is able to return it to existence after death. In this sense, the return of beings to life during resurrection is no different from the initial creation.[64]

Nursi, too, believes that material resurrection is possible.[65] However, he also notes that "there is no deficiency in Divine power, and the things necessitating it are extremely powerful. The matter is within the realm of the possible. And if a possible matter has something extremely powerful necessitating it, and there is no deficiency in the power of the agent, it may be regarded not as possible, but as actual."[66]

Nursi feels that the cause of disbelief or difficulty in belief in great matters such as resurrection is that people consider them irrational or impossible. "True impossibility, absurdity and irrationality," he notes, "pertain to the path of misbelief and the road of misguidance, whereas true possibility, facility and rationality are characteristics of the path of faith and highway of Islam."[67] Nursi, who considers belief in the pillars of Islamic faith to be a real possibility and rationality, says that resurrection's status of "possible" should not suggest any doubt about its occurrence.[68]

When discussing the impossibility of denial or negation of the pillars of Islamic

---

60. Ibid., 74, 78–80, 84.
61. Ibid., 514, 676–77.
62. Ibid., 514.
63. Nursi, *Kastamonu Lahikası*, 210–211.
64. al-Ghazzalī, *al-Iqtisad fi al-i'tiqad*, 155; al-Taftazānī, *Sharḥ al-maqāsid*, 5:83; al-Ghazzalī, *The Incoherence*, 214, 220, 223; Hermansen, "Eschatology," 319; Nursi, *The Rays*, 163, 165, 571, 625; Nursi, *The Words*, 154, 440, 716–18; Nursi, *The Letters*, 56, 291; The Qur'an 36:78–79. For the explanation of al-Ghazzalī's saying, "First creation is totally different from the second," see Nursi, *Barla Lahikası*, 257.
65. Nursi, *The Flashes*, 125.
66. Nursi, *The Words*, 552.
67. Nursi, *The Words*, 77. Nursi, *The Flashes*, 125.
68. Nursi, *The Words*, 286, 635.

faith, Nursi divides denial into two types. The first type of denial is the belief that "a certain thing does not exist at a certain place or in a particular direction."[69] It is possible to substantiate this type of denial. For example, if it is said that there are no walnuts in this room now and one searches the entire room only to discover that, indeed, there are no walnuts to be found, then this denial is proven, since the denial is restricted to a particular space and time. The second type of denial "consists of negating and denying those doctrinal and sacred matters, general and comprehensive, that concern this world, all beings, the hereafter, and the succession of different ages."[70] For Nursi, this type of negation, which is based on the condition that something is not inherently impossible,[71] "cannot in any fashion be substantiated."[72] This is due to the fact that "a non-particularized denial, not directed to a particular locus, cannot be proven."[73] For this reason, the number of the deniers, their level of knowledge, etc., cannot strengthen the denial, nor can individual denials fortify each other. Each denier can, at most, say, "I do not see it; therefore, in my opinion and belief, it does not exist," but they cannot claim, "It does not exist in actuality" since these claims are personal and not universal.[74] What Nursi means in this example is that the conclusions based on the denial depend on the self, reason, and observation of the denying person. Therefore, those who claim universal denial towards the pillars of belief can only do so due to their ignorance, obstinacy, or unwillingness to see.[75]

According to Nursi, it is essentially possible that the sun will not rise tomorrow or will not set today. But this essential possibility does not affect our certainty of its setting today and rising tomorrow and cannot lead to a rational doubt,[76] because, in Nursi's words, "a probability not originating from any indication or sign has no importance; it cannot induce doubt in a matter that is definite. It cannot shake the certainty that is based on sound judgment."[77] Such an essential possibility can rise to the level of reasonable possibility if there is evidence for it. Otherwise, an essential possibility cannot harm the certainty of belief.[78]

Nursi sees each pillar of belief supporting the others and, thus, supporting the possibility of resurrection. For example, all of the miracles proving the prophethood of Muhammad and all of the evidences of his truthfulness also prove the existence of resurrection. After the unity of God (*tawḥīd*), Prophet Muhammad's second greatest teaching was resurrection. Similarly, all of the miracles and evidences proving the teachings of the previous prophets can be seen as proofs of resurrection, as all the prophets are understood in Islam as having shared the same truth regarding the afterlife.[79] The evidences and miracles regarding the truth of the Qur'an point to the occurrence of resurrection, as nearly one-third of the Qur'an speaks about it.[80] Similarly,

69. Nursi, *The Rays*, 128.
70. Ibid.
71. Ibid., 234.
72. Ibid., 128.
73. Ibid., 126.
74. Ibid.

75. Ibid., 143.
76. Nursi, *The Words*, 286.
77. Nursi, *The Flashes*, 109; Nursi, *The Words*, 286, 635.
78. Nursi, *The Words*, 286, 635.
79. Nursi, *The Rays*, 205
80. Ibid.

the parts of the previously revealed books and that talk about resurrection support the Qur'an on this matter.[81]

Again, all the evidences of the existence of God also prove the existence of the afterlife. It is only through the coming of the afterlife that, according to Nursi, "perfections are saved from decline, absolute justice from mocking cruelty, universal wisdom from foolish absurdity, all-embracing mercy from jeering torment, and the dignity of power from abased impotence."[82] Therefore, "most of the evidences for the existence and unity of the Necessary Existent testify indirectly to the existence and opening up of an eternal realm of bliss, which will be the supreme manifestation of dominicality and divinity."[83]

Moreover, all of the evidences for Divine Destiny (*qadar*) are also valid for resurrection and the afterlife. According to Nursi, the record of details of the life of every single being through memories, seeds, and the Preserved Tablet "could surely only be the result of a general judgment in a supreme tribunal set up to deal out permanent reward and punishment."[84] If there was no resurrection and no afterlife, then it would be futile and contrary to wisdom to keep records of everything.

Similarly, all of the evidences for the existence of angels, their duties and communication with the prophets and some other people, in turn, prove the existence of resurrection and the afterlife. This is further proven by the words of Gabriel and other high-ranking angels who tell that they traveled in the realms of the afterlife.[85]

## CONCLUSION

The following conclusions can be made regarding Nursi's approach towards resurrection:

- In Nursi's opinion, resurrection and the afterlife cannot be understood without referring to the Divine Names. So, besides the existence of the Necessarily Existent One, the existence of his Names must be recognized in beings in the universe before proceeding to the proof of the afterlife.

- All of the Divine Attributes and Names are regarded as absolute and unlimited. Due to the restrictive conditions of this world, these absolute Names manifest only partially and in a very limited way amongst beings in this world. Therefore, all Divine Names require a never-ending place of manifestation that is appropriate to their essential qualities and magnificence.[86]

- As shown by the beings and actions in the universe, the Divine Names have requirements befitting them. The requirement for infinite generosity is infinite bounty; the requirement for mercy is infinite grace; the requirement for justice is the proper allocation of rights; the requirement for beauty and perfection is seeing and being seen through the art in beings. In order to comprehend the concepts of resurrection and the

---

81. Ibid.
82. Ibid., 210.
83. Ibid., 208.
84. Ibid., 211.

85. Ibid.
86. Ibid., 620–21.

afterlife, one must figure out the requirements of the Divine Names as reflected throughout creation from microscale to macroscale. This is necessary because the necessity of the existence of the afterlife is substantiated through the requirements of these names. One who cannot see justice governing over creation cannot understand that the justice that exists among human beings is a requirement for the same justice in creation as a whole. Similarly, one who cannot see the name Generous as the source of the service and care provided for each being cannot comprehend paradise, which is the place of ultimate and endless generosity.

- In order to understand the necessity of the existence of resurrection and the hereafter, one needs to look at the disproportionate relation between the perfection of the art and duty of beings and their limited purposes in this world. This disproportion must be analyzed in the context of wisdom and justice. For example, creating something that has numerous senses but then abandoning it to nothingness is against wisdom and justice. Similarly, having a human being worship with his material and spiritual aspects but then sentencing him to eternal death without rewarding his physical body and senses is against wisdom and justice.

- The relationship between the Divine Names and the existence of resurrection and the afterlife is crucial. If the One, whose names are described as the most Beautiful Names (al-Asmā al-Ḥusnā),[87] actually wastes everything by destroying it, overrides all the rules of justice, annihilates all the beauties permanently, rejects the prayers of even the most beloved servants, kills all of his admiring servants with no return, and, by doing all these, confirms the claims of those who deny and disrespect him, that One is going to be reduced to "a wile gambler or treacherous tyrant" in the eyes of his servants.[88] This situation would mean a discrepancy regarding the One whose absolute perfection and beauty is testified by the universe and a "total reversal of truths."[89]

## BIBLIOGRAPHY

Abdel Haleem, M. A. S. "Qur'an and Hadith." In *The Cambridge Companion to Classical Islamic Theology*, edited by Tim Winter, 19–32. Cambridge: Cambridge University Press, 2008.

Fakhr al-Din al-Rāzī, *Muhassal afkar al-mutaqaddimin wa-'l-muta'akhkhirin*. Edited by Taha `Abd al-Rauf Sa`d. Al-Qahira: 'Maktaba Kulliya al-Azhariya, n.d.

Gardet, L. "Ilm al-Kalam." In *Encyclopedia of Islam*, 2nd ed., edited by P. Bearman et al.. The Leiden: Brill, 2008. Online: http://dx.doi.org/10.1163/1573-3912_islam_COM_0366.

Ghazzalī, Abu Hāmid al-. *al-Hikmah fi makhluqat Illah,*. Edited by Mohammed Rashid Qabbani. Beirut: Dar Ihya' Al-Ulum, 1978.

———. *al-Iqtisad fi al-i'tiqad*. Edited by Insaf Ramadan. Beirut: Dar Qutayba, 2003.

———. *The Incoherence of the Philosophers*. Translated by Michael E. Marmura.

87. Qur'an, 59:24.
88. Nursi, *The Words*, 67.
89. Ibid., 98.

Islamic Translation Series. Provo, UT: Brigham Young University, 2000.

———. *Tahafut al-falasifah*. Translated by Sabih Ahmad Kamali. Lahore: Pakistan Philosophical Congress, 1968. Publisher?

Hermansen, Marcia. "Eschatology." In *The Cambridge Companion to Classical Islamic Theology*, edited by Tim Winter, 308–24. Cambridge: Cambridge University Press, 2008.

Ibn Sina. *Kitāb al-Najāt*. Edited by Majid Fakhry. Beirut: Dār al-Āfāq al-Jadīda, 1982.

Mahdaly, Al-Sayyid Muhammad Aqil al-. *Dirāsa fi al-samʿiyāt*. Al-Qahira: Dar al-Hadith, 1996.

Nursi, Said. *Asār-ı Badiʿiyya*. Istanbul: Ittihad, 1999.

———. *al-Mathnawī al-ʿarabī al-nūrī*. Istanbul: Sőzler, 1994.

———. *Barla Lahikası*. Istanbul: Envar, 1994.

———. *Kastamonu Lahikası*. Istanbul: Envar Publications, 1994.

———. *The Letters*. Translated by Şükran Vahide. Istanbul: Sőzler, 2010.

———. *Ishārāt al-iʿjāz*. Edited by Ihsan Qasim. Istanbul: Sőzler, 1994.

———. *Muhākemāt*. Istanbul: Envar, 1995.

———. *The Rays*. Translated by Şükran Vahide. Istanbul: Sőzler, 2002.

———. *Signs of Miraculousness*. Translated by Şükran Vahide. Istanbul: Sőzler, 2004.

———. *The Words*. Translated by Şükran Vahide. Istanbul: Sőzler, 2004.

al-Razi, Fakhr al-Din. *Muhassal afkar al-mutaqaddimin wa-'l-mutaʾakhkhirin*. Edited by Taha ʿAbd al-Rauf Saʿd. Al-Qahira, Egypt: ʿMaktaba Kulliya al-Azhariya, undated

Taftazānī, Saʿad al-Din Masud ibn Umar ibn Abd Allah al-. *Sharḥ al-maqāsid*. Edited by ʿAbdurrahman ʿAmira. Vol. 5. 2nd ed. Beirut: ʿAlam al-Kutub, 1998.

Vahide, Şükran. *Islam in Modern Turkey*. New York: State University of New York Press, 2005.

Ziai, Hossein. "Islamic Philosophy (*falsafa*)." In *The Cambridge Companion to Classical Islamic Theology*, edited by Tim Winter, 55–76. Cambridge: Cambridge University Press, 2008.

# 7

# The Problem of Evil in the Writings of Bediüzzaman Said Nursi

## Cüneyt Şimşek

### INTRODUCTION

The subject of evil makes up a large portion of Nursi's *Risale-i Nur*. He examines this topic from many different perspectives, both directly and indirectly, in the *Collection*. Through holistic evaluation, one recognizes two distinct approaches that he uses to address this issue. The first is a general view, in which he evaluates evil at the cosmological level. The second approach is more specific, involving responses to questions posed. At times, he describes evil as a necessary principle, as its existence allows for universal laws to be carried out according to some divine purposes behind the creation. At other times, however, he looks at it from the view of progress of the human spirit.

In this article, I will discuss Nursi's ideas regarding the concept of evil, organizing them under seven headings. These headings represent a chain of the successive phases of the creation of the universe. This paper will, on the one hand, try to show step by step how evil originates in the ongoing process of creation and, on the other hand, explore the essence, wisdom, and duties of evil based on Nursi's thought. It will not provide an overarching history of the problem of evil but will use a descriptive narrative to give a short summary of the subject as discussed in Nursi's *Risale-i Nur*. Due to the complexity of the subject, this work does not claim to convey the author's ideas about evil in its entirety but it is a short introduction.

Nursi describes the existence of evil[1] as being the result of infinite divine

---

1. For a very systematic approach to the problem of evil, see, Çoban, "Nursi on Theodicy: A New Theological Perspective." Also, for a

activity and divine will in a universe that is created by bringing together opposites.² He analyzes evil under the two headings of "necessitating cause" and "ultimate cause." What is seen behind these concepts is a continuous struggle to understand the reasons for the infinite divine activity that becomes apparent through creation, revitalization, dissolution, change, transformation, and the like. Moreover, Nursi describes these two concepts as the fundamental reason of all of the activity that occurs in existence, be it good or bad.³

He explains these concepts as follows:

> If a person performs a natural function or social duty enthusiastically, anyone who observes him carefully will certainly understand that there are two things that make him act in this way: The First are the benefits, fruits, and advantages resulting from the duty, which are called the ultimate cause. The Second: Such things as love, desire, and pleasure cause him to perform the duty enthusiastically, and these are called the necessitating cause and reason.⁴

For example, the real motivation that drives a person to eat is the pleasure and longing that arises from appetite. It is the "necessitating cause." Providing nutrition to the body and thus sustaining one's life is the "ultimate cause."⁵ It is in this way that Nursi ties, through his examination of the creation of the universe, the manifestations of continuous creation, change, transformation, death, life, and the like, to the concepts of necessitating cause and ultimate cause. In addition, these concepts result in the continuous manifestation of two types of divine attributes, those pertaining to God's glory (*jalālī*) and those pertaining to God's beauty (*jamālī*). Now, let's take a closer look at these two concepts.

## NECESSITATING CAUSE (*DĀĪ AND MUQTAZĪ*)

According to Nursi, "necessitating cause" is the main reason behind divine activity. He describes the features of this concept under three headings:

## PERFECT ESSENTIAL QUALITIES (*SHUŪNĀT*)

Throughout his works, Nursi refers to *shuūnāt*, a concept best defined as "perfect essential qualities of God," such as boundless sacred compassion, infinite holy eagerness, infinite holy pleasure, and infinite sacred gratification, which are the first part of necessitating cause that requires the Divine Names relevant to the governance and control (*tadbīr*) of the universe to manifest in the world. These attributes (*shuūnāt*) exist in the divine essence.⁶ According to Nursi, since these divine attributes are unlimited and absolute, they require boundless activity; this boundless activity in the universe, in turn, requires boundless change and transformation, alteration and destruction; and this boundless change and transforma-

---

very short summary of the ideas concerning the problem of evil as discussed in the history of Islamic thought, see, Aydın, "The Problem of Evil in the *Risale-i Nur*." (accessed April 11, 2012).

2. Nursi, *The Letters*, 336–52.
3. Ibid., 336–51.
4. Ibid., 113.
5. Ibid.

6. Nursi, *The Words*, 620–25, 650–53, 667, 698.

tion requires death and extinction, decline and separation in the world.⁷

## DIVINE BEAUTY AND PERFECTION AND DESIRE TO SEE AND BE SEEN

Divine beauty and perfection is the second part of necessitating cause, which is the reason for the activity in the universe. According to Nursi, it is the desire of the divine to see his own perfect art and show it "to the gaze of angels and jinn, of humans and animals."⁸ Thus, everything in the universe is created both as a mirror, reflecting the beauty and perfection of creation to some degree depending on its capacity, and, at the same time, as a letter describing all the Divine Names stemming from the divine attributes of beauty and perfection.⁹

## PLEASURE IN ACTIVITY

The third aspect of necessitating cause, which acts as the governor behind the curtain of infinite divine activity, is the pleasure in that activity. Nursi describes this concept of pleasure as encompassing all animate and inanimate creatures throughout the universe. According to him, there is pleasure in all activity. Pleasure in activity exists in the divine essence in a way that is appropriate to the holiness of the Names and Attributes, dispatching a continuous manifestation of Divine Names and attributes.¹⁰

## ULTIMATE CAUSE (AL-"ILLA AL-GHĀIYYA)

Nursi describes the ultimate cause as being the reason for an activity sought to attain benefit, fruit, and advantage. In this frame of reference, he categorizes the ultimate cause of all existence and life under three purposes.

## THE FIRST PURPOSE PERTAINS TO THE CREATOR

The most important purposes of continuous creation and the results of the endless activity of the Divine Names in the universe pertain to God. Through their life and existence, all things exhibit the miracles of his divine artistry to his divine view. As Nursi articulates, it is enough for this aim to be realized simply at the level of ability or seed alone.¹¹

---

7. Nursi, *The Letters*, 339.
8. Nursi, *The Words*, 86.
9. Ibid., 133, 656; Nursi, *The Rays*, 83–84.
10. The author explains the concept of pleasure in activity in this way: "Every sort of activity, whether particular or universal, yields pleasure. Rather, there is a pleasure in all activity. Indeed, activity is pure pleasure. Or, activity is the manifestation of existence, which is pure pleasure and is the shaking off and becoming distant from non-existence, which is pure suffering. Everyone with ability follows with pleasure the unfolding of his ability through activity. The revealing of innate talents through activity arises from a pleasure and results in a pleasure. Everyone who possesses some perfections follows with pleasure their disclosure through activity." Nursi, *The Flashes*, 450, 169; Nursi, *The Letters*, 347–50.
11. Nursi says, "The seeds and grains of plants are their intentions. . . . Since Almighty God knows how future things will come about, He accepts their intention as actual worship." Nursi, *The Words*, 86–87 [20th fn], 371.

## THE SECOND PURPOSE PERTAINS TO HUMANS, SPIRITUAL BEINGS AND ANIMALS

In Nursi's words, the second major purpose of living beings is to be presented to one another as a profoundly meaningful letter for the purpose of reading and contemplation. From this perspective, everything is a letter written to reflect the Divine Names and attributes.[12]

## THE THIRD PURPOSE PERTAINS TO THE SOUL OF THE THING ITSELF

The third purpose of the existence of everything consists of minor consequences such as "the experience of pleasure and joy and living with some degree of permanence and comfort."[13] Nursi says that "If we consider the purpose of a servant employed as a steersman on some royal ship, we see that only one hundredth of that purpose relates to the steersman himself, the wage he receives; ninety-nine hundredths of the purpose relate to the king who owns the ship. A similar relation exists between the purpose of a thing related to its own self and its worldly existence, and its purpose related to its Maker."[14]

According to the author, these three purposes serve as the reason behind "the wisdom in the existence of all things, the aims of their natures, the benefits in their creation, and the results of their lives."[15]

In summary, he views divine activity in the universe as having perfect essential qualities (*Shuūnāt*), such as sacred compassion and holy eagerness. This divine activity also contains a desire for the divine beauty and perfection to see and be seen and pleasure in activity. These characteristics are found in divine essence "in a way befitting the sacredness and perfect self-sufficiency of the Necessarily Existent Essence."[16]

The second fundamental reason for endless activity in the universe is what is called as the ultimate cause, the intended results, fruits, and consequences of divine activity. The most exalted purpose behind divine activity in the universe pertains to the Creator. The secondary purpose is to allow for the contemplation and understanding of conscious beings and being with emotions and divine instinct. The third purpose of the existence constitutes only one percent of divine activity.

As mentioned above, the necessitating cause and ultimate cause require the manifestation of two types of Divine Names, *jalālī* and *jamālī*. Here I will briefly discuss these two different types of Divine Names.

## THE REQUIREMENTS OF JALĀLĪ AND JAMĀLĪ NAMES

In his description of the third phase of divine activity, Nursi categorizes the Divine Names as either *jalālī*, pertaining to the glory of God, or *jamālī*, pertaining to the beauty of God. As a whole, both sets of names are described as *asmā al-ḥusnā*, the Most Beautiful Names of God, in

---

12. Ibid.

13. Nursi, *The Words*, 86–87 [20th fn]; Nursi, *The Letters*, 345; Nursi, *The Flashes*, 446.

14. Ibid.

15. Nursi, *The Letters*, 345; Nursi, *The Flashes*, 446.

16. Nursi, *The Flashes*, 452–53.

the Qur'an.¹⁷ However, the requirements of these two categories differ from one another, and these differences reveal themselves as different manifestations in creation. For example, the Names of Glorious (*Jalīl*), Almighty (*'Azīz*), and All-Compelling (*Jabbar*) are *jalālī*, and Beauteous (*Jamīl*), The Most Compassionate (*Rahīm*), The Most Generous (*Karīm*), The Most Gentle (*Latīf*), and The Most Patient (*Halīm*) are *jamālī*.¹⁸

Nursi points out that the desire for the Divine Names to manifest themselves comes not out of necessity but from the concept of requirement.¹⁹ According to the concept, *the Necessitating Cause* and *Ultimate Cause* require endless activity of Divine Names, and endless activity, in return, requires manifestations of *jalālī* and *jamālī* names, with respect to the distinct requirements of these names. The different and equally distinct manifestations required by the two distinct types of names occur through the creation of opposites in the universe.²⁰

## CREATION OF OPPOSITES

Nursi describes the fourth phase of activity of the Divine Names as the creation of opposites in the universe. This creation of opposites is a requirement for the existence of *jalālī* and *jamālī* names which are briefly mentioned above. He explains this as follows:

> The All-Glorious Creator of the universe has two sort of Names, those pertaining to his glory and those pertaining to his beauty. Since these Names require to demonstrate their decrees through different manifestations, the Glorious Creator blended together opposites in the universe. Bringing them face to face, he gave them aggressive and defensive positions, in the form of a sort of wise and beneficial contest. Through making the opposites transgress one another's bounds, He brought conflict and change into being, and made the universe subject to the law of change and transformation and the principles of progress and advancement. In human kind, the comprehensive fruit of the tree of creation, he made that law of contest in even stranger form, and opening the door to striving, which would be the means of all human progress....²¹

He notes that creation has two faces, an inner (*mulk*) and an outer face (*malakūt*),²²

---

17. Qur'an 59:24; Nursi, *The Flashes*, 280.

18. Nursi, *The Letters*, 114; Nursi, *The Words*, 343. İzzet Çoban claims that, since Nursi constructs the problem of evil based upon God's Names and Attributes, he "offers a new theological perspective on theodicy centered on Divine Names Theology." Çoban, "Nursi on Theodicy," 111, 115–16, 118.

19. Nursi, *The Words*, 658.

20. Nursi, *The Letters*, 80; Nursi, *The Flashes*, 115–16.

21. Nursi, *The Flashes*, 115. See also, Nursi, *al-Mathnawī al-'arabī al-nūrī*, 86, 113, 152, 215, 319, 335; Nursi, *Ishārāt al-i'jāz*, 219.

22. "The universe has two faces like a mirror. One is its external face, which resembles the coloured face of the mirror, the other is its face which looks to its Creator. This resembles the mirror's shining face. Its external face is the arena of opposites. It is where matters like beautiful and ugly, good and evil, big and small, difficult and easy appear. It is because of this that the All-Glorious Maker has made apparent causes a veil to the disposal of His power, so that the hand of power should not appear to the mind to be directly concerned with matters that on the face of it are insignificant or unworthy. For majesty and dignity require it to be thus. But He did not give a true effect to causes and intermediaries, because the unity of oneness requires that they have none. As for the face of beings which looks to its Creator, in everything it is shining, it is

and that only the outer face has been an arena of opposites due to the trial and examination.[23] By combining opposites in the creation, the universe is exposed to the law of constant permutation, change and transformation, which are famously named as "the law of contests" by Nursi.[24]

## EMERGENCE OF RELATIVE REALITIES

The result of combining opposites in the creation, which is the forth phase, causes the emergence of relative realities (in the entire creation, including humans).[25] According to Nursi, "the degrees of strength and weakness that a thing possesses are determined by the intervention in that thing of its opposite. For example, degrees of heat are determined by the intervention of cold; degrees of beauty, by the intervention of ugliness; stages of light, by the intervention of darkness."[26]

The existence of creation and all of its qualities are incidental. In other words, existence and its qualities do not come from themselves but are given to them subsequently. This is why, according to the author, a physical or metaphysical quality of contingent beings can easily interfere with the very opposite quality, and thus emerge various grades and levels in a contingent thing.[27]

Now, amongst contingent beings, through this interference of opposites, emerge in varying degrees and measures, relative realities. Different levels yield conflicts, which, in turn, result in transformations and metamorphisms in the cosmos. In this context, Nursi highlights the constant nature of the sequence that results from "relative realities." He adds to this sequence the concept of order and establishes the link between these three concepts, constant nature, sequence, and order, and the relative realities. Furthermore, he describes conflict, transformation, and order as the three productive principles in the universe.[28] Let's look at these concepts briefly.

## CONFLICT

Nursi asserts that conflict, which is described as being all the differences and variances resulting from multiplicity and as having arisen from the inscription of opposites in creation, acts to cause relative truths to appear in the universe. Moreover, relative truths are found more abundantly in the universe than real truths. According to Nursi, in order for relative realities to emerge, evil, which is only found lightly scattered throughout the universe, is allowed to exist amidst the purposeful beauty, goodness, and perfection of creation. Furthermore, evil is created as a unit of measurement for

---

clean. The colours and distortions of individuality do not intervene in it. This aspect faces its Creator without intermediary. There are no chains and disposition of causes in it. Cause and effect cannot intrude on it. It contains nothing contorted or askew. Obstacles cannot interfere in it. A particle becomes brother to the sun." Nursi, *The Words*, 547.

23. Bediüzzaman Said Nursi, *Sayqal al-islāmiyya*, 341, 344.

24. Nursi, *The Words*, 195, 552; Nursi, *The Letters*, 80; Nursi, *The Flashes*, 115; Çoban, "Nursi on Theodicy," 125–27.

25. Nursi, *The Letters*, 80; Nursi, *al-Mathnawī al-'arabī al-nūrī*, 86, 113, 152, 215, 319, 335.

26. Nursi, *The Words*, 104.

27. Nursi, *The Words*, 547; Nursi, *Sayqal al-islāmiyya*, 341, 344.

28. Nursi, *Mesnevi-i Nuriye*, 718; Nursi, *Ishārāt al-i'jāz*, 164, 219, 194.

and an introduction to the emergence of relative truths, which pertain to universal goodness and perfection.[29] Thus, relative truths exist for the purpose of instilling beings with different degrees.[30] In a world where everything is known by its opposites, light with darkness and warmth with the cold, health with illness and joy would have been jaded without tribulation.[31] Thus, *jalālī* and *jamālī*, names and perfect essential qualities (*shuūnāt*), require the existence of opposites, and this requirement is a law that is enforced throughout the universe.

For Nursi, each general law of the universe operates according to the requirements of the *jalālī* and *jamālī* names. For instance, while the name of *Jamāl* requires that created beings reach out to one another for assistance ("the law of cooperation"), the name of *Jalāl* requires that they compete with each other over things ("the law of competition").[32] This is why, as part of the requirement of the law of competition, opposites are combined within the human as well. While this competition opens the door for strife and struggle, it is also the main reason for progress among humanity as a whole.[33] While causing inspiration and whims and whispers of the human heart, the law of competition requires the struggle between Satan and the angels in heavens.[34] Just as the competition of opposites yields relative realities, it brings about varying degrees of relative realities in human strife, struggle, and competition of opposites, such as good morals, virtues, and grace.[35] The universe is subjected to transformation and change as a direct result of combined opposites. This, in turn, results in progress and perfection.

## EMERGENCE OF CHANGE AND EVIL

The conflict of opposites that results from the emergence of relative realities opens the way to change and transformation in this world.[36] Nursi explains the principal of change, which is seen in creation as transformation, metamorphosis, and progress towards perfection, as being based on regular and routine divine action and emphasizes how it manifests itself as a principal law. He further explains that the purpose of change in this universe is, in short, to multiply instances of relative realities and, thus, enable different manifestations of the Divine Names.[37]

As Nursi articulates, everything that is subordinated to the principal of progress towards perfection is subjected to the law of growth and development, and everything under this law has a limited

---

29. Nursi, *Sayqal al-Islāmiyya*, 219; Nursi, *Ishārāt al-i'jāz*, 35, 87.

30. Nursi, *Ishārāt al-i'jāz*, 35, 164; Nursi, *The Letters*, 80; Nursi, *Sayqal al-islāmiyya*, 341, 344.

31. Nursi, *The Words*, 141; Nursi, *The Letters*, 209; Nursi, *The Flashes*, 270–71.

32. Nursi, *The Words*, 195.

33. Nursi, *The Letters*, 80; Nursi, *The Flashes*, 115; Nursi, *The Words*, 553.

34. Nursi, *The Words*, 195.

35. Some of the common opposites that exist in the universe include the relative realities of perfection-impairment, light-darkness, life-death, beauty-beast, benefit-loss, many-few, big-small, existence-nonexistence, proof-disproof. In humans, they include health-illness, pleasure-pain, comfort-struggle, good-bad, belief-disbelief, obedience-rebellion, love-hate, knowledge-ignorance, good morals-bad morals, good deeds–bad deeds. See Nursi, *The Letters*, 80; Nursi, *The Flashes*, 115.

36. Nursi, *Sayqal al-islāmiyya*, 219.

37. Nursi, *Sayqal al-islāmiyya*, 219; Nursi, *Mesnevi-i Nuriye*, 718; Nursi, *The Words*, 553.

lifespan. Everything that has a limited lifespan has death.[38] For this reason, evil such as death and despair, grief, illness, and struggle carve out a place at this point in the universe. The manifestation of *jalālī* and *jamālī* Divine Names opens ways to constant and endless activity as a result of competing opposites, constant activity that results in transformation, metamorphosis, progress towards perfection and pathways to growth and development, and death and despair. As a result, Nursi sees death, despair, and tribulations as direct outcomes of the Divine Order in the universe that is also a platform of *relative realities*. Nevertheless, this leads to the questions, since God is absolute goodness, is it expected that only good should come from him; since he has absolute beauty, should he create only what is beautiful; and since he has absolute wisdom, should he have nothing odd, absurd, or useless in his actions and operations? What we see and experience in this life shows otherwise. Nursi offers several explanations for the imperfections of this life despite the relationship between the Divine Names, especially the *jamālī* names, and evil.

## EVIL IS FROM NONEXISTENCE

Contrary to those who deny the ontological existence of evil, Nursi accepts the existence of evil, albeit minimal, but states that evil stems from non-existence. In most cases, non-existence does not depend on the elimination and nonexistence of all of the elements that make up a being. For this reason, nonexistence, defined as true evil, is so much easier than existence. Unlike nonexistence, existence, defined as true good, could only take place with all the elements and conditions coming together all at once.[39] Thus, according to the author, evil depends more on the absence or abandoning of at least one of the conditions required for existence than it does on any other apparent reason. For instance, a human body is required to have all its organs and life-supporting faculties operating in order to live, while only one of these organs or faculties must cease to function for death to occur.[40] He argues that there is negation, abandoning, and denial at the root of evil, due to this great and fundamental difference between existence and nonexistence.[41]

## EXISTENCE DEMANDS A REASON; NONEXISTENCE DOES NOT

More often than not, goodness, beauty, and progress towards perfection depend on existence. Nursi, too, sees the essence of these concepts as being pertinent to existence, even as they seem to be stemming from nonexistence. On the contrary, the root of evils like calamities, tribulation, and ugliness is negation, and they stem from nonexistence, even when it seems that they are of existence. While existence always depends on and demands a cause, things that stem from nonexistence precede, are subject to, and are subordinate to nonexistence.[42] Likewise, absence of only one condition is a predecessor to

---

38. Nursi, *The Words*, 550.

39. Nursi, *The Letters*, 72–73; Nursi, *The Flashes*, 106; Çoban, "Nursi on Theodicy," 116, 120, 125.

40. Nursi, *The Letters*, 70; Nursi, *The Flashes*, 103–4.

41. Nursi, *The Letters*, 72–73.

42. Nursi, *The Letters*, 73; Nursi, *The Flashes*, 106.

numerous nonexistences, while, existence "yields results in accordance with itself."[43]

## EVIL IS A UNIT OF MEASUREMENT

According to Nursi, one of the reasons that evil exists is the fact that its existence allows for the emergence of good and progress towards perfection. As discussed above, the presence of opposites within creation facilitates the existence of *relative realities*, and change and transformation is willed in order to add variety to *relative realities*. Combining these opposites gives birth to *relative realities* along with *constant realities*, not only in the universe but also in human beings. Based on this understanding, every reality would have stayed as one had there not been a unit of measure, and other degrees of reality would have stayed hidden.[44] Therefore, Nursi explains, there is much less evil in the world than there is goodness. Furthermore, because evil enables the emergence of the varying degrees of beauty and goodness and helps one understand the multiple realities manifested in different forms, evil is goodness and ugliness is beauty.[45] For example, the introduction of cold enables degrees of heat to emerge and ugliness makes different levels of beauty apparent.[46]

## EVIL IS BEAUTIFUL AND, AS A RESULT, GOOD

Nursi says that everything has a real beautiful side, even that which seems to be the ugliest. He describes beauty as being divided into two categories, that which is beautiful in its essence, "Essential Beauty," and that which is beautiful in its result, "Relative Beauty."[47] According to him, ugliness that is openly seen is actually a veil hiding the real beauty underneath. What seems to be utterly chaotic and ugly does, in fact, have order and beauty hidden underneath. For instance, hidden beneath the veil of springtime rainstorms and mud are "innumerable beautiful flowers and well-ordered plants."[48] Moreover, beneath the veil of seemingly disastrous events like storms, earthquakes, and plague, is the unfolding of numerous wonderful possibilities that have not yet developed, as though general upheavals and comprehensive changes are all like rain.[49] Thus, insignificant ugliness that results in or enables substantial beauty is defined as relative beauty, and the absence of this seemed ugliness, which makes an immeasurable amount of beauty visible, is real ugliness many times over. Furthermore, the creation of what is ugly is not ugliness, because the

---

43. Nursi, *The Words*, 182; Çoban, "Nursi on Theodicy," 120.

44. Nursi, *The Rays*, 39.

45. Nursi, *The Letters*, 331; Nursi, *The Flashes*, 429.

46. Nursi, *The Words*, 754.

47. Nursi, *Ishārāt al-I'jāz*, 35; Nursi, *The Rays*, 39; Nursi, *The Words*, 240.

48. Nursi, *The Words*, 240. For some descriptions of and comments about Nursi's personal experience of evil in this context and the lessons he gained from these experiences, see: Mermer, "Bediüzzaman Said Nursi"s Scriptural Approach to the Problem of Evil" and Aydın, "The Problem of Evil in the *Risale-i Nur.*"

49. For insight into the aspects of divine justice and compassion in disasters, such as earthquakes, floods, etc., see Michel, "God's Justice in Relation to Natural Disasters."

majority of the outcomes of that creation are beautiful.[50]

## THE INSIGNIFICANCE OF EVIL AND THE UPHOLDING OF COMPREHENSIVE LAWS

According to Nursi, tribulation and evil are sporadic, insignificant outcomes of the universal laws that represent the all-encompassing divine will.[51] They are not deliberately intended, and they are infrequently created secondarily within goodness and beauty.[52] Therefore, comprehensive goodness, beauty, benefits, and blessings become apparent as a result of this insignificant evil.[53] As a result, divine mercy, wisdom, and justice demand the existence of evil for the greater good.[54] The existence of evil is an insignificant consequence of the comprehensive divine laws that are themselves a reason for all-embracing divine favors. An insignificant amount of evil is permitted to exist in order to uphold these laws. For example, if only good and innocent people miraculously survived in natural disasters, the comprehensiveness of the laws would be harmed and, furthermore, it would be inconsistent with the wisdom and secret of the examination and test. Moreover, anybody witnessing this privilege would be forced to believe in the Creator, and that would be contrary to the reason behind creation of humanity. Thus, natural calamities such as earthquakes and floods do not take people's beliefs or moral standings into consideration. Good people are also hurt along with bad people during such disasters. Nursi explains, however, that God directly helps those who cry out from the universal laws, within the exceptions of laws as a requisite of God's mercy. He describes these instances as out-of-the-ordinary benevolence and help.[55]

## EVIL ENABLES THE DIVINE NAMES TO BECOME APPARENT

According to Nursi, the main reason every human faces tribulations, illnesses, and evil is to enhance the essence and experience of life by making human nature become a mirror to the Divine Names. Each Divine Name demands a truly reflective and different mirror.[56] For instance, just as the name "Healer" demands illness, the name "Sustainer" requires creatures needing sustenance.[57] The nature and

---

50. Nursi, *The Rays*, 39.

51. According to Fakhr al-Din al-Razi (1149–1209), philosophers divide existence, in respect to good and evil, into two categories. While the intelligences and heavens of the first category are regarded as absolute good, our physical realm is described as a place in which good is dominant. Even though there is much illness here, health is far more dominant. Since it is impossible to create this realm completely devoid of evils, the amount of good that may result from the way this world is created is much greater than the amount of lesser evils that may result due to the abandoning of that creation. The abandoning of the greater good because of the lesser evil will lead to a greater evil. Therefore, from the point of wisdom, it is necessary to create this world in the way it is. See Fakhr al-Din al-Razi, *Muhassal afkar al-mutaqaddimin wa-'l-muta'akhkhirin min al-'ulama' wa-'l-hukama' wa-'l-mutakallimin*, 202; Çoban, "Nursi on Theodicy," 126.

52. Nursi, *The Rays*, 40; Nursi, *Ishārāt al-i'jāz*, 35; Nursi, *Muhakemat*, 40.

53. Nursi, *The Rays*, 39.

54. Nursi, *The Letters*, 71; Nursi, *The Flashes*, 105.

55. Nursi, *The Rays*, 40; Nursi, *The Words*, 684.

56. Nursi, *The Letters*, 109.

57. Ibid.

experience of life is enhanced through illness, trials, and tribulations as a consequence of reflecting the embroidery of Divine Names more comprehensively. Thus, anything that happens in life is seen as beautiful.[58]

## EVIL AS AN INDIVIDUAL CONTACT

As Nursi discusses the kind of contact humans have with evil, he explains that evil is dependent on the way each person is engaged with it. Since God is the Creator of everything, he is also the Creator of evil. Nonetheless, while the creation of an evil is for many beings good and its outcomes relevant to all, one's committing an evil act results in consequences appropriated for that person. As a result, the committing an evil action by free will is defined as a personal "contact" (*mubashara*), and with this contact, private, individual outcomes arise. For instance, it is not even a question as to how much good is intended by the creation of fire, but one who sticks his hand in fire, be it from not paying attention or sheer clumsiness, not only cannot claim that fire is evil, but also cannot ignore the many benefits and good that come from fire in general. Without a doubt, fire is created not to hurt that person, but to provide benefit to all of creation. Likewise, the responsibility for the devastation caused by natural disasters such as earthquakes and floods, particularly when it results from human negligence and the disregarding of ecology, belongs entirely to human beings. Having said that, if the catastrophes occur that are beyond human control and capacity, they too may have positive outcomes for people and may play a role in enabling the spiritual and physical progress of humankind, inciting more awareness, and warning against rebellion.[59]

## ILLNESS, PAIN, TRIBULATION, AND STRUGGLE AS FORMS OF ESCAPE FROM NONEXISTENCE

Nursi says that "Since non-existence is pure evil, circumstances that either result in non-existence or give an inkling of it, also comprise evil."[60] It is for this reason that life is enriched and purified by being exposed to various and, at times, conflicting situations. As a result, the desired outcomes take place and life shows the embroideries of the Divine Names of the Life Giver by means of having it go through multiple venues. The pains, troubles, tribulations, and misfortunes endured by living beings occur for the sake of renewing the light of existence and moving away from the darkness of nonexistence. This, in turn, results in the purification of their lives. According to Nursi, "Arrest, repose, silence, idleness, rest, and monotony are all non-existence, both in quality and in state. Even the greatest pleasure is reduced to nothing by monotony."[61] He notes that the human being understands the value and pleasure of life by struggling and that health and comfort make life bitter and make people want time to pass more quickly. More importantly, a life spent in constant health and comfort could be nothing more than a limited mirror to the manifestation of Divine Names; the constant change in life accentuates its meanings and plea-

---

58. Nursi, *The Words*, 487.
59. Ibid., 185–90.
60. Ibid., 487.
61. Ibid.

sures.⁶² Thus, the purpose of all ailments, pains, and tribulations is to introduce and demonstrate the different manifestations of Divine Names. Moreover, the body is outfitted with physical senses and spiritual faculties such as the eyes, ears, intellect, and soul and is subjected to many different circumstances that reveal the manifestations of the Divine Names.⁶³

Nursi goes on to use an analogy to explain the seemingly evil things such as ailments, trials, and tribulations. In this analogy, he describes a wealthy and skillful tailor who represents the manifestations of the Divine Names in creation and a poor man whom he hires as a model. The masterful tailor tries the suit he made on the poor man to show his skill and artistry. Just as the man who is hired to act as a model does not have any right to criticize the master tailor as to how he designs, cuts, and stitches or why he makes him pose in certain positions, all beings have been created by God to serve as models of the manifestations of the Divine Names. They exist for the purpose of seeing and showing the magnificent examples of beauty appropriated by the embroideries of the Divine Names in all of his artistry.⁶⁴ God clothes each existent being, especially those with life, with a body adorned with tools like eyes, ears, intellect, and soul "in order to display the impresses of His Most Beautiful Names. He changes it within very many situations. Among these are circumstances in the form of suffering and calamity which show the meanings of some of His Names, and the rays of mercy within flashes of wisdom, and the subtle instances of beauty within those rays of mercy."⁶⁵

Nursi underlines the fact that God rewards his creation for the services it renders and the troubles it endures while performing the duty of manifesting the Divine Names with perfection, pleasure, and splendor as wage.⁶⁶ For this reason, no creation that has already received a wage has a right to complain to God, who is the real Owner of all things, by saying, "You are giving me trouble and disturbing me."⁶⁷

The author brings attention to human negligence in regards to ailments and illnesses and infers that many of the illnesses of the human condition could be avoided. Like many evils that result from nonexistence, many illnesses are the direct result of abusing organs through poor diet, drinking, wasting, and going against the prescriptions of God.⁶⁸

## ILLNESS AND TRIBULATION AS NEGATIVE WORSHIP

In Nursi's view, illness and all kinds of trials and tribulations are considered "negative worship." He describes worship as being both positive and negative, with ritual prayer (*salat*) and fasting (*sawm*) being of the former, and drawing closer to God by feeling powerless with illness and tribulations as the latter.⁶⁹ In this context, worship is defined as a declaration of one's poverty and impotence to God, and

---

62. Nursi, *The Letters*, 216–7; Nursi, *The Flashes*, 280–1.

63. Nursi, *The Words*, 488; Nursi, *The Letters*, 207, 217; Nursi, *The Flashes*, 268–9, 281.

64. Nursi, *The Words*, 212–13.

65. Nursi, *The Words*, 487–88; Nursi, *The Letters*, 337–38.

66. Nursi, *The Letters*, 337.

67. Ibid.

68. Ibid. 217; Nursi, *The Flashes*, 267.

69. Nursi, *The Letters*, 206; Nursi, *The Flashes* 267; Çoban, "Nursi on Theodicy," 130.

illness plays a great role in forming this language. In fact, the purpose for poverty and impotence is to encourage humankind to take refuge with and supplicate to God through the languages of both tongue and condition.[70]

## ILLNESS AS A GUIDE

Nursi describes illness as a guide, a teacher who warns of this world being transient. In fact, since it awakens one from heedlessness, it is actually equivalent to health.[71] He further explains that physical illness serves as a form of retribution in this world for spiritual illnesses of heart, conscience, and soul. Through the window of impotence and weakness, it awakens the soul from heedlessness and reminds us of the divine power[72] and mercy lying underneath everything.[73]

## THE REALITY OF THE PRESENT AND THE ILLUSION OF THE PAST AND FUTURE DURING TRIBULATIONS

Humans have the ability to feel multifaceted pleasure and pain of the past, present, and future. During times of tribulation, the pain felt in the present is relatively real, while perceived pains from the past and future are mere illusions. According to Nursi, "the conditions you suppose to be life are only the minute in which you are. All the time previous to the present minute and the things of the world within that time are dead in the present minute. And all the time subsequent to the present minute and all it contains is nonexistent in it, and nothing. That means the physical life on which you rely is only one minute."[74] One thing that subjugates humans to rebellion, unnecessary sorrow, and pain is their spending of their currency of patience and perseverance for the nonexistent past and future.

## ILLNESSES OF CHILDREN AND THE INNOCENT

Nursi explains that there are two benefits to children's illnesses and suffering that are pertinent to both this world and the hereafter. The one relevant to this world is an exercise of the immune system and asceticism, a vaccination and a form of divine discipline that prepares the tender bodies of the young for the challenges to come in this world. Thus, in the case of children and the innocent, illnesses are a form of vaccination for physical and spiritual development, as opposed to a retribution for sins, as is the case for adults. In addition, "the merits accruing from such illnesses [the illnesses of innocent children] pass to the book of good works of the parents, and particularly of the mother who through the mystery of compassion prefers the health of her child to her own health."[75]

---

70. Nursi, *The Letters*, 211; Nursi, *The Flashes*, 274.

71. Nursi, *The Letters*, 206, 208; Nursi, *The Flashes*, 268, 269.

72. For the relation between Divine Unity (*tawḥīd*), the comprehensiveness of Divine Power and Compassion, and evil, see Mermer, "Bediüzzaman Said Nursi's Scriptural Approach to the Problem of Evil" http://www.nur.org/en/intro/nurlibrary/Nursi_s_Scriptural_Approach_To_The_ProbleOf_Evil_116.

73. Nursi, *The Letters*, 210; Nursi, *The Flashes*, 272.

74. Nursi, *The Words*, 489.

75. Nursi, *The Letters*, 219; Nursi, *The Flashes*, 284.

## DISSOLUTION—EPHEMERAL—DEATH

As all living beings are ephemeral and will face death as a consequence of the divine law of continuous progress. Nursi considers the possibility of God's complete annihilation of creation and his driving it to nonexistence. This, however, would be infinite and absolute ugliness, oppression, and mercilessness, concepts that run contrary to the absolute beauty and mercy that God has.[76] Thus, he explains that the main reality in creation is immortality (*al-baqā*).[77] He further articulates that only "relative determination" (*al-taayyunāt al-'itibāriyya*) changes with development and progress to manifest the meanings of the Divine Names. In line with this, the disposition/essence (*mahiyya*) of creation, which acts as a mirror to the Divine Names, is constant and immortal.[78] Therefore, the ephemeral side of a creature, that which is prone to death, is merely physical, nothing more than an effigy that serves as an envelope and shell of its essence.[79] Hence, the death and apparent dissolution of God's beautiful creations actually serves as a dismissal from duty once the duty is accomplished, an opening up of space for the arrival of new creations, a preparation for those who are charged with a duty, and a warning to those who are oblivious to the divine truths.[80]

Nursi formulates that opposites that reveal themselves in the outer face of creation (*mulk*), such as good-bad and beauty-ugliness, leave a pure and spotless picture of existence in the inner side (*malakūt*). Yes, there is death and transience, pain and struggle. However, creation in what Nursi describes as the shell and form of the mighty reality of the universe, that is to say the visible universe, does not arrive at nonexistence and dissolution through death as it appears to us. On the contrary, beings stream down from the divine power to divine knowledge, from the seen world to the unseen, from the world of change and transience to that of light and immortality.[81] He underlines the fact that the beauty and perfection in creation belong to God, and since the Divine Names are eternal and perpetual, the reflections and manifestation embroidery of these are also continuous. As mentioned above, the essence of everything is made as a model. Based on this, the model of the essence of each creation is continuously changed in its relative determination depending on divine intent as a result of endless activity with the manifestation of divine attributes. As a result, non-existence, dissolution, change, and metamorphosis in creation are only changes in relative determination on the physical aspect of beings.[82] Nursi likens the body of each living being, especially those with a soul, to a spoken or written word that is later lost. Just as this seemingly lost word leaves behind many forms of existence, including its meaning, similitude, result, and, especially if it is a blessed word, rewards, living beings,

---

76. Nursi, *The Words*, 120–21.

77. Nursi, *al-Mathnawī al-'arabī al-nūrī*, 96, 114, 184, 188, 243, 355.

78. Nursi, *The Words*, 575.

79. Nursi, *The Letters*, 345; Nursi, *The Flashes*, 447.

80. Nursi, Nursi, *al-Mathnawī al-'arabī al-nūrī*, 96

81. Nursi, *The Letters*, 340.

82. Ibid.

who depart this world through death and dissolution,

> ... leave behind them their spirits, if they possess them, and their meanings, and realities, and similitudes, and the worldly results and fruits of the hereafter produced by them individually; they leave their forms and their identities behind in memories and on the Preserved Tablet, and in the films displaying eternal vistas, and in the exhibitions of pre-eternal knowledge; and they leave the Divine glorifications offered by their essential beings, which represent them and give them permanence, in the notebooks of their deeds; and their innate responses to the manifestations of the Divine Names and what the Names necessitate, and their being existent mirrors to them, they leave in the sphere of the Names. They leave behind in their places numerous non-physical existences like these, more valuable than their external existences, then they depart.[83]

From this perspective, Nursi organizes death into three categories: death of existence without spirit, death of existence with spirit but without conscience, and with spirit and with conscience. He indicates that the beauty of existence without spirit belongs to the Divine Names, and praise and glory is due to these Divine Names. The transformation that takes place through dissolution does not hurt those without a spirit; whereas the death of animals that have a spirit but no conscience is not annihilation. In fact, these creatures continue to exist in the form of eternal spirits which rely on a Divine Name, freed from physical existence and the struggles of this life, while passing the gains earned in this world on to their eternal spirits. They go not to nonexistence, but to the eternal bliss suitable to them.

Beings with spirit and conscience, like humans and jinn, go, after this life, to eternal bliss and the permanent world of physical and spiritual perfection. Through death they experience worlds better than this one, like the intermediate realm, the world of similitudes, and the spirit world. Hence, their death is not ephemeral nonexistence. Quite the contrary, their death, in this context, is the indication of reaching respective perfection specific to them in those worlds.[84]

Moreover, Nursi conveys that creation experiences not only dissolution and death-prone physical existence but also metaphysical existence in various worlds that represents its immortal existence. It is through the existence and singularity (*Wahda*) of God, who is the Necessarily Existent One (*Wājibu'l-Wujūd*), that everything that associates with him and whose connection is known will have a connection with all of creation through its continuous existence.[85] It is through this association with God that the death, dissolution, and separation that sever one's connection to physical existence cease to exist. If the Necessarily Existent One is not acknowledged, the darkness of nonexistence and pains of dissolution will besiege that creation. In the perspective of the one who does not acknowledge the Necessarily Existent One, the world becomes a desolate land of fear and terror. Real evil and ugliness surfaces with the severance of the connection with or acknowledgement of

---

83. Nursi, *The Rays*, 79–80; Nursi, *The Letters*, 340.

84. Nursi, *The Letters*, 340.

85. Ibid., 342.

the Necessarily Existence One, because without this connection, everything will face separation as many as the number of affinity it has with other creation. As a result, a life of a million years without this connection would not be equal in value to a single moment with it.[86]

## ORDER

According to Nursi, order is the third productive principle in the universe. It is the result of the relative truths[87] that come into existence through the introduction of opposites.[88] Order is like a rope to which all benefits and wisdom are tied. It is a collection of ubiquitous laws that affect every species of creation,[89] and it establishes the connection between cause and effect.[90] According to Nursi, this order is God's general practice that is in effect in creation.[91] It is a discipline that is imposed on creation and a representation of the ubiquitous laws of nature. It is logical, relative, and rational.

As mentioned above, Nursi refers to the law of contest, which involves change, transformation, and the seeking of perfection. This law results from the clash of opposites that occurs throughout the universe. Nursi emphasizes that it is this law that opens the door for the tests and trials that are the key for continuous progress in human beings, for it is humans who are created as the most comprehensive fusion of opposites.[92] Now, let us investigate the relationship between opposites and relative truths and the testing of humankind.

## THE EMERGENCE OF STRUGGLE AND MORAL DECAY

We have mentioned above that the reflection in humankind of the clash of opposites in the universe is a "struggle." Nursi explains this as follows:

Yes, however many degrees there are from a seed to a huge tree, the *abilities* lodged in human nature are more numerous. There are degrees from a minute particle to the sun. For these *abilities* and *potentialities* to develop, *action* is required, a *transaction* is necessary. The action of the mechanism of progress in such a transaction is brought about through *striving*. And striving occurs through *the existence of evil spirits and harmful things*. Otherwise man's station would have been constant like that of the angels. There would have been no classes in humankind, which resembles thousands of species. *And it is contrary to wisdom and justice to abandon a thousand instances of good so as to avoid one minor evil.*[93] [Italics mine.]

In other words, the results attained in the universe through *change* and *transformation* by the introduction of opposites in creation are attained through the *striving of humankind*.[94] This is where the existence of evil comes into play, as

---

86. Ibid.

87. Nursi, *Ishārāt al-i'jāz*, 35.

88. Nursi, Nursi, *Ishārāt al-i'jāz*, 35; Nursi, *Sayqal*, 219; Nursi, *Mesnevi-i Nuriye*, 718.

89. Nursi, *Ishārāt al-i'jāz*, 150, 153.

90. Ibid., 29.

91. Ibid., 154.

92. Nursi, *The Letters*, 80; Nursi, *The Flashes* 115; Nursi, *The Words*, 553.

93. Nursi, *The Letters*, 74; Nursi, *The Flashes*, 104.

94. Nursi, *The Letters*, 71; Nursi, *The Flashes*, 104.

this striving could only happen through the existence of evil spirits and harmful things.

The tests and trials that occur in order to bring about the relative truths in humankind require not only the existence of nonexistential harmful acts like denial, rebellion, and selfishness and existential beings like evil humans and spirits but also the existence of complete good like mercy, wisdom, and justice.[95] According to Nursi, there are many reasons for man's bad behavior that are explained through divine wisdom. Some of these reasons are as follows:

## THE HUMAN BEİNG AS A MIRROR TO THE DIVINE NAMES

Nursi believes that man, with his comprehensive nature, is created to understand, find pleasure in, and serve as a mirror for all of the Divine Names. For example, sustenance is a point of focus for the manifestation of many Divine Names. Thus, man's experience of sustenance helps him understand those Names. Angels, however, cannot understand them from this perspective.[96] He explains that man is a mirror for the Divine Names from three perspectives.

First: Man becomes a mirror to the Divine Names through the opposites existing within him. In other words, his perspective of not having the nonexistent elements makes him a mirror. For instance, through his infinite poverty, he reflects infinite divine bounty, and through infinite powerlessness, he reflects infinite divine power. These visible deficiencies, which are regarded as evil, are, in fact, tools that can be used to understand God. Thus, man, with his free will but without the power to create, can see the deficiencies in himself, become aware of the Divine Names, and reach a higher knowledge of God.[97]

Second: Man becomes a mirror to the Divine Names through the limited abilities given to him. For example, it is his limited and deficient knowledge, volition, sight, and life that reflect God's infinite divine knowledge, volition, and sight, and it is through his deficient attributes that he learns the Divine Names of Perfect, Complete, and Infinite. In other words, the reason these deficient attributes are given to him is to reach the knowledge of God, which is absolute good.[98]

Third: Nursi categorizes the third perspective in two parts: First is that man mirrors the beauty of the Divine Names in his physical body. For example, the Divine Name of Creator is mirrored in God's beautiful and perfect creation, and the names such as The Controller (*al-Mudabbir*), The Orderer (*al-Munazzim*), and The Omniscient (*al-'Alīm*) are reflected in the order in the human body. In short, the human serves as a mirror for the Divine Names through the examples of Divine art that exists in the body.[99] Second is that man is a mirror for the perfect essential qualities (*shuūnāt*) like love, anger, and mercy. According to the author, since man is created as a unit of measurement, each ability, emotion, and sense has

---

95. Nursi, *The Letters*, 71; Nursi, *The Flashes*, 104; Nursi, *The Rays*, 89–90.

96. Nursi, *The Letters*, 353; Nursi, *The Flashes*, 456.

97. Nursi, *The Letters*, 354; Nursi, *The Flashes*, 457; Nursi, *The Rays*, 81–82.

98. Nursi, *The Letters*, 354; Nursi, *The Flashes*, 458; Nursi, *The Rays*, 82.

99. Nursi, *The Rays*, 82.

the ability to enable the understanding of these Divine Names and attributes.[100]

## VEILS WITH AND WITHOUT CONSCIOUSNESS

According to Nursi, angels act as supervisors to the divine laws ('*Adatullah*) and represent the laws of the good matters (*al-qawanin al-khayrīa*) in the universe. On the opposite end of the spectrum, Satan and demons serve as the reason behind and support for evil, as wisdom and truth require the existence of evil creatures.[101] Nursi explains this as follows:

> The existence of the angels, who are like the representatives and supervisors of the laws of the good matters in the universe, are established and agreed upon by all the religions. So too, the existence of evil and satanic spirits, who are the representatives and ushers of evil matters and the means of the laws of such matters, is required by wisdom and reality, and is certain. Indeed, in evil matters, a conscious screen is more necessary . . . since everyone cannot see the true good of everything, the All-Glorious Creator has made apparent intermediaries as a screen in respect of apparent evils and defects, so that objections should not be levelled at Him, nor His mercy be accused, nor his wisdom criticized or unjustly complained about, and so that objections, criticisms, and complaints should be directed at the screen, and not turned to the Generous Creator, the Absolutely Wise One. Just as He has made illness a screen to the appointed hour of death in order to save Azra'il from the complaints of His servants who die, so too He has made Azra'il a screen to the seizing of the spirits of the dying so that the complaints at that situation, which is fancied to be lacking in compassion, should not be directed to Almighty God. And even more certainly, dominical wisdom demanded the existence of Satan, so that objections and criticisms in the face of evils and bad things should not be directed to the All-Glorious Creator.[102]

While human and *jinnī* satans and demons represent veils with consciousness, physical causes like calamities, tribulations, accidents, illnesses, and earthquakes represent veils without consciousness.[103] Just as illnesses act as veils for death, which is the responsibility of the angel of death, the angel is a veil with consciousness who becomes the target of complaints in seemingly merciless situations that do not bode well with the perfection of mercy. In sum, wisdom requires the existence of human and *jinnī* satans and demons in order to curtail rebellion against and criticism of God.[104]

## SATAN AND THE PROBLEM OF EVIL

Nursi also touches upon how Satan makes misdeeds happen. Just like any other created being, Satan does not have the ability to create. Furthermore, he emphasizes that Satan does not have any power apart from his free will and ability to do things without creating. Nursi further explains

---

100. Nursi, *The Letters*, 354–56; Nursi, *The Flashes*, 458–59; Nursi, *The Rays*, 82.

101. Nursi, *The Letters*, 82; Nursi, *The Flashes*, 117–8.

102. Nursi, *The Words*, 301.

103. Nursi, *The Letters*, 82; Nursi, *The Flashes*, 118; Nursi, *The Words*, 524.

104. Nursi, *The Letters*, 82; Nursi, *The Flashes*, 118.

that human satans and demons accomplish things not with power and action, but with nonexistential behavior[105] like neglect and idleness or preventing good deeds from taking place.[106] Through not allowing good to take place, they commit evil, and by committing evil, they become evil.[107] Satan finds strength by guiding man into destruction. In so doing, much evil is committed with little effort.[108] Man's egoistic soul always listens to Satan,[109] and carnal desires and emotions such as anger,[110] which are placed in the essence of man to ensure the soul"s survival, act as a receiver for his whispers.[111]

## NONEXISTENCE AND ABANDONMENT AS THE BASIS OF EVIL

As Nursi articulates in the *Risale-i Nur*, there is no action in the essence of evil. Instead, there is abandonment that translates into inaction, thus, it is very easy to do evil things.[112] He describes the human as a creature with a propensity for good and evil. As he explains, there are two types of laws in effect in the universe. The first law (*sharīʿa*) involves the continuous manifestations of the Divine Names over creation, such as a stone that has been thrown falling to the ground under normal conditions. The second is the law which is in the form of injunctions of religion through revelations. There could be obedience to and rebellion against both sets of laws, with that of the former generally seen in this world and that of latter is generally being left for the hereafter.[113] For instance, if a person abandons his work, an act that translates as abandoning the general practice of God (*ʿAdatullah*), the punishment, in this case, failure, is executed here in this world. However, the punishment of not abiding by the commands and prohibitions of religious laws is usually left for the hereafter. As mentioned earlier, while all kind of evils take place by not having even one component of the whole, positive and existential happenings have to have all the components to be present for the whole to exist. For example, since belief is an indivisible single truth, to be a believer according to Islam, one has to accept and believe all the contingent elements of that belief, whereas non-belief happens by not believing only one of those elements. In Islamic belief, denial and rejection of one single contingent element is enough to step out of Islamic belief.[114]

Nursi uses one particular allegory to prove that the reason behind human evil is abandonment. In this allegory, a steersman of a ship abandons his post, and, as a result, the ship crashes and sinks along with its entire load and crew. Despite the fact that the steersman is the one responsible for the entire wreckage, in reality, he does not perform any particular action

105. Nursi, *The Letters*, 74; Nursi, *The Flashes*, 108.

106. Nursi, *The Letters*, 70, 73; Nursi, *The Flashes*, 103, 106–7; Çoban, "Nursi on Theodicy," 123.

107. Nursi, *The Letters*, 73; Nursi, *The Flashes*, 107.

108. Nursi, *The Letters*, 72, 77; Nursi, *The Flashes*, 105, 112.

109. Nursi, *The Letters*, 74; Nursi, *The Flashes*, 107–8.

110. Nursi, *Ishārāt al-iʿjāz*, 32.

111. Nursi, *The Letters*, 74, 83; Nursi, *The Flashes*, 107–8, 118.

112. Nursi, *The Letters*, 217; Nursi, *The Flashes*, 281.

113. Nursi, *The Words*, 760.

114. Nursi, *The Rays*, 256.

to cause the wreck. Thus, the entire loss is due to a lack and abandonment of the required action on his part. As a result, the steersman is responsible for the damage to the ship and its cargo, the loss of life, the potential profits from the sale of the cargo, and the crew. In the end, the outcome of the steersman's abandonment of his duty would not change even if the rest of the crew did its job perfectly and the condition of the vessel was perfect.[115]

Moreover, Nursi says that since it is so easy to cause massive destructions with small actions and, thus, to transgress the rights of much of creation, especially in modern times, weak and foolish people tend to opt for destruction in order to be seen as strong and worthy of respect.[116] In fact, he claims that "the number of destructive, harmful humans who have become like monsters through lack of religion is increasing."[117]

## THE ACQUISITION (VS. THE CREATION) OF EVIL AS EVIL

Nursi notes that it is not the creation of evil (*khalq*) by God, but rather people's acquisition of evil (*kasb*) that is evil. Accordingly, to be able to make choices freely, human beings are given a power of choice, or free will: "Apparent actions are generally the result of a succession of acts that end in a person's "inclination" (*mayalān*), called will (*al-juz al-ikhtiyārī*)."[118]

According to Nursi, the power of choice does not have any power of creation. Once a person selects something with his power of choice and God wills to create it, that thing is created through God's divine will and power. Everything created in the universe, including choices made through man's power of choice, is created according to divine laws and consequences. Since the creation of an evil has very auspicious consequences, the creation of that evil is the equivalent of good. For instance, the creation of satans, with challenges they construct for humanity, provides people with a means of attaining spiritual development and, ultimately, eternal happiness. Thus, if a person uses his own free will[119] to serve evil and is deceived by satanic wiles, the person cannot simply say, "The creation of Satan is evil." There are several reasons for this.

> [T]he creation of evil is not evil, the desire for or inclination towards evil, rather, is evil. For creation and bringing into existence look to all the consequences, whereas such desire looks to a particular result, since it is a particular relation. For example, there are thousands of consequences of rain falling, and all of them are good. If through ill choice, some people receive harm from the rain, they cannot say that the creation of rain is not mercy, they cannot state that the creation of rain is evil. Rather, it is due to their ill choice and inclination that it is evil for them. Also, there are numerous benefits in the creation of fire, and all of them are good. But if some people receive harm from fire through their misuse of it and their wrong choice, they cannot say that the creation of fire is evil, because it

---

115. Nursi, *The Words*, 182.

116. Nursi, *The Letters*, 72–73; Nursi, *The Flashes*, 105.

117. Nursi, "Hutbe-i Şamiye" http://ebooks.rahnuma.org/religion/Said_Nursi/DamascusSermon%20-%20Said%20Nursi.pdf (accessed July 3, 2017).

118. Nursi, *Signs of Miraculousness*, 80.

119. Nursi, *The Letters*, 76; Nursi, *The Flashes*, 110; Çoban, "Nursi on Theodicy," 122.

was not only created to burn them. Rather, they thrust their hands into the fire while cooking the food through ill choice, and made that servant inimical to themselves. . . . Thus, the creation and bringing into existence of evils, harms, tribulations, satans, and harmful things, is not evil and bad, for they are created for many important results. For example, satans have not been set to pester the angels, and the angels cannot progress; their degrees are fixed and deficient.[120]

God created Satan as a "conscious screen" over the evils done by people with their free wills. The most important role of Satan is to protect the dignity and sacredness of God against people's criticisms and disputes, for all the atrocities, injustices, and immoralities are caused by Satan and the evil-commanding souls (nafs) of people who follow Satan.[121] Thus, the conscious screens of immoralities, such as Satan and evil-commanding souls, as well as unconscious screens, such as ills and disasters, to be regarded as evil depends on the form of human relation with them. This is because evil is created for the sake of endless prosperity and bounty, none of which are evil in reality. Therefore, the acquisition of evil is regarded as a "particular relation/contact" (mubāshara) of a human, for it is linked only to its perpetrator.[122]

## HUMAN FREE WİLL

God is the creator of good deeds, but human free will, which has no ability to create, is the source of immoralities. Nursi says that, while the nature of human free will is unknown, its existence is known consciously.[123] He defines human free will as "a rational and relative matter" (al-amr al-'itibārī), a matter that has a rational, spiritual, and intellectual existence but does not have an external, material existence.[124] Rational and relative matters cannot perform the act of creating, which is the exclusive feature of divine power.[125]

Although human free will has a weak existence and no ability to create, Nursi notes that, Almighty God, the Absolutely Wise One, made that weak and partial will a condition for the connection of His universal will."[126] On the other hand, "the power of choice may provoke [man] through a rational matter and cause terrible consequences," as "disbelief and rebellion are non-existence and destruction."[127] In other words, since evils, being of nonexistential nature, are easier to bring into existence than existential (wujūdī) good deeds, they do not require an existent power and active creativity.[128] For this reason, the power of choice of a human being who has only rational/intellectual existence will cause great destruction, not by power and action, but rather through neglect of duty, as in the case of a steersman leaving the helm of his ship.[129]

120. Nursi, The Letters, 62; Çoban, "Nursi on Theodicy," 123.

121. Nursi, The Letters, 331; Nursi, The Flashes, 429.

122. Nursi, The Letters, 76; Nursi, The Flashes, 110; Nursi, The Words, 666.

123. Nursi, The Words, 480; Çoban, "Nursi on Theodicy," 122.

124. Nursi, The Words, 482; Çoban, "Nursi on Theodicy," 123.

125. Nursi, Ishārāt al-i'jāz, 87; Nursi, The Letters, 186; Nursi, The Flashes, 243.

126. Nursi, The Words, 483; Nursi, Ishārāt al-I'jāz, 207.

127. Nursi, The Words, 479 (I made some modifications in Vahide's translation).

128. Nursi, The Flashes, 73.

129. Nursi, The Letters, 84.

"Man is totally responsible for his evils,"[130] for it is his evil-commanding soul that wants the evil and it is he who opens the door to that evil with his own free will. Just the same, since evil and atrociousness originate from nonexistence, man merely becomes their agent (*fāil*). When man perpetrates evils by his own free will, "it is Almighty God Who creates the evils through a Divine law which comprises numerous benefits."[131]

## HUMAN ACQUISITION OF GOOD

According to Nursi, while man bears full responsibility for causing the evils that stem from nonexistence, he plays no role in good and grateful work other than wanting that good deed with his free will. This is because "what wants and requires the good deeds is Divine mercy, and what creates them is dominical power. Request and reply, reason and cause, are both from God. Man only comes to have them through supplication, belief, consciousness, and consent."[132] Since the human's evil-commanding soul does not desire good deeds and good deeds can only be created by divine power, human free will cannot be the source of these deeds. Man can be in possession of his good deeds only through "supplication, belief, consciousness, and consent."[133]

## HUMAN SPIRITUAL DEVELOPMENT AND GROWTH

In Nursi's view, human development occurs as a result of one's struggles, namely, his striving against the evil-commanding soul and the satans. Through this development, human dispositions become apparent, and with human dispositions becoming apparent, man's abilities become evident. These abilities then cause relative truths to occur. These relative truths include things that emanate through the collision of opposite tendencies in humans, such as good and evil, cruelty and justice, and sin and reward. It is as a result of these relative truths that man is able to manifest in his/her actions various Divine Names. For instance, man's sins require his manifestation of the name Oft-Forgiving, and his injustices make him manifest the name All-Just.[134]

Now, the law of change and transformation in the universe requires the change of all of creation, including man, who is the fruit of the universe. There is no innate limitation placed on the faculties of man and *jinn* when a change takes place, so a trial and test for man's endless rise and fall is opened.[135] Due to this rise and fall, there will inevitably be a grading of the people who participate in this test.[136] Therefore, people will have different spiritual degrees varying from pharaohs to prophets.

According to Nursi, the development of abilities is not limited to humans alone. The emergence and development of the abilities in all beings, from

---

130. Nursi, *The Words*, 478.

131. Nursi, *The Words*, 478; Nursi, *The Letters*, 84–85.

132. Ibid.

133. Nursi, *The Words*, 478.

134. Nursi, *The Words*, 553, 574–75; Nursi, *al-Mathnawī al-'arabī al-nūrī*, 708.

135. Nursi, *The Words*, 193–94; Nursi, *Ishārāt al-I'jāz*, 32; Nursi, *Signs of Miraculousness*, 29.

136. Nursi, *The Words*, 194.

potentiality to actuality, happen in two ways: First, by using animate-inanimate things for precious duties such as being a mirror to the Divine Names. Second, by giving a higher degree to those who perform their assigned duties. The second occurs in four manners: 1) Elements such as air, water, earth are raised to the degree of minerals; 2) Minerals are raised to the degree of plants; 3), plants are raised to the degree of animals through provision; 4) Animals are raised to the degree of people, the possessors of intellect and consciousness.[137] Through this test and trial, diamond-like souls are distinguished from the coal-like souls.[138]

## CONCLUSION

Nursi elucidates upon the existence of evil according to the general purposes established by God. These purposes include the desire of the Divine Names to be manifest in creation, as well as man's sophisticated nature, his knowledge of God, and his role in the universe as the greatest reflection of the Divine Names. From this perspective, that which results from evil is based on general purposes related to God and to man's relationship with God as a mirror to his names in the broadest way. According to Nursi, minute evils originate from nonexistence and such evils serve as a greater good; thus, God's creation is free from evil, ugliness, and tyranny. Furthermore, with respect to man's committing of evil by his own free will, any such evil is confined to its perpetrator. Satans, evil-commanding souls, and harmful beings are created to serve as screens between man and evil. It is in situations inappropriate to the dignity and perfection of God, that they divert the complaints of people, who judge according to the outward face of events, away from God. These screens can be conscious, such as devils, or unconscious, such as accidents and illness.

## BIBLIOGRAPHY

Aydın, Mehmet. "The Problem Of Evil in the *Risale-i Nur.*" Online: http://nursistudies.com/teblig.php?tno=288 (accessed April 11, 2012).

Çoban, İzzet. "Nursi on Theodicy: A New Theological Perspective." In *Classic Issues in Islamic Philosophy and Theology Today*, 4, part 3, edited by A-T. Tymieniecka and Nazif Muhtaroğlu, 111–35. New York: Springer, 2010.

Mermer, Yamina. "Bediüzzaman Said Nursi's Scriptural Approach to the Problem of Evil." Online: http://www.nur.org/en/intro/nurlibrary/Nursi_s_Scriptural_Approach_To_The_ProbleOf_Evil_116 (accessed April 11, 2012).

Michel, Thomas. "For You, Illness is Good Health": "Said Nursi's Advice in Time of Illness" Online: http://www.thomasmichel.us/Nursi-advice.html (accessed April 11, 2012).

———. "God's Justice in Relation to Natural Disasters." Online: http://www.thomasmichel.us/natural-disasters.html (accessed April 11, 2012).

Nursi, Bediüzzaman Said. *Asār-ı Badi'iyya*. Istanbul: Ittihad, 1999.

———. *al-Mathnawī al-ʿarabī al-nūrī*. Istanbul: Sözler, 1994.

———. *The Flashes*. Istanbul: Sözler, 2004.

———. *Ishārāt al-i'jāz*. Edited by Ihsan Qasim. Istanbul: Sözler, 1994.

———. *The Letters*. Istanbul: Sözler, 2010.

———. *Kastamonu Lahikası*. Istanbul: Envar, 1994.

———. *Muhākemāt*. Istanbul: Envar 1995.

---

137. Nursi, *The Letters*, 350; Nursi, *The Flashes*, 453.

138. Nursi, *The Words*, 553; Nursi, *al-Mathnawī al-ʿarabī al-nūrī*, 708.

## Section Two: Theology

———. *The Rays*. Istanbul: Sözler, 2002.

———. *Signs of Miraculousness*. Translated by Şükran Vahide. Istanbul: Sözler, 2004.

———. *The Words*. Istanbul: Sözler, 2004.

al-Razi, Fakhr al-Din. *Muhassal afkar al-mutaqaddimin wa-'l-muta'akhkhirin*. Edited by Taha ʿAbd al-Rauf Saʿd. Al-Qahira: ʻMaktaba Kulliya al-Azhariya, n.d.

# 8

# A Graceful Reconciliation
## Said Nursi on Free Will and Destiny

### ÜMEYYE ISRA YAZICIOĞLU

*And though you've travelled many roads*

*There's but one way—and that's the one you chose ...*
YUSUF, "BE WHAT YOU MUST," *ROADSINGER* ALBUM

WITH THE IMPRESSIVE ADVANCEMENT of science and technology in our age, the question of human freedom and destiny has become a more intriguing one. Indeed, the basic methodological assumption of modern science, natural determinism, yields puzzling results when applied to human actions. If we embrace the assumption that every event can be explained exclusively by referring to natural causes and natural laws, then it means that our actions are also determined by natural causes and forces around and within us. As the famous formula of biology goes, we are products of "our genes plus environment." In such a picture, it is assumed that natural laws work with precision, our past produces our future, and we are all part of an immense machine run by various natural and social causes. Given these deterministic implications of the scientific approach, William James was not exaggerating when he talked about the "wrath" of modern science against human free will.[1]

[1] "The wrath of science against miracles, of certain philosophers against the doctrine of free-will, has precisely the same root—dislike to admit any ultimate factor in things which may rout our prevision or upset the stability of our outlook." *The Writings of William James*, 327. To be sure, even the scientific principles can be rearticulated to make more room for free will. As quantum physics also reveals, natural

Fortunately, we are not obliged to take the wrath of modern science to heart. Instead, we just need to recognize the use of determinism in certain scientific contexts without turning it into a metaphysical principle. Hence, while it is understandable that making room for free will would hopelessly complicate the scientific purposes of predicting and controlling natural phenomena in many cases, we need not be constrained with such purposes in treating all issues. The question of free will and destiny thus exceeds the scope of scientific inquiry and brings us to the realms of theological and philosophical reflection.

Similar to other world traditions, Islamic tradition offers a rich engagement of the question of human freedom as well as destiny. The case of Said Nursi's approach to the issue of free will and destiny reflects both a distillation and a refinement of the traditional Islamic approaches to the issue. It also is impressive how Nursi keeps a focus on the pragmatic implications of belief in free will and destiny throughout his analysis, rather than letting it become an abstract intellectual exercise. He is clearly interested in the question of how belief in free will and destiny can properly inform our choices and nourish a mature and creative response to life.

Not surprisingly, the question of free will and destiny arises in the Islamic context especially because of the central concept of *tawḥīd*, oneness of God: the recognition that there is only one source of all power, beauty, and perfection. And the question is, if all traces of power, wisdom, beauty and goodness on earth are fully dependent on only One, how are we to make sense of human agency? Is there a genuine difference between a tree that grows with divine power and will, and a human being who acts through the aid of the same power and will?

The Qur'anic discourse also seems to raise some questions regarding the issue of human free will. On the one hand, the Qur'an is unequivocal about the unique human potential: having had God's spirit breathed into them (e.g., Q. 15:29; 38:72), human beings are clearly expected to take responsibility for their lives and make existential decisions thoughtfully (e.g., Q.18:29; 73:19; 74:55; 76:29; 78:39; etc.). On the other hand, there are also passages in the Qur'an that refer to divine planning and "measuring out" (*taqdīr*) of everything: nothing happens without divine will—not even a leaf falls without God's permission; everything "fresh or dry," dead or alive, is known (e.g., Q. 3:26; 6:59; 15:21; 36:12, etc.). Indeed, the Qur'an makes repeated references to a clear book in which all is recorded before and after it comes into existence: "And there is no living creature on earth but depends for its sustenance on God; and He knows its time-limit [on earth] and its resting-place [after death]: all [this] is laid down in [His] clear decree" (Q 11:6; also see: 22:70, 27:75, 34:3; 36:12; 50:4, etc.).[2] Thus, for instance, Adam's choice of eating from the forbidden fruit appertains to the divine plan to place human beings on earth (see Q. 2:30).

Belief in destiny or divine planning of everything also figures in prophetic traditions or *hadith* literature. For

---

phenomena simply exhaust the scope of natural determinism even in the scientific context. Also, see for instance, the work of the scientist and philosopher, Charles S. Peirce discussed in Corrington, *An Introduction to C. S. Peirce*, 174 ff.

2. Unless otherwise noted, the English translation of Qur'anic verses is from Muhammad Asad, *The Message of the Qur'an*.

instance, there are many sayings attributed to Prophet Muhammad which emphasize that God guides and misguides whomever he wills, that everyone's *rizq* or provision is fixed, and that there is a "book" in the presence of God in which everything is written down beforehand.[3] These traditions highlight the primacy of the divine plan so much that, if one focuses on them at the expense of other traditions, it would seem that human free will is completely irrelevant. Yet even in the case of such traditions, one must read between the lines keeping the broader thrust of *hadith* literature in mind. Given that the prophetic traditions are narrated to inform and persuade the believer to follow the prophetic example, such apparently predestinarian traditions are also narrated precisely to make a difference in believers' *choices*. That is, according to these *hadiths* a believer is expected to choose surrender to God and trust him in response to such providential arrangement. Thus, even such destiny *hadiths* aim to elicit a particular choice and response from the audience and thus implicitly accede to the notion of free will.

Given the emphasis on *tawḥid* as entailing God's comprehensive agency, as well as the apparently conflicting depictions of human agency and destiny in the sacred texts, it is perhaps not surprising that in the history of Islamic thought, the first intellectual debate to arise was on the issue of free will and destiny.[4] Interestingly, the debate was first opened up in a political context, during the period of the Umayyad dynasty, (41–132 AH/ 661–750 CE), whose rulers promoted a predestinarian view in order to vindicate themselves before the public.[5] According to their predestination propaganda, if the caliph seemed to act unjustly, one had to think twice before blaming him because the caliph was merely a tool that God was using to punish the people; he was not acting wickedly on his own.[6] To be sure, even this fatalistic propaganda worked with an implicit assumption of human free will and moral responsibility: after all, if no one had responsibility for their actions, why would God punish the people through unjust rulers?

Jahm bin Ṣafwān (d. 128 AH/ 745 CE) is regarded as the first one to argue that human beings are utterly devoid of choice and free will. Such a claim later became labelled the "Jabriyya" position, according to which human beings are compelled in their actions.[7] According to him, human actions are predestined by God in such a manner that actions can be attributed to human beings only in a figurative sense, no more than the way we ascribe "the bearing of the fruit to the tree, flowing to the stream, motion to the stone, rising or setting to the sun, blooming and vegetating to the earth."[8] That is, just as the natural world is continuously being created and sustained by God, the human being is made to sin or do good by God without having any will, power or choice in the matter whatsoever. Not surprisingly, such a deterministic position selectively emphasized the scriptural passages that talk about destiny and comprehensive divine will, conveniently

---

3. For some examples of the *hadiths* that emphasize the concept of destiny, see: Wensinck, *The Muslim Creed*, 55–56.

4. Fakhry, *A History of Islamic Philosophy*, 57.

5. Ibid.

6. Ibid.

7. Schwarz, "'Acquisition' (*Kasb*) in Early *Kalām*," 355.

8. Fakhry, *Islamic Philosophy*, 62.

overlooking the passages that affirm human free will. Perhaps more importantly, it flatly contradicted the very core of prophetic message, that people have the capacity to respond to the divine call. After all, if everything were merely a puppet show, why would God send messengers to invite people to belief? It is not surprising that such a view did not become accepted either among the learned or among the masses.[9] The Jabriyya view was not even endorsed by the strictest theologians with literalist inclinations, and eventually died out.[10] Now, while such a view did not survive, it did open up the discussion of *how* to reconcile belief in destiny with belief in human free will.

As a response to the predestinarian approach, the defenders of free will, who were called "qadarites," came to the fore. They asserted that human beings are responsible for their acts, and argued quite justifiably that if human beings were predestined to sin, God's punishment of wrongdoers would be meaningless and unjust. These proponents of free will suffered at the hands of the Umayyad rulers, who were aware of the political implications of the doctrine of free will, and carried out one of the rare inquisitions in Islamic history.[11] Later, the Mu'tazilites furthered the qadarite legacy of defending human moral responsibility. Their basic idea was that "God has entrusted (or delegated, *fawwaḍa*) action to men and has given them capability of fulfilling the duties which have been imposed on them. They are capable of both belief and unbelief.... *Men's actions are not created by God.*"[12] It is the very last sentence, which offered a particular interpretation of the relation between human agency and divine agency that was new and provocative.[13] As a reaction to the Mu'tazilite assertion that God is *not* the creator of human actions, Hasan al-Ash'ari (d. AH 935/324 CE) broke off from the Mu'tazilite party. He argued that God's all encompassing power and will pertained to human actions as well. His views were developed by later theologians, and the Ash'arite school emerged. Around the same time with the emergence of the Ash'arite school, the Maturidī school was being formed independently in Transoxiana, whose approach concurred with the Ash'arite school for the most part in terms of the relation between destiny and free will. A nuanced account of human agency within the framework of *tawḥīd* thus eventually emerged in what became the predominant view in Islamic theology.

The conclusion that became accepted by the Sunni schools, to which

---

9. Tritton, *Muslim Theology*, 58.

10. Frank, "The Structure of Created Causality according to Al-Ash'ari," 14; Watt, *Free Will and Predestination in Early Islam*, 167.

11. Fakhry, *Islamic Philosophy*, 57.

12. Abu'l Hasan al-Ash'ari, *Maqālat al-islāmīyīn wa'khtilaf al-muṣallīn*, quoted in Schwarz, "'Acquisition,'" 354. (Emphasis added)

13. Schwarz, "'Acquisition,'" 355. Since most Mu'tazilites also acknowledged occasionalism, such theory on the creation of human actions raised serious problems. For instance, they had to answer questions such as, if one is the creator of one's acts, does one also create all the consequences of his/her act? And, if I am not the creator of those acts outside my body, then could I be said to be the real creator of the action? Besides, if I am not the creator of the consequences of my action, then who is? Some Mu'tazilites said it is nature, others said it is God, and it was even said that it had no maker, it happened by itself! That is why, the Mu'tazilite view on human actions was "much more complex and paradoxical than is generally realized." Fakhry, "Some Paradoxical Implications of the Mu'tazilite View of Free Will," 98.

majority of Muslims ascribed,[14] was that human beings have a limited free will, with which they freely choose between alternatives, and God creates the consequences of the choices for them, which means that God is the creator of human acts while human beings *acquire* the responsibility of the act created as a result of their choice of that act. Acquisition (*kasb*), a term derived from the Qur'an, thus became a theological term denoting this idea that while the human being does not actually create her actions, she is the one who is morally responsible because she opts for them.[15] While the conclusion may seem quite straightforward, the discussions that led to it involved addressing a number of key questions: Why cannot human beings be considered genuine creators of their actions? How do we know that we have a choice even though we are not the creator of our acts? How do destiny and human freedom interact? How is it that the results of our bad choices are also created by a merciful God? Nursi's approach to the issue reflects both a keen understanding of these crucial questions discussed in Islamic theology as well as a creative contemporary contribution to it.

## NURSI ON HUMAN FREE WILL AND DESTINY

> For there is nothing [so deeply] hidden in the heavens or on earth but is recorded in [His] clear decree. (Q 27:75)

Since Nursi's approach to *tawḥīd* has been analyzed in detail in another article in this volume, it shall suffice for us to only briefly summarize his understanding of *tawḥīd* and focus on his references to human actions within that context. In the light of the Qur'an, Nursi analyzes natural causality and interprets it as either a veil or a mirror to divine agency.[16] For instance, Nursi argues, water isn't the cause of life, for it is lifeless, and also lacks the power, wisdom, and intentionality to create life. Instead, Nursi argues, the interaction between water and life—that is, the emergence of life in the presence of water—reveals the existence of a Life Giver who is giving life *through* water.[17] Just as water *appears* to be the cause of life, while in reality it is not, so too human beings are not the creators of their actions, even though they may seem to be so at first sight.

To be sure, Nursi says, the "noblest apparent cause" among all other "apparent causes" is the human being. For, human beings have the most comprehensive will compared to other living beings and elements of nature. Yet even human

---

14. While the Muʿtazilite school was a phenomenon that emerged among Sunnis, it lost appeal in the Sunni theological tradition and continued as a school among Shiite minority.

15. The term *kasb* is a frequently misunderstood term in modern scholarship as a thinly veiled predeterminism. In reality, as we shall discuss, the term has been used to denote the human relation to the act chosen by him and created by God; hence while God is the Creator, the person acquires responsibility because he chose it. See for instance, al-Juwaynī, *Kitab al-irshād ilā qawāṭīʿ l-adilla fī uṣūl al-iʿtiqād*, 42–45; al-Taftazānī, *A Commentary on the Creed of Islam*, 83. See also Frank, "Created Causality," 2.

16. That is, according to Nursi, natural causality is either a thin veil behind which God's agency is discernible for those who take time to meditate or a mirror that reveals God's attributes to those who are willing to look at nature carefully. In any case, for Nursi, it is the divine power and will that makes the natural causality possible at all times.

17. See for instance, Nursi, *The Flashes: From the Risale-i Nur Collection*, 182.

beings' agency pertains to only a fraction of their simplest acts.[18] When one talks, for instance, one only chooses to talk and has no idea how the voice is produced, how the utterance reaches through the airwaves to the listener, and how it is finally perceived as meaningful speech by an audience.[19] Similarly, in our other common voluntary acts, such as eating and drinking, we have no input on how what we eat is digested and utilized in the body, and in fact we are usually not even aware of how our act of chewing happens. Nursi also gives the example of thinking, which is also helpful because the act of thinking is even more elusive for us as a process than eating or speaking. As a result, Nursi argues, it is clear that even our most basic voluntary actions are not created by us, since we are only aware of a fraction of the process and oblivious to the rest of it. We simply intend to eat or think, and the results are created for us by God. Nursi's argument is reminiscent of classical theological arguments, as seen in al-Juwaynī's and al-Taftazānī's works, for instance.

In regards to the issue of destiny, Nursi highlights the Qur'anic notion that everything that transpires in the world is "written" both before and after it comes into existence. Typical of his hermeneutical style, Nursi turns to nature to see evidences for the existence of such a "written record" (*kitāb al-mubīn*) mentioned in the Qur'an. Regarding the recording of everything *after* it comes into existence, Nursi notes that our memory, for instance, provides crucial evidence. That we can recall things and images after they transpire is an indication that our actions are recorded and will be revealed to us in the Day of Judgment.[20]

As for the presence of a "written record" that *precedes* the existence of things, Nursi argues that the fact that a living being, such as a tree, flourishes in a particular pattern and goes through wisely measured shapes and forms shows that there is a plan that precedes its existence. Nursi notes that the "codes" in seeds and eggs, which today we call as DNA or genes, is a physical expression of that plan, or *qadar*. According to Nursi, if there is a plan for the simplest forms of existence, such as plants, then a plan exists for nobler forms of existence, that is, for human lives as well. It is interesting that Nursi understands there being a *qadar* for someone as an asset rather than a limitation. Existence of destiny for human beings indicates the care and importance with which the person is created.[21]

Now, as he affirms the comprehensive power and knowledge of God pertaining to all events, including human actions, Nursi also confirms that human free will is genuine. Indeed, Nursi's "Treatise on Destiny" (henceforth "Treatise")[22] is precisely aimed at showing how these two notions actually support each other.

---

18. Nursi, *Risale-i Nur Külliyatı*, vol. 1, 277; 644. Henceforth, this collection of Nursi's works will be referenced with the abbreviation *RNK*. Also see: Nursi, "Thirty-Second Word, Addendum to Second Station," in *Words*, 636; Nursi, "Seventeenth Flash, Fifth Note," in *Flashes*, 162.

19. Nursi, *RNK*, 277; *Words*, 636.

20. Nursi, *RNK*, 207; *Words*, 484.

21. Nursi, *RNK*, 208; *Words*, 485.

22. This treatise corresponds to *RNK*, 204–12; and in English translation, "Treatise on Destiny" ("Twenty-Sixth Word"), in *Words*, 477–94.

## CONTEXTUALIZING THE FREE WILL AND DESTINY DISCUSSION

It is noteworthy that Nursi starts the "Treatise" with a crucial note on the scope and use of such analysis. He notes that unlike discussions regarding other articles of belief, such as belief in God or hereafter, the discussion of destiny and free will does not lend itself to a theoretical analysis; rather it directly relates to conscience and attitude.[23] That is, the notions of destiny and free will are results of certain convictions and commitments and directly inform one's way of being in life. They are not theoretical premises to be discussed on their own.[24] According to Nursi, only when a person honestly admits all power, mercy, wisdom, and beauty is from God will the importance of the reality of free will emerge. Such a believer will be aware that his surrender to God does not absolve him from responsibility because he does have free will. And, once he admits his responsibility, there is also another pitfall: he may be deluded into taking credit for the good that is created as a result of his choices. It is in such a context that destiny "confronts him," reminding him that the real agent is God, and what befits the believer is gratitude instead of pride.[25] In other words, destiny and human freedom are both contextual, and pertain to an ultimate unfolding of belief in *tawḥīd*. Only when placed in such proper contexts are they meaningful and truthful.

To be sure, Nursi admits that even for people who do not have such a refined existential stand, the concept of destiny may have a limited truthful use. When used in reference to the past, belief in destiny can allow one to come to terms with calamities and painful events. Such belief in destiny can give hope and consolation about past sad events by showing them as part of a wise plan of God.

In contrast, when taken out of these existential contexts, Nursi argues, the very same concepts of destiny and free will would only be abused to perpetuate false pretensions: the person then will brag about the good consequences of his actions by invoking his free will, while appealing to the concept of destiny for justifying his laziness, and to avoid responsibility for his faults. Such use is a distortion and has nothing to do with the truth of belief in destiny and free will.[26]

Nursi's emphasis on the contextual, relational and spiritual aspect of destiny and free will is insightful in that it right away clears up much of the clutter that would arise in an abstract and isolated discussion of these concepts. Such an approach focused on actual implications of these concepts also speaks more directly to the needs of the audience. Of course, an immediate question also arises: Why is it that human beings should take full responsibility for their bad actions, while praising the Creator for their good actions?

## GOOD, EVIL, AND THE HUMAN SHARE

> Whatever good happens to thee is from God; and whatever evil befalls thee is from thyself. (Q 4:79)

---

23. Nursi, *RNK*, 204; "Treatise," *Words*, 477.
24. Ibid.
25. Ibid.
26. Nursi, *RNK*, 205; *Words*, "Treatise," 479–80.

According to Nursi, while everything, including the consequences of our actions, both good and bad, are created by God, we are fully responsible for our evil actions and get only partial credit for our good actions. How is that fair? Here, Nursi's distinction between the responsibility for the good and the bad actions seems to be guided by the Qur'anic concept of *fitra*, the notion that human nature is essentially wired for goodness (e.g., Q. 30:30). To give an illustration: let's assume that you are walking down the street and see a person lying on the ground, bleeding. You will instantly feel the need to help—you will want to call 911, try to get the person to a hospital, and so on. Compare such an instinct to save life to the inclination to kill: killing a person is utterly counterintuitive and much harder to carry out. In other words, in terms of one's natural instincts and conscience it is much harder to intend to kill someone than to intend to save his life. Hence, when a human being makes a bad choice and goes against her *fitra*, she takes complete responsibility for it. Whereas, when she follows her *fitra*, she gets credit only insofar as she did not block the goodness wired in her; she does not have the right to brag about it.[27]

Moreover, Nursi contrasts the nature of a good and a bad act so as to highlight the distinction between human responsibility for each. He argues that bad actions are essentially acts of destruction or negation: negating your inner instincts, you undermine something good, such as in the case of breaking someone's heart, or killing. While harder on the conscience, destroying as an act requires much less energy than building something; burning down a house requires just lighting up a match, while constructing it needs much more energy.[28] As Nursi explains elsewhere, there are *many* conditions for something to exist while the absence of only *one* of these conditions will result in its absence.[29] Thus, for instance, a garden will dry up when I fail to open the water canal, and it will flourish when I open the water canal. While I take the blame for the garden drying up, I do not get all the credit for its flourishing. After all, a garden grows in the presence of many things at once, such as sunshine, water, minerals, etc., while it will dry up at the absence of one thing only. Similarly, while just one person can take the blame for sinking a ship when he does not carry out his task, he alone cannot take the credit for making it sail well. After all, even when he does his part well, the entire crew still plays its role in the proper sailing of the ship.[30]

Therefore, Nursi concludes, we are fully responsible for our evil choices and the evil consequences that befall us as a result, while our input in the construction of good is only partial. Indeed, a human being can only be associated with the good that is created as a result of his choices through his attitude and intention. It is only through "prayer, belief, awareness and acceptance" that one can have a connection to the good that God

---

27. As Nursi notes, "Yes, as the Qur'an states, man is totally responsible for his evils, for it is he who wants the evils." Nursi, "Treatise," *Words*, 478; *RNK*, 204.

28. Ibid.

29. Nursi's use of "condition" seems intentional here. For, as he argues repeatedly, natural causes are not genuine creators. Rather, they are simply conditions, which the Creator takes into account in his unaided creative action of bringing the results into existence.

30. Nursi, *RNK*, 205; "Treatise," *Words*, 479.

creates as a result of his choices.³¹ Thus, Nursi confirms the Qur'anic passage that "Whatever good happens to thee is from God; and whatever evil befalls thee is from thyself" (Q 4:79).³²

While human choice of evil goes against their *fiṭra* and they are fully responsible for the consequences of such a free choice, according to the perspective of *tawḥīd*, all things are *created* by God. That is, as far as the creation aspect of things is concerned, everything is created by God, including our very ability to choose between good and evil, and the consequences of our evil choices. Nursi further explains how this fact does not bring any "blame" on the Creator.

## CREATING EVIL VS. ACQUIRING EVIL

Wherever you may be, death will overtake you—even though you be in towers raised high. Yet, when a good thing happens to them, some [people] say, "This is from God," whereas when evil befalls them, they say, "This is from thee [O fellowman]!" Say: *"All is from God . . . ."* (Q 4:78, emphasis added)

According to Nursi, from the perspective of creation, God's creation of our capacity to choose as well as its consequences is not evil because it has a bigger purpose that is good. While traditional theological discussions would typically note this much, Nursi, like Sufi masters, elaborates on this notion further. Reminiscent of Sufi masters such as Muhyiddin Ibn 'Arabi (d. 1240) and Jalal ad-Din al-Rumi (d. 1273), Nursi explains that both our capacity to choose between good and evil, and the whole spectrum of events that take place in the world, including apparently ugly and evil ones, are essentially good from the broader perspective of divine agency.

To start with human capacity to choose between good and evil, Nursi argues that it is good, notably in the context of his discussion of the "fall" of Adam, in the "Twelfth Letter." He notes that the immense human potentials need a place of challenge and choice (*dār al-taklīf*) to flourish in, a context where both encountering and choosing evil is possible. Precisely by being taken out of paradise onto earth, the human beings have been given the chance to develop their capacities and witness a variety of Beautiful Names of God in display.³³ Even the creation of satans is good, Nursi says, because they pose challenges that are necessary for human beings to develop their potentials.³⁴

Furthermore, Nursi suggests that whatever happens in life has a purpose and beautiful potential, even if an event seems to be out of the blue, uncomfortable or unjust. Indeed, Nursi argues, "Anything that befalls life is good."³⁵ Sickness reveals the beauty of healing, hunger is needed to perceive the beauty of sustenance, and injustices become venues for us to appreciate justice and opportunities to stand up for it, and so on. Thus, the Beautiful Names of God, such as Healer, Provider, Merciful, Just, etc., become revealed in various shades and colors through the various challenges

---

31. Nursi, *RNK*, 204; "Treatise," *Words*, 478.

32. This verse is also quoted in Nursi, *RNK*, 211; "Addendum" of the "Treatise," *Words*, 492.

33. Nursi, *RNK*, 364; Nursi, "Twelfth Letter," in *Letters*, 62.

34. Nursi, *RNK*, 365; "Twelfth Letter," *Letters*, 63.

35. Nursi, *RNK*, 209; "Treatise," *Words*, 487.

and difficulties in life.[36] This is a theme that many parts of the *Risale* are devoted to explaining, and to which Nursi also returns toward the end of the "Treatise."

Nursi concludes, therefore, that God's creation of evil is not bad, for it intends and achieves broader good purposes. In contrast, the human being who commits evil does not intend such good ends. Rather, he has a shortsighted vision and often a selfish intention that inform his bad choices. Thus, he bears moral culpability, and what he *acquires* is evil.[37] Hence, Nursi invokes the classical Islamic formula: God's creation of evil (*khalq al-sharr*) is not evil, while human acquisition of evil (*kisb al-sharr*) is evil.

Making such a distinction between human choice of evil and God's creation of its consequences, and noting the bad and limited motivation of the former and the broader good purpose of the latter, not only relieves a theological puzzle of theodicy, but also offers a precious consequence for human life. Indeed, as we shall observe, such a distinction offers an antidote to the victim mentality.

## ANTIDOTE TO THE VICTIM MENTALITY: EMBRACING DESTINY AND FREE WILL TOGETHER

The victim mentality suggests that one's circumstances can be so negatively influenced by outside factors that he or she loses the capacity to do anything about it, except for suffering its consequences. Now, if we affirm human free will at the expense of destiny, such a victim mentality prospers. For if everyone's will is the only factor in the equation, with no broader divine purpose and destiny in effect, then an evil result that I suffer because of other people's choices means that I am their helpless victim. In contrast, Nursi's approach suggests that freedom and destiny are intimately linked, and one person's freedom is part of someone else's wisely planned destiny. All events actually have two sides to them: an aspect that looks to a person's choices and a second aspect that looks to divine planning. From the perspective of people's free will, there is justice and injustice, while from the perspective of *qadar* or destiny there is pure justice and wisdom.[38] As far as the unjust person is considered, he is responsible for his injustice, and as far as the person who was exposed to injustice is concerned, she is relieved to know that no one can genuinely ruin her life, and that whatever befalls her has a wise purpose and message.

As an illustration of how belief in destiny can offer an antidote to the victim mentality, Nursi gives the example of someone being sentenced to prison because of an unjust accusation of theft. Now, Nursi says, the person may well be innocent of such a charge, but perhaps he has secretly committed another crime. In that case, while the judge who found him guilty of theft was indeed being unjust, from the perspective of his destiny

---

36. For a specific treatment of the theodicy in Nursi's works, see Mermer, "Bediüzzaman Said Nursi's Scriptural Approach to the Problem of Evil" and Yazıcıoğlu, "Affliction, Patience and Prayer: Reading Job (p) in the Qur'an."

37. Nursi, *RNK*, 204; "Treatise," *Words*, 487. "Since life displays [manifestations] of the Most Beautiful Names, everything that happens to it is good."

38. Nursi, *RNK*, 204. *Words*, 479.

it was fair that he ended up with such a sentence.[39]

In other words, if someone does evil to me, as far as she is concerned she is fully responsible because she has free will. At the same time, I am no victim of such choices that occur beyond my control; from my perspective, her treatment of me becomes my divinely planned challenge. While the person who hurt me cannot escape responsibility by saying, "Well, you were meant to be hurt as part of your destiny," I can refer to my destiny in interpreting the situation that happened to me and say: "I am not a victim of her choice; rather, I was meant to encounter this, and there is a message here for me to understand and respond to; my destiny is traced out by my Lord with justice, mercy and wisdom."

Here, Nursi's approach seems to be inspired by the Qur'anic concept of doing injustice to oneself (Q 3:117, 3:135, 4:64, 7:23, 11:101, etc.). According to this view, people can only do evil to their own selves, and not genuinely to others. While someone's attack on me may be beyond my control, I am not a loser because of it and I still retain agency for my purposes; hence, such a person is eventually harming himself only. In other words, my response to the hurtful situation is in my control and does matter: by trusting in the wisdom of my divinely planned destiny, I *can* approach the situation with a sense of responsibility and choose how to respond to it. Moreover, since it is God's agency that brings all things into existence, rather than apparent causes, I can trust that as I do my part in responding to the situation, God can protect me from being genuinely harmed. That is, if I choose to respond to the situation with full trust in destiny, rather than with a victim mentality that considers the oppressor's actions as decisive, then even the worst intentions and actions of my attacker can be transformed into a moment for growth and cleansing for me, by God's will.

Furthermore, Nursi insightfully argues that free will becomes meaningful only when connected with belief in destiny. Indeed, rejecting destiny, that is, the existence of a special wise and merciful plan laid out by God for each person, eventually undermines the concept of free will itself. After all, given that we are part of an immense and intricate web of relationships, my free will becomes negligible in the midst of the total sum of all other people's choices around me. Indeed, in such a picture without destiny, our free will is not only hopelessly competing with other people's choices but also the entire web of relations in nature and the universe that is beyond our control: "For, the human being is related to the entire universe. He has endless wishes and needs. Yet, his power, will and freedom cannot even suffice [to accomplish] a fraction of them, and thus his burden will be incredibly taxing and scary [if he denies destiny] . . . ."[40]

Thus, Nursi suggests, if one does not believe in destiny, then within that tiny feeling of autonomy and a limited sense of freedom, he will feel immense burdens on his weak spirit.[41] If all we have is our free will and limited power, then we need to somehow convince the entire world to adjust to and yield to our needs and wishes—an extremely stressful and

---

39. Ibid.

40. Nursi, *RNK*, 208 (my translation); "Treatise," *Words*, 486.

41. Ibid.

overwhelming idea, and, of course, an impossible task.

In contrast, belief in destiny allows one to see the events befalling him as purposeful and something that is intended for him to respond to. Moreover, in attaining his goals, he is only responsible to do his part and entrust the rest to the One to arrange and take care of.[42] Since in the worldview of *tawḥīd* things are related to each other only through God's power and will, the person can fully trust that things will be worked out by the One with power, and wisdom, as long as she does her part in having constructive intentions and making choices accordingly.

With such an affirmation of destiny and free will together, one does not act out of fear of forces beyond his control, and feel overwhelmed by perceiving himself as a product of his environment and stimulants. Rather, the person can act with confidence and hope. He can be sure that the posture that he takes in response to the world is what matters before God, who alone can grant his wishes and fulfill his needs.[43] Belief in God's control of events thus frees the person to act by relieving her burdens.[44] Thus, in Nursi's view, the concepts of free will and destiny gracefully become two sides of the same coin, supporting one another rather than competing with each other.

## NUANCES OF THE INTERACTION BETWEEN FREE WILL AND DESTINY

In addition to urging that free will and destiny be embraced together, Nursi addresses various subtle aspects of the connection between human free will and divinely planned destiny. Following classical theological views, he notes that just because we cannot fathom precisely how free will and destiny interact, it does not mean that they are irreconcilable. We all feel deep down a sense of free will, and that intuition is valid, though we do not comprehend its exact nature.[45] After all, there are many beings whose existence is obvious to us but whose natures are hard to define or pin down clearly. After these helpful disclaimers that break the ice, Nursi moves on to offer noteworthy observations highlighting how destiny does not precondition human freedom. As examples, let us look at some them.

To start with, Nursi highlights that destiny is an aspect of divine knowledge (*'ilm al-ilahī*), and that divine knowledge acknowledges human will. In other words, knowledge is dependent on the object known, and not vice versa. You may know for instance that a book is a hundred pages, but it is not so because you know it to be as such. Your knowledge does not determine the situation; rather it acknowledges it. Similarly, God's knowledge of human choices acknowledges them instead of determining them.

Of course, there is often an implicit assumption that we make when we think of the relation between an action and one's knowledge of it. We assume that we are in the same time zone with the agent, and if

---

42. Ibid.

43. Nursi's move seems to reflect the Qur'anic verses such as, "Verily, God does not change men's condition unless they change their inner selves; and when God wills people to suffer evil [in consequence of their own evil deeds], there is none who could avert it: for they have none who could protect them from Him" (Q 13:11; also see: Q. 8:53).

44. Nursi, *RNK*, 208; "Treatise," *Words*, 486.

45. For a similar view, see: al-Taftazānī, *Creed of Islam*, 84.

we can know *for sure* how he *will* act in the *future*, it means that the person is not really free in his action. For the person and I are both in the same present and both of us are looking out at the future from the same vantage point. Yet Nursi precisely questions this assumption of thinking of time as linear and God as part of that linear timetable with us, anticipating our future like we do. Rather, he notes that God's eternity means that what is past, present and future for us is viewed by him from a comprehensive perspective.[46] On the basis of a *hadith*, Nursi explains the comprehensiveness of God's knowledge with a metaphor of a mirror. He suggests that we assume that we hold a mirror and things reflected on the right side of the mirror represent the past and on the left side represent the future. When held low, the mirror can only reflect some of the things across it, and one would have to move it along so as to get the whole view of things. In such a case, we can talk about certain things preceding the other and the sequence of things as they show up in the mirror. In contrast, when held very high the mirror will reflect all the things across it all at once, and from that high vantage point, the events across the mirror cannot be said to be before or after each other. Similarly, divine knowledge sees all events at once; it does not involve a temporal sequence, as is the case with us.[47]

Besides, another interesting clarification Nursi offers regarding the connection between free will and destiny is that destiny pertains to both the cause and effect of an event at the same time. This contrasts with the Jabriyya view that sees the connection between an apparent cause and its consequence as completely arbitrary, as well as with the Mu'tazilite view that considers the connection between causes and their effects as necessary in itself. Nursi gives the example of someone killed with a gunshot. Now, the deceased person's destiny was precisely that, no less and no more. One may not say, "If it was his destiny to die, why is the person who fired the gun responsible? The person would die even if the gun was not fired." Such a conclusion assumes that from the perspective of destiny we can separate the murderer's choice—the cause— from the victim's death—the effect—and assume that the death was part of destiny in a way that the murderer's choice was not. Yet the moment you disconnect the cause from being part of destiny, you move the destiny perspective out of the picture completely. In Nursi's words, "If you assume that the man did not fire the gun, then you are assuming that destiny does not pertain to the event; hence, on what basis will you say that the man was destined to die? Only if you imagine a separate destiny for the causes and a different one for the effects, like Jabriyya does, or you reject destiny like the Mu'tazilites," would you succumb to such illusions.[48] That is, according to Nursi, in this scenario Jabriyya would say that the man still would have died even if no gun was fired, and the Mu'tazilites would say that the man would not have died if the murderer did not choose to kill.[49] While the Jabriyya view denies genuine responsibility to the murderer, the Mu'tazilite view gives him such a terrible agency that it seems

46. Nursi, *RNK*, 206; "Treatise," *Words*, 481.
47. Ibid.

48. *RNK*, 206 (my translation); "Treatise," *Words*, 481–82.
49. *RNK* 206; "Treatise," *Words*, 482.

to control the life span of someone else, to cut short someone's life. In contrast, Nursi argues that the right thing to say about *destiny* in such a hypothetical situation is: "If there was no gun shot, we do not really know what would have happened."[50] That is, one should affirm *both* that there is individual responsibility and that there is a destiny for everyone. Such affirmation requires admitting that the particular interaction of the two escapes an abstract hypothetical analysis.

Nursi also highlights how human free will is effective, despite its inability to create. As noted earlier, Nursi follows the traditional mainstream Sunni position that the human being chooses to act in a certain way and it is the divine will and power that gives existence to the acts. To be sure, from one perspective, this "partial free will" is too weak: it cannot create anything,[51] or necessitate the existence of anything.[52] We might add that even its ability to choose is limited: the alternatives from which it selects are not always under its control, and of course we have no choice over many things, such as when the sun will rise. Yet, Nursi notes, human free will is effective because of the divine will that makes human choices effective. To illustrate this interaction between human will and divine will and power, he gives the example of a child getting a ride from someone. Even though the child is unable to get to where she wishes on her own, her choice matters because the person giving her a ride is willing and powerful enough to honor it. Similarly, "the Almighty God, the Most Just of All Judges, makes the [limited] will of His utterly weak servant a simple condition for His all-comprehensive will."[53]

Nursi also resists the temptation to undermine human free will by requiring an explanation or a reason for all choices.[54] It is tempting to think that, for instance, if I selected coffee over tea this morning, it must have an explanation other than my free will: the chemical situation of my taste buds, the smell of the coffee, my habits, or some other reason external to my will must have compelled me toward coffee instead of tea. According to Nursi, such an idea that all choices are actually the result of a determining factor is simply not true. The whole point of having free will is to differentiate between two things without being *compelled* by one reason over another, as the famous theologian al-Ghazali (d. 505 AH/ 1111 CE) also emphasized.[55] Hence, despite all the factors weighing me toward coffee, I *can* choose tea over coffee "just like that"—that is the whole point of my having free choice.

What is perhaps most distinctive in the "Treatise" is that while treating subtle issues of Islamic theology or *kalām*, Nursi always keeps the actual implications for daily life in the foreground. What is at stake for him is not a theoretical reconciliation of apparently conflicting concepts, but an understanding that enables a conscious life, filled with an appropriate

50. Nursi, *RNK*, 206 (my translation); "Treatise," *Words*, 482.

51. Ibid.

52. Actually, according to Nursi, our very inability to necessitate anything allows room for our freedom. He seems to suggest that interpreting human actions within a deterministic view would actually contradict human freedom. (See: *RNK*, 206; "Treatise," *Words*, 482.)

53. Nursi, *RNK*, 206 (my translation); "Treatise," *Words*, 483.

54. Nursi, *RNK*, 206; *Words*, 482.

55. Al-Ghazali, *Tahāfut al-Falāsifa*, 25–27.

sense of gratitude, responsibility, and appreciation of the profound wisdom of situations one encounters in life. Hence, Nursi's analysis not only starts with a detailed introduction which sets the proper context and "use" of destiny and free will, but also ends with two extended notes (in the Conclusion and the Addendum), both of which are directed to the edification of the person.

## ULTIMATELY IT IS ABOUT SELF-EDIFICATION: FREE WILL, DESTINY, AND SPIRITUAL GROWTH

In agreement with classical Islamic spirituality, Nursi notes that there is a part within each human being that likes to brag about things that are gifted to it, instead of being grateful for them, and refuses to take responsibility for its faults. That aspect, more specifically denoted as *al-nafs al-ammāra* in the Sufi tradition,[56] is inclined to deny the Creator's manifestations of power, will, wisdom, and mercy. For Nursi, the ultimate purpose of discussing the issue of destiny and free will is to edify this *nafs* or ego.

In the Conclusion and the Addendum of the "Treatise," Nursi especially emphasizes how the human being is completely mistaken if he arrogantly appropriates the goodness that is created through him. Nursi argues that such an attitude is as ridiculous as a dry grapevine branch bragging about the grapes that grow through it.[57] Just as the dry branch in reality has no genuine input into the creation of such sweet nourishment from mud, the human being has no right to be boastful about the good created as a result of her choices. For the good results and situations are created through the will and the power of the One. Yet, with no justification the *nafs* has the tendency to worship itself, appropriating the good that manifests through it and constantly denying any shortcomings and faults it has. Indeed, when not controlled, such illusionary tendency can take over the innate human capacity (*fiṭra*) to praise and adore the source of power and beauty, God, and misuse that capacity to praise its own self. Such is the attitude noted in the Qur'anic passage: ". . . the one who makes his own desires his deity" (Q 25:43).[58]

A person who deludes himself with such claims and ridiculously idolizes himself needs constant stressful efforts to maintain his fake idol. Moreover, he finds himself in a dark world, devoid of overall purpose, wisdom and mercy. Here, Nursi refers to the Qur'anic passage, "And be not like those who are oblivious of God, and whom He therefore causes to be oblivious of their own selves" (Q 59:19).[59] He suggests that when the person claims to be the creator of her actions, she will find herself stuck in the moment in which she thinks she has control—after all, the moments before and after that very present moment are too obviously beyond her control. Nursi addresses such a person by saying, "What you consider as life is merely the moment you live in. Your time before that moment as well as the things of the world within that past is dead. And all

---

56. Literally, "the commanding soul," which "commands evil," as alluded in Q. 12:53.

57. Nursi, *RNK*, 209; "Treatise," *Words*, 488. Also see *RNK*, 89; "Eighteenth Word," *Words*, 239–40.

58. Nursi, *RNK*, 211; "Addendum" of the "Treatise," *Words*, 492.

59. Ibid.

the time after that moment and all what is contained in that future time is nothing at that moment."[60] To imagine yourself living precariously between the darknesses of past and future is a nightmare. Being stuck with finitude is the cost of claiming to be the creator of the good manifested through oneself. Indeed, when the soul

> trusts its own being, and ignores the Real Creator [*Mujīd al-Haqīqī*], its tiny light like a firefly will be drowned out in endless darknesses of non-existence [*adam*] and separation. But if it gives up its egoism, and sees that on its own it is nothing, and he is a mirror on which the Real Creator is manifest, then it gains the [presence] of entire beings and has access to a limitless reality. For, the one who finds the Necessarily Existent One, whose manifestations of Beautiful Names [*asmā' al ḥusna*] the entire beings reflect, then, he finds everything.[61]

In other words, even when we pretend to have control over ourselves, it is impossible to pretend that the world is under our control. Since we cannot remedy our own finitude, let alone the finitude of the beings around us, the price of such self-conceit is to settle with the view that the world is passing and the constant death and separation is what the world is about. Only when one gives up such pretension, and believes in destiny, and admits that there is an Eternal One who is in control, and who has a divine, wise, and merciful plan for each being, will he find himself in an enlightened world. In such a world, the flux of the events and beings is no longer painful reminders of death, but renewed manifestations of the Eternal.[62] The person, through acknowledging the One, will raise up to the levels "the heart, the spirit and the inner mystery [*sırr,*]" and enjoy the expanse of their vision, for which past and future are both alive and present.[63] Admitting its finitude and weakness, the soul will now recognize the blessings showered on him, and respond with praise and gratitude, instead of vain pride and deluded self-praise in relation to its agency.

## CONCLUSION

Because of the limitations of space, we skipped many of Nursi's subtle points in the "Treatise." Even from the scope of our limited discussion, I trust that it is clear how Nursi insightfully places such a classical issue of theology within a pragmatic context of a believer's attitude toward life, and also connects it to the purpose of spiritual transformation and awakening. Hence, in Nursi's analysis, what may seem to be a troubling implication of modern scientific formulas about human agency, and what is treated often in a dry manner in Islamic theology, becomes a venue for reaffirming the profound human potential to connect to the Eternal. Building on the rich legacy of Islamic tradition, and

---

60. Nursi, *RNK*, 209 (my translation); "Treatise," *Words*, 489.

61. Nursi, *RNK*, 211 (my translation); "Addendum" of the "Treatise," *Words*, 493.

62. In discussing the complete change in the perception of the world through belief, Nursi uses the metaphor of "gallows" transforming into an exciting "movie screen." The painful finitude of the world becomes an enjoyable screen to various colors of the beautiful manifestations of the Names of the One. See *RNK*, 11; "Seventh Word," *Words*, 41–42. Also, for a noteworthy example of his contrast between the perspectives of belief and disbelief, see *RNK*, 132–35; "Twenty-third Word, First Station," *Words*, 319–27.

63. Nursi, *RNK*, 209–10 (my rendering); "Treatise," *Words*, 489.

combining theological and Sufi considerations, Nursi's *Risale* offers an accessible and notable reconciliation of free will and destiny in the modern age.

# BIBLIOGRAPHY

Asad, Muhammad. *The Message of the Qur'an*. Gibraltar: Dar al-Andalus, 1984.

Corrington, Robert S. *An Introduction to C. S. Peirce*. Lanham, MD: Rowman & Littlefield, 1993.

Fakhry, Majid. *A History of Islamic Philosophy*. New York: Columbia University Press, 1970.

———. "Some Paradoxical Implications of the Mu'tazilite View of Free Will." *The Muslim World* 43 (1953) 95–109.

Frank, Richard M. "The Structure of Created Causality according to Al-Ash'arī: An Analysis of the *Kitāb al-Luma'* §§ 82–164." *Studia Islamica* XXV (1969) 82–64.

Al-Ghazālī, Abū Ḥamīd. *The Incoherence of the Philosophers: "Tahāfut al-falāsifa"; A Parallel English-Arabic Text*. Translated and annotated by Michael E. Marmura. Provo, UT: Brigham Young University Press, 2000.

James, William. *The Writings of William James: A Comprehensive Edition*, edited by John J. McDermott. New York: Random House, 1967.

Al-Juwaynī, 'Abdalmalik ibn 'Abdallāh. *al-'Aqīda al-niẓāmiyya fī al-arkan al-islāmiyya*. Cairo: al-Maktabah al-Azhariyah, 1992.

———. *Kitab al-irshād ilā qawāṭī l-adilla fi uṣūl al-i'tiqād*, Cairo: Maktabat al-Sa'āda, 1950.

Mermer, Yamina. "Bediüzzaman Said Nursi's Scriptural Approach to the Problem of Evil." *The Journal of Scriptural Reasoning* 4.1 (2004). Online: http://etext.lib.virginia.edu/journals/ssr/issues/volume4/number1/ssr04-01-e02.html.

Nursi, Bediüzzaman Said. *Letters*. Translated by Şükran Vahide. Istanbul: Sözler, 1994.

———. *The Flashes: From the Risale-i Nur Collection*. Translated by Şükran Vahide. Istanbul: Sözler Neşriyat, 1995.

———. *Risale-i Nur Külliyatı*. Vols. 1 & 2. Istanbul: Yeni Nesil Yayınları, 1996.

———. *The Words: From the Risale-i Nur Collection*. Rev. ed. Translated by Şükran Vahide. Istanbul: Sözler, 2004.

Peirce, Charles S. *The Collected Papers of Charles Sanders Peirce*. Vols. 1–6 edited by Charles Hartshorne and Paul Weiss. Vols. 7–8 edited by Arthur W. Burks. Cambridge: Harvard University Press, 1931–58. Online edition: http://www.nlx.com.

Schwarz, M. "'Acquisition' (*Kasb*) in Early *Kalām*." In *Islamic Philosophy and the Classical Tradition: Essays Presented by His Friends and Pupils to Richard Walzer on his Seventieth Birthday*, edited by S. M. Stern, Albert Hourani, and Vivian Brown, 355–87. Columbia, SC: University of South Carolina Press, 1972.

al-Taftazānī, Sa'd al-Dīn. *A Commentary on the Creed of Islam: Sa'd al-Din al-Taftazānī on the Creed of Najm al-Dīn al Nasafī*. Translated, with introduction and notes, by Earl Edgar Elder. New York: Columbia University Press, 1950.

Tritton, A. S. *Muslim Theology*. Bristol, UK: Luzac, 1947.

Watt, Montgomery. *Free Will and Predestination in Early Islam*. London: Luzac, 1948.

Wenscik, A. J. *The Muslim Creed: Its Genesis and Historical Development*. 2nd ed. New Delhi: Oriental Books Reprint Co., 1979.

Yazıcıoğlu, Isra. "Affliction, Patience and Prayer: Reading Job (p) in the Qur'an." *The Journal of Scriptural Reasoning* 4.1 (2004). Online: https://jsr.shanti.virginia.edu/back-issues/vol-4-no-1-july-2004-the-wisdom-of-job/affliction-patience-and-prayer-reading-job-p-in-the-Qur'an/.

# 9

# Supplication as Agent and Fruit of Transformation for Bediüzzaman Said Nursi

## Lucinda Allen Mosher

Transformation—change in composition, structure, outward appearance, character, or condition—is at the core of the story of Bediüzzaman Said Nursi. Repeatedly during the course of his long life, war and politics would transform his homeland.[1] Repeatedly, imprisonment or exile would transform his living situation. Internally, he himself would undergo "a strange revolution of the spirit" from which he would emerge as "the New Said."[2] The fruit of this deliberate embrace of the life of illumination and contemplation, the *Risale-i Nur*,[3] would transform the spiritual and devotional lives of millions. Spiritual transformation, it has been argued, is the process of "becoming new" by means of struggle. Struggle is itself a process by which change leads to isolation, darkness, vulnerability, exhaustion, and scarring. From this process emerges hope—itself a process whose elements include faith, courage, surrender, and endurance.[4] These elements (isolation, darkness, vulnerability, exhaustion, and scarring; faith, courage, surrender, and endurance) are patently obvious in all accounts of Nursi's life. Obvious also is the importance of supplication as an agent of his own spiritual transformation and in

1. Nursi's life spanned the last decades of the Ottoman Empire and its collapse after WWI, the establishment of the Turkish Republic, the twenty-five-year reign of the Republican Peoples' Party, and the beginning of the post-Republican era.

2. Şükran Vahide, *Bediüzzaman Said Nursi: The Author of the Risale-i Nur*, 164. Hereafter, Vahide, *Bediüzzaman Said Nursi*.

3. Throughout, any quotations from the *Risale-i Nur* will be Şükran Vahide's translation, and hereafter will be cited simply as *Words*, *Letters*, *Flashes*, and *Rays*.

4. Thanks are due to Roman Catholic social psychologist, communications theorist, and spiritual visionary Joan D. Chittister for her outline of the processes from which spiritual transformation results. See her *Scarred by Struggle, Transformed by Hope*.

## BECOMING THE "NEW SAID"

Nursi's early adult years—what he would later call the period of the "Old Said"—were fraught with political activism. Imprisonment was not a new experience for him when, during World War I, he was injured and captured by Russian forces in eastern Turkey.[5] Eventually, having been transferred to a camp in northwestern Russia, he transformed a portion of the prison into a place for prayer and study for himself and his fellow prisoners. In 1918, after two years of captivity, he escaped and returned to Istanbul—famous, but scarred; depleted physically and distracted spiritually.[6]

Toward the end of his imprisonment near the banks of the Volga River, Nursi had experienced what he described as a temporary arousal "from a deep sleep of heedlessness" and pledged to spend the remainder of his life in solitude.[7] Only in 1920 would he make good on this commitment and withdraw from public life. From the self-imposed isolation, deep introspection, and theological writing of the period 1920–21, Bediüzzaman emerged as the "New Said."

Nursi's transformation from Old to New Said occurred, as he himself described it, in three stages:[8] Stage One, his own personal reassessment of the value of philosophy to his spiritual health (and finding philosophy wanting); Stage Two, the "bitter medicine" of his close reading of ʿAbd al-Qadir al-Jilānī's *Futūḥu'l-ghayb* (*Revelations of the Unseen*);[9] and Stage Three, the inspiration he took from Shaykh Ahmad Sirhindī's *Maktūbāt* (*Letters*)—that his sole guide and orientation should be the Qurʾan.[10]

Regarding the first stage, biographer Şükran Vahide notes that Nursi's "process of 'spiritual awakening'" was triggered initially by "a few flashes ... [which] took the form of realizing the stark realities of death and separation, old age and the transitoriness of things," coupled with the realization that his years of study of the philosophical sciences had failed to provide "consolation and a ray of light," but rather "had 'dirtied his spirit,' and been an obstacle to his spiritual progress."[11]

The second stage of transformation began when, soon after settling into a house in Sarıyer, on the European side of the Bosphorus, Nursi came into possession of ʿAbd al-Qadir al-Jilānī's *Futūḥu'l-ghayb* (*Revelations of the Unseen*). Opening this book at random, Nursi came upon lines which he took to mean that, before he could be about the business of curing the spiritual sickness of others, he would first need to find a doctor for himself! Thus Nursi "hired" al-Jilānī as his physician, and set to reading *Futūḥu'l-ghayb* as if it were addressed to him directly. The effect was "severe,"

---

5. For an account of Nursi's early activism, see Şükran Vahide, *Islam in Modern Turkey*, chapters 1–6; for an account of his capture, see particularly pp. 120–25.

6. Vahide, *Islam in Modern Turkey*, 154.

7. Nursi, *Flashes*, 299–301.

8. Vahide, *Islam in Modern Turkey*, 166.

9. ʿAbd al-Qadir al-Jilānī, also transliterated Abdulkadir Geylani or Gilani; also known by the honorific *al-Ghawth al-Aʿzam* (The Greatest Helper).

10. Nursi often refers to Shaykh Ahmad Sirhindī as Imām al-Rabbānī.

11. Vahide, *Islam in Modern Turkey*, 164. See also, Nursi, *Flashes*, 205.

he says. In his "Twenty-eighth Letter," he explains:

> [Futūhu'l-ghayb] carried out the most drastic surgery on my soul. I could not stand it. I read half of it as though it was addressing me, but did not have the strength and endurance to finish it. I put the book back on the shelf. Then a week later the pain of that curative operation subsided, and the pleasure came in its place. I again opened the book and read it right through; I benefited a lot from that book of my first master. I listened to his prayers and supplications, and profited abundantly.[12]

Here is a clue to the nature of Nursi's spiritual discipline: the crucial role of supplication in his devotional life and in his teaching. Having been transformed himself, he would now provide for the transformation of countless others through his exegetical and inspirational masterwork, the multi-volume *Risale-i Nur*, and its seedbed—the dozen or so Arabic-language essays composed during his retreat, published in 1922 and 1923,[13] which would become the single-volume anthology, *Al-Mathnawī al-nūrī*.[14]

The third stage of transformation came some time later, upon opening at random a copy of the *Maktūbat* (*Letters*) of Shaykh Ahmad Sirhindī (to whom Nursi more often referred as Imām Rabbānī). From this he took advice Imām Rabbānī had "persistently recommended in many of his letters" as meant for him personally: "... which was: 'Make your *qiblah* one.' That is, take one person as your master and follow him; do not concern yourself with anyone else." Upon reflection, he realized that ultimate guidance was not to be had from any of the great mystics such as al-Ghazali, or Rumī, or al-Jilānī (to whose writings he had turned earlier in his retreat) or Imam Rabbānī

---

12. Nursi, *Letters*, 418–19.

13. Mardin, *Religion and Social Change in Modern Turkey*, 177. The titles of Nursi's Arabic treatises from this period are: *Lama'āt min shamsi'l-tawḥīd* (*Sparks from the Realm [lit., Sun] of Tawḥīd*); *Rashaḥāt min baḥri ma'rifati 'l-Nabi'* (*Splashes from the Prophet's Sea of Knowledge*); *Lā Siyyamā* (*In Particular*)—i.e., "particular arguments for the Resurrection;" *Qatrah min baḥri'l-Tawḥīd* (*A Drop from the Sea of Tawḥīd*); *Habābun min 'ummāni'l-Qur'an al-ḥakīm* (*Grain from the Depth of the Wise Qur'an*); *Habbah min nawatāt thamarah min thamarat jinān al-Qur'an* (*A Seed from Pits of the Fruit from the Gardens of the Qur'an*); *Zahratun min riyad al-Qur'an al-ḥakīm* (*A Flower from the Meadows of the Wise Qur'an*); *Dharratun min shu'ā' hidāyat'l-Qur'an* (*An Atom from the Rays of the Guidance of the Qur'an*); *Shammatun min nasimi hidāyat'l-Qur'an* (*A Whiff from the Breeze of the Guidance of the Qur'an*); *Al-Qit'atu'l-thalithatu min shammah* (*A Third Fragment from "A Whiff"*; sometimes published as part of treatise *Shammatun*); *Shu'latun min anwāri shamsi'l-Qur'an* (*A Torch from the Lights of the Sun of the Qur'an*); *Nuqtah min nūrī ma'rifati'llahi* (*A Point from the Light of the God's Knowledge*); *Nūrun min anwāri nujumi'l-Qur'an* (*Light from the Lights of the Stars of the Qur'an*). Throughout the present essay, the first mention of a treatise will give its full title; subsequent mentions will be by the first word only.

14. Şükran Vahide, "A Chronology of Said Nursi's Life" in *Islam at the Crossroads*, ed. İbrahim M. Abu-Rabi', xix. Unless otherwise indicated, all citations of *Al-Mathnawi al-nūrī* will refer to the Arabic-language edition: Badī'uzzamān Sa'īd al-Nursi, *Al-Mathnawi al-'Arabī al-Nūrī*—hereafter, *Al-Mathnawī al-nūrī*. Note that the title is often transliterated *Mesnevî-i Nûriye* by Turkish authors and editors. Unless otherwise noted, all paraphrasing and translation of *Al-Mathnawī al-nūrī* is my own, and most of this was prepared in consultation and collaboration with Hashim Al-Tawil, PhD, of the faculty of Henry Ford Community College, Dearborn, Michigan, to whom I extend my deepest thanks. Where there are errors, they are mine alone. Some half-dozen of these Arabic essays included in *Al-Mathnawī al-nūrī* are also considered the "Thirty-third" of *The Flashes*.

himself (to whom he had just turned); rather, the Qur'an itself provides "the true single qiblah" and "is also the most elevated guide and most holy master." Therefore, Nursi explains, "I clasped it with both hands and clung on to it."[15] The concrete consequence of the third stage of Nursi's transformation—his embrace of the Qur'an as "most elevated guide and most holy master"—is, of course, the *Risale-i Nur* itself: some 6,000 pages, mostly Qur'anic exegesis or Qur'an-based theological reflection.

## NURSI AS MUFAKKIR

Nursi's self-outlined three stages of transformation may well provoke the question: was Bediüzzaman a mystic?[16] As William Chittick has pointed out, rightly, the term "mysticism" has accrued unfortunate associations—that it is something peripheral; that is has to do with "psychic extravagance"—and argues against its use as a synonym for Sufism.[17] But "Sufism" as a term does not serve us well when describing Said Nursi or analyzing his spiritual progress and practice. While his "Twenty-ninth Letter" provides a warm-hearted description of the nature and practice of Sufism, Nursi vigorously shunned the label of Sufi for himself. His practical motive was the Turkish government's 1925 ban on Sufism. Repeatedly, Nursi would be charged with violation of this ban; repeatedly, he would argue strenuously that he was neither a Sufi nor a political activist.[18] But for Nursi, the pastoral motive for eschewing the Sufi label was at least as strong. The Sufi Way, he explained, luminous and radiant though it might be, was an elite path; he preferred to be known for advocating a pathway open to all.[19]

Yet, even taking Chittick's concerns seriously, descriptions of Bediüzzaman's three-stage transition from Old to New Said are consonant with definitions of mysticism such as that offered by Andrew Louth: a "search for and experience of immediacy with . . . the object of the soul's longing . . . [and] an unwillingness to be satisfied with anything less than [that immediacy]."[20] Mysticism is often described in terms of "metaphors of pilgrimage to a goal," notes Evelyn Underhill, whose study remains broadly influential; in terms of "a road followed, distance overpassed, fatigue endured [as] the traveling self in undertaking the journey is fulfilling a destiny, a law of the transcendental life, obeying an imperative need."[21] Underhill stresses that, while paradigms for the mystic's "journey" vary in number of stages and labels for those stages, most account for sustained periods of purgation and illumination on the way to profound awakening to the fullness of divine beauty.[22]

---

15. Nursi, *Letters*, 419.

16. This question is taken up in my earlier essay, "The Spirit of Worship and the Result of Sincere Belief: Nursi's *Mathnawi al-'Arabi al-Nuri* as a handbook for the contemplative life," in *Islamic Spirituality in the Modern World*, ed. İbrahim Abu-Rabi', upon which this section of the present essay draws substantially.

17. See Chittick, *Faith and Practice of Islam*, 167ff. See also Murata and Chittick, *The Vision of Islam*, 238.

18. Vahide, *Bediüzzaman Said Nursi*, 202, 239–40. See also, Nursi, *Letters*, 84–85, 518–35.

19. Vahide, *Bediüzzaman Said Nursi*, 168.

20. Andrew Louth, *The Origins of the Christian Mystical Tradition from Plato to Denys*, xiii–xiv.

21. Underhill, *Mysticism*, 132.

22. Ibid., 169–70. Underhill prefers a five-stage schema of the mystic's progress, but does

In fact, *Purgation* and *Illumination*—which figure in the oldest paradigms of mysticism—are well-suited to an outline of the stations of Said Nursi's spiritual progress and the form of guidance he gives his disciples. For Station Three in the Nursi context, I prefer to borrow language from Underhill and name it "joyous apprehension of the Absolute: that which many ascetic writers call 'the practice of the Presence of God.'"[23] This stage might also be called *Contemplation*—which many spiritual masters define in terms of *tranquility in focus upon the Real*.[24] And, rather than *mystic*, we may do well to call Said Nursi a *contemplative* instead—especially in light of references to contemplation [*tefekkür*] in accounts of his devotional practice.[25]

For Nursi, the *Way of Purgation* began with reflection on death and the material world's transitory nature—an occupation he likened to travel through a subterranean tunnel and across a suffocating desert. Having sought guidance in devotional materials from many great spiritual masters, and found valuable aid in some—particularly, as we've seen, *Futūhu al-ghayb* (*Revelations of the Unseen*) of "Abd al--Qādir al-Jīlānī, and the *Maktūbat* (*Letters*) of Imām Rabbānī—he emerged from the "tunnel" and the "desert," turned decisively from the "Way of Naturalism" and the "Way of the Philosophers" (i.e., reason alone) and declared that henceforth he would travel exclusively on the "Way of the Qur'an."[26]

The very effort of writing his Arabic treatises during a withdrawal and reflection (1920–21) would be a major factor in Nursi's triumph over what he described as the "idols" of "ego within humanity" and "nature in the outer world."[27] Near the end of his treatise *Zahrah*, Nursi explains why (although he admits he ought to keep them private) he commits his supplications to writing: "I write the entreaties of my heart to my Lord . . . in a hope that the Almighty's Mercy will accept the speech of my book, once death has silenced my tongue . . . ." He concludes the treatise with a four-part supplication in the voice of an elderly man—even though (as the text of the prayer eventually confirms) he is but in his forties: "O my Merciful Lord, O my Generous God! My life and youth have been wasted in calamity of my own accord." He thrice claims already to be clothed in his burial shroud, already in (or on the verge of climbing into) his

---

not dismiss the value of classical three-stage paradigms.

23. Underhill, *Mysticism*, 240. As I have explained elsewhere, *Unitive* is the label given mysticism's Stage Three in the oldest paradigms. In Islamic thought, this is sometimes explained in terms of *fanā'* (annihilation). However, even though *fanā'* figures prominently in Jīlānī's discourses (which Nursi had studied well), *Unitive* is not the best descriptor of Stage Three as it can be discerned in Nursi's biography and literary legacy. See Lucinda Allen Mosher, "The Spirit of Worship . . ." in *Islamic Spirituality in the Modern World*.

24. See the many uses and explanations of the term "contemplation" by the masters highlighted by Louth, *Origins of the Christian Mystical Tradition*.

25. See, for example, Vahide, *Islam in Modern Turkey*, 178.

26. Nursi, *Letters*, 418–19; Vahide, *Islam in Modern Turkey*, 10–11. For Nursi, "Naturalism" is preoccupation with the study of nature or with the notion that nature is the cause of its own existence. (cf. Nursi, *Al-Mathnawi al-Nuriye al-'arabī*, 184.) It is important to realize that this awakening was informed by earlier profound Qur'an study. See the discussion of the Way of Joyous Apprehension, below.

27. Vahide, *Islam in Modern Turkey*, 11; See also, Nursi, *Al-Mathnawi al-Nuriye al-'arabī*, 220.

grave or ready to climb in. Forgiveness and admission to Paradise cannot be demanded, but have come to be expected of the God the Most Compassionate, Nursi concludes.[28]

On the one hand, this is demonstrative of the mystic's *Way of Purgation*. On the other hand, by embedding such a supplication in a treatise destined for publication and distribution, the still comparatively young Nursi demonstrates for his growing circle of students the boldness with which they are to call upon God as they travel the Illuminative Way. And, with the publication of these dozen or thirteen treatises (later to be collated as *Al-Mathnawī al-nūrī*), we see that Nursi himself has entered the *Way of Illumination* ("the luminous highway of the people of the Qur'an," as he put it).[29] Supplication as key to the illumined life would become a major theme of the *Risale-i Nur*. Heeding the Qur'an's many instructions to the faithful to call upon God,[30] the New Said would maintain for himself and commend to his students an ardent discipline of devotional practice.[31]

We might say that Nursi commenced on the *Way of Contemplation*—the way of *tranquility in focus upon the Real*—with his withdrawal from Van to Mount Erek for the summer and autumn of 1924, where, says his biographer, "he was able to devote himself entirely to prayer and contemplation."[32] Nursi was known to prefer high places as venues for prayer, supplication, and contemplation—be that a mountain, the highest point of Van's citadel, a tree-house, or the roof of a mosque.[33] In fact, tree-houses became a hallmark of the New Said, says his biographer; for him, study, prayer, and contemplation—"reading the book of the universe," as he sometimes characterized it—was best accomplished in a tree-house.[34]

For Nursi, the *Way of Contemplation* is also the *Way of Joyous Apprehension of the Absolute*, involving sheer delight in the mystery, beauty, and efficacy of the Qur'an itself. While still in the Purgative Stage, he had already published significant examples of Qur'anic exegesis and commentary in Arabic: *Muhākamah* (*Proceedings*), in 1911; and *Isharat al-i'jaz* (*Signs of Miraculousness*), in 1913.[35] The Arabic treatises of 1920–21 would provide a seedbed; for the next several decades Nursi would expand on their themes and ideas, but would do so in Turkish.

## THE WAY OF CONTEMPLATION AND THE BEAUTIFUL NAMES[36]

Recalling our definition of *contemplation* as tranquility in focus upon the Real, we find the *Way of Contemplation* leading Nursi quite naturally to delight in God's Beautiful Names (*al-asmā' al-husnā*)—God's attributes as mentioned in the

28. Nursi, *Al-Mathnawi al-Nuriye*, 281–82.

29. Nursi, *Words*, 569. See also Vahide, *Islam in Modern Turkey*, 11.

30. See, for example, Qur'an 2:186, 7:29, 17:110,; 25:77, 27:62, 40:60, 40:65.

31. Nursi, *Al-Mathnawi al-Nuriye*, 178.

32. Vahide, *Islam in Modern Turkey*, 177.

33. Ibid., 178, 179.

34. Ibid., 179.

35. Vahide, *Chronology*, xviii. *Muhâkemat* and *İşārātū'l-Ī'caz* are the common Turkish iterations of these titles.

36. This section is informed by my discussion of Nursi's attitude toward the Beautiful Names and the *Jawshān al-kabīr* in my essay, "The Spirit of Worship and the Result of Sincere Belief: Nursi's *Mathnawī al-'Arabī al-Nurī* as a handbook for the contemplative life," in *Islamic Spirituality in the Modern World*.

Qur'an. Insight into Nursi's method of reflection on the Beautiful Names can be found in the treatise *Qatrah*, the earliest of the treatises incorporated into the *Al-Mathnawī al-nūrī*. "All things other than God, that is, the universe, should be looked at as signifying something other than themselves (*māna-yi harfī*) and on His account," Nursi explains therein. "It is an error to look at them as signifying only themselves (*māna-yi ismī*) and on account of causes . . . when looking at causes, one should think of the True Causer of Causes."[37] Many Qur'an verses conclude with one or several of God's Beautiful Names, Nursi asserts, in order to reinforce our attention to the origin of the divine work just described. "Thus it spreads out before humanity the textiles of [God's] design, then envelops this in the Names. And [again], thus it categorizes [God's] acts, then sums them up through the Names."[38]

Nursi would have been familiar with the great al-Ghazali's definitive study of the traditional list of God's attributes: *Al-Maqsad al-asnā fī sharh asmā' Allāh al-husnā* (*The Most Radiant Import, consisting in an Explanation of the Beautiful Names of God*). Al-Ghazālī works with the list found in a *hadīth* transmitted by Abū Hurayrah, submitting it to meticulous analysis. Because al-Ghazali embraces the notion of ninety-nine Divine Names, and is well aware that the Islamic tradition has put forth more than one list, he considers how to reconcile them to yield a list of Names totaling only ninety-nine. For this reason, he is also concerned with whether two forms of the same tri-literal root (or similarly, whether synonyms) are to be considered two names or one.[39]

Nursi, on the other hand, is never particularly concerned with Abū Hurayrah's list, nor with "ninety-nine" as the definite quantity of God's Names. His favorite vehicle for contemplation of God's Names is the one-hundred-stanza supplication *Jawshān al-kabīr* (The Greater Armor)—a *hadīth* of the Prophet transmitted through Ali[40]—which encourages conception of Divine Beautiful Names in much broader terms than does Abū Hurayrah's hadīth. It seems that, for Nursi, the *Jawshān* figures second only to the Qur'an itself as a personal devotional aid.

While he may have known of it beforehand, Nursi cultivated his deep and abiding fondness for the *Jawshān al-kabīr* during his profoundly transitional sojourn of 1920–21. According to his biographer, Şükran Vahide, it became from then on a source of inspiration for his writing projects.[41] In his *Rays*, Nursi himself calls the *Jawshān* "worship in the form of reflective thought;" it is "a won-

---

37. Vahide emphasizes this point. See her *Islam in Modern Turkey*, 11.

38. *Al-Mathnawī al-nūrī*, 339.

39. Abu Hamid Muhammad ibn Muhammad al-Ghazālī, *The Ninety-Nine Beautiful Names of God*, 24–26, 51.

40. See Nursi, *Rays*, 596. The chain of transmission has been traced (albeit somewhat weakly) through Zayn al-'Ābidīn (Ali ibn al-Husayn: a grandson of the Prophet) and his father Husayn to Alī. For a scholarly analysis of the *Jawshān al-kabīr*, see Kademoğlu, *The Textual and the Spiritual Structure of the Jawshān al-Kabīr*.

41. The *Jawshān al-kabīr* was readily available to Nursi by virtue of its inclusion in *Majmu'at al-ahzāb*, a supplication collection from which he drew other items included in the *Mathnāwī al-Nūrīye* and the *Risale-i Nur*. See note 79, below. See also, Vahide, *Islam in Modern Turkey*, 235. In the introduction to her translation of the *Jawshan*, Vahide notes Nursi's role in popularizing it in the twentieth century. See Vahide, *A Supplication of the Prophet Muhammad (PBUH)*, 3.

drous supplication that in one respect proceeds from the Qur'an; [and] is superior to all the other invocations recited by those who advance in knowledge of God," asserting that—in a sense—the *Jawshan* gave birth to the *Risale-i Nur,* and is the source of the *Risale's* brilliance.⁴² The *Third Ray,* said by Nursi to be both a supplication and something of a commentary" on Sūrah 2:164,⁴³ is actually a study of the *Jawshān,* as is Nursi's treatise *Al-Qit'atu 'l-thalithatu min shammah.*⁴⁴

Given that its title means "the great armor," the *Jawshān al-kabīr* is the sort of prayer to be chanted while arming oneself for a physical or spiritual battle. In *The Rays,* Nursi explains that it was during a military expedition that the Prophet received the *Jawshān* directly from the angel Gabriel, who said to him: "Cast away your armour and in its place read this 'armour'!" Armor for daily spiritual battle seems to be the purpose to which Nursi put the *Jawshān* and the reason he commended to his disciples.

Nursi's disciples report that it was his routine to arise at 3:30 each morning to pray the hour-long *Jawshān al-kabīr.*⁴⁵ The sole reason for such arduous discipline, he insists to his students, is to please God in hope for "fruits and benefits" of the next world. This-worldly fruits and benefits from recitation of the *Jawshān* are acceptable and may even be encouraging, "so long as they are not the ultimate reason and not intentionally sought." When this-worldly fruits and benefits are the sole (or even partial) reason for such a spiritual practice, it becomes mere recitation rather than valid worship.⁴⁶

Nursi refers to the *Jawshān al-kabīr* as a *wird* (litany),⁴⁷ a genre closely related to (or even synonymous with) the *hizb.*⁴⁸ Typically, a *wird* or *hizb* is through-composed rather than broken into sections by a recurrent refrain. This is the case with Al-Shādhilī's litanies. We see Nursi composing in this style as well—in his treatise *Habbah,* for example, the appendix to which begins with a *hizb.* Nine pairs of clauses on the theme "There is no force and strength save God" are followed by a transitional assertion that trust and reliance on God yields experience of God's sufficiency, then nine more vocatives—each beginning with and elaborating on the statement, "God is sufficient for us and what a good Guardian He is."⁴⁹

A survey of the entirety of the Nursi corpus reveals the importance of the role played by litanies in his own devotional discipline, and in the life of contemplation he advocates. In the *Rays,* Nursi quotes part of al-Ghazzālī's *Hizb al-masūn* (Litany of Innocence).⁵⁰ As well, he mentions the *Hizb al-nūrī* (Litany of Light), a forty-five page Arabic supplication which he considered "a luminous proof of the *Risale-i Nur,* a supreme in-

---

42. Nursi, *Rays,* 596.

43. A rather long verse, *Sūrah* 2:164 begins, "Behold! In the creation of the heaven and the earth..." and concluding, "Here indeed are signs for a people that are wise."

44. *Al-Qit'atu 'l-thalithatu min shammah* is, in some editions of *Mathnāwī al-Nūrīye,* considered the third section of the Ninth Treatise (of twelve); in other editions, it is considered the Tenth Treatise (of thirteen).

45. At least an hour is required to recite the *Jawshān* once in its entirety.

46. Nursi, *Flashes,* 180.

47. Ibid.

48. While some might argue that while there is a distinction between the *hizb* and the *wird,* they are often used interchangeably. See Padwick, *Muslim Devotions,* 20–25, 98, 170.

49. *Al-Mathnāwī al-Nūrīye,* 248–49.

50. Nursi, *Rays,* 329;

vocation springing from it, and a small sample of it."⁵¹ He also mentions the *Hizb anwār al-ḥaqā'iq al-nūrīyya* (*Litany of the Luminous Truths of Light*), a collection of supplications including the *Jawshān al-kabīr*.⁵² In the *Flashes*, Nursi commends Shah Naqshband's *Awrad-i qudsiya-i* (*Holy Litanies*), but notes that recitation of it has but one-tenth the value attainable from the *Jawshān al-kabīr*.⁵³ Mention is also made of *Hizb al-Qur'an*, which seems to have been a selection of Qur'an verses brought together as a supplication manual by Nursi and his students. According to Şükran Vahide, this small handbook's contents "form the basis of, and are expounded in, the *Risale-i Nur*."⁵⁴

In fact, Nursi's treatise *Qatrah*'s second, third, and fourth chapters may be construed as litanies themselves. Chapter 2 features a series of twelve exclamations of praise, each beginning *Subhan Allah*; Chapter Three, nine—each beginning *Al-Hamdu li-llah*; and Chapter 4, fourteen—each beginning *Allahu Akbar*.⁵⁵

The one-hundred-stanza structure of the *Jawshān al-kabīr* contrasts interestingly with most others in the genre of Islamic litany. The stanzas, each made up of ten invocations in parallel format, are grouped in quartets. Every stanza concludes with "Praise be to You, than whom there is no god! Security of the security: save us from the Fire!" (or a variant of this);⁵⁶ each quartet of stanzas is inaugurated by, "O God! I beseech You by means of Your Names." By virtue of these two regularly recurring refrains, a unique rhythm is established for the litany as a whole. In every quartet, the first stanza consists of "single names"; in the subsequent three stanzas, the names consist of two or more words, thus are increasingly more complex. A set of ten is unified by the honorifics' length and the word order, word endings, and other techniques by which they have been created. Thus, a particular rhythm and rhyme is created for each stanza; sound patterns and grammatical devices, rather than any traditional list, determine the order of the Beautiful Names in this supplication. And rather than the traditional ninety-nine, the *Jawshān* provides a list of God's 1001 Names "both explicitly and allusively," says Nursi; and the thousand-and-one in turn provide "a thousand and one proofs of *tawḥīd*."⁵⁷

Nursi provides commentary on the *Jawshān al-kabīr* in several of his Arabic treatises from his 1920–21 retreat. In his treatise *Al-Qiṭ'at'l-thalthah min shammah*,⁵⁸ to take one example, Nursi equates the *Jawshān*'s one hundred stanzas to as many jewel-cases, each containing "gems of *tawḥīd*." He also argues that, since God's existence penetrates all lev-

---

utmost security."

57. Nursi, *Rays*, 51, 593, 596; also, Nursi, *Words* 344.

58. *Al-Qiṭ'at'l-thalthah min shammah* may be translated "A Third Fragment from 'A Whiff'"—i.e., from Nursi's treatise *A Whiff from the Breeze of the Guidance of the Qur'an*. This treatise has appendices labeled "A First Fragment" and "A Second Fragment." The Kaynak English translation (1999) treats "A Third Fragment" as yet another appendix to "A Whiff." The Sözler edition refers to this material by the shorthand "Whiff (3)."

51. See note 78 in Nursi, *Rays*, 501.

52. Nursi, *Rays*, 620 note 46; 300.

53. Nursi, *Flashes*, 180.

54. See Nursi's own comments and translator's note in *Rays*, 322.

55. *Al-Mathnawi al-Nuriye*, 132–39.

56. "Security of the security" translates *amānu'l-amānu*, a construct which might also be paraphrased, "You who are the provider of

els—and since God's Names reflect each other, and God's many ways of acting correspond to and resemble each other, and since God's many manifestations corroborate each other—inevitably, if we know God by one of the Divine Names or manifestations, we cannot help but know God by the others as well.[59] Praying the *Jawshān* helps us to internalize this understanding. And, such internalization of understanding has transformative potential. Human beings have the potential to reflect God's Beautiful Names—a point Nursi makes several times in his writings. In his "Eighteenth Letter," he argues that, just as a mirror show us something true of the original—at least to an extent; so, human beings may reflect God's attributes (one or several at a time), but never all of them—nor any of them completely.[60] In the *Words*, he notes that human beings manifest many of the Divine Names, and invoke many of them in supplication.[61] Thus, it would seem better one knows them, and the more of them one knows, the greater one's potential to be such a mirror.

Related to Nursi's discussions of comparative and superlative Beautiful Names of God is his teaching about God's (unknown) Greatest Name; for example:

The Beautiful Names—each one of them—each contain the whole in general. Just like white light contains the "seven colors" [i.e., the whole of the color-spectrum], so each name contains the whole list. Therefore, each one is itself a reference to, and a result of, all of them. [God's Beautiful Names] reflect each other like mirrors. So, they can be invoked in a manner similar to the way measurement can lead to sequential results. And, just as a verdict emerges from solid evidence, so the Greatest Name contains the whole of the list [the whole of the general included information]. Some can reach the light of the Greatest Name through the other Beautiful Names. In this reaching, the Greatest Name would be relative to the level of the seeker reaching it. And God knows best![62]

The commentary on the *Jawshān al-kabīr* begun in the Arabic treatises of 1920–21 would be expanded in the *Risale-i Nur*. Therein, in a number of places, Nursi declares that the *Jawshān* is a summary of and commentary on the Qur'an (at least to an extent).[63] In the *Flashes*, he also asserts that, as a *hadīth*, the *Jawshān* not only reports on the Prophet's practice, but also exhibits the depth of the Prophet's knowledge of God. By commending it to his disciples, Nursi infers that to pray the *Jawshān* is to participate in such joyous apprehension of the divine.[64]

## SUPPLICATION AS SEED AND FRUIT OF SPIRITUAL TRANSFORMATION

Nursi's persistent point is that to pray the *Jawshan al-kabīr* regularly and systematically has transformative potential. Further, by example and word, he asserts the value of supplication as seed and fruit of

---

59. *Al-Mathnawi al-Nuriye*, 343.

60. See "Eighteenth Letter"; see also "Twentieth Letter: Second Station: Eighth Phrase" in *Letters*, 286.

61. Nursi, *Words*, 344.

62. *Al-Mathnawi al-Nuriye*, 236.

63. See, for example, "Appendix Four to the Nineteenth Letter," in *Letters*, 259; see also "The Eleventh Ray: Tenth Topic: A Flower of Emirdağ," in *Rays*, 266; also published as an addendum to the "Twenty-fifth Word," in *Words*, 468.

64. Nursi, *Flashes*, 436.

his own transformation, thus its potential for the transformation of others.

While Nursi's commitment to regular performance of *salāt*, even under duress of imprisonment or exile, is affirmed by all his biographers,[65] he is also acclaimed as one who spent legendary numbers of hours in supererogatory *du'ā'* (supplication). For example:

> [Nursi's] sister-in-law, Rabia, notes that he never slept at night while staying with them, from his room came the continuous sound of prayer and supplication. . . . Molla Hamid, who spent the most time with him on Mount Erek, states that Nursi was never for a moment idle, but was always occupied, mostly in prayer and supplication. He spent hours on his knees, so that his toes became raw.[66]

By Nursi's own account, supplication was an agent of the "strange revolution of the spirit" which began beside the Volga River (while still a prisoner of war) and which would culminate in his declaration that he was now the "New Said." In that riverside moment of despair, he recalls:

> . . . succor arrived from the All-Wise Qur'an; my tongue said: "God is enough for us; and how excellent a guardian is He!" (Qur'an, 3:173). Weeping, my heart cried out: "I am a stranger, I am alone, I am weak, I am powerless: I seek mercy, I seek forgiveness, I seek help from You, O my God!"[67]

Nursi may have taken the Qur'an as his only *qiblah*; yet, in his treatise *Rashahāt*, he still commends an impressive (albeit not exhaustive, he says) list of great spiritual masters who are informed by and continue to transmit the Prophet's light of guidance. The Qur'an is the *qiblah*, but these learned leaders offer aid in focusing on it, thus advancing spiritual transformation.[68] Similarly, Nursi's own literary legacy includes vast resources for those who wish to take up or enhance the practice of supererogatory prayer—including at least two hundred supplications. Some are his own compositions; many come from other sources, including the Qur'an.

The Qur'anic supplication appearing most frequently in Nursi's writings is Sūrah 2:32 ("Glory to You! We have no knowledge except that which You have taught us . . ."); it occurs some seventy-four times in the *Risale-i Nur*. Next often in appearance is Sūrah 2:286 ("Our Lord! Do not take us to task if we forget or unwittingly do wrong. Overlook our trespasses and forgive us, and grant us Your mercy"). At least eight times, we can find Sūrah 3:8 ("O our Sustainer! Let not our hearts deviate after You have guided us, and grant us Mercy from Your presence, for You are the Granter of bounties without measure"). At least a dozen other Qur'anic supplications can be found a time or two. Occasionally, Nursi offers a supplication which combines verses from

---

65. See Vahide, *Bediüzzaman Said Nursi*; see also Reed, *Anatolia Junction*.

66. Vahide, *Islam in Modern Turkey*, 178–79.

67. Nursi, *Flashes*, 299–301.

68. In addition to the already-mentioned al-Jīlānī, Imam-ı Rabbani, and Abū Hamid al-Ghazālī, Nursi's list includes: Abu Hanīfah (700–768 CE), al-Shāfi'ī (767–820 CE), Abū Yazid al-Bistāmī (802–873 CE), Junayd al-Baghdādī (d. 910 CE), Muhyiddīn ibn al-'Arabī (1165–1240 CE), 'Ali Abu'l-Hasan al-Shādhilī (1196–1258 CE), Shah al-Naqshband (1316–89 CE); see *Al-Mathnawi al-Nuriye*, 64–65 and footnotes. Elsewhere, Nursi commends Sufyān ibn 'Uyaynah (726–814 CE), Abu'l-Husayn Muhammad ibn Ahmad ibn Sam'un (913–97 CE), and Jalāludin Rūmī (1207–73 CE); see *Al-Mathnawi al-Nuriye*, 182, 314, and 315 respectively.

several sūrahs. A single supplication in the "Thirty-third Word," for example, makes use of Q. 2:286, 3:8, 2:127, and 2:128. In other places, the "Twenty-Eighth Word" being but one example, he may include a supplication comprising two or more Qur'an verses[69] plus other supplicatory texts (borrowed, or of his own composition).[70]

The *Risale-i Nur* also mentions or includes the texts of various supplications associated with particular Qur'anic prophets. For example, the *Prayer of Jonah* can be found in the "First Flash," with interpretation. In the "Second Flash," we find the *Supplication of Job*. The *Prayer of Ibrahim* (Sūrah 2:201) is included in the "Twenty-third Letter." The supplication concluding the "Twenty-sixth Letter" speaks of the *Prayer of Zakariya*.[71] Each of these many supplications derived from the Qur'an gives voice to *transformation*—the process of "becoming new" by means of struggle.

Nursi also quotes or mentions supplications from the hadīth and from the writings of a number of great spiritual masters. An adaptation of a supplication of the Prophet concludes the "Second Ray."[72] A long supplication of Uways al-Qarānī[73] can be found in the "Twentieth Letter"; a shorter one, in the "Twenty-Ninth." Twenty-two Letters conclude with a Naqshbandī supplication: "The Everlasting One, He is the Everlasting One."[74] 'Abd al-Qadir al-Jīlānī is the source of supplications in the "Seventeenth Word" and in the treatise *Shammatun min nasimi hidāyat'l Qur'an*.

In fact, the *hizb* (litany) attributed to al-Jīlānī which closes treatise *Shammatun* is said to be one of Nursi's favorite supplications—and one which, like the *Jawshan al-kabīr*, he would recite daily. In *Shammatun*, he prefaces al-Jīlānī's words with some of his own:

> Sins have reduced me to silence, and the copiousness of my disobedience puts me to shame, and the greatness of my negligence reduces my voice to silence. I pound on the door of Your Mercy and summon you at the door of Your Pardon in the voice of my master and support, Shaykh 'Abd al-Qādir al-Jīlānī ([may God] sanctify his secret, and may his summons be acceptable and familiar in the opinion of the Door-Keeper).[75]

Nursi's point here seems to be that he has more confidence calling upon God in the strong voice of a great master, thus with words with which God is already quite familiar. There seems also to be

---

69. In this case, Sūrah 2:32 and 2:286. See Nursi, *Words*, 519.

70. This paragraph draws on observations included in Mosher, "The Marrow of Worship and the Moral Vision: Said Nursi and Supplication," in Abu-Rabi', *Islam at the Crossroad*, 181.

71. Some two dozen of 'Abd al-Qadir al-Jīlānī's discourses include or close with the *Prayer of Ibrahim*. Nursi's acknowledgement of al-Jīlānī's profound influence is extensive. (See, for example, the "Seventeenth Word"; the "Tenth Flash"; the "Seventeenth Flash"; the "Twenty-Sixth Flash." See as well, treatise *Shammatun*.) Thus it is interesting that Nursi does not include the *Prayer of Ibrahim* in the *Risale-i Nur*, with similar frequency.

72. The traditional text is expanded to include supplication on behalf of the *Risale-i Nur* itself.

73. Uways al-Qarānī was a Yemeni Muslim mystic and philosopher, a contemporary of the Prophet Muhammad—although the two never met. He is also known for his allegiance to Ali against Mu'awiyah.

74. Nursi labels this prayer "a Naqshi supplication" in the "Thirteenth Flash."

75. *Al-Mathnawi al-Nuriye*, 331–32.

implied here a suspicion on Nursi's part that his students are vulnerable—an element of struggle characteristic of spiritual transformation. They may need their own confidence bolstered, thus his expectation that they put to use the devotional material he provides.

"Supplication is a mighty mystery of worship," explains Nursi in his "Twenty-fourth Letter"; "indeed, it is like the spirit of worship."[76] In the same essay, he later asserts:

> Supplication is the spirit of worship and the result of sincere belief. For one who makes supplication shows through it that there is someone who rules the whole universe; One Who knows the most insignificant things about me, can bring about my most distant aims. Who sees every circumstance of mine, and hears my voice. In which case, He hears all the voices of all beings, so that He hears my voice too. He does all these things, and so I await my smallest matters from Him too. I ask Him for them.[77]

In his earlier treatise *Shu'lah*, Nursi had taught that all creatures make supplication to God their Creator—either with the tongue of speech, the tongue of necessity, or the tongue of readiness by which he means the natural process of developing and growing, of transformation and progression.[78] Human beings may and should supplicate in the tongues of consciousness and neediness. Nursi had alluded to this when he asserts (in his addendum to the treatise *Habābun*) that God "has created you surrounded by concentric circles of needs." God, he continues, has equipped us with means by which we can satisfy the smallest circle of needs through reliance on our own will and power. However, other needs comprise a circle so large that its diameter stretches eternally from past to future, and its radius from the center of the earth to the throne of God. To deal with these needs, Nursi explains, "God has provided [us] with *du'ā'*."[79]

Having commended "the luminous highway of the people of the Qur'an," Nursi demonstrates through the supplications he gleans from many sources or writes himself the vulnerability which brought him to this path, and the faith, courage, surrender, and endurance which propelled him along it, that his disciples' own strange revolutions of the spirit might result in their own attainment of the Way of Contemplation: joyous apprehension of God marked by tranquility in focus upon the Real.

## BIBLIOGRAPHY

Abu-Rabi', İbrahim M. ed. *Islam at the Crossroad: On the Life and Thought of Bediüzzaman Said Nursi*. Albany, NY: State University of New York Press, 2003.

———, ed. *Islamic Spirituality in the Modern World: Spiritual Dimensions of Said Nursi's Risale-i Nur*. Albany, NY: State University of New York Press, 2008.

Abu-Rabi', İbrahim M., and Bilal Kuşpınar, eds. *Theodicy and Justice in Islamic Thought: The Case of Said Nursi*. Farnham, UK: Ashgate, 2010.

Baktiar, Laleh. *Sufi Expressions of the Mystical Quest*. New York: Thames and Hudson, 1987.

Chittick, William C. *Faith and Practice of Islam: Three Thirteenth Century Sufi Texts*. Albany, NY: State University of New York Press, 1992.

---

76. Nursi, *Letters*, 353.
77. Ibid., 357.
78. *Al-Mathnawi al-Nuriye*, 403.
79. Ibid., 210.

Chittister, Joan D. *Scarred by Struggle, Transformed by Hope.* Grand Rapids, Michigan: Eerdmans, 2003.

Cilacı, Osman. "The Concepts of Supplication and Worship in the *Risale-i Nur.*" In *Third International Symposium on Bediüzzaman Said Nursi: The Reconstruction of Islamic Thought in the Twentieth Century and Bediüzzaman Said Nursi* (September 1995), Vol. 2, translated by Şükran Vahide, 84–100. Istanbul: Sözler, 1997.

al-Ghazālī, Abū Hāmid. *Invocations & Supplications: Book IX of The Revival of the Religious Sciences* (Iḥya al-'ulūm al-dīn: Kitāb al-adhkār wa al-da'awāt). Translated by Kojiro Nakamura. Cambridge: Islamic Texts Society, 1990.

———. *The Ninety-Nine Beautiful Names of God* (Maqsad al-asnā: fī sharh asmā' Allāh al-husnā). Translated with notes by David B. Burrell and Nazih Daher. 1992. Reprint. Cambridge: The Islamic Texts Society, 1995.

Gilani, Abdul-Qādir. *The Endowment of Divine Grace and the Spread of Divine Mercy (Al-Fathu Rabbāni),* Vol. 1. Translated by Muhammad M. Al-Aliki. Philadelphia: Pearl, 1990.

———. *Futuh al-Ghaib (The Revelations of the Unseen).* Translated by M. Aftab-ud-Din Ahmad. Lahore: Muhammad Ashraf, 1979.

Ibn Qayyim al-Jawziyah, Muhammad ibn Abi Bakr. *A Handbook of Islamic Prayers.* Compiled by Hafiz Ibn al-Qayyim. Edited by Khalil Ahmad Hamidi. Translated by Muhammad İbrahim and Abdul Hameed Siddiqi. Lahore: Islamic Publications, 1991.

al-Jīlānī, 'Abd l-Qādir. *The Removal of Cares (Jalā' al-Khawātir).* Translated by Muhtar Holland. Fort Lauderdale, FL: Al-Baz, 1997.

———. *Revelations of the Unseen (Futuh al-Ghaib): A Collection of Seventy-eight Discourses.* Translated by Muhtar Holland. Houston: Al-Baz, 1992.

———. *The Secret of the Secrets (Sirr al-Asrār).* Interpreted by Shaykh Tosun Bayrak al-Jerrahi al-Halveti. Cambridge: The Islamic Texts Society, 1992.

———. *The Sublime Revelation (Al-Fath ar-Rabbānî): A Collection of Sixty-Two Discourses.* Translated by Muhtar Holland. Houston: Al-Baz, 1992.

———. *Sufficient Provisions for Seekers of the Path of Truth* (Al-ghunya li-talibi tariq al-haqq): *A Complete Resource on the Inner and Outer Aspects of Islam.* Translated by Muhtar Holland. Vol. 4. Hollywood, Florida: Al-Baz, 1997.

———. *Utterances (Malfūzāt): Collected Sayings of the Crown of the Saints.* Translated by Muhtar Holland. Fort Lauderdale, FL: Al-Baz, 1992.

Kademoğlu, Ahmet Eren. *The Textual and the Spiritual Structure of the Jawshān al-Kabīr: A Study on Jawshān al-Kabīr and Its Translation.* Phd diss., Pontificio Instituto di Studi Arabi e d'Islamistica, Rome, 2000.

Kuşpınar, Bilal. "Nursi's Evaluation of Sufism." In *Third International Symposium on Bediüzzaman Said Nursi: The Reconstruction of Islamic Thought in the Twentieth Century and Bediüzzaman Said Nursi,* 24th-26th September, 1995, Vol. 2, translated by Şükran Vahide, 72–83. Istanbul: Sözler, 1997.

Louth, Andrew. *The Origins of the Christian Mystical Tradition from Plato to Denys.* Oxford: Oxford University Press, 2007.

Mardin, Şerif. *Religion and Social Change in Modern Turkey: The Case of Bediüzzaman Said Nursi.* Albany, NY: State University of New York Press, 1989.

Mosher, Lucinda Allen. "The Marrow of Worship and the Moral Vision: Said Nursi and Supplication." In *Islam at the Crossroad: On the Life and Thought of Bediüzzaman Said Nursi,* edited by İbrahim M. Abu-Rabi', 181–98. Albany, NY: State University of New York Press, 2003.

———. "The Spirit of Worship and the Result of Sincere Belief: Nursi's *Mathnawi al-'Arabi al-Nuri* as a Handbook for the Contemplative Life." In *Islamic Spirituality in the Modern*

## Section Two: Theology

*World: Spiritual Dimensions of Said Nursi's Risale-i Nur*, edited by İbrahim Abu-Rabi', 103–24. Albany, NY: State University of New York Press, 2008.

Murata, Sachiko, and William C. Chittick. *The Vision of Islam*. St. Paul, MN: Paragon House, 1994.

al-Nursi, Badī'uz-zamān Sa'īd. *Al-Mathnawī al-'Arabī al-Nūrī*. Istanbul: Sözler Yayınevi, 1999.

Nursi, Bediüzzaman Said. *Al-Mathnawi al-Nuri: Seedbed of the Light*. Translated by Hüseyin Akarsu. Somerset, NJ: Light, 2007.

———. *Epitomes of Light* (Mathnawi al-Nuriya): *The Essentials of the Risale-i Nur*. Translated by Ali Ünal. Konak-Izmir, Turkey: Kaynak, 1999.

———. *Risale-i Nur 3: The Flashes Collection*. Translated by Şükran Vahide. Istanbul: Sözler, 1995.

———. *Risale-i Nur 4: The Rays Collection*. Translated by Şükran Vahide. Istanbul: Sözler, 1998.

———. *Risale-i Nur Collection 1: The Words: On the Nature and Purpose of Man, Life, and All Things*. Translated by Şükran Vahide. 1992. Rev. ed. Istanbul: Sözler, 1998.

———. *Risale-i Nur Collection 2: Letters (1928–1932)*. Translated by Şükran Vahide. 1994. Rev. ed. Istanbul: Sözler, 1997.

Padwick, Constance E. *Muslim Devotions: A Study of Prayer-Manuals in Common Use*. 1961. Reprint. Oxford: Oneworld, 1996.

Reed, Fred A. *Anatolia Junction: A Journey into Hidden Turkey*. Burnby, BC: Talonbooks, 1999.

Underhill, Evelyn. *Mysticism: The Nature and Development of Spiritual Consciousness*. 12th ed. Oxford: Oneworld, 1999.

Vahide, Şükran. *Bediüzzaman Said Nursi: The Author of the Risale-i Nur*. Istanbul: Sözler, 1992.

———. "A Chronology of Said Nursi's Life." In *Islam at the Crossroads*, edited by İbrahim M. Abu-Rabi', xvii–xxiv. Albany, NY: State University of New York Press, 2003.

———. *Islam in Modern Turkey: An Intellectual Biography of Bediüzzaman Said Nursi*. Edited by İbrahim M. Abu-Rabi'. Albany, NY: State University of New York Press, 2005.

———. "The Life and Times of Bediüzzaman Said Nursi." *The Muslim World* 89.3–4 (1999) 208–44.

———. *A Supplication of the Prophet Muhammad (Peace and blessings be upon him): Al-Jawshan al-Kabīr*. Istanbul: Sözler Neşriyat, 2003.

# 10

# The Moral World of Said Nursi

## M. Salih Sayilgan

### INTRODUCTION

This chapter examines morality in the writings of Said Nursi. It shall begin with a brief introduction to the word morality and its usage in the *Risale-i Nur* (henceforth *the Risale*) which will be followed by an outline of the foundations of Nursi's morality and his methodology. The next section of this article attempts to address Nursi's perspective on forming moral individuals in society. What specifically threatens the morals of individuals and what are the remedies? The last section shall focus on Nursi's understanding of morality in a pluralist society.

In its general sense, the word morality often appears in conjunction with the words ethics and virtues. While these three words are occasionally employed interchangeably, they signify distinctive implications. Morality originated from the Latin word *mores*, meaning manner or character, while the word ethics emanated from the Greek word *ethos*, which also refers to character or manners. The general distinction is that "morality seems to focus on human actions and practices, whereas ethics is primarily concerned with study and reflection on morality."[1] The word virtue slightly differs from both morality and ethics in its signification. It is known as a "particular moral excellence."[2]

The three words have been associated with concepts such as *akhlāq* and *ādāb* in Islamic literature. The former is generally translated as ethics, while the latter, as manners.[3] In fact, Nursi abides by the tradition in this sense and whenever he addresses any issue with regard to morality, ethics or virtues, he mainly

---

1. Diener, *Religion and Morality*, 9.

2. "Virtue" in *Merriam_Webser Dictionary*.

3. The Arabic word *akhlāq* is the plural version of the word *khuluq* and the word *ādāb* is the plural version of the word *ādab*.

uses the words *akhlāq* and *ādāb*.[4] He also talks of immorality (*ahlaksızlık*) in various parts of the *Risale*.[5] In this context, he posits that faith plays a considerable role in sustaining a moral society and preserving it from immorality and anarchy. The following analysis examines Nursi's foundations of morality, which are the Qur'an, Prophet Muhammad's *sunna* or exemplary model and behavior, the universe, and major prominent saints and theologians in the history of Islam.[6]

## THE FOUNDATIONS OF NURSI'S MORALITY

### The Qur'an

It is essential to remark that Nursi does not particularly dedicate any of his treatises to morality in his *Risale*; instead, his focus on morality is stretched throughout the entire collection. Furthermore, the sources of his morality are fairly noticeable in his writings.[7]

The Qur'an as Nursi's foundation of morality is one of the most pervasive themes in the *Risale*. Nursi repeatedly affirms that the *Risale* is an interpretation of the Qur'an for the understanding of modern people.[8] He goes further and asserts that the *Risale* is the property of the Qur'an.[9] For Nursi, the Qur'an is eternal; its principles do not age, unlike the law of civilizations.[10] Responding to a Western intellectual's negative remarks, he claims that the Qur'an accommodates all of the ethical principles which can potentially protect individuals from all sorts of immoralities.[11]

Nursi also focuses on the prophetic stories in the Qur'an as a basis for his narrative ethics in the *Risale*. In these accounts, Nursi pays attention to faith as a virtue.[12] Indeed, his mainly introspective readings of the prophetic stories in the Qur'an are distinct from the ones to be found in classic exegetical literature. One could even argue that his resembles a Sufi reading of the Qur'an by concentrating on the esoteric meanings of the passages. From these narratives, Nursi evolves moral principles that have implications for contemporary people.

One of the instances is his expansion on the story of Jonah in the Qur'an. According to the Qur'anic narration, Jonah was thrown into the sea and was

---

4. The precise Turkish words are *ahlak* and *edeb*.

5. See Bediüzzaman Said Nursi, *Şualar*, 681; Nursi, *Asa-yı Musa*, 326; Nursi, *İman Küfür Muvazeneleri*, 196; and Nursi, *Sözler*, 548. The Turkish *Risale* references are all from the *Risale-i Nur* edition published by Söz Yayınevi in 2009 in Istanbul. Online access is available through http://www.erisale.com/.

6 Nursi, *Emirdağ Lahikası*, 14.

6. Prophet Muhammad's daily life and practice are known in Islam as the *sunna*. On the role and significance of Prophet Muhammad in Muslim piety, see the phenomenological study of Annemarie Schimmel *And Muhammad is His Messenger: The Veneration of the Prophet in Islamic Piety*. See also, Hanson, "The *Sunna*: The Way of the Prophet Muhammad," in *Voices of Islam*, ed. Cornell, 1:125–45.

7. Ian S. Markham's article on the ethical system of the *Risale* is one of the first articles that outlines Nursi's ethics. For more details, see Markham, "Secular or Religious Foundations for Ethics" in *Globalization, Ethics, and Islam*, 69–78.

8. Nursi, *Emirdağ Lahikası*, 35.

9. Ibid.

10. Nursi, *İman Ve Küfür Muvazeneleri*, 131.

11. Nursi, *İlk Dönem Eserleri*, 167–68.

12. For other examples, see Nursi's interpretation of the story of Job (Eyyub) in *Lem'alar*, 1–9; the story of Moses (Musa) in *Sözler*, 335–41; of Joseph (Yusuf) in *Mektubat*, 399–400.

swallowed by a big fish.[13] While in the belly of the fish, Jonah prayed as follows: "There is no god but you; glory be to you; I have certainly been one of the wrongdoers."[14] Commentating on the narration, Nursi articulates that the ethical principle of the story is linked to Jonah's faith and trust in God.[15] He goes further and posits that people potentially are in a more delicate state than Jonah, although he was swallowed by a fish. In this case, Nursi suggests that our ego or soul (*nefs*)[16] is likely to be more harmful than the fish that swallowed Prophet Jonah. The former, Nursi continues, threatens a person's eternal life;[17] while the latter was merely harming Jonah's ephemeral short existence on earth. For Nursi, in the first state people are unconscious of God and may completely forget him.[18] Nursi's view on this matter lies in the deep internalization of Jonah's sincere supplication made by him while in the belly of the fish. This powerful prayer is also part of the verse 21:87 in the Qur'an. Like Jonah, Nursi states one should constantly refresh his/her faith (*iman*) and trust (*tevekkul*). These are the two cardinal virtues in the *Risale*. This way, as in the case of Jonah, one will be safe amidst all spiritual dangers both in this world and the hereafter.[19]

The practice of reflecting on the divine by means of these meaningful supplications and thus strengthening one's faith is deeply connected to Prophet Muhammad's *sunna*. Traditionally, the model behavior of Muhammad is the major secondary source after the Qur'an and it comes therefore with no surprise that Nursi embraces it strongly in his notion of morality.

## The *Sunna*

In the *Risale*, Nursi mentions the Prophet Muhammad and his *sunna* frequently in the context of morality. For him, Muhammad's character embodied the best morality. That is why even his opponents called him by the name of "al-Amin" (the trustworthy).[20] Nursi explains that a person who actualizes a high morality in his character has virtues of "personal dignity, gravity, and self-respect, and these do not permit a person to stoop to trivial inanities."[21] Hence, Muhammad was the best exemplar with regard to morality.[22] It is important to note that the moral excellence of the Prophet and the authority of the *sunna* are established by the Qur'an itself. In this context, Nursi refers to one of the verses in the Qur'an: "And you are truly a man of noble character."[23] This verse confirms, Nursi highlights, the Prophet's best moral character.[24] Nursi also mentions one of the narrations in

13. The Qur'an, 21:87, 61:48. The references from the Qur'an are from Majid Fakhry's modern English edition (Beltsville: Amana, 2003).

14. The Qur'an, 21:87.

15. Nursi, *Lem'alar*, 1–9.

16. There have been various translations of the word *nafs* (*nefs*, Turkish version). In this article, it is used in the context of the lower self. In her English translation of the *Risale-i Nur*, Şükran Vahide translates the word "*nefs*" as "soul."

17. Nursi, *Lem'alar*, 1–9.

18. Ibid.

19. Ibid.

20. Nursi, *Signs of Miraculousness*, 183. The references from the English translation of the *Risale-i Nur* are based on Şükran Vahide's translation published by Sözler Publications in 2008 in Istanbul.

21. Ibid.

22. Nursi, *İlk Dönem Eserleri*, 242.

23. The Qur'an, 68:4.

24. Nursi, *İlk Dönem Eserleri*, 270.

tradition; once Aisha, the wife of the Prophet, was asked about his character. She answered that his character was the Qur'an (*khuluquhu al-Qur'an*).[25]

For Nursi, one of the many proofs that the Prophet was indeed an embodiment of perfect morality and reflected the highest ideal of ethical behavior was his radical transformation of a society which was, morally speaking, extremely deficient. Muhammad replaced inhumane practices such as female infanticide with high virtues and the strongest respect towards even animals and insects. If he would not have embodied these morals in his personality, he would have never been able to actualize such an individual and social revolution.[26] Muhammad's transformation of that tribal society was not a superficial, but rather a permanent one, as he continued to conquer the hearts of people.[27]

Nursi believes that paying mere lip service to the Prophet's outstanding character is not sufficient. One needs to emulate and implement his *sunna* into daily life as much as possible, for this is the only way to gain divine love. This he bases on the Qur'anic injunction of 3:31: "Say: If you love God, follow me; then God will love you and forgive your sins."[28] Nursi remarks that it is God's will that people follow the Prophet and his *sunna*.[29] Therefore, it is not surprising that Nursi dedicates two major treatises to the Prophet in his *Risale*.[30] One of the major themes of these treatises are Muhammad's high morals as reflected in his actions, sayings and inner attitudes.

According to Nursi, Prophet Muhammad's most important miracle after the Qur'an is *himself*, because of his high moral character. This was, Nursi notes, even confirmed by his friends and opponents.[31] The Prophet's courage, for instance, as narrated by Ali, the cousin and son-in-law of the Prophet, was so great that during the most heated moment in battle, the companions would take refuge in the Prophet.[32]

According to Nursi, every detail of the *sunna* contains wisdom, light, and a moral lesson.[33] This is strengthened by his reference to a prophetic statement: "My Sustainer taught me good conduct, and how well he taught me."[34] Doubtlessly, following the Prophet's *sunna*, will form strong moral individuals.[35]

As evident throughout his collection, Nursi often supports his statements with regard to *sunna*ic morality by citing sayings of the Prophet. For instance, his assessment on filial piety and the ethics of care-taking of non-related elderly persons is supported by *hadith* such as: "If it were not for your elderly folk with their bent backs, calamities would have descended on you in floods."[36]

---

25. Ibid.
26. Nursi, *İşaratül İ'caz*, 227.
27. Ibid., 228.
28. The Qur'an, 3:31.
29. Nursi, *Lem'alar*, 106.
30. See Nursi, *The Words* 243–53 and *The Letters*, 112–261. From Vahide's translations (2009).

31. Nursi, *Mektubat*, 258.
32. Ibid.
33. *Lem'alar*, 108.
34. Nursi, *The Flashes*, 87.
35. Nursi, *Lem'alar*, 108.
36. el-Beyhakî, *es-Sünenü'l-Kübrâ*, 3:345 in Nursi, *Lem'alar*, 373.

## Saints and Scholars

Examples from the life of saints and theologians play a significant role in Nursi's moral foundations. In various parts of the *Risale*, Nursi speaks of some of the great saints and theologians in the history of Islam as his masters. He shows a high esteem for them and refers to them in his writings on moral issues. Some major saints whom Nursi repeatedly refers to are Mawlana al-Rumi, Imam Abu Hanifa, Imam Shafii, Abu Yazid al-Bistami, Junayd al-Baghdadi, Shaykh 'Abd al-Qadir al-Gilani, Muhyiddin al-Arabi, Imam al-Ghazali, Abu'l-Hasan al-Shadhali and Shaikh Ahmad Sirhindi. According to Nursi, these pious leaders lived a life of moral conduct inspired by the ethical teachings of the Prophet and have illuminated centuries.[37]

Before giving some examples from the *Risale*, it is important to turn to one of Nursi's treatises on *ijtihād*, where his position with regard to the morality of the great saints becomes clearer.[38] In this treatise, Nursi is asked about whether the gate of *ijtihād* is open or not. Needless to say, it remains outside the scope of this paper to discuss Nursi's position on *ijtihād*. What matters for the present purpose is Nursi's high esteem of the first generations of Islam who came after the companions of the Prophet:

> And at the time of the first generations of Islam and in the market of that age, deducing from the Word of the Creator of the Heavens and the Earth His wishes and what He wants of us were the most sought-after goods, and obtaining the means to gain through the light of prophethood and the Qur'an eternal happiness in the world of the hereafter, which had been revealed to such a degree it could not be concealed. At that time, since people's minds, hearts and spirits were directed with all their strength towards understanding the wishes of the Sustainer of the Heavens and the Earth, the discussions, conversations, events, and circumstances of social life all looked to that.[39]

For Nursi, this distinctive high moral attitude of the great saints in the first generations of Islam made them capable of doing *ijtihād*. Having situated these great saints and scholars in a high position, Nursi derives moral instructions from their teachings and writings. Their complete commitment to the will of God by prioritizing the hereafter and the teaching of the Qur'an, including the *sunna* of the Prophet, makes them morally reliable for Nursi. Moreover, Nursi believes that the writings and teachings of the first generations was likely to be sound since they "lived close to the time of the companions of the Prophet, the age of light and age of truth. They were able to receive a pure light and make pure interpretations."[40] These favorable circumstances gave them the opportunity of profoundly understanding the Qur'an and *sunna*.

## The Universe

The universe appears as another significant source of Nursi's morality in

---

37. Nursi, *Nurun İlk Kapısı*, 117.

38. *Ijtihād* refers to sound and balanced personal reasoning with regard to law in Islam. For more details, see Fareed, "*Ijtihād*" in *Encyclopedia of Islam and the Muslim World*, ed. Martin, 1:344–45.

39. Nursi, *The Words*, 496.

40. Ibid., 499.

his *Risale*. He frequently employs some examples from the universe and deduces moral conclusions. In his treatise on elderly people, for instance, Nursi utilizes some analogies from the universe in order to build a base for the virtue of hope. First, he states the principle of embracing weakness as a means of coming closer to the Divine. Thus, the more one is in need and feels impotence, the more s/he enjoys God's mercy. Nursi refers to the example of hatchlings. He states that while hatchlings are in their nest on top of a tree, their mothers work as their servants and strive to provide food for them. But when hatchings grow and develop the ability to fly, the mother does not feed them anymore. The moral lesson in consequence is to embrace weakness and acknowledge one's impotence to the Creator. These then are in truth the means to be connected with the infinite power and compassion of God.[41]

This also holds true in the case of the relationship between a mother and her infant child. Since the infants are impotent, they are shown mercy in a great way. This applies likewise to elderly people: "I have had experiences which have led me to form the unshakeable conviction that just as the sustenance of infants is sent to them in wondrous fashion by divine mercy on account of their impotence, being made to flow forth from the springs of breasts; so too the sustenance of believing elderly who acquire innocence, is sent in the form of plenty."[42]

Nursi also reflects on the virtue of sacrifice by drawing attention to some examples in the animal world. He brings up the examples of a rooster and a chicken. A rooster prefers to give its food to a chicken while the rooster itself is hungry. There is exaltation and joy in this virtue for the rooster as there is more joy in the virtue of sacrifice than eating. Otherwise the rooster, Nursi concludes, would not prefer to give its food to a chicken while it is hungry.[43] The same virtue can be observed between a chicken and its hatchling. When a dog attacks its hatchling, the chicken sacrifices itself to protect the hatchling without any hesitation.[44] Nursi also gives the example of a lion that is hungry but gives the meat to its cubs.[45] By giving these examples from the universe, Nursi draws focus on the virtues of solidarity, sacrifice, and sharing as evident in the universe and by its creatures. Furthermore, human beings are on earth to live out their highest potential of morality. Outward attacks or challenges are only to be considered positive since they bring out and develop the moral and spiritual faculties such as unconditional love for the other or sacrifice.

Another of the many moral examples found in nature is the attitude and disposition of trees. By looking at them, humans are reminded of the glory and eternal beauty of God and as a result, a deep sense of hope and optimism is instilled in them.[46] Nursi narrates this personal experience as follows. Several years after World War I, Nursi returned to Van. He visited his *medrese* and saw that just like the other buildings in the city, it had been completely destroyed by the Armenians during the Russian occupation. He

41. Nursi, *Lem'alar*, 373.
42. Nursi, *The Flashes*, 300.
43. Nursi, *Şualar*, 749.
44. Ibid.
45. Ibid.
46. For more details about Nursi's view of positive action, see Sayılgan "Constructing an Islamic Ethics of Non-Violence," 43–47.

began to remember his friends, brothers, and close students who had studied in his *medrese*. Most of them had lost their lives in the war, and recalling the past events made Nursi cry, putting him in a state of deep despair.[47] He then reflected on the verses of Qur'an 57:1–2. These verses helped Nursi find a way out of such a desolate situation. He saw that the fruits at the tops of the fruit-trees were looking at him, smiling and saying, "Note us as well. Do not only look at the ruins."[48] The reality depicted by the verses brought the following thought to his mind:

> Why does an artificial letter written in the form of town by the hand of man, who is a guest on the page of Van's plain, being wiped out by a calamitous torrent called the Russian invasion sadden you to this extent? Consider the Pre-Eternal Inscriber, everything's True Owner and Sustainer, for His missives on this page of Van continue to be written in glittering fashion, in the way you used to see. Your weeping over those desolate ruins arises from the error of forgetting their True Owner, not thinking that men are guests, and imagining them to be owner.[49]

This very emotional moment in Nursi's life shows how he derived moral lessons from the universe.

Giving the examples from Nursi, one might situate him within the natural law moral theory. According to this theory, the universe functions through the laws of nature and physics. In fact, natural law theory goes back to Greek and Stoic philosophers who paid attention to the fact that there are higher laws than the ones arranged by human beings for the society. Influenced by Aristotle's natural theology, the medieval theologian Thomas Aquinas developed this theory much further.[50] Through observing the universe and human nature, like Nursi, Aquinas derived moral duties.

## NURSI'S METHODOLOGY

It is important to note that Nursi's *Risale* is a thematic commentary on the Qur'an. However, his Qur'anic commentary does not resemble the classical ones. Nursi's treatises with regard to morals usually start off with a Qur'anic verse. However, he does not continue with the context, epistemological or linguistic traces of the verse; rather he develops moral reasoning with analogies.[51] Also, as already stated, Nursi relies on the *sunna*, the teachings of major saints and scholars in the history of Islam, and the universe. After having laid out Nursi's foundations of morality and methodology, we will now attempt to answer the question of how Nursi envisioned the development of moral individuals.

## FORMATION OF MORAL INDIVIDUALS

### Self-Reflection and Introspective Analysis of the *nefs*

For Nursi, self-reflection is key to one's personal moral development. He believes in the principle of first advising and educating one's self before asking others to

---

47. Nursi, *The Flashes*, 316.
48. Ibid., 317.
49. Ibid.
50. Diener, *Religion and Morality*, 29.
51. Markham, *Engaging with Bediüzzaman Said Nursi*, 13–14.

do it. In his eyes, this way of teaching is much more effective.

In his *Risale*, Nursi remarks that a person who cannot "reform his own ego cannot reform others."⁵² Therefore, it comes as no surprise that Nursi addresses his own self (*nefs*) with the following phrases in various parts of his *Risale*: Oh who is listening to this complaint with my soul; Oh my ignorant soul; Oh my helpless soul; Oh my gluttonous soul; Oh my impatient soul; Oh my soul that worships the world; Oh my soul that worships itself; Oh my arrogant soul; Oh my hypocrite soul; Oh my soul that does not want to do the prayers; Oh my blind soul; Oh my imperfect soul; Oh my soul that is hopeless because of delusional thinking/confused thoughts; and Oh my soul that is screaming.

## Belief in God

Nursi believes that belief in God plays a significant role in forming moral individuals. For him, it is impossible to hire a guardian observing each and everyone's acts in society. A strong unshaken belief in God, reminding the person that he is watched carefully, will have a positive impact on individuals' behavior. Belief creates an enduring awareness of God and thus influences one's moral conduct.⁵³ Even though Nursi considers belief in God as "the highest aim of creation and its most important result," he states that merely believing in God is not adequate.⁵⁴ One needs to seek the knowledge of God—in particular, the attributes of God (*asmā al-ḥusnā*). The more one knows about the attributes, the more s/he acquires knowledge of God. Ultimately, this journey, according to Nursi, results in the love of God.⁵⁵ In order to demonstrate one's love for God, one should act as "a mirror to the Ever-Living and Self-Subsistent One and His qualities and all-embracing attributes."⁵⁶ At this level, one starts to display and imitate the attributes of God, to reflect and embody them as much as possible. For instance, the attribute of *al-quddus*, the most Holy and Pure, is reflected by creatures in the universe who strive to be the mirror of God:

> This palace of the world and factory of the universe displays greatest manifestations of the divine name Most Holy whereby it is not only the carniverous cleaners of the seas and the eagles of the land which obey the commands proceeding from that sacred cleansing, but also its cleansing officials which gather up corpses, like worms and ants. Like the red and white blood-corpuscles flowing in the body obey those sacred commands and do the cleaning in the body's cells, so does breathing purify and clean the blood.⁵⁷

Likewise, Nursi states, human beings should be part of the circle of purification and cleanliness in order to reflect and be a mirror of God's attribute *al-quddus* in the universe. Indeed, this approach may be a major contribution to works related to environmental ethics. In a similar vein, human beings should attain a profound knowledge of God's beautiful attributes (*marifetullah*) and live in accordance with them by displaying them in their attitudes and lives. Such a human being attains the

---

52. Nursi, *The Words*, 276.
53. Nursi, *Lem'alar*, 215.
54. Nursi, *The Letters*, 262.
55. Ibid.
56. Nursi, *The Flashes*, 452.
57. Ibid., 394.

highest moral character and gains value since one is connected with God's qualities and perfections. The same holds true for emulating all other Divine Names and implementing them in one's individual and social behavior, such as compassion, as exemplified by the Divine Name al-rahman, or concealing the personal faults of others by displaying the name *al-sattār* (The Concealer), or being just by following God's justice, *al-'adl*, etc.

## Observance of Faith Rituals

Throughout his *Risale*, Nursi states that observing faith rituals, as is strongly encouraged in Islam, plays a major role in training one's soul (*nafs*) and forming moral individuals. He draws attention, for instance, to fasting, which is one of the five pillars of Islam. Enumerating the various wisdoms of the practice of fasting, Nursi remarks that it disciplines the soul (*nafs*). The soul sometimes tends to forget that it is the servant of God and that all blessings are given by God. In this context, Nursi refers to one of the *aḥadīth* of the Prophet Muhammad. According to this narration, God created the *nafs* and said,

> "O *nafs* come forth," yet it didn't. Then He said "O *nafs* go back," and it didn't. Then He said "O *nafs* who am I?" and it said, "You are you and I am I." [The soul] was tormented in fire and then He imposed hunger upon it . . . ." He said, "O *nafs* who am I?" and it said, "You are God, the Lord of the worlds."[58]

Hunger reminds the *nafs* of its limits as well as its duties and protects it from immorality.[59]

In addition, Nursi states that people have been created in different conditions. Therefore God invites the rich to help the poor. The ritual of fasting leads the rich to understand what it really means to be poor and in dire need. Without this deep internal experience, the wealthy may not be able to fully understand the conditions of poverty.[60]

In a similar mode, Nursi reflects on the daily prayer performed five times a day. He states it is like training in the field of battle and protects individuals against any immorality.[61] Fundamentally, prayer reminds one of inherent human weakness (*'ajz*) and impotence (*faqr*) and leads consequently to a strong sense of humility and deeper affirmation of *tawḥīd*, or monotheism. Through the various postures during the *ṣalāt* and the inner attitude, the servant declares and acknowledges that it is only God who can provide for all material and spiritual desires; thus prayer strengthens the bond with God.

## Belief in the Hereafter

Nursi counts belief in the hereafter among one of the major elements of forming moral individuals. With a strong belief in the hereafter, people will be potentially happier, for the concept of paradise instills a sense of hope in a reunion with friends and relatives who passed away. Young children who lost their loved ones in an early age or elderly people who feel

---

58. El-Havbevî, *Dürretüt'l-Vâizîn*, 11 in Nursi, *Mektubat*, 574.

59. Nursi, *Mektubat*, 569.
60. Ibid.
61. Nursi, *Sözler*, 50.

they are coming closer to death are relieved by the knowledge of the existence of an afterlife. Individuals who faced oppression and injustice may be able to live a more balanced life by hoping for the resurrection and absolute judgment of God. To Nursi's mind, faith in the hereafter occupies a major role in saving these people from their desolate and desperate situation.[62]

In addition, belief in an afterlife increases a deep sense of responsibility and accountability in youth. Knowing that each and every act will be recorded and judged might have a positive, educating impact on youth. Otherwise, they might become involved in immoral acts because of their passionate desires. Nursi's position is highlighted and appreciated by the theologian Ian Markham. He states the fact that for many Christian theologians, believing in hell is morally offensive.[63] The majority of non-evangelical Christian theologians who are affiliated with traditions such as Anglican, Lutheran, Methodist, and Presbyterian, etc., are "deeply suspicious of the doctrine of hell."[64] For Markham, there is a danger in this approach as "the elimination of hell has led to a universe which does not hold individuals accountable for their actions."[65]

To sum up this section, in order to form moral individuals Nursi starts off with the self and then reaches out to individuals. In this regard, Nursi differs from contemporaries such as Sayyid Qutb.[66] In trying to form a moral society, Nursi's starting point is the individual. He believed that the main reason for the backwardness of a society is the decline of personal ethics. Once individual ethics are cultivated and nurtured, society will inevitably transform into a community of ethically and morally good persons and ultimately move forward.

Qutb believed that the world is in the stage of *jāhiliyya*.[67] Unlike Nursi, he focused very much on the transformation of society as a whole rather than on the individual. A human soul, according to Qutb, is so strongly connected to society and his environment that he will not be able to be a moral individual if the external does not permit him to do so. If society does not allow the spiritual to come into practice, man cannot engage with other human beings on a spiritual level. He will not be able to reveal his spiritual potential, as he cannot benefit from the blessings of a spiritual community that combines Islam into every phase of life. It is this spiritual community which God has determined to exist. When man's atmosphere is Islamic, "every good value becomes well established and begins to yield fruit."[68]

Qutb emphasized the power of Islamic social influence. For him this was a great means to eventually eradicate evil and sin. Muslims, therefore, must create

---

62. Nursi, *Şualar*, 297.

63. Markham, *Engaging with Bediüzzaman Said Nursi*, 36.

64. Ibid.

65. Ibid.

66. This comparison of Nursi and Qutb with regard to morality is based on a section of my MA thesis. For more details, see Sayılgan, "Constructing an Islamic Ethics of Non-Violence," 67–76.

67. In the traditional understanding of Islam, the phrase *jāhilīya* was usually used to understand the "era of ignorance" which had preceded the advent of Prophet Muhammad. See Mawdudi, *A Short History of the Revivalist Movement in Islam*. Sayyid Qutb developed his definition of *jāhilīya* (ignorance) to become the cornerstone of belief of many Islamic resurgent movements.

68. Qutb, *Zilal*, 96.

a fully Islamic society, as without such an establishment they could not reach the situation of spiritual perfection and full submission to God. That is to say, instead of trying to change individuals or to create a spiritual tendency in the individual, the societal settings and conditions first need to be changed in order to ensure that humans can morally flourish. He thought, as Yvonne Haddad rightly puts it, that "salvation can only come through promoting an Islamic system that tolerates no differences and no compromise with alternate options or solutions to social problems[;] . . . only then will they [Muslims] be able to restore justice and virtue and implement their agenda of Islamizing the world."[69]

## THREATS TO MORALITY AND REMEDIES

As stated in the beginning of this chapter, Nursi refers to immorality (*ahlaksızlık*) from time to time in his writings. He usually uses this word in the context of a threat to the morality of individuals. In fact, the word immorality is ambiguous in Nursi's writings. There is no doubt that Nursi held the position that removing belief from society might cause immorality.[70] In this regard, Nursi was critical of some principles of modern civilization. He remarked that the new civilization made unnecessary things necessary and promoted a harmful materialistic consumer culture. In previous times, for instance, a person might be in need of four things; modern civilization increased these needs to one hundred things. Earned income is not considered sufficient anymore, so people are tempted to earn more through impermissible and immoral ways. This characteristic of modern civilization violates the principles of morality.[71]

Reflecting on the principles of the Qur'an and their roles in shaping and preserving a moral society, Nursi pays attention to its command of giving the obligatory alms-tax, *zakāt*.[72] He argues that the conflicts within society are rooted in all sorts of immoralities and can be subsumed under two basic thoughts: 1) If I am full and satisfied, I do not care about someone who dies due to hunger; and 2) You work and I will eat.[73]

The moral decline in the Muslim world was one of the particular concerns of Nursi, as evident in his renowned Damascus Sermon. He diagnosed six major threats to morality in the Muslim community: despair, deceit, enmity, disunity, despotism, and egotism. As a remedy to these sicknesses, he provided an ideal of an ethically upright Muslim shaping his/her life according to the morals of Islam. The following characteristics are identified as elements of this perfect model.

### Hope and Self-Confidence

Considering the tragic conditions of the Muslim community, Nursi believed that hope was one of the most significant remedies that might save Muslims. He assured Muslims that a great future is awaiting them.[74]

---

69. Haddad, "Ghurbah as Paradigm for Muslim Life," in *Islam at the Crossroads*, ed. İbrahim Abu-Rabi', 239.

70. See Nursi, *İlk Dönem Eserleri*, 418.

71. Nursi, *Sözler*, 967.

72. The Qur'an, 2:275, 2:43.

73. Nursi, *İman ve Küfür Muvazeneleri*, 131.

74. Nursi, *the Damascus Sermon*, 27.

Nursi urged Muslims to be self-confident in practicing their religion. It is essential to note that some Ottoman intellectuals saw the backwardness of the Islamic world as rooted in religion itself. Europe's rise and progress was due to its Christian faith, those figures believed. Nursi reflected on this position and stressed that such reasoning did not apply to Islam. History testified that Muslim societies flourished as long as Islam was properly observed. However, some leaders turned their backs on Islam; "they fell into savagery and decline, and disaster and defeat amidst utter confusion to the degree of their weakness in adhering to the truths of Islam."[75] Islam cannot be blamed and its adherents should be self-confident in their religion even in the most unfortunate times of turmoil and distress.

## Honesty

Nursi identified deception as one of the main threats to morality within the Muslim community. Society lacked truthfulness, which is "the basis and foundation of Islam."[76] He stated that in the Era of Bliss, referring to the period of the first Muslim generation, with the inspiration of faith and the truths of the universe "truthfulness became the most valuable merchandise in the market of human society, and the goods most in demand."[77] Furthermore, in the Era of Bliss, there was a great distance between honesty and dishonesty, similar to the distance between belief and unbelief.[78] However, over the course of time the gap between both has been drastically shortened. This went further: "political propaganda has sometimes given greater currency to lies, and evil and lying have to some degree taken the stage."[79] For Nursi, truthfulness and honesty is the key to the salvation of Muslims.[80] This is the only way to revive Islamic morals in the contemporary Muslim world.

## Love and Compassion

Nursi considered love as a remedy for the sickness of enmity in the Islamic world. In fact, for him love should not only be restricted to fellow Muslims but needs to be shown to the non-Muslim world as well. The two major World Wars happened because of the lack of love. Enmity dominated people's desires and the two destructive wars became inevitable. He urged Muslims to replace enmity with compassion in their personalities.

Nursi believed that human beings have the potential to be destructive and hateful. He remarked that what is most worthy of being hated is hatred itself. His motto was "Love love and hate hatred."[81] Nursi reflected in detail in his writings on the significance of being a loving Muslim and put this into practice. As he stated, "We are the competitors of love; we have no time for enmity."[82]

Compassion was an essential aspect of Nursi's thought. If one encounters an enemy or a person who has shortcomings, the way of approaching such a person is by means of compassion rather

75. Ibid., 29.
76. Ibid., 45.
77. Ibid., 46.
78. Ibid.

79. Ibid.
80. Ibid. 48.
81. Ibid., 49.
82. Nursi, *İlk Dönem Eserleri*, 426.

than hatred; as he said, "They [students of the *Risale-i Nur*] feel not anger at their enemies, but pity and compassion. They try to reform them; in the hope they shall be saved."[83] Nursi saw compassion as a highly significant faculty in the hearts of human beings. If respect and compassion are taken out of human hearts, "reason and intellect would make human beings such horrible and cruel monsters to the extent that they would not be able to be ruled by politics anymore."[84]

There are many occasions in Nursi's life that clearly reflect his compassionate attitude. One event occurred during his years in the prison in Denizli, a city in the southwestern part of Turkey. According to Süleyman Hünkar, one of Nursi's students who spent time with him in Denizli, there were around 350–400 prisoners and most of them were guilty of murder. The rest were imprisoned either because of criminal activities or attempted murder. Frequent conflicts and quarrels among the inmates often ended in violence. Hünkar narrates that from 1939, the year when he was put into prison, until 1943, eighteen people were killed.[85] In 1943, Nursi, along with 126 of his students, was put into the same prison in Denizli. According to Hünkar, Nursi had such an impact on the inmates that they made a remarkable personal transformation. Even those who had committed murder were hesitant to kill little insects out of their new understanding of compassion and love for God's creatures, as one account tells.[86]

Another incident highlighting his deep compassion even for his oppressors happened during Nursi's years in the prison of Afyon, a city in the western part of Turkey. The winter season in Afyon is known for being very harsh and cold. As Sabri Halıcı, one of Nursi's close students and fellow prisoners recalls, Nursi was intentionally put into a room which had no windows so that he would eventually die due to the severe cold. Nursi himself admitted that he could not bear this torture anymore and was about to curse the prosecutor. Halıcı quotes Nursi as follows: "The prosecutor intentionally put me in this room so that I would die. I cannot stand this oppression anymore and I shall imprecate him. As he raised his hands, he realized a little girl was passing by the window. Nursi asked his student Halıcı "Do you know this girl?" Halıcı said that "she is the prosecutor's daughter." Once he knew that she was the prosecutor's daughter, he changed his mind. Nursi then said, "I am concerned that later on, the girl will cry and ask what happened to her father." This was Nursi's way of compassion. He even had pity for his oppressors.[87]

The final example stems from the period of the Old Said. During the Russian occupation in the Eastern province of the Ottoman Empire, Armenians were attacking villages like Isparit, a place close to Nursi's hometown of Nurs. The forces Nursi was leading were able to suppress the Armenian forces. Nursi gathered the Armenian women and children in the area and handed them over to the Armenian forces.[88] In a time of major

83. Nursi, *The Rays*, 290.

84. Nursi, *Şualar* in *Risale-i Nur Külliyatı I*, 888.

85. Necmettin Şahiner, "Süleyman Hünkar Maddesi," in *Son Şahitler* II, 268–73.

86. Ibid.

87. Ömer Özcan, "Said Özdemir Maddesi," in *Risale-i Nur Hizmetkarları Ağabeyler Anlatıyor* III, 286–88.

88. Abdurrahman, *Tarihçe-i Hayat*, 36, cited

upheavals and tensions between Muslims and Armenians in the region, Nursi did not take the opportunity to kill innocent Armenian civilians. According to Abdurrahman, the author of Nursi's biography (*Tarihçe-i Hayat*), the Armenians were so impressed by his compassionate behavior that they refrained from killing innocent civilians on the opposing side.[89]

As shown, Nursi urges Muslims to be loving and compassionate. These manners did not remain mere theory in Nursi's life, but were put into action.

## Search for Unity

Nursi believed that Muslims who are seeking unity would play a significant role in saving Muslims from their dire state. Muslims should struggle against the sickness of disunity with the instrument of unity. He considered the whole Muslim *umma* as one tribe. Therefore, a mistake of one individual within the tribe would affect all of the members. Division weakens the strength of the *umma*.[90]

Elsewhere, Nursi constantly encouraged his students to promote peace and harmony in society. Nursi called this manner positive action *(müsbet hareket)*: "Our duty is 'positive action,' not 'negative action.' It is solely to serve belief [in the truths of religion] in accordance with divine pleasure, and not to interfere in God's concerns.... The positive service to belief, which results in the preservation of public order and security...."[91] In another letter Nursi wrote to his students that "the most important duty of the Risale-i Nur students at this time is taking *taqwa*[92] as the basis of their actions against the moral destruction."[93] Nursi did not leave room for conflict which might lead to disorder, chaos and anarchy. That would ultimately contradict with God's will of order and unity. He believed that Muslims are obliged to seek for unity.

## Establishment of Consultation

Nursi believed that one of the sicknesses of the Muslim world is despotism. It is one of the major reasons for being backward compared to the West.[94] He says, "Belief necessitates not humiliating others through oppression and despotism and not degrading them, and secondly, not abasing oneself before tyrants. Someone who is a true servant of God cannot be a slave to others. Do not make anyone other than God lord over yourselves."[95] Islam does not leave room for despotism. Consultation is an instrument in order to deal with this sickness in the Muslim world. For Nursi, "the key and discloser of the continent of Asia and its future is mutual consultation *(şura ve meşveret)*."[96]

## MORALITY WITHIN A PLURALIST SOCIETY

It is important to note Nursi's statement of distinguishing between one's personality and his/her attributes.[97] He points out that

in Vahide, *Islam in Modern Turkey*, 116–17.

89. Ibid.
90. Nursi, *The Damascus Sermon*, 52–54.
91. Nursi, *Emirdağ Lahikası*, 630.

92. *Taqwa* means abstaining from sin and what is prohibited and acting within the bounds of good works.
93. Nursi, *Kastamonu Lahikası*, 186.
94. Nursi, *The Damascus Sermon*, 34.
95. Ibid., 56–57.
96. Ibid.
97. This section is mainly based on a chapter

"a person is loved not for his personhood, but for his character."[98] Nursi goes further and elaborates on some negative characteristics of Muslims that are not Islamic and do not deserve to be loved. He says that "it is not necessary that every attribute of every Muslim is Muslim; as it is not necessary that every attribute of every non-Muslim is non-Muslim."[99] Nursi does not pay attention to the person or the "label" per se but rather to the attributes which represent the moral character.

For instance, after the declaration of the constitution (II. Meşrutiyet) of the Ottoman State in 1908, Nursi travelled to different parts of the Eastern Province of the Empire in order to "enlighten" people about freedom. Many tribes were concerned about the new amendments, such as the right of an Armenian to become a governor. Indeed, Nursi's response in this situation is an answer to the question of morality within a religiously pluralist society. He did not believe that the religious affiliation of a person should be held as detrimental to their opportunities for leadership and government. At that time, he explained, "The Armenians have certain jobs such as horologer or machinist in this country; likewise they can become governors. The governors are the paid servants of the people if there is a precise constitution."[100] The principles based on the constitution need to be observed and followed in any case. Again, the issue is not the person but the skills and the moral characteristics.

Moreover, Nursi urged people of different religions to promote moral values in society. He particularly urged Muslims and Christians to unite their forces in order to work for social justice and combat unbelief.[101]

## CONCLUSION

In this chapter, I tried to provide an overview of the foundations and themes of Nursi's concept of morality. First, Nursi does not present his view of morality in a systematic way. There is not one specific chapter that is dedicated to morality in his writings. His view of morality is a recurring theme throughout his collection. This should not come as a surprise, since the *Risale* follows the Qur'anic method of constantly reminding readers of fundamental truths. Repetition is thus welcomed and employed frequently. Nursi himself claims that his writing is in line with the Qur'anic style and themes. Second, Nursi's notion of morality is mainly based on the religious framework of Islam, even though he often utilizes philospical reasoning to support his arguments. The Qur'an, the *sunna* of the Prophet, writings of great Muslim saints and scholars who appeared in the history of Islam, and the universe form the foundation of Nursi's morality.

Third, Nursi believes educating one's soul (*nafs*), belief in God, observing the rituals of Islam, and belief in the hereafter play a significant role in forming moral individuals for society. Through these elements, the individuals will be more cautious with regard to their roles and responsibilities within the community.

---

of my MA thesis. For more details, see Sayılgan "Constructing an Islamic Ethics of Non-Violence," 51–53

98. Nursi, *İlk Dönem Eserleri*, 483.

99. Ibid.

100. Nursi, *Tarihçe-i Hayat*, 108. See also Nursi, *Münazarat*, 478.

101. Nursi, *Emirdağ Lahikası*, 265.

Fourth, reflecting on the threats to the morality of Muslim society, Nursi enumerates selfishness as one of the major immoralities which causes conflicts. He summarizes these threats with these phrases: "If I am full and satisfied, I do not care about someone who dies due to hunger"; "You work and I will eat." Despair, deceit, enmity, disunity, and despotism are the other threats to morality explored by Nursi. Hope and self-confidence, honesty, love and compassion, unity, and establishing consultation are Nursi's remedies to counter these threats. Fifth, Nursi develops a moral theology which is based on a person's character, regardless of her/his religion. This approach of morality may be useful in pluralist societies. Finally, it is important to remark that this article does not do full justice to Nursi's understanding of morality, even though it is the first comprehensive study in this sense. Our hope is that this article will be an introductory step for further studies on Nursi's notion of morality.

## BIBLIOGRAPHY

Diener, Paul W. *Religion and Morality: An Introduction.* Louisville, KY: Westminster John Knox, 1997.

Fareed, Muneer Goolam. "Ijtihad." In *Encyclopedia of Islam and the Muslim World*, Vol. 1, edited by Richard C. Martin, 344–45. New York: Macmillan Reference USA, 2004.

Haddad, Y. Yvonne. "Ghurbah as Paradigm for Muslim Life: A *Risale-i Nur* Worldview." In *Islam at the Crossroads: On the Life and Thought of Bediüzzaman Said Nursi*, edited by İbrahim Abu-Rabi', 237–54. New York: State University of New York Press, 2003.

Hanson, Hamza Yusuf. "The *Sunna*: The Way of the Prophet Muhammad." In *Voices of Islam*, Vol. 1, edited by Vincent Cornell, 125–45. Westport, CT: Praeger, 2006.

Markham, Ian S. *Engaging with Bediüzzaman Said Nursi: A Model of Interfaith Dialogue* Farnham: Ashgate, 2009.

———. "Secular or Religious Foundations for Ethics: A Case Study of Bediüzzaman Said Nursi." In *Globalization, Ethics, and Islam: The Case of Bediüzzaman Said Nursi*, edited by Ian S. Markham and İbrahim Özdemir, 65–78. Aldershot, UK: Ashgate, 2005.

Mawdudi, Sayyid Abul A'la. *A Short History of the Revivalist Movement in Islam.* Translated by Al-Ash'ari. Lahore: Islamic Publication, 1976.

Nursi, Bediüzzaman Said. *Asa-yı Musa.* Istanbul: Söz Yayınevi, 2009. Online: http://www.erisale.com/.

———. *The Damascus Sermon.* Translated by Şükran Vahide. Istanbul: Sözler Publications, 1996.

———. *Emirdağ Lahikası.* Istanbul: Söz Yayınevi, 2009. Online: http://www.erisale.com/.

———. *The Flashes.* Translated by Şükran Vahide. Istanbul: Sözler, 2008.

———. *İlk Dönem Eserleri.* Istanbul: Söz Yayınevi, 2009. Online: http://www.erisale.com/.

———. *İman Küfür Muvazeneleri.* Istanbul: Söz Yayınevi, 2009. Online: http://www.erisale.com/.

———. *İşaratül İ'caz.* Istanbul: Söz Yayınevi, 2009. Online: http://www.erisale.com/.

———. *Kastamonu Lahikası.* Istanbul: Söz Yayınevi, 2009. Online: http://www.erisale.com/.

———. *Lem'alar.* Istanbul: Söz Yayınevi, 2009. Online: http://www.erisale.com/.

———. *The Letters.* Translated by Şükran Vahide. Istanbul: Sözler Publications, 2008.

———. *Mektubat.* Istanbul: Söz Yayınevi, 2009. Online: http://www.erisale.com/.

———. *Münazarat.* Istanbul: Söz Yayınevi, 2009. Online: http://www.erisale.com/.

———. *The Rays.* Translated by Şükran Vahide. Istanbul: Sözler, 2008.

———. *Signs of Miraculousness.* Translated by Şükran Vahide. Istanbul: Sözler Publications, 2008.

———. *Sözler.* Istanbul: Söz Yayınevi, 2009. Online: http://www.erisale.com/.

———. *Şualar.* Istanbul: Söz Yayınevi, 2009. Online: http://www.erisale.com/.

———. *Şualar.* In *Risale-i Nur Külliyatı I.* Istanbul: Nesil Publications, 1996.

———. *Tarihçe-i Hayat.* Istanbul: Söz Yayınevi, 2009. Online: http://www.erisale.com/.

———. *The Words.* Translated by Şükran Vahide. Istanbul: Sözler, 2008.

Qur'an. Translated by Majid Fakhry. Beltsville, MD: Amana, 2003.

Qutb, Sayyid. *Zilal.* Translated by Adil Salahi. Vol. 6. London: The Islamic Foundation, 2002.

Şahiner, Necmettin. "Süleyman Hünkar Maddesi." In *Son Şahitler II*, 268–73. Istanbul: Yeni Asya, 1981.

Sayılgan, Salih. "Constructing an Islamic Ethics of Non-Violence: The Case of Bediüzzaman Said Nursi." MA thesis, University of Alberta, 2011.

Schimmel, Annemarie. *And Muhammad is His Messenger: The Veneration of the Prophet in Islamic Piety.* Chapel Hill, NC: University of North Carolina Press, 1984.

Vahide, Şükran. *Islam in Modern Turkey: An Intellectual Biography of Bediüzzaman Said Nursi.* New York: State University of New York Press, 2005.

# 11

# Morality and Ethics in the Risale-i Nur

## SUENDAM BİRİNCİ PİRİM, HARUN PİRİM

SAID NURSI WAS A leading twentieth-century Muslim intellectual. The primary sources of Islam, the Qur'an and *hadīth*, stand as the main foundations of his theology. He addresses his first and foremost source and teacher to be the scripture of Islam, the Holy Qur'an.[1] He considers Islam and its truths to be the very sources of progress, not only in matters of spirituality, but also in physical, material, and moral fields.[2] Based on logical reasonings, he rejects secular foundations for ethics.[3]

This chapter is a survey of Nursi's thought on morality and ethics. It will provide a brief summary of his views on the matter chiefly based on his writings in the *Risale-i Nur*. His biography and his students' memoirs will be used as secondary sources along with scholarly works on Nursi that are applicable to the topic. A brief mention of Nursi's methodology will be followed by his views on the matter. His approach on morality and ethics will be analyzed with a closer look at his thoughts on divine, personal, social, and environmental ethics.

## NURSI'S METHODOLOGY OF ETHICS

According to Said Nursi, the human mind is incapable of comprehending countless different circumstances, simply because it is restricted with each person's worldview and tends to be colored by self-interest. Based on this reasoning, he sees a crucial need for "a general or universal intellect" to lay down a just ethic, from which all huhumankind may benefit. Nursi describes this intellect as "the universal law," which is "the *sharī'ah*," Islamic injunctions based on divine guidance.[4] This conviction is one of the key elements shaping both his view and his methodology of ethics.

1. Nursi, *Letters 1928–1932*, 410.
2. Nursi, *The Damascus Sermon*, 28.
3. Nursi, *Signs of Miraculousness*, 161.
4. Ibid.

It is important, however, to note that Nursi refers to the ontological meaning of the *sharīʿah* in relation to the Creator of the universe and does not use the term only as a set of rules. For him, "ninety-nine percent of the *sharīʿah* consists of ethics, worship, and afterlife, and virtue." Only the remaining "one percent is related to politics."[5]

Three aspects of his methodology strike attention. First, Nursi's ethical arguments are grounded in the main sources of Islamic knowledge, the Qur'an and *Hadīth*. Second is his use of logic and reason, which complement the former aspect on a crucial point that Nursi's respect and adherence to Islam, along with its essential sources, are not based on a blind imitation. Third, Nursi initially identifies a problem, provides its definition, and then offers a solution. His analysis of the inevitable shortcomings of the individual mind, for instance, leads him to a conclusion that a universal intellect is needed for the cultivation of a just ethical system.

## MORALITY AS A NECESSITY OF CREATION

Nursi's understanding and interpretation of morality is based on and reflects his theology of the Divine Names.[6] He believes that knowledge of God is gained through a sound understanding of the Divine Names revealed in the Qur'an and taught in *Hadīth*. The reality of each being, he asserts, is "based on one Name or on many."[7] Nursi describes the universe, along with all the forms of creation within it, as a "divinely-penned" book,[8] in which every creation stands as a letter, word, or verse mirroring the names and attributes of its Creator.[9] The Name *al-Fāṭir*, the Originator, who creates awesome and unique things out of nothing, is an oft-mentioned Divine Name in the *Risale-i Nur*, in relation to the nature of human beings. The Divine Name *al-Fāṭir* shines in God's act of creation as he endows every being with the most appropriate *fiṭrah*, its innate nature. He provides each being with a program perfectly fitting its nature.

## Human Nature

In order to consider morality in respect to the creation, one needs a proper understanding of the spiritual anatomy of human beings and their inner faculties. Nursi describes human beings as the most comprehensive fruit of the universe that is created with a potential to reach its perfection.[10] He notes that human beings and the universe have distinctive similarities.[11] A human is interested in a small flower as well as the eternal paradise; serious troubles worry him or her, as do the

---

5. Nursi, *Divan-ı Harbi Örfi*, 1922.

6. See Nursi, "The Twenty-Fourth Word" in *The Words,* Also see *Jawshan al-Kabīr*, the famous supplication of the Prophet Muhammad consisting of 1,001 Divine Names, which is one of the most referred sources by Nursi. An available translation is *A Supplication of the Prophet Muhammad: al-Jaushan al-Kabîr*, trans. Şükran Vahide.

7. Nursi, *The Words*, 655.

8. Turner and Horkuc, *Said Nursi*, 53.

9. For Nursi on the Divine Names and manifestations of the Names in the cosmos, see Nursi, "The Twenty-Fourth Word," "The Third-Stopping Place of The Thirty-Second Word," and "The Tenth Word" in *The Words;* and Nursi, "The Thirtieth Flash" in *The Flashes*.

10. Nursi, *The Words*, 586.

11. Ibid., 52.

insignificant. Regarding human beings' relation with the universe, Nursi writes:

> Man stands in need of most of the varieties of beings in the universe and is connected to them. His needs spread through every part of the world, and his desires extend to eternity. As he wants a flower, so he wants the spring. As he desires a garden, so does he also desire everlasting Paradise. As he longs to see a friend, so does he long to see the All-Beauteous One of Glory. Just as in order to visit one he loves who lives somewhere else, he is in need for his beloved's door to be opened to him, so too in order to visit the ninety-nine per cent of his friends who have travelled to the intermediate realm and so be saved from eternal separation, he needs to seek refuge at the court of an Absolutely Powerful One. For it is He Who will close the door of this huge world and open the door of the hereafter, which is an exhibition of wonders, remove this world and establish the hereafter in its place.[12]

Human beings, for Nursi, are provided with intellect and imagination that expand their outlook to embrace all aspects of life. He explains the relation of reason to other human faculties:

> [B]y reason of the mind and thought, man's senses and feelings have greatly developed and expanded. And numerous emotions have come into being because of the multiplicity of his needs. And his senses have become extremely diverse. And because of the comprehensiveness of his nature, desires have appeared turned towards numerous aims. And because he has numerous duties due to his nature, his members and faculties have expanded greatly. And since he has been created with a nature capable of performing every sort of worship, he has been given abilities which embrace the seeds of all perfections.[13]

The comprehensiveness of their nature keeps humans in relation with all beings, animate and inanimate.

In *Al-Mathnawī al-nūrī*, Nursi illustrates the distinctiveness of human nature by describing the sensitivity of some of these faculties, which cannot bear even a small amount of weight. Some of them, he states, may fade or die with the weight of a sin:

> Know, O Friend, that the All-Wise Creator has implanted within human nature a strange characteristic: Since the world cannot contain you, you frequently utter, as if in a suffocating dungeon, a sound of disgust. Yet something as small as a mustard seed, a cell, a memory, a minute of time so absorbs you that you are lost in it and passionately attracted to it. The Creator has given you such faculties that some of them would not be satisfied even if they could swallow the world. Some others are bored even with microscopic particles and cannot tolerate even a hair out of place. You know that your eye cannot work properly if there is a hair in it. So be alert and careful of what you do so that you will not ruin yourself and your most subtle faculties. An (unlawful) morsel or a word, an (illicit) glance, beckoning, or kiss can ruin you. Everything has an aspect of non-existence that can ruin and swallow you.[14]

In a parable, Nursi mentions two people who are given twenty-four gold pieces to use during their journey to a

---

12. Ibid., 328.
13. Ibid., 334.
14. Nursi, *Al-Mathnawī al-nūrī: Seedbed of the Light*, 214.

royal farm, where they are supposed to settle.[15] Regarding earthly life as a part of huhumankind's journey to the eternity, he emphasizes the significance of worship during this voyage. The twenty-four gold pieces represent the twenty-four hours of a day constituting the main capital of humans in this life. Nursi draws attention to the amazing wealth a human being is given compared to other creatures. He implies that such wealth requires instructions for its disposal. So, human beings would be able to utilize the capital entrusted to them without wasting it. He points out with a comparison that the human faculties are given not only for use in this worldly life, but also for a much greater cause:

> For example, someone gave one of his servants twenty gold pieces, telling him to have a suit of clothes made out of a particular cloth. The servant went and got himself a fine suit out of the highest grade of the cloth, and put it on. Then he saw that his employer had given another of his servants a thousand gold pieces, and putting in the servant's pocket a piece of paper with some things written on it, had sent him to conclude some business. Now, anyone with any sense would know that the capital was not for getting a suit of clothes, for, since the first servant had bought a suit of the finest cloth with twenty gold pieces, the thousand gold pieces were certainly not to be spent on that. Since the second servant had not read the paper in his pocket, and looking at the first servant, had given all the money to a shopkeeper for a suit of clothes, and then received the very lowest grade of cloth and a suit fifty times worse that his friend's, his employer was bound to reprimand him severely for his utter stupidity, and punish him angrily.[16]

A smartphone may be given as an explanatory example illustrating morality regarding creation. Let's think about a smartphone with perfect predefined features and capabilities. If the phone functions in the way it is described, its producer will be regarded as an excellent designer and a moral person doing what is promised and described. The phone itself, in this case, would be regarded as an efficient—moral, if it had consciousness—and a most beneficial device. Similarly, human beings become moral agents if they submit their will power to the divinely revealed moral law and reflect it in their behavior. This moral code is imparted to huhumankind through two means: the universe and the divine texts. In Nursi's thought, the universe is a Mighty Qur'an which is expounded by the revealed verses of the Qur'an: "Yes, the All-Wise Qur'an is a most elevated expounder, a most eloquent translator of the Mighty Qur'an of the Universe."[17] Each is understood by the elucidation of the other.

Nursi interprets the aim of the creation of human beings to be vicegerents of God, to whom *amānah*, the divine trust, was offered. Undertaking this role elevated them to a rank above the rest of the creation at which they were assigned the role of caretaker.[18] Their *fiṭrah* is bestowed with the qualities to comprehend the astonishing beauty of the divine acts and to respond with belief, submission, and worship to the awe-inspiring works of their Sustainer. He states that, "the

---

15. Nursi, *The Words*, 32.
16. Ibid., 139.
17. Ibid., 145.
18. Nursi, *The Damascus Sermon*, 42.

elevated purpose of the universe is man's universal worship and submission to God."[19] He defines human beings as "the choice result of the universe and the most important creature in the view of the Creator."[20] The Almighty created the human being "to manifest all his names and their inscriptions, in the form of a [miniature specimen of the universe."[21] Having the gift of "divine breath,"[22] Nursi writes that humans were equipped with "a unit of measurement,"[23] that is the ego (*anā*), allowing them to understand qualities of their Creator, his Divine Names and attributes. Trust and vicegerency load huhumankind with moral responsibilities.

## The Middle Way

An important reason requiring humans to act morally, Nursi states, is the creation and existence of evil in the world.[24] Based on a *Hadīth* meaning, Nursi mentions that every human's heart has a point from where the "diabolical suggestions" of a satanic tongue and angelic inspirations are perceived.[25] In the face of such challenges, human beings are tested as to their ability to distinguish good from evil and voluntarily choose good deeds and abandon evil acts.

This is closely linked with three unlimited innate human powers: the power of animal appetites to attract benefits," "the power of savage passion to repulse harmful and destructive things," and "the power of angelic intellect to distinguish between benefit and harm."[26] The significant feature of these powers is that no "innate limitations" are set on them.[27] Divine guidance reveals the limits of these powers. It calls human beings to submit themselves to the divine principles and limit these powers by their free will. Nursi writes,

> In the absence of any innate limitation, three degrees arise in the three powers: the degree of deficiency, which is negligence; the degree of superabundance, which is excess; and the middle way, which is justice.... deficiency in the power of intellect is stupidity and foolishness, and its excess, perfidious deception and overmeticulousness in trivialities, and its middle way is wisdom....
> 
> Deficiency in the power of animal appetites is apathy and want of appetite, while its excess is profligacy, which is to desire whatever is encountered whether lawful or unlawful. Its middle way is uprightness, which is desiring what is licit and shunning what is illicit.... Deficiency in the power of savage passion is cowardice, that is, fear of what is not to be feared and delusive imagining. Its excess is uncontrolled anger, which is the progenitor of despotism, domination, and tyranny. And its middle way is courage, which is giving freely of oneself with love and eagerness for the defense of the laws of Islam and the upholding of the Word of divine unity.[28]

Upon these explanations, Nursi defines the six extremes as tyranny and the

19. Nursi, *The Words*, 272.
20. Nursi, *The Damascus Sermon*, 43.
21. Nursi, *The Words*, 320.
22. Qur'an 38:72.
23. Nursi, *The Words*, 558.
24. See Nursi, "The Thirteenth Flash" in *The Flashes*.
25. Nursi, *The Flashes*, 119.
26. Nursi, *Signs of Miraculousness*, 29.
27. Ibid., 29.
28. Ibid., 29–30.

three middle ways as justice.²⁹ Unlimitedness of these three powers is among the mysteries of the earthly trial of human beings. It is involved with a struggle to refrain from evil and involve with moral acts. If these powers were left uncontrolled, they would lead human beings either to excess or negligence. Divine guidance shows the middle way for each of them.

Since the innate nature of human beings is programmed for and necessitates moral acts, Nursi looks on immoral behavior as a sickness disturbing the heart and spiritual life of the individual.³⁰ To combat these threats, and the deterioration of morality, he advises that the Qur'anic precepts of "good works and *taqwa*" piety, be adopted.³¹ Nursi explains *taqwā* in relation to human nature:

> Will, mind, emotion, and the subtle inner faculties, which constitute the four elements of the conscience and four faculties of the spirit, each have an ultimate aim. The ultimate aim of the will is worship of God; that of the mind is knowledge of God; that of the emotions is love of God; and that of the inner faculties is the vision of God. The perfect worship known as taqwa comprises the four.³²

These four elements and faculties, for Nursi, are cultivated, corrected, and led towards their ultimate goals best by the Qur'anic guidance.³³

## DIVINE ETHICS

It is understood that huhumankind's creation with a unique nature confirms the chief purpose of their existence, which is to mirror the Divine Names and attributes. Human beings are expected to discover the meaning of their existence and life on earth. This follows on from belief in the Unseen,³⁴ whose overwhelming presence may be understood through a holistic acknowledgment of the manifestations of his names and attributes. Nursi explains that these stages of realization ultimately reach the level of "true happiness." He writes:

> Be certain of this, that the highest aim of creation and its most important result is belief in God. The most exalted rank in humanity and its highest degree is the knowledge of God contained within belief in God. The most radiant happiness and sweetest bounty for jinn and human beings is the love of God contained within the knowledge of God. And the purest joy for the human spirit and the sheerest delight for man's heart is the rapture of the spirit contained within the love of God.³⁵

If humans follow their creational program, that involves believing in One God and strengthening this belief by obtaining the knowledge of God, it would result in the humble assumption of "God-given ethics." Nursi's identifies this as a prophetic principle guiding huhumankind: "Be distinguished by God-given morals and turn towards God Almighty with humility recognizing your impotence, poverty, and defectiveness, and so be a

---

29. Ibid., 30.
30. Nursi, *Al-Mathnawī al-nūrī*, 85–87.
31. Nursi, *The Words*, 759.
32. Nursi, *The Damascus Sermon*, 117.
33. Ibid., 117.

34. Qur'an, 2:3.
35. Nursi, *Letters*, 262.

slave in His presence."[36] Knowledge of God and consequently of the names are crucial components of the discovery of and being molded by God-given ethics. Another is following the example of the Prophet Muhammad.

By showing that knowledge of God may be attained by witnessing the manifestations of the Divine Names and acts in the cosmos, Nursi discloses a "mysterious principle" to be in force in the universe.[37] This is, *sunnatullāh*, or the laws of "divine practice."[38] An example is frugality, an important principle in Nursi's thought. He asserts that the sciences testify that "there is no waste in creation."[39] Their discoveries continue to surprise scientists since sciences demonstrate that there is an amazing system at work encompassing the entire universe, which allows for no excessive use of energy, neither causes pollution, nor harms any of the creatures. Sciences prove the perfect balance of the cosmic ecosystem.

Enlightened with knowledge of the names, human beings are required to follow the codes of these names in their actions. That is to say, his name *al-Hakem*, All-Wise instructs frugality; *al-'Adl*, All-Just, commands acting justly; and so on. Nursi writes,

> Yes, the universal wisdom of the universe, which is the greatest manifestation of the divine name of All-Wise, turns on economy and lack of waste. It commands frugality. And the total justice in the universe proceeding from the greatest manifestation of the Name All-Just, administers the balance of all things and enjoins justice on man.... [J]ust as there is no wastefulness in anything, so in nothing is there true injustice or imbalance.[40]

Another example of divine practice is justice in regard to the afterlife, which is the realm of reward and punishment. Nursi is very clear that abandoning the creation of an eternal realm would be contrary to divine wisdom and justice. Concisely, denial of resurrection and afterlife is conflicting with the morality of the divine acts, to which this moral universe is testimony.[41]

Following the example of the Prophet is another way to be formed by God-given ethics. At the beginning of his Damascus Sermon, Nursi's *salwala*, the greetings and prayers for the Prophet, includes the *Hadīth*, "I came to perfect morality." The *Hadīth* continues with the Prophet's announcing that a significant cause for his prophecy is to "perfect good conduct and morality, and deliver humankind from immorality and vice."[42] In his exegesis on the verse "And you [stand] on an exalted standard of character,"[43] which is one of the numerous Qur'anic verses describing the virtuous characteristics of the Prophet,[44] Nursi cites sound reports which state that the Prophet's character was the Qur'an.[45] The Prophet, he explains, is "the exemplar of the fine

---

36. Nursi, *The Words*, 564.
37. Nursi, *The Flashes*, 171.
38. Ibid., 171.
39. Nursi, *Signs of Miraculousness*, 61.
40. Nursi, *The Flashes*, 399.
41. See Nursi, "The Tenth Word" in *The Words*.
42. 'Ajluni, *Kashf al-Khafa*, i, 211 as noted in Nursi, *The Damascus Sermon*, 25.
43. Qur'an, 68:4.
44. See Qur'an, 2:151, 4: 80, 7:158, 33:21.
45. Muslim, *Salat al-Musafirin*, 139; Abu Da'ud, *Tatawwu'*, 26; Nasa'i, *Tatawwu'*, 2; *Musnad*, vi, 54, 91, 163, 188, 216; al-Munawi, *Fayd al-Qadir*, v, 170; Ibn Hibban, *Sahih*, i, 345; iv, 112 as noted in Nursi, *Letters*, 93.

moral qualities described by the Qur'an."[46] Pointing out the importance of being on "*aṣ-ṣirāṭ al-mustaqīm*," the straight path, Nursi quotes a Qur'anic verse instructing the Prophet to "stand firm [in the Straight Way] as you are commanded."[47] For Nursi, the account of the Prophet's life proves that he followed this divine order to the letter, fulfilled his duty not only as a messenger, but also a vicegerent. Related to the three unlimited powers, Nursi points to the Prophet as guide, who stood "at the degree of maximum virtuousness."[48] He emphasizes that moderation prevailed in all his actions, speech, and conduct. He always chose moderation and avoided excess and deficiency. He was careful to avoid wastefulness and was completely frugal, even in his speech, eating and drinking.[49]

## PERSONAL ETHICS

Personal ethics in Nursi's view is an investment in the betterment of society. Change of the individual is a crucial component of social transformation. Hence, the progress of the individual is the focal point of his writings. His thought and writings are directed towards a genuine social revolution starting from the grassroots level. His contributions towards the advancement of contemporary Turkey have become a subject of research and study due to recent developments in the country.[50] It is not difficult to discern his legacy as one of the factors leading to the decline of despotism in the Middle East.

Scholars both from the East and the West, Muslim and non-Muslim, have evinced interest in discovering the incentives leading people in Turkey to practice their religion in spite of the country's secular regime and the environment in which they live. The number of young people embracing religion continues to increase despite the belittling of religion and piety by most of the popular currents.[51]

An example in Nursi's thought of individual ethics that would have social impact is the avoidance of backbiting. Nursi warned his students not to gossip even about animals.[52] Based on its Qur'anic description as "eating the flesh of one's dead brother,"[53] Nursi considers backbiting to be "poisonous to social life," explaining it as repulsive behavior harming the individual's "social and civilized responsibility."[54] He urges individuals to comply with the Qur'anic prohibition, describing slander and backbiting as "repugnant to the intelligence and the heart, to humanity and conscience, to nature and social consciousness."[55] In its place, he states, love, fraternity, and companionship should be embedded in personal and social lives.[56]

---

46. Nursi, *Letters*, 93.
47. Qur'an, 11:112.
48. Nursi, *The Flashes*, 94.
49. Ibid., 94.
50. Akyol, *Gayri Resmi Yakın Tarih*, 161.

51. See Kaymakcan, *Gençlerin Dine Bakışı: Karşılaştırmalı Türkiye ve Avrupa Araştırması*, 109.

52. His students left some meat unattended and a dog ate it. When Nursi heard his students talking about the dog, he said that the dog did what it supposed to do. Gently, he warned his students to not to get used to backbiting, even if it was of an animal. Atasoy, *Van Hayatının En Yakın Şahidi: Molla Hamid Ekinci*, 174.

53. Qur'an, 49:12.
54. Nursi, *Letters*, 321.
55. Ibid., 322.
56. See "The Twenty-Second Letter" in *Letters*.

Other moral qualities Nursi mentions in his writings are sincerity, patience, compassion, gratitude, frugality, staying away from gossiping, positive thinking in place of unfavorable thinking, positive action as opposed to violent or harmful acts, humility, loyalty, love, hopefulness, forgiveness, truthfulness, and so on. Examples of immoral characteristics that Nursi elucidates are pride, egotism, arrogance, love of fame, greed, enmity, ingratitude, despair, hypocrisy, wastefulness, stinginess, laziness, ignorance, deceit, and so on.

While detailed explanations of these qualities are found in the *Risale-i Nur*, the purpose and span of this chapter will allow us to briefly mention only a few of them. Sincerity in Nursi's thought, for instance, entails that every action should be for God's pleasure alone, with no expectation of anything from anyone.[57] He writes, "in this world sincerity is the most important principle in works pertaining to the hereafter; it is the greatest strength, the most acceptable intercessor, the firmest point of support, the shortest way to reality, the most acceptable prayer, the most wondrous means of achieving one's goal, the highest quality, and the purest worship."[58]

Nursi is very particular about attaining pure sincerity in every act, having no concerns other than *ridhā-i īlāh*, winning divine pleasure. Hence, he strongly recommends students of the *Risale-i Nur* to read the section on sincerity frequently, "at least once a fortnight."[59]

Concerning the importance of honesty, Nursi claims that belief is "truthfulness and honesty."[60] He urges the Muslim community to cling to these virtues writing that "truthfulness is the basis and foundation of Islam, and the bond between people of good character, and the basis of elevated emotions. Since this is so, as the foundation of the life of our society, we must bring to life truthfulness and honesty, and cure our moral and spiritual sicknesses with them."[61] Honesty and truthfulness are vital features of the divine revelation and the Prophet, hence they should be reflected in personal life and social life.[62]

Gratitude and offering thanks are also examples of moral precepts. Nursi epitomizes thanks as the divine aim of the creation and purpose of the existence of life in the cosmos. Thanks, in his thought, is "the most important fruit of the tree of creation," and gratitude is "the most elevated product of the factory of the universe."[63] Divine guidance instructs humanity to offer thanks in the most appropriate ways. From enjoyment and pleasure to supplications and acts of worship, there are various forms of offering thanks.[64] Ingratitude, on the other hand, is a fault that belittles the high purposes of creation by considering them valueless and degrades their elevated results.[65] Nursi identifies "the measure of thanks" as "contentment, frugality, and being

57. Nursi, *The Flashes*, 214.
58. Ibid., 213.
59. Ibid.
60. Nursi, *The Damascus Sermon*, 45.
61. Ibid.
62. See Nursi, *The Damascus Sermon*, 45–49 and "The Twenty-Fifth Word" in *The Words*, 375–477.
63. Nursi, *Letters*, 419.
64. See Nursi, "The Fifth Matter of The Twenty-Eight Letter," *Letters* and "The Fourth Word" and "The Twenty-First Word" in *The Words*.
65. Nursi, *Letters*, 421.

satisfied and grateful." The measure of ingratitude, he writes is "greed, wastefulness and extravagance; it is disrespect; it is eating whatever one comes across, whether lawful or unlawful."⁶⁶ In some places, Nursi associates gratefulness with frugality and ungratefulness with excess and wastefulness. While the former lead huhumankind to contentment, the latter lead them to dissatisfaction and greed, which consequently "destroys sincerity and damages actions in regard to the hereafter."⁶⁷ He writes,

> Excess and wastefulness lead to lack of contentment. And lack of contentment destroys enthusiasm for work; it causes laziness, opens the door to complaining about life, and makes the dissatisfied person grumble continuously. . . . Also, it destroys sincerity, and opens the door to hypocrisy. And it destroys self-respect, and points the way to begging.⁶⁸

Frugality and economy, however, result in contentment which gives rise to self-esteem. It also encourages effort and work. It increases enthusiasm, and induces striving. Also, the contentment arising from frugality opens the door of thanks and closes the door of complaint. Throughout his life, the contented person is thankful. And in so far as he is independent of others due to his contentment, he does not seek their regard. The door of sincerity is opened and the door of hypocrisy closed.⁶⁹

Nursi's exposition of *jihād* has a moral approach. In one account, he defines *jihād* as "the struggle against the soul and its desires, and against the satans among jinn and men, to deliver them from sin and bad morals, and save the heart and spirit from eternal perdition."⁷⁰ The *Risale-i Nur*'s method, he explains, is "positive action," which is "the patient and silent struggle to save and strengthen belief in God and the other truths of religion by peaceful means—primarily the written word—and non-involvement in politics."⁷¹ Nursi also refers to the method of the *Risale-i Nur* and the Nur movement as *mānevī jihād*, nonmaterial or moral *jihād*, which is, "the struggle against aggressive atheism and irreligion."⁷²

Forgiveness, along with peacemaking, is another moral principle Nursi emphasizes strongly in his writings and adhered to throughout his life. His biography notes a number of occasions when he forgave those who oppressed him cruelly. In his writings, he advises his students to follow the path of forgiveness and discourages them from attempting to take revenge or engage in violent acts.⁷³

An important aspect of personal ethics in Nursi's thought is that he does not necessarily evaluate manners as positive or negative; instead he cautions by stating, "if qualities change places, their natures change."⁷⁴ He illustrates this with the different roles a person performs. While a person of authority's "gravity" is considered to be "dignity" in his office and his "humility" at work to be "abasement," in his house his gravity is considered

---

66. Ibid.
67. Nursi, *The Flashes*, 196–197.
68. Ibid., 198.
69. Ibid.
70. Nursi, *The Words*, 35.
71. Vahide, *Islam in Modern Turkey*, 323.
72. Ibid.
73. Michel, "The Ethics of Pardon and Peace" in *Globalization, Ethics and Islam*, 37–47.
74. Nursi, *The Words*, 759.

"arrogance," and his humility at home is "modesty."[75]

## SOCIAL ETHICS

Nursi's hopes for society were not based on institutional strategies or structured social proposals. Deeply concerned with the moral and spiritual "destruction" caused by material philosophies, he concluded that only the adoption of the ethical values of Islam could help the individual and society disturbed and negatively affected by these ideologies.[76]

He identifies two phrases as the source of all immorality, corruption, and instability in social life. The first is, "So long as I'm full, what is it to me if others die of hunger?" And the second is, "You suffer hardship so that I can live in ease; you work so that I can eat."[77] He elaborates on the sources and cures of these mind-sets:

> That which perpetuates these two is the prevalence of usury and interest on the one hand, and the abandonment of *zakāt* on the other. The only remedy able to cure these two awesome social diseases lies in implementing *zakāt* as a universal principle and in forbidding usury. *Zakāt* is a most essential support of happiness not merely for individuals and particular societies, but for all of humanity. There are two classes of men: the upper classes and the common people. It is only *zakāt* that will induce compassion and generosity in the upper classes toward the common people, and respect and obedience in the common people toward the upper classes. In the absence of *zakāt*, the upper classes will descend on the common people with cruelty and oppression, and the common people will rise up against the upper classes in rancour and rebellion. There will be a constant struggle, a persistent opposition between the two classes of men.[78]

Prohibition of usury and interest, along with the careful payment of *zakāt* alms, are Nursi's essential principals towards the betterment of social ethics. He sees *zakāt* as a much-needed bridge connecting different classes of society and a means establishing tranquillity in social life.[79]

In his article outlining the five macro crises currently affecting our globe, Rodrigue Tremblay, a prominent Canadian economist, marks the fifth one as "the moral crisis." The underlying reason for the moral decline, he notes, is the rise of a Machiavellian ideology justifying the means according to their results. Machiavellianism is the cause of other crises and is a most destructive ideology in his view. A small elite justifies all the means to enrich itself "at the expense of the rest of society." He warns that world civilization will decline unless humanity claims back its moral values immediately.[80] Showing the growing gap between social classes to be the source of the moral crisis, Tremblay's analysis alarmingly proves that huhumankind has not yet overcome its main social problem, which affects the entire globe.

---

75. Ibid.

76. Hörküç, "Said Nursi's Ideal for Human Society," 257–58.

77. Nursi, *Letters*, 533.

78. Ibid., 319.

79. Nursi, *Signs of Miraculousness*, 51.

80. Tremblay, "The Five Macro Crises of Our Times: The Financial, Energy, Political, Moral and Demographic Crises."

Related to this is despotism and tyranny. The source of these issues in Nursi's thought is the philosophical principle approving might as right and right residing in power. He writes that such norms have given "moral support to tyranny, encouraged despots, and urged oppressors to claim divinity." The principle of prophethood, he notes, gives power to right. It says: "Power is in right; right is not in power." Hence, it puts an end to tyranny and safeguards justice for all.[81]

Along with tyranny and oppression, enmity and greed are personal inclinations that have bad consequences for the life of society. He describes greed as an "awesome disease, as harmful for the life of Islam as enmity. Greed brings about disappointment, deficiency, and humiliation; it is the cause of deprivation and abjection."[82] But he points out that prophetic guidance requires justice for all as the remedy of tyranny and oppression, and love and brotherhood as opposed to enmity and greed. In this famous utterance, he concisely summarizes his social experience and the wisdom of his lifetime study:

> [T]he thing most worthy of love is love, and that most deserving of enmity is enmity. That is, love and loving, which render man's social life secure and lead to happiness are most worthy of love and being loved. Enmity and hostility are ugly and damaging, have overturned man's social life, and more than anything deserve loathing and enmity and to be shunned.[83]

Nursi places great emphasis on securing the life of the family, caring for one another, being considerate of each other's rights, and avoiding backbiting and slander. He points out the social outcomes of such conduct. In his exegesis of the verses related to backbiting and slander, he writes that the most horrifying form of backbiting is ascribing adultery to people without bringing out four eyewitnesses as the Qur'an requires.[84] He evaluates this manner as a poisonous betrayal to the life of society. The testimony of anyone making accusations of adultery without bringing four eyewitnesses is eternally rejected, he recalls, because they are liars. Nursi interprets that the Qur'anic challenge to bring four eyewitnesses guides humanity to avoid gossip about these things and closes the door of slander.[85]

Belief is the most essential component of ethical renewal in Nursi's view, as it is belief which "places in the heart and mind a permanent 'prohibitor'; when sinful desires emerge from the soul, it repulses them, declaring: 'it is forbidden!'"[86]

Belief in the hereafter sustains social life with "true respect, earnest compassion, disinterested love, mutual assistance, honest service and social relations, unhypocritical charity, virtue, modest greatness, and excellence." It teaches children self-control, encourages them with to be worthy of paradise; warns youth with hell-fire, cautions oppressors with the outcome of their acts and invites them to justice, gives hope to the elderly with the awaiting eternal happiness and immortal youth.[87] Nursi invites sociologists and moralists to take particular and universal

---

81. Nursi, *The Words*, 563.
82. Nursi, *The Letters*, 316.
83. Nursi, *The Damascus Sermon*, 49.
84. Qur'an, 24:16–19.
85. Nursi, *Barla Lahikası*, 372–73.
86. Nursi, *The Damascus Sermon*, 69.
87. Nursi, *The Rays*, 247.

benefits of belief in the hereafter into serious consideration.[88]

## ENVIRONMENTAL ETHICS

Nursi reads creation as a form of divine book and ponders on the manifestations of the divine acts and attributes of them. The vicegerency has the meaning in his writings of the custodianship of creation. His biography recounts many instances of his kind conduct towards creatures of the creation.

In a section dedicated to the wisdom in the creation of flies, in his words "miniature birds," he describes his sadness at witnessing some people applying chemical sprays to eliminate them.[89] He calls the flies as "health workers and cleansing officials and chemists," while ants are also employed as "cleansing officials."[90]

When he learned that one of his students had killed a lizard, he told him sadly that he had destroyed its home, and invited his students to speak about this act. The conversation among them reported by his student is as follows:

> Did this animal attack you?
> No.
> Did it bite you?
> No.
> Did it take anything form you?
> No.
> Did it trespass on your territory?
> No.
> Did it walk around your property?
> No.
> Did it live on your livelihood?
> No.
> Do you know why it was created?
> No.
> Did God Who create this animal for you to kill it? ...
>
> He asked many questions after one another and pointed out that there are thousands of benefits and wisdoms in the creation of these animals. I understood that I made a mistake by killing it. Throughout my life, I never killed another living creature after this lesson.[91]

Nursi was deeply respectful towards all creatures, for they mirror and constantly glorify their Creator, and they perform to perfection the particular duties with which they are charged. He would never allow his students to disturb an animal or insect, as he never did himself.[92]

## CONCLUSION

Human nature necessitates moral behavior, which is learned through divine guidance. Belief is an essential component of morality in Nursi's thought. He suggests a faith-based moral system starting from the individual level and resulting in a social, and finally global, transformation. Responsibility and accountability are two essential factors completing Nursi's approach to ethics.[93] Humans are created as responsible agents of God and consequently, they are accountable for everything they do in the course of their lives, which is the period of trial. Belief in the hereafter has a particular importance with respect to morality, for it constantly recalls the consequences of worldly actions.

88. Ibid.
89. Nursi, *The Flashes*, 337.
90. Ibid., 339.
91. Atasoy, *Van Hayatının En Yakın Şahidi: Molla Hamid Ekinci*, 178–79.
92. Ibid., 160.
93. Nursi, *Letters*, 118–19.

Nursi's ethics could be concisely summarized as, abstaining from extremes and following divine guidance, which leads to the straight path.[94] The Prophet is the guide and role model whose life reflects a perfect balance of moderate actions, avoiding any form of excess or deficiency. Nursi believes strongly in the harmony of the threesome for the human being: human condition; the Qur'an, the Prophet's guidance, and the book of the universe; promoting a purposeful life at both the individual and societal levels.

## BIBLIOGRAPHY

Akyol, Mustafa. *Gayri Resmi Yakın Tarih*. İstanbul: Etkileşim, 2011.

Atasoy, İhsan. *Van Hayatının En Yakın Şahidi: Molla Hamid Ekinci*. İstanbul: Nesil, 2011.

*The Holy Qur'an*. Translated by Abdullah Yusuf Ali. Ware, UK: Wordsworth, 2000.

Hörküç, Hasan. "Said Nursi's Ideal for Human Society: Moral and Social Reform in the *Risale-i Nur*." PhD diss., University of Durham, 2004.

Kaya, Faris. "The Concept of Morality in the Writings of Said Nursi: The *Risale-i Nur*." In Challenges to Contemporary Islam: The Muslim World 100 Years after Nursi's Damascus Sermon. Conference at John Carroll University, October 23–25, 2011.

Kaymakcan, Recep. *Gençlerin Dine Bakışı: Karşılaştırmalı Türkiye ve Avrupa Araştırması*. Istanbul: Dem, 2007.

Michel, , Thomas. "The Ethics of Pardon and Peace." In *Globalization, Ethics and Islam: The Case of Bediüzzaman Said Nursi*, edited by Ian Markham and İbrahim Özdemir, 37–47. Farnham, UK: Ashgate, 2005.

Nursi, Bediüzzaman Said. *Al-Mathnawī al-Nūrī: Seedbed of the Light*. Translated by Hüseyin Akarsu. Clifton, NJ: The Light, 2007.

———. *Barla Lahikası*. İstanbul: Söz, 2006.

———. *The Damascus Sermon*. Translated by Şükran Vahide. Istanbul: Sözler, 1996.

———. *Divan-ı Harbi Örfi* in *Risale-i Nur Külliyatı*, Istanbul: Nesil, 2002.

———. *The Flashes*. Translated by Şükran Vahide. Istanbul: Sözler, 2010.

———. *Letters 1928–1932*, Translated by Şükran Vahide. Istanbul: Sözler, 2010.

———. *The Rays*. Translated by Şükran Vahide. Istanbul: Sözler, 2010.

———. *Signs of Miraculousness: The Inimitability of the Qur'an's Conciseness*. Translated by Şükran Vahide. Istanbul: Sözler, 2007.

———. *The Words*. Translated by Şükran Vahide. Istanbul: Sözler, 2010.

*A Supplication of the Prophet Muhammad (Peace and blessings be upon him): al-Jaushan al-Kabîr*. Translated by Şükran Vahide. Istanbul: Sözler, 2002.

Tremblay, Rodrigue. "The Five Macro Crises of Our Times: The Financial, Energy, Political, Moral and Demographic Crises." *Global Research*, October 7, 2011. Online: http://www.globalresearch.ca/index.php?context=va&aid=26983.

Turner, Colin, and Hasan Horkuc. *Said Nursi*. London: I.B. Tauris and Oxford University Press, 2009.

Vahide, Şükran. *Islam in Modern Turkey: An Intellectual Biography of Bediüzzaman Said Nursi*. New York: State University of New York Press, 2005.

---

94. Kaya, "The Concept of Morality in the Writings of Said Nursi: The *Risale-i Nur*."

# 12

# The Importance of the *Sunna* in Islamic Spirituality

## Said Nursi's Approach

### M. SALİH SAYILGAN

IN THIS CHAPTER, WE shall shed light on SaidNursi's view of the *Sunna* as an important component of Islamic spirituality. It proposes that for Nursi, the *Sunna* of the Prophet cannot be overestimated in Muslim life because of its comprehensive nature covering thought and action in Islamic spirituality. We will begin by locating Nursi in the historical context of modern Turkey and an overview of the challenges posed to the *Sunna* in Muslim spirituality in the new republic. This will be followed by a brief outline of Nursi's view of the *Sunna* in relation with the Qur'an. The chapter then examines the *Sunna* as informing the worldview of Muslim believers. In the final section, we will assess the *Sunna* as guidance for moral conduct and ritual practice in Muslim spiritual life.

## LOCATING NURSI IN THE HISTORICAL CONTEXT

Writing about the century prior to Nursi's birth, the renowned scholar of Islamic history Marshal Hodgson describes the situation of the Muslim world in his *Ventures of Islam* as follows: "Though the eighteenth century was not without its interesting and creative figures, it was probably the least notable of all in achievement of high-cultural excellence; the relative barrenness was practically universal in Muslim lands."[1] The Muslim world was in decline almost in all aspects; militarily, culturally, economically, and socially. In addition, a psychological regress occurred. A small portion of the Muslim lands were occupied in the eighteenth century by the European powers, yet the dominant presence of the West

1. Hodgson, *The Venture of Islam*, 134.

was felt everywhere in the Muslim world. By the turn of the nineteenth century, the Western powers along with the Russians were overwhelmingly dominating most of the rest of the world, in particular the Muslim territories.[2]

The situation of the Muslim world in the early 1920s was even more dramatic. Almost the entire Muslim territory was controlled by the European powers.[3] The state of the Ottoman territories was not much different. The situation of the Ottomans was as dramatic as in other parts of the Muslim world.

Within this context, Ottoman intellectuals were seeking solutions to save the empire. As İbrahim Abu-Rabi' rightly highlights, there were several intellectual reactions in the nineteenth century to the "question of modernity and the threat it posed to the integrity of the Ottoman state."[4] The first one was a nationalist response aimed to unite all of the Turks under one umbrella. This school was represented by Turkish nationalists. They were not concerned about the empire and Islam. They intended to unite all the Turks in order to have one language, one ethnicity, and a shared tradition under the Empire. The nationalists initiated a new understanding of Turkish civilization and emphasized pre-Islamic Turkish history. Turkish history would no longer begin with their conversion to Islam. They focused very much on a "purification" of the Turkish language to eliminate the influence of Arabic and Persian vocabulary. The nationalists even attempted to remove Arabic and Persian elements in Turkish in order to create a national literature.

The second reaction aimed to preserve the Ottoman Empire. The representatives of this response are called the Westernists. They dismissed "any central role to Islam in either society or politics."[5] For them, the only way to save the empire was through a process of westernization. This was, in their eyes, a journey to make "a radical moral and mental transformation" in order to "develop a new morality based upon the Western system of values."[6]

The third response to save the empire, called the Islamist, was to some extent a reaction to the Westernist school. The Islamists aimed to modernize the Empire while "preserving the status of Islam in that society."[7] Said Nursi initially belonged to this group and advocated for Islamic values to be maintained in order to save the empire.

According to Şükran Vahide, Nursi himself was exposed to the discussions concerning means of saving the empire and the Muslim *umma* during his time with the government officials in Van in 1895. Nursi spent around twelve years there before he made his first visit to Istanbul in 1907.[8] It was in Van where he was alarmed at the extent of Westernization and secularization, and the doubts about Islam among the Ottoman elites. While in İstanbul from 1907 to 1909 for his *Medresetü'z Zehra* project and during his time as the member of Darü'l Hikmetü'l İslamiye after his captivity in

2. Ibid., 177.
3. Sonn, *Islam: A Brief History*, 115–14.
4. Abu-Rabi', ed., *Spiritual Dimensions of Bediüzzaman Said Nursi's Risale-i Nur*, vii.

5. Ibid., vii.
6. Berkes, *The Development of Secularism in Turkey*, 338.
7. Abu-Rabi', ed., *Spiritual Dimensions of Bediüzzaman Said Nursi's Risale-i Nur*, vii.
8. Vahide, *Islam in Modern Turkey*, 27.

Russia, Nursi was also able to engage in conversations seeking answers for the problems of the Muslim community.[9] In addition, in 1922 Nursi was invited to Ankara at the invitation of Mustafa Kemal Atatürk to deliver a talk to the members of the newly established Grand National Assembly. Nursi was initially highly respected by Mustafa Kemal and the members of the assembly because of his support for the national movement. In Ankara, however, Nursi saw the direction of the new republic. He was deeply disappointed with the situation after observing that the government was pursuing the politics of secularization, a pursuit that has been described in the following terms: "Atheistic ideas of philosophic materialism were being propagated, and deputies were demonstrating a lax attitude towards Islam and their religious obligations."[10]

The new republic adapted nationalism and westernism as its ideologies. This adaptation along with its attitude towards Islam mainly came at the expense of dismantling institutions teaching the *Sunna* and banning the practices linked to the example of the Prophet Muhammad.

## CHALLENGES TO THE *SUNNA* IN THE NEW REPUBLIC

In order to make the new state, secular, national, and Western, Mustafa Kemal enforced reforms from top-down. In 1924 the caliphate was abolished. All the religious orders (*tarīqas*) were dismantled and their properties were confiscated. Some of the locations of the *zaviyas* (sufi lodges) were turned into museums including some of the mosques. The *medreses* were shut down and the *waqf* (foundation) endowments were seized by the new state. The *shari'ah* law was eliminated and replaced by the European law codes.[11] Here, we should point out that the *Sunna* of the Prophet had been transmitted to the generations mainly through the religious orders and *medreses*. In addition, one of the major sources of Islamic Law was the *Sunna* of the Prophet.

The new republic also enforced a dress code. In order to be part of the civilized world, all men were required to wear a brimmed hat. The fez that was introduced by Mahmud II was forbidden including any brimless hat. Wearing a brimless hat had been common among Muslims for centuries as part of following the *Sunna* of the Prophet Muhammad. As a sign of following the Prophetic example, the brimless hat has also been worn during the prayers. It was convenient compared to a brimmed hat considering Muslim believers would put their forehead on the ground as part of the *salat* (five daily prayer) during the prostrations. Introducing the brimmed hat as a requirement was an attempt from the regime to reject Islamic heritage

---

9. The *Darü'l-Hikmeti'l-Islamiye* was a leading institution founded to find solutions to the problems facing the Muslim world and to respond to attacks upon it; to disseminate publications informing the people of Turkey concerning their religious duties; and to uphold Islamic morality. Branches were opened in all provinces and major towns. Its members included Mehmed Akif, its first Secretary (baş katip); Izmirli Ismail Hakkı; Elmalılı Hamdi Yazır; Mustafa Sabri Efendi; and Saadettin Pasha. All of them were prominent religious scholars; the members were divided into three committees: jurisprudence (*fiqh*), ethics (*akhlaq*), and theology (*kalam*).

10. Turner and Horkuc, *Makers of Islamic Civilization: Said Nursi*, 21.

11. Hodgson, *Venture of Islam*, 262.

and adapt to new Western habits.¹² The hat law also outlawed all other types of turbans, caps, and other head coverings worn by various groups in the Ottoman Empire, particularly the scholars (*ulema*) and the members of the religious orders (*tarīqas*).¹³

According to Hodgson, the enforcement of the hat also "served as a psychological *coup*. Even in language, 'the hatted man' had meant a European, and 'to put on a hat' had, as a phrase, meant 'to Europeanize'—that is, 'to desert Islam, or the state' (which came to the same)."¹⁴

In one of his speeches in Kastamonu, Mustafa Kemal singled out a man in the crowd who was wearing a fez wrapped with a green turban. The man was having a smock on his back and wearing a modern jacket on it. Referring to this man he saw in the crowd, Mustafa Kemal then remarked: "Would a civilized man put on this preposterous garb and go out to hold himself up to universal ridicule?"¹⁵

There was also opposition to the enforcement of wearing a brimmed hat. However, as noted by Carter Findley, "the Independence tribunals (*istiklal mahkemeleri*) repressed their resistance with a reign of 'political-judicial terror,' denying prisoners legal counsel and overstepping the terms of the penal code."¹⁶ By the time of the closure of the two tribunals in 1927, more than 7000 people have been arrested and 660 people had been sentenced to death.¹⁷

Among those who were sentenced to death was İskilipli Atıf Hoca (d. 1926), a contemporary of Nursi. He became the symbol of the opposition to the hat reform and also the tragedy of Muslims in modern Turkey. In December 1925, one day the police knocked on his door and asked him to go with them to their headquarters. Atıf Hoca was a prominent scholar of Islam wearing a white beard and a turban, which have been regarded as the symbols of following the *Sunna* of the Prophet by Muslims. Known for his piety among the people in his region, he was teaching at a *medrese* in Fatih. Atıf Hoca was kept in custody and then taken to the court. His family learned later on that the reason for his custody was the booklet that Atıf Hoca had written. In the booklet, Atıf Hoca criticized those who were following the western dress style. It was published a year and a half before the hat reform. Atıf Hoca was making the point that Muslims should not blindly imitate the West. While acquiring Western science and technology, Muslims should also preserve their identity.¹⁸

Because the booklet was written before the hat reform, he was initially released. But the new regime rearrested Atıf Hoca.¹⁹ After a short trial, he was sentenced to death and hung on the gallows on February 4, 1926.²⁰ In fact, one of the accusations against Nursi was that he did not comply with the hat law. Nursi remarked that he did not wear the brimmed hat in order to preserve the *Sunna* of the Prophet.²¹

---

12. Ibid., 264.
13. Ibid.
14. Ibid.
15. Findley, *Turkey, Islam, Nationalism, and Modernity*, 253.
16. Ibid.
17. Ibid.

18. Akyol, *Islam Without Extremes*, 177–78.
19. Ibid., 79.
20. Ibid.
21. Nursi, *Sikke-i Tasdik-i Gaybi*, 84.

As a follow up to the new reforms, the Qur'anic letters used for the alphabet were replaced with the Latin alphabet in 1928. This was a further attempt for the new republic to disconnect itself from both the Ottoman and Islamic heritage. Using the Qur'anic letters in printing was forbidden. According to Hodgson, "what the new alphabet did achieve was twofold: it ensured that the reform should be psychologically complete and irreversible; and that the younger generation should be abruptly cut off from all the printed books then in the libraries—from the Ottoman literary heritage."[22] In addition, there were attempts to remove the Arabic and Persian words in Turkish. These words were technically replaced with "French and Gallicized Latin" words. There was a special focus on the words with Turkish origins.[23] Using the Qur'anic letters were also a means to understand the Prophet's legacy, his *Sunna*, better. With the Qur'anic letters, it was easier for Muslims to engage with the Qur'an and the hadith collections, the most important sources of the *Sunna*.

We should note, nevertheless, that the new state did not completely dissociate itself with religion. It continued to appoint religious staff, imams and *muezzins* (associate imams), for the mosques. However, the state required that the *ezan* (the call to prayers) should be in Turkish rather than in Arabic. The form of *ezan* in Arabic dates to the Prophet's time and it is part of his *Sunna*. Requiring *ezan* to be in Turkish was part of the project of nationalizing the religion and making it less dependent on Arabic. A more dramatic step was to use some of the mosques as munitions depots.[24] Nursi regarded *ezan* in its original form as an important symbol of Islam (*şeair*) and part of the Prophetic tradition.[25] He pointed out that having the *ezan* in Turkish would not serve the intended purpose. Because the Arabic phrases that are part of the *ezan* are based on the *Sunna* of the Prophet. It is a well-established practice of the *Sunna* and with a translation meanings are not entirely preserved. The *ezan*, therefore, should be kept in its Arabic original.[26] In fact, one of the accusations against Nursi was that he did not adhere to the form of *ezan* in Turkish in his private place during the prayers.[27]

The reforms of the new regime that came at the expense of many practices of the *Sunna* of the Prophet were present almost in all cities. In his memoirs, Mehmet Kırkıncı (1928–2016), a student of Nursi from Erzurum, remarks that in Erzurum all of the *medreses* and mosques were shut down. The Kurşunlu Mosque, for example, was turned into a prison. There were three mosques in Erzurum that remained open for worship for certain times. The *ezan* (the call to prayer) was in Turkish and it was forbidden to study the Qur'an and other Islamic sciences. Learning how to recite the Qur'an and seeking knowledge are also parts of the *Sunna* of the Prophet. Kırkıncı notes that as a teenager, he would get up in the early morning and go to the house of his teacher, Hacı Mustafa Efendi, to study the Qur'an and Islamic sciences. Kırkıncı would finish the lecture and return to his

22. Hodgson, *Venture of Islam*, 265.

23. Ibid.

24. Zürcher, *The Young Turk Legacy and Nation Building*, 267.

25 Nursi, *Emirdağ Lahikası II*, 388.

26 Nursi, *The Letters*, The Twenty Sixth Letter, 401.

27 Nursi, *The Rays*, The Thirteenth Ray, 369.

house before the police would get up and return to the streets. Because studying religion was banned.[28] Although, they were very cautious in not getting any attention, Kırkıncı narrates, his teacher's house was often investigated by the police. When the situation became unbearable, Hacı Mustafa Efendi decided to immigrate to Medina and made the following remarks: "I cannot live in this country anymore. I will immigrate. We study our religion here in secret and those who study are imprisoned. The Qur'an is forbidden and there is no *ezan*."[29]

It is within this context that Nursi attempts to reemphasize the importance of the *Sunna* of the Prophet in Islamic Spirituality. Following the *Sunna* of the Prophet is a recurring theme in his *Risale*. In his treatises on the Prophet and his *Sunna*, the Qur'an is a departure point.[30] A brief introduction to the *Sunna* in relation to the Qur'an, thus, would be essential.

## THE *SUNNA* IN RELATION WITH THE QUR'AN

The *Sunna* of the Prophet has been regarded by Muslim scholars as the most important source to understand the Qur'an. In fact, the Qur'an itself emphasizes the significance of following the Prophet. Many verses of the Qur'an repeatedly instruct Muslim believers to follow and obey the Prophet. The most cited verses from the Qur'an by Muslim theologians including Nursi in this context is "Say, 'if you love God, follow me, and God will love you and forgive you your sins; God is most forgiving, most merciful."[31] Reflecting on this verse in his treatise on the following the *Sunna* of the Prophet, Nursi attempts to derive principles by using a hypothetical syllogism in logic: "'If the sun comes out, it will be daytime.' For a positive result it is said: 'The sun has come out. One may therefore conclude that it is daytime.' For a negative result, it is said: 'It is not daytime. One therefore draws the conclusion that the sun has not come out.' According to this logic, these two conclusions, negative and positive, are definite."[32] Nursi then applies the same logic to the teachings of the same verse:

> In just the same way, the above verse says: "If you love God, you will follow God's Beloved (the Prophet). If you do not follow him, it points to the conclusion that you do not love God." If a person loves God, it entails following the practices of God's Beloved. Yes, the person who believes in Almighty God will certainly obey Him. And the most acceptable, the most direct, and the shortest among the ways of obeying Him is without doubt the way God's Beloved showed and followed.[33]

In light of the Qur'anic verse, Nursi comes to the conclusion that love of God requires following the *Sunna* of the Prophet. The Qur'an also characterizes the Prophet as the "excellent model" for Muslim believers.[34] In another verse, the Qur'an refers to the Prophet as embodying an "exalted

---

28. Kırkıncı, *Hayatım-Hatıralarım*, 24.

29. Ibid., 26.

30. These treatises are the Nineteenth Word, the Eleventh Flash, and the Nineteenth Letter.

31. The Qur'an 3:31. The translations are based on Haleem's *The Qur'an: English Translation and Parallel Arabic Text*.

32. Nursi, *The Flashes*, The Eleventh Flash, 84.

33. Ibid.

34. The Qur'an 33:21.

character."[35] Based on the interpretations of these Qur'anic references, Muslim scholars have positioned the Prophet's words and actions "as the archetype of a life lived in full submission to God."[36] Living in accordance with the Prophetic example both in conduct and practicing the rituals has been regarded as a way of remembering[37] and loving God.[38]

## THE *SUNNA* AS INFORMING THE WORLDVIEW OF MUSLIM BELIEVERS

Nursi did not only believe that love of God necessitates following the *Sunna* of the Prophet, but also had the conviction that the *Sunna* informs the worldview of Muslim believers concerning their relationship with God.[39] Nursi identifies three major sources to know God in Islam. The first one is the book of the universe, the second one is the Qur'an, and the third one is the Prophet Muhammad.[40] In focusing our discussion on the third source, Nursi believes that with his mission the Prophet Muhammad is answering the most existential questions. He invites the readers, for instance, to imagine that they are traveling to the Arabian Peninsula, at the time of the Prophet. Nursi wants them to visit the Prophet during the proclamation of the divine message. He then refers to the Prophet's character and sermon through a miraculous book addressing all beings. The prophetic message uncovers the mystery of the world's creation and answers the most fundamental existential questions: "Where do I come from? What am I doing here? What is my destination?"[41]

Nursi believes that the Prophet provides satisfying answers to the question of the purpose of creation and meaning of life. He then presents his reasons for this conviction. In his treatise on the Prophet, the Nineteenth Word, Nursi imagines the universe without the teachings of the Prophet. For him, the universe would turn into a public mourning space; everything becomes estranged from each other and even hostile towards each other. The world is full of corpses and people are weeping because of the many unavoidable separations. With the message of the Prophet, the universe turns into a peaceful and meaningful place. With his message the public mourning place turns to an abode of joy and prayer. Through the message of the Prophet, the entire creation is seen as servants of God and seeking their assigned tasks. With this perspective, Nursi regards the entire creation as one community. Prayer, as Nursi describes it, is performed by all beings in the universe. The Qur'an stresses that each and every creature, animate and inanimate objects, are members of a praying congregation, each glorifying, praising and adoring God in their own unique way and capability. In this vein Qur'an 22:18 reads: "Do you not realize that everything in the heavens and earth submits to God: the sun, the moon, the stars, the mountains, the trees, and the animals? So do many human beings, though for many others

---

35. The Qur'an 68:4.
36. *The New Study Qur'an*, ed. Nasr, 1025.
37. Ibid.
38. The Qur'an 3:31.
39. The most related treatise in *the Risale* in this context is the Nineteenth Word of *The Words*.
40. Nursi, *Sözler*, On Dokuzuncu Söz, 319. See also, *The Words*, The Nineteenth Word, 243.
41. Nursi, *Sözler*, On Dokuzuncu Söz, Üçüncü Reşha, 321. See also, *The Words*, The Nineteenth Word, Third Droplet, 244.

torment is due. Anyone disgraced by God will have no one to honor him: God does whatever He will." This Qur'anic teaching conveyed by the Prophet thus infuses the human being with a view that regards the universe as sanctified and meaningful. In this sense, for instance, stones, trees, cows, and human beings are different members of this community with different responsibilities.[42] In prayer then, one is reminded of these sacred bonds, their duties towards the creation and the call to respect and maintain the inherent dignity of every being. Those who embrace these Prophetic teachings would ideally not feel disconnected to their surroundings as each and every thing is a mirror of the divine attributes reflecting God's beauty in a dim and limited manner. No one is a stranger to one another, but friends and brothers. There is no weeping because of separation. The departures and deaths are releases from one realm to an eternal realm.[43]

Moreover, the *Sunna* defies a dichotomy between sacred and profane. The *Sunna* demonstrates that all human acts can be extraordinary acts of worship such as smiling, dressing, studying, etc. Hence, life with all its aspects becomes a life of worship and meaning. God values all human deeds and by following the *Sunna* human beings add sanctity and meaning to their lives. As Nursi puts it, emulating the Prophet leads to remembrance of God, who is the Most Compassionate and Sovereign of the world. He is the One who sends messengers as moral ideals and human models to be emulated. Practicing a simple *Sunna* like entering the house with your right foot, thus connects the observant believer to the heavenly realm and to God—knowing that God is observing and creating the very act of walking into the house. One is then led to a life of constant God-awareness and is conscious that God cares about every single act and is in the center of human life. This creates a deep connection to the divine, knowing that God concerns Himself with His creation in every act. A human being then feels valued and honored. A sense of meaning and sacredness infuses human life then. As one famous Qur'anic verse stresses: "Who remember God while standing, sitting, and lying down, who reflect on the creation of the heavens and earth: 'Our Lord! You have not created all this without purpose, -You are far above that!- so protect us from the torment of the Fire."[44]

Such an approach becomes also apparent in Nursi's own life as a faithful person. During the most challenging time the *Sunna* of the Prophet brings a positive perspective to the worldview of Nursi. In the trying moments of prison and exile, the *Sunna* of the Prophet becomes a spiritual lifeboat for Nursi:

> At a time this poor Said was struggling to emerge from the Old Said, his intellect and heart were floundering among truths in a terrible spiritual storm resulting from lack of a guide and the pride of his evil-commanding soul. They were being tossed around, rising and falling, sometimes from the Pleiades to the ground, sometimes from the ground to the Pleiades.[45]

---

42. The First Word of *The Words* in the *Risale* is a good example for Nursi's understanding of community in the context of being assigned with different tasks.

43. Nursi, *Sözler*, On Dokuzuncu Söz, Dördüncü Reşha, 321. Also, *The Words*, The Nineteenth Word, Fourth Droplet, 244.

44. The Qur'an 3:191.

45. Nursi, *The Flashes*, The Eleventh Flash,

Nursi continues by saying that during this spiritual turmoil, conducts based on the *Sunna* of the Prophet were like a compass for him: "At that time I observed that like qibla-directing compasses showing the course to be followed in ships, each of the matters of the practices, even small points of conduct, were like electric switches among innumerable hazardous, dark ways."[46] Nursi, also stresses how the Prophetic conduct lifted all of the pressures, doubts and scruples from him,

> Whenever in the course of that spiritual journeying, I saw myself under awesome pressure overwhelmed by truly burdensome loads, I followed the matters of the practices touching on the situation; I experienced a lightness as though all my burdens were being lifted from me. By submitting to them, I was saved from doubts and scruples, that is, from such anxieties as: "is this course of action right, is it beneficial?"[47]

The example of the Prophet even brings comfort to the worldview of Nursi for the question of death. The topic of death and the meaning of life have often been related. For Nursi as a follower and advocate of the Prophetic example, life in regards to death is more meaningful. In his treatise on the Hereafter, the Tenth Word, one of Nursi's arguments for life after death is the prayer of the Prophet Muhammad. Nursi remarks that the Prophet was wholeheartedly asking for eternal life in his prayer. This was the major concern of his supplications. If God answers even a minor need such as hunger and thirst with millions of material blessings like food, why would God not accept his most beloved servant's prayer who is asking for an eternal life after death.[48] In this case, it is not only the Prophet's desire to live eternally but also humanity's in general. Muhammad is simply presenting the most fundamental need of human beings—namely to be granted an eternal life.

Nursi finds peace and comfort by following the teachings of the Prophet Muhammad. Within severe spiritual turmoil, sufferings, and the reality of death, it is not only faith in God, but also following the *Sunna* of the Prophet, which becomes a safe refuge for him.

## THE *SUNNA* AS GUIDANCE FOR MORAL CONDUCT

The *Sunna* of the Prophet is also presented as guidance for moral conduct in the *Risale*.

Nursi describes Prophet Muhammad as the moral embodiment of the Qur'an. For him, Muhammad displayed the best morality through his character. That is why even his opponents called him by the name of "al-Amin" (the Trustworthy).[49] Nursi explains that people who actualize a high morality in their character have virtues of "personal dignity, gravity, and self-respect, and these do not permit a person to stoop to trivial inanities."[50] Hence, Muhammad was the best exemplar with regard to morality.[51] This moral excellence of the Prophet and the authority of the *Sunna* are established

---

81.

46. Ibid., 81–82.
47. Ibid., 82.

48. Nursi, *Sözler*, Onuncu Söz, 113. Also see, Nursi, *The Words*, the Tenth Word, Fifth Truth, 81–84.
49. Nursi, *Signs of Miraculousness*, 183.
50. Ibid.
51. Nursi, *İlk Dönem Eserleri*, 242.

by the Qur'an itself. In this context, Nursi refers to one of the aforementioned verses in the Qur'an: "Truly you have a strong character."[52] This verse confirms the Prophet's unique moral character.[53] Nursi also draws attention to one of the narrations in the Islamic tradition; once Aisha, the wife of the Prophet, was asked about the Prophet's character. She answered that his character was the Qur'an (*khuluquhu al-Qur'an*).[54]

For Nursi, one of the many proofs that the Prophet was indeed a Qur'anic embodiment of perfect morality and reflects the highest ideal of ethical behavior was his radical transformation of a society which was morally speaking extremely deficient. Muhammad replaced inhumane practices such as female infanticide with high virtues and strongest respect even towards animals and insects. If he had not embodied these morals in his personality, he would have never been able to actualize such a large-scale social revolution.[55] Muhammad's transformation of that tribal society was not a superficial but rather a permanent one as he did continue to conquer the hearts of people.[56]

Nursi believes that by following the *Sunna* every human act and habit becomes a prayer, in other words sacred and meaningful for a Muslim believer.[57] Following the *Sunna* is not just a simple imitation; he points out that every detail of the *Sunna* contains wisdom, light, and a moral lesson.[58] This is strengthened by his reference to a Prophetic statement: "My Sustainer taught me good conduct, and how well he taught me."[59] In addition to presenting the *Sunna* as guidance for moral conduct, Nursi also brings it up as guidance for Islamic ritual practices.

## THE *SUNNA* AS GUIDANCE FOR ISLAMIC RITUAL PRACTICES

While Islamic rituals are based in the Qur'an, Muslim scripture does not provide the details about how a ritual should be conducted. Therefore, Muslims from the beginning followed the Prophetic example in conducting the Islamic practices such as five daily prayers, fasting, and pilgrimage, etc. As rightly pointed out by Ingrid Mattson, in the case of the five daily prayers, for example, the Qur'an commands the believers in various verses to "establish prayer," however these verses do not provide the guidelines about how the prayers should be conducted.[60] In this vein, following the prophetic example in establishing prayers becomes essential in Islam. Such reasoning convincingly put by the prominent jurist Imam al-Shafi'i (d. 820) as following:

---

52. The Qur'an 68:4. There is a consensus among Muslim scholars that this refers to the beautiful, noble, moral character of Prophet Muhammad. For some details about the interpretations of this verse see Nasr, ed., *The New Study Qur'an: A New Translation and Commentary*, 1401. The same study translates this verse as "And truly thou art of an exalted character."

53. Nursi, *İlk Dönem Eserleri*, 270.

54. Ibid.

55. Nursi, *İşaratül İ'caz*, 227. Also see *Signs of Miraculousness*, 185–86.

56. Nursi, *İşaratül İ'caz*, 228. Also see *Signs of Miraculousness*, 185–86.

57. Nursi, *Lem'alar*, On Birinci Lem'a, 108. Also see, *The Flashes*, the Eleventh Flash, Sixth Point, 85.

58. Ibid.

59. Nursi, *The Flashes*, the Eleventh Flash, Seventh Point, 85.

60. Mattson, *The Story of the Qur'an*, 211.

The Prophet specified that daily prayers shall number five, that the number of cycles in the noon, afternoon and evening prayers shall number four repeated twice in the towns and that the cycles at the sunset prayer are three and the dawn prayer two. He decreed that in all the prayers there should be recitation from the Qur'an, audible in the sunset, evening and dawn prayers, and silent in the noon and afternoon prayers. He specified that at the beginning of each prayer, the *takbir* should be said and at the end, the *taslim*, and that each prayer consists of *takbir*, recitation, bowing and two prostration after each inclination but beyond that, nothing is obligatory [only recommended]. He decreed that the prayer made on a journey can be shorter, if the traveler so desires, in the three prayers that have four cycles, but he made no change in the sunset and dawn prayers.[61]

Here, al-Shafi'i demonstrates the crucial role of the Prophetic example in conducting the rituals commanded in the Qur'an. It is in this light that Nursi repeatedly emphasizes establishing the five daily prayers based on the *Sunna*. In *The Words*, for instance, Nursi underlines the cornerstones of the spiritual path put forward for his followers. He remarks that the means to this spiritual path are following the *Sunna* of the Prophet, fulfilling the requirements, avoiding the major sins. Nursi then emphasizes the importance of establishing the five daily prayers according to the *Sunna* of the Prophet and doing the supplications after each prayer, which are also based on the example of the Prophet.[62]

In fact, it is fair to say that there is no ritual practice that is not related to the *Sunna* of the Prophet in Islam. Nursi remarks that there are three sources of the *Sunna* of the Prophet. These are his "words, his acts, and his conduct" and each of them are divided into three categories which are "obligatory, voluntary, and laudable."[63] Some are compulsory for Muslim believers. For example, the five pillars of Islam are part of this category. The other sorts are voluntary. These types of practices are divided into two: the practices of the *Sunna* that are related to worship and the ordinary practices known as conduct (*adab*). Leave aside compulsory practices of the *Sunna*, Nursi remarks, even practicing usual conduct such as eating, drinking, and sleeping with the intention of following the *Sunna* "imparts a light to the heart" of a Muslim believer.[64] Nursi also points out that among the practices of the *Sunna* the most important ones are those that became the symbol of Islam and representing the Muslim community as a whole. Nursi regards fasting, for instance, as one of these symbols. Likewise, the five daily prayers, mosques, and the call to prayer (*ezan*) are also considered as the symbols of Islam (*şeair*). In order to make a point about the significance of the symbols, Nursi gives the example of the call to prayer (*ezan*). He points out that one should imagine a person coming with the idea that "the wisdom and purpose of the call to prayer is to summon Muslims to prayer; in which case, firing a rifle would be sufficient."[65] Nursi

---

61. Al-Shafi'i, *Islamic Jurisprudence*, 158–60 cited in Mattson, *The Story of the Qur'an*, 211.

62. Nursi, *The Words*, The Twenty Sixth Word, 641.

63. Nursi, *The Flashes*, The Eleventh Flash, 91.

64. Ibid.

65. Nursi, *The Letters*, The Twenty-Ninth Letter, 465.

responds by highlighting that summoning Muslims to prayers is just one among the many benefits of the call to prayer. He continues by remarking that even if the sound of a rifle fulfills one aspect of the purpose of the call to prayer, the others remain missing. Such a practice would not provide the very essential meaning of the call to prayer such as "proclaiming worship before Divine dominicality and the proclamation of Divine Unity."[66] Nursi, thus, did not only practiced the Islamic rituals according to the *Sunna* of the Prophet, but also repeatedly advised his followers to do so.

## CONCLUSION

Nursi lived in a time when the Muslim world was facing a dramatic stagnation and decline almost in all aspects. The Ottoman Empire representing the glorious times of the Muslim *umma* was falling apart. Many nations, both Muslims and non-Muslims, had parted their ways from the Empire and became independent states. There was also the feeling of psychological inferiority among Muslims against the progress of the West. As shown, Ottoman intellectuals were seeking solutions to stop the stagnation and compete with Europe in many ways. Three positions become apparent among these intellectuals as solutions: Islamism, westernism, and nationalism. While Islamism was favored by many including Nursi as a lifeboat to save to the *umma*, ultimately it was westernism and nationalism that made their ways into the new republic of Turkey. For the new republic,

Islam was not a solution anymore. Adapting westernism and nationalism as its ideologies, the new republic needed to do some reforms in order to clear the way for the implications of the new ideologies. Many of these reforms came at the expense of dismantling the institutions teaching the *Sunna* of the Prophet. With the new reforms, some of the practices based on the *Sunna* were also outlawed. It was within this spiritually challenging context that Nursi wrote his treatises on the Prophet Muhammad and his *Sunna*. As shown, Nursi advocated the importance of the *Sunna* in Muslim spiritual life with three aspects. First, Nursi points out that the Qur'an itself emphasizes the significance of the *Sunna* and following the prophetic example is a means to show one's love to God and his messenger in Islam. Second, in time of spiritual turmoil, the *Sunna* serves as a compass. It provides a meaningful perspective for a Muslim believer. Third, the *Sunna* is a guide for moral conduct and ritual practices.

## BIBLIOGRAPHY

Abu-Rabi', İbrahim M. ed. *Spiritual Dimensions of Bediüzzaman Said Nursi's Risale-i Nur*. New York: State University of New York Press, 2008.

Akyol, Mustafa. *Islam Without Extremes*. New York: Norton, 2011.

Berkes, Niyazi. *The Development of Secularism in Turkey*. London: Routledge, 1968.

Brown, A. C. Jonathan. *Misquoting Muhammad: The Challenge and Choices of Interpreting the Prophet's Legacy*. London: Oneworld, 2014.

Findley, Carter Vaughn. *Turkey, Islam, Nationalism, and Modernity: A History, 1789-2007*. New Haven: Yale University Press, 2010.

Hodgson, Marshal G. S. *The Venture of Islam: Conscience and History in a World*

---

66. *Pew Research Center*, "Muslims and Islam: Key findings in the U.S. and around the world," December 7, 2015.

Civilization, Vol. 3. Chicago: University of Chicago Press, 1977.

Kaya, Faris. "The Concept of Morality in the Writings of Said Nursi: The *Risale-i Nur*." Paper presented at *Challenges to Contemporary Islam: The Muslim World 100 Years after Nursi's Damascus Sermon*, John Carroll University, October 23–25, 2011.

Kırkıncı, Mehmet. *Hayatım-Hatıralarım* Istanbul: Zafer, 2013.

*The New Study Qur'an: A New Translation and Commentary*. Edited by Seyyed Hossein Nasr. New York: HarperOne, 2015.

Turner, Colin, and Hasan Horkuc. *Makers of Islamic Civilization: Said Nursi*. London: I. B. Tauris, 2009.

Mattson, Ingrid. *The Story of the Qur'an: Its History and Place in Muslim Life*. Oxford: Wiley-Blackwell, 2013.

Nursi, Bediüzzaman Said. *The Flashes*. Translated by Şükran Vahide. Istanbul: Sözler, 2004.

———. *İlk Dönem Eserleri*. Istanbul: Söz Basım, 2010.

———. *İşaratül İ'caz*. Istanbul: Söz Basım, 2010.

———. *Lem'alar*. Istanbul: Söz Basım, 2010.

———. *The Letters*. Translated by Şükran Vahide. Istanbul: Sözler, 2001.

———. *Mesnevi-i Nuriye*, Habbe. Istanbul: Söz Basım, 2010.

———. *Muhakemat*. Istanbul: Söz Basım, 2010.

———. *The Rays*. Translated by Şükran Vahide, Istanbul: Sözler, 2002.

———. *Signs of Miraculousness*. Translated by Şükran Vahide. Istanbul: Sözler, 2004.

———. *Sözler*. Istanbul: Söz Basım, 2010.

———. *Şualar*. Istanbul: Söz, 2010.

———. *Tarihçe-i Hayat*. Istanbul: Söz Basım, 2010.

———. *The Words*. Translated by Şükran Vahide. Istanbul: Sözler, 2004.

*The Qur'an: English Translation and Parallel Arabic Text*. Edited and translated by M. A. S. Abdel Haleem. Oxford: Oxford University Press, 2010.

Al-Shafi'i, Muhammad ibn Idris. *Islamic Jurisprudence: Shafi'i's Risala*. Translated by Majid Khadduri of al-Risala. Baltimore: John Hopkins University Press, 1961.

Sonn, Tamara. *Islam: A Brief History*. Oxford: Wiley-Blackwell, 2010.

Vahide, Şükran. *Islam in Modern Turkey: An Intellectual Biography of Bediüzzaman Said Nursi*. New York: State University of New York Press, 2005.

Zürcher, Erik J. *The Young Turk Legacy and Nation Building: From the Ottoman Empire to Atatürk's Turkey*. London: I. B. Tauris, 2010.

# 13

# The Prophetic Virtue of Compassion as a Core Principle of the Risale-i Nur

## Zeyneb Sayılgan

### INTRODUCTION

VIOLENCE, FEAR AND TERRORISM are words that are increasingly associated with Islam in the public discourse. The perception seems to be that Muslims are anything but compassionate. A recent survey conducted by the Pew Research Center asked residents of the United States, Russia, and Western Europe which traits they associate with Muslims. A median of 50 percent view Muslims in general as violent. 58 percent regard them as fanatical.[1] The modern phenomenon of Muslim extremism and the lack of ethical journalism which has led to a one-sided portrayal of the general Muslim population contribute to these negative opinions.

The notion of *jihad* (literally meaning struggle or effort)—often understood as a holy war raged by Muslims against the West—dominates the public image of Islam. Contrary to the popular perception, many Muslims today consider *jihad* as the spiritual and intellectual struggle to overcome egotistic or selfish desires and interests.[2] *Jihad* understood in this light functions as an instrument to achieve certain objectives.[3] The physical *jihad* or the *jihad* of force was only allowed by Muslim authorities to be carried out under special circumstances and had very limited application. It certainly did not mean that every ordinary Muslim could simply declare war as that would have resulted in anarchy and chaos—a condition strongly

---

1. *Pew Research Center*, "Muslims and Islam: Key findings in the U.S. and around the world."

2 A quick look on the popular website www.myjihad.org is sufficient to see how the diverse American Muslim community endorses *jihād* in order to attain spiritual and intellectual goals.

3. Asghar Ali Engineer, "Compassion in Islam—Theology and History," , 101.

condemned by standards of Islamic law.[4] As Asghar Ali Engineer has argued, while compassion occupies a strong and central theological position in Islam, physical *jihad* with minor historical appearances occupied a lesser theological role.[5] The latter served as a means to attain certain goals while the former continues to stand as a value.

In this essay, I would like to examine how Said Nursi relates to the central Qur'anic virtue of compassion (*rahma*) as embodied through Prophet Muhammad's life. In the beginning, I will briefly highlight the Qur'an's treatment of compassion and how scripture relates it to the Prophet. I will then turn to Nursi's *Risale-i Nur* (henceforth *Risale*) in order to offer a close reading of some relevant text passages dealing with compassion. This will however not be a full-fledged analysis of all instances in which compassion is mentioned but it will still help us to uncover the significance of it in his writings. In addition, I shall briefly highlight some acts of compassion carried out by Nursi himself during his lifetime. For this task, I will focus on a popular hagiographic work which has collected some of the compassionate acts carried out by Nursi. Some of those are also mentioned in the *Risale* itself.

This two-fold approach demonstrates that Nursi not only wrote on a theoretical and abstract level about the virtue of compassion but also offered through his own life example a practical model to be emulated. Such a holistic teaching continues to have a great impact on those who are drawn to his writings. It lends credibility to his teachings since he embodied a compassionate attitude in his own conduct.

## *AL-RAHMA*—COMPASSION IN THE QUR'AN

A cursory glance into the Qur'an, reveals quickly that compassion is central to the Islamic tradition. All but one of the 114 chapters of the Qur'an begin with the formula "In the Name of God, the Most Compassionate (*al-Rahmān*), the Most Merciful (*al-Rahīm*)." As William C. Chittick explains, in the Qur'anic worldview *rahma* is the most common term when talking about God's loving care for his creation. *Rahma* generally denotes the meaning of mercy, benevolence, and compassion and is derived from the same root as *rahīm* (womb). It therefore calls to mind the attributes of a caring and compassionate mother.[6] Compassion is most closely connected with God as the following verse in the Qur'an states: "Call upon God, or call upon the Most Compassionate—whichever you call upon, to Him belong the Most Beautiful Names" (Q 17:110). In another instance we read in the Qur'an that God's "compassion embraces all things" (Q 7:156). In Islamic theology, the divine reality is described not only as compassionate but also as wrathful. Nonetheless, as Prophet Muhammad stressed and as many verses confirm, "God's mercy takes precedence over His wrath." God's wrath even serves the purpose of a wise and caring Creator.[7]

---

4. For more on the different interpretations of *jihād* see Asma Asfaruddin, *Striving in the Path of God: Jihad and Martyrdom in Islamic Thought*.

5. Engineer, "Compassion in Islam," 101.

6. Chittick, "Divine and Human Love in Islam," 169.

7. For more on the hermeneutics of mercy

In a similar vein, Prophet Muhammad is described in the Qur'an as "a mercy sent to the worlds" (*raḥma lil-'ālamīn*).⁸ Though often depicted in non-Muslim circles as a prophet of war and violence, there are many instances in Muhammad's prophetic career demonstrating how he expressed compassion not only towards fellow Muslims but also to the creation as a whole.⁹

## COMPASSION AS A CORE PRINCIPLE OF THE *RISALE-I NUR* WAY

In turning to Said Nursi, we see that he considers his monumental work, the *Risale*, as being closely connected to Qur'anic teachings. The simple exercise of looking at the index of his collection demonstrates that *rahmet* (compassion) and *şefkat* (compassion) are the most common terms used throughout his writings. The richness of words describing this powerful virtue only shows too well how significant of a concept it is in the Islamic tradition. While both terms denote compassion, Nursi uses the former mostly when he discusses compassion related to God. *Şefkat* is often used when referring to human compassion. Both terms can however be used synonymously and also appear as such in his writings.¹⁰

As noted above, Nursi understands the *Risale* to be strongly related to Qur'anic ideals. On occasion he emphasizes that the sole inspiration for his works was the Qur'an.¹¹ It should therefore come as no surprise that he endorses the central Qur'anic and Prophetic virtue of compassion (*al-raḥma*) as a core principle of the *Risale* path. According to my own reading of his works, we do not hear him state explicitly *why* he concentrates so much on compassion and declares it as a major principle of the *Risale* path. Yet, from a holistic reading of his writings in which God is at the center, Nursi approaches his choice from a theocentric perspective. Not only the Qur'an—the verbatim word of God—but also the Book of the Universe (*kitab-ı kâinat*) draw attention to the most important of God's qualities—namely compassion (*raḥma*). The Second Station of his Fourteenth Flash is solely dedicated to a treatment of the famous Qur'anic formula "In the Name of God, the Most Compassionate (*al-raḥman*), the Most Merciful (*al-raḥīm*)."¹²

Through unveiling the six mysteries in this Flash, Nursi emphasizes the importance of compassion in the universal divine scheme. In the third mystery, for instance, he explains how divine compassion makes all the earth subservient to humanity. Human beings who intellectually, emotionally, and physically speaking stand on the highest level in the hierarchy of creation, are still incapable of making the earth submissive to themselves. While they have innumerable needs and desires, it is only divine compassion that satisfies endless human necessities. Nursi

---

see Chittick, *Ibn 'Arabī: Heir to the Prophets*, 133.

8. Qur'an 21:107.

9. For an overview see the seminal phenomenological study by Schimmel, *And Muhammad is His Messenger: The Veneration of the Prophet in Islamic Piety*.

10. See for example, Nursi, *The Words*, The Tenth Word, Fifth Truth, 81.

11. See for example Nursi, *Barla Lahikası*, 10: "The All-Wise Qur'an is our spiritual master (*mürşid*), our teacher (*üstad*), our imam, and our guide (*rehber*) in all affairs." See also Nursi, *Barla Lahikası*, 242.

12. Nursi, *The Flashes*, The Fourteenth Flash, Second Station, 134.

describes the human being to be at the center of the creation. The rest of beings are basically in constant motion and activity to gratify humanity's wants. What then, if not divine compassion, is it which orders the universe to rush to human needs? People obviously cannot communicate with planets, animals, plants, minerals, etc., in order to make them work in a way which is desirable and beneficial to human flourishing and growth. For Nursi the answer is simple. It is only God's all-embracing compassion that educates and dictates the rest of creation to help and assist huhumankind.[13] Or in his explicit words:

> O human being! Come to your senses! Is it at all possible that the All-Glorious One, who causes all the varieties of creatures to turn towards you and stretch out their hands to assist you, and to say: "Here we are!" in the face of your needs—is it possible that He does not know you, is not acquainted with you, does not see you? Since He does know you, He informs you that He knows you through His mercy. So you should know Him too, and with respect let Him know that you know Him, and understand with certainty that what subjugates the vast universe to an absolutely weak, absolutely impotent, absolutely needy, ephemeral, insignificant creature like you, and dispatches it to assist you, is the truth of divine mercy (*rahmet*), which comprises wisdom, favour, knowledge, and power.[14]

Such thinking is reiterated over and over throughout his writing. For instance, in the Twenty-Second Word, Nursi attributes the extraordinary workings in the universe to God's wisdom and compassion. All beings—animate and inanimate—rush to the needs and help of one another. In the great diversity of creation, he sees an extraordinary unity manifested—a unity which, as Nursi argues, points again to the existence of the One Creator. He portrays the creation as being in enduring "mutual assistance, help and support" of one another. Of course, as a believer, he dismisses the notion of "the survival of the fittest." Instead, in his view, there is a constant attitude of sacrifice, giving, and embrace. This law of mutual assistance and mutual embrace testifies to God's vast compassion since human beings are unable to direct and perform these vast workings in the universe.[15]

In fact, Nursi argues on many occasions that God has made this earth subservient to human beings because of their weakness and impotence. Divine compassion rushes to human needs whereas human beings claim in their arrogance and ignorance, greatness and strength. As he puts it:

> This means that man's domination and human advances and the attainments of civilization, which are to be observed, have been made subject to him not through his attracting them or conquering them or through combat, but due to his weakness. He has been assisted because of his impotence. They have been bestowed on him due to his indigence. He has been inspired with them due to his ignorance. They have been given him due to his need. And the reason for his domination is not strength and the power of knowledge, but the compassion and

---

13. Nursi, *The Flashes*, The Fourteenth Flash, Second Station, 136.

14. Ibid.

15. Nursi, *The Words*, The Twenty-Second Word, Second Station, Seventh Flash, 310. See also *The Words*, The Thirty-Third Word, Tenth Window, 691–92 and Sixteenth Window, 695.

clemency of the Sustainer and Divine mercy and wisdom: they have subjugated things to him. Yes, what clothes man, who is defeated by vermin like eyeless scorpions and legless snakes, in silk from a tiny worm and feeds him honey from a poisonous insect is not his own power, but the subjugation of the Sustainer and the bestowal of the Most Merciful, which are the fruits of his weakness. O man! Since the reality of the matter is thus, give up egotism and arrogance. With the tongue of seeking help proclaim your impotence and weakness at the Divine Court, and with the tongue of entreaty and supplication, your poverty and need. Show that you are His slave.[16]

Such statements shatter all human claims to declare ownership of technological advancement and progress. On the moral plane, they call the human being back to humility and reliance on God. Human self-sufficiency and arrogance are condemned by Qur'anic standards and likewise in Nursi's writings. To Nursi's mind, this does not mean though that human beings deserve no credit for their achievements. Following Qur'anic thinking, he puts emphasis on the sincere intention (*niyya*) regardless of the outcome on any deeds. God will reward people for their sincere struggles and efforts. Nursi's concern is rather the complete denial of God in these undertakings.

That human beings can equally refuse to see divine compassion as the real cause of these universal favors is also admitted by Nursi. As far as he is concerned these observations are self-evident truths confirming the existence and compassion of God. Yet, as the Qur'an also states, people can attribute these compassionate actions in the universe to anything other than God and can become truth-concealers (*al-kāfirūn*). Such a possibility naturally exists and this is why divine revelation serves as guidance and reminder. Nursi follows these Qur'anic explications and acknowledges that those two perspectives—the self-referential (*mânâ-yı ismî*) and the Other-indicative (*mânâ-yı harfî*)—exist among huhumankind.[17] The former does not attribute the beings and events in the world to an All-Powerful Maker and Causer by looking at the things in themselves and makes them devoid of meaning. The latter concept instead does acknowledge in everything the existence of the Most Compassionate Creator and perceives wisdom and divine artistry in all creatures. Through this view one understands that the universe is nothing but a self-disclosure of God, though in a limited way.

Divine compassion is not simply a quality confined to this earthly life. It also occupies a prominent role with regard to the existence of the hereafter. When Nursi writes about the necessity of an afterlife in his Treatise on Resurrection or the Tenth Word, he argues that God's vast compassion cannot allow for the hereafter not to exist. This would simply counter God's very quality of being the Most Compassionate. The Creator who answers to human hunger and thirst with innumerable blessings and bounties, will certainly respond to the greatest of human needs—namely immortality. As he writes in his section of the "Gate of Compassion, (*bâb-ı şefkat*)"

---

16. Nursi, *The Words*, The Twenty-Third Word, Second Chapter, Fourth Remark, 337.

17. See for instance Nursi, *Barla Lahikası*, 306–307.

Is it at all possible that a Lord possessing infinite compassion [*kemâl-i şefkat*] and mercy, Who most compassionately fulfills the smallest need of His lowliest creatures in the most unexpected fashion, Who heeds the muffled plea for help of His most obscure creature, and Who responds to all the petitions He hears, whether vocal or mute—is it at all possible that such a Lord should not pay heed to the greatest petition of the foremost among His servants, the most beloved among his creatures, that He should not hear and grant his most exalted prayer? The kindness and ease manifested in the feeding and nurturing of weak and young animals show that the Monarch of the cosmos exercises his dominicality with infinite mercy [*rahmet*].[18]

Nursi continues in the same vein, when he explains in his Twenty-Ninth Word that the non-existence of an afterlife would not befit God's compassion. Human beings who are in love with numerous bounties in creation desire that these blessings should be endless. Since separation and death does not permit for ceaseless pleasure, an eternal life must exist. Otherwise, as Nursi puts it, life itself would be nothing but torment and pain. Again, for him, divine compassion is so self-evident in the universe that he regards it as foolish not to believe in it. The greatest expression of divine compassion is eternal happiness through a life with never-ending delights.[19] Of course, this is a circular argument since one can only believe in an afterlife if the existence of an Eternal Creator and his compassion is acknowledged. A non-believer might find this approach less than convincing. Nevertheless, we recognize that the divine quality of compassion is key in Nursi's grand scheme of contemplating both on the earthly and heavenly realm.

Simply knowing and reflecting about the divine attributes in the creation such as compassion, is not sufficient. The believer is also called to live in conformity with these divine qualities.[20] Nursi, following mainstream Muslim theologians like Ibn 'Arabī or Imam Ghazzalī (d. 1111), emphasizes that it is the duty of every human being to become mirrors of the divine. In fact, all what is perceived as beauty (*cemal*), perfection (*kemal*), and goodness (*ihsan*) are only pale reflections of God's attributes displayed through beings in a dim and limited manner. Human beings who are naturally drawn to these qualities, love God already—even if they are in denial of God. They simply attribute these divine qualities to secondary causes which are only mirrors of the divine.[21]

In the above mentioned section of the Fourteenth Flash he stresses several times that human beings are created according to the "form of the Most Compassionate One" (*sūrat al-raḥmān*).[22] Surely, humans are only shadowy, partial reflections of these attributes while God is the absolute and ultimate source of all goodness and perfection. God's all-embracing compassion calls humanity to live in accordance with the Divine Name of *al-raḥmān* by expressing compas-

---

18. Said Nursi, *The Words*, The Tenth Word, Fifth Truth, 81.

19. Nursi, *The Words*, The Twenty-Ninth Word, Second Aim, Second Fundamental Point, Sixth Point, 540.

20. Nursi, *The Words*, The Eleventh Word, 140–41.

21. For Nursi's discussion on love, see for example Nursi, *The Flashes*, The Third Flash, 31.

22. Nursi, *The Flashes*, The Fourteenth Flash, Second Station, Fifth Mystery, 139–40.

sion to all creation. This teaching goes back to a Prophetic statement in which Muhammad is believed to have said: "Become characterized by God's character traits (takhallaqu bi-akhlāq Allāh)!"[23] On many occasions, Nursi emphasizes that human compassion is merely a pale reflection of God's vast compassion.[24]

It is in this light that Nursi singles out compassion (şefkat) to be one of the most single important virtues of the *Risale* way because it is more inclusive and accessible to all individuals. As the Qur'an gives emphasis to this particular attribute of God's nature, Nursi as well stresses it in his own writings. As he says,

> The ways leading to Almighty God are truly numerous. While all true ways are taken from the Qur'an, some are shorter, safer, and more general than others. One of these is the way of impotence, poverty, compassion [şefkat], and reflection, from which, with my defective understanding, I have benefited. Indeed, like ecstatic love, impotence is a path which, by way of worship, leads to winning God's love; but it is safer. Poverty too leads to the Divine Name of All-Merciful. And, like ecstatic love, compassion leads to the Name of All-Compassionate, but is a swifter and broader path. Also like ecstatic love, reflection leads to the Name of All-Wise, but it is a richer, broader, and more brilliant path.[25]

By cultivating and practicing compassion towards others, one is not only all-embracing but also can reach God's love most swiftly. In another section, Nursi remarks, that God takes great pleasure in expressing compassion towards his creation. He, "the Merciful and Compassionate One, experiences exalted, pure, holy, and beautiful meanings, like fondness and love, in a manner appropriate to Him, that may be described through qualities which are proper to Him."[26] If compassion is so valued by God and key in his treatment of the creation, then surely he desires his servants also to be compassionate and caring to one another. For honoring his creation would mean to honor God. Embodying compassion through word and deed is therefore crucial in gaining proximity to God.

To whom should compassion be expressed? Compassion needs to be shown to all creation as a reading of Nursi's works suggests since divine compassion does not exclude anything or anyone from receiving God's care. Most importantly, compassion should be demonstrated to those who are considered the weakest in society and who are in great need of loving care. Nursi begins with the immediate environment and directs particular attention to aging parents and elderly.[27] Once they enter old age, often this distinct needy group can be perceived as burden to individuals and society. However, following the Qur'anic model, Nursi highlights the important role they play in receiving God's favor and pleasure. Those who continue to show compassion and selfless love to the needy refrain from a widespread egotism. They demonstrate that they truly love God because they do prioritize others over themselves even if it

---

23. See Burrell, *Al-Ghazali on the Ninety-Nine Most Beautiful Names of God*.

24. Nursi, *The Letters*, The Seventeenth Letter, Fifth Point, 99.

25. Nursi, *The Words*, Addendum, 491.

26. Nursi, *The Words*, The Thirty-Second Word, Second Stopping-Place, Third Aim, Fourth Indication, 651.

27. Nursi, *The Letters*, The Twenty-First Letter, 303–5.

is burdensome. This, according to Nursi, is the ideal attitude of a pious person who claims to love God.

It is interesting to read that Said Nursi singles out women to be the most loyal and dedicated students of the *Risale*. Women who characteristically are equipped with a stronger sense of compassion and selfless love are therefore ideally suited to serve the *Risale* way which means to hear, read or write and most importantly to live and disseminate its teachings.[28] Nursi shares with his audience how strong of an influence his own mother was in his spiritual formation. He writes:

> I am eighty years old and have received lessons from eighty thousand people. Yet I swear that the truest and most unshakeable lessons I have received are those inculcated in me by my late mother, which have always remained fresh for me. They have been planted in my nature as though they were seeds planted in my physical being. I observe that other instruction has been constructed on those seeds. That is to say, the lessons instilled in my nature and spirit by my mother when I was one year old, I now see at the age of eighty to be fundamental seeds amid great truths. For instance, I consider it certain that I learnt from the compassionate behaviour and acts of my mother and from her teaching, to be compassionate, which is the most important of the four principles

of my way, and to be kind and clement, which is the greatest truth of the *Risale-i Nur*.[29]

In one of his many letters in the *Kastamonu Lahikası* collection, he stresses again that women are naturally drawn to the *Risale* because they share its main principle—namely compassion.[30]

Not only did God create human beings with the capacity to show compassion to one another, but he also established the basic practices of Islam as a means to cultivate compassion. As Nursi explains, the fundamental ritual of performing the fast in the month of Ramadan also serves as a basis to cultivate a social ethic of compassion. The believer is invited to existentially feel the deep hunger many poor people experience around the globe.[31] Such an exposure deepens the bonds between different members of society and invites them to mutual assistance and embrace—similar to the diverse creation which takes divine compassion as its departure point.

In reading the *Risale* as a whole and considering Nursi's context and overall concerns, it is safe to say that he is also writing against the backdrop of an increasing egotistic and materialist culture.[32] Nursi hopes to challenge this spiritual sickness with the most fundamental and needed human response—namely compassion. It is only selfless love and mercy that prioritizes others' needs over one's ego. A compassionate heart will first have the best interests in mind for the hu-

---

28. Nursi, *The Flashes*, The Twenty-Fourth Flash, First Point, 259: "Since one of the fundamental principles of the Risale-i Nur is compassion and women are champions of compassion, they are by nature more closely connected with the Risale-i Nur than others. Praise be to God, this natural sympathy is felt in many places. The self-sacrifice within such compassion seeks nothing in return and expresses true sincerity, and so is of the greatest importance at this time."

29. Nursi, *The Flashes*, The Twenty-Fourth Flash, First Point, 260.

30. Nursi, *Kastamonu Lahikası*, 122.

31. Nursi, *The Letters*, The Twenty-Ninth Letter, The Second Section, Fifth Point, 459–60.

32. Nursi, *The Letters*, The Twenty-Ninth Letter, Sixth Section, Fifth Satanic Stratagem, 488.

man family and will attempt to be a positive and transformative force in society.

## ACTS OF COMPASSION IN SAID NURSI'S LIFE

In looking at Nursi's life, we see that he not only preached these above teachings but he also strived to embody compassion throughout his life. This he did in full embrace of the Prophetic *sunna*—the living example of Prophet Muhammad who was described by his wife Aisha as "embodying the Qur'an" (*kāna khuluquhu al-qur'ān*).[33]

A couple of interesting instances from his life demonstrate only too well how compassionate Nursi was towards his fellow beings. In the following, I would like to point to some examples collected in the popular book on Nursi entitled *Başkasının Günahına Ağlayan Adam* (The Man Who Shed Tears for the Sins of Others) written by Vehbi Vakkasoğlu. The author, an avid reader of the *Risale*, provides a useful overview of Nursi's compassionate acts drawn from his writings and eye witnesses. Vakkasoğlu is a popular writer and speaker in Turkey and the diaspora and has a wide reach when it comes to explaining the *Risale* to a general audience. My choice in selecting this non-academic contemporary book for this purpose is to demonstrate that Nursi's living example continues to inspire many people who seek for religious and moral guidance.

Nursi did not only show compassionate care to human beings but also to animals and plants. For him, all creation were manifestations of the divine attributes as noted earlier. He therefore treated them with the utmost respect while affirming their inherent sacredness. Since all beings glorify and praise God in their own unique language of disposition, he strived to maintain their holiness and value.

In terms of vegetation for example, he did not allow for any fresh greenery to be destroyed or collected since that would mean to end their distinct remembrance of God. He refused to cut off fresh trees when he needed firewood and instead tried to look for dried one.[34] In one of his encounters with a baker, Nursi again expresses his discomfort of cutting off green, fresh trees to use them as firewood. He urges the baker to change his profession saying that he would pray to God for him so that he will be blessed with enough provisions and good health. The baker, initially resistant, followed Nursi's plea and looked after another source of income.[35]

On another occasion, one of his close students named Molla Hamid from Van narrates, that Nursi would not allow his companions to consume the fruits found in the mountains. He would explain to them that God created those for the animals in the wilderness. Human beings should therefore take their provision from their immediate urban area and

---

33. The Qur'an declares in Q 68:4, "Truly, you have a strong character (*wa innaka la 'alā khuluqin 'azīm*)." Likewise, Q 33:21 states, "The Messenger of God is an excellent model (*uswatun ḥasanatun*) for those of you who put your hope in God and the Last Day and remember Him often." According to a report on the authority of Qatāda, ʿĀʾisha said the mannerism and character of the Prophet was whatever was stated in the Qur'an. See *Saḥīḥ Muslim* http://sunnah.com/muslim/6/168

34. Vakkasoğlu, *Başkasının Günahına Ağlayan Adam*, 94.

35. Ibid., 92–93.

should respect the rights of animals.³⁶ In addition, Nursi also advised his students to leave some of the slaughtered meat behind for those animals in need. His compassionate care included hence wild animals who were not even living in his close proximity. His view of the creation was a sacred one and therefore led him inevitably to express compassion to all beings. Molla Hamid shared another incident involving a dog who one day entered their house and ate all the cooked meat kept in a pot. Molla Hamid became not only upset about the fact that all their meal was gone but also that the dog had destroyed the cooking pot. While complaining about the dog and trying to find ways to catch and punish him, Nursi intervened and admonished him for making such plans. He defended the dog and explained to his students that the dog was only hungry. Animals, as he went on, could not distinguish between right and wrong and simply followed their natural desires. After some more explanations he advised his students to forgive the dog and not to keep backbiting about him any further. Molla Hamid and Molla Resul were convinced that they were in the wrong and forgave the dog for he was only following his natural inclination.³⁷

In another instance, Nursi asked his students to build a small woodhouse in the mountains. Once they discovered several anthills, Nursi did not allow for any construction to be built in that area. He explained to his students that a house cannot be built while another one is being destroyed for it. According to these eye witnesses, he even offered bread crumbs, bulgur wheat and sugar to these little beings.³⁸ When he encountered hunters during his hikes in the mountains, he counseled them not to kill any rabbits and deer for mere play. In fact, one of these passionate hunters whom he persuaded not to go after these animals, Abdulkadir Badıllı, became one of his close students.³⁹ At another incident, we see him saddened by the fact that his student Molla Hamid killed a grasshopper while strolling in the forest. Nursi admonished him by saying that he did not create the little being and that only God is the true Creator who can give and take away life. He added further that the creation of the grasshopper contains unlimited divine wisdom and hence this being deserved care.⁴⁰

Kinyas Kartal, a past member and head of the Turkish parliament shared following incident happened during Nursi's lifetime: It was the month of Ramadan and a very cold winter day during which no one kept the fast except Nursi. Due to an uprising in the Eastern provinces, officials decided to bring a number of people to Erzurum and from there send them into exile as punishment to other western provinces. These people were all grieving about the fact that they had to forcefully leave their beloved home. The group was taken on cow carriages for the journey. One of the cows suddenly started to bleed on its leg. Nursi noticed this and immediately urged all people to leave the carriage by saying that "Cow *Efendi's* (meaning Mr Cow's) leg has been hurt. We all need to get off from this carriage." Kinyas Kartal objected to this by claiming that he had paid the owners of these animals a lot of money and that they should

---

36. Ibid., 94–95.
37. Ibid., 95–96.
38. Ibid., 97–98.
39. Ibid., 98.
40. Ibid., 96–97.

continue carrying them. However, Nursi refuted his argument by saying that only God is the sole Owner of these beings and that they had to be treated with utmost dignity.[41]

Stories like this abound and considering the harsh context of this particular moment (the cold winter day, the physically burdensome fast, the sadness and grief because of exile) it is quite impressive that he does not seem to be self-absorbed. Rather, his compassion and care towards all fellow beings is unshaken even in such difficult circumstances. Given also the simple mindedness of people around him, such views and attitudes seemed strongly alien to his contemporaries.

Nursi's compassion and care was not confined to his own fellow believers. In one letter we hear him cry about the millions of innocent lives lost during World War II. He was particularly in grief about the pure children who had passed during these senseless conflicts. At the end, Nursi found solace and comfort in his faith by reaffirming that those who died in an innocent state will be given the high rank of martyrdom and eternal happiness in the hereafter. While stating that the majority of these victims were Christians he does not compromise on his belief that Islam is the one, final and true religion. Instead, he justifies his compassion for these innocent non-Muslims by maintaining a traditional orthodox belief which grants possible salvation for those who were not reached by Muhammad's message.[42] They simply did not have access to the complete and undistorted message, therefore their possibility of being "people of salvation" (*ehl-i necat*) remains.[43]

The point here is not to discuss Nursi's stance on religious pluralism. Rather, his attitude demonstrates that a believer's compassion and selfless love should not only be limited to one's own faith group but should ideally include all beings. It also shows that he was genuinely concerned with the happiness of all people in this world and the hereafter. Considering that God is Most-Compassionate to all on this earth without excluding anyone, Nursi's attempt to be a mirror of this divine attribute can be appreciated.

Such limitless compassion is displayed in many other situations. In the wake of the inner turmoil between Armenian Christians and Muslims in the eastern part during World War I, Nursi protected thousands of Armenian children who were taken captive and about to be killed. The Muslim side argued that it would be only just and fair to execute these children since the Armenians had done the same to their offspring. Nursi, however, protested against such injustice and prevented these innocent children from being murdered. He ordered the soldiers to send them back to their families. It is told that the Armenians were so moved by this gesture that they too decided not to kill any more Muslim children.[44] Needless to say that we cannot independently verify these accounts but they are alive within the collective memory of the community which still draws important lessons out of it on how to follow an ethical conduct even in war situations.

---

41. Vakkasoğlu, *Başkasının Günahına Ağlayan Adam*, 98–99.

42. Nursi, *Kastamonu Lahikası*, 141–42.

43. Nursi, *The Letters*, The Twenty-Sixth Letter, Fourth Topic, Fifth Matter, 386–87.

44. Vakkasoğlu, *Başkasının Günahına Ağlayan Adam*, 90–91.

Another act of compassion narrated from Nursi's life is his encounter with an alcoholic man. While he was spending some time outside in the city of Isparta to read some supplications and contemplate on the creation, a drunk person attempted to approach him. Nursi's close students wanted to keep the man away from him but Nursi insisted to let him come. The man came and started to hold Nursi's hands. Over and over he would ask Nursi to forgive his sins and to pray for his recovery from addiction. Out of his compassion, Nursi embraced the man stroking affectionately his head and promised to offer special supplications for him. "Oh my Lord, please rescue this man from his distress," he said and continued by adding, "God-willing you will be saved." It is reported that this man recovered from his addiction after a short period.[45] There are several other reports involving similar occurrences in which Nursi did not condemn or judge the sinner, but is rather concerned to express a compassionate approach by embracing everyone through prayer and support. Out of his compassionate care he did not exclude anyone. Instead, he tried to find ways to bring them back to the fold of faith and its related rituals.[46]

It was quite common that Nursi cried for the sins of others. Out of his compassion, he did not only care for the worldly comfort of his fellow human beings but was seriously concerned for their wellbeing in the hereafter. In one instance occurring during his imprisonment in the Emirdağ penitentiary in 1935, he recounted an interesting incident. He shared his sorrow and grief about a group of young female high school students which he observed from his prison window. The school was located on the opposite side to the prison. In what we could describe as a true vision of the future shown to him, he shed tears over the fact that some of these young women will suffer torment in their graves due to their immoral acts committed during their lifetime. Further, some of these women will not receive compassion during their old age from the people they expected them to love. Due to their vices many had distanced themselves from them. Nursi cried so hard that inmates finally had to inquire about his wellbeing.[47] This occurrence is instructive in that Nursi exemplified that a true follower of the *Risale* path has to be compassionately preoccupied with people's final state in the world and the hereafter.

Interestingly, not only fellow beings felt his loyalty, care and compassion but also inanimate objects. One case in point, is his broken teaspoon which, as Nursi described it, "was his close friend of forty years."[48] Nursi, who enjoyed drinking tea, had a little tea set in his possession. After his spoon broke apart, he asked his close student Zübeyir Gündüzalp to take it to the city for repair. Gündüzalp inquired about this possibility but quickly had to found out that it would be difficult to fix the damage since the spoon was made out of aluminum. He then decided to buy a new spoon for Nursi who is only saddened by that. He again requested for his broken spoon to be repaired which Gündüzalp finally manages to get done. Such narrations about close belongings of Nursi which had accompanied him throughout

---

45. Ibid., 127.
46. Ibid., 128–33.
47. Nursi, *The Rays*, The Eleventh Ray, The Third Topic, 219.
48. Vakkasoğlu, *Başkasının Günahına Ağlayan Adam*, 83.

his life abound in the collection. They not only teach his community that compassion is not merely limited to living beings but can be also extended to inanimate objects. Further, contentment (*kanaat*) and loyalty (*sadakat* or *vefa*) also feature as important virtues in these important accounts. Nursi wrote about these issues in length in his *Risale*.[49]

Certainly, these hagiographic writings might appear to an outside reader uncritical or too reverential. It is however undeniable that they offer us a valuable record of how Nursi continues to be perceived by a large Muslim community which takes these compassionate acts as moral inspiration in shaping their lives. Such popular hagiography therefore needs to be taken seriously in understanding how Nursi's piety continues to impact the hearts of the faithful.

There are far too many compassionate acts from Nursi's life to cite them all in this limited space. We will have to confine ourselves with these few examples. Suffice it to say that compassion as the *Risale*'s major principle and virtue was a backbone of his life. The way he engaged with his fellow beings was marked by limitless compassion. On many occasions, he reiterates that the Qur'an and the *sunna* of the Prophet was his sole inspiration. The Prophet was for him as well as for many billions of other fellow Muslims, most importantly an embodiment of compassion. He felt a deep loyalty to these two foundational sources of Islam and was keen to practice their interrelated teachings in every context. One of his letters from the *Emirdağ Lahikası* collection puts it quite succinctly how seriously he took the compassionate approach:

> Compassion is the pillar of the *Risale-i Nur* path and since thirty years has been the unshaken principle of my life. Due to that I cannot reprimand those tyrants who have oppressed me throughout my life, let alone curse on them. For I fear that I could harm an innocent person in that process. Although I was very distressed about the injustices afflicted on me, compassion has prohibited me from not only physically rebuking these oppressors but also not to curse on those evildoers verbally. For I do not want to cause injury to the innocent and guiltless fathers, mothers or children of these criminals. I do not want those innocent people to be hurt by any physical or emotional detriment. This is why I have refrained from reproaching these tormenters in any way, and sometimes have sincerely forgiven them.[50]

## CONCLUDING REMARKS

In examining Nursi's works and life we have uncovered how central compassion was not only in his writings but also in his overall behavior and attitude towards other fellow beings. Such a dual approach has demonstrated that Nursi taught his followers from a holistic perspective. What he put in writing was also first exemplified by his own personal example. Theory and practice walked hand in hand and gave credibility to his works. This actually fits very well to his overall understanding that one should first start changing one's own limited, weak and faulty self. Throughout the *Risale*, he states time and again that the Qur'an and

---

49. See for example his treatise on frugality in Nursi, *The Flashes*, The Nineteenth Flash, 189–200.

50. Nursi, *Emirdağ Lahikası*, 354.

the Prophetic *sunna* have guided him in this compassionate conduct.

Sadly, today, many non-Muslims associate anything but compassion with Islam and its Prophet. It remains therefore critical to underscore the contribution and legacy of Said Nursi which continues in raising generations who are equally committed to the way of unlimited and uncompromising compassion. Millions of followers today within the Nur community find a strong appeal in Nursi's teachings because of the way he practiced this wisdom in his personal life. His piety in which compassion is foundational in drawing the attention of Muslims is scripture lived and nothing but emulating the Prophetic *sunna*. As Jacob Neusner has noted, most followers of the world's religions rely on scholars and revered leaders to interpret their sacred texts for them:

> Even now, when literacy is widespread but not ubiquitous, it is not clear that most practitioners of the [major world's religions] "read" the sacred texts of their religion in any systematic or disciplined way. More typically, religious intellectuals and virtuosi, read, understand, interpret, mediate, and exemplify the texts in the life of a religious community.... These "living" texts become models of behavior—of ethics, piety, learning, compassion, and discipline. People who practice those religions turn to these "living texts" to learn what to do and what their religion teaches.[51]

Nursi, thus, did not only practiced the Islamic rituals according to the *Sunna* of the Prophet, but also repeatedly advised his followers to do so.

---

51. Neusner, *Sacred Texts and Authority*, xv.

# BIBLIOGRAPHY

Asfaruddin, Asma. *Striving in the Path of God: Jihad and Martyrdom in Islamic Thought*. Oxford: Oxford University Press, 2013.

Burrell, David. *Al-Ghazali on the Ninety-Nine Most Beautiful Names of God*. Cambridge: Islamic Texts Society, 1992.

Chittick, William C. "Divine and Human Love in Islam." In *Divine Love: Perspectives from the World's Religious Traditions*, edited by Jeff Levin and Stephen G. Post, 163–200. West Conshohocken, PA: Templeton, 2010.

———. *Ibn 'Arabī: Heir to the Prophets*. Oxford: Oneworld, 2005.

Engineer, Asghar Ali. "Compassion in Islam—Theology and History." In *Compassion in the World's Religions: Envisioning Human Solidarity*, edited by Anindita Balslev and Dirk Evers, 101–8. Berlin: LIT Verlag, 2010.

www.myjihad.org

Neusner, Jacob. *Sacred Texts and Authority*. Cleveland, OH: Pilgrim, 1998.

Nursi, Said. *Barla Lahikası*. Istanbul: Sözler Publications, 2012.

———. *Emirdağ Lahikası*. Istanbul: Söz Publications, 2010.

———. *The Flashes*, translated by Şükran Vahide. Istanbul: Sözler Publications, 2010.

———. *Kastamonu Lahikası*. Istanbul: Söz Publications, 2010.

———. *The Letters*, translated by Şükran Vahide. Istanbul: Sözler Publications, 2010.

———. *The Rays*, translated by Şükran Vahide. Istanbul: Sözler Publications, 2010.

———. *The Words*, translated by Şükran Vahide. Istanbul: Sözler Publications, 2004.

Pew Research Center. "Muslims and Islam: Key findings in the U.S. and around the world." December 7, 2015. Online: http://www.pewresearch.org/fact-tank/2015/12/07/muslims-and-islam-key-findings-in-the-u-s-and-around-the-world/

Schimmel, Annemarie. *And Muhammad is His Messenger: The Veneration of the Prophet in Islamic Piety.* Chapel Hill, NC: The University of North Carolina Press, 1985.

Vakkasoğlu, Vehbi. *Başkasının Günahına Ağlayan Adam.* Istanbul: Nesil, 2013.

# Section Three

# Nursi and Society

# 14

# An Outline of the Social Theology of Said Nursi

SYED FARID ALATAS

## INTRODUCTION

THE CONSTRUCTION OF THE social theology of Said Nursi is based on the presupposition that there is a social dimension to his thought and that this dimension is significant enough to warrant the effort at such a construction. In fact, Nursi's theology was oriented towards issues of societal reform in several ways. He lived in a time when there was much consciousness of the decline of Muslim civilization and the backwardness of Muslims in certain areas vis-à-vis the West. At the same time, Nursi was very critical of what he understood to be the ills of Western civilization. Even Nursi's didactic approach had a social dimension to it. The many theological lessons that fill the *Risale-i Nur* are conveyed to the reader via analogies that involve accounts of relations between individuals in a modern setting. Indeed, it can be said that Nursi's work belongs to the evolving but nascent Ottoman social theology (*ictimāī ilm-i kelām*) project associated with Mehmed Şerafeddin Yaltkaya (1879–1947),[1] although there are important differences between the two scholars.

The task of constructing and presenting in a systematic manner the social theology of Said Nursi requires a statement of the subject matter of such a social theology, its methods, and its aims. For the purpose of this work, the subject matter of Nursi's social theology is said to be modern civilization and its ills (*al-amrāḍ*)[2] and, in particular, the relative backwardness of Muslim society as Nursi saw it. Nursi's methods were traditional, rooted in the sciences of Muslims as they developed centuries before Nursi's time,

---

1. Özervarlı, "Said Nursi's Project," 317–34.

2. Nursi used the metaphor of illness (*marīḍ*, pl. *amrāḍ*) and refers to the pharmacy of the Qur'an when discussing the lessons of the six "words." See Nursi, *The Damascus Sermon*, 26–27.

and include various types of analogical reasons such as allegorical comparisons (*kiyas-ı temsili*). The aim of Nursi's social theology was no less than the reform of Muslim society via the revitalization of faith in Islam.[3] Nursi believed that modern society required the demonstration of the truths of religious beliefs, such as God's existence, prophethood, resurrection, justice, and so on. The strengthening of those beliefs was necessary in order to deliver humans from the modern pathologies of unhappiness, despair, individualism, and isolationism.

I proceed as follows: The next section discusses in broad strokes social theology as a field. The purpose here is to define social theology in order that the thought of Nursi can be readily identified as belonging to this field. This is followed in the same section by a discussion of the structure or architectonics of social theology. This basic structure is derived from a reading of contemporary social theology and theory. I then turn to the elaboration of Nursi's theology, covering his assessment of Western and Muslim civilizations, his delineation of their problems and prognosis for the future. I argue here that it is useful to draw from European as well as Russian thought in order to elaborate on some of Nursi's ideas. This is in order to show that much of Nursi's assessment of the problems of modern civilization accord with the views of some Europeans and Russians of his time. The section after this deals with Nursi's ideas on the emancipation of modern society from the problems that it created for itself. The last section introduces Nursi's methodology, which I maintain has implications for his social theology. I conclude this chapter with a discussion of areas for further development.

## THE DEFINITION AND STRUCTURE OF SOCIAL THEOLOGY

Social theology can be defined as theology that takes as its point of departure the reality of the social, that is, the reality of human social organization and the myriad of problems that this organization creates, faces and attempts to solve. Social theology is not necessarily opposed to traditional theological doctrines. Rather it merely emphasizes the social dimension in human life and requires traditional theology to engage with the challenges presented to us by life in society. It does so in two ways. First of all, it emphasizes the relevance of theology for social life. An example would be the impact that the divine attributes have or should have on human thought and action. Secondly, theological issues are discussed in terms of social categories such as class, the elite, the state, intellectuals, or social issues such as corruption, economic exploitation, political oppression, alienation, and so on. Social theology, unlike traditional theology, is not confined to the personal or spiritual dimension of a human's relationship with God. It is concerned with the implications of the religious understanding of God for how we may understand the nature of human society and its problems. Social theology as a field of study and reflection is a modern

---

3. Nursi has been said to belong to the *iḥyāʾ* or revitalization tradition of Islam but, nevertheless founded his thought on the traditional Islamic sciences. See Özervarlı, "Said Nursi's Project," 319; and Leaman, "Nursi's Place in the *Iḥyāʾ* Tradition," 314–24, cited in Özervarlı, "Said Nursi's Project," 319, n. 17.

phenomenon, having emerged in the context of the rise of capitalism and the responses of theologies to the challenges presented by this rise. Social theology developed in both Christian and Muslim societies, but it is more developed in the former, where it takes the form of liberation theology.

The theology of liberation attempts to reflect on the experience and meaning of the faith based on the commitment to abolish injustice and to build a new society; this theology must be verified by the practice of that community, by active, effective participation in the struggle which the exploited social classes have undertaken against their oppressors.[4]

This introduces another element in social theology, that of social injustice. Social theology is not merely concerned with the social dimension of human life but with problems related to the poor, economic exploitation, political oppression, corruption, and so on. Social theology is not neutral about these problems and takes a definite stance with regards to their genesis, development and solution. Furthermore, because social theology is concerned with the social in ways that traditional theology is not, it makes use of the concepts and theories of the social sciences. In the case of liberation theology, this use has been selective. Certain frameworks in the social sciences, such as structural functionalism, were rejected, while others such as dialectical or historical structural analyses, derived from the neo-Marxist tradition, were embraced, as they resonated with the position taken by social theology regarding social issues.[5]

What are the basic elements that make up social theology, or more generally, social thought? Any systematic thinking on the nature of the social world usually comprises the following elements:

1. A concept of the human being
2. An understanding of the human construction of the social world that emerges from this concept of humans.
3. An understanding of the central problems of this world or of the human condition.
4. An understanding of the variety of responses to these central problems.
5. An assessment of the prospects of dealing with or overcoming these problems.

Let us take the example of Karl Marx's sociological theory. Marx was first and foremost a theorist of capitalist society. His is a theory about what capitalist society is, how it functions, what its essential features are, and what its future is. Capitalism is a system in which wage labor is sold to capitalists. As capital expands with technological advances and increases in plant size, labor becomes more specialized, routinized, and interdependent. Workers become alienated in a number of ways from the work process, from fellow workers, from their product and, ultimately, their human potential. Alienation is one of the more important sociological concepts developed by Marx. Workers also develop what Marx called class consciousness and enter into a hostile relation with the state. The state performs the function of perpetuating the capitalist system through a number of mechanisms. The system is also

---

4. Gutierrez, *A Theology of Liberation*, 307.

5. Smith, *The Emergence of Liberation Theology*, 28–29.

perpetuated through ideological domination by the ruling class. At the same time, overproduction and underconsumption result in periodic crisis, manifested in the decline in profits, wages, and employment. This leads to a final crisis in which labor takes over the means of production and initiates the transition to socialism. Each of these aspects of Marx's theory are important sociological topics. The identification and elaboration of Nursi's social theology requires, in the initial stages, our having a picture of his overall conception of society, its central problems, his view of the human condition and his prognosis for humanity.

## NURSI'S SOCIAL THEOLOGY

Before discussing Nursi's social theology, it is necessary to explore the definition of theory. This is because we are saying that Nursi's social theology is a social theory about the nature and characteristics of modern civilization. What do we mean by theory? In general, there are four types of theories: empirical, ethical, theological, and metaphysical. Metaphysical theories are concerned with the ultimate nature of reality which transcends the observable or phenomena, that is, things observable by the senses. A metaphysical theory of the development of modern science and technology may explain this in terms of one stage in the unfolding of reason. The ultimate nature of reality is pure reason, that is, that whose existence is not dependent on anything and which is the cause of all existence. Theological theories explain reality by recourse to theories about the nature of God. For example, outbreaks of war may be explained in terms of the degree of sin in certain societies or natural disasters in terms of the fact that revelation was not accepted or heeded. Ethical theories express preference or distaste for reality in accordance with certain standards of evaluation, and they specify the ideal goal toward which reality should be changed. An example is the view that the charging of interest for financial transactions is bad for society, resulting in a ban on such interest.

Nursi's work does contain metaphysical, theological and ethical theories. In this work, however, we are concerned with Nursi's empirical theory. Empirical theories offer generalizations about observable reality—in our case, observable social reality. The theory of Nursi that we are interested in here is his theory of the nature and characteristics of modern civilization. In matters concerning jurisprudence and its principles (*fiqh* and *uṣūl al-fiqh*), Nursi adopts a more holistic approach. To my mind, Nursi's important role here was to give a social dimension to *kalām* or theology. It is interesting to note that the attempt to establish a social theology in the Muslim world took place as early as the 1910s in the Ottoman empire, decades before it became popular in the form of liberation theology in Latin America and the Philippines. Özervarlı notes the example of Mehmed Şerafeddin Yaltkaya's (1879–1947) *ictimāī ilm-i kelām* (social theology) project.[6] I believe it would be accurate to state that there is a social theology to be found in Nursi's works and that this social theology does not occupy an insignificant place in his overall thought. While Nursi was not a *mutakallim* in the classical sense of the term,[7] he was very much concerned with

---

6. Özervarlı, "Said Nursi's Project," 319.
7. Ibid., 322.

the relevance of theology for the social life of humans. On the divine attributes, Nursi emphasized their consequences for human action in this world, particularly in relation to the contest between good and evil.

> The All-Glorious Creator of the universe has two sorts of Names, those pertaining to His Glory and those pertaining to His Beauty. Since these Names require to demonstrate their decrees through different manifestations, the Glorious Creator blended together opposites in the universe. Bringing them face to face, he gave them aggressive and defensive positions, in the form of a sort of wise and beneficial contest. Through making the opposites transgress one another's bounds, He brought conflict and change into being, and made the universe subject to the law of change and transformation and the principles of progress and advancement. In humankind, the comprehensive fruit of the tree of creation, he made that law of contest in even stranger form, and opening the door to striving, which would be the means of all human progress, He gave Satan's party certain faculties with which to be able to challenge God's party.[8]

In other words, the basic nature of social reality is conflict. Conflict is the primary factor that explains change and progress in human society. Society progresses as a result of successfully struggling against the people of misguidance. Progress is essentially a struggle between two types of groups, the party of Satan and the party of God. Here Nursi relates theology to social relations, as he does also in the following:

> For one of the greatest results of the universe's creation is man's worship and his responding to Divine dominicality with belief and submission. However, due to the denial of unbelief, the people of unbelief and misguidance reject that supreme result, which is the ultimate cause of beings and the reason for their continued existence, and therefore perpetrate a sort of transgression against the rights of all beings.[9]

Here, the consequences of unbelief are described not in terms of the fate of the individual soul, but in terms of the transgression against the rights of all beings. Nursi sees his task to chart a "new way in the life of human society" and to "act in conformity with the natural laws in force in the universe." Failure to do so would mean that he would not "be successful in beneficial works and in progress."[10] In fact, Nursi sets his agenda in very social terms:

> Yes, by birth and the way I have lived I am from the class of common people, and I am one of those who by temperament and intellectually have accepted the way of "equality of rights." And due to compassion and the justice proceeding from Islam, I am one of those who for a long time have opposed and worked against the despotism and oppression of the elite class called the bourgeouisie. I therefore support total justice with all my strength, and oppose tyranny, oppression, arbitrary power, and despotism.[11]

Thus, Nursi builds a moral and spiritual basis for social existence which cannot simply be established or determined by rules, regulations or law.

8. Nursi, *The Flashes Collection*, 115.
9. Ibid., 119.
10. Ibid., 225.
11. Ibid., 226.

The subject matter of Nursi's social theology is the pathology of modern civilization. We have already noted that Nursi used the term illness or sickness in *The Damascus Sermon* when speaking of the problems of Muslim society. A similar term, pathology, has been used in Western discourses on modern civilization, the idea here being to draw upon the body metaphor to talk critically about the human condition. Nursi's critique of modern civilization involved the critique of Muslim society as well. By Nursi's time, the Ottoman Empire and other Muslim nations were thoroughly integrated into the world capitalist system and international political economy and were being affected culturally by the West as well. Nevertheless, Nursi differentiated between the problems of the modern West and Muslim societies.

For Nursi, the West was European civilization or Europe, as noted by Thomas Michel.[12] Nursi's critique of modern civilization was first and foremost a critique of Europe, as Europe was the most direct manifestation of what went wrong with modernity. Muslim societies were struggling during Nursi's time to be modern, with their own pathologies functioning as obstacles in the path to the modern world. It should not be understood that Nursi saw no value in Western civilization. Nursi saw two sides to modern Europe. His famous statement "Europe is two" refers to the distinction between the first Europe founded on true Christianity and the second Europe that was corrupt and founded on the philosophy of naturalism.[13] As Michel noted, Nursi did not spend much time talking about the first Europe as he had no quarrel with it.[14] The Europe that was problematic for modern civilization was the one informed by the philosophy of naturalism and atheism.

Much of Western social thought during Nursi's lifetime was concerned with the problem of freedom. They questioned the assumption of the inherent positive relationship between reason and freedom. Thinkers of the European Enlightenment believed in the supremacy of reason and that it could solve all problems. On the other hand, the classical social thinkers who came later did not accept this view. The phenomenon of alienation as discussed by Marx, the rationalization of increasing spheres of life that concerned Max Weber, and the experience of anomie that preoccupied Emile Durkheim all testify to the miscalculation of the Enlightenment and to the idea that reason can be ultimately unreasonable. Nursi, like his contemporaries in the West, also identified what he considered to be a central problem of modern civilization. In discussing Nursi's views on modern civilization, it is necessary to point out that he had different criticisms for European and Muslim societies. We deal first with Nursi's critique of the West.

## Second Europe and Its Harmful Philosophy

Nursi clearly saw the benefit of science and technology and European civilization's contribution to these. He also recognized the virtues of European civilization. At the same time, however, he found Europe to be a "noxious, dissolute

---

12. Michel, "Grappling with Modern Civilization," 79–108; 81.

13. Nursi, *Flashes*, 160.

14. Michel, "Grappling with Modern Civilization," 82.

civilization" informed by a "meaningless, harmful philosophy." To this Europe, he said,

> Know this, O second Europe! You hold a diseased and misguided philosophy in your right hand and a harmful and corrupt civilization in your left, and claim "Humankinds' happiness is with these two!" May your two hands be broken and may these two filthy presents of yours be the death of you! . . . And so they shall be![15]

These sound like very harsh words. However, we must remember that Nursi was not calling for the destruction of Western or European civilization as a whole, but only for what he saw to be its harmful philosophy and outlook. In fact, Nursi refers to the influence of the European outlook on Muslims:

> At this time, however, due to the dominance of European civilization and the supremacy of natural philosophy and the preponderance of the conditions of worldly life, minds and hearts have become scattered, and endeavor and favor divided. Minds have become strangers to non-material matters![16]

As we shall soon see, Nursi is not merely critiquing the materialist outlook on life, but also the deceptive nature of this outlook. At the same time, Nursi recognized that there was an emerging awareness in the West of destructive philosophy:

> Because of the extreme tyranny and despotism of this last World War and its merciless destruction, and hundreds of innocents being scattered and ruined on account of a single enemy, and the awesome despair of the defeated, and the fearsome alarm of the victors and their ghastly pangs of conscience arising from the supremacy they are unable to maintain and the destruction they are unable to repair, and the utter transitoriness and ephemerality of the life of this world and the deceptive, opiate nature of the fantasies of civilization becoming apparent to all, and the exalted abilities lodged in human nature and the human essence being wounded in a universal and awesome manner, and heedlessness and misguidance and deaf, lifeless nature being smashed by the diamond sword of the Qur'an, and the exceedingly ugly, exceedingly cruel true face of world politics becoming apparent, which is the widest and most suffocating and deceptive cover for heedlessness and misguidance, most certainly and without any shadow of a doubt, since the life of this world—which is the metaphorical beloved of humankind—is thus ugly and transient, man's true nature will search with all its strength for eternal life, which it truly loves and yearns for, just as there are signs of this occurring in the North, the West, and in America.[17]

Furthermore, Nursi asks us to realize that it cannot be that the "sole aim of the delicate and subtle senses, the sensitive faculties and members, the well-ordered limbs and systems, the inquisitive feelings and senses included in the machine of your life is restricted to satisfying the low desires of the base soul."[18]

Nursi's summary of the problem of European civilization is presented in the collection of aphorisms entitled "Seeds of Reality." Here Nursi states that modern

---

15. Nursi, *Flashes*, 160.
16. Nursi, *The Words*, 496.
17. Ibid., 167.
18. Ibid., 139.

civilization is founded on five negative principles:

1. Its point of support is force, the mark of which is aggression.
2. Its aim and goal is benefit, the mark of which is jostling and tussling.
3. Its principle in life is conflict, the mark of which is strife.
4. The bond between the masses is racialism and negative nationalism, which is nourished through devouring others; its mark is collision.
5. Its enticing service is inciting lust and passion and gratifying the desires. But lust transforms man into a beast.[19]

Michel restates these principles as follows:[20]

1. Might makes right.
2. Self-interest and competition.
3. The law of the jungle, everyone for himself.
4. My race and nation are superior.
5. I have a right to whatever I want.

How can one conceptualize Nursi's statement of the central problem of modern civilization? I propose that at the heart of Nursi's claim is the marginalization of God from humanity's concerns, or what we may refer to as the phenomenon of desacralization. This follows logically from Nursi's criticism of the dominance of naturalism in modern civilization, a philosophy according to which everything is explained in terms of natural causes. As a result, "minds become strangers" to non-material explanations. Throughout Nursi's writings it is possible to identify various problems discussed or touched upon by Nursi that are manifestations of the desacralization of life. These include problems such as alienation and anomie. However, a more general problem that subsumes those of alienation and anomie is that of nihilism.

I am not suggesting here that Nursi directly addressed the problem of nihilism or that he was consciously engaging the philosophy of nihilism that had already developed in his time, particularly in Europe and Russia. I would say, however, that Nursi was acutely aware of the problem of meaninglessness in life and that he related this meaninglessness to the expunging of spiritual matters from the concerns of modern humans. By nihilism I refer to both moral nihilism in the sense of the idea of the removal of moral restrictions on behavior, as well as existential nihilism, which has to do with the idea of the purposelessness or meaninglessness of life.[21] Nursi has hinted at the problem of meaninglessness on various occasions. The aphorism "If there is no imagined goal, or if it is forgotten or pretended to be forgotten, thoughts perpetually revolve around the 'I'" refers to the meaninglessness of life.[22]

Nursi's concern with the problem of meaninglessness is also indicated by his continual references to its opposite, that is, the meaningfulness of creation. This comes across unambiguously in Nursi's discussion on the distinction between two types of meaning, that is, nominal (*mana-yı ismî*) and significative (*mana-yı*

---

19. Nursi, "Seeds of Reality," 541–54; 548.
20. Michel, "Grappling with Modern Civilization," 88.
21. In this connection, see Özdemir, "Said Nursi and J. P. Sartre."
22. Nursi, "Seeds of Reality," 546.

*harfî*) meanings.[23] Indeed, the meaningfulness of our existence is derived from this distinction. Consider the following statement of Nursi:

> According to the apparent meaning of things, which looks to each thing itself, everything is transitory, lacking, accidental, non-existent. But according to the meaning that signifies something other than itself and in respect of each thing being a mirror to the All-Glorious Maker's Names and charged with various duties, each is a witness, it is witnessed, and it is existent. The purification and cleansing of a person at this stage is as follows:
>
> In his existence he is non-existent, and in his non-existence he has existence. That is to say, if he values himself and attributes existence to himself, he is in a darkness of non-existence as great as the universe. That is, if he relies on his individual existence and is unmindful of the True Giver of Existence, he has an individual light of existence like that of a fire-fly and is submerged in an endless darkness of non-existence and separation. But if he gives up egotism and sees that he is a mirror of the manifestations of the True Giver of Existence, he gains all beings and an infinite existence. For he who finds the Necessary Existent One, the manifestation of Whose Names all beings manifest, finds everything.[24]

We find meaning in our existence by recognizing the significative meaning of our lives as a mirror to the divine attributes, and gain an infinite existence.

The five negative principles that form the basis of modern civilization are related to the problem of nihilism. To the extent that moral restrictions on behavior are removed and to the extent that life is seen as purposeless and meaningless, people will live by the five principles, particularly principles one, two, three, and five. What Nursi was referring to here are principles such as self-interest, the gratification of desires and the use of force to realize these interests and desires. While these characteristics and traits are to be found in all civilizations in all times, Nursi is saying that they are principles of modern civilization. This reminds us of what we may refer to as the negative principles of Russian society as captured by Fyodor Dostoevsky's *The Brothers Karamazov*.

Dostoevsky's *The Brothers Karamazov* tells the story of what in Nursi's terms would be the negative principles of Russian society. Through the characters Ivan Karamazov and Zossima the Monk, Dostoevsky discusses how the influence of Enlightenment ideas paradoxically leads to authoritarianism, individualism, despair, and the loss of values, all of which are disguised in a Roman Catholic reform orientation espoused by the Westernized Russian elite, and the response to this from the supporters of Russian orthodoxy. The context is nineteenth-century Russia in the midst of the breakdown of the feudal system and the influx of Western Enlightenment ideas.

The promises of science to liberate man, as noted by Zossima the Monk, are false. Science's denial of spirituality and the proclamation of the reign of freedom only resulted in the multiplication of desire, envy, isolation, and even suicide. The problem is with the elite who want to base justice on reason alone and dispense with

---

23. Nursi, *Al-Mathnawī al-'arabī al-nurī*, 62. See also Özdemir, "Said Nursi and J.P Sartre," 22–23.

24. Nursi, *The Words*, 493.

Christ. Rationalists like Ivan no longer have faith in God because God failed to live up to his promise of saving humanity. Instead, God allowed suffering and misery on earth to run its course. If God were truly just, he would allow for perfection on earth by ordering the world in such a manner to as to eliminate suffering and provide comfort for all. Furthermore, since God is unjust there is no morality, since morality can only come from a good God. Ivan, therefore, advocates the leading of immoral lives founded on self-interest and worldly desires, and the rejection of God. This is his nihilistic outlook. From Nursi's point of view, self-interest, the pursuit of worldly desires, the excessive faith in reason, and egoism would be among the traits that make up the negative principles of Russian society.[25]

## Nursi's Critique of the Muslim World

Nursi's critique of modern civilization was not one-sided and biased. He did not reserve moral critique for the West alone. Nursi did not deny that Muslim societies were also adopting the negative principles of modern civilization.[26] At the same time, he believed that there were other problems that beset Muslim societies and which accounted for the material backwardness of the Muslim world in comparison to Europe. He referred to these collectively as the six dire sicknesses of Muslim nations:[27]

1. The rising life of despair and hopelessness in social life.
2. The death of truthfulness in social and political life.
3. Love of enmity.
4. Not knowing the luminous bonds that bind the believers to one another.
5. Despotism, which spreads, becoming widespread as though it was various contagious diseases.
6. Restricting endeavor to what is personally beneficial

Here I shall focus on two of the sicknesses, despair and ignorance of the luminous bonds. Nursi's reference to the pervasiveness of despair is very instructive.

Despair is an important theme in social theory, particularly since the nineteenth century, and continues to be an important phenomenon today. In European thought, despair is often treated under the category of anomie. Anomie refers to a state in which society fails to exercise sufficient regulation or constraints over the desires of individuals such that they are tormented at not being able to satisfy these desires. The unlimited desires and their insatiability due to the nature of things constantly renews the torture of individuals, finally resulting in despair. This is the condition of the anomie discussed by Emile Durkheim.[28] It is interesting to inquire how despair (*al-yā's*) in Nursi differs from the same in Durkheim. Despair and related concepts such as anomie are important themes in Western thought and have spawned important theories and empirical research. Although despair and anomie are important phenomena in the Muslim world, they are under-researched. Nursi's identification of the phenomenon

---

25. Dostoevsky, *The Grand Inquisitor*.
26. See Michel, "Grappling with Modern Civilization," 89.
27. Nursi, *The Damascus Sermon*, 26–27.
28. Durkheim, *Suicide*, 241–48.

should result in serious conceptual and empirical attention to the problem.

One of the sicknesses identified by Nursi is the ignorance of the special bonds that bind believers, or what Nursi calls the luminous bonds (*al-rawābiṭ al-nūrāniyyah*).[29] While the terminology differs, what Nursi has in mind resonates with Ibn Khaldūn's concept of *'aṣabiyyah*. Only a society with a strong *'aṣabiyyah* could establish domination over one with a weak *'aṣabiyyah*.[30] In this context, *'aṣabiyyah* refers to the feeling of solidarity among the members of a group that is derived from the knowledge that they share a common descent. However, the social cohesion expressed by the concept of *'aṣabiyyah* is only partly derived from agnatic ties in tribal social organizations. While all tribal groups have stronger or weaker *'aṣabiyyah*s based on kinship, religion can also bring about such social cohesion, as was the case with the Arabs who needed Islam in order to subordinate themselves and unite as a social organization.[31]

Although Nursi used the term *rawābiṭ* and not *'aṣabiyyah* to refer to bonds uniting people, it is likely he had in mind what Ibn Khaldūn meant by an overarching *'aṣabiyyah* determined by religion. Nursi says that through the bond of sacred nationhood "All the people of Islam become like a single tribe."[32] Here Nursi is using "tribe" in a metaphorical sense. He is saying that Muslims lack the solidarity that can only come about if "all the groups of Islam are bound to each other with a luminous chain."[33] Nursi is chastising the congregation at the Umayyad Mosque during his sermon for taking the view that they are powerless to act for the sake of morality or their material interests. An important theme in Nursi's work, therefore, is the role of social solidarity and unity in the progress of the Muslim world. Essentially, he is saying that the solidarity had dissipated and its potential forgotten. Nursi did not elaborate on the theme but we may develop a better understanding of the importance of the "luminous bonds that bind believers" by referring to Ibn Khaldun.

## The Problem of Extremism

The problem of extremism in the Muslim world was not listed as one of the six sicknesses of the Muslims by Nursi. However, Nursi's reference to the Prophet's saying to the effect that he was sent by God to perfect morality (*akhlāq*)[34] implies that he placed great emphasis on morality as a defining feature of Islam. A Nursian approach that is relevant today would stress the need to reintroduce *akhlāq* as the core of religion. This is necessary in order to reclaim the space occupied by extremism.

Muslim modernism is a consequence of the contact between Islam and Western modernization in the nineteenth century and after. It is based on the idea of the need for reform in law, society, and politics, as well as moral and spiritual issues, in order for Muslims to progress in science and technology. Modernism has two streams. One is modernist

---

29. Nursi, *Al-Khuṭbah al-shāmiyyah*, 28.

30. Ibn Khaldūn, *Muqaddimat Ibn Khaldūn*, 139; 154 [vol. 1: 284–85; 313]. Page numbers in brackets refer to Franz Rosenthal's English translation, *The Muqaddimah*, 3 vols., from which these quotations are taken.

31. Ibid., 151 [vol. 1: 305–6].

32. Nursi, *The Damascus Sermon*, 52.

33. Ibid.

34. Ibid., 25.

accommodationism. According to this orientation, Islam should inform public life, but is interpreted as being congruent with Western ideologies and systems such as democracy and capitalism. Modernist accommodationism does advocate a return to the Qur'an and *sunna* to seek fresh interpretations that are compatible with modern times. Furthermore, it is flexible because it limits the authoritative sources to the Qur'an and *sunna*, the latter itself being limited by a strict *ḥadīth* criticism. Also, modernist accommodationism supports a radical reinterpretation of sources on polygamy, *hadd* punishments, *jihad*, and the treatment of non-Muslims. An example is the view that the requirement of four witnesses voids *hadd* punishment in practice; or the condition of equal treatment of wives as stated in the Qur'an as impossible to fulfill in practice, thereby establishing monogamy as the ideal. At the same time, Islam is flexible enough to allow polygamy when circumstances call for it.

The other stream of modernism is modernist extremism. This refers to those orientations that are often labeled fundamentalist, Islamist or radical Islamist. It is represented by activists such as Sayyid Qutb and Mawdudi. There is no identification of Islam with Western thought. Extremists place more emphasis on implementing *sharīʿah* (which they understand in narrow terms as a system of rules and regulations codified by jurists of the past).[35] The modernist extremists share with the modernist accommodationists the quest for progress as defined in terms of the modern economy, political systems, etc., but differ from them in terms of the following traits:

1. intolerance of others
2. overemphasis on rules and regulations
3. forbidding of what is allowed by others
4. non-contextual/historical interpretation of Qur'an/*ḥadīth*
5. literalism

Examples of extremist orientations are Wahhabism, some orientations to be found among various ideologues of the Muslim Brotherhood, as well as those of the Jemaat–i Islami. A more elaborate account of Nursi's social theology would attempt to conceptualize his notion of extremism as well as reconstruct his idea of the antidote to the pathology of extremism.

## Nursi and the Theme of Laziness

There is one further area that arises from Nursi's discussion of the six dire sicknesses of the Muslim world. Nursi had made several references to the laziness of the Muslims. For example:

> And because of this despair, Muslims even suppose the indifference and despondency of others to be an excuse for their own laziness and say: "What is it to me?" Saying, "Everybody is contemptible, like me," they abandon the courageousness of belief and fail to perform their Islamic duties.[36]

Nursi also tells the congregation at the Umayyad Mosque:

---

35. See Shepard, "Islam and Ideology," 307-36.

36. Nursi, *Damascus Sermon*, 44.

Do not make apologies, saying: "We do no harm, but neither do we have the power to do anything beneficial; therefore, we are excused." Such an apology is not acceptable. Your laziness and saying: "What is it to me?," and your displaying no effort and not getting into the working spirit through Islamic unity and true Islamic brotherhood, have done much damage and are an injustice to you.[37]

Nursi says that the sin of the Muslims is great due to their laziness, although much could be expected of them should the different Muslim groups unite.[38] Now, it is interesting that the accusation of laziness hurled by colonial scholarship against the peoples of Asia and Africa resulted in responses that exposed the myth of the lazy native.

The Filipino thinker, José Rizal (1861–96), noted that the Spaniards blamed the backwardness of the Filipinos on their indolence. The Spaniards charged that the Filipinos had little love for work. As Syed Hussein Alatas noted, the unwillingness of the Filipinos to cultivate under the *encomenderos* was interpreted out of context and understood to be the result of indolence, which was in turn attributed to their nature.[39]

Rizal noted that the "miseries of a people without freedom should not be imputed to the people but to their rulers."[40] That the Filipinos are an inherently lazy people was not true. Although there was some indolence, it was not a cause of backwardness. Rather it was the backwardness and disorder of Filipino colonial society that caused indolence.

Prior to the colonial period, they were not indolent. They controlled trade routes, were involved in agriculture, mining and manufacturing. But when their destiny was taken away from them, they became indolent.

The theme of indolence in colonial scholarship is an important one that formed a vital part of the ideology of colonial capitalism. Rizal was probably the first to deal with it systematically.[41] This concern was later taken up by Alatas in *The Myth of the Lazy Native*. It is interesting that while Rizal and Syed Hussein Alatas debunk the myth of the lazy native, Nursi affirms laziness as a reality. This suggests further areas of research in Nursi studies which can benefit from the approaches of Rizal and Alatas in which laziness is conceptualized and its discourses critically studied.

## LESSONS FROM THE PHARMACY OF THE QUR'AN

Our introduction to Nursi's social theology would be incomplete without an exposition of the solutions he proposed for overcoming the problems and obstacles to the spiritual and material progress of the Muslim world. If we could summarize Nursi's perspective on this with a single concept, it would be that of *akhlāq*. Related to *akhlāq* is the concept of justice, including social justice.

Said Nursi's thinking on the question of social justice is intimately linked to his theodicy. In *The Words*, life is conceived as a journey of partaking of God's bounty, of receiving instruction or gaining knowledge from him, and of

37. Ibid., 52.
38 Ibid., 53.
39. Alatas, *The Myth of the Lazy Native*, 125.
40. Rizal, "The Truth for All," 31–38.

41. Rizal, "The Indolence of the Filipino," 111–39.

remembering and thanking him. If we are true believers, we would believe in God's mercy and be certain that there is another realm or abode beyond this transient life. Said Nursi provides twelve proofs of the existence of such a realm. Basically, the provision of an afterlife for us is a matter of God's generosity, mercy and justice. But to receive the gift of a goodly ending (*ḥusn al-khātimah*), we have to live this life in line with divine law. We are required, indeed, to emulate the attributes of God, one of them being that of justice (*'adālah*). As Nursi says, the believer affirms Almighty God and views this world as an abode where the Names of God are recited, and an abode in which to gain knowledge from contemplating the Names. Nursi did not only speak of God's justice but of social justice, that is, justice conceived of and established, with God's instruction, by humans in this world. Nursi himself represents a type of man with a particular ideal of excellence that is characterized by a certain vision of justice.

Any discussion of justice in the Islamic context must be prefaced by the definition of key concepts relevant to the area of enquiry. For the purpose of this paper, the concepts of *'adālah* and *mīzān* are relevant. In Islamic discourse, the term that is usually translated as justice is *'adālah*. In the work of Nursi, in keeping with the Qur'an and with Islamic thought in general, it appears alongside the concept of *mīzān*, or balance. When Nursi discusses the justice of God, he speaks of both justice and balance. For example, he suggests that it is impossible that God, who established justice and balance in the cosmic order, would not favor those who believe in that justice and who worship him.[42]

In Islamic jurisprudence, the majority view has been that *'adālah* refers to a qualification according to which one abides by the prescribed obligations and recommendations of the *sharī'ah*, or Islamic code of morality and conduct, and avoids what it prohibited and disapproved of.[43] A specific attribute of *'adālah* is *mīzān*. This is in line with the Qur'anic view of God's justice: "And we shall set up balances (*al-muwāzīn*) of justice for the day of resurrection, then none will be dealt with unjustly in anything. And if there be the weight of a mustard seed, we will bring it. And sufficient are we to take account."[44]

Writing a few centuries later, Ibn Khaldūn noted earlier scholars' treatment of the social function of law. For example, he refers to the speech of the Persian priest, Mobedh, before King Bahrām bin Bahrām, as related by Mas'ūdī:

> O king, the might of royal authority materializes only through the religious law, obedience toward God, and compliance with His commands and prohibitions. The religious law persists only through royal authority. Mighty royal authority is accomplished only through men. Men persist only with the help of property. The only way to property is through cultivation. The only way to cultivation is through justice. Justice is a balance set up among huhumankind.

42. Nursi, *The Words*, 77. See also the Arabic translation of *The Words*, which more accurately reflects the use of Islamic terminology in the Turkish original—Nursi, *Al-Kalimāt*, 68.

43. Ibn Rushd, *The Distinguished Jurist's Primer*, 556. See also the Arabic original, *Bidāyat*, 678.

44. Qur'an 21:47.

The Lord set it up and appointed an overseer for it, and that (overseer) is the ruler.[45]

Of particular interest to us here is the statement, "Justice is a balance set up among huhumankind." (*Al-adl al-mīzān al-manṣūb bayn al-khalīqah*). This is in reference to human justice. If we take all three quotations above into consideration, it is clear that the concepts of *'adālah* and *mīzān* refer both to God's as well as human justice. Although the notion of justice among humans has always been paramount in Islamic jurisprudence as an ideal to be achieved, the actual study of justice as achieved in society had rarely been systematically studied by Muslims. In other words, it is the theological dimension of justice that had usually been given precedence over the sociological dimension. The sociological dimension, however, cannot be neglected. It has been observed by many that the main factor in the hierarchy of cause and effect is the quality of leadership. To the extent that leaders lacked the qualities of justice, balance and morality (*akhlāq*), they would not be effective in creating a just social order. Instead, society would be ruled by what Syed Hussein Alatas called the *bebalians*[46] (*Malay*) or the fools. Among the traits of the fool are (i) the inability to recognize a problem; (ii) the inability to solve a problem if told to him; (iii) the inability to learn what is required; (iv) the inability to learn the art of learning; (v) not admitting that he is a fool.[47]

Thus, Nursi's overall notion of the key to progress, I believe, is the concept of *akhlāq*. Indeed, *The Damascus Sermon* begins with a reference to a *ḥadīth* that is similar to the following: "Verily God sent me to complete the nobility of morality (*makārim al-akhlāq*) and practice."[48] The mind that possesses the nobility of morality (*makārim al-akhlāq*) never fears to constantly differentiate between truth and falsehood and is not fearful of losing wealth, prestige and position as a result of standing on principle.

## The Dialogue with Christianity

Nursi's hope for change, reform, and progress was not directed solely at Muslim societies. He also believed that Europe would change for the better, and that this change would come about as a result of dialogue with the Muslim world. As he once said famously:

> So, supported by the fact that the clever fields of Europe and America have produced crops of brilliant and exacting scholars like Carlyle and Bismarck, I say with all assurance: Europe and America are pregnant with Islam; one day they will give birth to an Islamic state. Just as the Ottomans were pregnant with Europe and gave birth to a European state.[49]

He further speculated that true Christianity, as a result of the dialogue, would unite with Islam.[50]

---

45. Ibn Khaldūn, *The Muqaddimah*, 39.

46. Derived from the word *bebal*, meaning stupid, indolent and stubborn. See Alatas, *Intellectuals in Developing Societies*, 30.

47. Alatas, *Intellectuals in Developing Societies*, 45.

48 Imam Malik, *al-Muwatta*, Book 47, Hadith 1643.

49. Nursi, *The Damascus Sermon*, 35.

50. Ibid., 36.

## THE METHODOLOGY OF THE RISALE-I NUR

In the previous section, reference was made to Nursi's methodology, specifically concerning his use of analogical reasoning. Nursi's analogical comparative method is extremely important because its cultivation in Muslim societies has important consequences for the development of the various fields of knowledge. The model of performing *ta'wīl* does not merely refer to a method of interpretation, but forms the basis of the culture and civilization of Muslims. In other words, the development of the arts and sciences and everything else associated with civilization is dependent on the pervasiveness of a traditionalist culture informed by the method of *ta'wīl*:

1. Where texts are concerned, the *ẓāhir* and *bāṭin* refer to the exoteric and the esoteric respectively, and the movement from literal to allegorical meanings. There is also a sense in which *bāṭin* refers to what Franklin Lewis defines as the "real experiential comprehension achieved through self-discipline and purity, not through easy or superficial or worldly understanding."[51]

2. Where the study of society is concerned, they refer to the facts, on the one hand, and to the laws and motive forces underlying social and historical change, on the other. This is the sense in which Ibn Khaldūn refers to the *ẓāhir* and *bāṭin*.

3. Concerning the study of history, the *ẓāhir* refers to overt action and behavior, while the *bāṭin* refers to the intentions underlying such acts. Such a distinction is needed for the adjudication between the positions of the Sunnīs and Shī'īs over the events at Ghadīr al-Khumm and the "Pen and Paper" incident.

4. The *ẓāhir* also refers to the overt practices of a religious community, while the *bāṭin* refers to their "hidden" practices and the rationalization that informs these practices. The example from this paper was taken from 'Alawī jurisprudence.

5. The *ẓāhir* refers to the outer form of rituals and other practices, while the *bāṭin* refers to the inner experience that accompanies these practices. The example is Sūfī rituals.

6. The *ẓāhir* and *bāṭin* also correspond to the distinction between *mana-yı ismî* and *mana-yı harfî*, the aspect of things that look to themselves, and the aspect that looks to God. As Nursi notes, this is explained in all books on Arabic grammar and is something basic.

Nursi's explanation of the distinction, by way of analogy, is very instructive:

> When you look in the mirror, if you look at it for the glass, you will intentionally see the glass; in it, Re'fet will strike the eye secondly, indirectly. Whereas if your purpose is to look at the mirror in order to see your blessed face, you will intentionally see lovable Re'fet. You will exclaim: "*So blessed be God, the Best of Creators!*" The glass of the mirror will strike your eye secondly and indirectly. Thus, in the first instance, the glass of the mirror is "the meaning which looks to the thing itself," while Re'fet is its "significative meaning." In the second instance, the glass of the mirror is "the significative

---

51. Lewis, *Rumi—Past and Present*, 405.

meaning," that is, it is not looked at for itself, but for another meaning; that is, the reflection. The reflection is "the meaning which looks to the thing itself." That is, it is included in one respect in the definition "it points to a meaning in itself." While the mirror verifies the definition of its 'significative meaning', which is "it points to the meaning of another."[52]

Nursi goes on to explain that according to the Qur'anic view, all things in the universe are letters that have *mana-yı harfî* or significative meaning. They point to the names and attributes of the Maker. This is to be contrasted with materialist, or what Nursi calls soulless, philosophy that points to a meaning in itself. The consequence of Nursi's method of allegorical comparison is the contribution to the development of a culture of multidimensional interpretation.

## CONCLUSION

The social theology of Said Nursi can be considered to be a theology of reform. This is because the two main aspects of this theology concerns the negative principles of Western civilization which Nursi thought had also infiltrated Muslim societies, and the six dire sicknesses of the Muslim world. Nursi's social theology, therefore, provides diagnoses of modern civilization and suggests areas for reform.

The task of reconstructing Nursi's social theology should not be confined to presenting what is already stated in the *Risale-i Nur*. There are concepts discussed and topics raised by Nursi that need to be further defined and elaborated. This can be done by recourse to the contributions of both Muslim and non-Muslim scholarship. For example, we may understand better Nursi's concept, *al-rawābiṭ al-nūrāniyyah* (luminous bonds) by bringing in a discussion of Ibn Khaldūn's *ʿaṣabiyyah*. Nursi's discussion on despair (*al-yāʾs*) can also benefit from, as well as enrich, discussions of concepts such as alienation and anomie that have been treated in European thought, or on the phenomenon of nihilism that preoccupied many Russian writers.

There are also themes and concepts in Nursi's work that have generally not been touched upon in Western thought. An example is the theme of laziness or indolence. Although this had been discussed by Rizal and explored exhaustively by Syed Hussein Alatas, it remains marginal to the interests of Western social science. Such themes and concepts in the work of Nursi should be identified and elaborated in order to contribute to original theorizing and research in the social sciences and humanities. This paper has merely provided an outline of Nursi's social theology. A more theoretically developed and nuanced presentation with references to historical and contemporary empirical cases for illustration would fill many more pages and should be the aim of future research in Nursi studies. Hence, more specific recommendations can be made.

## The Definition of Social Theology

To further refine and elaborate on the definition of social theology, there are at least three areas of work to be undertaken. First of all, more aspects of the social in Nursi's writings need to be identified. I am referring to those aspects that have

---

52. Nursi, *Flashes*, 155–56.

to do with the social context, causal factors that are social such as class, ethnicity and tribe, or the social consequences of religious factors. Secondly, comparisons and contrasts should be made between Nursi and other Ottoman/Muslim thinkers. I have in mind those associated with the Ottoman *ictimāī ilm-i kelām* project or thinkers from other traditions such as 'Ali Sharī'atī. Thirdly, there is much to be learnt from the Catholic tradition of liberation theology.

## Reconstructing Nursi's Social Theology

The reconstruction of Nursi's social theology covers his critique of both European and Muslim societies. As I have suggested, the elaboration and further refinement of Nursi's critique of the second Europe requires mastery of many non-Muslim classics that deal with similar issues. I have brought in the words of Marx, Durkheim, Rizal, and Dostoevsky. There is much scope to include many other seminal thinkers such as Max Weber, Franz Kafka, Ivan Turgenev, Alexander Herzen, Nikolai Gogol, Ortega Y Gasset, and others, to make them conceptually relevant to Nursi's concerns in a mutually enriching project.

The same is true for Nursi's critique of Muslim civilization. The six dire sicknesses that he listed and the six words he elaborated with inspiration from the pharmacy of the Qur'an require some conceptual contribution and even intervention from many important Western and other works. This provides opportunities for the further refinement of the ideas and concepts of not only Nursi but all the thinkers concerned. I also suggested the need to introduce new topics and concerns that may not have been addressed by Nursi but to which Nursi's approach is extremely relevant. The examples I gave are the themes of Muslim extremism and indolence, but many others can be identified, as well.

## Lessons from the Pharmacy of the Qur'an

There is much scope for the development of Nursi's thought in the area of the solutions he proposed for overcoming the problems of modern civilization. First of all, it is necessary to establish the key concepts and factors around which revolve Nursi's solutions and his vision for a better order. Such concepts include *akhlāq* (morality), *'adālah* (justice), divine mercy and power, evil, *al-marḍ* (illness, pathology), *sharī'ah*, *insān* (huhumankind), society, and many others. Indeed, one of the successes of Nursi studies to date is the proliferation of conference papers and articles that discuss many of these concepts. What remains to be done is the integration of these concepts in a systematic fashion into a theoretical framework. One possible theoretical framework is that of social theology.

Secondly, it is necessary to work through systematically all the solutions discussed in the *Risale-i Nur* and *The Damascus Sermon* and to relate them to historical and contemporary empirical cases to facilitate their translation into programs of action. One such area in this respect is dialogue between Islam and Christianity. Interreligious dialogue is very popular these days, but a specifically Nursian approach to practical dialogue has yet to be conceived, let alone implemented. Another area of research that needs to be developed is the study of extremism, especially its control and arrest. Again, a specifically Nursian approach related to his *ta'wīl* method and his emphasis on *akhlāq* as a corrective to extremism has yet to be developed.

## Nursi's Methodology

The reconstruction of Nursi's social theology requires not only the development and formation of concepts, themes and topics, but also the elucidation of his methodology. It is necessary to describe Nursi's methods, particularly his use of various forms of analogical reasoning. This is a very important area of development in Nursi studies because it provides a resource to train graduate students to think systematically and logically. Indeed, a worthy project would be to outline the field of logic, using Nursi's definitions, concepts and illustrations. This outline could include conception and assent (*taṣawwur* and *taṣdīq*) and the five modes of argumentation, that is, *burhān* (demonstration), *jadal* (dialetics), *shi'ir* (poetics), *khiṭābah* (rhetorics) and *safsaṭah* (sophistics).

This is the framework for the reconstruction of the social theology of Said Nursi. Ultimately, the delineation of Nursi's social theology, his critique of the pathology of modern civilization, his vision of change and progress, all point towards Nursi's concept of *tajdīd* and *iṣlāḥ*. Nursi said that "ninety-nine percent of the *sharī'ah* is concerned with morality, worship, the hereafter, and virtue."[53] Clearly, Nursi did not reduce the *sharī'ah* to rules and regulations. He was not legalistic in his approach. He considered virtue, love, mutual attraction, cooperation, unity, and solidarity to be among the principles underlying the *sharī'ah*.[54] More can be said elsewhere on the relationship between the *sharī'ah* and morality, and religion and modern science. Furthermore, there are other themes in Nursi's work such as freedom that are also related to the theme of justice. Nursi regarded Islam as a vital force that should underlie the planning of a society's development. Only Islam could hold greed, extravagance and corruption in check. Nursi saw the problems of Turkey as resulting from a moral crisis that could only be resolved via the implementation of the *sharī'ah*, understood in the broader sense as a code of ethical conduct. This should not be confused with the clamoring for a vaguely conceived "Islamic" state that is often found among many modernist agitators. These are some of the ingredients that would go into the definition and conceptualization of Nursi's understanding of the reform of Muslim societies. That should be understood as the goal of Nursi's social theology, for he was, after all, a *mujaddid*.

## BIBLIOGRAPHY

Alatas, Syed Hussein. *Intellectuals in Developing Societies*. London: Cass, 1977.

———. *The Myth of the Lazy Native: A Study of the Image of the Malays, Filipinos and Javanese from the 16th to the 20th Century and its Function in the Ideology of Colonial Capitalism*. London: Cass, 1977.

Dostoevsky, Fyodor. *The Grand Inquisitor—With related chapters from the Brothers Karamazov*. Indianapolis: Hacket, 1993.

Durkheim, Emile. *Suicide: A Study in Sociology*. London: Routledge, 1989.

---

53. Vahide, *Islam in Modern Turkey*, 67.

54. Nursi, *The Words*, 745–46.

Gutierrez, Gustavo. *A Theology of Liberation.* Maryknoll, NY: Orbis, 1973.

Leaman, Oliver. "Nursi's Place in the *Iḥyā'* Tradition." *Muslim World* 89 (1999) 314–24.

Ibn Khaldun. *Muqaddimat Ibn Khaldun.* Beirut: Dar al-Qalam, 1981.

———. *The Muqaddimah.* 3 vols. New York: Pantheon, 1958.

Lewis, Franklin D. *Rumi—Past and Present, East and West: The Life, Teachings and Poetry of Jalāl al-Din Rumi.* Oxford: Oneworld, 2000.

Michel, Thomas. "Grappling with Modern Civilization: Said Nursi's Interpretive Key." In *Said Nursi's Views on Muslim-Christian Understanding,* Thomas Michel, 79–108. Istanbul: Sözler, 2005.

Nursi, Bediüzzaman Said. *Al-Khuṭbah al-shāmiyyah.* Istanbul: Sözler, 2007.

———. *Al-Mathnawī al-'Arabī al-Nurī.* Istanbul: Sözler, 1999.

———. *The Damascus Sermon.* Translated by Şükran Vahide. Istanbul: Sözler, 2001.

———. *The Flashes Collection.* Translated by Şükran Vahide. Istanbul: Sözler, 2004.

———. "Seeds of Reality." In Bediüzzaman Said Nursi, *Letters 1928–1932,* translated by Şükran Vahide, 541–56. Istanbul: Sözler, 2001.

———. *The Words: On the Nature and Purpose of Man, Life, and All Things.* Translated by Şükran Vahide. Istanbul: Sözler, 2004.

Özdemir, İbrāhīm. "Said Nursi and J. P. Sartre: Existence and Man—A Study of the Views of Said Nursi and J.P. Sartre." Online: http://iozdemirr.blogspot.com/2009/12/said-nursi-and-j-p-sartre.html.

Özervarlı, M. Sait. "Said Nursi's Project of Revitalizing Contemporary Islamic Thought." In *Islam at the Crossroads: On the Life and Thought of Bediüzzaman Said Nursi,* edited by İbrahim Abu-Rabi' 317–34. Albany, NY: State University of New York Press, 2003.

Rizal, José. "The Indolence of the Filipino." In *Political and Historical Writings,* José Rizal, 111–39. Manila: National Historical Institute, 1963.

———. "The Truth for All." In *Political and Historical Writings,* José Rizal, 31–38. Manila: National Historical Institute, 1963.

Ibn Rushd. *Bidāyat al-mujtahid wa nihāyat al-muqtasid.* Beirut: al-Ilmiah, 1997.

———. *The Distinguished Jurist's Primer: Bidāyat al-mujtahid wa nihāyat al-Muqtasid.* Vol. 2. Reading, UK: Garnet, 1996.

Shepard, William E. "Islam and Ideology: Towards a Typology." *International Journal of Middle East Studies* 19 (1987) 307–36.

Smith, Christian. *The Emergence of Liberation Theology: Radical Religion and Social Movement Theory.* Chicago: University of Chicago Press, 1991.

Vahide, Şükran. *Islam in Modern Turkey: An Intellectual Biography of Bediüzzaman Said Nursi.* Albany, NY: State University of New York Press, 2005.

# 15

# The *Risale-i Nur* as an Epistemological Ground for the Framework of a Sociology of Science

## Alparslan Açıkgenç

Our present study is concerned with the sociology of science, which is a relatively new field. Most discussions in the West concerning this new discipline are unproductive because they seem to neglect the epistemology upon which scientific activities are built. We shall argue that science is the result of a dynamic process in history which reveals its sociological characteristics with regard to a community of scholars and customs, called "scientific tradition." This paper is an attempt to elaborate this aspect of science based on its epistemology, in relation to the well-known Muslim thinker, Bediüzzaman Said Nursi's (d. 1960) magnum opus, *Risale-i Nur (Risale)*. I need to introduce first the aim and purpose of the *Risale* and show how it can be taken as an epistemological basis for the sociology of science. In my attempt I shall try to utilize Nursi's general epistemology as my theoretical framework, which is in fact needed for the epistemology of science.

## SOCIOLOGY OF SCIENCE AS A NEW DISCIPLINE

The epistemology of science in history presents a process which inevitably assumes a social context in two perspectives: One is the fact that scientists live in a society, in other words, a social environment which in some respects shapes their minds and in turn their activities; the other is the smaller community of scholars and scientists together with their students within that society, who, all together, carry out the scientific activities. Of course, the social environment does affect the scientific activities through many channels, all of which need to be investigated in the sociology of science. But in a similar fashion the smaller community of scholars, scientists, and their students form a *social environment* that is now commonly called a "scientific community" in the Western scientific tradition; but in Islamic scientific tradition we have the term *ulemā'* (pl. of *'ālim*, i.e., scholar, or scientist) to express the same idea in a different way. Actually this aspect together with the historical perspective constitutes what is known as the "sociology of science," as I understand it. One of the purposes of this study is to emphasize the link between the epistemology and sociology of science and thus posit a thesis that science cannot be explained without paying attention to both of these aspects.[1]

In the first place, we would like to defend the idea that science is not just a cognitive activity or sociological phenomenon. Science is not merely a historical process taking place within a social context which determines its rules, customs and mores. Both the cognitive and sociological aspects must be combined in order to examine how the epistemology of science is actively at work in history in a particular environment represented by a civilization. In the second place, in the approach to science from this perspective, the sociology of science reveals three phenomena: first, science is the product of a community working actively in a certain mental framework acquired through their scientific training; second, science needs an *environment* in which it can flourish. Our contention is that this is a mental environment which flourishes within a particular social context. Hence, the concept of environment combines the mental with the social. Finally, science is the product of a historical process and it needs this process in an uninterrupted chain of scholars to sustain its vitality.[2] Therefore, the third phenomenon is the historical movement of the epistemology of science, which is called "*scientific process*."[3] The first two phenomena are sociological and as such they will be examined in this section. The third phenomenon is the historical manifestation of this social aspect as governed by an epistemology in two senses: as pure epistemology expressed as the anatomy of the human knowledge system; and as applied epistemology which reveals the mental frameworks of the scientists utilized in their scientific activities, called the "epistemology of sciences." It is this scientific process that gives us access to what we have termed elsewhere "historical epistemology."[4]

In that case we are basically arguing that as a knowledge acquisition activity, science is based on an epistemology which governs its processes that take place in a double social context with a long history. Since pure epistemology is an analysis of the anatomy of the human knowledge system, we apply it to scientific activities

---

1. The pioneers of this new discipline in the West pay attention to primarily the sociological aspect of science. What we are trying to defend in this brief study is that even in sociology of science the cognitive aspect of science should not be neglected. These Western sociologists are Robert K. Merton (*The Sociology of Science* and also *Social Theory and Social Structure*), Pitirim Sorokin (*Social and Cultural Dynamics*, 4 vols.), and Bernard Barber (*Science and the Social Order*).

2. In our previous work these subjects were analyzed under two separate chapters as "epistemology of science" and "sociology of science." See *Scientific Thought and its Burdens*, chapters 2 and 3.

3. See Açıkgenç, "The Emergence of Scientific Tradition in Islam," 91–114.

4. See Açıkgenç, *Islamic Scientific Tradition in History*, chapter 1.

in order to come up with an epistemology of science. Pure epistemology is unified in all knowledge processes and thus will be the same in scientific activities, as well, keeping in view the general human knowledge system. In that case, the epistemology of science as an applied epistemology is solely concerned with the specific mental frameworks utilized by scientists in their scientific activities. It is these mental frameworks that will act as the ground of the sociology of science.[5] We cannot, therefore, discuss anything that is transpiring in the social community of scientists claiming that we are doing sociology of science; we must pay attention to the epistemology of science as the ground of all scientific activities as processes of acquiring scientific knowledge. How can we determine these mental frameworks?

We may utilize an analogy in this case. Since the primary purpose of scientific inquiry is to try to investigate phenomena and the nature of things in order to explain them, in a sense it is just like an artist's work; for the artist observes things in the environment and then depicts them on his canvas. There is however a significant difference between the scientist's work and the artist's painting: the former uses concepts to depict his projections whereas the latter uses paint and brush. As a result, in the former case only words as concepts appear, but in the latter case, a concrete painting. Keeping this difference in mind we may use this analogy to uncover the frameworks in the mind of a scientist. In this case we are applying pure epistemology to scientific activities. Pure epistemology attempts to analyze the process of knowledge acquisition; and therefore, its application to scientific activities shall not question the same process in epistemology of science but rather decipher the framework in the mind of a scientist applied in the process of acquisition of scientific knowledge. We may now attempt to briefly analyze this application on the basis of our analogy.

In the first place, the artist will try to choose a *location* which would provide him a good perspective to view the object or scenery he is trying to paint. The perspective he chooses will be very wide and thus includes all the things he wants to see in his painting. The scientist also has to choose a perspective for his scientific activities. This perspective is not a *location* like that of the painter because his *painting* is not concrete, but conceptual; and as such his perspective will have to be mental. In this regard if we ask for the largest perspective in our mind which we utilize in all our activities, we can give only the *worldview* as an answer. For, everyone's worldview is the largest conceptual framework that gives him his perspective. Obviously the scientist will have to utilize his worldview as his perspective in order to carry out his scientific studies. The perspective is an epistemological necessity without which no activity at all is possible. In fact, if there is not a proper worldview as a perspective, a human being cannot be engaged in scientific research.

For the sake of argument, assume that every worldview does not provide the appropriate mental environment for

---

5. Collins defends this approach which does not neglect the epistemology of science. See Collins, *The Sociology of Philosophies*. We may also mention in this context Hans-Jörg Rheinberger who has a historical approach which does not also neglect the cognitive aspect of science and thus tries to develop a historical epistemology. See his *On Historicizing Epistemology*.

carrying out scientific activities. But if a worldview that is not properly developed may not be suitable for scientific activities, what kind of a worldview would provide such a perspective? We may answer this if we pay attention to the nature of knowledge acquired in scientific inquiries. Since science is essentially an organized body of theoretical knowledge, this means that within that worldview there should arise certain concepts that can support such a kind of knowledge activity. If we turn back to the painter analogy, we may assert that after the painter chooses a location for himself as a perspective, he will then try to determine a *frame* in order to fit the object of painting onto his canvas, because what he wants to paint may not have a limit, whereas his canvas is limited. Hence, he must identify a *frame* for his painting.

This is the same for the scientist, except that the frame of the scientist is again conceptual. This *frame* exists in the mind of the scientist as a structure in which we find a well-developed network of concepts which supports his scientific activities more directly than the *perspective*, i.e., the worldview. That structure in our worldview is called "knowledge structure." But still the perspective and frame are not sufficient to support each activity in their respective scientific fields. Knowledge structure may sustain knowledge activities but it must also develop in a peculiar way to give rise to what we shall call a "scientific conceptual scheme" which is general at this stage. A conceptual scheme is a web of logically interconnected concepts organized in the mind of the scientist according to the structure of human knowledge system as scientists receive their scientific training. It is this web of concepts that determines his scientific activities to a large extent. But this conceptual web is sustained by another structure of concepts which we have termed "knowledge structure" within the worldview of the scientist. We do admit that a thorough analysis of worldview and knowledge structure is required to explain how they function and sustain the scientific conceptual scheme.

Leaving this analysis for a later study, if we continue based on our analogy, the painter is ready to paint because he has set his *perspective* and *frame*. But then he needs an understanding of painting, as he learnt from his masters, which he will now apply to the actual act of painting. He may, like his master(s) and other followers, belong to a specific school of painting according to which they all paint. Of course, they will have their own individual approaches, too. This will determine the way they actually paint. Now this understanding also forms a third mental framework in the mind of the painter as well as the scientist. But since it is directly connected to the act of performing whatever the activity is, it is more directly visible to the mind. As such it can be called a "specific conceptual scheme" and since in case of the scientist the activity is science, we term it a "specific scientific conceptual scheme." On the other hand, since this scheme as a network of concepts form a frame in the mind, we shall call it an "outlook." All these mental frameworks of *perspective*, *frame* and *outlook* constitute our epistemology of science. These mental frameworks as epistemological concepts may be termed: 1. Worldview, which is the perspective; 2. Knowledge structure and more specifically the general scientific conceptual scheme, which is the frame; and finally 3. The specific scientific conceptual scheme, which is the outlook.[6]

Our analysis brings us to a fresh concept that I shall try to briefly elucidate here, as "scientific process" which, I believe, will shed light also on our understanding of science, as well. We have argued that science is essentially a knowledge acquisition process; as such it should be defined on the basis of our system of knowledge. When we examine any scientific activity we find that there is a community (of scientists) involved in the activity and as such it also has a social character. But the activity carried out by this community is basically a knowledge acquisition activity, and as such it is fundamentally epistemological, which stresses the cognitive aspect of science. Moreover, since this socio-epistemological activity continues through a span of time, it is historical at the same time and as such has the character of a (historical) process. Our analysis reveals three aspects of science which emerge as a result of this complex phenomenon. The first aspect is represented by the scientist as an individual involved in the knowledge acquisition activity. This aspect is epistemological because it can be explained on the basis of a theory of knowledge. The second aspect is represented by the group of scientists who set up their own tradition and as such it is social. The third aspect brings out the scientific activity as essentially a socio-epistemological activity progressing through a historical process.

We now imagine a society at a point in history where there is no science; let us imagine in this society that there is no learning activity either. How can a process begin to yield in the first place a learning tradition that will lead to the emergence of sciences? In order to explain this, we need to develop a theory of contextual causes taking place at the initial stage of the historical process. At this stage we find nothing but moral struggle. Moral struggle is *sunnatullah* (divine law), to borrow our term from the Islamic scientific tradition; as such it will always be there. But for this moral struggle to lead to a learning and knowledge tradition, there should emerge in the mind of individuals a concept of knowledge that would perform a fundamental function in their worldview. If this leads to a structural element in their worldviews, then together with the moral struggle there will be intellectual activities in that society.

In the meantime, when there is moral struggle, those who are involved in the struggle will try to shape the society in accordance with their moral ideals. Therefore, social movement may begin simultaneously with moral struggle or it may start at a later period and perhaps even after the intellectual movements begin. This way there will be moral, intellectual and social dynamism within that society, all of which will gradually lead to economic, political and legal reforms. The whole society will begin to reshape itself.

At some point in history we begin to see, however, that there arose those who are simply interested in *knowing* certain problems in a way others do not *know*. There are many *modes* in which we can know things; but there is one way of knowing things, which is not only systematic and organized, but also it questions its own findings. In other words, this way of knowing is not satisfied by just

---

6. For a detailed discussion and clarification of these concepts, see Açıkgenç, *Islamic Scientific Tradition in History*, chapter 1.

having information about the subject of inquiry, it rather questions it and analyzes its findings, if any, or else its own mode of handling the inquiry so that it can actually know the thing as it is. If in this way someone establishes himself, there usually grows around him a group of interested disciples who are also interested knowing things the way the *Master* knows things. As soon as this happens, then this group of people has a good chance of establishing a tradition of studying things in order to know them in a way that is different from the ordinary way of knowing things.

Let us suppose that this group of people who are interested in knowing things as they really are have established a tradition. Usually, we name something in order to be able to communicate about it, as this is also one natural operation of our intellect to name things in order to produce concepts about them. The knowledge produced in this tradition of learning will also be *named* because as we have said these groups of people are interested in knowing things in a way that is different from other types of knowing. In that case they will give a name to it, i.e., they will produce a concept expressing their activity so that they can distinguish it from other activities of knowing. We usually choose names or concepts from the related activity; since the activity is *knowing* the best name for this tradition is also *knowing*. That is why in the Greek tradition Aristotle gave the name *episteme* for science; in Islam first, as we shall see, the term *fiqh* (to grasp, comprehend, which still means "to know *differently*"), then *'ilm* is used to name sciences; in the Western scientific tradition also the Latin term *scientia* is used for this purpose. This way, individual sciences emerge at some stage of this process and the study of these sciences gradually turns the existing tradition of knowledge and learning into a "scientific tradition."

We have described here the path sciences take in history with respect to their tradition. It is this historical path which we identify as a "scientific process" which is a civilizational phenomenon, and as such we cannot say "scientific process of a scientific tradition" because it is the route that the tradition itself takes. In this analysis of scientific process what concerns us are the frameworks utilized in these activities; we shall try to see whether the *Risale* provides any such framework and, if so, how. This leads us to discuss the nature of the *Risale* in order to explain this issue.

## THE RISALE AS AN EPISTEMOLOGICAL FRAMEWORK OF THE SOCIOLOGY OF SCIENCE

The main goal of this paper is to discuss the *Risale* as an epistemological framework for the sociology of science. In this section I shall try to develop the general perspective of the classification of knowledge in order to determine the place of the *Risale* in such a classification. Since the fundamental aim of the *Risale* is to develop an Islamic state of mind as a perspective, in this context the Qur'an and *ḥadīth* will be used as basic sources in defining and classifying knowledge.[7] A careful study of the Qur'an and *ḥadīth*

---

7. This section is based on my previous work entitled "An Evaluation of the *Risale-i Nur* from the Point of View of Knowledge and the Categorization of Knowledge." This work is originally in Turkish and it is translated into English by Şükran Vahide for the proceedings.

reveals that they both attach a central importance to knowledge. The Qur'an, in the first place, stresses that knowledge possesses distinctive characteristics. For, by saying that "Those truly conscious about God among His servants are the ones who have knowledge" (Q 35:28),[8] the Qur'an is not only emphasizing the importance of knowledge, it is also pointing out the highest level that scholars have to reach. The verse, "Are those equal, those who know and those who do not know?" (Q 39:9) shows clearly the value of knowledge. Moreover, God's Messenger was commanded to pray: "O my Lord! Advance me in knowledge" (Q 20:114). It is possible to extract meanings pointing indirectly to the importance of knowledge from many other verses similar to the above (See for example, Q 3:18, 4:157, 6:119, 140–44, 16:25, 31:20, etc.).

In the second place, there are also a large number of *hadīths* which emphasize the importance of knowledge (*'ilm*) as knowledge. If we take a look at only a few of these, we see that in Bukhari, for example, the Prophet is reported to have said "decline in knowledge and increase in ignorance" is a sign of the end of the world (*ashrat al-sa'a*).[9] God's Messenger also said: "When no scholars remain, people will choose the ignorant as their leaders. When these are asked something, they will reply despite being ignorant, and will therefore lead astray both themselves and others."[10] And in many books of *hadīth*, it is related that God's Messenger said,

> Since those who seek knowledge are happy with what they do, the angels overspread them with their wings. Whatever there is on the land and in the heavens, and even the fishes in the seas, pray for forgiveness for those with knowledge. The superiority of the learned over the one who worships, is the superiority of the moon (due to its light) over the other stars. The scholars are the heirs of the prophets. For the prophets left not riches and possessions as their legacy, but knowledge. Let those who desire to acquire this, hasten after it gratefully.[11]

In another *hadīth*, it says, "When a person dies, everything he has done comes to an end (with respect to merit) with the exception of three things: ongoing charity, knowledge that is profited from, and a righteous child who prays for him."[12] While another is: "The ink of the scholars is superior to the blood of the martyrs."[13]

---

8. Translations of the Qur'an are based on and may not in all instances be taken verbatim from A. Yusuf Ali, *The Holy Qur'an*.

9. Muhammad ibn Ismā'īl al-Bukharī, *Saḥīḥ*, "Kitab al-'Ilm," 71, 72. All the six books of hadith are printed in the collection *Al-Kutub al-Sittah wa Shuruhuha*. I shall refer to these books by the name of their collector.

10. Ibid, 86.

11. Abu Daw'ud, al-'Ilm, 1. See also Tirmidhi, al-'Ilm, 19; Nasa'i, al-Tahara, 112; Ibn Maja, al-Muqaddima, 17; Ahmad b. Hanbal, iv, 239, 241; v, 196.

12. Muslim, al-Wasiyya, 1631; see also Bukhari, *al-Adab al-Mufrad*, ed. by Kamâl Yûsuf al-Hût, hadith no. 38.

13. 'Ali al-Muttaqi al-Hindi. *Kanz al-'Ummal* ed. by Mahmud Umar al-Dumyati, , x, 14, Nos: 28714–15. Al-Khatib al-Baghdadi states that this *hadīth* is unreliable (*mawdū'*); see *Ta'rikh al-Baghdad*, ed. by Bashar 'Awwad Ma'ruf, ii, 193. Abu al-Faraj Ibn al-Jawzi is of the same opinion: see *al-'Ilal al-Mutanahiyya*, i, 71–72. It is said there are numerous fabricated *hadīths* on this subject. But in my view, even if they are not *hadīths*, they were accepted without difficulty by Muslims, since they reflected the attitude towards knowledge which had been instilled in the people of that time. This is mentioned in order to highlight the importance of knowledge

In the *Sunan* of Abu Daw'ud are the following *hadīths*, in summary: "The path leading to knowledge is the path leading to Paradise." "As the full-moon shines brighter than the stars, so the scholars are superior to the pious who worship day and night." "The scholars are the heirs of the prophets." "If knowledge is asked of someone and he does not impart what he knows, he shall be punished in the hereafter with Hell-fire." In the section *Kitab al-'ilm* in his *Sahīh*, Tirmidhi includes the following *hadīths*: "To seek knowledge is to push open the door of Paradise." "So long as one on the way of knowledge does not leave that way, he is on God's way." Although there is no *Kitāb al-'ilm* in the *Sunan* of Ibn Maja, we find this important *hadīth*: "It is obligatory for every Muslim to seek knowledge."[14]

In the above-mentioned verses and the *hadīths* which show the great importance of knowledge (*'ilm*), the word *'ilm* has been interpreted as "knowledge" in a special sense. For instance, it is said in the verse, "Were you to follow their desires after the knowledge that has reached you, then would you find neither protector nor helper against God" (Q 2:120). Since what was sent to God's Messenger was revelation, the knowledge here must refer to "revelation." We can observe this in many other verses of the Qur'an that knowledge (*'ilm*) refers to the knowledge brought by revelation: "If anyone disputes in this matter with you now after knowledge has come to you . . ." (Q 3:61). We may also cite the following verses: "Thus We have revealed it to be a judgment of authority in Arabic. Were you to follow their [vain] desires after the knowledge which has reached you, then would you find neither protector nor defender against God (Q 13:37). Qur'an 11:14 states, "Know that this revelation is sent down [replete] with the knowledge of God." And Qur'an 27:15: "We gave [in the past] knowledge to David and Solomon."

We cannot conclude from all these verses that the Qur'an identifies revelation with all classes of knowledge. Similarly, there are verses which show clearly that there are also other classes of knowledge which are not the same as revelation. For example, "Verily We have brought them a scripture [*kitāb*] which We expound with knowledge, a guidance and mercy for those who believe" (Q 7:52). This verse demonstrates the importance of knowledge as knowledge, and states that revelation brought "a particular knowledge as a *book*." While in Surat al-Ra'd verse 43, the phrase "such as have knowledge of the Book" distinguishes between revelation and the knowledge revelation has brought. This distinction is to be understood from numerous other verses as well (for example, Q 19:43, 27, 40, 6:143).

If we distinguish the general knowledge from the revealed knowledge, we may posit another class of knowledge in between, based on the above verses and the *ahadīth*. For all the above verses make a very subtle connection between knowledge and revelation. We may then point out two more aspects of knowledge which emerge as the result of analysis. The first we may call "revelational knowledge" which is the knowledge brought by the Qur'an itself. The second is the knowledge we acquire in whatever form, which is illumined through revelational knowledge. It is this kind of knowledge which

---

in Islamic circles.

14. Ibn Maja, al-Muqaddima, 17, No: 224; 1, No: 81 (Egypt 1951). For other narrations, see, *Kanz al-Ummal*, x, 131, Nos: 28651–54.

we put in between the revelation and the general class of knowledge. But we shall enumerate them in the following order as basically four classes of knowledge, distinguished on the basis of revelational sources:

1. General knowledge which we possess in our daily life;
2. Revealed knowledge, either as scripture, (*kitāb*, namely the Qur'an) or merely divine knowledge as given to a prophet;
3. Knowledge received by inheritance from the Prophet, as indicated in the *ḥadīth* that "scholars are the heirs of Prophets," quoted above. Since such knowledge is generally used for guiding others, just like its correlate revelation, and is known in the Islamic terminology as *tablīgh*, namely communicating the teachings of the Qur'an, I shall call this "*tablīgh* knowledge";
4. Knowledge based on revelation and/or *tablīgh* knowledge, which may be called "illumined knowledge."

It is possible to add the term Qur'anic *jahl*, ignorance, as the fifth class of knowledge here because on the basis of the Qur'anic terminology, ignorance as *jahl* does not mean lack of knowledge; on the contrary people may be very knowledgeable in the first sense of the class of knowledge but may be "ignorant" because of heedlessness to the revealed truth. In that case, knowledge in the general sense as we use it in everyday life may be the source of ignorance, as well. Therefore, no matter how knowledgeable a person is, and of whatever knowledge he is informed to the very highest degree, if he does not reach to the level of enlightened knowledge, his knowledge is the equivalent of ignorance and harmful to huhumankind as the Qur'an states in the following verses:

> But many do mislead [people] by their appetites unchecked by knowledge. (Q 6: 119)

> Lost are those who slay their children, from folly, without knowledge, and forbid the sustenance which God has provided for them, inventing [lies] against God. (Q 6:140)

> But who does more wrong than one who invents a lie against God, to lead astray men without knowledge? (Q 6:144)

If these verses are considered in the moral context, what is meant by "without knowledge" (*bi-ghayri 'ilm*) or "ignorant" is not people who are totally devoid of knowledge. They are rather people with the knowledge which is not illuminated by belief and revelation. This is also clarified in numerous other verses (see Q 46:23, 6:111, 25:63). But now we face a significant question which is directly related to our theme: Can we derive the concept of scientific knowledge also from the Qur'an and *ḥadīth*, as a fifth class of knowledge? I would like to argue that this is possible although the Qur'an does not clearly refer to such a class of knowledge, especially by the term *'ilm*. The term scholar (*'ālim*) may be interpreted as "scientist" today but the Qur'an means only the scholar who is expert in the last two classes of knowledge, i.e., in the *tablīgh* and illumined knowledge, as only the prophets are given revelational knowledge. Of course, all human beings possess the first class of knowledge. Based on this interpretation of the textual evidence we cannot interpret the Qur'anic term *'ālim* as "scientist." How can we then derive the meaning of scientific knowledge from the Qur'an or *ḥadīth*, and with what word refer to the person who possesses this kind of knowledge?

There is a term in the Qur'an which refers to human understanding; *fiqh*. In this sense, *fiqh* signifies human knowledge based on cognitive understanding and hence it refers to knowledge of the rational kind. That is why *'ilm* is used by both the Qur'an and *ḥadīth* to refer to revealed knowledge which is definite and absolute; while *fiqh* refers to human understanding which may err, just like scientific knowledge. The Prophet's prayer for Ibn 'Abbas combines the verbal form of both terms in a single sentence referring thus to their different signification: "O God, provide him with the *[rational] understanding* of religion and give him the *knowledge* of interpretation" [italics mine].[15] In this *ḥadīth*, the term *'ilm*, i.e. knowledge, is used in relation to interpretation (*ta'wīl*) which is not allowed in case of revelation.[16] Whereas, since religion is to be *understood* by us with an effort of the mind in order to live in accordance with its injunctions, in relation to religion, *fiqh* is used. I drive from this usage the understanding that *'ilm* is absolute knowledge revealed by God, as such it cannot be interpreted. Whatever is understood (*fiqh*) by individuals it should be applied in life; whereas *fiqh* is human knowledge acquired by an effort to learn and understand something. The following usages in the *ḥadīths* are also meaningful:

"An intellectual [*faqīh*] is more vehement to the Satan than one thousand devout persons [*'ābid*]."[17] "If God wants to do good to a person, He makes him an intellectual (*faqīh*) in religion."[18] This means that *'ilm* is understood as a definite piece of knowledge which is either directly taken from a revealed source, or derived from it on the basis of a precedent practice of the Prophet. Another term may be introduced here to support our interpretation: *ra'y*, which means "theory." We should assert that *ra'y*, meaning "provisional opinion," also expresses a rational argumentation because a scientific theory is based on reasoning. Moreover, since the human mind is not authoritative in understanding the revelation, the Prophet says that "if one interprets the Qur'an on the basis of his theory (*ra'y*), he has committed an error even if he is correct in his interpretation," since no knowledge (*'ilm*) can be based on a theory.[19]

Now, the knowledge based on a rational argumentation is reached as a result of *ra'y* (theory), and such knowledge is actually defined as *fiqh* in the Qur'an and *aḥadīth*. This is clear in the above quotations of the *aḥadīth* in which *fiqh* occurs. Since such a knowledge is in fact science per se, in certain early sources it was used

---

15. Ismā 'īl ibn Muḥammad al-'Ajlūnī. *Kashf al-Khafā' wa Muzīl al-Ilbās*, Vol 1: 220–21.

16. This is attested by the verse of the Qur'an 2:7: "He it is Who has sent down to you the Book. In it are verses of established, clear meaning; they are the foundation of the Book. Others are not entirely clear (*mutashābihāt*). But those in whose hearts is perversity follow the part thereof that is not clear, seeking discord, and searching for their interpretation, but no one knows its interpretation except God. And those who are firmly grounded in knowledge say: 'We believe in the Book; the whole of it is from our Lord, and none will grasp the Message except people of understanding.'"

17. Ibn Mājah, "Muqaddimah," 222.

18. Al-Bukhari, "Kitab al-'Ilm," chapter 14.

19. Abu Dawud Sulaymān ibn al-Ash'ath al-Sijistani, *Sunan Abu Dawūd*, 1036.

exactly in the same manner, such as in the title of a book written by al-Tha'ālibī, *Fiqhu'l-lughah*, i.e., *The Science of Lexicography*. Later developments, however, diverted this usage, and perhaps as an influence of the Greek scientific tradition, this usage was dropped and thus replaced by the term *'ilm*. Moreover, according to Abu Hanifah, *fiqh* meant "speculative thinking" which is clear in the title of his book *Al-Fiqh al-akbar*. Furthermore, al-Dhahabi says of 'Abdullah ibn al-Mubarak that he "recorded knowledge [i.e., *ḥadīth*] in chapters and concerning *fiqh* ["*dawwana'l-'ilm fi'l-abwāb wa'l-fiqh*"]."[20] Of course, this usage of the term has a basis in the Qur'anic expression "to rationally understand the religion" (Q 9:122; "*li yatafaqqahu fi al-dīn*"). This is why the early *muhaddithūn* used the term *'ilm* to refer to *ḥadīth*.

In that case we may argue that the Qur'an does not use terms which are not utilized towards its main purpose, which is *guidance par excellence* (*al-hidāyah*). Its purpose is not therefore scientific discussion. If a scientific truth can be utilized for guidance, such as opening a door for a human mind for belief in God, it may utilize that scientific truth, such as the creation of mountains and the earth. It is not a book on cosmology and therefore it may utilize cosmological phenomena to show God's majesty and relation to the cosmos but it will not give detailed cosmological information. However, since guidance is based on truth, the information it utilizes is also based on truth, hence, cannot be false. Under this consideration the term *fiqh* was utilized in early Islamic scientific tradition to refer to scientific knowledge and it is only in this sense that we may argue for the existence of the concept of scientific knowledge in the Qur'an. But later this term lost its significance and was confined to its legalistic usage alone; namely today it means only the science of law. Based on our above discussion, we come up with six classes of knowledge which may be derived from the Qur'an:

1. General knowledge;
2. Revealed knowledge;
3. *Tablīgh* knowledge;
4. Illumined knowledge;
5. Scientific knowledge; and finally
6. Ignorance as dark knowledge.

We would like to first try to determine which class or classes of knowledge the *Risale* belong to. Based on our definitions of each class, we may already eliminate some of these classes. They obviously do not belong to the class of general knowledge because they do not pretend to give us everyday knowledge. They cannot belong to revealed knowledge, either, as the author is not a prophet; nor do they belong to the class of dark knowledge. Hence, they belong to one of these three classes: *tablīgh* knowledge, illumined knowledge or scientific knowledge. I would like to argue that the *Risale* belong primarily to *tablīgh* knowledge. As we have defined illumined knowledge as that state of mind and knowledge based on revealed and *tablīgh* knowledge, we may eliminate this class also. For in a sense *tablīgh* knowledge is derived from and based on revelation; as such it can be regarded as illumined knowledge in relation to the revelation, but in itself (*bi'l-dhāt* or *bi dhātihi*) since it is based on the revelation, *tablīgh* knowledge will share its purpose,

---

20. Muhammad ibn Ahmad ibn 'Uthman ibn Qayyum 'Abu 'Abd Allah Shams ad-Din al-Dhahabi, *Tadhkirat al-Huffaz*, 1:275.

method, means and scope. Based on this result, we can safely infer that the purpose of *tablīgh* knowledge is also primarily *guidance par excellence* (*hidāyah*); hence, it will also utilize scientific knowledge for this purpose but with one difference that since the locus of *tablīgh* knowledge is not a prophet, he must be an *'ālim* (scholar) of religious sciences, on the one hand, and be knowledgeable of other sciences of his time, on the other. There will necessarily be a scholarly approach, as well, in his works. In that case, there will be only one difference of method: that when the *tablīgh* knowledge utilizes scientific knowledge for its purpose, its approach will be scholarly; whereas the approach of revelation in scientific issues is "analogical," rather than scientific.

We may now embark upon the *Risale* to see how its author, Said Nursi, perceives the whole corpus compiled by him. First of all, he points out to the aim of the revealed knowledge, the Qur'an, as *guidance par excellence*, which we mentioned above: "The Qur'an's chief function is to teach about the perfections and acts of the sphere of dominicality and the duties and circumstances of the sphere of worship."[21] In a memoir, he alludes to the main purpose (*vazife-i asliye*) of the *Risale*, as following the Qur'an, being guidance in the manner of revelation:

> Tahir Pasha, the Governor of Van, assigned me a room in the upper storey of his residence. I used to stay there. Every night when I retired to my room I would recite for three hours the ninety books, concerning true sciences (*haqāiq*), I had memorized. It used to take three months to get through all of them. Thanks be to God, my brothers, what I had memorized and my repetition of them became the steps to ascend to the truths of the Qur'an. Some time later I ascended to those truths and I saw that each of the Qur'an's verses encompasses the universe. The Qur'an was then sufficient for me; no need remained for anything else, any other book.[22]

He also tells us how he experienced a crisis of *tablīgh* in his life:

> Thirty years ago dreadful blows descended on the heedless head of the Old Said and he pondered over the assertion "Death is a reality." He saw himself in a muddy swamp. He sought help, searched for a way, tried to find a savior. He saw that the ways were many; he was hesitant. He took an omen from the book *Futuh al-Ghayb* of Gawth al-A'zam, Shaykh Gilani (May God be pleased with him). It opened at these lines: "You are in the *Dar al-Hikma*, so find a doctor who will heal your heart." It is strange, but at that time I was a member of the *Darü'l-Hikmeti'l-Islamiye*. It was as though I was a doctor trying to heal the wounds of the people of Islam, but I was sicker than they. A sick person must look to himself first, then he may look to others. . . . So I said: "You be my doctor!" . . . I again opened the book and read it right through; I benefited a lot from that book of my first master. . . Then I saw the *Letters* (*Mektubat*) of Imam-i Rabbani and took it in my hands. I opened it with pure intention to take an omen. . . . Only, the Imam persistently recommended in many of his *Letters* what he wrote in these two, which was: "Make your *qibla* one." That is, take one person as your master and follow him; do not concern

---

21. Nursi, *Sözler*, 358; Nursi, *The Words*, 273.

22. Quote from Erdem, *Davam*, 94–95. Trans. Şükran Vahide in the *Third Symposium*, op. cit., 2:110.

yourself with anyone else. This most important recommendation did not seem appropriate to my capacity and mental state. However much I thought: "Should I follow this one, or that one, or that other one?," I remained in a state of bewilderment. Each had different characteristics which drew me, one was not enough for me. While thus bewildered, it was imparted to my heart by God's mercy that "the head of these various ways and the source of these streams and the sun of these planets is the All-Wise Qur'an; the true single *qibla* is to be found in it. In which case, it is also the most elevated guide and most holy master." So I clasped it with both hands and clung on to it.... That is to say, the words and those lights, which proceed from the Qur'an, are not only scholarly matters pertaining to the intellect, they are rather matters of belief which pertain to the heart, the spirit, and spiritual states. They resemble most elevated and valuable knowledge of God.[23]

It is clear that in this memoir Nursi emphasized the difference between revealed knowledge and *tablīgh* knowledge, which we explained above as the scholarly approach in his work. He thus describes the *Risale* above as "scholarly matters pertaining to the intellect."[24] But as a corollary of the revelation, "they are rather matters of belief which pertain to the heart, the spirit, and spiritual states," which are the marks of revealed knowledge as guidance inherited by the *Risale*. For, Nursi points out that "the truths and perfections in the *Risale* are not mine; they are the Qur'an's and they have issued from the Qur'an. The Tenth Word, for instance, consists of a few droplets filtered from hundreds of verses. The rest of the treatises are all like that."[25]

Once we identify the *Risale* as belonging to the class of *tablīgh* knowledge, we need to treat them accordingly. On this basis we shall try to see how they can be utilized as a framework for the sociology of science. In order to determine this, we need to compare and contrast three classes of knowledge: revealed knowledge, *tablīgh* knowledge, and scientific knowledge. But as the aim and scope of the first two classes coalesce, we may consider them as one in kind and compare them with scientific knowledge. As this paper does not intend to dwell upon this issue I shall briefly enumerate their differences:

| TABLĪGH KNOWLEDGE | SCIENTIFIC KNOWLEDGE |
| --- | --- |
| 1. Primary purpose is "guidance." | 1. Primary purpose is real nature of things (*haqā'iq al-ashyā'*). |
| 2. Its epistemology is based on the psychology of the heart. | 2. Its epistemology is based on the mind and other rational faculties and senses. |
| 3. Its main principle is "renewal" (*tajdīd*). | 3. Its main principle is "accumulation." |
| 4. Its essence is *light* (*nūr*) and thus enlightens. It is thus like the sun. | 4. It needs the *light* of the *tablīgh* in order to enlighten. It is thus like the moon. |
| 5. It is *given* knowledge, Divine Grant. | 5. It is acquired knowledge. |
| 6. It addresses all human beings alike. | 6. It addresses only the specialist. |

---

23. Nursi, *Mektubat*, 355–56; Nursi, *Letters 1928–1932*, 418–19.

24. Ibid.

25. Nursi, *Mektubat*, 369; Nursi, *Letters*, 419.

We may give brief examples from the *Risale* pointing to these characteristics. As we have described the *tablīgh* knowledge as "renewal" (*tajdīd*), so the one representing this knowledge is a "renewer" or "regenerator" (*mujaddid*). Renewal is the restatement of the truths of revelation without their being changed, on the level of and in the style of the sciences of the century in question. That is to say, renewal is not change or substitution; it is merely expression of the truth in conformity with the understanding of the age. But of course it means that the truth expressed in this way will be renewed in some respects. In consequence of this renewal, knowledge which had become inadequate and therefore ineffective is once again made adequate and effective. We observe this characteristic of renewal clearly in the *Risale*:

> Furthermore, the great majority of the works that have been written, the treatises, have been bestowed instantaneously and suddenly in consequence of some need born in my spirit, not from any outside cause. Then when afterwards I have shown them to some friends, they have said that they are the remedy for the wounds of the present time. After they have been disseminated, I have understood from most of my brothers that they meet the needs of the times exactly and are like a cure for every ill.[26] Formerly, the fundamentals of belief were protected, submission was strong. Even if the intuitive knowledge of those with knowledge of God lacked proof, their expositions were acceptable and sufficient. But at this time, since the misguidance of science has stretched out its hand to the fundamentals and pillars [of belief], the All-Wise and Compassionate One of Glory, Who bestows a remedy for every ill, in consequence of my impotence and weakness, want and need, mercifully bestowed in these writings of mine which serve the Qur'an a single ray from the comparisons of the Noble Qur'an, which are a most brilliant manifestation of its miraculousness. . . . Whatever beauty and effectiveness are found in my writings, they are only flashes of the Qur'anic comparisons. My share was only my intense need and my seeking, and my extreme impotence and my beseeching. The ill is mine, and the cure, the Qur'an's.[27]

As to the method of *tablīgh* knowledge, Nursi clearly refers to its usage in the *Risale*:

> Most of the corpora of the blessed persons of that time, and some of the works of the religious scholars, discuss the results, fruits, and effulgences of the belief and knowledge of God. In their time, there was no attack on the fundamentals of belief, and the pillars of faith were not being shaken. Now, however, there is a severe and concerted attack on those fundamentals. Most of those corpora and those scholarly works addressed particular believers and individuals; they were not repulsing the awesome assaults of this age. As for the *Risale-i Nur*, as a miracle of the Qur'an, it saves the fundamentals of belief, and not utilizing the already existent belief (of the believers), assists through its many and brilliant proofs, in demonstrating, proving, and preserving belief, and thus saving that belief from doubts and scepticism. For this reason, those who study it carefully declare that everyone has need of it

---

26. Nursi, *Mektubat*, 375; Nursi, *Letters*, 441.

27. Nursi, *Mektubat*, 376–77; *Letters*, 443–44.

at this time, like [they have for] bread and medicine.... Also, the *Risale-i Nur* does not only teach by means and the eye of the reason like the works of other scholars, nor does it only move with the illuminations and inspirations of the heart like the saints, it rather flies to the loftiest peaks by progressing with the feet of the uniting of the reason and heart, and assistance of the spirit and other subtle faculties. It rises to places where not only the feet, but the eye of aggressive philosophy as well cannot reach, and thus demonstrates the truths of belief to eyes that are blind even.[28]

It is thus emphasized that the epistemology utilized in the *Risale* takes the route of combining mind and heart. This combination gives us an epistemology which takes three ontological realms: The absolute realm, to which the Qur'an refers with the term *ghayb*; the transcendental realm, to which the Qur'anic expression *īmān bi'l-ghayb* refers; and finally the world of the senses, to which the Qur'anic term *shahādah* refers. The absolute realm is totally closed to the human faculties of knowledge and therefore, only revelation is the authority that imparts knowledge from this realm (*'ālam*). The only method to ascertain the knowledge of the absolute realm (*'ālam al-ghayb*) is to surrender to the revelation, and thus *tablīgh* knowledge is not authoritative in this realm because it is itself dependent on the authority of the revelation with regard to the knowledge of this realm.

The method of acquiring the knowledge of the second realm with *īmān bi'l-ghayb* is to utilize our faculties connected with the heart under the guidance of the revelation. In fact, this is the main purpose (*vazife-i asliye*) of the revelation as guidance. *Tablīgh* knowledge may utilize here the method of the revelation as it inherits from the Prophet and assumes the role of guidance, as well. As for the knowledge of the third realm, *'ālam al-shahādah*, which is open to our senses and rational faculties, sciences of the *kawn*, called in Western scientific tradition "natural sciences," are authority in providing knowledge concerning things and phenomena therein.

But in all of these realms the ultimate decision depends on the disciplined human intellect, which is thus accepted in Islamic epistemology as the "ruler." For it is the intellect that will eventually give the decision. Nursi emphasizes this fact and also enunciates a general rule that the intellect (*'aql*) should not be left alone; it must be followed by the senses in the *'ālam al-shahādah* and by the heart in the realm of *īmān bi'l-ghayb*. Otherwise, it will suffer bad consequences, expressed by Nursi as, "Without the light of the heart the light of the mind will not shine; so long as the two lights are not combined, all is darkness."[29] The following fact, emphasized strongly by Bediüzzaman, throws light on the subject:

> The light of conscience is religious sciences [*ulûm-u diniye*]. The light of the mind is modern sciences [*fünûn-u medeniye*]. The reconciliation of both manifests the truth. The student's skills develop further with these two (sciences). When they are separated, from the former superstition and from the latter corruption and skepticism is born.[30]

28. Nursi. *Kastamonu Lahikası*, 27–28.

29. Nursi, *Sözler*, 958; Nursi, *The Words*, 739.

30. Nursi, *Muhakemât*, present author's translation, printed in his collected works in Nursi, *Risâle-i Nur Külliyâtı*, vol. 2, 1956.

It is at his junction that the *Risale* brings an epistemological basis for the sociology of science outlined above. Now that we have outlined the nature of Nursi's corpus and its methodology as a class of *tablīgh* knowledge in order to show how it acts as a frame of mind for the contemporary Muslim scientist and sociology of science, we may attempt to show what kind of an epistemological basis it provides for the *kawnî* sciences (*'ulûm-u kevniye*).

## THE *RISALE* AS AN EPISTEMOLOGICAL BASIS FOR THE SOCIOLOGY OF SCIENCE

In the above discussion we have provided a comparison on a table between scientific knowledge and what we have called *tablīgh* knowledge. This comparison also tells us their differences. It is clear that the essential purpose of *tablīgh* knowledge is to provide *guidance* in the Qur'anic sense. Otherwise it cannot furnish *light* for the guidance of scientific knowledge in general. This may bring forth the awesome question of objectivity for scientific undertakings. But we should not be worried at the moment about this question, as we shall try to show that guidance in this case is related to values, on the one hand, and mental frameworks, on the other. Both of these cannot be dispensed with (even if we avoid the guidance of *tablīgh* knowledge); in other words, neither the mental frameworks nor the values can be omitted in order to be objective in scientific search. In that case what we are suggesting is that we should let the divine guidance provide a mental framework for us as well as values because if this guidance is avoided, some other values and frameworks will replace them, endangering thus the objectivity of scientific activities. We may give the following example in this case from the *Risale* in order to explain how the divine guidance may act as a mental attitude for scientific activities:

> All attainments and perfections, all learning all progress, and all sciences, have an elevated reality which is based on one of the divine names. On being based on the Name, which is concealed under numerous veils and has various manifestations and different spheres, the sciences and arts and attainments find their perfection and become reality. And this is not some incomplete and deficient shadow.[31]

*Tablīgh* knowledge is thus the knowledge penetrating all other knowledge, qualifying it, and raising it to the level of enlightened knowledge. This conclusion shows us too that it is necessary that the revelational aspect is incorporated into the knowledge of all Muslim scholars, either directly from the Qur'an, or through a teacher who achieved this. A striking example from the *Risale* shows how revelational knowledge is made to penetrate and suffuse philosophical knowledge, raising it to the level of enlightened knowledge:

> O world-worshipping person! Although you conceive of your world as very broad, it resembles a narrow grave. But since the walls of that narrow grave-like dwelling are of glass, they are reflected one within the other and stretch as far as the eye can see. While being narrow as a grave, your world appears to be as large as a town. For despite both the right wall, which is the past, and the left wall, which is the future, being non-existent, they are reflected one within the other,

---

31. Nursi, *Sözler*, 262–63; Nursi, *The Words*, 270.

unfolding the wings of present time, which is extremely brief and narrow. Reality mixes with imagination, and you suppose a non-existent world to be existent. Like on being spun round at speed, a line appears to be broad like a surface, despite in reality being a fine line, your world is in reality narrow, but due to your heedlessness, delusions, and imagination, its walls have drawn far apart. If driven by a calamity you stir in that narrow world, you will hit your head on the wall, which you supposed to be distant. It will dispel the illusions in your head and banish your sleep. Then you will see that that broad world of yours is narrower than the grave, finer than the Bridge of Sirat. Your life passes faster than lightning, it pours away more swiftly than a stream gushing through. Since worldly life and the life of the flesh and animal life are thus, shake free of animality, leave behind corporeality, and enter the level of life of the heart and spirit! You will find a sphere of life, a world of light, broader than the world you imagined to be broad. The key to that world is to make the heart utter the sacred words 'There is no god but God,' which express the mysteries of Divine Unity and knowledge of God, and to make the spirit work them.[32]

Here, a psychological error is indicated which results from the concepts of existence and non-existence being applied to the fact of time, and the sorts of disasters this error can drive human beings are examined extremely effectively from the angle of revelational knowledge. Thus, both philosophy and psychology are employed in *tablīgh*. If the basic aim here had been philosophy or psychology, the nature of the concepts of existence and non-existence would have been studied from the philosophical angle, and how the errors occurred explained perhaps by experimental and observational methods. However, without paying much attention to these questions, it moved on to explain *tablīgh* knowledge, which is necessary for Islam to be reflected in life. The aim of *tablīgh* knowledge is to prevent the sciences being broken off from one another and becoming unrelated to each other, and particularly to prevent their relations with revelation being severed. It is this that the *Risale* aims to do, since it is *tablīgh* knowledge which illuminates human beings spiritual and inner aspects, while it is the physical sciences that illuminate his reason. Nursi refers to the former as "the sciences of religion," and to the latter as "the sciences of civilization." It is through the blending of the two that the truth is revealed. If they are separated, it leads to bigotry in the former, and skepticism and trickery in the latter.[33]

Since its aim is guidance, *tablīgh* knowledge generally addresses all classes of people without distinction. For this reason, it employs every sort of subject and means from the simplest to the most profound, and from the most straightforward manner of exposition to the most precise and scholarly methods. Thus people from all sectors may benefit from it in proportion to their endeavor and abilities. Nevertheless, of course, there will be a difference between the degree to which a learned person profits and an illiterate one does.

> I shall tell you about a conversation between my elder brother Abdullah and myself forty to fifty years ago: my

---

32. Nursi, *Lem'alar*, 136–37. Nursi, *The Flashes*, 186.

33. Nursi, *Munazarat*, translated by the author for this study, 72.

late brother was the special disciple of Hazret Ziyaeddin, one of the great saints. Even if it is to excess, the followers of the *tariqats* consider acceptable tremendous love and good will towards their spiritual guides. My late brother said: "Hazret Ziyaeddin knows all the sciences. He has knowledge of everything in the universe like the supreme spiritual pole." He described his truly wondrous stations in order to bind me to him. I said to my brother: "You are exaggerating. If I was to see him, I would silence him in numerous matters. Moreover, you don't in fact love him as much as I do. For you love a Ziyaeddin you imagine as a supreme spiritual pole who knows all the sciences in the universe; that is, you are bound to him because of that title. . . . If the veil of the unseen was to be drawn back and the truth was to become apparent, your love would either evaporate or it would be reduced fourfold. Whereas I earnestly love that holy person like you, and appreciate him. For he is a sincere, effective, and important guide for the people of belief, in the way of reality within the sphere of the *sunna* of the Prophet. I would sacrifice my spirit for him for this service of his, whatever his personal station and rank. If the veil was to be drawn back and his true station was to become apparent, I would not withdraw or give him up or my love diminish, on the contrary I would adhere to him with even greater respect and appreciation. That is, I love a true Ziyaeddin, while you love an imaginary one!" Being a fair-minded and exacting scholar, my brother accepted my point of view and applauded it.

O valuable students of the *Risale-i Nur* and my brothers more fortunate and self-sacrificing than myself! Perhaps your excessively favorable views of my person will not harm you, but perspicacious persons like you should look to your service and duties, and from that point of view. If the veil was to be drawn back, my altogether faulty nature would cause you to flee from me. So as not to make you flee from my brotherhood and for you to regret it, do not bind yourselves to stations you imagine in my person which are far higher than my due. In relation to you I am a brother; to be spiritual guide is beyond my due. I am not your teacher either, but your fellow student. Because of my faults I am in need of your compassionate prayers and your support. It is not your awaiting help and support from me, it is my right that you help me. Through Almighty God's grace and munificence, and according to the rule of the division of labour, I share in a most sacred, most important, and most valuable service, of benefit to all believers. The extraordinary importance, worth, guidance, and teaching of the collective personality obtained through our solidarity is sufficient for us.[34] It is understood from this that enlightened knowledge can be attained only deficiently and partially without revelation, and this is not something that Islam wants. For revelation is not only an aspect which qualifies knowledge, it is itself also knowledge. For numerous matters like God's existence, His essence, the hereafter, the nature of revelation, and human freedom, which the Qur'an calls "the Unseen," can only be known through revelation. Thus, knowledge of them is revelational knowledge. And this shows that revelation comprises knowledge. "Medicine is a science, and also an art; it is ultimately based on the Absolutely Wise One's Name of Healer, and through seeing

---

34. Nursi, *Kastamonu Lâhikası* in the *Külliyât*, 1605, letter number 58. Trans. Şükran Vahide in the *Third Symposium*, op. cit., 115.

the compassionate manifestations of that Name in the vast pharmacy of the face of the earth, medicine finds its perfection and becomes reality."[35] It is thus saved from being sophistry. Again, relying on this fact it is stated that "philosophy without religion is a sophistry divorced from reality and an insult to the universe."[36]

It is understood from this that the qualification of knowledge gives rise to a moral dimension. *Ḥadīths* have dealt with this dimension to a greater extent, thus implanting in the heads of Muslims a mentality springing from Islamic knowledge. For example, it is said in a *ḥadīth* which illustrates this moral dimension: "A person who teaches knowledge to one unworthy of it will have draped a necklace of precious stones, gold and emeralds on a pig."[37] It is also related that God's Messenger prayed: "O God! I seek refuge with you from useless knowledge."[38] That is to say, knowledge that is not enlightened by revelation causes harm to people rather than benefit. It is understood from this that in the Islamic context, if knowledge is indifferent towards life and the living of it and it is not qualified, it is considered unimportant. It should be repeated that since being qualified adds a moral dimension, all these warnings about unbeneficial knowledge should be heeded by people. For it is again human beings who produce useless knowledge. However, the knowledge revelation teaches does not bear this characteristic. For the knowledge that comes in that way is itself enlightened. We may mention the following *ḥadīth* which emphasizes this moral dimension: "One who seeks knowledge for worldly aims will go to Hell."[39] Thus, enlightened knowledge advances a fundamental attitude which has to be adopted in relation to knowledge.

It is thus clear that enlightened knowledge is a state qualified by experiential knowledge which we may reach through either revelational knowledge permeating all our other knowledge directly, or through *tablīgh* knowledge, which is based on revelation, permeating it. In fact, although numerous subjects that belong to *kalām* (theology) are discussed in detail in the *Risale*, the work's purpose is not to teach *kalām*.[40] This shows us that essentially the *Risale* should be considered within the framework of *tablīgh* knowledge. So in order to demonstrate this more clearly, we may discuss the characteristics of this knowledge, giving examples from the *Risale*.

---

35. Nursi, *Sözler*, 262–63; Nursi, *The Words*, 270–71.

36. Nursi, *Sözler*, 132; Nursi, *The Words*, 145.

37. Ibn Maja, al-Muqadimma, 17, No. 224; 1, No: 81 (Egypt, 1951). For other narrations, see *Kanz al-'Ummal*, x, 131, Nos: 28651–54.

38. Muslim, Kitab al-Dhikr, 73; Abu Da'ud, Witr, 32; Tirmidhi, Dawat, 68; Nasa'i, al-Isti'adha, 13, 18, 21, 64; Ibn Maja, al-Muqaddima, 23; al-Du'a, 2, 3; Ahmad b. Hanbal, *Musnad*, ii, 168, 198, 340, 365, 451; iii, 192, 255, 283; iv, 371, 381.

39. *Kanz al-'Ummal*, x, 196, No. 29034.

40. He describes the difference between the science of *kalām* approach and the *Risale* as follows: "Yes, the knowledge of God gained by means of theology does not afford a complete knowledge and a complete sense of the Divine presence. However, when gained in accordance with the method of the Qur'an of Miraculous Exposition, it affords both complete knowledge and gains a total sense of the Divine presence. God willing, all the parts of the *Risale-i Nur* perform the duty of an electric lamp on that light-filled highway of the Qur'an of Miraculous Exposition." In Nursi, *Mektubat*, 1928–32. Nursi, *The Letters*, 388.

## CONCLUDING REMARKS

As may be understood from our explanations, *tablīgh* knowledge forms the basis of Islam being reflected in life. Our demonstrating that the *Risale* has to be knowledge of this sort is also an indication of its existence. Therefore, I have not considered it necessary to examine it in detail from this point of view. Moreover, in Islamic history, there have been works that may be placed in this category, the best examples of which are Abu Talib al-Makki's *Qūt al-qulūb* and Ghazzali's *Ihya' 'ulūm al-dīn*. If this fact is borne in mind, both the nature of the *Risale* will be better understood, and it will put a stop to the many irrelevant disputes about the work. We also should not forget that like other Islamic scholars, Nursi strove for Islam to be reflected in life and wrote his work for this purpose, in the understanding of its being the duty of a Muslim scholar. Any criticisms that are to be made of him should be made with this same understanding, as is not only the requirement of science, but is also a characteristic of the enlightened knowledge which Islam itself seeks in scholars.

What we may infer from the above discussion is that *tablīgh* knowledge does not aim at developing a scientific theory because its aim is guidance, just as its basis, which it inherits from the revealed source is the Qur'an. But it has a fundamental difference from its revealed source in that its locus is not the Prophet but the scholar, *'ālim*. Because of this locus of *tablīgh* knowledge, it utilizes scholarly methods, as well, and thus some of the knowledge contained in it may lead to a *partial* formulation of a scientific theory. What I mean by this is that there may be some scientific theories in *tablīgh* knowledge, but this is only rudimentary, not essential to its character. As a result, we should not attempt to show in the *Risale* a complete theory of knowledge, or a theory of matter, or a complete doctrine of being. But we may utilize it as a basis for such theories because they do provide such frameworks, as explained in the first section of this study.

## BIBLIOGRAPHY

Açıkgenç, Alparslan. *Bilgi Felsefesi*. Istanbul: İnsan Yayınları, 1992.

———. "The Emergence of Scientific Tradition in Islam." *Kultur: The Indonesian Journal for Muslim Cultures* 1 (2001) 91–114.

———. "An Evaluation of the *Risale-i Nur* from the Point of View of Knowledge and the Categorization of Knowledge." In *Third International Symposium on Bediüzzaman Said Nursi*, 101–16. Istanbul: Sözler, 1995.

———. *Islamic Scientific Tradition in History*. Kuala Lumpur: Institute of Islamic Understanding (IKIM), 2014.

———. *Scientific Thought and its Burdens*. Istanbul: Fatih University Press, 2000.

Al-'Ajlūnī, Ismā'īl ibn Muḥammad. *Kashf al-Khafā' wa Muzīl al-Ilbās*. Beirut: Mu'assasat al-Risālah, 1985.

Barber, Bernard. *Science and the Social Order*. New York: Free, 1952.

———. "The Sociology of Science" In *The International Encyclopedia of Social Sciences*, edited by David L. Sills, Vol. 14: 92–100. New York: Macmillan and the Free Press, 1968.

Al-Bukhari, Muhammad ibn Ismā'īl. *Al-Adab al-Mufrad*. Edited by Kamāl Yūsuf al-Hūt. Beirut: Ālam al-Kutub, 1984. English translation by Rafiq Abdur Rahman as *Manners in Islam*. Lebanon: Dar Al-Kotob Al-Ilmiyah, 2011.

———. *Sahih* in *Al-Kutub al-Sittah wa Shuruhuha*. Istanbul: Çağrı Yayınları and Dar Sahnun, 1992.

Collins, Randall. *The Sociology of Philosophies: A Global Theory of Intellectual Change.* Cambridge: Belknap, 2000.

Al-Darimi, Abu Muhammad Abdullah ibn Abd al-rahman ibn Fadhl ibn Bahran ibn Abd al-Samad al-Tamimi. *Sunan* in *Al-Kutub al-Sittah wa Shuruhuha.* Istanbul: Çağrı Yayınları and Dar Sahnun, 1992.

Al-Dhahabi, Muhammad ibn Ahmad ibn 'Uthman ibn Qayyum 'Abu 'Abd Allah Shams ad-Din. *Tadhkirat al-Huffaz.* Hyderabad: The Dairatu'l-Ma'arif-il-Osmania, 1955.

Erdem, Rahmi. *Davam.* Istanbul: Timaş Yayınları, 1993.

Fuller, Steve. *Philosophy of Science and Its Discontents.* London: Guilford, 1993.

Giere, Ronald N. *Explaining Science: A Cognitive Approach.* Chicago: University of Chicago Press, 1990.

Gjertsen, Derek. *Science and Philosophy: Past and Present.* London: Penguin, 1989.

Al-Hindi, 'Ali ibn 'Abd al-Malik Husam al-Dīn al-Muttaqi. *Kanz al-'Ummal.* Edited by Mahmud Umar al-Dumyati. Beirut: Dār al-Kutub al-'Ilmīyah, 1998.

Ibn Hanbal, Ahmad. *Musnad* in *Al-Kutub al-Sittah wa Shuruhuha.* Istanbul: Çağrı Yayınları and Dar Sahnun, 1992.

Ibn al-Jawzi, 'Abd al-Raḥmān ibn 'Alī Abu al-Faraj. *Al-'Ilal al-Mutanahiyya.* Faysalabad, Pakistan: Idarat al-'Ulum al-Athariyya, 1981.

Istanbul İlim ve Kültür Vakfı. *Third International Symposium on Bediüzzaman Said Nursi.* Proceedings, translated from Turkish by Şükran Vahide. 2 vols. İstanbul: Sözler Publications, 1995.

Al-Khatib al-Baghdadī, Abu Bakr Ahmad ibn 'Ali. *Tarīkh Baghdād.* Edited by Bashar 'Awwad Ma'ruf. Beirut: Dār al-Gharb al-Islami, 2001.

Laudan, Larry. *Science and Values: The Aims of Science and Their Role in Scientific Debate.* Berkeley: University of California Press, 1984.

Longino, Helen E. *Science as Social Knowledge.* Princeton: Princeton University Press, 1990.

Merton, Robert K. *Social Theory and Social Structure.* 2nd ed. New York: Free, 1968.

———. *The Sociology of Science: Theoretical and Empirical Investigations.* Edited by Norman W. Storer. Chicago: University of Chicago Press, 1978.

Nursi, Bediüzzaman Said. *The Flashes Collection.* Translated by Şükran Vahide. Istanbul: Sözler, 1995.

———. *Kastamonu Lahikası.* Istanbul: Söz Basım Yayın, 2006.

———. *Lem'alar.* Istanbul: Envar Neşriyat 1990.

———. *Letters 1928–1932.* Translated by Şükran Vahide. Istanbul: Sözler, 1994.

———. *Mektubat.* Istanbul: Envar Nesriyat 1991.

———. *Muhakemât*, printed in his collected works as *Risâle-i Nur Külliyâtı*, 2 vols. Istanbul: Nesil Basım Yayın, 1996.

———. *Munazarat*, printed in his collected works as *Risâle-i Nur Külliyâtı*, 2 vols. Istanbul: Nesil Basım-Yayın, 1996.

———. *The Words.* Istanbul: Sözler, 1993.

———. *Sözler.* Translated by Şükran Vahide. Istanbul: Söz Basım Yayın, 2006.

Rheinberger, Hans-Jörg. *On Historicizing Epistemology: An Essay.* Translated by David Fernbach. Stanford: Stanford University Press, 2010.

Sorokin, Pitirim A. *Social and Cultural Dynamics*, 4 vols. New York: American Book Co., 1937.

Al-Tirmizī, Abū 'Īsa Muḥammad ibn 'Īsá al-Sulamī al-Ḍarīr al-Būghī. *Sunan.* In *Al-Kutub al-Sittah wa Shurūhuha.* Istanbul: Çağrı Yayınları and Dar Sahnun, 1992.

Whitley, Richard. *The Intellectual and Social Organization of the Sciences.* Oxford: Clarendon, 1987.

# 16

# Said Nursi's View on Materialism, Positivism, and Sciences

## Yunus Çengel

### SUMMARY

MATERIALISM, WHICH DATES BACK to ancient Greek philosophers, maintains that everything is made of matter and matter only, and all phenomena including life, consciousness, and happiness are simply due to interactions of matter. Implicit in materialism is atheism since materialism has no room for metaphysics or any supernatural being. Positivism, which is formulated in early nineteenth century after the establishment of the scientific method and the scientific developments, asserts that the only legitimate means of acquiring knowledge is through sensory experiences. Knowledge acquired by other means is nonsense. According to materialism, all existence is random, meaningless, and purposeless, and positivism declares all non-matter things as unknowable. Positivism limits true knowledge to that acquired by the observation-based scientific method and thus by the *five senses*. For positivists, to express simply, "*what you see is what there is*" and "*what you see is what it is*," and anything else is unknowable. This rather strict interpretation of empiricism has played a major role in shaping the nineteenth-century thought, and is adopted and later imposed as an ideology especially by the natural scientists. But positivism is criticized for not being based on observations and thus not being true knowledge itself by its own definition.

Rationalists cite *reason* as a significant source of knowledge, and give mathematics, morality, and induction as examples. Religious studies as a branch of learning relies generally on testimony and interpretation, like history. Theology, which is a study of the divine, beliefs, the

## INTRODUCTION

During the Middle Ages, which lasted a millennium, from the fall of Rome in the fifth century to the fall of Constantinople in the fifteenth, Western Europe suffered a general stagnation and backwardness in all areas, from economy to intellectual output in literature, art, and the sciences. Religion was the dominant influence in daily life, and clergy held a monopoly on truth. This age was characterized by a strong faith in the church and the absolute authority of clergy. The claims of Aristotle (384–322 BC) concerning the physical universe, such as the earth being the center of the universe and the planets moving in circular motions around it, were adopted as part of the doctrines of the church. But the pioneering works of Nicolaus Copernicus (1473–1543), Johannes Keppler (1571–1630), and Galileo Galilei (1564–1642) in the sixteenth century, based on careful observations and experiments, followed by the formulation of the three fundamental laws of physics in the seventeenth century by Isaac Newton (1643–1727), disproved the Aristotelian claims and shook the church's credibility. This new method of acquiring knowledge about the universe on the basis of observation, experimentation, and reason laid the foundations of the scientific method and the era of modern science. The revolt against religious authority unwilling to loosen its grip on knowledge was later named the "scientific revolution" and resulted in the church losing more and more ground as the sciences progressed. The continued scientific discoveries shattered the centuries-old notions, changed the worldview of the public, and established the reason-based modern way of thinking.

nature of God, and religious truths relies mostly on testimony and the teachings of religious authorities, with rational arguments serving in a supporting role, and investigates the relation between the divine and other beings.

Nursi can be portrayed as a new-age religious scholar and a theologian as he has chosen observation and reason as his main platform of study, with testimony serving in a supporting role. Instead of taking scripts as indisputable facts, Nursi uses observations and reason to prove the stated facts in the scripts. That is, he closed the door to blind submission that sidesteps the mind, and opened the way for convincing via rational arguments by fully engaging the mind. It can even be said that Nursi combined natural theology and revealed theology, and merged revelation with reason. In his approach which is unique in theology, Nursi combines the best of empiricism, rationalism, and testimony and sets the stage for inference by appealing to the mind and conscience of the reader. Therefore, Nursi's approach resembles in many ways the modern scientific method of inquiry. He demonstrates in his *Risale-i Nur* collection that faith and sciences are not adversaries but rather allies. He also mentions that all sciences continuously speak of God and make known of the Creator in their particular tongues. Nursi maintains that there can be no contradiction between confirmed scientific facts and religion, and that careful observations and objective thinking that form the platform of positive sciences necessitate belief rather than disbelief. Despite the common thought, Nursi asserts that sciences that maintain objectivity and logical consistency confirm belief and not refute it.

The scientific discoveries that refuted long-held beliefs, such as the earth being the center of the solar system, offered reasonable explanations of natural phenomena, casting a serious doubt on biblical authority, and resulting in a growing skepticism about all religious truths. Everything was being questioned critically, and new questions led to new discoveries. As the era of faith and submission gave way to the era of reason, the basis of knowledge shifted from religious authority inspired by revelation to scientific claims based on observation and reason. Eventually, the entire physical universe was declared the domain of science, and religion was forced to retreat into the realm of metaphysics and morality. But the church's stand was weakened, and trust in religious truths was deeply shaken. The dominance of science shed doubts on everything that violated the natural laws, such as miracles and scriptures that spoke of the supernatural. At the beginning of the twentieth century, there was a highly successful and just as arrogant scientific establishment that denigrated religion and all forms of the divine. There was even talk that a reasonable person could not possibly believe in God; and with the expanding dominance of science and materialistic philosophy, some argued, religions and faith would become things of the past.

Similar changes were occurring in the same time frame in applied sciences and engineering. During the eighteenth and nineteenth centuries, the world underwent a revolution in industrialization termed the "industrial revolution." The construction of the first commercially successful steam engine by Thomas Newcomen in 1712 (patented in 1698 by Thomas Savory) marked the beginning of the switch from manual labor to machine power, and the invention in 1775 of James Watt's efficient steam engine that reduced coal use by 75 percent accelerated the change. With the demonstration of a steam locomotive by Robert Trevithick in 1801, the electromagnetic rotation used in the electric motor by Michael Faraday in 1821, and the gasoline engine by Etienne Lenoir in 1859, industrialization was on its way to infusing all segments of society. This period witnessed the mechanization of all industries from steel-making to ship-building, textile machinery, transportation and agriculture, and the establishment of technology as the dominant source of power and wealth. Industrialization and the establishment of a working class eventually had a profound effect on all aspects of social and personal life, from political systems to individual thinking. The economic and social changes gave rise to individualism and individual freedoms, and entangled the moral fabrics of societies. All attention was turned to the world and to things that provided material gain and enjoyment, and the regard for spiritual matters and the hereafter was on the decline.

Newton's discovery of universal gravitation in the seventeenth century opened the door for a new understanding that the universe was governed by the laws of nature. This and the works of early natural philosophers such as Keppler, Copernicus, and Galileo inspired some to apply the reason-based approach to religion, also, and fueled the thought that God created the universe, set it in motion in accordance with the laws of nature, and then abandoned it. In the words of Alfred

Montapert, "Nature's laws are the invisible government of the earth."[1]

Materialism and positivism were firmly established at the beginning of the twentieth century, but this did not last long. First, Einstein's theory of relativity established that mass and energy are equivalent, and one can be converted to the other according to Einstein's famous formula. The essence of physical beings is energy, not mass, and mass is simply a special form of energy. The subatomic particles exhibit the dual character of waves and particles, and quantum mechanics established that electrons are simply waves of probabilities. In the subatomic world, being in more than one place at the same time was the rule, and existence at the subatomic level was anything but firm. All these developments shook the claims of materialism, and it became necessary to give a new interpretation of it. In the 1930s, the term "physicalism" was introduced by Otto Neurath and Rudolf Carnap, replacing matter in materialism by the broader term "physical being," i.e., existence that complies with the laws and principles of modern physics. Today materialism and physicalism are used interchangeably to conceptualize matter in a modern sense.[2]

The widely-accepted big bang theory about the origin of the universe gave rise to the notion that this is an all-material universe, and everything is made of matter (more correctly, mass-energy) and matter only. This notion still forms the foundation of modern scientific thought, and any suggestion that implies otherwise is often discarded as being non-scientific. Positivism declares unmeasurable things to be nonexistent. This is a very narrow definition of existence, as it limits existence to things that can only be seen via the naked eye or instruments. We typically rely on our five senses and instruments to assess existence. However, another way of seeing existence is through the mental eye, by examining the influences exerted on beings, with the conclusion that the source of influence must exist even if it cannot be sensed or detected directly.

Calculations show that it is not possible for visible mass to account for the gravitational force that holds the stars together in galaxies. Therefore, some kind of invisible mass called "dark matter" must provide the additional gravitational force. Dark matter does not give off, absorb, or reflect light; and it is not made of electrons, protons, neutrons. One of the objectives of the highly publicized experiments at CERN is to detect dark matter. In 1998, the Hubble Space Telescope observations of very distant supernova showed that the expansion of the universe has not been slowing due to gravity as commonly thought, but accelerating. The astrophysicists concluded that this must be caused by a mysterious form of energy unknown to anyone, called "dark energy," since this acceleration effect cannot be caused by anything that already is already known to exist in the universe. It turns out that roughly 70 percent of the universe is dark energy, 25 percent is dark matter, and the "normal" universe that contains everything ever observed with all instruments makes up only the

---

1. Laughlin, *A Different Universe*. This notion formed the foundations of the philosophy or belief called *deism*, which is in contrast to theism in narrow sense (believing in a God that intervenes in worldly affairs), polytheism (believing in the existence of many gods), and atheism (denying the existence of God altogether).

2. Stoljar, "Physicalism."

remaining 5 percent.[3] This means that most of the universe that we live in exists in "our knowledge" rather than in the familiar "physical form." Therefore, it is ironic that physics itself invented the concept of mental existence that coexists with physical existence, which is in sharp contrast with materialism and positivism. Today many prominent physicists have abandoned materialism and embraced alternative theories like parallel universes that posit simultaneous existence in an infinite number of universes.

## NURSI'S REASON-BASED APPROACH TO RELIGION

What looked to most like the peak of enlightenment and awakening for humanity and the apex of civilization was viewed by Said Nursi as abatement and animalism. He saw this captivating wave of scientism and materialism that was side-stepping the divine and promising a joyous worldly life as a serious threat for the eternal life of people, and wanted to attract attention to this great danger. Being a realist, Nursi knew that faith in the divine was weak, and thus basing his case on the verses of the Qur'an would be ineffective. Also, people were highly inclined towards worldly comfort and pleasures, and asking people to give up the certain of the present for the probable of the future would fall on deaf ears. Therefore, there was only one thing to do, and it was to counter reason-based disbelief with reason-based belief, and to demonstrate that the purest, highest, and longest lasting pleasures even in this world are in faith—to distinguish it from belief in science and in leading a virtuous life. Nursi proved the matters of faith quite convincingly by refuting all alternatives on the basis of observation, reason, and logical consistency.

The developments during the era of the scientific and industrial revolution showed that nothing would remain the same, and religion was no exception. Said Nursi was a contemporary religious scholar who recognized the realities of his time and addressed them rather than ignoring or opposing them. He approached religion like a scientist by challenging the mind with deep-probing provocative questions related to theology and religion, then seeking answers to them using rational arguments based on logic and observations. Therefore, it can be said that Nursi adopted the scientific approach to religion in general and theology in particular, and contributed to the qualification of these branches of learning as sciences. He did not hesitate to raise the most mind-boggling questions and resolve them in a reasonable fashion.

Nursi's approach is very much in line with the scientific approach. He builds his case on objective observations and universally accepted facts, and subjects his case to all sorts of scrutiny by heavily engaging reason. He asks that his analysis be accepted as true knowledge only after showing that it passes all the tests for reasonableness, compliance with observations, and conformity with known facts. Therefore, the *Risale-i Nur* "proves" the cases it makes to satisfy the mind. In instances when the direct proof of a case is not possible, Nursi uses the indirect approach and disproves the

---

3. "Dark Energy Changes the Universe." The NASA web site provides detailed information on dark matter and dark energy.

opposing alternatives to show the validity of his case. He then appeals to conscience for validation.

Nursi views the universe as a major book, and the creatures as the lines or pages of that book. The discussions in the *Risale-i Nur* are based to a large extent on observations and reasoned arguments, and thus they are fully compatible with the scientific approach. Therefore, although his writings are religious pamphlets, they also resemble scientific articles. Among those who view the universe as a book is also Einstein: "We are in the position of a little child entering a huge library filled with books in many languages. The child knows someone must have written those books. It does not know how. It does not understand the languages in which they are written. The child dimly suspects a mysterious order in the arrangement of the books but doesn't know what it is."[4] In his book *Il Saggiatore*, Galileo, who was condemned by the church for heresy, described the position of a scientist as a person trying to read the book of the universe and make some sense out of it: "Philosophy [i.e., science] is written in this grand book—I mean the universe—which stands continually open to our gaze, but it cannot be understood unless one first learns to comprehend the language and interpret the characters in which it is written."[5]

Nursi, like Einstein, sets up his experiments in the mental, rather than physical, world. Many treatises start with a claim and end with a proof. For example, the "Twenty-third Flash" on Nature starts with four hypotheses regarding creation and continues as follows:

> Indeed, since beings exist and this cannot be denied, and since each being comes into existence in a wise and artistic fashion, and since each is not outside time but is being continuously renewed, then, O falsifier of the truth, you are bound to say either that the causes in the world create beings, for example, this animal; that is to say, it comes into existence through the coming together of causes, or that it forms itself, or that its coming into existence is a requirement and necessary effect of Nature, or that it is created through the power of One All-Powerful and All-Glorious. Since reason can find no way apart from these four, if the first three are definitely proved to be impossible, invalid and absurd, the way of Divine Unity, which is the fourth way, will necessarily and self-evidently and without doubt or suspicion, be proved true.[6]

Nursi supports this thesis with a thought experiment such as this:

> Imagine there is a pharmacy in which there are hundreds of jars filled with quite different substances. A living potion and a living remedy are required from those medicaments. So we go to the pharmacy and see that they are to be found there in abundance, yet in great variety. We examine each of the potions and see that the ingredients have been taken in varying but precise amounts from each of the jars, one gram from this, three from that, seven from the next, and so on. If one gram too much or too little had been taken, the potion would not have been living and would not have displayed its special quality. Next, we study the living

---

4. Isaacson, *Einstein—His Life and Universe*, 386.

5. Galilei, *The Assayer*, 183–84.

6. Nursi, "The Twenty-third Flash," *The Flashes*, 233.

remedy. Again, the ingredients have been taken from the jars in a particular measure so that if even the most minute amount too much or too little had been taken, the remedy would have lost its special property. Now, although the jars number more than fifty, the ingredients have been taken from each according to measures and amounts that are all different. Is it in any way possible or probable that the jars should have been knocked over by a strange coincidence or sudden gust of wind and that only the precise, though different, amounts that had been taken from each of them should have been spilt, and then arranged themselves and come together to form the remedy? Is there anything more superstitious, impossible and absurd than this?[7]

Starting with this example, Nursi states that each living being may be likened to the living potion in the comparison, and each plant to a living remedy that is composed of matter taken in most precise measure from numerous and various substances. He declares the claim "causes created these" and the attribution to causes and the elements to be as unreasonable and absurd as the claim that the potion in the pharmacy came into existence through the jars being knocked over by accident. At the end, he states that all living creatures can only come into existence "through a boundless wisdom, infinite knowledge and all-encompassing will."[8] With such reason-based arguments, Nursi aims to satisfy the mind by overcoming all possible objections and to establish contentment in the heart.

Unlike the traditional religious scholars, Nursi does not invite people to embrace faith by dropping reason and unconditionally surrendering to the commandments in the undisputable Holy Scriptures. That is, he does not appeal to the conscience or hearts of people alone and bypass the mind. Instead, he directs any religious matter to the mind, and challenges the mind to examine the matter most critically, using the most stringent criteria for scientific information. He is not afraid of opening religious matters to all sorts of questioning and criticism, since he contends that there can be no contradiction between the sound mind and true messages of religion. The mind may not be able to fully comprehend some realms of religion; but lack of comprehension is not rejection.

By carefully analyzing what is observed and making logical inferrals, Nursi went further than the natural scientists in opening tunnels into the phenomena governing ordinary events behind the scenes, and describing those invisible phenomena fully with logical consistency. For example, Nursi makes the following inferrals on the basis of the observation that all existence, individually and collectively, exhibits signs of great wisdom:

> It is obvious that perfection in a work points to the perfection of the act which is the source and origin of the work. And the perfection of the act points to the perfection of the name, and the perfection of the name, to the perfection of the attribute, and perfection of the attribute to the perfection of the essential qualities, and the perfection of the qualities point necessarily and self-evidently to the perfection of the essence possessing those qualities.[9]

---

7. Ibid., 234.
8. Ibid., 235.

9. Nursi, "The Twenty-second Word," *The Words*, 313.

## KNOWLEDGE AND ITS RELATION TO THE ALL-KNOWING ONE

From atoms to galaxies, everything has a firm existence woven into a web of knowledge. Scientific research is merely an attempt to expose this body of knowledge correctly and completely. This is done by observing the glitters of knowledge in the structures of beings and by seeing the sun of knowledge that is the source of these glitters with the mental eye. For example, the mass of a cell is about one-billionth of a gram. But the knowledge that is contained within this cell fills volumes of books, and the amount is ever increasing. Hundreds of scientists have been walking through a cell whose length is one-hundredth of a millimeter for years, and still there is no end in sight. In short, the universe is a feast for knowledge, and a mysterious book filled with wisdom waiting to be read and understood. Nursi repeatedly emphasized this aspect of the universe with the phrase "the grand book of universe." He relates the precise measuredness in beings and this all-encompassing invisible universe of knowledge to the Divine Name, "All-knowing":

> A balance so perfect and measure so regular and unfailing govern in all living creatures and sorts of creatures from minute particles to the planets of the solar system that they prove conclusively an all-encompassing knowledge and testify to it with complete clarity. This means that all the evidences for knowledge are evidences also for the existence of the All-Knowing One. Since it is impossible and precluded that there should be an attribute without the one it qualifies, all the proofs of knowledge form a powerful and completely certain supreme proof of the Pre-Eternal All-Knowing One's necessary existence.[10]

Also, Nursi introduces knowledge as a prominent attribute of God, and states that knowledge indicates a being that knows everything, just like light indicates the sun:

> Yes, just as mercy shows itself as clearly as the sun through the wonders of sustenance and proves decisively a Most Merciful and Compassionate One behind the veil of the Unseen; so too, through the wisdom, purposes, and fruits of order and balance in things, knowledge, which is reined in hundreds of Qur'anic verses and in one respect is the chief of the sacred seven attributes, displays itself like the light of the sun, making known with certainty the existence of One Knowledgeable of All Things. Yes, the comparison between ordered, measured art, which points to man's consciousness and knowledge, and man's fine creation, which indicates the knowledge and wisdom of man's Creator, resembles the comparison between the tiny glow of the fire-fly on a dark night and the encompassing light of the sun at noon.[11]

Nursi stresses that point of view, like intention, may transform ordinary acts into worship: "Just as permissible habitual actions may become worship through intention, so too the physical sciences may become knowledge of God through the right point of view."[12] When a group of high-school students in Kastamonu visited Nursi and asked him to tell them about their Creator because their teachers did not speak of God, he responded as follows: "All the sciences you study con-

---

10. Nursi, "The Fifteenth Ray," *The Rays*, 615.
11. Ibid., 609.
12. Nursi, "Gleams," *The Words*, 757.

tinuously speak of God and make known the Creator, each with its own particular tongue. Do not listen to your teachers; listen to them."[13] That is, to Nursi, the science books and documentaries that do not seem to be mentioning God are indeed mentioning of God constantly—just like a book or article written about a painting is talking about the artist and describing him or her indirectly.

Nursi views the presence of numerous branches of sciences as evidence for the presence of order, and the presence of order as the presence of an orderer: "A science has been formed about every field in the universe and is being formed. The sciences consist of universal laws. The universality of the laws discloses the fine order in the field concerned. That is to say, each and every science is a faithful witness to the fine order."[14] Nursi attracts attention to the knowledge and consciousness of beings by pointing to a microbe, which is a technological wonder micro-machine, and states that the existence of beings cannot be explained by the mindless and ignorant cause-and-effect relations and natural laws in the background:

> A microbe that is invisible to the eye, a tiny animal, possesses a rather delicate and peculiar divine machine. Since that machine's existence is a mere possibility, its chances of existence and nonexistence are equal. It cannot come into existence without a necessitating cause. It is essential that that machine comes into existence with due cause. But that necessitating cause is not the natural causes. Because the delicate order in that machine is the result of knowledge and consciousness. The natural causes are inanimate things with no knowledge and consciousness. One who claims that intricate machine that amuses the minds to originate from natural causes should bestow Plato's consciousness and Calino's knowledge on every bit of natural causes. In addition, he should believe that communication is present among the particles. Those who are heedless of all wisdom and benefits in the grand order of the universe pointing to a perfect will, an all-encompassing knowledge, and a supreme power were obliged to attribute the real motive to the inanimate causes.[15]

To give a modern example, cell phones function in full compliance with the mechanical, electrical, and electromagnetic laws and principles. But the presence of cell phones is not the natural result of such natural laws. If there were no people in the world with knowledge, artistry, will, and consciousness, there would be no such thing as a cell phone today. The claim, "Even if there were no conscious human beings in the world, in time there would form cell phones that were capable of duplicating each other, and aliens that land on earth would collect cell phones from the ground like pebbles" has no scientific backing and no validity.

As a second example, when someone looks at the hundreds of dissimilar chimney rocks in Cappadocia valley in Turkey with such glasses, he may conclude that these sculptures may have formed by erosion under the influence of natural events like rain, hale, and wind that are not related to purpose and will. This is because there is no order in the

---

13. Nursi, "The Thirteenth Word," *The Words*, 169.

14. Nursi,, *Muhakemat* (Rational Arguments, in Turkish), 40.

15. Nursi, *İşârâtül İ'caz* (Signs of Miraculousness, in Turkish), 87–88.

arrangement among chimney rocks, no apparent purpose or utility is observed, no diligence is noticed, and no rules or conventions are used in their formation. The same can be said about the underground caves. But when someone enters the underground cities and observes the houses, stairs, columns, paintings, and other art work on walls and ceilings, and even the ventilation channels, he or she will immediately know that these are made by beings that possess intelligence and knowledge like human beings, even if there is no one around. This is because crafting and constructing purposely and diligently using concise measurement can be done only with consciousness, will, and knowledge. This approach shows some parallelism with the intelligent design theory. But Nursi goes beyond and makes the connection to the designer by arguing that "if there is a design, there must be a designer."

The primary sources of knowledge are observation and experimentation that rely on the five senses, reason, written and oral communication, perception, and association. Therefore, the acquisition of knowledge involves the five senses, as well as the sixth sense (inspiration) and the mental thought process. In humans, the acquisition of knowledge develops an innate understanding and growing awareness. Knowledge differs from opinions and beliefs in that mere beliefs involve personal biases, opinions involve personal biases together with doubt. Knowledge, on the other hand, involves a high level of certainty and is free of personal biases and doubt. Therefore, knowledge is often characterized as justified true belief. It is something that the mind admits and the heart affirms.

In *The Evolution of Physics,* Albert Einstein argues that we may never be able to acquire certain knowledge of the seen and the unseen and thus reach absolute reality through the inference of facts:

> Physical concepts are free creations of the human mind, and are not, however it may seem, uniquely determined by the external world. In our endeavor to understand reality we are somewhat like a man trying to understand the mechanism of a closed watch. He sees the face and the moving hands, even hears it's ticking, but he has no way of opening the case. If he is ingenious he may form some picture of a mechanism which could be responsible for all the things he observes, but he may never be quite sure his picture is the only one which could explain his observations. He will never be able to compare his picture with the real mechanism and he cannot even imagine the possibility or the meaning of such a comparison.

There is certainty and unanimity in what is observed (the face and the moving hands of the watch), but uncertainty and differing opinions on the nature of the unobservable (the sealed mechanism that runs the watch). Therefore, even in observation-based natural sciences, opinions can easily be confused with plain facts and be perceived as facts since they often come packaged together.

Sciences that are based on certified facts can prevent nonfactual interpretations in religion while religion can shed light on science to progress in the right direction. As expressed by Albert Einstein in his famous quote, "Science without religion is lame, and religion without science is blind."[16] Denying one another is

16. Einstein, "Religion and Science" *New York Times Magazine*, November 9, 1930, 1–4.

harmful to both religion and sciences. For example, if modern medicine subscribed to the notion that every being is in its highest creation, rather than the notion that every being is the outcome of a chain of random events, it would not fall into the mistake of searching for a baby food superior to mother's milk or viewing menopause as an illness and attempting to treat it with estrogen supplements, with apparent adverse results. Scientists would rise up and view creation from the perspective of the Creator, like Einstein did, and would produce innovative theories about how the universe is running.

## EMPIRICISM AND RATIONALISM AS SOURCES OF KNOWLEDGE

The ultimate source of knowledge has long been a topic of dispute between empiricists and rationalists. Empiricists hold that the only, or at least the most, reliable source of knowledge is the sense experience by means of observation and experimentation. Rationalists find this approach too limiting and hold that the reliable source of knowledge extends well beyond the knowledge acquired by perception through the five senses. Rationalists cite reason as a significant source of knowledge, and give mathematics, morality, and induction as examples. Empiricists express skepticism about knowledge that is not based on experience. Empiricists consider sense experience as the only reliable source for concepts, knowledge, and ideas, and thus knowledge as a posteriori—something that occurs after the relevant experience. Rationalists counter by claiming that it is possible to have a priori knowledge—knowledge gained before having a relevant experience.

Natural scientists are of course closely involved with the material universe. They rely on the scientific method to generate knowledge, and thus they tend to primarily use empiricism in their studies. In their scientific inquiries, they resort to carefully designed and conducted experiments, and are open to confirmation or falsification by others. They also tend to view existence as comprised of matter subject to physical laws, and thus search for answers in the motion and changes of material beings, as expected. But there are notable exceptions. Einstein, for example, derived the knowledge that formed the basis of his theories from logical empiricism via mental arguments and mathematical rigor, to be confirmed later by others with actual physical experiments. Therefore, Einstein can be said to be a rationalist since he resorted to rational intuition and reason to discover new knowledge. Likewise, as mentioned before, calculations show that visible mass cannot account for the gravitational force that holds the stars together in galaxies. Therefore, based on rational arguments alone, it is widely believed by physicists that some kind of invisible mass called "dark matter" exists that provides the additional gravitational force. Despite the lack of any direct empirical evidence for its existence, calculations show that dark matter constitutes 25 percent of the universe.

Unlike empiricism, which requires direct experience with reality and rejects other claims of truth, rationalism is not of a uniform shade, and different approaches to it exist. Some rationalists see pure reason and thought sufficient for acquiring knowledge while others require some experiential evidence. One reason for the bitter dispute between empiricism and rationalism lies in confusing the areas of applicability of each approach. The conflicts will be minimized if the two methods are pulled within their rightful boundaries.

The five senses are associated with the material world, and thus physical sciences such as physics, chemistry, and geology are prime areas of inquiry by empiricism. Still, any generalizations and understanding of what is sensed require rationalism in the form of intuitive induction. A similar argument can be given for social sciences such as psychology and sociology. Subject areas such as mathematics that are not directly associated with the physical universe are best suited for study by rationalism. For subject areas such as the philosophy of science, both empiricism and rationalism are relevant, and the two approaches should be used as appropriate to complement each other. The scientific method dwells on empiricism, and thus it is appropriate for the sciences. But denigrating information generated in non-scientific areas because the scientific method is not utilized is simply prejudice.

Empiricism and rationalism should be taken as complementing each other rather than competing with or even denying each other, and these two methods should never be in conflict during the search for truth. For example, information generated by reason and rational arguments should never be in conflict with information based on confirmed empirical studies. Therefore, information obtained in fact-based scientific fields (areas of study that are suitable for observations) using the scientific method should be taken as the base, and rational arguments should be used in a supporting role to scrutinize the observed data, to fill in the gaps, and to generalize the findings. Of course, empiricism is not infallible, and what we see is not necessarily what is. For example, for many centuries it was thought that the earth was at the center of the universe and the sun was revolving around the earth, based on plain observations. But later, unbiased careful observations refuted this old science and established the opposite as the truth. Therefore, raw data yielded by empiricism should always be checked for reasonableness and consistency, and be scrutinized in the light of confirmed facts.

Pluto used to be one of nine planets in the solar system since its discovery in 1930. But on August 24, 2006 the International Astronomical Union General Assembly in Prague passed a resolution redefining the planets using a new rationale, and the new definition excluded Pluto. That is, a rationalist approach in this case took precedence over an empirical approach, since there was no new empirical information about Pluto to justify this change of status. Again there is no guarantee that the criteria for planets will not change, and thus the good old Pluto may appear in the list of planets again in the future.

In medical sciences and pharmacology, it is not uncommon for the medical "truths," which are based on empiricism and serve as the basis for treatment and prevention of diseases, to be overturned, and yesterday's justified true belief to become medical misinformation. Judgments passed on the basis of limited observations or studies are like guessing the whole picture of a puzzle board based on a limited number of pieces in place; and thus care should be exercised when attempting to construct truths on the foundation of a limited number of empirical facts—especially on multi-faceted comprehensive matters. Therefore, empirical findings also are prone to error, no matter how carefully the experiments are conducted in well-controlled environments. Being based on empiricism is no guarantee for a widely believed fact not to turn out to be actually false. Rationalism can be a valuable tool in weeding out fiction from facts.

Also, the realm of empiricism cannot reach the non-scientific areas of knowledge. Therefore, rejecting knowledge in those areas is not rational at all since empiricism is not applicable in those areas. Of course it is compulsory to accept scientific knowledge, since the evidence is external and can be demonstrated to all. But this is not the case for non-scientific knowledge, since the evidence is internal, and the rational arguments presented can be found convincing for some and non-convincing for others, and universality cannot be expected.

Nursi attracts attention to the importance of both the general branches of knowledge based on reason and the sciences based on observation and experiments, and emphasizes their future dominance: "At the end of time, humankind will spill into science and learning. It will obtain all its strength from science. Power and rule will pass to the hand of science."[17] In his work *Ishārāt al-I'jāz*, Nursi states: "The source of Islam is knowledge (*al-'ilm*) and its base is reason or intellect (*al-'aql*)"; and it is the reputation of Islam 'that it accepts the truth and rejects fallacy and delusion.'"[18] He often makes reference to Qur'anic phrases like "So will they not think,"[19] "So will they not reason,"[20] and "So will they not ponder on it"[21] to show that Islam values reason and knowledge as witness. Like a rationalist, Nursi emphasizes the importance of passing the tests for logic, consistency, and coherence in the evaluation of propositions: "Logic and coherence should be taken as a guide. . . . The guides that will point to the path of moderation and stir away from extremism on both sides are the philosophy of religion, lucidity, logic, and sciences."[22] Therefore, Nursi views both empiricism and rationalism as valid approaches so long as they are used in their rightful places. He uses both methods himself as he finds them appropriate.

## POSITIVISM

Positivism is the strict form of empiricism that limits genuine knowledge to that which is based on sense experience alone. Founded primarily by the French philosopher Auguste Comte in the 1830s and spread throughout Europe in the second half of the nineteenth century, positivism holds that the only authentic knowledge is scientific knowledge acquired by the scientific method using observations. Positivism requires knowledge to be testable, logical, and the outcome to be observable with the human senses. Any

17. Nursi, "The Twentieth Word," *The Words*, 272.
18. Nursi, *İşârâtül İ'caz*, 180.
19. Qur'an, 36:68. http://kuran.diyanet.gov.tr Accessed July 1, 2013.
20. Qur'an, 6:50.
21. Qur'an, 4:82.
22. Nursi, *Muhakemat*, 36.

proof should be made by empirical means only and not by rational arguments, and the statements must possess universal validity. It declares any knowledge based on other sources such as innate faculties and intuition as meaningless, and rejects all forms of metaphysics and inquiries about the ultimate causes or origins of events. Therefore, positivist philosophy is confined to observable "positive" facts verified empirically by actual senses. Also, scientific information is subject to change when warranted by new evidence.

It is plausible that positivism itself does not qualify as genuine knowledge since it cannot be verified empirically. Therefore, positivism better fits into the domain of ideology, and the positivistic view labeled "scientism." Positivists label all knowledge not directly tied to observations and verification not as wrong but as meaningless, and thus ignore it. But many philosophers respond by critiquing positivism and labeling this highly confining approach nonsense. At first look, the positivist approach may seem appropriate for hard sciences such as physics, chemistry, and geology since they are based on observations; but even this is debatable in the light of quantum mechanics, since the position of the observer influences the outcome of the observation. Extending the positivistic approach to other fields of learning, even social sciences, has met with resistance, and most social scientists and historians have long disregarded positivism in their line of work. Also, based on physical laws, we precisely know what time the sun will rise tomorrow morning. Yet positivism will reject this knowledge since it cannot be tested (our senses are limited to the current time, and cannot extend to the future). Therefore, positivism is irrelevant for most knowledge, and thus cannot be used as a general criterion for true knowledge.

Nursi uses the expression "understand no further than their eyes see, have no heart, are blind, and have grown distant from spiritual matters"[23] to describe those who subscribe to the positivist movement and limit knowledge to what is acquired on the basis of observation and experiments. He points out that the sphere of the mind is much larger than that of the eye, and the sphere of the heart is much larger than that of the mind.

Empiricism (in particular positivism), with its focus on the five senses, is just one of the mechanisms of acquiring knowledge. Declaring knowledge that is not suitable for testing in laboratories, and thus whose truth or falsehood cannot be ascertained on the basis of measurements, as unscholarly is not scholarship, but rather, prejudice and bigotry. The positivist approach can be suitable for sciences that are based on observation and laboratory testing, but learning will be limited to the scientific. The scale of the grocer can measure only things that have weight and thus things that respond to gravity. Ignoring and even denying things like temperature, length, electric charge, time, and light because they cannot be measured by a grocer's scale is not scholarship; it is "grocer-ship." The scale that receives and measures the light of knowledge is the mind; both knowledge and the mind are non-matter. It is unfair to limit knowledge to that which reflects on matter; this is an attempt to materialize knowledge and its processing center, the mind. And this is opposite to the

---

23. Nursi, "The Eleventh Ray," *The Rays*, 234.

nature of things—wishing for the impossible—since there is neither knowledge nor mind in the basic building blocks of matter.

Consider a person who found a box of chocolate gift-wrapped in a bag, hanging on the doorknob of his house when he opened the door in the morning after a stormy night. There is no question about the presence of the box of chocolate, and any bypasser will agree that there is a box of chocolate hanging at the door, since the five senses will positively confirm it. But the answer to the question, "How did this box of chocolate ended up on the doorknob?" is not easy to answer since the five senses cannot confirm it (unless there was a security camera recording the vicinity of the door the night before). One possibility is for someone to have left it there intentionally as a sign of love, with the element of surprise to enhance the effect. Another possibility is to presume that someone walking in the neighborhood dropped off the box of chocolate, which was already gift-wrapped and conveniently put in a bag, after which a gusty wind blew it away and lifted it in the air, with the chocolate box finally ending up on the doorknob of the house by accident. A third possibility is that the rain and the wind moved the debris and matter around and lightening struck, initiating chemical reactions, so that the molecules merged that made up the chocolate, the wrapping material, and the bag, and then somehow arranged themselves so as to assemble a box of gift-wrapped chocolate in a bag; and finally a strong wind moved it to the doorknob.

When let loose, there is no end to the possibilities the human imagination can generate. It is up to the human mind to sort out these possibilities and choose the most probably one. In this particular case, probably all people will reject the third possibility, and almost all will think that this is a surprise gift by a loving person. This belief will be reaffirmed if the same thing happens the following night. Of course, there will always be some, especially those with no concept of love, care, and generosity, who will refuse to accept that actually a thinking being is leaving those gifts unless they see "positive proof"; i.e., the identity of the person who has done it. It is ironic that those who chose to subscribe to the notion that those gifts are due to the passers-by who are dropping the boxes or the random winds never ask for a proof for it.

For example, scientifically it is well-established that tobacco is one of the strongest cancer-causing agents. Tobacco use is closely associated with lung cancer, with 90 percent of lung-cancer deaths among men in the United States attributed to smoking. Men who smoke one pack a day are 10 times more likely to suffer lung cancer compared with nonsmokers. Also, smokers are up to six times more likely to suffer heart attacks than nonsmokers.[24] For an ordinary person looking at these statistics, it is clear that smoking causes cancer and a rational person should abstain from smoking.

For a rationalist, the proposition "smoking causes cancer" is true knowledge since it is certified on the basis of an overwhelming amount of observational evidence. Yet for a positivist, this proposition is false since there are some smokers who never get cancer, thus falsifying the proposition. Similarly, from the

---

24. U.S. National Institutes of Health, National Cancer Institute, "Smoking."

positivistic view, the proposition "drunk driving causes accidents" is also false since there are so many people who drive while drunk without getting involved in a traffic accident. These examples reaffirm that the positivist approach based on the strict scientific method is limited to inanimate beings only, and is not applicable to animate beings, especially human beings. Adopting a rational approach, the whole world is unanimous in discouraging smoking because of its harm to smokers themselves and banning drunk driving because of its potential harm to others.

Governments appeal to the minds of their citizens with facts based on data obtained from observational studies to change citizens' behavior regarding smoking and drunk driving. Nursi does the same thing in the *Risale-i Nur* on matters of belief and religion by presenting facts on the basis of reasoned arguments stemming from observations. Nursi strongly argues that a rational person should choose belief over disbelief, just like choosing non-smoking over smoking, using statistics:

> A single hour a day is sufficient for the five prayers together with taking the ablutions. So what a loss a person makes who spends twenty-three hours on this fleeting worldly life, and fails to spend one hour on the long life of the hereafter; how he wrongs his own self; how unreasonably he behaves. For would not anyone who considers himself to be reasonable understand how contrary to reason and wisdom such a person's conduct is, and how far from reason he has become, if, thinking it reasonable, he gives half of his property to a lottery in which one thousand people are participating and the possibility of winning is one in a thousand, and does not give one twenty-fourth of it to an eternal treasury where the possibility of winning has been verified at ninety-nine out of a hundred?[25]

Also, the deterministic positivist approach is not suitable to the general philosophy of religion as it would result in compulsion, whereas religion is a choice, just like smoking. A person does not have a choice when it comes to obeying gravity.

## NATURAL SCIENCES AND THE SCIENTIFIC METHOD

Science can be defined as the continuing process of acquiring knowledge about the universe in a systematic manner and reducing that body of knowledge into general principles that are open to testing by others. Science constitutes the branch of knowledge that is related to observed phenomena in both animate and inanimate worlds. As such, scientific information is universal in nature and it is common to all people since we all share the same universe. Historically, "science" was used as a synonym for "knowledge." The term science acquired its modern meaning in the nineteenth century with the development of the experiment-based scientific method.

Sciences may broadly be subdivided into the categories of natural sciences (called natural philosophy until the modern era) which study natural phenomena, and social sciences which study human behavior and societies (formerly called moral philosophy). The natural sciences consist of physical sciences (physics, chemistry, astronomy, etc.), earth sciences (physical geography, geology, hydrology, meteorology, etc.), and life

25. Nursi, "The Fourth Word," *The Words*, 33.

sciences (biology, zoology, botany, genetics, medicine, etc). Social sciences include psychology, sociology, anthropology, and economy. Each branch is divided into sub-branches (like mechanics, optics, electricity, particle physics, thermodynamics, etc. under physics). Sciences such as biology and social sciences that rely heavily on statistics are called soft sciences.

Scientific knowledge is condensed into testable (and thus falsifiable) theories and laws. The scientific method involves the elements of (1) the collection of data and evidence through experimentation and observation, (2) the formulation of hypotheses by the reduction of data and evidence, (3) testing of the hypotheses, (4) elimination of any inconsistencies through reasoning, and (5) verification of hypotheses by further testing, examinations, and reasoning. The body of knowledge acquired using the scientific method is also referred to as science. Further, the word science is used commonly as a label for fields that are studied systematically. The goal of science is to acquire knowledge in order to better understand and describe natural phenomena. This is done by revealing the intricacies of the inner workings of beings, and thus exposing the invisible machines that govern natural phenomena behind the scenes.

The testing ground for material beings is the modern laboratory equipped with state-of-the-art equipment and well-trained technicians. Hypotheses are verified or falsified on the basis of data obtained from careful measurements. Verified knowledge is then accepted as fact, and falsified knowledge is discarded as fiction. Therefore, the data collected from experiments is the deciding factor.

Even after being well-established, scientific theories are subject to falsification by new contradictory data obtained by more careful measurement. Therefore, absolute certainty in sciences is a rarity. For observational studies, the entire earth becomes an observatory. Scientific knowledge about the fields of psychology and sociology is derived by carefully observing the common traits in the behaviors of individuals and groups of individuals, respectively. Medical science involves both laboratory studies and observational studies in acquiring knowledge related to health and medication.

Science pertains to perceived reality, and it is a valuable tool for trying to describe *what is*. But it does not deal with untestable matters. The objective of science is to understand, describe, and formulate physical phenomena (usually as physical laws or theories) underlying occurrences in the natural world which can predict similar future occurrences. Once a working knowledge of a phenomenon is gained through observations, predictions for the future and generalizations can be made even if an adequate explanation for the phenomenon cannot be given.

Science is often mixed with opinions, beliefs, and extensions, and thus unscientific information is often presented as science. To avoid confusion and mix-up, it should be remembered that science refers to objective knowledge and deals with *what is*. Scientific knowledge is based on observable phenomena, and it is open to testing by others for verification or falsification. The objective of science is to describe what is on the basis of sensation filtered through reason, but not to deduce. The conclusions drawn or deductions made from the studied phenomena on the basis of what is observed is philosophy and not science. Still, the line between science and non-science is not clearly drawn. Therefore, when it is done right, there is unanimity in science since all unbiased observers will observe the same, but conflict in philosophy since the deductions made often reflect personal biases.

Nursi accepts the sciences being based on the five senses as part of their nature, and states that sciences are the senses of humanity. He calls on people to interpret the knowledge that comes via the sciences and points to the high order behind the scenes to make the right inferrals: "O humankind! If your thinking and your vision prove inadequate to discover this high order, and if you are unable to see that order even after a general investigation or a comprehensive research, examine the universe and read its pages via the sciences that result from the joining of ideas of people and are like the senses of humanity so that you see that high order that leaves the minds astonished."[26] According to Nursi, if the world were a human being, the sciences would have been its senses through which to perceive the environment.

The scientific method relies on observations and careful reasoning. Science analyzes what is sensed on the basis of reason and logic, and any deductions that go beyond what is observed are not scientific. Studying the behavior of living organisms systematically under varying conditions is science, but theorizing about how life started on earth is non-science. So it is no surprise that there is general agreement among all manuscripts on cell biology, but widespread dispute on the origin of life. Of course this does not mean that searching for the origin of life is not a legitimate learned activity. All efforts that produce useful knowledge are part of scholarship, and the success of non-scientific information depends on the degree of consistency with observed phenomena, compliance with logical rules, and appeal to reason. Non-scientific information that is inconsistent with science and does not appear to be reasonable will obviously not find much acceptance. Well-supported non-scientific information with convincing arguments and logical consistency will be perceived by the human mind as "fact"—just like scientific information based on observations and laboratory experiments.

Consistency with an existing body of knowledge, conformity to observed phenomena, and compliance with reason and logical consistency are important tools for testing hypotheses. Logical consistency can be used as an effective means of identifying and eliminating falsehood. This is commonly done by thought experiments even in the fields of hard natural sciences like physics. The motivation behind thought experiments is clear: they are fast, inexpensive, easy to devise, and very effective, especially in falsifying hypotheses. Besides, sometimes it is impossible to set up real experiments in the lab for certain phenomena (like those associated with black holes), and experimental work is time-consuming and expensive. Albert Einstein is famous for well-done thought experiments in physics. Said Nursi is also a master in setting up vivid scenarios and analyzing them in the light of knowledge and reason. With oft-used expressions like "Is it at all possible . . . ?"

---

26. Nursi, *İşârâtül İ'caz*, 86.

Nursi invites people repeatedly to weigh differing ideas with the scale of logic.

## PHYSICAL AND SOCIAL SCIENCES

Scientific investigations rely on experimentation, observation, and reason. They involve the collection of raw data that contain unprocessed information, the analysis and classification of facts, checking for logical consistency, and generalization—like the supply-and-demand law in economics. Experimentation constitutes a major part of scientific investigations that involve matter, such as physics and chemistry. But sciences that involve the behavior of humans and human societies are characterized as observational, and proceed mostly via observation and reason.

Physical and earth sciences deal with inanimate matter, which is fully governed by the laws of physics, and always gives the same reaction to a specific action. The motion of a piece of wood dropped in a river, for example, can be predicted accurately using the relevant physical laws and principles. Therefore, the cause-and-effect relationships hold well for natural sciences, and the general conclusions drawn are verifiable and universally applicable. Also, natural sciences are well-suited for observational and experimental studies, and thus the scientific method in the strict modern sense. This is also the case for animate beings like plants that lack free will, but not so for human beings that possess free will together with a physical body that is subject to physical laws—the subject of social sciences. Despite some common traits like playing in water or swimming towards either side of the river, no one can predict with precision what a particular person will do when dropped into a river. Social sciences deal with societies made up of free-thinking individuals rather than mindless molecules. As a result, social sciences are often labeled soft sciences, and use a distinct form of the scientific method in the broad classical sense as their methodology.

Natural theology is the branch of theology based on reason and rational arguments alone, with no recourse to revelation and scriptures. Natural theology holds that knowledge about the existence and nature of God may be acquired on rational grounds by merely observing creation, reasoning, and contemplating. It differs from revealed theology, which is based on scriptures. Many theologians are skeptical about natural theology because of the limitations of human faculties and reasoning power, and view divine guidance as an essential component. Judging from the imaginative mental scenarios created and the rational arguments presented to demonstrate his cases in his *Risale-i Nur* collection, Said Nursi can be labeled a natural theologian. He uses natural theology as a platform to arrive at revealed theology and to establish the proper framework for the interpretation of revelation, thus merging these two branches of theology and combining reason with revelation.

Nursi states that the critique of religion and theology by those who are involved in the positive sciences do not carry much weight since these two fields are so different—just as the words of an engineer on medicine do not have much value. With respect to a problem subject to discussion in science or art, those who stand outside that science or art cannot speak authoritatively, however great, learned and accomplished they may be, nor can their judgments be accepted as decisive. They cannot form part of the learned consensus of the science. For example, the judgment of a great engineer on the diagnosis and cure of a disease does not have the same value as that of the lowliest physician. In particular, the words of denial of a philosopher who is absorbed in the material sphere, who becomes continually more remote from the non-material or spiritual and cruder and more insensitive to light, whose intelligence is restricted to what his eye beholds—the words of such a one are unworthy of consideration and valueless with respect to non-material and spiritual matters.[27]

He also states elsewhere:

> A person who is far from something cannot see that thing as clearly as the one who is close. Whenever there is disagreement about the nature of something, the opinion of the person closely is valued no matter how intelligent the far person is. Therefore, one cannot say that the philosophers that discovered technological things like lightening and steam can also discover the lights of the Qur'an and the secrets of truth. Because his mind is at his eyes. And the eye cannot see what the mind and the heart see.[28]

## CONCLUSION

We sense many things—including force, love, and even life—only when they are manifest in matter, so naturally we think matter to be the source of everything. This prejudgment that we've held since childhood without much questioning still forms the main platform on which sciences are built. Nursi did not show any interest in the one-dimensional view that the universe and everything in it are made entirely of matter (or energy), and criticized those who have. To those who raised the objection "Who do you think you are to challenge these famous philosophers? You are like a mere fly and yet you meddle in the flight of eagles!" Nursi responded by saying, "The matter in which they got drowned did not even wet my toes."[29]

Like a natural philosopher, Nursi does not refrain from attacking the most perplexing matters; he even questions the nature of the most fundamental concepts of physics, like natural law and force, which are closely associated with existence and the concept of nature. While the materialistic thinkers present the familiar physical universe that formed after the big bang as the whole of existence, Nursi views this universe as the "corpse of creation" which he terms the "manifest universe." He describes nature as the laws and principles of creation that regulate the motions of the parts and elements of this material body and maintain order, and sees nature as a divine printing machine that prints the works of the Creator in the form of books: "There exists divine laws of creation that keep the motions of the elements and parts of the corpse of creation, known as the manifest universe, in line and in order. It is this set of the laws of creation that is called 'nature' or 'divine printing machine.' Yes, nature consists of the assembly of the immaterial

---

27. Nursi, "The Seventh Ray," *The Rays*, 127.
28. Nursi, *Mesnevî-i Nuriye*, 239.
29. Nursi, "The Thirtieth Word," *The Words*, 568.

laws that are in effect in the creation of the universe."³⁰

To Nursi, what is called natural law is a section or article of this constitution of creation that is called nature, and force is the enforcement of these laws. The law of gravity, for example, is part of nature. The force of gravity, on the other hand, is the enforcement of the law and thus for everything to be pulled towards the center of the earth was foreseen by the law of gravity. The fact that the laws of nature are in effect since the beginning of the universe and the tendency of people to confuse illusion with reality set the stage for human imagination to give nature a real external existence. This is done as if there is an invisible very powerful hand that controls everything from subatomic particles to galaxies, and enforces the laws with no tolerance. In reality, what are known as laws and general forces do not have the ability to serve as the cause and the source for this universe. But because of the unawareness about the Artist of the universe and the forcing of the undeniable order, thinking that the astonishing works of wonder are the making of nature which is nothing more than a printing press is the result of an invalid argument which claims that a book is the natural product of a printing machine. According to Nursi, nature is nothing more than a channel of water, but somehow it is confused with being the source of water because of the over-involvement of our imagination. The superficial view that looks at a printing machine as the author of printed books has paved the way for shallow and amusing situations.³¹

Similar to the scientific and industrial revolutions witnessed in the later part of the past millennium, Nursi has initiated a rational and open approach to religion at the dawn of the new millennium by opening up even the most sensitive theological matters to criticism and scientific scrutiny. As a result of this bold approach, the *Risale-i Nur* has put an end to the presumed clash between sciences and religion, and turned them into allies. Nursi maintains that careful observations and objective thinking that form the platform of positive sciences result in a strong belief rather than disbelief, and past experience is indicative of this.

## BIBLIOGRAPHY

Einstein, Albert, and Leopold Infeld. *The Evolution of Physics*. Edited by C. P. Snow. New York: Touchstone, 1967.

———. "Religion and Science." *New York Times Magazine*, November 9, 1930, 1–4.

Galilei, Galileo. *The Assayer*. Rome: Giacomo Mascardi, 1623.

Laughlin, R. B. *A Different Universe: Reinventing Physics from the Bottom Down*. New York: Basic, 2005.

Isaacson, Walter. *Einstein—His Life and Universe*. New York: Simon and Schuster, 2007.

NASA. "Dark Energy Changes the Universe." Online: http://www.nasa.gov/missions/deepspace/f_dark-energy.html. Accessed July 1, 2013.

Nursi, Bediüzzaman Said. *The Flashes*. Translated by Şükran Vahide. Istanbul: Sözler Neşriyat, 2009. Online: https://www.dur.ac.uk/resources/sgia/imeis/3Fl09157-253.pdf. Accessed July 1, 2013.

———. *Işârâtü'l İ'caz* (Signs of Miraculousness, in Turkish; Translation by Yunus Çengel). Istanbul: Envar Neşriyat,1998.

---

30. Nursi, *Muhakemat*, 138.

31. Nursi, *Muhakemat*, 139.

———. *Mesnevî-i Nuriye* (Seedbed of Light, in Turkish; Translation by Yunus Çengel). Istanbul: Envar Neşriyat, 1998.

———. *Muhakemat.* (Rational Arguments, in Turkish; Translation by Yunus Çengel). Istanbul: Envar Neşriyat, 1998.

———. *The Rays.* Translated by Şükran Vahide. Istanbul: Sőzler Neşriyat, 2007. Online: https://www.dur.ac.uk/resources/sgia/imeis/15Ray07.pdf Accessed July 1, 2013.

———. *The Words.* Translated by Şükran Vahide. Istanbul: Sőzler, 2008. Online: https://www.dur.ac.uk/resources/sgia/imeis/words19-22_07_.pdf. Accessed July 1, 2013.

*Qur'an.* Translated into Turkish by Yunus Çengel. Online: http://kuran.diyanet.gov.tr Accessed July 1, 2013.

Stoljar, Daniel. "Physicalism." *The Stanford Encyclopedia of Philosophy.* Fall 2009. Edited by Edward N. Zalta. Online: http://plato.stanford.edu/archives/fall2009/entries/physicalism/. Accessed July 1, 2013.

U.S. National Institutes of Health, National Cancer Institute. "Smoking." Online: http://www.cancer.gov/cancertopics/smoking. Accessed May 10, 2012.

# 17

# The *Medresetü'z-Zehrâ*—Explorations into Its Nature and Significance

## Zeyneb Sayılgan

**INTRODUCTORY REMARKS**

Recent conversations within the Nur community on the notion of the *Medresetü'z-Zehrâ* ("The School of Brilliance")—Said Nursi's lifelong ambition of establishing an institute of higher education—have also gained prominence in the public discourse.[1] Considering current reform efforts in the educational sector and the attempt to improve the rights of ethnic groups in Turkey, it comes as no surprise that alternative concepts on schooling are sought out.[2] Nursi hoped that the institution of the *Medresetü'z-Zehrâ* could strengthen alliances between Turks, Kurds, and Arabs. It is therefore no coincidence that one academic symposium, in October 2012, focusing on Said Nursi's educational philosophy as reflected through the concept of the *Medresetü'z-Zehrâ*, had taken place in the eastern city of Van.[3] Nursi had envisioned the university in this region and hence the city bears symbolic significance.

Within this public discourse, the exact nature of the *Medresetü'z-Zehrâ*, its purpose, and its realization still remain unclear. Based on Nursi's own defining parameters as articulated in his *Risale-i Nur* (henceforth *Risale*), many argue in a literal fashion for the establishment of formal institutes of higher education.[4] Other

---

1. See Bulut, "*Medrese*tü'z-Zehrâ modeli" or Çalışlar, "Said-i Nursi, Atatürk ve Van'a üniversite."

2. See Çalışkan, "10 neden: Eğitim reformu ertelenmeli" and Laçiner, "Seçmeli Kürtçe: Yetmez ama Evet."

3. See the official symposium website, "*Me*dresetüz Zehra Sempozyumu: Said Nursi Eğitim Felsefesi" (http://www.*medrese*tuzzehrasempozyumu.com/).

4. See Özcan, "Risale-i Nur'da İttihad-ı İslâm, siyasetsiz bir siyasettir," 164.

voices express that the mass scale implications of the *Medresetü'z-Zehrâ*— again as outlined in the *Risale*—are too broad to be manifested in a sole institutional fashion. Instead, the *Medresetü'z-Zehrâ* must be perceived as a large informal enterprise: either as a mentality, visionary mindset or outlook for lack of a better term[5] (*zihniyet/bakış açısı*) or as a far-reaching civilizational program[6] (*medeniyet projeksiyonu*) setting up the foundation for a healthy social order and human progress.

This essay aims to be a modest contribution to the ongoing conversation by offering a more nuanced reading of the 400 passages dealing with the *Medresetü'z-Zehrâ* in the *Risale*.[7] As will be evident, Nursi did not neglect the founding of an institution of higher learning in the future but rather left it open. As he states in one key passage: "But God—the Most Exalted and Compassionate One—established the *mânevî* (informal, spiritual, immaterial) form/essence of that *medrese* in the city of Isparta. He made the (written) Risale-i Nur an embodiment of it. *God willing, the Risale-i Nur students will succeed in establishing the maddî (material/physical/formal) form of this exalted truth (the medrese) in the future.*"[8] This statement belongs to Nursi's Kastamonu period, lasting seven years, from 1936–43 and as such points to the later stage in the evolution of the *Medresetü'z-Zehrâ*.

Yet his effort in drawing out the characteristics of the *mânevî Medresetü'z-Zehrâ* stood out and encompassed human civilization as a whole. I argue therefore that the establishment of a formal institution of higher learning does not need to be excluded but presents only a branch in this wider civilizational program of the *mânevî Medresetü'z-Zehrâ*. This will become evident by looking closely at whom Nursi identified as "the student body."

A solid comprehension of the *Medresetü'z-Zehrâ* will provide insights into several questions: Given the centrality of this concept in his life, what did Nursi aim to accomplish with the establishment of the *Medresetü'z-Zehrâ*? Considering some of the negative outcomes of modernity, how did Nursi confront the increasing disintegration of human beings from themselves, their societies and the world? How did he challenge the fragmentation of knowledge resulting in a bifurcation of religious and natural sciences? In addition to these issues being still relevant for our own time, can we discern some early postmodern elements in Nursi's portrayal of the *Medresetü'z-Zehrâ*? And if so, can these guide us in our present quest for a holistic understanding and education of human beings?

The subsequent analysis attempts to answer these questions. First, I shall briefly examine the historical context in which the idea of the *Medresetü'z-Zehrâ* emerged. Second, I will outline the features of the formal *Medresetü'z-Zehrâ* as an institute of higher learning proposed by Nursi. This section cannot be engaged critically given the limits of this essay. Next, the evolution to the informal *mânevî Medresetü'z-Zehrâ* and how it navigated around the secular

---

5. See Yıldız, "Bediüzzaman, düşüncesi ve aksiyonuyla evrenseldir," 76.

6. See Kaplan, "*Medresetü'z-Zehrâ*: Üniversite projesi mi, medeniyet projeksiyonu mu?"

7. Simple keyword search on *e-risale* "medrese," accessed May 20, 2012, www.erisale.com.

8. The term *mânevî* connotes meanings such as metaphorical, spiritual, immaterial, informal or invisible. To retain this range of meanings I will remain with the original use of *mânevî*.

framework will be drawn out. In this context, I will reflect briefly on how the *mânevî Medresetü'z-Zehrâ* went beyond the classic understanding of the Ottoman *medreses*.

Throughout the transformation from the institutional to the *mânevî Medresetü'z-Zehrâ*, Nursi's guiding framework remained unchanged. As has been stated elsewhere, he employed the foundational Qur'anic concept of *tawḥīd* which informed his worldview.[9] This *tawḥīdī* paradigm will be addressed at the end of this study. The concluding section shall identify some early postmodern elements discernible in Nursi's approach.

## BRIEF HISTORICAL CONTEXT: EDUCATION IN THE TANZIMAT AND HAMIDIAN ERA

Nursi entered the world scene during a period in which Islamic societies had to face their decline in the technological, scientific and legal fields. Thus, many Islamic modernists proposed changes in the realm of education.[10] In fact, the modernist Islamic movement (1840–1940) pioneered the reformation of educational institutions.[11] Islamic modernism in itself was never a monolithic discourse, showing deep disagreements on virtually all subjects.[12] Without characterizing Nursi upfront as a modernist—a question which remains outside the scope of this essay—he nonetheless engaged with elements of modernity. It is in this intellectual milieu where the early origin of the *Medresetü'z-Zehrâ* as a formal institution of higher learning can be found.

In the Ottoman Empire the first educational reforms were carried out during the Tanzimat era (1839–76).[13] Reformation included the reordering of the government, administration, and many areas of Ottoman life along Western lines.[14] The intention was to restore the empire's fast-declining power and deliver it from subjection to Europe.[15] Despite all efforts, the Tanzimat reforms did not solve the empire's burning issues, but it did set the future course of Turkish history. As a consequence of these wide reforms, religious institutions were neglected and Islam was taken from the center of life. The upper rank of the *'ulamā* (the religious scholars) was supportive of this new direction; the lower ranks and *medrese* (religious schools) students, however, remained fiercely hostile to it.[16] With the founding of new secular schools, the empire experienced a flow of European ideas. Frequently, students were sent to Europe and foreign languages were increasingly taught at these new institutions.[17]

The Hamidian era (1876–1909) continued the reform efforts of the Tanzimat

---

9. Yıldız, "Bediüzzaman, düşüncesi ve aksiyonuyla evrenseldir," 64.

10. For an overview of the modernist Islamic discourse see for instance *Modernist Islam (1840–1940): A Sourcebook*.

11. Kurzman, Introduction to *Modernist Islam*, 4.

12. Ibid., 5.

13. For the educational reform efforts in the late Ottoman Empire, see Somel, *The Modernization of Public Education in the Ottoman Empire 1839–1908*.

14. Ibid., 1.

15. On the Tanzimat era, see Ahmad, *The Making of Modern Turkey*; Findley, *Bureaucratic Reform in the Ottoman Empire*; and Goffman, *The Ottoman Empire*.

16. Heyd, "The Ottoman 'Ulema," 29–33; 33–35 and 39–53.

17. Evered, *Empire and Education under the Ottomans*, 2 and Somel, 22–23.

period. Throughout the empire, Sultan Abdulhamid II established hundreds of new schools, along with institutes of higher learning in Istanbul.[18] However, the outcome of these efforts was anything but desired. The secular education did create obstacles for the goal of implanting the official Islamic ideology and raising loyal servants.[19] Institutions like the Military School of Medicine and the War College turned into a breeding ground of opposition to the government.[20] Medical students were drawn to books discussing scientific materialism and positivism.[21]

The expansion of the press had also unforeseen consequences.[22] Since political issues could not be discussed publicly, mainstream publications increasingly printed articles on popular science and the new discoveries of Europe and America. These writings were more and more consumed by the public and led publishers to increase the printing of such material. While the greater amount of these publications could hardly be described as serious, it introduced the readership to the developments in the Western world and its material progress.[23]

Looking at the condition of the *medreses* by the end of Sultan Abdulhamid's rule, one could only feel distress. The course material remained unchanged since the fifteenth century, buildings were basically crumbling apart, student facilities were not available, and the pious foundations—the main independent financial sources—had been appropriated by the administration in 1840.[24] Western type educational models replaced the classic *medrese* systems and other institutions—a process started in the Tanzimat era and continued by Abdulhamid. In this endeavor, the educational policies centered on Islamization and pan-Islam. The 'ulamā had expected support from the ruling government to raise the new generation of scholars. Instead, they were entirely ignored and *medreses* as a result perished even further.[25] It seems likely that the class of the 'ulamā was ignored largely because of fear of their growing influence.[26] The Sufi order of Khalidi/Naqshi, existent with its *medreses* in Eastern Anatolia, helped to maintain the presence of scholars; otherwise the learned class would have been diminished.

After the Constitutional Revolution ending Abdulhamid's power, *medrese* reform was approached anew. Earlier a

---

18. Vahide, *Islam in Modern Turkey*, 35.

19. Somel, 4–5, 268, 275–76.

20. Berkes, *The Development of Secularism in Turkey*, 275–76.

21. Hanioğlu, *Bir Siyasi Düşünür Olarak Doktor Abdullah Cevdet ve Dönemi*, 9–14; Hanioğlu, *The Young Turks in Opposition*, 20–21; and Mardin, *Religion and Social Change in Modern Turkey*, 354.

22. Lewis, *The Emergence of Modern Turkey*, 187ff.

23. Berkes, 276–82.

24. Sarıkaya, *Medreseler ve Modernleşme*, 79, 82 and 191–92.

25. In a newspaper article published in March 1909, Nursi described to the sultan in an imaginary conversation how he should act as a caliph in the new age of constitutionalism: "Raise Yıldız Palace to the Pleiades by filling it with leading 'ulamā like angels of mercy in place of the former demons of hell, and by making it like a university and reviving the Islamic sciences, and by promoting the offices of Şeyhü'l-Islam and the caliphate to their rightful positions, and by curing with your wealth and power the weakness in religion that is the nation's heart disease and the ignorance that is the disease of its head." "Bediüzzaman Kürdi'nin Fihriste-i Maksadı ve Efkârının Programı," *Volkan Gazetesi*, no. 84 (Mart 12/1325/March 24, 1909), in Düzdağ, *Volkan Gazetesi*, 407, cited in Vahide, *Islam in Modern Turkey*, 360.

26. Sarıkaya, 76–77.

number of scholars had expressed their ideas on this matter in articles and treatises. Their suggestions, though, were never put into practice. Ali Suavi[27] and Hoca Muhyiddin need to be mentioned in particular.[28] Similarities can be identified between Nursi's thoughts and Hoca Muhyiddin.

## THE EMERGENCE OF THE *MEDRESETÜ'Z-ZEHRÂ*

In 1898, Nursi moved to Van and stayed there until he was sent into exile in 1925.[29] He was hosted by the governor Tahir Pasha in his residence. Tahir Pasha, who early on noticed the extraordinary intelligence and potential in Nursi, was a proponent of education, followed developments in science, and was in possession of an extensive library.[30] His residence was a frequent destination of government officials, teachers of the new secular schools (*mektebs*), and various thinkers who were able to discuss a number of issues. As Şükran Vahide notes, Nursi joined these discussions, "but the new environment soon opened his eyes to the effects on the thinking and attitudes of these officials of the secularizing reforms of the Tanzimat, and the chasm that had opened up between them and traditional views."[31] Numerous educated Ottomans now believed that Islam was blameworthy for putting the empire behind in terms of true progress.[32]

Nursi realized that in its traditional form, Islamic theology (*kalām*) was incapable of answering the criticisms that had been raised about Islam. This led him to learn the modern sciences—something unprecedented among the *'ulamā* in the Eastern provinces. He engaged with the scientific literature available in Tahir Pasha's house and began a deep self-study.[33] One day, Nursi read the report of a speech made by a British politician who declared that, "so long as the Muslims have the Qur'an, we shall be unable to dominate them. We must either take it from them, or make them lose their love of it."[34] Nursi was shaken up by this declaration and challenged to develop his own thoughts in response to such a threat. An inner revolution occurred guiding him to the aims he would now pursue. He declared: "I shall prove and demonstrate to the world that the Qur'an is an undying, inextinguishable Sun!"[35] Based on the knowledge he had gained, he was determined to prove the Qur'an's truths and its being the source of true knowledge and progress. This was the way to defend Scripture against the intentions to discredit it. In 1955, Nursi explained that he found two means of doing this: one was the *Medresetü'z-Zehrâ*, which took him to Sultan Abdulhamid's court, and the second was the *Risale*.[36]

---

27. Sarıkaya, 95–96; Çelik, *Ali Suavi ve Dönemi*, 650–56.

28. Sarıkaya, 96–100.

29. In *Islam in Modern Turkey*, 27 Vahide first stated that Bediüzzaman moved to Van in 1895 or 1896. In a personal correspondence from February 11, 2013, she highlighted that "subsequent research has shown that it was actually around 1898 that Nursi moved to Van. Ömer Pasha was Governor of Bitlis 1896–98; Tahir Pasha, Governor of Van, 1898–1906."

30. Nursi, *Tarihçe-i Hayatı*, 50.

31. Vahide, *Islam in Modern Turkey*, 27.

32. Ibid., 33.

33. Nursi, *Tarihçe-i Hayatı*, 48–49.

34. Ibid., 53–54.

35. Ibid.

36. Nursi, *Emirdağ Lahikası*, 2:195.

In the first period of his life, Nursi cooperated with the Committee of Union and Progress (CUP), a revolutionary underground movement. The members were united in their opposition to the Hamidian despotism by being firm believers in constitutionalism and representative government. The CUP aimed to preserve the unity of the empire and led the Constitutional Revolution of 1908.[37] Nursi quickly became disenchanted with the CUP, yet he equally aspired for the unity of the empire.[38] However, as he said, "unity cannot occur through ignorance. Unity is the fusion of ideas, and the fusion of ideas occurs through the electric rays of knowledge."[39] His major effort was therefore dedicated to the area of education, particularly for his native Kurdistan.

## FEATURES OF THE FORMAL *MEDRESE*TÜ'Z-ZEHRÂ

To win support by the authorities for his Islamic university, Nursi travelled to Istanbul in November 1907.[40] He named this institution the *Medresetü'z-Zehrâ*, after the Azhar university in Cairo, as it was to be its sister university in the center of the eastern Islamic world. He later extended his project to include three such institutions—in Van, Bitlis, and Diyarbakır.[41] Fighting against prevalent ignorance, backwardness of the eastern provinces and other social and political problems was only possible by providing access to large scale education.[42] For him, the strengthening of the Ottoman Empire was the primary goal for spreading education in Kurdistan. Material and cultural development would inevitably come along with that. Charges against him that he was a Kurdish nationalist were therefore baseless.[43]

In May or June 1908, Nursi presented his appeal on educational reform. The proposal focused on synthesizing "the three main branches" of the educational system—the *medreses* or traditional religious schools, the *mektebs* or new secular schools, and the *tekkes* of Sufi establishments—and the disciplines they represented.[44] The second element in Nursi's plan concentrated on restructuring *medrese* education completely and was highly modern in its outlook. As Vahide notes, "these consisted of what might be described as the democratization of the *medrese* system, and its diversification so that the 'rule of the division of labor' could be applied."[45] Another element was concerned with the role of the preachers, who had a major influence on the general population.

In his petition, Nursi emphasized that the *Medresetü'z-Zehrâ* and its two sister institutions should be called by the well-known name of *medrese*, and the lessons should be taught in familiar languages.[46] As he explained in his *Münâzarat*, the instruction should be trilingual, with Arabic being "compulsory," Kurdish "permissible," and Turkish necessary.[47]

37. On the CUP see Ahmad, *The Young Turks*; Arai, *Turkish Nationalism in the Young Turk*; and Heyd, *Foundations of Turkish Nationalism*.

38. Vahide, *Islam in Modern Turkey*, 37.

39. Nursi, *Münâzarat*, 61.

40. Vahide, *Islam in Modern Turkey*, 33.

41. Nursi, *Risale-i Nur Külliyatı*, vol. 2, 1886, 2130, 2131.

42. Nursi, *Tarihçe-i Hayatı*, 72.

43. Vahide, *Islam in Modern Turkey*, 37.

44. Ibid., 45.

45. Ibid.

46. Ibid.

47. Nursi, *Münâzarat*, 71.

Kurdish scholars who had gained the trust of both Kurds and Turks and those who were well-versed in the languages should be assigned as instructors. Furthermore, they should also be alerted to the competence and cultural background of the student body they were to guide. In addition, the *medreses* should be treated in an equal manner with official secular schools. Nursi stressed the importance of religion (*din*) in the eastern part and that an agenda of progress necessitates the inclusion of religious sciences.[48] The East (*şark*), as Nursi stated, was the center of the Islamic world, and he called for the recognition of the high intellectual potential in this region which seemed to be neglected.[49]

An idea developed later, as reflected in Nursi's letter to the President and Prime Minister in 1956, was that the *Medresetü'z-Zehrâ* should serve also as a venue to counter negative nationalism among the various ethnic groups. Nationalism did not arise among the Kurds until after the First World War. The preservation of the integrity and unity not only of the individual but also of the nation (*ferdî ve millî saadet*) would then be ensured.[50]

After the Second World War, Nursi was convinced that the institution of the *Medresetü'z-Zehrâ* would furthermore help the West to find a more constructive relationship with the Muslim world since "secular" sciences prominent in the Western world would also be included into the curriculum.[51] A unification of the religious and natural sciences taking place within the folds of the *Medresetü'z-Zehrâ* would open avenues of collaboration between Muslims and non-Muslims. It remains unclear how exactly Nursi envisioned such a relationship. Would he be open to including non-Muslims in the university? For the moment, suffice it to say that the totality of the *Risale* was addressed to human beings in general and as such bears a strong sense of inclusiveness.

Nursi built on the principles of all he had studied, along with his knowledge of teaching religious (*ulûm-u diniye*) and scientific subjects (*funûn-u cedide/funûn-u akliye*), and then articulating them according to the needs of his time.[52] The main focus was to "combine" the religious sciences and modern sciences and showing that the positive sciences corroborate and strengthen the truths of religion.[53] To Nursi's mind, this would then in due course result in moral and material progress.[54]

Over time, *medrese* syllabi had become static and distant from modern developments in science, which sometimes were discarded altogether. At the beginning of the twentieth century, the *medreses* were raising scholars who were convinced—just as Europeans were—that Islam was at odds with certain matters of science. This caused feelings of despair within the Muslim community and had closed the door of progress.[55] "Whereas," as Nursi pointed out, "Islam is the master and guide of the sciences, and the chief and father of all true knowledge."[56]

---

48. Nursi, *Risale-i Nur Külliyatı*, vol. 2, 1887.
49. Ibid., 2133.
50. Ibid., 1905, 2224.
51. Nursi, *Emirdağ Lahikası*, 612.
52. Vahide, *Islam in Modern Turkey*, 29.
53. Nursi, *Risale-i Nur Külliyatı*, vol. 2 (1887), 2138.
54. Ibid., 2133.
55. Vahide, *Islam in Modern Turkey*, 45.
56. Nursi, *Muhâkemat*, 8.

From a human perspective, Nursi considered religion as symbolizing the heart and conscience, and science, the reason; both were indispensable for progress to be achieved.[57] On a broader level, the *Medresetü'z-Zehrâ* should aim to create a fusion of the three traditions in the educational structure by representing "the most superior *mekteb* (secular school) by the reason, the very best *medrese* (religious school) by the heart, and the most sacred *zawiye* (Sufi order) by the conscience."[58] In due course, the *Medresetü'z-Zehrâ* would acquire financial independence by way of the donations and pious bequests it would obtain.

The advantages of such a structure would guarantee the future of the scholars in the eastern region. Moreover, this would initiate a process toward the unification and reform of the general educational system. Finally, it would free Islam from the bigotry, superstitions, and false beliefs that had covered some branches of it over time. Above all it would introduce modern learning into the *medreses* and encourage the *'ulamā* to dispose of their suspicions concerning modern science.[59] At the same time, it would "open the door to spreading the beneficial aspects of constitutionalism."[60]

Nursi envisioned Islam operating like a consultative council. Through the mutual consultation (*shura*) of the three branches of Islamic education—those of the *medreses* (religious schools), the *mektebs* (secular schools), and the *tekkes* (Sufi orders)—"each would complete the deficiencies of the other." He regarded the *Medresetü'z-Zehrâ* as a possible reflection of this.[61] Transforming the *medreses* from being "single—faculty" institutions into being "multifaculty" and putting into practice "the rule of division of labor" was in harmony with the wisdom and the laws of creation. The lack of following such a practice had led to despotism and the exploitation of learning in the *medreses*. Unqualified teachers had guided the *medreses* toward their decay.[62]

Another interesting element in Nursi's educational proposal was his view that "public opinion" should reign among both the *'ulamā* and the students. In other words, he believed that it was "scholastic despotism," an outcome of political despotism, "that has opened the way to blind imitation (*taqlīd*) and barred the way to searching for the truth." The challenges of modernity could only be overcome by instituting "constitutionalism among the *'ulamā* in the *'ulamā* state." In a similar vein, "public opinion" among students or the widespread ideas arising from debate and the exchange of ideas on different subjects should be taken as the norm. Nursi believed that this would stimulate and spur progress.[63]

In 1913—the year in which he started to write his Qur'anic commentary *Isharat al-i'jaz fi mazann al-ijaz* (*Signs of Miraculousness*)—Nursi stressed his vision of combining and teaching the religious and modern sciences, specialization, and mutual consultation.[64] Again, he highlighted that the Qur'an's truths are displayed through the discoveries of

---

57. Nursi, *Münâzarat*, 72.

58. Ibid.

59. Vahide, *Islam in Modern Turkey*, 46.

60. Nursi, *Münâzarat*, 74–76.

61. Ibid., 76.

62 Nursi, *Muhâkemat*, 46–47.

63. Nursi, "Bediüzzaman Kürdi'nin Fihriste-i Maksadı" (March 11, 1325/March 24, 1909) Düzdağ, *Volkan Gazetesi*, 403.

64. Nursi, *Signs of Miraculousness*, 14–15.

science. Consequently, in the modern period when the cosmos is being opened up and its workings are being revealed by science, commentaries on the Qur'an must keep pace with these giant strides science is taking. An individual alone or even a small group can never be knowledgeable on all matters of science, and a commentary should therefore be written by a board of scholars who are experts in a number of sciences, both religious and modern.[65]

Active participation in the process of study on the part of students was essential. The emphasis on the instrumental sciences (grammar, logic, syntax) in place of the sacred sciences (*tafsīr* or Qur'anic exegesis, *hadīth* or the teachings of the Prophet, *kalām* or theology) had resulted in a backwardness of the *medreses*. Dynamic discussions and the role of competition along with the importance of the fundamental sacred sciences were foundational for revitalizing the *medreses*. Nursi also drew attention to the need for specialization. Students should focus on one subject alone while studying other areas as long as they would deepen their main subject. That way they would gain solid depth.[66] Nursi analyzed the causes for the discrepancy between the different streams of the educational system and stated as follows: "The people of the *medreses* [religious schools] accuse those of the *mektebs* [secular schools] of weakness in belief because of their literalist interpretation of certain matters, while the latter look on the former as ignorant and unreliable because they have no knowledge of modern science. Then the scholars of the *medreses* regard the people of the *tekkes* [Sufi orders] as followers of innovations."[67]

He stressed that the obstacles should be broken down and that modern science should be taught in the *medreses* "in place of obsolete ancient philosophy," religious sciences should be taught "fully" in the secular schools, and scholars from the *medreses* should be attending the Sufi *tekkes*. The ineffectiveness of the preachers who played such a vital role in educating the mass of the people was also addressed. Nursi envisioned the preachers "to be both searching scholars, so that they can prove what they claim, and subtle philosophers so that they do not spoil the balance of the *sharia*, and to be eloquent and convincing. It is essential that they are thus."[68] He would reiterate these statements in his "Address to Freedom," a public speech given after the announcement of the new constitution in July 23, 1908.[69]

After much political turmoil, repeated imprisonment, and disenchantment with the authorities, Nursi left Istanbul for the eastern provinces in 1909.[70] It is in 1911 that he returned to Istanbul in order to renew his efforts to establish the *Medresetü'z-Zehrâ*. After his travels with Sultan Mehmed Reşad, he resolved to get official support for the construction of the university, which he began in the winter of 1912–13.[71] However, the outbreak of

---

65. Vahide, 107.

66. Vahide, *Islam in Modern Turkey*, 48.

67. Ibid.

68. Ibid.

69. Nursi, "Divan-ı Harb-i Örfî," in *Asar-ı Bedi'iyye*, 56–70, cited in Vahide, *Islam in Modern Turkey*, 361.

70. For a more detailed account of the events preceding and following the proclamation of the new constitution in 1908, see Vahide, *Islam in Modern Turkey*, 51–81.

71. Letter to Minister of Education Tevfik İleri, dated August 19, 1951, cited in Abdülkadir Badıllı, *Bediüzzaman Said-i Nursi: Mufassal*

the First World War and other events prevented the realization of his project.[72]

## NAVIGATING AROUND AGGRESSIVE SECULARISM— THE TRANSFORMATION TO THE *MÂNEVÎ MEDRESETÜ'Z-ZEHRÂ*

After the War of Independence, Nursi was invited to Ankara in November 1922. After his arrival, he was dismayed to find a lax and indifferent attitude toward religion.[73] He strongly disapproved of the new course taken by the new rulers, who believed that the time had come to dispense with the religious sciences and for education to be Westernized and concentrated on the modern sciences.[74] After realizing that he could not work alongside the new leaders, he withdrew to Van, from where—as a result of the baseless suspicions of the politicians—he was sent into exile and endured many years of imprisonment.[75]

During his time in Ankara, Nursi tried to gain support for the building of the *Medresetü'z-Zehrâ* in the eastern province. Vahide summarizes the bureaucratic procedure by referring to Badıllı in the following way:

> On February 2, 1923, a bill proposing the founding of the university, signed by 167 deputies including Mustafa Kemal, was presented to the president of the assembly. On February 17, it was sent before the relevant committee. It proposed that 150.000 liras be assigned to the project in that year's budget. On September 12, 1923, having passed through the necessary procedures, it was sent to the education and sharia committees, and there it remained. Once again, the building of the *Medresetü'z-Zehrâ* was overtaken by events. Finally, two years later, on November 29, 1925, it was rejected by the committee and sent back to the assembly. It was put to the vote and rejected. By then the law for the unification of education and closing of the *medreses* had been passed (March 1924).[76]

With the establishment of the Republic, resulting in a radical removal of Islam from public life, Nursi now had to give up the idea of the construction of the *Medresetü'z-Zehrâ*. Against the intangible threats of aggressive atheism, materialism, and secularism, he increasingly moved on to a depiction of the *mânevî Medresetü'z-Zehrâ* and accommodated his educational project into the new secular framework. He was convinced that a spiritual counter-response was needed.[77] His work is filled with depictions of the *manevî Medresetü'z-Zehrâ* and the characteristics of its sincere students whom he considered as his heirs, representatives and pillars, strongly relying on each other.[78]

The *Medresetü'z-Zehrâ* was now represented through the informal collective

---

*Tarihçe-i Hayatı*, vol. 1 (Istanbul: n.p., 1998), 352–53, cited in Vahide, *Islam in Modern Turkey*, 369

72. For a closer assessment of these events, see Vahide, *Islam in Modern Turkey*, 101–10.

73. *Risale-i Nur Külliyatı Müellifi*, 129, cited in Vahide, *Islam in Modern Turkey*, 169.

74. Vahide, *Islam in Modern Turkey*, 172.

75. Ibid., 238.

76. Badıllı, *Bediüzzaman Said-i Nursi*, vol.1, 563–71, cited in Vahide, *Islam in Modern Turkey*, 172.

77. Nursi, *Risale-i Nur Külliyatı*, vol. 2, 1888.

78. Ibid., 1736, 1775, 1815, 1826, 1827, 1851, 1852, 1857, 1899, 1901, 1909.

council of the Nur students.⁷⁹ Its visible shape was non-existent but the content surely was not. In his writings we see how the *medrese* became alive.⁸⁰ In this sense, the *manevî Medresetü'z-Zehrâ* had its center in Isparta.⁸¹ All other cities or villages like Sav (elsewhere also mentioned as Sava) were described as sections of the center.⁸² In calling his followers to turn their private homes into a *medrese* he went beyond the classic understanding of the *medrese*.⁸³ This reminds one of the Qur'anic passage in which Prophet Moses is ordered by God to turn his people's houses into places of worship.⁸⁴ Nursi, stating that he took the Qur'an as his sole guide, seemed to have been inspired by this model.⁸⁵ This practice was also carried out by the early Muslim community, which suffered persecution in the Meccan period and therefore met in the safe space of *Dar al-Arqam* (The House of Arqam–a companion of the Prophet).⁸⁶

To Nursi's mind, solitary reading of the text was beneficial but collective reading helped to deepen understanding, and for this to be realized the foundation of *medreses* were crucial.⁸⁷ Furthermore, the dissemination of the *Risale* through the venues of the *medreses* would lead to the preservation of society.⁸⁸ One passage made reference to two hundred *medreses* in Diyarbakır only; among those, four or five were solely dedicated to women.⁸⁹ Father, mother, child—each family was encouraged to participate in the learning enterprise.⁹⁰ This was an impressive move of Nursi in transforming the private realm into a public sphere and unifying them. He maneuvered around the restrictions of the oppressive regime which had prohibited any religious activity.

One feature of Nursi's *mânevî Medresetü'z-Zehrâ* was its strong inclusiveness of all members of society.⁹¹ He integrated women as students of the *medrese* and saw them as equal to their male peers.⁹² He addressed them constantly as his sisters—*hemşirelerim*⁹³—emphasizing his care and compassion. Nursi regarded his female students in high esteem, for by their natural disposition they possessed one specific element of the *Risale* path, namely selfless, unconditional love (*şefkat*).⁹⁴ Especially those who were often regarded as belonging to the periphery, elderly women for instance, were addressed in high regard.⁹⁵ His integrative method was stressed through separate treatises for women, youth and the elderly—showing his maximum effort and concern in reaching out to all members of society.⁹⁶

Nursi assigned major importance to children as being his students and took

---

79. Ibid., 1783.

80. Nursi, *Risale-i Nur Külliyatı*, vol. 1, 1087 and *Risale-i Nur Külliyatı*, vol. 2, 1795.

81. Nursi, *Risale-i Nur Külliyatı*, vol. 2, 1751.

82. Ibid., 1749, 1788, 1832, 1863, 1901, 2222.

83. Ibid., 1852, 1855, 1908, 2251.

84. *The Qur'an*, trans. Abdullah Yusuf Ali, Qur'an 10:87.

85. Nursi, *Mesnevî-i Nuriye*, 16 and Nursi, *Şuâlar*, 711.

86. "The Prophet and the Muslims in Dar al-Arqam."

87. Nursi, *Risale-i Nur Külliyatı*, vol. 2, 2061.

88. Ibid., 2251.

89. Ibid., 1907.

90. Nursi, *Risale-i Nur Külliyatı*, vol. 1, 964 and vol. 2, 2277.

91. Nursi, *Risale-i Nur Külliyatı*, vol. 2, 2223.

92. Ibid., 1891, 1775, 1796.

93. Ibid., 1826, 1827.

94. Ibid., 1828.

95. Ibid., 1900.

96. Ibid., 1828.

them seriously in spreading and understanding the *Risale*.[97] Children, women, and men should all be involved in the dissemination of the *Risale*.[98] Another aspect was that his students could be from any profession: they were barbers, teachers, doctors, lawyers, villagers, carpenters—once again this went beyond the classic notion of the *medrese*, in which students were entirely dedicated to the scholarly pursuit.[99]

What also stood out was his emphasis on the worldly and spiritual benefits in engaging with the *Risale*: it did not only bring blessings (*baraka*) into one's livelihood and time, creating peace within the inner soul, heart, and body, but also granted divine reward in the hereafter for spreading religious knowledge in a time of great distress.[100] Many of his students were professionals, and the *Risale medreses* also allowed them to pursue a significant religious task in less time. A typical education in a classic *medrese* would have required a student at least five to ten years.[101] An engagement with the *Risale* equipped the sincere student with an education equaling twenty years of the *medrese*.[102] On another occasion, Nursi stated that a student committed to the *Risale* did not have to invest five to ten years but only five to ten weeks to become a scholar.[103] Needless to say, those claims require substantial investigation and comparison between the contents and teaching outcomes of the *Risale* and the classic *medrese* system. They cannot be discussed here given the limitations of this essay.

Nursi explained that reading or listening to the writings for five to ten minutes granted a person the high rank of the *talebe-i ulûm*, the esteemed rank of the students of religious sciences. The worldly provisions of the *talebe-i ulûm* would be secured by divine will.[104] Nursi was certainly aware of the fact that in a time of materialism, worldly concerns were of utmost interest. He took those seriously and assured the material benefits in engaging with the works.

Again, maximum access with minimum time and effort would yield fruits in the world and the hereafter. These were elements clearly going beyond the classic *medrese* institution. Moreover, the followers were not centered on a charismatic teacher but instead around an everlasting textual entity.[105] They were equal in membership and each was invited to offer their personal observations on the text. Even the prisons were transformed into a *medrese-i Yusûfiye*—a school of Prophet Joseph who spent years in prison. Criminals were elevated to the rank of students.[106]

In a time in which the mass population became illiterate overnight through the introduction of the Latin alphabet and was denied access to religious education, Nursi attempted to provide maximum access to knowledge under minimum conditions. Those who were not able to read or write were encouraged to listen to

97. Ibid., 1776, 1783, 1788, 1795.
98. Ibid., 1736, 1852.
99. Ibid., 1795.
100. Nursi, *Risale-i Nur Külliyatı*, vol. 1, 1076.
101. Nursi, *Barla Lâhikası*, 213–14.
102. Nursi, *Risale-i Nur Külliyatı*, vol. 1, 214.
103. Nursi, *Risale-i Nur Külliyatı*, vol. 2, 2061.

104. Ibid., 1852.
105. Nursi, *Risale-i Nur Külliyatı*, vol. 1, 1076.
106. Ibid., 722, 1003.

the *Risale* and disseminate its content.[107] Literate and illiterate people were unified in this common effort. Students like the famous Bekir Ağa (1869–1961) from the eastern village of Adilcevaz, who was *ümmî*, illiterate and travelled to even far villages to spread the *Risale* works, were assigned a rank among the *'ulamā* by Nursi himself—a sign of the importance of simply listening and sharing the works with others.[108] In short, Nursi provided a mass scale religious education while also unifying different societal classes with each other. There were no formal requirements, no specific curriculum and no strict hierarchy.

Within the fold of the *mânevî Medresetü'z-Zehrâ*—with the *Risale* remaining its central focus and guiding principle—we can detect more unifying and integrative features. It has been argued that Nursi aimed to make every reader his own religious authority and that he challenged the traditional religious elite.[109] As shown earlier, he was certainly critical of the prevailing methods in the *medrese* institutions which had also contributed to the decline of the Muslim world, and he sometimes challenged religious authority.[110] Yet a more nuanced reading of his writings reveals that he was deeply rooted in the scholarly tradition, embracing it fully and seeking the support of the *'ulamā*.[111] That is why he insisted on the attention of the Ministry of Religious affairs, the *Diyanet*, and referred to the importance of scholars in Konya.[112] In the case of the former, he believed that it occupies a representative function for Islamic and Western countries, and in order to reflect a genuine understanding of Islam, its support of the *Risale* was indispensable.[113] In the years to come, students of Nursi also worked within the Diyanet, another sign of the inclusion and support of the formal authority.[114] Furthermore, he advocated the translation of his works into Arabic, sent several copies of his works to the scholars of the al-Azhar institution,[115] and delivered his Damascus sermon to a large scholarly audience. On another occasion, he requested copies of his *Asâ-yı Mûsâ* and *Zülfikar* to be sent to the scholarly authorities in Damascus.[116] In one instance, he called upon the *'ulamā* around the *Rawda al-Mutahhara*—scholars living in the Prophet's city of Medina—to compassionately support the *Risale*, which was a *mahdum*, a servant and a student of their large *medrese* in these times of struggle.[117]

As outlined above, in bringing together the best of the tradition, Nursi regarded the *Medresetü'z-Zehrâ* as a powerful means of unifying the *ehl-i tarikat* or *ehl-i tekke* [people of the Sufi orders], *ehl-i mektep* [people of the secular schools] and *ehl-i medrese* [people of the religious schools].[118] The fragmentation of these influential forces would lead

---

107. Nursi, *Risale-i Nur Külliyatı*, vol. 1, 1076 and *Risale-i Nur Külliyatı*, vol. 2, 1775.

108. Nursi, *Barla Lâhikası*, 582.

109. Yavuz, "Nur Study Circles (*Dershanes*), 306, 310, and 313.

110. Nursi, *Risale-i Nur Külliyatı*, vol. 2, 1935.

111. Nursi, *Risale-i Nur Külliyatı*, vol. 1, 1080.

112. Nursi, *Emirdağ Lâhikası*, 171 and *Risale-i Nur Külliyatı*, vol. 2, 1811.

113. Nursi, *Risale-i Nur Külliyatı*, vol. 2, 1886.

114. Ibid., 1821.

115. Ibid., 1755, 1833.

116. Ibid., 1789.

117. Ibid., 1783, 1755.

118. Ibid., 1658 1830, 1935.

to a weakening in education. Instead, he strove for the unification of spiritual and rational knowledge in hand with religious authorities.[119]

Reconciliation, integration, unification, and forming alliances—these were the guiding principles in Nursi's educational vision, bringing together various streams of knowledge and members of society. This is specifically seen in his approach towards Sufism as a branch of knowledge. With this in mind, Nursi depicted the *Risale* path as the summation of the twelve great *ṭarīqas* and underlined the importance of all of them.[120] This is a recurring statement in Nursi's works, still awaiting an in-depth study, and cannot be discussed here. Nursi stated repeatedly that the Nur circle provided the benefits of the *ṭarīqas* and that one did not need to look for them somewhere else.[121] The *Risale* way did offer the highest degree of the *ṭarīqa*, the *velayet-i kübra*. The holder of this rank was not concerned with the showings of *keramet* or *keşf*—wonderworks of saints—but instead occupied the highest degree in sincerity equally to the companions of the Prophet.[122] The two aspects of the Prophet were his *veraset-i nübüvvet* and the *velayet-i Ahmediyye*, the former referring to his prophetic role, the latter to his saintly dimension, from which numerous *evliya*—the saints—followed. Nursi unified the *walaya* and *warasa* stream and presenting the *Risale* path as the highest rank of *walaya*.[123] The *Risale* was infused with references to the spiritual support of the founders of *ṭarīqas*, like Imam Rabbani, Imam Ghazali, Ibn Arabi, Shah-i Naqshiband, Abd al-Qadir al Gilani, and Rumi, and some of their *awrad* [supplications and prayer formulas] were incorporated into the reading of the *Jawshan al-kabir*. This is a collection of Prophetic supplications which is often recited within the Nur community.[124] Their spiritual degrees were all contained in the *Risale* works.[125] According to Nursi, Rumi's work, the *Mathnawi*, became a mirror of reflecting one *ḥaqīqat* (truth) among seven, whereas the *Risale* became a mirror of all seven *ḥaqīqas*.[126] Nursi was furthermore pleased with the fact that students from the secular schools who were engaged in studying the *hikmet-i cedîde* (the new sciences) joined the *Risale* circle—which indicated a growing unifying enterprise.[127] They were in need of the *Risale* works, as Nursi believed.[128]

Nursi also paid attention to the division between Sunnism and Shi'ism and was concerned with reconciling these sometimes conflicting groups.[129] He considered Imam Ali as one of the masters of the *Risale* and the love for the *ahl al-bayt* (the family of the Prophet) as an essential characteristic of his community. All of this—Nursi's effort to embrace the knowledge of the various Sufi orders and integrating different groups into the educational project—shows that the elements

119. Ibid., 1935.
120. Ibid., 1935.
121. Nursi, *Risale-i Nur Külliyatı*, vol. 1, 734 and vol. 2, 1783.
122. Nursi, *Risale-i Nur Külliyatı*, vol. 2, 1785.
123. Nursi, *Risale-i Nur Külliyatı*, vol. 1, 734.
124. Nursi, *Risale-i Nur Külliyatı*, vol. 2, 1751.
125. Nursi, *Barla Lâhikası*, 215.
126. Nursi, *Risale-i Nur Külliyatı*, vol. 1, 743.
127. Nursi, *Risale-i Nur Külliyatı*, vol. 2, 1796.
128. Ibid., 1754.
129. Nursi, *Risale-i Nur Külliyatı*, vol. 1, 588–90.

of reconciliation and unification were strong pillars in Nursi's vision.

## THE TAWḤĪDĪ PARADIGM—APPROACHING KNOWLEDGE, INDIVIDUALS, AND SOCIETY HOLISTICALLY

Nursi's understanding of the universe and consequently his educational vision was deeply informed by a *tawḥīdī* paradigm—a holistic approach—rooted in the conviction that unification, alliance and mutual support on the micro and macro level of human life is essential in order to raise higher beings. This included the individual in his wholeness, the totality of society with its various members, and knowledge in its different manifestations as outlined above. Nursi's theo-centric life was so infused by the notion of *tawḥīd* that his only aim was to declare the Oneness of God and integrate everyone and everything into it.[130] Nursi's worldview was utterly informed by the example of the Book of the Universe in which unity in diversity, based on *tawḥīd*, is constantly and harmoniously displayed. His writings made clear that it was on the basis of *tevhid* and *ittihad* (unification and alliance) that life could exist and persist, and by definition also any intellectual, spiritual, or societal life.[131]

The previous assessment made clear how this *tawḥīdī* paradigm or the process of unification was manifested on a micro and macro level of human life within the broad notion of the *Medresetü'z-Zehrâ*. Based on the textual evidence one could hardly argue that a formal institution alone could carry out such a wide teaching enterprise. The audience was not a student audience in the usual sense. More than anything, these elaborations point to a civilizational program in which a holistic education was perceived as a strong foundation. The *mânevî Medresetü'z-Zehrâ* expressed how the various elements of knowledge, the individual and society had to be understood and related to each other. The aim was not only to provide education in order to attain healthy material progress, but to also achieve spiritual and moral formation for this world and the afterlife.

On a micro level, Nursi sought to nurture all realities within a human being and addressing these human dimensions to an equal degree. If the human heart, soul, and intellect would not be nourished in a sufficient way, society would be doomed to failure. On the other hand, he aimed to maintain a healthy balance between society and the nucleus of it—the family. On the basis of the *tawḥīdī* paradigm, the individual, his family and society were strongly connected. This is a challenge faced by modern education today—the inclusion of families into the learning process and assurance of its continuation.

As explained earlier, a strong feature in Nursi's *mânevî Medresetü'z-Zehrâ* was its inclusiveness and integration of all members of society, which only reiterates the notion of unification. No formal requirements of literacy, no specific curriculum and no distinct hierarchy were required. Nursi maintained his deepest respect towards the transnational

---

130. The terms *tevhid*, *ittihad*, *vahdet*, all defining oneness, unity and unification, are mentioned throughout the *Risale*. See www.erisale.com, where *vahdet* alone is mentioned 445 times, accessed April 4, 2013.

131. Nursi, *Risale-i Nur Külliyatı*, vol. 2, 1901.

scholarly community and preserved the bonds of unity between them and the lay population.[132] By way of mentioning classic scholars of the past, he not only upheld the scholarly tradition and showed the continuity of his work within this lineage but also marking the boundaries of the solitary and communal exercise of reading the *Risale*. Any exegetical exercise was hereby maintained within the confines of traditional Islam. Nursi therefore attempted to bring positive change within the tradition, and did not position himself outside of it. His writings rejected a wholesale critique of the scholarly community[133] and preserved the reputation of scholars.[134] This served as an important reminder to his followers not to break with orthodoxy, but rather to unify with it and further it in the best sense. In this light, the *mânevî Medresetü'z-Zehrâ* took the best elements of the tradition, revived and furthered them.

## CONCLUDING REMARKS: DISCERNING EARLY POSTMODERN ELEMENTS

John O. Voll has shown that in much of what Nursi wrote, one can see his articulation of a postmodern "middle-way" for the Islamic faith.[135] A close assessment of Nursi's *mânevî Medresetü'z-Zehrâ* certainly revealed some "postmodern" elements, even though as a devout Muslim he would have rejected some of its assumptions, such as the relativity of truth.

The postmodern emphasis on holism was certainly articulated within Nursi's understanding of knowledge, the individual, and society. "Postmodern holism entails an integration of all the dimensions of personal life—affective and intuitive as well as cognitive," as Grenz explains.[136] Nursi did not regard human beings simply as rational beings but also as spiritual creatures whose souls, hearts, and emotions should be nourished as well. The postmodern mind refuses to limit truth to its rational dimension but includes emotions and the intuitions as other paths to knowledge besides reason.[137] In Nursi we see the effort to bring those streams of knowledge together which were represented in their strongest form through the *mektebs* (secular schools), *medreses* (religious schools), and *tekkes* (Sufi orders). Unifying these intellectual forces became then a cornerstone of the educational enterprise.

Postmoderns are conscious of the importance of community, of the social dimension of existence.[138] Wholeness in this sense entails a consciousness of the indelible and delicate connection to what lies beyond one's self, in which the personal existence is embedded and from which it is nurtured. Nursi had the conviction that each person is embedded in the human community and that this should lead to a corporate understanding of truth. Each and every individual was an important member of the collective personality of believers (*şahs-ı mânevî*).[139] As it became evident, different members of society were seen as potential students of the *mânevî Medresetü'z-Zehrâ*. Women, children, men, elderly, literate,

132. Ibid., 1782–83, 2133.
133. Ibid., 1957.
134. Ibid., 2130.
135. Voll, "Renewal and Reformation," 61.
136. Grenz, *A Primer on Postmodernism*, 14.
137. Ibid., 7.
138. Ibid., 4.
139. Nursi, *Lem'alar*, 256.

illiterate, professionals, farmers, scholars, lay people, and even criminals—no one was left out in this wider educational endeavor.

Yavuz has argued that the informal settings of the *medreses* also provided opportunities for economic activity.[140] Since the *medreses* fostered bonds of trust, honesty and reliability, better business relationships came into existence, created stronger networks and thickened civil society. In addition, Salih Sayılgan describes the *medreses* as safe Islamic havens helping students arriving from rural Anatolia to make their transition into a modern urban setting, while strengthening their religious character.[141] The informal *medreses* thus fulfill to the present day many functions: they preserve a collective religious identity, facilitate social and economic participation, create new networks, and are platforms for the dissemination of information.

Nursi even called for an intellectual engagement and reconciliation between the Western and the Islamic World. Human beings and their moral and material progress are interconnected and this global vision was clearly manifested in the depiction of the *Medresetü'z-Zehrâ*.

The spread of postmodernism parallels and has been dependent on the transition to an information society.[142] This meant a shift from the modern technique of centralized control to the new model of "networking." Hierarchical structures have been replaced by a more decentralized, participatory form of decision making.[143] Nursi's *mânevî Medresetü'z-Zehrâ* seemed to seriously engage with the mass culture that this age of information is creating. There are no longer formal hierarchies, no specific curricula, no clear charismatic figures who lead the educational enterprise. Instead, the students are gathered around an everlasting textual entity accessible anywhere and anytime. Yet, orthodoxy is upheld and the relationship with the traditional scholarly heritage is preserved. Students are informally connected in this global network of the *mânevî Medresetü'z-Zehrâ* while also preserving the principle of consultation and collaborative work. Numerous students of Nursi early on established *medreses* in every city and country. While it is generally understood that the postmodern ethos is centerless and that "no clear shared focus unites the diverse and divergent elements of postmodern society into a single whole," the *mânevî Medresetü'z-Zehrâ* proved the contrary.[144] The *Risale* was the common denominator creating a unified perspective among its diverse followers and providing a shared vocabulary.

As obvious, some elements of the postmodern outlook are clearly evident in the notion of the *mânevî Medresetü'z-Zehrâ*. Once again, considering the broader perspective of Nursi's educational agenda, it seems difficult to argue that its realization can be carried out in a sole institutional fashion. For Nursi, something greater was at stake. Based on his *tawḥīdī* notion or his emphasis on holism he set out the parameters for a healthy human civilization in which a solid education of the individual and society was

---

140. Yavuz, "Nur Study Circles (*Dershanes*) and the Formation of New Religious Consciousness in Turkey," 308.

141. Sayılgan, "Constructing an Islamic Ethics of Non-Violence," 83–85.

142. Grenz, *Primer on Postmodernism*, 17.

143. Ibid., 18.

144. Ibid., 19.

a key factor. His quest was guided by the conviction that all influential forces for shaping a strong moral being must be integrated and interconnected so that human life can flourish to its fullest.

## BIBLIOGRAPHY

Ahmad, Feroz. *The Making of Modern Turkey*. London: Routledge, 2002.

———. *The Young Turks: The Committee of Union and Progress in Turkish Politics, 1908–1914*. Oxford: Clarendon, 1969.

Arai, Masami. *Turkish Nationalism in the Young Turk Era*. Leiden: Brill, 1992.

Berkes, Niyazi. *The Development of Secularism in Turkey*. New York: Routledge, 1998.

Bulut, Mehmet Ali. "*Medrese*tü'z-Zehrâ modeli." *Haber 7*, October 4, 2012. Online: http://www.haber7.com/yazarlar/mehmet-ali-bulut/936027-medresetuz-zehra-modeli. Accessed January 26, 2013.

Çalışkan, Koray. "10 neden: Eğitim reformu ertelenmeli." *Radikal*, March 30, 2012. Online: http://www.radikal.com.tr/Radikal.aspx?aType=RadikalYazar&ArticleID=1083340. Accessed April 30, 2013.

Çalışlar, Oral. "Said-i Nursi, Atatürk ve Van'a üniversite." *Radikal*, December 26, 2012. Online: http://www.radikal.com.tr/radikal.aspx?aType=RadikalYazar&ArticleID=1113904&Yazar=ORAL-CALISLAR&CategoryID=98. Accessed January 26, 2013.

Çelik, Hüseyin. *Ali Suavi ve Dönemi*. Istanbul: İletişim, 1994.

"Dertlere deva *Medrese*tü'z-Zehrâ'dır." *Haber Diyarbakır*, October 14, 2012. Online: http://www.haberdiyarbakir.com/dertlere-deva-medresetuz-zehradir-54169h/.

*E-risale*. Online: www.erisale.com. Accessed May 20, 2012.

Evered, Emine Ö. *Empire and Education under the Ottomans: Politics, Reform, and Resistance from the Tanzimat to the Young Turks*. London: I. B. Tauris, 2012.

Findley, Carter V. *Bureaucratic Reform in the Ottoman Empire: The Sublime Porte, 1789–1922*. Princeton: Princeton University Press, 1980.

Goffman, Daniel. *The Ottoman Empire and Early Modern Europe*. Cambridge: Cambridge University Press, 2002.

Grenz, Stanley J. *A Primer on Postmodernism*. Grand Rapids: Eerdmans, 1996.

Hanioğlu, M. Şükrü. *Bir Siyasi Düşünür Olarak Doktor Abdullah Cevdet ve Dönemi*. Istanbul: Üçdal, 1981.

———. *The Young Turks in Opposition*. New York: Oxford University Press, 1995.

Heyd, Uriel. *Foundations of Turkish Nationalism: The Life and Teachings of Ziya Gökalp*. London: Harvill, 1950.

———. "The Ottoman 'Ulemā and Westernization in the Time of Selīm III and Maḥmūd II." In *The Modern Middle East: A Reader*, edited by Albert Hourani, Philip S. Khoury and Mary C. Wilson, 29–59. London: I. B. Tauris, 1993.

Kaplan, Yusuf. "*Medrese*tü'z-Zehrâ: Üniversite projesi mi, medeniyet projeksiyonu mu?" *Platin Haber*, March 16, 2012. Online: http://www.platinhaber.com/medresetuz-zehra-universite-projesi-mi,-medeniyet-projeksiyonu-mu-2328yy.htm. Accessed January 24, 2013.

Kurzman, Charles, ed. *Modernist Islam (1840–1940): A Sourcebook*. Oxford: Oxford University Press, 2002.

Laçiner, Sedat. "Seçmeli Kürtçe: Yetmez ama Evet." *Star*, June 18, 2012. Online: http://haber.stargazete.com/yazar/secmeli-kurtce-yetmez-ama-evet/yazi-613091. Accessed March 31, 2013.

Lewis, Bernard. *The Emergence of Modern Turkey*. London: Oxford University Press, 1968.

Mardin, Şerif. *Religion and Social Change in Modern Turkey: The Case of Bediüzzaman Said Nursi*. Albany, NY: State University of New York Press, 1989.

"*Medrese*tüz Zehra Sempozyumu: Said Nursi Eğitim Felsefesi." Online: http://www.medresetuzzehrasempozyumu.com. Accessed March 31, 2013.

Nursi, Bediüzzaman Said. *Barla Lâhikası.* Istanbul: Söz, 2010.

———. *Emirdağ Lahikası.* Istanbul: Söz, 2008.

———. *Emirdağ Lahikası.* Istanbul: Sinan, 1959.

———. *Kastamonu Lâhikası.* Istanbul: Söz, 2008.

———. *Lem'alar.* Istanbul: Söz, 2010.

———. *Mesnevî-i Nuriye.* Istanbul: Söz, 2010.

———. *Muhâkemat.* Istanbul: Sözler, 1977.

———. *Münâzarat.* Istanbul: Sözler, 1977.

———. *Risale-i Nur Külliyatı.* Vols. I and II. Istanbul: Nesil, 1996.

———. *Signs of Miraculousness: The Inimitability of the Qur'an's Conciseness,* Translated by Şükran Vahide. Istanbul: Sözler, 2004.

———. *Şuâlar.* 2nd ed. Istanbul: Envar, 2005.

———. *Tarihçe-i Hayatı,* 9th ed. Istanbul: RNK, 2012.

Özcan, Mustafa. "Risale-i Nur'da İttihad-ı İslâm, siyasetsiz bir siyasettir." In *Gelenekle Gelecek Arasında Bediüzzaman,* edited by Metin Karabaşoğlu, 163–69. Istanbul: Nesil Karakalem, 2012.

Sarıkaya, Yaşar. *Medreseler ve Modernleşme.* Istanbul: Iz, 1997.

Sayılgan, Salih. "Constructing an Islamic Ethics of Non-Violence: The Case of Bediüzzaman Said Nursi." MA thesis, University of Alberta, 2012.

Somel, Selçuk Akşın. *The Modernization of Public Education in the Ottoman Empire 1839–1908: Islamization, Autocracy and Discipline.* Leiden: Brill, 2001.

*The Qur'an.* Translated by Abdullah Yusuf Ali. New York: Alavi Foundation, 2000.

"The Prophet and the Muslims in Dar al-Arqam." *Questions On Islam,* March 9, 2011. Online: http://www.questionsonislam.com/article/prophet-and-muslims-dar-al-arqam. Accessed April 1, 2013.

Yavuz, Hakan M. "Nur Study Circles (*Dershanes*) and the Formation of New Religious Consciousness in Turkey." In *Islam at the Crossroads: On the Life and Thought of Bediüzzaman Said Nursi,* edited by İbrahim M. Abu-Rabi', 297–316. Albany, NY: State University of New York Press, 2003.

Yıldız, Ahmet. "Bediüzzaman, düşüncesi ve aksiyonuyla evrenseldir." In *Gelenekle Gelecek Arasında Bediüzzaman,* edited by Metin Karabaşoğlu, 59–97. Istanbul: Nesil Karakalem, 2012.

Vahide, Şükran. *Islam in Modern Turkey: An Intellectual Biography of Bediüzzaman Said Nursi.* Albany, NY: State University of New York Press, 2005.

Voll, John. O. "Renewal and Reformation in the Mid-Twentieth Century: Bediüzzaman Said Nursi and Religion in the 1950s." In *Globalization, Ethics and Islam: The Case of Bediüzzaman Said Nursi,* edited by Ian Markham and İbrahim Ozdemir, 48–62. Burlington, VT: Ashgate, 2005.

# 18

# Spiritual and Moral Reform of Muslim Inmates
## The Model of Said Nursi

### Benaouda Bensaid

## INTRODUCTION

THIS PAPER DISCUSSES SOME of the fundamental concepts and strategies pertaining to the reform of Muslim inmates in light of Nursi's perspective of change. Nursi lays the foundation for the comprehensive spiritual and moral reform of Muslim inmates, based on a set of concepts and themes such as the purpose of life, human nature, the notion of the "expansion of time," and good and evil. Nursi's plan of reform for Muslim inmates makes use of the *Risale-i Nur* to provide both a cognitive and moral shaping of inmates, in addition to an enhancement of their personality in the context of spiritual remembrance and brotherhood between inmates. A comprehension of Nursi's program of inmates' reform first enhances our understanding regarding the best approaches towards the effective therapy, reform and rehabilitation of inmates, while highlighting the distinct characteristics and methodology of the *Risale-i Nur* in the process of inmate reform, in addition to the enrichment of our understanding of inmates from the perspective of cross-cultural settings.

Today, one finds extensive efforts being made to improve the cognitive, social and spiritual well-being of inmates so that they would positively reintegrate with society. Such efforts help inmates regain the ability of self-reflection while encouraging the scrutiny of their life story, development of a personal ethical and moral character, entrenchment of personal responsibility for one's own actions and the consequent development of choices and skills for daily living. In overview, new methods and theories are being developed at a surprising rate, all contending with the issues presented by the reform of inmates. Muslim inmates today continue to be subjected to diverse approaches of rehabilitation, reform, and training, affected often by chaplains or counsellors' personal emotional, religious, and cultural experiences. As a result, this causes a drift, leading away from studied programs tailored to their original religious and cultural needs or considerate of their many complex issues and convoluted problems. An approach to Muslim inmates however, has yet to be thoroughly explored. In order to fill the seemingly empty void that this particular field presents, this paper attempts to develop a general framework for the spiritual and moral reform of Muslim inmates based on the *Risale-i Nur* of Said Nursi. The reader of the *Risale-i Nur* quickly picks up on the background of prison in which Nursi has formulated many of his insights and reflections.[1] In prison, he not only was able to provide a full account of his own spiritual, intellectual and religious experience reflecting some of the stressful circumstances found in prison but also formulated an approach for the spiritual and moral reform of Muslim inmates. In such a formulation, however, Nursi was able to address various questions critical to the reform of Muslim inmates, not strictly from a theoretical perspective, but emerging from an operational level where prison was transformed into a Josephic School of education, reform, and training.

## NURSI'S VIEW ON PRISON

Prison appears to have had a large influence on Nursi's thought and development. In one of his narrations, Nursi tells the story of how he was captured as a prisoner during the First World War and how he made a commitment to spend the rest of his life in caves away from political and social life, having had enough of mixing with them. Nursi then realizes that the "Divine Grace" transformed the caves he had imagined into prisons, the sought-after seclusion and loneliness into places of ordeal and solitary confinement; thereby granting him "Josephic Schools" which furnished him with benefits pertaining to the hereafter and provided him with the services of belief and the Qur'an.[2] Nursi, however, throws prison into sharp contrast by drawing parallels between it and life. His views on prison are formed in light of the tradition of the Prophet Muhammad which states: "This world is the prison of the believer and the Paradise of the disbeliever.[3]" For Nursi the world would turn into a prison when dissociated from religion;[4] the grave would either be a dark, dank individual prison or a gate to eternal gardens after one's release from life's prison.[5] The mundane world is seen as a guest-house where humans act as guests, and whereby they are given the most essential matters to prepare for the hereafter, yet continue to view the world through a veil of heedlessness, hence

---

1. Şükran Vahide writes: "During the events in Eastern Turkey of 1925, Nursi was sent into exile in Western Anatolia. Following this, for the next twenty-five years—and to a lesser extent for the last ten years of his life—he suffered nothing but exile, imprisonment, harassment and persecution by the authorities. See Nursi, "*Who was Bediüzzaman Said Nursi?*" 8. This fact is easily discernible in his signature: "Said Nursi: who is being held in total isolation and solitary confinement in Denizli Prison." Nursi, *The Rays*, 312.

2. Nursi, *The Flashes*, 336.
3. Naysuburi, *Sahih Muslim*, 2956, 1991.
4. Nursi, *The Words*, 45.
5. Nursi, *The Rays*, 243.

perceiving it as an eternal abode.⁶ In the course of his ideas on life and purpose of creation, Nursi emphasizes the fragility and shortness of life, effectively giving life a stark and austere feel with his words. This harsh texture creates an effect comparable to that of a prison in the reader's mind.

In a discussion on the merits of prison and its impact on the lives of inmates, Nursi states that in addition to the good deeds acquired through spiritual cooperation, inmates' faith transforms their hardships into mercy. Charity given by wealthy inmates, amounts to the reward of multiple almsgivings, their time being transformed into multiple worships. As for the needy inmates, their lives outside of prison afford them merits with no benefit, as well as hardships for which they are responsible. Their hardships within the prison, however, are more rewarding and entail no responsibilities, in addition to the fact that their difficulties are alleviated through the companionship of their inmates.⁷ Thus prison should be viewed as bounty and mercy as well as a hurdle for sinning.⁸ For him, when tyranny and oppression are added to the circumstances of inmates, prison becomes even more comfortable and beneficial⁹ (i.e., prison should be considered one of the best places to be, particularly during periods of trouble, propaganda, doubt and suspicion).¹⁰ In prison, Nursi narrates, it is possible for students of the *Risale-i Nur* to gather without being exposed to harm due to the fact that their gatherings outside of prison were costly and often deemed suspicious.¹¹

Nursi believes that the reform brought about by the *Risale-i Nur* would not have been possible otherwise. In his discourse, Nursi painted reflective illustrations which engage both the heart and mind of Muslim inmates, along with intense rational interactions intended to affect their cognitive and behavioral conditioning. This, Nursi does through delving into some fundamental themes that would, in his view, affect inmates' perceptions, thinking and behaviors, including issues such as the spiritual effects of human actions, the question of good and evil, morality for youth offenders, and the understanding of guidance, misguidance and misfortune. In addition to having devised engaging methods for cognitive rectification of inmates, Nursi addressed the emotional and physical effects of specific series of actions on the human soul. For Nursi, the effects of hostility are devilish and even cause noble spirits to feel the torment of conscience affecting both the heart and spirit. Showing respect, compassion, and help are good deeds enfolding great pleasures, gratification and positive feelings in anticipation of the rewards of the hereafter.

According to Nursi, pessimism and negative suspicions are the cause for immediate worldly punishment.¹² At a point during Nursi's imprisonment, following a certain unpleasant incident in Eskişehir Prison which he attributes to distress, Nursi reminded inmates that out of his perfect divine munificence, compassion, and justice, God associated good deeds with immediate rewards, and evil actions

6. Nursi, *The Words*, 274.
7. Ibid., 340–41.
8. Ibid, 163–64.
9. Nursi, *The Flashes*, 330.
10. Nursi, *The Rays*, 565.
11. Nursi, *The Flashes*, 337.
12. Nursi, *The Flashes*, 363–64.

with immediate punishment. In other words, God integrated spiritual pleasures with good deeds in such a way that they evoke the rewards of the hereafter, and created spiritual penalties for evil deeds in such a way that they recall the torments of hell.[13] Nursi's idea is that each committed sin or doubt inflicted upon the mind causes wounds on the heart and spirit.[14]

## ON YOUNG OFFENDERS

On the issue of young offenders, Nursi can be seen to devote considerable attention. He exhorts them to undertake a series of reflective exercises for their own benefit. According to Nursi, the flowering of youth is a most precious and delightful divine bounty when combined with knowledge of religious duties and proper usage of time. Youth with sound hearts and minds are most powerful, agreeable and pleasant, especially when preoccupied with worship, good actions and preparation for the hereafter. This implies that when youth is spent in ways other than that of moderation, uprightness, and fear of God, eternal happiness and worldly life become damaged.[15] Specifically, Nursi stresses that thoughts of hell-fire are what check the turbulent emotions and excesses of youth, restraining them from committing aggression, oppression and destruction, and ensuring that social life continues in peace. Should such a fear be absent, then the rule of "might is right" would cause those drunken youth to turn the world of the weak and helpless into hell and that of the higher humanity into base animality.[16]

Nursi argues that young age can be potentially abused, resulting in consequences that go beyond the expectations of the abuser during the moment of his vice. For example, Nursi draws on the action of murder in a moment's anger, which causes the murderer a longer period of imprisonment. Nursi believes that the pains of jealousy, separation, and unreciprocated love transform the limited pleasures of illicit love into "poisonous honey." This implies, according to Nursi, that when youthful afflicted hearts and spirits fail to perform their functions properly, they can often be found ill in hospitals or placed in prisons, bars, dens of vice, or in graveyards as a result of their unnourished hearts and spirits.[17] Such damages cause the loss of youth as a result of their failure to observe the bounds of the licit.

Nursi believes that instead of gaining pleasures in this life, youth will be afflicted by calamities and suffering in this world, the grave, and in the next life.[18] Nursi further argues that the majority of the grave torments result from squandered youth.[19] This he explains in terms of youthful turbulent emotions, due to their inability to control their intelligence and the ease with which they are overcome by passions. When youth fail to observe their beliefs or recall the torments of hell, they endanger the property and honor of society as well as the peace and respect of the weak and elderly.[20]

---

13. Ibid., 363–64.
14. Ibid., 22.
15. Ibid., 298.
16. Ibid., 204.
17. Nursi, *The Rays*, 225.
18. Nursi, *The Words*, 158.
19. Ibid., 160.
20. Nursi, *The Rays*, 245–46.

Unfortunately, not only do youth destroy their agreeable lives and futures through their impulsive actions, but they also ruin their happiness in the eternal life, and instead transform it into an abode of torment and suffering.[21] According to Nursi, Muslim inmates, particularly young offenders, are in dire need of consolation from the *Risale-i Nur*.[22] Nursi urges them to equip themselves with "The Fruits of Belief" and "The Guide for Youth" from the *Risale-i Nur*.[23]

## INMATES' COGNITIVE DEVELOPMENT

In addition to the cognitive development of Muslim inmates, Nursi addresses potential issues concerning their understanding of divine generosity. He first tackles the issues found in the inmates' perception of good and evil and their proper understanding of human acquisition (*al-kasb al-insani*). For him, the divine determining and the power of choice are integral aspects of belief. Human power of choice confronts believers in such a way that they do not neglect their obligations, thereby leading them to acknowledge their responsibilities. The divine determining has been integrated with the articles of belief, not to relieve believers from their obligations and responsibilities, but rather to save them from pride and conceit.[24] In fact, according to the Qur'an, humans are completely responsible for their wrongdoings, as they are the ones who wanted them and initiated them in the first place.

Therefore, the "acquisition" (*kasb*) of evil, namely, the desire for evil, is evil; but the creation of evil is not evil.[25] Nursi believes that misunderstanding the role played by human influence may lead to confusion and may justify evil deeds under the pretext of human incapacity to acknowledge one's faults and misdeeds.[26]

Nursi argues that divine generosity expresses the amount of compassion that God holds for his creation, his given example being that God counts one sin as one and one good deed as one or ten, or multiplies it by seventy, seven hundred, or seven thousand.[27] In this regard, Nursi raises the question: how do believers with past grievous sins still retain their belief? His answer is simply that when emotions dominate a person, they do not completely heed the reasoning of the mind. This yields an influential state of desires and delusions in which the person would prefer the slightest instant of pleasure than an immense future reward. Nursi, however, confirms that sins and crimes do not necessarily result from lack of faith, but rather from the defeat of the heart and mind because of dominating emotions, desires and illusions.[28]

Another detrimental effect is regret, which Nursi labels as another deadly disease often caused by the pain of separation from past pleasures. For Nursi, instant pleasures can cause the person everlasting pain. To persist in thinking about it, however, is like lancing a wound and causing regrets to gush forth.[29] Nursi is of the thought that for a believer, if the

---

21. Nursi, *The Words*, 161.
22. Ibid., 161.
23. Ibid.
24. Ibid., 477–78.
25. Ibid., 478.
26. Nursi, *The Rays*, 252.
27. Nursi, *The Words*, 330.
28. Nursi, *The Flashes*, 111.
29. Ibid., 24.

previous day held misfortune, then the distress should have gone in the present with only tranquility remaining, the pain having vanished and the pleasure in its cessation ubiquitous; the trouble is gone and the reward is all that remains. This, according to Nursi, is because it would be foolish to think of illnesses or misfortunes that have yet to occur. Nursi even considers it to be stupid to suffer the pains of non-existent misfortunes or sicknesses or to show impatience and oppress oneself without any need.[30]

While Nursi devoted a large portion of his attention to the cognitive development of Muslim inmates, he never limited himself to specific reform strategies; rather, his methodology was wide and varied, touching on inmates' problems in a number of ways. One of the concepts that Nursi sought to ingrain in the consciousness of Muslim inmates is that of the importance of faith in their lives. According to him, the spiritual merits of believing in the hereafter are critically essential to society and human life, effectively constituting the basis of human happiness, prosperity and achievement.[31] Nursi states that in circumstances where belief in the hereafter is absent from the lives of Muslim inmates, their despair at losing property or children, or their distress for having to suffer the pain of the prison sentence turns their world into a prison and their life into an agonizing torment. Conversely, when faith comes to the inmate's assistance, they breathe freely; and depending on the strength of their faith, their distress, despair, anxiety, anger and desire for vengeance partially or completely decline.[32]

Having touched upon the effect of faith on inmates' lives, Nursi goes on to address the significance of time in relation to religious meanings and purposes. The act of prayer for example, plays a central role in the concept of timing. Prayer times mark the start of important revolutions, and are considered to be mirrors of the divine bestowment of power and the universal divine bounties.[33] Nursi also points out that when the future is attached to disbelief, it becomes a non-existent, dead, blackened and desolate wasteland.[34] On the other hand, a union made in God's name even for a moment can be considered a permanent window of divine union.[35]

While addressing the question of inmates' grasp of the concept of time, Nursi touches on the issue of long-lasting emotional effects of time on human beings in the physical world. He argues that when thinking of happy and enjoyable days in the past, one may experience regret and longing, yet one may also experience pleasure while recalling unhappy days in the past. This proves that a temporary pain and sorrow may leave a pleasured spirit, while one pleasant moment can potentially leave behind permanent pain.[36] Nursi sought to rectify this problem by proposing a new perspective of time which does not cause humans a great deal of pain or panic. Nursi insists that inmates should not preoccupy themselves in the present with a future that has yet to

---

30. Ibid., 25.
31. Nursi, *The Rays*, 203.
32. Ibid., 245–46.
33. Nursi, *The Words*, 51.
34. Nursi, *The Rays*, 219–20.
35. Nursi, *The Flashes*, 32.
36. Nursi, *The Words*, 163–64; *The Rays*, 474.

arrive.[37] His argument is that the past has departed and shall never return, while the future has yet to come and is not yet in possession, and therefore, true life only pertains to the present.[38] For Nursi, each new day should be perceived as a gate to a new world.[39]

Nursi also discusses the notion of "time expansion," which involves the immeasurable reproduction of time spent in association with the divine or in perfecting one's spiritual and moral character. Nursi repeatedly applies this notion in the context of prison, probably to generate a balanced emotional state for inmates, where neither regret nor victimization continue to cause pain or unrest for their loss of time, which may also disturb their well-being and performance. The proper understanding of "time expansion" may lead inmates to a better, more moderate use of time and even to an improved state of mind. This altered state would draw focus on inmates' present duties rather than the loss of their selves in the past or in worrying about the future. According to Nursi, belief in the hereafter expands the present, encompasses the past and future and is as broad as the world, making apparent the bounds of existence which stretch from pre-eternity to post-eternity. As a consequence of their newly formed sincerity and loyalty, inmates become the most eminent and happy guests in the universe, superior to all and the most loved servants of the Creator.[40]

For Nursi, numerous occurrences of "time expansion" have been previously experienced by Muslim saints.[41] It must be noted, however, that while Nursi denotes the expansion of time in the physical sense; he does not always use it in that respect; quite often Nursi can be seen to use it in a metaphorical sense, where more can be done not due to the stretching of time, but as a result of the increased value of worship and remembrance in prison. Nursi states that each day spent in prison may amount to as much as ten days of worship, and may transform a few years of imprisonment into salvation from millions of years in an eternal prison.[42] However, the condition for gaining such an invaluable advantage is to perform the obligatory prayers, repent from sins and crimes leading to imprisonment and offer thanks.[43] This equally applies to young offenders who repent from their misdeeds and abstain from sins through daily prayers; thus benefiting their lives, relatives, future, country and nation.[44] In regards to their passing youth, they shall gain many years of eternal and brilliant youth.[45] In the case of unjustly sentenced inmates, each hour shall equal a day of worship, provided the obligatory prayers are performed. Also, they will be marked among the pious hermits of olden times who retired to caves for worship. For inmates who are poor, aged or ill, and are eager to embrace the truths of belief, each hour of worship will be multiplied by twenty; their prison becoming a resthouse, on the condition that they repent and perform their obligatory prayers.[46]

---

37. Nursi, *The Words*, 278.
38. Ibid., 280.
39. Ibid., 280.
40. Nursi, *The Rays*, 243–44.
41. Nursi, *The Flashes*, 33.
42. Nursi, *The Rays*, 474.
43. Ibid., 474.
44. Nursi, *The Words*, 162.
45. Ibid., 162.
46. Nursi, *The Rays*, 476–77.

Nursi puts forward the idea that human love and fear cause one to turn to either the Creator or the creature.[47] For him, love is the secret of existence and the light of life and the universe. Nursi maintains that humans are the most comprehensive creation and therefore a love that will conquer the universe has also been implanted into their hearts. For him, human love should be perceived as a tribulation; this is because humans love themselves first, then their relations, nation, living creatures, universe and the world. In their attachment to the spheres of creation, humans remain in constant distress or plunge into heedless drunkenness. On the other hand, fear of the 'creature' is either a grievous affliction or a supreme pleasure when it comes to God. It is also a whip that drives humans into the vicinity of the divine mercy.[48]

In light of the above, Nursi argues that when humans give their love to its true owner, they shall love everything without any distress. On the other hand, the opposite will turn love from a delicious bounty into a grievous affliction, which is the severe torment and penalty for unlawful or abused love.[49] According to Nursi, the Divine Names and attributes enfold thousands of degrees of love, perfection, bounty, and beauty. As for friends and associates, their love can only relate to the divine when they befriend one another for the sake of God Almighty through acts of faith and good deeds. This implies that spousal love and cherishment is a gracious gift of divine mercy and is not strictly based on a women's physical beauty, but rather on their fine character and refinement.[50] Nursi associates love with being the true object of worship. When it is used to appreciate and preserve life, it becomes the most precious wealth and capital guiding one to an eternal life, only to be used in God's service. Therefore, it should be for God's sake that one loves this world. This will then cause them to restrict the type of love which enters into their heart, supplicating: "Oh God, grant us love for You, and love for that which shall draw us closer to You."[51]

## INMATES' SPIRITUAL AND MORAL DEVELOPMENT

Throughout his analysis of the different issues associated with the reform of Muslim inmates, Nursi shows serious preoccupation with the role and position of human nature and life in the cognitive, spiritual and behavioral remedies of Muslim inmates. Such a preoccupation led him to provide extensive discussion of humans and nature. For him, at the most basic levels, humans are superior to animals, yet pose a dire desire for immortality amidst other mixed yearnings. For Nursi humans' interest in tranquility and peace of the heart is nearly insubstantial, secret, and particular while their aims for immortality and the satisfaction of spirit are immense, comprehensive, and universal.[52] Humans are extremely weak, demanding, and are easily saddened and grieved. They are also insignificant with respect to their souls and forms, yet when viewed from a perspective of responsibility, act as observing spectators and

---

47. Ibid., 367–69.
48. Ibid., 367–69.
49. Ibid.
50. Nursi, *The Rays*, 667–70.
51. Nursi, *The Words*, 667–70.
52. Nursi, *The Rays*, 24.

discerning readers of the "book of the universe."⁵³

Interestingly, Nursi points out two distinct states of humanhood: one that heeds the whispers of Satan and the soul (*al-nafs al-'ammara* [the commanding soul]) and falls to the lowest of the low (*asfal safilin*), and another that heeds the truth and the Qur'an, rising to the most excellent pattern in the universe (*ahsan taqwim*).⁵⁴ According to Nursi, humans are created in the most extraordinary patterns, hence should not constrain their thoughts to the realms of worldly life.⁵⁵ Nursi argues that the very existence of the human's spiritual faculties reveals their purpose of creation, namely worship of God.⁵⁶ To better illustrate the ultimate objective of creation, Nursi draws on the Qur'an, according to which the purpose of human creation rests in the recognition, belief and worship of the Creator, and also in the ability of humans to ascend and to unite with the divine through submission and certainty.⁵⁷ According to Nursi, this world is transient and perishable, in which beings travel in succeeding convoys to disappear, the grave being the first stopover on the way to an everlasting separation and eternity.⁵⁸

In the reform of Muslim inmates, Nursi underscores the importance of understanding the creation of the Prophet Muhammad, who embodied the most moderate character, and whose actions proceeded according to a moderate and peaceful course. Nursi argues that the biography of the Prophet Muhammad shows moderation in all of his actions, words, and conduct. It also demonstrates that the Prophet avoided excess and negligence, wiliness, and stupidity, and proceeded in the middle way of moderation.⁵⁹ While it is true that Nursi emphasizes the importance of understanding the Prophet Muhammad, he also draws on other Prophets as well. In a discussion of the modelling of inmates according to the example of Prophets, Nursi mentions Prophets such as Job, Joseph, Jonah, and Muhammad. For example, Nursi selects the invocations made by Prophet Jonah: "There is no god but You, Glory be unto You! Indeed, I was among the wrongdoers. Glory be unto You! We have no knowledge save that which You have taught us; indeed, You are All-Knowing, All-Wise,"⁶⁰ and the supplication of Job which is described in the Qur'an as follows: "When he called upon his Sustainer saying: "Verily harm has afflicted me, and You are the Most Merciful of the Merciful."⁶¹

Nursi also exhorts inmates to recite Jonah's supplication, "But he cried through the darkness, (saying): None has the right to be worshipped but you. Truly, I have been of the wrong doers. So We

---

53. Ibid., 337.

54. Ibid., 338. This is made in reference to the Qur'an, which states: "Surely We created the human being in the best stature. Then we reduced him to the lowest of the low. Save those who believe and do good works, and theirs is a reward unfailing." (Q 95:4–6). Unless otherwise noted citations are from Hilālī and Khan, *Translation of the Meanings of the Noble Qur'an in the English language*.

55. Ibid., 333.

56. Ibid.; *The Words*, 35.

57. Nursi, *The Rays*, 125.

58. Nursi, *The Flashes*, 178.

59. Ibid., 92–93.

60. Qur'an 2:32.

61. Qur'an, 21:83. Nursi, *The Flashes*, 20–21.

answered his call, and delivered him from the distress."[62]

The examination of Nursi's approach to inmates' reform, however, reveals how he uniquely engages inmates in a constant stream of reflections and thinking. His reflective thought can be said to originate from both heart and mind. This is alluded to in the Qur'anic instruction found in verses such as the following:

> In the creation of the heavens and the earth, and in the alteration of night and day, there are indeed signs for people of understanding.[63]

> Those who remember God, standing, sitting, and lying down on their sides, and think deeply about the creation of the heavens and earth, (saying): "Our Lord! You have not created (all) this without purpose, glory to You!"[64]

> Do they not think deeply (in their ownselves) about themselves? God has created the heavens and the earth ....[65]

> Verily, in things, there are signs for those who consider.[66]

Nursi also quotes the following *hadīth* in support of his reflective approach, the meaning of which goes as follows: "An hour of reflective thought is better than a year of [voluntary] worship." This implies that on occasions, an hour of reflective thought can equal a year of worship.[67]

A method of reflection which assists Muslim inmates internalize values and acquire sincerity, this requires contemplation on death as a step in their spiritual journey. Sincerity, according to Nursi, may be cultivated through worship of God, and through letting the pleasure of God vanquish the pleasures of the soul and ego. Nursi believes that awareness and remembrance of death causes disgust with hypocrisy and cultivates sincerity, eventually leading inmates to realize that this world is transient, assisting them against the tricks of the soul. In this, however, Nursi differs from the Sufis' approach and the instructions of the "People of the Truth" which are induced from verses such as "Everyone shall taste death. Then unto Us you shall be returned."[68] "Verily you will die, and verily they (too) will die."[69] According to Nursi, Sufis imagine and perceive themselves as dead and already placed in their graves. Such imaginations, contemplations, and morose thought sadden and affect the evil-commanding soul to an extent it gives up its far-reaching ambitions and hopes. The *hadīth* stating "Frequently mention death which dispels pleasure and makes it bitter" illustrates the function of this contemplation.[70] Nursi also maintains that attaining the sense of divine presence is made through the strength of belief and the lights emanating from reflective thought on creatures, which inevitably guides to the Creator, and the thought that God the all Compassionate is All-Present and All-Seeing. It further enables inmates to devote their attention to none

---

62. Qur'an, 21:87–88.
63. Qur'an, 3:190.
64. Qur'an, 3:191.
65. Qur'an, 30:8.
66. Qur'an, 13:3.
67. Ibid., 380. See Al-'Iraqi, *Al-Mughni 'an Haml al-Asfar*, 5:161.
68. Qur'an, 29:57.
69. Qur'an, 39:30.
70. Nursi, *The Flashes*, 217. Hadith recorded by al-Baghawi in *Sharh al-Sunnah*, 3:198.

other than God, and to realize that looking to others in his presence or seeking help from them infringes upon the right conduct in his presence.[71]

Nursi's approach to contemplation differs, however, from that of the Sufis because it follows the path of reality, unlike the Sufis, who perform this contemplation in an imaginary and hypothetical way. Nursi's contemplative approach does not require the mind to draw the future to the present by thinking of its demise, but rather, starts out in thought from the present and progresses to the future; all these are held in terms of reality. Without the need for perception, inmates could examine their own corpses and think of their own deaths. If they travel a little further, they may see the death of this century, and going further still, observe the death of this world, effectively opening up the gates for complete sincerity.[72] The following call illustrates this point well:

> O my Compassionate Sustainer and Munificent Creator! Through making the wrong choice, my life and youth are lost and gone, and all that has remained are grievous sins, abasing sorrows and misguiding doubts and scruples. I am drawing closer to the grave, shame-faced with this heavy load and sick heart. My friends, peers, and relationships are all dying before me. I am also nearing the door of the grave. O my Compassionate Sustainer and Munificent Creator! I see now that soon I will have donned my shroud, mounted the bier, bade farewell to my friends. Approaching my grave, I call out to the Court of Your Mercy through the mute tongue of my corpse and the articulate tongue of my spirit: "Mercy! Mercy! O Most Kind, Most Clement! Deliver me from the shame of my sins!" Now I have reached the brink of my grave. I am standing at the head of my corpse stretched out beside it.[73]

It must be noted however, that Nursi does not exclude the crucial role of self-criticism from his reflective process. For him, Satan's wiles inhibit humans from acknowledging their own defects in order to shut the door of seeking forgiveness or taking refuge in God. That is because Satan incites human egotism so that the soul may defend itself, thus acquitting itself of all faults. According to Nursi, people fail to see their own faults when they become satisfied with their own souls.[74] Nursi's writings tend to explore a new approach to spirituality and moral change. For him, God requires three things in return for his blessings and bounties, namely remembrance, thanks, and reflection.[75] It is only through knowledge of God that the human spirit and heart can be relieved from confusion and distress, finding thereby assurance through the remembrance of God.[76]

According to Nursi, prayer plays a central role in the process of spiritual reform. The spiritual movement of the heart involves remembrance of God (*dhikr*) and contemplation (*tafakkur*). Nursi argues that the circle of remembrance is held through three sacred phrases, namely the pillars of faith, the five daily prayers and the Qur'an. Moreover, Nursi considers these to be the true sources and foundations of the *Risale-i Nur*. Nevertheless, Nursi puts forward the notion that

---

71. Nursi, *The Flashes*, 217.
72. Ibid.
73. See Nursi, *The Flashes*, 178.
74. Ibid., 124.
75. Nursi, *The Words*, 17.
76. Ibid., 692.

through remembrance, the believer is included in a wider orbit of remembrance called the "large circle of remembrance." Nursi writes in this regard: "These phrases are the invocations of the Muhammadan way where, following each daily prayer, they are repeated collectively in a large circle of remembrance by one hundred million believers. They declare Glory be to God! Thirty-three times, All praise be to God! Thirty-three times, and God is Most Great! Thirty-three times."[77]

For Nursi, the paths leading to God are achieved through impotence, poverty, compassion and reflection. Unlike some Sufi orders' use of silent recollection, however, Nursi's proposed method is based on both the reality commonly known as (*haqiqat*) and *sharī'a* (Islamic Law).[78] For him, the shortest path to God is the path of the Qur'an whose uprightness and all-inclusiveness are ever-distinct.[79] Nursi's method requires inmates to follow the practice of the Prophet Muhammad, perform religious obligations and abstain from serious sins. Nursi, however, places extreme emphasis on the need for inmates to perform the prescribed prayers correctly and with proper attention, and follow them with the *tesbihat* (invocations held after regular prayers).[80]

## THE EFFECTS OF THE RISALE-I NUR

Nursi often highlights the effective and comforting effects of the *Risale-i Nur* in the positive change of hundreds of Muslim inmates. Nursi reports that because of the students of the *Risale-i Nur*, about forty to fifty inmates had begun prayer.[81] He relates that as a result of the prison's transformation into a *medrese* (religious school), students of the *Risale-i Nur* took the role of teachers.[82] According to Nursi, the *Risale-i Nur* demonstrates that sins enfold eternally spiritual ailments, as well as spiritual pleasures similar to those found in paradise, which can also be found in good deeds and qualities, and in the embodiment of Islamic truths.[83] For Nursi, the *Risale-i Nur* intends to rescue inmates from the distresses of prison and worldly harm, to save them from wasting their lives in grief or sorrow, to provide them with true comfort, and to safeguard them from a miserable future in the hereafter.[84] For him, the *Risale-i Nur* helps inmates realize that their endured worldly hardships are transitory and irrelevant, but rewarding, and helps them transform their fleeting difficulties into permanent moments of mercy.[85] Nursi argues that compassion constitutes the basic principle of the *Risale-i Nur*; this means that neither innocents nor tyrants should be cursed or harmed. Even in what appears to be a state of anger, Nursi's compassion prevented him from cursing or acting violently towards oppressors or tyrants.[86]

Nursi even goes to the point of considering the *Risale-i Nur* as a moral barrier. He doubts that fear of prison or detection alone would thwart people from sins or crimes such as murder, adultery, theft, gambling, or drinking. Had

---

77. Nursi, *The Rays*, 255.
78. Nursi, *The Words*, 493.
79. Nursi, *Al-Mathnawi*, 427–28.
80. Nursi, *The Words*, 493.
81. Nursi, *The Rays*, 331.
82. Ibid., 338.
83. Nursi, *Sayqal al-Islam*, 483.
84. Nursi, *The Words*, 166.
85. Nursi, *The Rays*, 320.
86. Ibid., 395.

that been the case, Nursi argues, police officers and detectives should have been permanently stationed in every home and at all corners so as to prevent people from committing evil. The *Risale-i Nur*, in Nursi's perspective, plays a better role in implanting good deeds and beliefs since it sets permanent mental barriers around everyone, effectively preventing people from committing evil through evoking remembrance of prison, hell and divine wrath.[87] Nursi goes on to say that due to the apparent benefits of the *Risale-i Nur*, and that since imprisonment is made for education and training purposes, authorities should have allowed inmates to meet with students of the *Risale-i Nur* so that they could acquire more training and education in a day or month's period of time than they would otherwise receive during a yearlong phase. This would have been better suited and more beneficial to helping them become better individuals, useful to the nation, and prosperous in their futures.[88]

To substantiate the moral power of the *Risale-i Nur*, Nursi quoted the testimony of some police officers whom he described as "fair-minded" who viewed the influence of the students of the *Risale-i Nur* as follows: "The students of the *Risale-i Nur* represent moral police who assist us in preserving the public order. Through belief, they leave in all who read the *Risale-i Nur* something that restrains them from misdemeanors."[89] To further consolidate his position, Nursi draws on a real life example in the Denizli Prison, where just in a short period of three or four months, more than two hundred inmates became extraordinarily obedient and developed good religious and righteous conduct, to a point that an inmate who had formerly murdered three or four people could not even kill bedbugs.[90] This reinforced Nursi's statement that if knives, Mausers and revolvers were given to Muslim inmates with orders to fire, they would not hurt anyone. It is through the guidance and command of the Qur'an, belief and Islamic brotherhood that these inmates have chosen to forgive and avoid offences, even when they have many reasons for enmity and hostility.[91] These inmates, we are told, became completely compassionate and harmless individuals.[92]

Nursi believes that Muslim inmates being discharged from prison will not act as murderers or thirst for revenge, but rather will be penitent, well-behaved and beneficial for the nation.[93] In reality, it appears that the study of the *Risale-i Nur* helped inmates in the Denizli prison become extraordinarily well-behaved in a short period of time. In another testimonial, some expressed the following: "Studying the *Risale-i Nur* for fifteen weeks is more effective in reforming inmates than fifteen years in prison." A comment worth mentioning is that not only did the *Risale-i Nur* affect inmates, but they also influenced prison officials who become inclined to the *Risale* with their hearts after studying confiscated copies of the *Risale-i Nur*.[94] The reach of the *Risale-i Nur* went so far that inmates would hope to remain in prison rather

---

87. Ibid., 310.
88. Nursi, *The Rays*, 331.
89. Nursi, *The Flashes*, 331.
90. Ibid., 331.
91. Nursi, *The Words*, 166.
92. Ibid., 331.
93. Nursi, *The Rays*, 476–77.
94. Ibid., 327.

than being free, due to their fear of confusion and susceptibility to sins outside of prison. Nursi adds that prison helps inmates acquire a complete education.[95] The testimony of some young inmates prior to their sentence, as quoted by Nursi, confirms the above: "Would the 'Nurjus' remain in prison, we will attempt to convict ourselves in order to learn from their teaching and example and change ourselves through their instruction."[96] Another small example that Nursi associates with the *Risale-i Nur* can be found in his story of how through the lessons of the *Risale-i Nur*, enemy inmates in the Denizli prison became closer brothers.[97]

Nursi's experience shows that the study of the *Risale-i Nur* affects inmates through the comfort of their heart, ease of their spirits, improvement of their health and supply of their sustenance.[98] Nursi considers the collective reading, study and discussion of the *Risale-i Nur*, particularly the last parts of "The Fruits of Belief" as an honor for inmates as they turn them into "students of religious sciences."[99] It is through the Qur'anic guidance, the teachings of the *Risale-i Nur*, and the enthusiasm of students that prison was turned into Josephic School and was the leading reason ignorant inmates were able to read the whole Qur'an.[100] The *Risale-i Nur* can be seen to effectively draw on stories, parables, analogies and examples of the sociocultural surrounding inmates themselves. This for Nursi, to a degree, reflects the teaching methodology of the Qur'an and *hadīth*, which use allegories in addition to familiar comparisons to teach profound matters and to express the most intense truths.[101] The *Risale-i Nur* also incorporates encouragement (*targhib*) and warning (*tarhib*) as mediums for expression. According to Nursi, these methods plant in the individual a pursuit for divine satisfaction instead of the desire for fame, replacing fear and doubts with belief in the divine decree; and substituting greed with belief in the power of divine sustenance. They also exchange feelings of discrimination with a stronger belief in Prophets; selfish love with acknowledgement of one's own shortcomings and weaknesses.[102]

## RESPONSIBILITIES OF INMATES

One of the interesting features of Nursi's reform program is that it prohibits inmates from interference in politics or the affairs of the government.[103] Inmates subscribing to Nursi's reform program act like brothers, whose brotherhood is based on the sacred program of "The believers are nothing else than a single brotherhood."[104] As a result, Muslim inmates hasten to assist one another with their prayers and spiritual gains. This means that they subscribe to a wider sacred society, possess a united interest in teaching the Qur'anic truths of belief and save believers from eternal annihilation and everlasting solitary confinement in the intermediate realm.[105] This

---

95. Nursi, *The Words*, 162.
96. Nursi, *The Flashes*, 331.
97. Nursi, *The Words*, 165.
98. Nursi, *The Rays*, 483.
99. Ibid., 338.
100. Ibid., 293.
101. Nursi, *The Flashes*, 129.
102. Nursi, *Al-Malahiq : Mulhaq Barla*, 55.
103. Ibid., 372.
104. Qur'an, 49:10.
105. Ibid., 337.

moral structure of reform necessitates the presence of close friendship, sacrifice of companions, appreciative comrades, and noble actions of brothers.[106]

For Nursi, the process of reforming Muslim inmates does not entertain the notion of the spiritual master Shaykh. For him, the Sufis use terms among themselves such as "annihilation in the Shaykh," "annihilation in the Prophet"; yet due to the fact that Nursi was neither a Sufi nor affiliated with Sufi orders, such Sufi principles would not make a good rule in his inmates' reform program, Nursi taking instead an altogether different form of "annihilation in the brothers." This occurs when inmates imagine or visualize the virtues and merits of their brothers in their own selves and take pride in their brother's glory. Among brothers, this may be called "*tafani*" [annihilation]; that is, the "annihilation in one another." It should be noted, however, that unlike the relationship between a shaykh and his disciples, this *tafani* in the context of prisons requires inmates to forget the feelings of their souls, and to live in their mind with their brothers' virtues and feelings. For Nursi, at the very best, the Master can be an intervening teacher (*ustad*).[107]

Nursi explains how time spent in worship, reflection, and service with the intent of preserving belief causes gratitude and pride.[108] Muslim inmates should utilize good deeds and actions to create a prime example, that they may transform prison officials into righteous individuals, giving them the role of masters and guards raising people for paradise as opposed to enacting their role as torturers standing over criminals and murderers.[109] Such an endeavor, in his view, requires collective learning, adherence to faith and good proper conduct, recitation of the Qur'an, abstinence from distressing fancies, absorbing meanings from friends who teach them, making up for missed prayers, and taking advantage of one another's good qualities. This, according to Nursi, would transform prison into a blessed garden that would raise the seedlings of good character.[110]

Nursi proposes a different approach in the field of spiritual development, one which focuses on mutual participation in deeds of sincerity, cooperation, brotherhood, and unity.[111] According to Nursi, students of the *Risale-i Nur* eventually adopt the way of love, brotherhood and "annihilation in each other."[112] In order to reach such a status, inmates should act positively and should preoccupy themselves with their own selves, show tolerance, unite with others in love and brotherhood, and create a collective force to preserve justice. They should also preserve the truth from falsehood, denounce the self and its ego, and cast away any negative feelings of rivalry.[113] Inmates should avoid despair, and should strengthen each other's morale, not be frightened, and meet the calamity of prison with trust in God.[114]

For Nursi, the major gains achieved through compassionate assistance require inmates to provide each other with needed sustenance and the soothing of

---

106. Nursi, *The Flashes*, 217.
107. Ibid., 217.
108. Ibid., 360.
109. Ibid., 222.
110. Ibid.
111. Ibid., 219.
112. Ibid., 343.
113. Ibid., 203.
114. Nursi, *The Rays*, 360.

each other's wounds. Providing inmates with food is thus seen as almsgiving, the reward of which is multiplied especially when inmates are old, ill, or poor. A condition exists, however—namely, that these helpers should perform obligatory prayers for God's sake, and hasten to assist with sincerity, compassion and joy.[115] In the course of assistance, however, extreme caution is essential so that one does not offend or be offended by seasoned inmates, thus avoiding all disagreements, and strengthening brotherhood and solidarity through humility and modesty.[116] It thus follows that inmates should not offend one another under the pressures of discomfort or distress, and should not use an insulted honor as a pretext for offensive behavior.[117] Rather, inmates should be thinking of and consoling one another, and should act as patient role models. In addition, inmates must show compassion, solidarity, and care; they must also behave intelligently during discussions, and reflect fine moral qualities.[118]

## CONCLUSION

It becomes clear that Nursi diversified the program in the reform of Muslim inmates. These included learning and study of the *Risale-i Nur* as a means of changing perceptions concerning essential concepts such as human nature, belief, life and time, worship, sinning and forgiveness, love and fear, and preoccupying oneself with the real issues of the present time. In Nursi's reform model, the study circle, exercise of God's remembrance, and recitation of the Qur'an, held through inmates' spiritual cooperation related to a wider circle of remembrance, are all critical. They provide Muslim inmates with a solid and encouraging environment for repentance, cultivating sincerity that removes evil impulses, and rectifying inmates' own character. Nursi's model engages Muslim inmates in a conscious, reflective exercise and meditation as a means of re-discovering oneself and traveling towards God; yet unlike secular meditation, it does not immerse inmates in reflection on their personal pains, but rather places them within the parameters of reality, without causing any regret, despair or pain.

What distinguishes Nursi's approach, however, is that it moves inmates to God throughout internal and external methods of observation and internalizing of positive meanings and values through spiritual journeys and cooperation. This collective force also provides inmates with new learning experiences and with the opportunity to acquire new characters within the moral foundation of brotherhood. This, however, requires sharing, forgiveness, brotherhood, love, care and kindness. In addition, inmates are continually encouraged to promote the teaching of the Qur'an and the *Risale-i Nur* which to limit the often-increasing rate of crimes and vices learned in prisons. The spiritual elements, however, rest at the core of the entire process of reform. Muslim inmates in Nursi's model perform their obligatory prayers, recite the Qur'an and supplications, constantly repent from sins, perform good deeds instead, become preoccupied with the perfection of their own selves, and act compassionately and brotherly with other inmates.

---

115. Ibid., 475.
116. Ibid., 339.
117. Ibid., 359.
118. Ibid., 330.

This remarkable success of the *Risale-i Nur* in the reform of inmates demonstrates its richness, as well as its all-encompassing nature and realistic approach towards inmates' problems, stress, pain, deficiencies and struggle. These lead us to believe that Muslim inmates today would greatly benefit from Nursi's model of reform, and consequently, from further analysis and examination of the *Risale-i Nur*. In such an endeavor, however, one should not forget about the exceptional character and personality of the chaplain designing and implementing such a reform program for inmates: Bediüzzaman Said Nursi.

## BIBLIOGRAPHY

Al-Baghawi, H. Bin Mas'ud. *Sharh al-Sunnah*, 1st ed. Beirut: Dar Al-Kutub al-'Ilmiyyah, 2003.

Hilālī, Taqī al-Dīn, and Muhammad Muhsin Khan. *Translation of the Meanings of the Noble Qur'an in the English Language* (Tafsīr ma'ānī al-Qur'ān al-Karīm bi-al-lughah al-Injilīziyah). Madinah, K.S.A.: King Fahd Complex for the Printing of the Holy Qur'an, 1998.

Al-'Iraqi, 'Abdul Rahim bin Husayn. *al-Mughni 'an Haml al-Asfar fi -Takhrij ma fi al-Ihya' min al-'Akhbar*. 1st ed. Beirut: Dar Sadir, 2000.

Al-Naysaburi, Imam Muslim bin al-Hajjaj al-Qushayri. *Sahih Muslim*. 1st ed. Edited by Muhammad Fu'ad 'AbdulBaqi. Cairo: Dar Ihya' al-Kutub al-'Arabiyyah 'Issa al-Babi al-Halabi, 1991.

Nursi, Bediüzzaman Said. *The Damascus Sermon*. 2nd ed. Translated by Şükran Vahide. Istanbul: Sözler, 1996.

———. *The Flashes*. Translated by Şükran Vahide. 2nd ed. Istanbul: Reyhan Ofset A.Ş. 1996.

———. *Al-Malahiq Mulhaq Barla*. Şükran Vahide. 2nd ed. Istanbul: Reyhan Ofset A.Ş. 1996.

———. *Al-Mathnawi al-'Arabī al-Nūrī*. Translated by Şükran Vahide. 2nd ed. Istanbul: Reyhan Ofset A.Ş. 1996.

———. *The Rays*. Translated by Şükran Vahide. 2nd ed. Istanbul: Reyhan Ofset A.Ş. 1996.

———. *Sayqal al-Islam: al-Khutbah al-Shamiyah*. Translated by Şükran Vahide. 2nd ed. Istanbul: Reyhan Ofset A.Ş. 1996.

———. *The Words*. Translated by Şükran Vahide. 2nd ed. Istanbul: Reyhan Ofset A.Ş. 1996.

# 19

# The Dissemination of the *Risale-i Nur* in Europe and the United States

## Zeyneb Sayilgan

### INTRODUCTION

It is remarkable to discover a significant number of statements vis-à-vis Europe and America made explicitly by Said Nursi and stretched all through his *Risale-i Nur*.[1] This goes sometimes as far as offering future predictions on specific countries.[2] A closer analysis reveals an ambivalent relationship characterized by a nuanced approach to Europe's and America's accomplishments as well as their less successful endeavors in serving human welfare and society. While a detailed examination of these important text passages remains out of the scope of this essay, it is important to keep in mind that Nursi's followers were already introduced to the notion that the *Risale-i Nur* is not confined to the Turkish territory alone or the Muslim world in particular. Rather, it is a worldwide venture challenging global threats like aggressive atheism, materialism, and secularism endangering a God-centered life of many

---

1. A simple look on the search engine *E-Risale* comes up with 251 passages naming "Europe" directly and 107 results for "America," accessed March 12, 2012, www.erisale.com. For Said Nursi's statements on "Europe," see, for instance *Sözler*, 549; *Mektubat*, 451–57; *İlk Dönem Eserleri*, 343; *Lem'alar*, 203. On "America," see, for example, *Sözler*, 220; *Emirdağ Lahikası* 424, 596.

2. See, for instance, Nursi's famous prediction that "Europe is pregnant with Islam" in *Emirdağ Lahikası*, 491 or that "well-known preachers (*hatipler*) in Sweden, Norway, Finland, and England will strive for the acceptance of the Qur'an and just like a very important religious faction in America looking out for the true religion will seek the Miraculous Qur'an and after comprehending its truth will accept it fully, similarly different regions and governments of the world will seek the Miraculous Qur'an and after understanding its truth will embrace it fully with all their souls and lives" (*Emirdağ Lahikası*, 316).

citizens. It comes therefore as no surprise that this vision has shaped the worldwide Nur community, whose members set out to countries in Europe and the United States to share their insights with people of different backgrounds. This spirit enables millions of Nur members to accommodate the *Risale* in new settings like Europe and America and develop a discourse that is receptive to these societies. The present essay seeks to examine the Nur community in its European and American context by outlining its history and development. Special attention will be given to Germany, as it is a good case study for the growth of the community in Europe. In this regard, I will rely heavily on the work of the sociologist Cemil Şahinöz, whose *Die Nurculuk Bewegung: Entstehung, Organisation und Vernetzung* provides a good in-depth study of the community.

## GERMANY

With the labor movement beginning towards the end of the 1950s, the first guest workers (German: *Gastarbeiter*) arrived in Europe. Approximately 9 million Turks live on this terrain, representing the largest Muslim immigrant community.[3] According to recent surveys, Germany's Muslim population is estimated between 3.8 and 4.3 million with Turkish Muslims, at 60 percent, being the largest ethnic group.[4] These numbers signify the importance of Islam as understood by the wider Turkish Muslim community in Europe. Jörn Thielmann duly argues that this has led to a "Turkish bias" in German scholarship which has not paid sufficient attention to the rich ethnic and national diversity of Islam in Germany.[5] Leaving these valid sentiments momentarily aside, one cannot be dismissive of the weight of the Turkish Nur community.

## Early Beginnings

Muslims in Germany often settled around the industrial areas of Berlin, Cologne, Frankfurt, Stuttgart, and other major cities. Only a few Muslims live on the territory of the former German Democratic Republic.[6] Along with the *Gastarbeiter*, the first members of the Nur community reached Germany.[7] As early as 1967, Abdul-Muhsin Alkonavi, who is a direct student of Said Nursi, founded the *Unabhängigen Islamischen Gemeindedienst e.V.* (The Independent Islamic Community Service) in West Berlin.[8] The activities of the center were limited to Berlin only. While a student at Humboldt University in Berlin, Alkonavi also wrote a doctoral thesis entitled "The Islamic Constitutional Societal Model in Bediüzzaman Said Nursi's Works For Confronting Dictatorship, Anarchy or Chaos," under the supervision of Dr. Serauky.[9]

With the guidance of Ali Uçar, one of the leading Nur members in Turkey, the community began in 1971 to expand

---

3. Cole, *Ethnic Groups of Europe*, 367.

4. Bundesamt für Migration und Flüchtlinge: *Muslimisches Leben in Deutschland*, 11.

5. Thielmann, "The Turkish Bias and Some Blind Spots," 174.

6. Motadel, "Islam in Germany," accessed March 8, 2012, http://www.euro-islam.info/country-profiles/germany/.

7. Wunn and Pınar, "Die Nurculuk Bewegung Jama'at un-Nur," 93.

8. Şahinöz, *Die Nurculuk Bewegung*, 132.

9. See "Nursi Studies," accessed March 8, 2012, http://www.Nursistudies.com/akademi.php?ctg=Academy&lng=English&aid=3.

its efforts to all parts of Germany. Uçar travelled extensively throughout the country, held *Risale* faith-sharing sessions (*ders*) at private homes and through his charisma was influential in establishing several *medreses* (study centers).[10] Based on the model of Said Nursi, he remained in regular correspondence with the attendants by exchanging personal letters and succeeded in mobilizing Muslims in every German city, as the following dynamic account testifies.

> My dear praiseworthy brother! We took the airplane from England to Mannheim. Immediately the next day, we visited brothers in Stuttgart and then drove to Munich. We visited the homes (*heim*), the congregations and mosques. Along with the *Risale* works and the *Risale* brothers we held faith sharing sessions (*ders*) everywhere. . . . I returned then to Mannheim and continued visiting homes (*heim*). We organized meetings, held lectures and wrote letters. . . . We were then in Alzey and from there drove to Mainz. Until morning prayer, we spent time together reading the *Risale-i Nur*. On the same morning we drove back to Mannheim, visited the mosque and stayed for giving another *Risale* lecture. After the mosque program we went to our *medrese* and read again together. On the same day we took off to Waldorf. There, we stayed longer and shared memories of our teacher (*üstad*) with our brothers. Then, we drove back to Mannheim and from there to Stuttgart. Upon our arrival we visited another *heim*. Just like everywhere else, we shared information on our activities in England. . . . On the next day we were in Urbach holding lectures again. On the evening we visited another mosque and read the *Risale-i Nur*. Everywhere we hear the same complaints: "You are not visiting frequently enough!" . . . This evening we will visit another *heim*. Every Saturday and Sunday we are in Sindelfingen und Böblingen. On Monday, there will be a lecture in Mannheim. Then, we will be in Aschaffenburg for a week. . . Then, we will be driving to Cologne, Duisburg and Düsseldorf; and afterwards to more distant places.[11]

The fact that eleven cities were visited within a short time is indeed a major accomplishment. In a first meeting taking place in the city of Aachen, Uçar gathered around 300–400 people, including Muslims from France, the Netherlands, and Switzerland. According to one attendant, this event strengthened the religious identity among participants who were strongly motivated to start the religious service (*hizmet*) in their own neighborhoods.[12] The members remained in contact through letters which were read publicly during the gatherings. This served as an important tool to create a sense of unity, solidarity and brotherhood. Uçar was a key figure in establishing the foundations of the Nur community in Germany. According to the Turkish newspaper *Hürriyet*, he gave no less than 400 conferences every year.[13]

In addition, Uçar, in trying to fulfill Nursi's wish to print the Qur'an in either Germany or Italy, founded a publication house named *Ittihad Druck–und Verlags GmbH* in Berlin in 1972, which also started to publish short treatises of the *Risale* and distribute them among the followers

---

10. Şahinöz, *Die Nurculuk Bewegung*, 133.

11. Letter from Ali Uçar to Hüseyin Aydemir cited in Şahinöz, *Die Nurculuk Bewegung*, 134–35.

12. Şahinöz, *Die Nurculuk Bewegung*, 134.

13. Ibid., 136.

of Nursi. To print in German was not yet regarded as necessary, as Mehmet Emin Birinci, a direct student of Said Nursi, explained.[14] Although the printing cost was higher than in Turkey, the community continued the task for two-fold reasons: the works of Said Nursi were still banned and bringing them from Turkey would cause difficulties at Turkish airports. Moreover, the printing house was a means to help Nur members deepen their sense of religious service.

The connection between the main base in Turkey and the German Nur communities remained strong. Along with Mehmet Emin Birinci (d. 2007), Mehmet Fırıncı, who was also an immediate student of Bediüzzaman, visited Germany regularly. While Birinci was in charge of observing the faith sharing sessions, Fırıncı resided half of the year in Turkey and the rest in Germany and was therefore fondly described as "the minister for foreign affairs."[15]

After having established a somewhat solid network, Uçar did return to Turkey in 1976. As the community grew, it caught the attention of the media. In 1977, rumors spread that Nur members were running the majority of Qur'an schools. This was a misunderstanding of their self-ascribed title: the *Nur talebeleri* (Nur students). The director of the *Islam Archiv* in Soest, Muhammad Salim Abdullah, clarified the issue. On July 8, 1978, Birinci gave a public interview on the radio station *Deutsche Welle* for the program, "Mosques in Germany—The *Nurculuk* Community." He described the work as follows: "Considering the fact that the presence of Islam in Germany is not a temporary one we deem our work here as important. . . . We are prepared to offer Islam to the West. Each of us is obligated to provide access to Islam for interested individuals."[16] He emphasized that the community does not follow any missionary endeavor. The only effort is directed inwardly to Muslims in order to address their religious concerns.

The publication task still continued and after bureaucratic efforts, the community founded the publishing house *Asya Verlags GmbH* in Cologne, which remained under the ownership of Zeki Şevkli until his death in 2006. The aim was to publish *Risale* treatises and only some portions were published in German. The publishing house was not as productive as one had hoped. On January 26, 1980 an article on the Nur community appeared in the *Berliner Stimme*:

> The fourth group is the *Risale-i Nur* community which is mystic in its cult, apolitical and liberal. The community decided to offer Islam to the West. They have three mosques in Berlin, a publishing house and prayer rooms at the two universities. The members provide the space of their *Unabhängigen Gemeindedienst* to all groups under the condition that no political ideas are spread. Since the community does not perceive itself as anti-Western, its members can be welcomed as conversation partners.[17]

Such public appearances increased the level of confidence among the adherents, who felt encouraged to participate in the public discourse on Islam.

---

14. Ibid.
15. Ibid., 138.
16. Ibid., 139.
17. Ibid., 140.

## The Secular Framework

While the Nur community tries to preserve some sense of Turkish identity, it does not promote nationalism, though it remains in healthy relation with the homeland. The members do not deem it integral to establish an Islamic state; instead they regard such a notion as a utopia. Observing Islam is not bound to a certain form of government, as the members believe.[18] Interestingly, Udo Steinbach and Nils Feindt-Riggers list the establishment of an Islamic state based on the Qur'an among the goals of the Nur community.[19] This mistaken assertion stems probably from statements made by intellectuals like Metin Gür, who described the community "as religiously fanatic struggling against the laicist Turkish republic."[20] As Wunn and Pınar duly point out, such claims contradict the community's work in public; in fact, German officials often welcomed Nur adherents as conversation partners.[21] Marfa Heimbach attests in her research on the community to the same transparency.[22]

Said Nursi himself did not directly confront the secular regime in Turkey; instead, he sought to practice Islam under the new rule while preserving the integrity of Muslim faith. In order to transform society positively, the establishment of an Islamic state was not seen as essential. Despite obvious challenges, Nur members in Germany seem to have no objection to living under secular rule since they emerged out of that Turkish experience.

## Diversity of Religious Service

Different branches of the Nur community in Germany, like Nesil or Yeni Asya, laid out different accents on their religious service (*hizmet*). This led each branch to highlight certain elements in their *hizmet*. All members were still centered on the text, the *Risale-i Nur*, and found legitimization in it for their emphasis on religious service. Some tended to focus more on the reading in the faith-sharing sessions (*Meşveret* branch) or writing and copying of the *Risale* in its original language (*Yazıcılar* branch), while others, such as *Nesil*, highlighted the dissemination of the *Risale* via popular publications like magazines or books, academic discourse and programs on radio and TV stations.

A visibly distinct hierarchy did not lie in the nature of the community and resulted in a positive dynamic in which voluntary work took a crucial role and new avenues of engagement remained constantly open. The emphasis on certain aspects of religious service was perceived as an overall enhancement of the community's endeavor. The *medreses* in Germany went along either with the activities of Nesil or Yeni Asya. There were different additional branches in Turkey, as well, but those were not present on German soil.

After having reached some degree of professionalism in its work, the community decided to publish a journal called *Nur-Das Licht*. In 1991, the director of the *Islam Archiv*, Muhammad Salim Abdullah, participated in the first international

---

18. Nursi, *Emirdağ Lahikası*, 338.

19. Steinbach and Feindt-Riggers, *Islamische Organisationen in Deutschland*, 20.

20. Gür, *Türkisch-Islamische Vereinigungen in der Bundesrepublik Deutschland*, 79.

21. Wunn and Pınar, "Die Nurculuk Bewegung Jama'at un-Nur," 85.

22. Heimbach, *Die Entwicklung der islamischen Gemeinschaft*, 103.

*Bediüzzaman Symposium* in Istanbul. He raised the question of how to introduce Nursi's ideas to the Western world and Mehmet Fırıncı suggested printing a German journal. Under the direction of the teacher Rüstem Ülker who lived in Germany, the first edition was published in 1992 by the group *Jama'at un-Nur Köln e.V.* The institute aimed to publish an edition every three months, following the model of the *Risale-i Nur Institute of America* in Berkley, California.[23] The same publication was printed later on in Istanbul in English, Turkish, and German. The members intended to publish a monthly edition and distribute it among leading German figures, universities and religious institutions. However, the work on the journal ceased in summer 1999 due to lack of financial resources and personnel.[24]

In October 1997, Ali Uçar and Bayram Yüksel decided to visit the groups in Europe and within one month they had visited numerous cities and also attended the opening ceremony of the *medrese* of the *Cultural Foundation of Bediüzzaman Said Nurs*i. Tragically, Ali Uçar, Bayram Yüksel, and their driver Mehmet Çiçek died in a traffic accident on November 19, 1997.

## From Faith-Sharing Sessions to *Medrese*s

Establishing a faith sharing session (*ders*) in Germany and developing it into a *medrese* follows the same global pattern of the Nur community worldwide.[25] Based on Nursi's directions as expressed in his *Emirdağ Lahikası*, everyone should strive to gather his family for a faith-sharing session (*ders*) in his own home.[26] If one lives alone, neighbors, friends or relatives should be invited. The members meet once or twice a week, read portions from the *Risale* and then attempt collectively to interpret it. When the number of Nur adherents increases, people run out of space and then decide to rent a bigger space, which then becomes the official *medrese*.[27] Such informal practice is also based on the instructions of Nursi.[28] Naturally, these gathering places are important platforms in creating a sense of identity, deepening moral and ethical virtues and developing a network among the members.

Nursi's sense of creating maximum access to theological discourse for a large audience of even illiterate participants, who also happen to have less time for any religious involvement, is remarkable. He states that even listening to the wisdom of the *Risale* for five or ten minutes on a daily basis is as valuable as writing or reading the collection.[29] Such needs to be emphasized since a large segment of the community belonged to a lower uneducated class who then felt more encouraged to engage with Nursi's thought.

It needs to be highlighted, however, that members also feel compelled to get together for the collective reading due to the language of the *Risale*. The younger generation is less familiar with the original Ottoman language in which the

---

23. Şahinöz, *Die Nurculuk Bewegung*, 141.
24. Ibid.
25. Ibid., 146.

26. For more on the structure and function of the study circles see Yavuz, "Die Renaissance des religiösen Bewusstseins in der Türkei," 121–46.
27. Şahinöz, *Die Nurculuk Bewegung*, 147.
28. Nursi, *Emirdağ Lahikası*, 217 or 445.
29. Ibid., 481.

works are written.[30] Mere solitary reading would be difficult and faith-sharing sessions fill this gap and satisfy the need for a proper understanding. These *medreses* act autonomously. Sometimes students reside in them and spend significant time together. The first *medrese* was officially founded in Remscheid in 1971 and a few months later another one was established in Cologne.[31] On January 14, 1979 the members founded the group Jama'at un-Nur Köln e.V., which with immense effort bought a community house in 1986. According to Rüstem Ülker, one of the founders of this group, thirty *medreses* existed in the beginning of the 1980s in various German cities such as Bremen, Duisburg, Düsseldorf, Frankfurt and Hamburg.[32] The majority of these *medreses* offer *ders* in Turkish. Recently, lectures in German have been provided, as well, since the younger generation considers German a native tongue and comprehension of the text is therefore made easier. Nur members of the group Lichtjugend e.V. in Berlin and a group in Offenbach under the direction of Hakan Çelik offer regular German *ders*. In the long run, it seems inevitable that the religious discourse be offered in German if the community wants to reach out to a larger segment of German society. For a commemoration of Said Nursi's death and legacy in March 2008 in Cologne, members of all Nur branches gathered together.[33] Such events are also welcoming occasions for emphasizing the overarching unity among the members.

On the basis of official statements made by the Yeni Asya group, currently 36 *medreses* do exist in Europe, of which 16 were founded in Germany. In addition, there are numerous faith–sharing sessions taking place in private homes. According to their own estimates, 1,000 members belong to the Yeni Asya branch. The most influential group, based in Ahlen, is called Islamisches Jugendzentrum e.V. The Moslemische Pfadfinder Deutschlands (BMPD) belongs to the Yeni Asya and is also an official member of the Islamrat, the German Islam Council. The group in Ahlen publishes the daily newspaper *Yeni Asya International*, a European edition of the newspaper *Yeni Asya*.[34] The Nesil branch oversees eight *medreses* in different parts of Germany. Members are estimated to be five hundred, yet it remains difficult to provide accurate numbers due to the informal organization of the community.[35] The *Jama'at-un Nur* in Cologne belongs to Nesil which is also in charge of translating the *Risale* into German and organizing the symposiums in collaboration with the *Istanbul Foundation for Science and Culture* (IIKV). *Meşveret* is the largest group among the German Nur community. It has formed itself around Nursi's immediate students like Sungur, Yüksel and Kırkıncı. The group owns 18 *medreses* in Germany and has its base in Aschaffenburg.

One small group in the city of Bochum feels drawn to one of the leading Nur figures, Hüsrev Altınbaşak. Followers of Nursi's immediate student, Abdullah Yeğin, can be found in nine German

---

30. This is also the reason why recent publishing houses have added footnotes to the *Risale* works, enabling readers to access the current vocabulary.

31. Şahinöz, *Die Nurculuk Bewegung*, 148.

32. Ibid., 157.

33. Ibid., 157.

34. Ibid.

35. Ibid.

cities.³⁶ In 2007, a group in Stuttgart founded the Stuttgarter Stiftung für Wissenschaft und Religion.³⁷ The Stuttgart community works often with Nesil and participates in their councils. The exact number of the *medreses* given in some publications varies. Akbulut mentions around 120 *medreses* belonging only to the Cologne based Jama'at an-Nur.³⁸

## Academic Discourse

The activities of the German division reached another level on December 4, 1999 with its first academic *Said Nursi Symposium* in Bonn under the title "A Contemporary Approach to the Understanding of Islam," organized by Nesil.³⁹ Inspired by the international symposiums in Turkey organized by the Istanbul Foundation for Science and Culture (IIKV) under the direction of Faris Kaya, the members invited non-Muslim academics to discuss the thought of Said Nursi and bring him into conversation with other German figures such as Alfred Delp, Dietrich Bonhoeffer or Leo Bäck.⁴⁰ Symposiums in Germany were organized in the year of 2004, 2005, and 2007 and were an important means to reach the non-Muslim public and academia. As noted earlier, besides the symposiums, events such as the commemoration of Said Nursi were organized for the Turkish speaking audience.⁴¹ To this end, Nesil or Yeni Asya invited speakers from Turkey.

In June 2000, another step was undertaken in order to further the academic approach towards the works of Nursi. Nesil aimed to raise a German-speaking generation of young Muslim academics who should be well-versed in the *Risale* as well as in the intellectual discourse of the West. This group of students meeting under the name *International Seminar Group* met until 2006 every three months. In these three-day workshops which had taken place twenty-three times in total, students had the chance to discuss present social, political or theological issues in the light of Nursi's work.⁴² The seminars were also held in Switzerland and Austria. Muslims from other Islamic organizations and non-Muslims attended, as well. According to Bünyamin Duran, who was one of the leading academics, the goal was to create an East-West synthesis by studying the thoughts of classic and contemporary Islamic thinkers such as Imam Ghazali, Razi, Nursi, and Muhammad Iqbal and bring them into conversation with past and present Western intellectuals like Immanuel Kant, Max Weber or Heidegger. Common values and ideas were to be analyzed and a "Muslim elite" to be formed in order to prepare public speakers for tomorrow and German society.⁴³ One group in Bielefeld existing since 2001 founded the Risale-i Nur Academy in 2008 with the purpose of translating the *Risale* collection into German.⁴⁴

One program which was attempting to take the lead in Nursi Studies on European soil and inspire young academics within the Nur community in Germany and elsewhere was founded in 1997. The

36. Ibid., 160
37. Ibid.
38. Akbulut, *Türkische Moslems in Deutschland*, 72.
39. Şen and Aydın, *Islam in Deutschland*, 60.
40. Şahinöz, *Die Nurculuk Bewegung*, 142.
41. Ibid.

42. Ibid., 143.
43. Ibid.
44. Ibid., 145.

University of Durham in the United Kingdom established the Risale-i Nur Studies program and supervised a number of students pursuing a degree in Nursi Studies. The Durham institution has organized one major international conference so far, entitled "God, Man and Mortality: The Perspective of Bediüzzaman Said Nursi," in 2008 and several other related seminars. It described its aims as follows:

> The long-term objective of the Durham Program in *Risale-i Nur Studies*, an inter-departmental initiative, is the scholarly study and analysis of the thought and teachings of Bediüzzaman Said Nursi, particularly as embodied by his *magnum opus*, the six-thousand-page work of Koranic exegesis known as the *Risale-i Nur*. The more immediate aim of the program is to facilitate and encourage debate, research and the growth of Nursian studies in the UK and overseas.[45]

Colin Turner, the leading academic of this program, has also co-authored with Hasan Horkuç the introductory book *Makers of Islamic Civilization: Said Nurs*i, published by Oxford University Press in 2009. The work divided into two parts provides an overview of the life and thought of Nursi covering various subjects, such as Nursi's view on the renewal of faith, his stance on politics and Sufism. Turner has also written several essays such as "Bediüzzaman and the Concept of ʿAdl: Towards a Nursian Ontology of Divine Justice," which appeared in the *Asian Journal of Social Science* in 2010 and attended many conferences organized by the IIKV. He is also the author of the publication, *Qur'an Revealed*.

## Network Structure

The community in Germany often turns to Turkey in order to seek guidance and assistance on various issues. Members in Turkey frequently visit the German community in the month of Ramadan, attend conferences in order to increase the motivation among people and help them to further the work. They serve as no more than advisers, refraining from imposing their own ideas.

Nesil in Turkey runs a major publishing house under the same name and frequently brings famous authors to Germany. These programs are aimed to inspire members to engage in more activities. As a second step, the Istanbul base organizes a European-wide meeting of *medrese* representatives every six months. This creates an opportunity for exchanging ideas and more importantly strengthening the network. Naturally, the Turkish network model cannot be applied as easily to the German framework as one might think. Compared to the Turkish context, different conditions exist in Germany and inevitably call for distinct approaches. In order to overcome these challenges, the Istanbul base created a German office overseeing the coordination of various activities and organizational matters.[46]

Once a month, Yeni Asya comes together at its advisory council.[47] Three times a year a European-wide meeting takes place and twice a year a general gathering is organized in Ahlen, with hundreds of members attending. The editor of the Yeni Asya newspaper, *Kutlular*, and various journalists participate at this meeting, where passages from the *Risale*

---

45. "Risale-i Nur Studies," accessed March 8, 2012, http://www.dur.ac.uk/sgia/imeis/risale/.

46. Şahinöz, *Die Nurculuk Bewegung*, 163.
47. Ibid.

are also read. Today, the members of the Nur community in Germany are estimated to be from 5,000 to 9,000.[48] While Pohl suggests a number of 5,000 followers,[49] Şahinöz's own estimate approaches 4,000 members.[50] The community is estimated to have between 5 and 6 million adherents worldwide.[51] Some numbers run as high as 9 million followers.[52] Other sources mention even 20 million members in more than 100 countries.[53] Again, the informal and open structure of the community makes it difficult to name exact figures.

## Social Participation and Activities

Nur members in Germany are increasingly making their contribution to the general Muslim population and cooperate with different Islamic organizations on various levels.[54] For instance, the community was co-founder of the Landesverband islamischer Gemeinschaften in North Rhine-Westphalia, an organization dedicated to represent Muslim interests to the German government. It was established in 1980. Members of the Nur community are also co-founders of the *Islamrat*, one of the major Muslim councils in Germany, working since 1986. Avni Altıner, the head of the Schura Lower Saxony and Haluk Yıldız, member of the Rat der Muslime in Bonn are also active within the Nur community. Both of these organizations have representative functions for the general Muslim population in Germany. The Nur community participates in the public discourse on Islamic religious education, the integration debate, issues on adult education, youth work and interreligious dialogue. In this regard, already in 1978 the Nur community in Germany along with two other Turkish Islamic organizations, the Millî Görüş and Süleymancı associations, turned to school authorities, requesting religious instruction according to Article 7 of the Basic Law.[55]

Involvement in interreligious dialogue is an important goal of the community.[56] It comes therefore with no surprise that Nur members in Germany are participating in dialogue programs and have initiated or helped in forming groups such as the Christlich-Islamische Gesellschaft e.V. (CIG) in Cologne, Dialog–Forum Stuttgart e.V. and FABIZ (Familien-und Bildungszentrum) in Mannheim, just to name a few. According to Salim Abdullah, Nur adherents, though refraining largely from active political involvement, favor the agenda of the German social democrats and unions who advocate social justice and equity for all.[57]

## Publications and Online Presence

Generally, German literature on Islamic theology and ethics published by Muslims can rarely be found. Due to the efforts of the IIKV, the works of Said

48. Hüttermann, *Islamische Mystik*, 114.
49. Pohl, *BRD und Dritte Welt*, 13.
50. Şahinöz, *Die Nuruculuk Bewegung*, 180.
51. Yavuz, *Islamic Political Identity in Turkey*, 11.
52. Michel, "Peaceful Movements in the Muslim World, 230.
53. Wunn and Pınar, "Die Nuruculuk Bewegung Jama'at un-Nur," 94.
54. Şahinöz, *Die Nuruculuk Bewegung*, 169.
55. Sovik, "Islamic Instruction in German Public Schools, 245.
56. Utermann, *Türkischer Islam in Deutschland*, 18.
57. Abdullah, *Was will der Islam in Deutschland?*, 41.

Nursi have been translated into over forty languages thus far.[58] As in the case of the English translations, the *Risale* works have not yet been entirely translated into German. However, eight out of the fourteen works of Nursi are now accessible for a German readership, and major books such as the *Words*, *Flashes*, and *Letters* provide a good understanding of the intellectual ideas of Nursi. Various booklets and short treatises published by the community itself are also available. Two German translations of the collection do exist. One project was led by the Jama'at un-Nur in Cologne and was published by Sözler publication. The other translation was done under the direction of Davut Korkmaz and was published by the Verein für Familien und Jugendhilfe in Europa e.V. in Cologne. The books cannot only be purchased on the Internet under their own homepage (www.lichtstr.de) but the collection is fully accessible online on different websites. Generally, the community does not aim for profit, but instead seeks to make Nursi's thought available to a large audience.

Besides the primary literature, the secondary literature remains equally scarce. This may be due to the fact that early members of the Nur community in Germany were not fully able to articulate themselves in the local language and secondly did not belong to a significant educated class. The task seems now up to the younger academic generation within the Nur community to publish considerable material in German. Some of the secondary works already available in English and published under the auspices of the IIKV at SUNY press have been translated into German. Some of these are *Islamische Theologie des 21. Jahrhunderts: Der aufgeklärte Islam, Aufkommen-Ideen-Niederschlag: Das Paradigma des Said Nursi* (2007) and *Der Islam in der modernen Türkei: Die intellektuelle Biografie des Bediüzzaman Said Nursi* (2009). Another introductory work on Nursi's life, *Islam und Aufklärung: Ein Islamdenker fur unsere Zeit—Bediüzzaman Said Nursi*, was written by Cäcilia Schmitt and Ali Demir, a couple both active within the community and based in Stuttgart. Already mentioned is Cemil Şahinöz, a sociologist and active member at *Nesil*, who did a major study entitled *Die Nurculuk Bewegung: Entstehung, Organisation und Vernetzung*. Collections of essays presented at the Nursi symposiums in Bonn in 2004, 2006, and 2007 were also published by the organizers Rüstem Ülker and Wolf A. Aries at LIT publications, with the assistance of the IIKV. The above mentioned works are the few ones made available by the community members themselves and thus are aimed to offer a self-description.

Besides these publications, a few descriptive studies and essays about the Nur community have been written by German scholars, usually included in works on Islam in Germany or, more specifically, Islamic organizations in Germany.[59] Sig-

---

58. For a full list of publications see the homepage of the *Istanbul Foundation for Science and Culture* (IIKV): http://www.Nursistudies.com/collection.php and for a selection of translations, see, for instance, "Nur.gen.tr" accessed March 8, 2012, http://www.nur.gen.tr/tr.html.

59. In this connection see for example Lemmen, *Islamische Vereine und Verbände in Deutschland*; Abdullah, *Was will der Islam in Deutschland?*; Wunn and Pınar, "Die Nurculuk Bewegung Jama'at un-Nur," 85–92; Akbulut, *Türkische Moslems in Deutschland*; Şen and Aydın, *Islam in Deutschland*; Heimbach, *Die Entwicklung der islamischen Gemeinschaft in Deutschland seit 1961*.

nificant quantitative and qualitative material is still missing and, as Thielmann rightly points out, research here is at the very beginning, if started at all.[60] Most notably among the scholarly works are three essays written by Ursula Spuler-Stegemann, professor of Islamic studies and comparative religion at the Philipps University of Marburg: *Nurculuk: Die Bewegung des Bediüzzaman Said Nursi in der modernen Türkei* (1973), *Nurculuk. Eine moderne islamische Bewegung* (1977) and *Zur Organisationsstruktur der Nurculuk-Bewegung* (1981). Spuler-Stegemann has been doing research on the Nur community for more than twenty years and was also presenter at the Nursi symposium in Istanbul in 1991. In some of the secondary sources, the community has been incorrectly characterized as a Sufi *ṭarīqa*, though elements of *tasawwuf* certainly had an influence on Nursi's thought.[61] However, Nursi constantly refrains from such attributions and does not regard his initiative as a mystical brotherhood.

On the Internet, the presence of the Nur community in Germany is very limited. There are a few private German language pages offering insight into Nursi's life and thought as well as some basic information on the activities and aims of the community.[62] Only a couple of *medreses* do have a webpage, a fact which seems to suggest that the emphasis lies more on the printed word.

## AMERICA

### Early Beginnings

While the establishment of the Nur community in Europe was realized and largely furthered by the significant presence of the Turkish Muslim immigrant community, which is mainly engaged in doing groundwork, the development in America is increasingly moving into the academic direction both through the work of Muslims who arrived in the United States as students in the 1970s, and through non-Muslim scholars.

The Risale-i Nur Institute of America, founded in 1975 by followers of Nursi in the United States, initiated the first English translations of some *Risale* treatises. The founder Osman Birgeoğlu narrates the early history of Nursi Studies in the United States as follows:

> It all started in the summer of 1970. I felt there was a big need to translate *Risale-i Nur* into English in order to reach people outside of Turkey. At that time, I was part of the team of proofreaders of *Risale-i Nur* books. Zübeyir Gündüzalp [an immediate student of Nursi] was leading this team of proofreaders. Due to poor health, he was unable to participate in the general meetings that were going on simultaneously, but instead he concentrated his energy on the proofreading task of the books which he felt was most important. Thus, I met with Zübeyir Gündüzalp

---

60. Thielmann, "The Turkish Bias," 181.

61. See, for example, Lemmen, *Islamische Vereine und Verbände in Deutschland*, 47 and Steinbach and Feindt-Riggers, *Islamische Organisationen in Deutschland*, 17–21.

62. See, for instance, "Said Nursi," accessed March 8, 2012, www.said-Nursi.de; "Said Nursi Symposion," accessed March 8, 2012, www.saidNursisymposion.de; "LICHTstr.de -Alles über Risale-i Nur und Bediüzzaman Said Nursi," accessed March 8, 2012, www.lichtstr.de; "Said Nursi Symposium," accessed March 8, 2012, www.said-Nursi-symposium.de; or public Nur forums such as "Misawa . . . Just the Truth," accessed March 8, 2012, www.misawa.de..

very frequently. Important to note is that only very rarely were people other than government officials able to leave Turkey. The general public simply could not purchase foreign currency to travel during the 60s and 70s. God answered my prayer by sending a fellow *Risale-i Nur* follower, Hüseyin Demirkan, who asked me to seek Zübeyir Gündüzalp's blessings for him to attend a master's program in the United States. This was also my perfect opportunity to personally discuss with Zübeyir Gündüzalp my burning desire to take *Risale-i Nur* to America.[63]

Hüseyin Demirkan went to the University of Iowa at Ames in 1971. Osman Birgeoğlu followed him in the summer of 1973 as a visiting scholar at the same university. He took courses at the university as well as met potential people who could help him facilitate the translations of Nursi's works into English. The two men teamed then with Mehmet Fırıncı to find the best English translator. They started translating the biography of Said Nursi. Ali Uçar came all the way from Germany to help with typing. In this early phase the team was able to locate Hamid Algar of the University of California-Berkeley to work with them on the translations, which he had previously agreed to do. The English translations started in 1970 and the first publication, the *Biography of Bediüzzaman Said Nursi*, appeared in March 1974. Due to the lengthy process of book printing, it was decided that *Risale-i Nur* could be delivered to readers faster in the form of a magazine. Four months later, the first issue of *Nur—The Light* magazine was printed in July 1974.

Copies were sent to seventy different countries. In March 1975 the team moved to El Cerrito, California and continued publishing the bi-monthly magazine *Nur—The Light*. After the biography and a small booklet, *Nationalism in the View of Islam*, the third book, *Fruits from the Tree of Light*, was published at the end of 1975. Demirkan, Fırıncı, Mehmet Buker, and Ümit Şimşek had come to help with printing and manual binding of the books at the end of 1975 for a brief time.

Birgeoğlu and his wife continued the *Risale-i Nur* service in California until they moved to Phoenix, Arizona in August 1993, where they reside and operate The Risale-i Nur Institute of America; its printing division, Nur Publishers; and the newest branch, the Nursi School of Theology, which was opened in March 2011. *Nur Publishers* prints and distributes the English translation of the *Risale-i Nur* books, not only for the United States, but also for other countries such as Canada, England and Australia, and various European countries.

## Publications

Hamid Algar continued translating the *Risale* until 1985 when Şükran Vahide took over and continued his work. Algar was the first academic to introduce Nursi and his *magnum opus* to the English-speaking world. In 1999, Algar attended a symposium on Nursi in Malaysia, arranged by the IIKV, where he presented a paper discussing Nursi in the context of the *tajdīd* tradition. He developed his presentation into an article which appeared in 2001.[64] The crucial point in Nursi Studies was Şerif Mardin's mono-

---

63. Birgeoğlu, "Our Story," accessed March 8, 2012, http://www.nurpublishers.com/about-us/our-story/.

64. Algar, "The Centennial Renewer."

graph, *Religion and Social Change in Modern Turkey: The Case of Bediüzzaman Said Nursi*, in 1989.⁶⁵ Mardin wrote the book while a visiting scholar at Oxford University, where he had conversations with Faris Kaya, who pursued his doctoral degree at Sussex University and led faith–sharing sessions on the *Risale*.

A pioneer was İbrahim M. Abu-Rabi', who was to become an expert in Nursi Studies. He not only authored and edited a number of books on Nursi, but also introduced his thought to the academy, especially in the United States.⁶⁶ One issue of *The Muslim World* was dedicated to Nursi Studies when Abu-Rabi' himself was the senior editor of the journal.⁶⁷ *Islam at the Crossroads: On the Life and Thought of Bediüzzaman Said Nursi* was Abu-Rabi's first book on Nursi, consisting of 19 articles written by a wide range of scholars, including Dale F. Eickelman, Barbara Freyer Stowasser, and Oliver Leaman. Abu-Rabi' was also the editor of *Islam in Modern Turkey: An Intellectual Biography of Bediüzzaman Said Nursi*, authored by Şükran Vahide. It is so far the most comprehensive intellectual biography of Nursi. Vahide uses primary sources to portray Nursi in as much detail and as genuinely as possible. Another scholar worth mentioning in the field of Nursi Studies is Hakan Yavuz, presently at the University of Utah. Besides his publication of a number of articles, Yavuz authored the work, *Islamic Political Identity in Turkey*.

Increasingly, Christian theologians like Ian Markham and Thomas Michel have turned to a closer analysis of Nursi's thought. Markham has published three books on Nursi thus far which were all published by Ashgate publications. His first book, *Globalization, Ethics and Islam: The Case of Bediüzzaman Said Nursi*, is co-edited with İbrahim Özdemir. Markham's second study on Nursi is *Engaging with Bediüzzaman Said Nursi: A Model of Interfaith Dialogue* and was published in 2009. He spent about eight years of deep theological engagement with Said Nursi, whom he regards as a mirror reflecting the challenges of every person of faith in the West. His most recent book on Nursi is *An Introduction to Said Nursi: Life, Thought, and Writings*, co-authored with Suendam Birinci Pirim.

Thomas Michel, another significant figure in bringing Nursi Studies forward, is a leading expert in Christian-Muslim relations who has served on the Pontifical Council for Interreligious Dialogue and published extensively on modern Muslim thinkers such as Said Nursi. In 1988, he became Head of the Office for Islam in the same Vatican department. His essays on Nursi deal mostly with ethical and theological themes and in collaboration with the IIKV he has presented numerous lectures on Nursi's thought in the United States and worldwide. Many of his essays appeared in works edited by Abu Rabi'.

Within the US context so far, a number of dissertations and Master theses have been written on Nursi and the *Risale-i Nur*.⁶⁸ In June 2003, the Nursi Chair

---

65. For an assessment of *Risale* related academic literature written in English see the Literature Review by Sayılgan, "Constructing an Islamic Ethics of Non-Violence."

66. For a full list of English written publications on Nursi, see "Nursi Studies," (http://www.Nursistudies.com/books.php).

67. For more details, see *The Muslim World*.

68. For a full list, see "Nursi Studies" (http://www.Nursistudies.com/akademi.php?ctg=Akademik&lng=English&aid=5 and http://www.

in Islamic Studies was established in the Religious Studies Department at John Carroll University in Cleveland.[69] While this branch offers a variety of courses on Islam it does not award academic degrees. Under the direction of the chair, Zeki Sarıtoprak, the university organized two conferences on Nursi so far, the recent one being held in October 2011 under the title "Challenges to Contemporary Islam: The Muslim World 100 Years After Nursi's Damascus Sermon." Members of the Nur community increasingly attend academic circles and conferences in order to develop the new field of Nursi Studies. Comparative works engaging Nursi with different intellectuals such as Paul Tillich, Reinhold Niebuhr, Rene Girard, and many others are at the forefront of this endeavor.

## The Istanbul Foundation for Science and Culture—Leading Academic Discourse

As the previous assessment makes evident, the IIKV has played an instrumental role in developing the academic discourse on Nursi and his *Risale-i Nur* within the European and American context, not to say worldwide. It has established itself as an important resource with its extensive archive, but also oversees global activities by maintaining contact with persons working in the community. Since the 1990s the IIKV has been leading the academic initiative and has served as a major point of resource for academics. Its goal to disseminate the thought of Nursi has brought numerous scholars from America and elsewhere to Istanbul to engage with the *Risale* on an academic level. The IIKV has inspired young academics attending graduate conferences in Istanbul to pursue Nursi Studies in Europe and the US. Its influential role cannot be underestimated. The international symposiums hosting participants from around the globe accelerated academic works in Nursi Studies significantly in the past years.[70] The first international symposium was organized in 1990 and many other conferences have been held in Europe, North Africa and Asia since then.[71] The foundation collaborates with institutions like Virginia Theological Seminary and Hartford Seminary in the United States. Scholars like Lucinda Mosher or Jeremy Walton, who did research on Nursi and his followers, turned to the IIKV as a resource. The national meeting of the American Academy of Religion and the World Parliament of Religion in Australia and the United States was also attended by the IIKV in order to draw attention to Nursi Studies. The IIKV also maintains numerous relationships with universities and academic institutions all around the globe. In this sense, the foundation has also participated in a series of conferences at the University of Alberta in Canada in 2010 and at the University of Calgary in 2011.

---

Nursistudies.com/akademi.php?ctg=Academy&lng=English&aid=3).

69. For more on the Nursi Chair in Islamic Studies at John Carroll University see "Nursi Chair in Islamic Studies," accessed March 8, 2012, http://sites.jcu.edu/Nursichair/about/about-2/.

70. For more on the *Istanbul Foundation for Science and Culture,* see "Nursi Studies," accessed March 8, 2012, www.Nursistudies.com or www.iikv.org.

71. For a full list of the international conferences and symposiums see "Nursi Studies," accessed March 8, 2012, http://www.Nursistudies.com/akademi.php?ctg=Akademik&lng=English&aid=4.

Faris Kaya, the director of the IIKV, remembers the dire need for a full accessible English translation of the *Risale* during his stay in the United Kingdom as a student from 1977 until 1981.[72] Besides a few translated pamphlets done by the Risale-i Nur Institute in America, Kaya did not have more *Risale* works available for the faith-sharing sessions he organized three times a week. In 1984, Kaya visited Durham University and attended the multi-national faith-sharing session led by Ali Mermer, who also wrote the first dissertation in Nursi Studies entitled, "Some Aspects of Religious Identity: The Nurcu Movement in Turkey Today" in 1985. Here, Kaya made acquaintance with the Muslim convert Mary Weld, known later on as Şükran Vahide, and scholars like Colin Turner and Yamina Mermer, who also contributed academically to Nursi Studies later on in their lives. Kaya invited Vahide to Istanbul and after a two week visit she decided to live in Istanbul dedicating her life to the translation of the *Risale*. She has done the first comprehensive translation of Nursi's work and continues to make his thought available for the English-speaking world.

Nur members. While Turkish immigrants in Europe with a lower educational background have focused more on spiritual transformation within the community, one discerns a stronger focus on the academic discourse initiated by young academics of the Nur community who came to the United States in the early 1970s. Yet this is only a matter of emphasis.

Second, the two initiatives are acting in complementary ways. The exchange and communication between the Nur members in Europe and the United States and the former's imitation of the academic enterprise suffices as evidence. It remains to see whether a balance of the inward and external discourse will be achieved in the future. As for Europe, it seems more likely that the academic discourse will be furthered given the emergence of a young Muslim academic group. In this regard, the IIKV continues its task as a driving force in furthering Nursi Studies worldwide. In closing, the community's endeavors within the American and European context only signify that the willingness to cope with new challenges and conditions is evidently present.

## CONCLUSION

Given the young stage of research, this essay was not able to do justice to a full portrayal of the Nur community in its European and American context. Yet the previous survey identified certain characteristics. First, the form and method of the *Risale-i Nur* service on the two respective continents have been largely shaped by the social background of the

72. Kaya, Personal Interview, March 11, 2012.

## BIBLIOGRAPHY

Abdullah, Muhammad Salim. *Was will der Islam in Deutschland?* Gütersloh: Gütersloher Verlagshaus, 1993.

Akbulut, Duran. *Türkische Moslems in Deutschland: Ein religionssoziologischer Beitrag zur Integrationsdebatte*. Albeck bei Ulm: Verlag Ulmer Manuskripte, 2003.

Algar, Hamid. "The Centennial Renewer: Bediüzzaman Said Nursi and the Tradition of Tajdid." *Journal of Islamic Studies* 12.3 (2001) 291–311.

Birgeoğlu, Osman. "Our Story." Online: http://www.nurpublishers.com/about-us/our-story/. Accessed March 8, 2012.

Bundesamt für Migration und Flüchtlinge. *Muslimisches Leben in Deutschland*. Nuremberg: Bundesamt für Migration und Flüchtlinge, Juni 2009.

Cole, Jeffrey. *Ethnic Groups of Europe: An Encyclopedia*. ABC-CLIO: 2011.

Gür, Metin. *Türkisch-Islamische Vereinigungen in der Bundesrepublik Deutschland*. Frankfurt a.M.: Brandes & Apsel, 1993.

Heimbach, Marfa. *Die Entwicklung der islamischen Gemeinschaft in Deutschland seit 1961*. Berlin: Klaus Schwarz Verlag, 2001.

Hüttermann, Jörg. *Islamische Mystik: Ein 'gemachtes Milieu' im Kontext von Modernität und Globalität*. Würzburg, Ergon Verlag, 2002.

Istanbul Foundation for Science and Culture. "Nursi Studies." Accessed March 8, 2012. www.nursistudies.com or www.iikv.org.

Kaya, Faris. Personal Interview, March 11, 2012.

Lemmen, Thomas. *Islamische Vereine und Verbände in Deutschland*. Bonn: Friedrich-Ebert Stiftung, 2002.

Michel, Thomas. "Peaceful Movements in the Muslim World." In *Religious Pluralism: Globalization and World Politics*, edited by Thomas Banchoff, 229–53. Oxford: Oxford University Press, 2008.

Motadel, David. "Islam in Germany." *Euro-Islam.Info: News and Analysis on Islam in Europe and North America*. Online: http://www.euro-islam.info/country-profiles/germany/. Accessed March 8, 2012.

Nursi, Bediüzzaman Said. *Emirdağ Lahikası*. Istanbul: Söz, 2008.

———. *Emirdağ Lahikası*. Istanbul: Yeni Asya, 2001.

———. *İlk Dönem Eserleri*. Istanbul: Söz, 2008.

———. *Lem'alar*. Istanbul: Söz, 2010.

———. *Mektubat*. Istanbul: Soz, 2010.

———. *Sözler*. Istanbul: Söz, 2010.

Nursi Studies. Online: http://www.nursistudies.com/akademi.php?ctg=Academy&lng=English&aid=3. Accessed March 8, 2012.

Pohl, Reinhard. *BRD und Dritte Welt* 59.6 (2004) 1–48.

Risale-i Nur Studies. Online: http://www.dur.ac.uk/sgia/imeis/risale/. Accessed March 8, 2012.

Sayılgan, Salih. "Constructing an Islamic Ethics of Non-Violence: The Case of Bediüzzaman Said Nursi." MA Thesis, University of Alberta, 2012.

Sovik, Margrete. "Islamic Instruction in German Public Schools: The Case of North-Rhine Westphalia." In *Islam and Muslims in Germany*, edited by Jörn Thielmann and Ala Al-Hamarneh, 241–65. Leiden: Brill, 2008.

Steinbach, Udo, and Nils Feindt-Riggers. *Islamische Organisationen in Deutschland: Eine aktuelle Bestandsaufnahme*. Hamburg: Deutsches Orient-Institut Hamburg, 1997.

Şahinöz, Cemil. *Die Nurculuk Bewegung: Entstehung, Organisation und Vernetzung*. Istanbul: Nesil, 2009.

Şen, Faruk and Aydın, Hayrettin. *Islam in Deutschland*. Munich: Beck, 2002.

*The Muslim World* LXXXIX.3–4 (1999).

Thielmann, Jörn. "The Turkish Bias and Some Blind Spots: Research on Muslims in Germany." In *Muslim Organizations and the State—European Perspectives*, Bundesamt für Migration und Flüchtlinge, 169–95. Nuremberg: Bundesamt für Migration und Flüchtlinge, 2010.

Utermann, Claudia. *Türkischer Islam in Deutschland*. Hamburg: DPA, 1995.

Wunn, Ina, and Sevil Pınar. "Die Nurculuk Bewegung Jama'at un-Nur." In *Muslimische Gruppierungen in Deutschland: Ein Handbuch*, edited by Ina Wunn, 85–92. Stuttgart: Kohlhammer, 2007.

Yavuz, Hakan M. "Die Renaissance des religiösen Bewusstseins in der Türkei: Nur-Studienzirkel." In *Islam in Sicht: Der Auftritt von Muslimen im öffentlichen Raum*, edited by Nilüfer Göle and

Ludwig Amman, 121–46. Bielefeld: Transcript, 2004.

Yavuz, Hakan M. *Islamic Political Identity in Turkey*. Oxford: Oxford University Press, 2003.

# 20

# Christian–Muslim Engagement

THOMAS MICHEL

## NURSI AND INTERRELIGIOUS DIALOGUE

ALREADY IN THE EARLY part of the twentieth century, Said Nursi proposed to his students that they should "unite also with the truly pious and spiritual Christians."[1] Nursi never spoke of "dialogue with Christians," for the term did not come into current usage until after his death in 1960. Consequently, one would search in vain in the *Risale-i-Nur* for references to Said Nursi's views about dialogue with Christians or the followers of any other religion. However, Nursi used a much stronger word: unity; Muslims should strive to be united with faithful, God-fearing Christians. Nursi's advocacy of Muslim-Christian unity was based on a conviction that Muslims and Christians had a God-given task in society that could only be achieved by working together. His awareness of the need for cooperation and friendship between the two communities of faith mark him as one of the pioneers of dialogue in the twentieth century.

For Nursi, the days of the "*jihād* of the sword" are over, so there is no question of any obligation to engage in warfare against the People of the Book. But questions regarding the proper way for Muslims to relate to the followers of the earlier religions remain. Was it determined by God that Muslims and Christians should live in enmity and rivalry, or that one community would be in full possession of the truth while the other was irredeemably in error? Are there any grounds on which Muslims might propose that the two communities of believers could live in a mutually beneficial way and together make a contribution to society and work for the good of all? What can be said concerning Qur'anic verses such as the following: "O you who believe! Do not take the Jews and the Christians for your

---

1. Nursi, *Lem'alar*, 146.

friends and protectors" (Q 5:51)? Nursi addressed such questions in the *Risale-i-Nur*, not in the form of a systematic treatise on the Islamic theology of religion, but variously, as events in his life and questions from students raised the issues.

If Nursi had held that Christians and Muslims were irreconcilable enemies, to be opposed by pen or sword, any real dialogue between the members of the communities would have been impossible. Similarly, if Nursi had believed that the teachings of the "heavenly" religions, as he called them, were so different and contradictory that no meaningful encounter was conceivable, or if he considered Christianity as being wholly corrupt and devoid of any holiness, truth, and goodness, he could not be said to advocate a dialogue of religions. However, it is clear from the *Risale-i-Nur* that Nursi regarded the other religions as possessing elements of holiness, truth, and goodness. These elements can be considered as legitimate bases for a real conversation and cooperation among the followers of the three religions.

This essay will be limited to Nursi's views about relations with Christians and the possibility of dialogue and unity with the true followers of Christ. Living most of his life in eastern and central Anatolia, Nursi rarely encountered Jews, and hence wrote relatively little about relations with Jews. The reasons for his silence concerning the religions of Buddhism, Hinduism, and other mainly Asian religions is still more obvious, for such were not encountered in Anatolia in his day. The *Risale* was written as practical information and advice aimed at forming devout Muslims and answering their questions; it was not written as a theoretical treatise on religions. The greatest number of non-Muslims the students of the *Risale-i-Nur* encountered in their daily lives were Christians, so Nursi focused on the relationship of Muslims to Christians.

## THE UNIVERSALITY OF WORSHIP OF GOD

Nursi affirms that not only Muslims, but also the followers of other religions worship God, each in their own way. Not only does the inanimate world worship the one God by performing the various natural functions commanded by God, but also the various religious communities seek to do God's will as they understand it. This is an argument, according to Nursi, for the existence of the One God. If the followers of the earlier religions perform a certain type of genuine worship of God, it follows that there is a kind of spirituality and holiness present in them. Nursi asserts:

> The involvement of each group of men in a mode of worship dictated by their innate dispositions, the species of worship engaged in by other animate beings, as well as inanimate beings, through the performance of their essential functions, the way in which all material and immaterial bounties and gifts in the cosmos become means inciting men to worship and thanks, to praise and gratitude; the fashion in which all the manifestations of the unseen and epiphanies of the spirit, revelation and inspiration, unanimously proclaim the exclusive fitness of one God to receive worship—all of this in most evidential fashion, proves the reality and dominance of a single and absolute Divinity.[2]

2. Nursi, *The Rays*, 172.

In holding that "the fashion in which all the manifestations of the unseen and epiphanies of the spirit, revelation and inspiration unanimously proclaim the exclusive fitness of one God to receive worship," Nursi is inviting Muslims to acknowledge some of the ways in which the One God might be active also in other religions. When taken up by Muslim scholars, such theological investigations could form the basis of an "Islamic theology of religions." Moreover, if evidence of spiritual, inspired, and revelatory experiences is to be found among the followers of other religions, as well as demonstrations of the unseen divine activity, or grace, a basis for religious communication between Muslims and adherents to the earlier religions is established.

## THE POSSIBILITY OF FRIENDSHIP

If there are genuine elements of holiness and goodness in the other religions, it follows that it is proper for Muslims to befriend and love their neighbors of the Peoples of the Book. Challenged that this was against the teaching of the Qur'an (Q 5:51), Nursi demonstrated that the Qur'anic verse in question was not a general ('*amm*) injunction to be applied to all times and places where Muslims cohabit with Jews or Christians, but rather a limited or specific (*mutlaq*) judgment whose application is determined by the concrete situation. Muslims can befriend Jews and Christians on the basis of the "Muslim" qualities that many individual Jews and Christians possess. Nursi makes his case by citing the human example of a Muslim man married to a woman from one of these communities. "Of course he should love her,"[3] states Nursi.

Nursi affirms, even in the most tragic of circumstances, that he had Christian friends. When Nursi visited Van after the destruction of the city as a result of the Russian invasion, he wept without distinction for both the Christian and Muslim victims, who had been his "friends and acquaintances." "Most of the people of those houses had been my friends and acquaintances. The majority of them had died in the migrations—may God have mercy on them—or had gone into wretched exile. In addition to the Armenian quarter, all the Muslim houses of Van had been leveled."[4]

## THE TWO SIDES OF EUROPE

Nursi accepts that because of the elements of goodness and truth in the earlier heavenly religions, Muslims can make friends with their adherents. Moreover, the challenges of modern life provide a positive impetus that should lead Muslims and Christians into dialogue and cooperation. Nursi adopts a nuanced approached to what he calls "Western" or "European" civilization. He acknowledges that modern civilization is not all bad and affirms that there are many good qualities to be found in Western civilization. The positive qualities to be found in European civilization derive "especially from the

---

3. Nursi, *Münazarat*, 70–71. The *Münazarat* [*Dialogues*] is a part of the *Risale-i-Nur* that has not been translated in full into English. First published in 1913, it relates the "dialogues" or question-and-answer sessions that Nursi held with tribesmen in Eastern Anatolia. I have used the partial translations made by Sarıtoprak in "Said Nursi's Teaching on the People of the Book, 325–28.

4. Nursi, *The Flashes*, 314.

guidance of the Qur'an, and from the preceding revealed religions."[5]

Historically, the greatest influence on the development of European culture has been from the Christian tradition. The European heritage from true Christianity is to be found in two areas: in those fields of study that promote justice and goodness, and in the sciences that are oriented toward social happiness. Nursi states: "There are two Europes. I am not criticizing the Europe of scientific works, of justice and equity, of useful and beneficial artwork for humanity and the welfare of people, with all its inspiration and enlightenment learned from true Christianity and Islam."[6] However, Nursi considers that these positive virtues beneficial for huhumankind are outweighed by a number of negative values that modern civilization has adopted from non-religious and antireligious philosophies. The result is a two-sided Europe. One current, inspired by the teachings of true Christianity, has worked to establish justice and to develop scientific thought for the benefit of society. The second current, rejecting Europe's Christian heritage, has pursued a variety of atheistic and materialistic philosophies to produce a selfish, impoverished, self-destructive civilization.

With the first current, that is, the Europe of faith, Nursi has no argument, but the second Europe he considers a danger, not only to Islam, but to all the revealed religions.[7] "I am addressing the second corrupt Europe which, through the darkness of the philosophy of Naturalism and supposing the evils of civilization to be its virtues, has driven humankind to vice and misguidance."[8] In opposing themselves to "the bases of all heavenly laws," those who promote the atheistic current of European civilization produce more harm than good and actually give false guidance to humanity.[9]

Since the divine and humane values beneficial to humanity are taught not only by the Qur'an, but also by the earlier religions, such values form the basis for dialogue and cooperation between the followers of the "revealed religions" of Judaism, Christianity, and Islam. One can conclude from the *Risale-i Nur* that dialogue among Jews, Christians, and Muslims is a legitimate and vital tool for the religions to carry out their mission to embody and bear witness in contemporary society to the spiritual values found in the divine Word.

## CRITIQUE OF ACTUAL BEHAVIOR OF CHRISTIANS

Although he believed that true Christianity had made a valuable contribution to the development of European civilization, Nursi sharply criticized the actual behavior of Christians and even some of the theological presuppositions of Christian faith. He felt that Christians were led astray by excessive love of the prophet Jesus, just as, in his view, the Shia deviated from the true path through their excessive devotion to Ali.[10] He cites a *hadīth*

---

5. Nursi, *The Words*, 421.
6. Nursi, *The Flashes*, 160.
7. Nursi, *Emirdağ Lahikası*, 270. The *Emirdağ Lahikası* is a collection of letters written by Nursi during his period of house arrest in Emirdağ between 1944 and 1951. The collection has not yet been translated into English.

8. Nursi, *The Flashes*, 160.
9. Nursi, *Emirdağ Lahikası*, 99–100.
10. Nursi, *The Words*, 673. Nursi makes a similar observation in regard to the way many Sufis are excessively devoted to their *shaykhs* and

in which Muhammad is reported to have said to Ali:

> As was true of Jesus, two groups of people will perish on your account: one because of excessive love, the other because of excessive enmity. Christians, on account of their deep love for Jesus, transgressed the limits and called him—God forbid!—"the son of God," while the Jews, because of their hostility, went to the other extreme by denying his message and virtue.[11]

This disproportionate love for Jesus is, according to Nursi, dangerous for Christians[12] because it leads them to overstep the bounds; discontent to accept him as a prophet of God, they affirm a belief in Jesus as Son of God. Nursi denies that Jesus was responsible for such an institutionalized personality cult,[13] for most of the dogmas, regulations, and religious practices were developments of a later age.

In the religion of Jesus, only the fundamentals of religion were taken from Jesus. Most of the injunctions concerning social life and the secondary matters of the Law were formulated by disciples and other spiritual leaders. The greater part was taken from former Holy Scriptures. Since Jesus was not a worldly ruler and sovereign, and since he was not the source of general social laws, the fundamentals of his religion were as though clothed in a garment of common laws and civil rules taken from outside, then given a different form and called the Christian law. If this form is changed and the garment transformed, the fundamental religion of Jesus may persist.[14]

It is worth noting that, according to Nursi, although the basic elements of Jesus' teaching ("the fundamentals of his religion") came to be dressed in man-made, earthly practices that came to be known as "the Christian law," that is, religion, it is still possible for the followers of Jesus to transform the evolved structures and restore the primordial prophetic faith brought by Jesus.

In regard to scripture, Nursi claims that the biblical texts have undergone change. The divine speech brought by the prophets has been adulterated by translations, additions, and human interpretations and, as a result, the biblical passages do not display the unique extraordinary power of the Qur'anic text. This charge of *taḥrīf*, or corruption of scripture, is not new with Nursi, but was a perennial feature of Islamic polemic in regard to the People of the Book. However, Nursi does not raise the issue in a polemical context so much as to underline the splendor of the Qur'an.

> The words of the Torah, the Bible, and the Psalms do not have the miraculousness of those of the Qur'an. They have also been translated again and again, and a great many alien words have become intermingled with them. Also, the words of commentators and their false interpretations have been confused with their verses. In addition, the distortions of the ignorant and the hostile have been incorporated into them. In these ways, the corruptions and alterations have multiplied in those Books.[15]

---

saints. Nursi, *The Letters*, 531–32.

11. Nursi, *The Letters*, 137.
12. Nursi, *The Flashes*, 41.
13. Nursi, *The Letters*, 510.
14. Nursi, "Twenty-Ninth Letter," *The Letters*, 508.
15. Nursi, "'The Miracles of Muhammad,' Sixteenth Sign, Second Proof," *The Letters*, 201.

It was not the fundamentals of faith but the later developments that occurred in Christian history that caused Islam and Christianity to diverge in many respects.[16] Nursi holds that the original, true Christianity has been corrupted by the writings of materialist philosophers, which have engendered self-centered and egoistic tendencies among Christians.[17] Under the influence of philosophical thought, Christians today understand others than God as being the actual causes of things, in contrast to the Islamic view of God as the only true cause of all that occurs.

At the popular level, the Christian acceptance of causality translates into a belief that their clergy and saints can independently intercede and bestow help and favors on devotees. To this popular perception, he contrasts the Islamic position in which prophets and holy persons are but manifestations of the power and qualities of the One God, unable to assist others or achieve anything without the unique enabling power of God.

> Because it has been corrupted, present-day Christianity considers causes and intermediaries to have an effect, and looks on them as signifying themselves. Their belief in Jesus as the son of God and in the priesthood demands and urges this. They regard their saints for their own sakes as though they do not signify another. ... We [Muslims] look on the saints as signifying the meaning of another, that is, as a place of reflection and manifestation, like a mirror spreads the sunlight.[18]

This provides the basis for Nursi's view, which runs throughout the *Risale-i Nur*, that there is a "true Christianity" brought by the prophet Jesus and still followed by a certain number of his disciples, and a "false, corrupted Christianity" that is the result of human interventions and innovations. When Nursi addresses "Europe," he is usually referring to those elements and currents of European civilization that have rejected the sound Christian teaching and inspiration that comes from the person and message of Jesus.[19]

Nursi admits that Muslims as well have not been immune from corrupting developments. Both through the introduction of *masīḥīyat* from early Christian converts to Islam[20] and of *isra'iliyat* introduced by converts from Judaism, as well as borrowings from Greek philosophy,[21] Muslims adopted views incompatible with Qur'anic teaching that sowed confusion in their ranks. In a criticism of the popular misperceptions concerning Islam that were prevalent in his day, Nursi wrote, "Abandoning the essence and kernel of Islam, we fixed our gaze on its exterior shell. Through misapprehension and ill-manners, we did not afford Islam its right nor pay it its due respect ... We mixed *isra'iliyat* with the fundamentals of belief, and stories with the tenets of faith,

---

16. Nursi, "Twenty-Ninth Letter, Seventh Section," *The Letters*, 510.

17. Nursi, "Second Addendum, Second Part," *The Damascus Sermon*, 119.

18. Ibid., 118. Cf. also, Nursi, "Twenty-Sixth Letter, Third Topic," *The Letters*, 384.

19. "O Europe corrupted with vice and misguidance and drawn far from the religion of Jesus!" Nursi, "Seventeenth Flash, Fifth Note," *The Flashes*, 161.

20. Nursi, "In the time of the Companions of the Prophet most of the Jewish and Christian scholars entered Islam, and their former knowledge became Muslim along with them. Some of their former knowledge which was contrary to the truth was imagined to be a part of Islam." The "Twenty-Fourth Word, Third Branch, Third Principle," *The Words*, 351.

21. Nursi, *Münazarat*, 7. Cited by Vahide, *Islam in Modern Turkey*, 162.

and metaphors with the truths of belief, and did not appreciate its value."[22]

Nursi saw lessons for Muslims in Turkey that could be derived from the unhappy religious history of Europe. In obvious references to Inquisition trials and the Galileo affair, he criticizes the Roman Catholic Church for having silenced its scholars and having demanded blind adherence to authority.[23] In the political sphere, the Catholic Church came to be an instrument of the ruling classes to maintain their power and control the poor. When the poor rose up against unjust rule, they rejected the church as well. For a long time in France, the Christian religion, and particularly the Catholic Church, had been a means of domination and despotism in the hands of the upper and ruling classes. By that means the upper class perpetuated its influence over the ordinary people. It was a tool for oppressing the patriots, who were those who were awakened among the common people and were called Jacobins, and a tool for oppressing the freedom-seeking thinkers, who attacked the despotism of the upper class tyrants. Since for nearly 400 years it had been considered to be a cause, through revolutions in Europe, of overturning the stability of social life, the Catholic Church was attacked, not in the name of irreligion, but by the other Christian sects.[24]

## POSSIBILITY OF VIRTUE AMONG CHRISTIANS

Despite his critique of the actual practice of Christianity, Nursi notes that Christians, even though they do not accept Muhammad as prophet, are not abandoned by God. They can experience a kind of divine grace (light, *nur*) that pervades their lives, giving rise to a type of religious faith and producing ethical behavior and good character. Nursi wrote: "Even if they cast out from their hearts the light of the Prophet Muhammad, lights of a sort may remain. They may continue to have a sort of belief in their Creator and in Moses and Jesus, which will allow them to attain good morals and character."[25] Thus, it is in their faith in God as Creator and their obedience to God's commands as they know them through the biblical Testaments of Moses and Jesus that Christians and Jews can arrive at pious and ethically upright lives.

To the pious and obedient Christian or Jew, Nursi contrasts the unbelieving Muslim who has rejected his Islamic faith and the Prophet and consequently has nothing to sustain and enrich his spiritual life. Such a person will not accept another prophet and will find himself lost and alone in a secular wasteland. However, the Christian, who has never known Muhammad as prophet, is still able to rely on his Christian faith and national heritage and in this way can continue to grow in virtue and hope. Nursi asks: "Do you not see that a Westerner who rejects the Prophet Muhammad can still console himself with his Christianity and his Western civilization, which contains elements of his nation's customs? It is possible for him to preserve

22. Nursi, *Münazarat*, 16–18. Cited by Vahide, *Islam in Modern Turkey*, 161–62.

23. Nursi, "Twenty-Ninth Letter, Seventh Section," *The Letters*, 510.

24. Nursi, "Twenty-Ninth Letter, Seventh Section," *The Letters*, 509.

25. Nursi, "Twenty-Fourth Word, Fifth Branch," *The Words*, 373.

in his spirit some laudable virtues and make praiseworthy efforts to improve his worldly life."[26]

Nursi's concern is obviously with those Muslims who have abandoned Islam and follow a secular, nonreligious way of life. He acknowledges that, by comparison, the lives of Christians who follow their religion conscientiously are more characterized by praiseworthy qualities and efforts to progress in virtue. It is not only the deeply devout believer who can display sensitivity to religious matters. Even a Christian who does not regularly follow the practice of his religion can provide positive input to social life and respond faithfully to God in many religious demands. "A Christian may still contribute to society, even if he is irreligious. He may accept some sacred matters and may believe in some of the prophets, and may assent to Almighty God in some respects."[27]

It is obvious that Nursi does not consider all Christians to be living distant from divine truth and ethical norms. Some have "good morals and character," display "laudable virtues," make "praiseworthy efforts to improve," and "accept some sacred matters, believe in some of the prophets, and assent to God in some respects." These realities form the basis for the kind of unity and cooperation to which Nursi calls conscientious Muslims and Christians.

## THE BATTLE AGAINST THE FORCES OF EVIL

Although his judgment could be harsh on what he regarded as theological corruptions and innovations, on the religious wars and forms of oppression found in Christian history, and on the sad realities of life and practice among many Christians, Nursi repeatedly expressed a hope that Christians would undergo a purification to live the true message of Christ more faithfully. He was convinced that as Christians come closer to practicing the faith they received from Jesus, they will in the process also come closer to the teaching of Islam.

The starting point for this hopeful expectation is a *hadīth* report from Muhammad that states that at the end of time, a purified Christianity will be transformed into a kind of Islam.[28] At that point, the renewed Christian community will overcome irreligious and atheistic ideas and behavior to live as faithful followers of Jesus.[29] They will oppose and overcome an antireligious and hedonist way of life represented by the figure of the *dajjal*, the Islamic equivalent of the Antichrist in Christian scripture and tradition.

An appreciation of Nursi's expectation of future times demands an understanding of the concept of corporate or collective personality. Unlike most Muslim scholars, who regard the *dajjal* as an individual who will be confronted by the man Jesus upon his return to earth, Nursi understands both "Jesus" and *dajjal*

---

26. Nursi, *Mathnawi al-Nūrīya* [*Epitomes of Light*], 466–67.

27. Nursi, "Twenty-Ninth Letter, Seventh Section," *The Letters*, 512.

28. Nursi, "First Letter," *The Letters*, 22.

29. "On the coming of Jesus and emergence of the true Christian religion, the Antichrist's irreligious way will be wiped out and will cease." Nursi, "Fifth Ray," *The Rays*, 101.

as collectives. According to this reading, *dajjal* represents not an evil individual but all those materialist, atheistic forces—human and demonic—that oppose faith and obedience to God's will on earth; whereas "Jesus" indicates the collectivity of all those who follow a purified, incorrupt Christian faith that remains faithful to Christ's sound teaching. Nursi expects to see a power struggle between these two human forces, with the eventual victory of the purified Christian community, represented by the collective personality of Jesus, over the powers of irreligion and immorality.

Nursi states that at the point when the current of *dajjal* appears to be very strong, the religion of true Christianity, which comprises the collective personality of Jesus, will emerge. It will descend from the skies of Divine Mercy. Present Christianity will be purified in the face of that reality; it will cast off superstition and distortion, and unite with the truths of Islam. Christianity will in effect be transformed into a sort of Islam.[30]

Also within the Islamic community there will be a struggle. Among Muslims there will appear a *dajjal*-like figure called Sufyan, who will seek to turn the Islamic community from its path of truth and uprightness and seek to sow discord, wrongdoing, and disobedience. Sufyan, the Islamic Dajjal will try to abrogate some of the eternal injunctions of the *shari'a* of Muhammad. Destroying the material and spiritual bonds of human life, and leaving headstrong, drunken, out-of-control souls, he will unfasten the luminous chains of respect and compassion. By giving people a freedom which is pure despotism so they fall on one another in a swamp of lust, he will open the way to terrible anarchy.[31]

Like the *dajjal*, Sufyan is not to be interpreted as an individual personality, but as a collectivity of all those within the Islamic *umma* who want to turn the community away from the straight path. It includes thinkers, movements, and governments that encourage Muslims to abandon and renounce Islamic teachings. Just as the true Christians will rise up to defeat the *dajjal* outside the Islamic community, so will the collective personality of *mahdi* lead the faithful Muslims to defeat the forces of unbelief in their midst.

In Nursi's understanding of the future, the true Christians and pious Muslims who are struggling against antireligious tendencies in society will not, on their own, be strong enough to defeat the forces of unbelief. But once the two communities unite and work together—which Nursi sees as happening under Muslim initiative—they will achieve a victory for true religion. Jesus, the representative of the unique perennial prophetic religion, having descended from his place in the heavens, will lead the religious current:

> True religion will become a mighty force. Although defeated before the atheistic current while separate, Christianity and Islam will have the capability to defeat and rout it as a result of their union. Then the person of Jesus, who is present with his human body in the world of the heavens, will come to lead the current of true religion.[32]

---

30. Nursi, "Fifteenth Letter," *The Letters*, 78.

31. Nursi, "The Fifth Ray, Second Station," *The Rays*, 114.

32. Nursi, "Fifteenth Letter," *The Letters*, 78.

## MUST CHRISTIANS CONVERT TO ISLAM?

Nursi anticipates that in the future true Christianity will reemerge, and "stripping off superstition and corrupted belief, will be transformed into Islam."[33] Two questions follow. First, it can be asked whether Nursi expects Christianity to go out of existence in the future when Christians, individually or as a community, adopt Islam. The second question regards Nursi's timeline. Is Nursi referring to a far-off eschaton in close proximity to Judgment Day, or is he envisioning Jesus' return and the battle against the *dajjals* as occurring during his lifetime or shortly after his death?

Concerning the question of the form that the union between purified Christianity and Islam will take, the ambiguity of Nursi's answer underlines the difficulties connected with speaking about the future. Nursi appears to have a complex scenario in mind. He is looking forward to a community of Christians coming to live in a faithful manner according to the message and example of Jesus. They will discard any superstitions that had crept into Christian faith and will reject the unhealthy influences originating in naturalist philosophy;[34] they will become a powerful force, in fact, the only spiritual force strong enough to be able to overcome the attacks of *dajjal*, or organized atheism. Nursi writes:

> He [*dajjal*] will be so powerful and long–lived that only Jesus will be able to kill him; nothing else will be able to. That is, it will only be a revealed, elevated, pure religion that will be able to overturn his way and rapacious regime, and eliminate them. Such a religion will emerge among the true followers of Jesus, and it will follow the Qur'an and become united with it.[35]

Nursi uses various phrases to express the kind of union that he expects between Muslims and Christians. Some expressions give the impression that the Christian community will simply enter Islam and follow the Qur'an.[36] Others imply that as Christians become more faithful in following the teaching and example of Jesus, they will "blend the essence of true Christianity with the essence of Islam,"[37] thereby becoming similar to and living near in friendship to Muslims. Elsewhere, he speaks of Christianity "accepting truths of Islam" and evolving into "a sort of Islam,"[38] with the implication of their retaining a distinctive Christian identity. Elsewhere, Nursi speaks simply of close cooperation between the two purified communities,[39] and of Jesus' returning to bring his religion to its proper conclusion.[40]

Perhaps Nursi's most intriguing insight is his expectation of the emergence of a unique community that maintains its Christian identity but whose faith and practice will be no different from the

---

33. Nursi, *The Damascus Sermon*, 36.
34. Nursi, "First Letter," *The Letters*, 22.
35. Nursi, "Fifth Ray," *The Rays*, 101.
36. Nursi, "First Letter," 22; cf. also "Fifteenth Letter," *The Letters*, 80.
37. Nursi, "Fifth Ray, Second Station," *The Rays*, 108.
38. Nursi, "Fifteenth Letter," *The Letters*, 78.
39. Nursi, "Twentieth Flash, 'On Sincerity,'" 203. See also, "In the continents of the future ... there will be only Islam and the real religion of the followers of Jesus, which will transform into Islam and get rid of superstitions and alterations. It will follow the Qur'an and ally [*ittifak eder*] with Islam." Nursi, *Damascus Sermon*, 36.
40. Nursi, "Fifteenth Letter," *The Letters*, 78.

reality of Islamic faith. It is this purified Christian community that Nursi expects to be instrumental in defeating the *dajjal*. He writes: "A zealous and self-sacrificing community known as a Christian community but worthy of being called 'Muslim Christians' [lit. 'Muslim followers of Jesus'] will be united with the reality of Islam, and will kill and rout that society of the *dajjal*, thus saving humanity from atheism."[41]

A second question regards when all this is to happen. Here Nursi is wisely vague. He appears to hold that after true Christianity emerges and unites with Islam, there will appear another period of nearly universal apostasy which will last almost until the approach of Judgment Day. With the emergence of the true religion of Christianity and its being transformed into Islam, it will spread its light to the great majority of people in the world, but when the end of the world is close an atheistic current will again appear and become dominant. . . . "Allah! Allah!" will not be uttered by a significant group which holds an important position on the earth. The people of truth will form a minority or will be defeated, but they will remain permanently till the end of the world. At the moment Judgment Day occurs, as a sign of divine mercy, the spirits of the believers will be seized first so that they do not see the terrors of the Last Day, but it will break forth over the unbelievers.[42]

When Jesus returns, not everyone will necessarily recognize him. Only those who have remained faithful to his teachings will "through the light of belief"[43] identify him. These views have led some contemporary students of the *Risale-i Nur* to the opinion that Jesus has already returned and that the struggle against the *dajjal* and Sufyan is not to be construed as occurring at some point in the distant future, but is taking place at the present time.

Some passages of the *Risale* would seem to support such a "contemporary" interpretation of Nursi's eschatology. He appears to refer to the struggles taking place in Turkey between the proponents of secular and religious society as instances of the conflict between the collective forces of faith and godlessness. It is tempting to read into Nursi's description of Sufyan as a veiled reference to Mustafa Kemal Atatürk.

Because both *dajjals* will win the assistance of a secret Jewish society which nurtures a terrible desire for revenge on Islam and Christianity, and that of another secret society which uses women's liberation as a screen, and because the Islamic *dajjal* will deceive even the Masonic lodges and win their support, they will be supposed to possess tremendous power. Also, it is understood from the divinations of some of the saints that the *dajjal* called Sufyan who will come to lead the Islamic world will be a leading politician who is extremely capable, intelligent, and active, who does not like ostentation and gives no importance to personal rank and glory. He will be a military leader who is extremely bold, forceful, energetic, and resolute and does not condescend to fame-seeking; and he will captivate the Muslims.[44]

---

41. Nursi, "Twenty-Ninth Letter, Seventh Section," *The Letters*, 515.

42. Nursi, "Fifteenth Letter," *The Letters*, 80.

43. Nursi, "Fifteenth Letter," *The Letters*, 78–79.

44. Nursi, "Fifth Ray, Second Station," *The Rays*, 115.

## GETTING AT THE ROOT OF THE PROBLEM

Nursi's advocacy of Muslim-Christian unity was not abstracted from the difficult realities of tense and even wartime relations. His formulations of peaceful coexistence arose from challenges posed by angry or worried interlocutors. In the early years of the Turkish Republic, subsequent to the First World War, some Kurdish tribesmen in Eastern Anatolia found the idea of freedom for Greeks and Armenians offensive. Memories of the massacres, betrayals, and retaliations that occurred on all sides were still fresh in their minds, and they asked Nursi's advice on the new republican government that was being formed to replace the defunct Ottoman state.

Nursi challenged the tribesmen to see the freedom of Christians as a constitutive element of the Muslims' own freedom.[45] He defended the right of a Christian to be a member of the constitutional assembly, and affirmed that, according to the *shari'a*, a Christian could also be appointed governor or military commander. He not only affirmed the right to liberty of these Christian peoples as something commanded by the *shari'a*, but went farther to turn the question back on the tribesmen, challenging them to recognize the deeper problem as one that lay at the heart of their own ignorance and hard-heartedness. "Their [the Christians'] freedom consists in leaving them in peace and not oppressing them," he said, "for this is what the *shari'a* enjoins. More than this is their aggression in the face of your bad points and craziness, their benefitting from your ignorance."[46]

Nursi went on to state that the real enemy is not this or that group of Christians, but rather the situation of degradation into which all had fallen. He stated, "Our enemy, that which is destroying us, is Lord Ignorance, his son Poverty Effendi, and grandson, Enmity Bey. If the Armenians have opposed us in hatred, they have done so under the leadership of these three corrupters."[47] This identification of the triple enemy facing not only Muslims, but conscientious followers of all religions, is one of the most oft-quoted lines from the *Risale*. The value Nursi placed on peaceful *convivenza* can be summarized in these words to the tribesmen: "I am telling you with a certainty that the happiness and salvation of this nation lies only in a friendly relationship with the Armenians. Relations with them are not to be forged in a despicable way, but by extending the hand of peace. . . . Enmity is completely the wrong approach."[48]

## CHRISTIANS AS MARTYRS

Nursi lived through one of the most disastrous periods of the history of the early twentieth century. World War I resulted in a population loss of more than 30 percent, 10 percent of whom emigrated, 20 percent of whom died. The death toll encompassed vast numbers of Armenians, Greeks, and Turks in a situation in which the secondary causes of war—disease,

---

45. Nursi, *Münazarat*, 20–21.

46. Nursi, *Münazarat*, 20.

47. Nursi, *Münâzarat*, (Ott. ed.) in *Asar-ı Bediyye*, n.p, n.d., 433. Cited in Vahide, *Bediüzzaman Said Nursi*, 95.

48. Nursi, *Münazarat*, 68. Cited by Sarıtoprak, "Said Nursi's Teaching," 326.

starvation, and exposure—accounted for a greater number of victims than did battles, raids, and massacres.[49] Writing during this tragic period, Nursi rose above sectarian allegiance to address the question of innocent Christians who fell victim to the times. "Even if those innocent people were unbelievers," he stated, "in return for the tribulations they suffered due to that worldly disaster, they will receive such a reward from the treasury of Divine mercy that if the veil of the Unseen were to open, a great manifestation of mercy would be apparent in relation to them and they would declare, 'O Lord, thanks be to You! All praise belongs to God.'"[50]

Nursi wrote that he was moved to intense compassion and pity when he saw the sufferings of innocent people, and he was "touched strongly by the affliction, poverty and hunger visited on unfortunates as a result of humankind's disaster and the winter cold, as well as by a harsh nonphysical, spiritual cold." He held that those innocent people who died in such circumstances "were martyrs of a sort, whatever religion they belonged to," and that "their reward would be great and save them from Hell." "Therefore," he concluded, "it may be said with certainty that the calamity which those oppressed Christians suffer, those connected to Jesus, is a sort of martyrdom for them."[51]

Not all those who died during the war years were innocent of wrongdoing. Those who oppressed others and perpetrated evil against their neighbors, declared Nursi, will be punished by God. By contrast, he said, "If those who suffered the calamity hastened to assist the oppressed, strove for the welfare of humanity, and struggled to preserve the principles of religion and sacred revealed truths and human rights," their rewards will be so great from God as to completely transcend their earthly sufferings.

## SINCERE RELIGION AND MUSLIM-CHRISTIAN RELATIONS

One of the passages of the *Risale-i Nur* to which Nursi attached special importance was his "Treatise on Sincerity." So central is this passage to his thought that Nursi recommended that his students read it at least once every two weeks. The essay, which could alternately be called the "Treatise on Pure Intention," consists of nine counsels by which Nursi's students could build and maintain a loving unity within their group.

Nursi perceived at times an element of rivalry and competition among his disciples. He recognized that such rivalry could easily lead, if left unattended and unchecked, to hard feelings, envy, resentment, and divisive factions in the community. Moreover, Nursi saw that although these tendencies are found among the students of the *Risale-i Nur*, they are even more evident in the broader Islamic community. These divisive inclinations must be taken seriously for, in Nursi's view, disunity—along with ignorance and poverty—amounts to the most serious enemy to be faced by modern society. Combating these destructive tendencies presents pious Muslims with their most pressing social challenges. Nursi's advises his students that the way to combat tendencies toward factionalism and personal

---

49. McCarthy, *Muslims and Minorities*, 120–21.

50. Nursi, *Kastamonu Lahikası*, 45.

51. Ibid., 75.

aggrandizement is through the practice of sincerity or purity of intention. His advice can be summarized in the form of nine rules:

Act positively with love for one's own point of view, but avoid enmity for other views; do not criticize the views of others nor interfere in their beliefs and practices. Build unity within the fold of Islam by recalling the numerous bonds of unity that evoke love, brotherhood, and harmony. Adopt the rule of conduct that the follower of any sound position has the right to say, "My outlook is true, or very good," but not, "My outlook alone is true," or "My outlook alone is good," implying the falsity or repugnance of other views. Consider that union with pious friends brings divine aid and supports one's faith. Remember that error and falsehood will be defeated through unity among pious believers, which depends upon their ability to create a united and collective force to preserve justice and right. Defend truth from the attacks of falsehood. Abandon self-centered egoism. Give up the mistaken notion of self-pride. Reject all trivial feelings aroused by rivalry.[52]

Nursi's point is that differing opinions and views need not cause factions and enmity within the community. If a Muslim is willing to admit that others have part of the truth, even when they disagree with one's personal view, unity can be maintained in spite of differences of opinion. However, one will only succeed in this if one does everything solely with the intention of sincerely worshiping God.

It is significant that Nursi adds a footnote to his Rules for Sincerity. He cites a *hadīth* from the Prophet Muhammad:

> It is recorded in authentic traditions of the Prophet that at the end of time the truly pious among the Christians will unite with the People of the Qur'an and fight their common enemy, irreligion. In our day, too, the people of religion and truth need to unite sincerely not only with their own brothers and fellow believers, but also with the truly pious and spiritual among the Christians, refraining temporarily from the discussion and debate of points of difference in order to combat their joint enemy, aggressive atheism.[53]

By linking the rules for sincerity with the Prophetic expectation of Muslim-Christian unity, Nursi ties the principles of sincerity not only to the way that Muslims should relate to one another, but also to the way that Muslims should act towards sincere and pious Christians. Read in the context of Muslim-Christian relations, Nursi's rules for sincerity provide sound guidelines for dialogue between the two communities of faith. He urges all to refrain from interfering in the beliefs and practices of others; to build unity by emphasizing those features of shared history that evoke love, brotherhood, and harmony; to affirm one's own belief without implying the falsity or inadequacy of others' beliefs; to recognize the value of associating with God-centered individuals; to work together with others for justice and right; to strive for humility in one's faith and life. These counsels, applied to relations between Muslims and Christians, offer a sound starting point

---

52. Nursi, "Twentieth Flash, 'On Sincerity,'" *The Flashes*, 203.

53. Nursi, "Twentieth Flash, 'On Sincerity,'" *The Flashes*, fn. 7, 203.

for the two communities to live together in harmony and cooperation.

## DISCUSSING FAITH WITH CHRISTIANS

Nursi approved of his students making contact and discussing religious topics with Christian missionaries. He felt that the dangers arising from atheistic communism were a common threat that should draw the two religious communities together. Through their contacts and discussions, Nursi felt that Muslims and Christians could better defend religious faith from intellectual attack and could build a greater unity that would foil attempts to drive a wedge among religious believers.

One of Nursi's students, Selahaddin Çelebi, was friends with some Christian missionaries in Istanbul. He read parts of the *Risale-i Nur* with them and gave them copies of some passages.[54] Nursi was asked whether this was acceptable. He answered: "In connection with Selahaddin giving the American *The Staff of Moses*, we say that it is essential that missionaries, Christian spiritual leaders, and Nurcus [students of the *Risale-i Nur*] be extremely careful. Sooner or later, the northern movement will try to break down the alliance of Muslims and missionaries, in order to defend itself from attacks by Islam and Christianity."[55]

## CONCLUSION

Nursi's views on living in peace with Christians and cooperating with them to defend religious values such as faith,

54. Nursi, *Emirdağ Lahikası*, 154, 179.
55. Nursi, *Emirdağ Lahikası*. 156.

justice, and moral uprightness were ahead of his time. He often had to defend his position as well as to challenge his Muslim interlocutors. He took practical initiatives, considered daring at the time, to promote greater understanding between the two communities. In 1951, he sent a copy of the *Risale-i Nur* to Pope Pius XII in Rome, and received a letter of thanks from the Vatican dated February 22, 1951. Two years later, he visited H. B. Athenagoras, the Greek Orthodox patriarch in Istanbul. Five years before his death, he supported the Baghdad pact, noting that by it not only would Turks gain 400 million brothers and sisters among Muslim peoples, but that the international accord would also gain for Muslim Turks "the friendship of 800 million Christians"[56] and be a step toward a much-needed peace and general reconciliation between the two communities of faith.

Knowledge of Nursi's views of Muslim-Christian relations will grow in international scholarship as the remaining parts of the *Risale-i Nur*—particularly the all-important collections of letters[57]—are translated into English and other European languages. His writings on the importance of unity between the pious followers of Islam and Christians who are seeking to follow the religion of Christ faithfully has inspired many to a greater openness toward the other religion. Nursi's exhortation to his followers to "unite also with the truly pious and spiritual Christians"

56. Nursi, *Emirdağ Lahikası*, II: 24, 56, cited in Vahide, *Islam in Modern Turkey*, 354.

57. These are the *Barla Lahikası*, the *Emirdağ Lahikası*, and the *Kastamonu Lahikası*. These are collections of letters sent by Nursi to colleagues and students written during his periods of house arrest in those cities.

to oppose together huhumankind's perennial enemies of ignorance, poverty, and disunity will remain a lasting legacy of his thought.

## BIBLIOGRAPHY

McCarthy, Justin. *Muslims and Minorities: The Population of Ottoman Anatolia and the End of the Empire*. New York: New York University Press, 1983.

Nursi, Said. *The Damascus Sermon*. Translated by Şükran Vahide. Istanbul: 2004.

———. *Emirdağ Lahikası*. Istanbul: Sinan Matbaası, 1959.

———. *The Flashes*. Translated by Şükran Vahide. Istanbul: 2004.

———. *Kastamonu Lahikası*. Istanbul: Sinan Matbaası, 1960.

———. *Lem'alar*. Istanbul: Sözler, 1986.

———. *The Letters*. Translated by Şükran Vahide. Istanbul: 2004.

———. *Mathnawi al-Nūrīya* [*Epitomes of Light*]. Izmir: Kaynak A.S., 1999.

———. *Münazarat*. Istanbul: Yeni Asya, 1996.

———. *The Rays*. Translated by Şükran Vahide. Istanbul: 2004.

———. *The Words*. Translated by Şükran Vahide. Istanbul: 2004.

Sarıtoprak, Zeki. "Said Nursi's Teaching on the People of the Book: A Case Study of Islamic Social Policy in the Early Twentieth Century." *Islam and Christian–Muslim Relations* II.3 (2000) 325–28.

Vahide, Şükran. *Bediüzzaman Said Nursi*. Istanbul: Sözler, 1992.

———. *Islam in Modern Turkey: An Intellectual Biography of Bediüzzaman Said Nursi*. Albany, NY: State University of New York Press, 2005.

# 21

# Roman Catholic Theological Engagement with Said Nursi

## Leo D. Lefebure

DURING THE LIFETIME OF Said Nursi (ca. 1877–1960),[1] Roman Catholic attitudes towards non-Christian religions and theologians were generally suspicious and hostile. All too often these attitudes were not well-informed. There were, to be sure, some exceptions. Figures of international renown such as Martin Buber and Mohandas Gandhi commanded widespread respect and were extremely influential across religious boundaries. There were also a few Catholics who studied other religious traditions, including Islam, with appreciation and respect during this period. For example, Nursi's contemporary Louis Massignon (1883–1962), a noted French Catholic scholar of Islam, did extensive studies of the Sufi mystical tradition, especially a multivolume work on al-Hallaj.[2] Massignon's attitude toward Islam was so positive that Pope Pius XI reportedly dubbed him "a Catholic Muslim" as a compliment.[3] Another Catholic contemporary of Nursi, the Trappist monk Thomas Merton (1915–68), engaged in a profound dialogue with Sufism.[4] However, it appears that neither Massignon nor Merton engaged Nursi's theology in a major way.[5] Apart from the few exceptions, most Catholic theologians during Nursi's

---

1. Said Nursi's birth has been variously dated from 1876 to 1878. His biographer Şükran Vahide places the date in 1877. Vahide, *Bediüzzaman Said Nursi*, 3; Vahide, *Islam in Modern Turkey*, 353, n. 1. Turner and Horkuc accept the date of 1876. See Turner and Horkuc, *Said Nursi, Makers of Islamic Civilization*. Markham and Birinci Pirim place the date in 1878. *An Introduction to Said Nursi*, 3–4.

2. Massignon, *The Passion of Al-Hallaj*.

3. Anawati, "Louis Massignon et le dialogue islamo-chrétien," 266.

4. Baker and Henry, eds., *Merton & Sufism*.

5. A comprehensive survey of Louis Massignon's relations to his contemporaries does not include Said Nursi. *Louis Massignon et ses contemporains*. In his writings on Islam, Merton does not refer to Nursi. Baker and Gray, *Merton & Sufism*.

lifetime did not undertake serious studies of Nursi or other Muslim theologians. Thus, Nursi received little or no attention from the major Catholic theologians of his day. Nonetheless, Nursi reportedly did enjoy one cordial exchange with Catholic leadership: in 1950, with Nursi's permission, Selahaddin Çelebi sent some of Nursi's writings to the Vatican, and Nursi received a handwritten note of thanks in response, dated February 22, 1951.[6]

There is no indication that Nursi himself studied Roman Catholic theology in any detail or depth. Şükran Vahide has carefully examined the development of Nursi's views on Christianity and the West, describing Nursi's comments on Christianity prior to World War I as "confined to the question of the Christian minorities of the Empire and their gaining equal rights under the 1908 Constitution, and to relations with People of the Book."[7] During and after World War I, Nursi argued that Christians who were innocent victims of atrocities should be viewed as martyrs alongside Muslims.[8] Later in his life, Nursi entertained the hope that Christians would purify Christianity, become allies with Muslims, and defeat *dajjal*, the manifestation of the Antichrist in the "collective personality" of materialism and irreligion.[9] Nursi called on Muslims and Christians to put aside debate over points of difference "in order to combat their joint enemy—aggressive atheism."[10]

Nursi does not appear, however, to have studied seriously or been influenced significantly by the works of Catholic theologians or philosophers. He views Jesus in light of traditional Islamic views and expectations, without examining Catholic discussions of Jesus' identity and significance. Though Nursi called on Muslims and Christians to make common cause against aggressive atheism, he did not discuss contemporary Catholic strategies of apologetics. Though Nursi's lifetime coincided almost exactly with the period of the dominant role of Thomas Aquinas in Roman Catholic theology, which decisively shaped most Roman Catholic responses to atheism during these years, Nursi did not discuss this movement. Despite the lack of direct theological engagement from either side during his lifetime, Nursi nevertheless shared many concerns with his Catholic contemporaries. Catholics reading his work today can find many points of convergence, as well as important points of difference.

Nursi could not have known how profoundly the atmosphere of Muslim-Catholic relations would change within just a few years of his death. The lifelong work of Massignon had quietly influenced Popes Pius XI, Pius XII, and Paul VI, preparing the way for a changed Catholic regard toward Muslims and Islam.[11] In October 1962, two years after Nursi's death and just a couple of weeks before Massignon died, the Second Vatican Council opened in Rome. All contemporary Roman Catholic theological engagement with Nursi takes place in the context of the changes initiated by Vatican II. The

6. Vahide, *Bediüzzaman Said Nursi*, 343–44; Vahide, *Islam in Modern Turkey*, 316.

7. Vahide, "An Outline of Bediüzzaman Said Nursi's Views on Christianity and the West," 110. See also Meryem Weld, *Islam, the West, and the Risale-i Nur*.

8. Vahide, "Outline," 112–13.

9. Ibid., 113–14.

10. Nursi, *The Flashes Collection*, 203–4;

cited by Vahide, "Outline," 115.

11. Gude, *The Crucible of Compassion*.

*Dogmatic Constitution on the Church* (commonly known by the opening words of the Latin text, *Lumen Gentium*, "*Light of Nations*"), issued by the Second Vatican Council in 1964, declared: "[T]he plan of salvation also embraces those who acknowledge the Creator, and among these the Moslems are first; they profess to hold the faith of Abraham and along with us they worship the one merciful God who will judge humanity on the last day."[12] In October 1965 the Council issued *The Declaration on the Catholic Church's Relation to Non-Christian Religions* (commonly referred to by the opening words of the Latin text as *Nostra Aetate*, "*In Our Age*"). This document developed the framework for a more appreciative Catholic stance toward Muslims, praising them for their faith in the one God, noting that they honor Abraham, Jesus, and Mary, and citing common values of prayer, almsgiving, and fasting. While Vatican II did not mention the Qur'an or Muhammad, the Council called on Muslims and Christians alike to move beyond the conflicts of the past in order to address together pressing contemporary concerns for social justice, moral values, peace, and freedom.[13]

In the decades since the Council, there have been numerous dialogues and theological encounters between Muslims and Catholics.[14] In recent years, some Catholic theologians have studied the work of Said Nursi, bringing awareness of his work into circles of Muslim-Catholic dialogue. Arguably the most extensive and appreciative Catholic engagement with Nursi's theology has come from Thomas Michel, S.J., who has widespread experience in Muslim-Catholic dialogue. Pim (Wilhelmus) Valkenberg has also studied Nursi's work and has posed important questions for exploration and critical reflection. In earlier essays, I have compared Nursi's perspectives on the resurrection to German Protestant theologian Jürgen Moltmann, and I have explored Nursi's view of reason, science, and faith in relation to German Catholic theologian Karl Rahner.[15] I have also related Nursi's perspectives on prophecy, wisdom, and the guidance of humanity to those of Pope John XXIII.[16]

## THOMAS MICHEL

Thomas Michel brings an extensive background for engaging the writings of Nursi. Michel wrote his doctoral dissertation at the University of Chicago on Ibn Taymiyya under the direction of the noted Islamic scholar Fazlur Rahman. After teaching at Sanata Dharma University in Yogyakarta, Indonesia, Michel worked with the Pontifical Council for Interreligious Dialogue and the Federation of Asian Bishops' Conferences; he has also served as the Secretary for Interreligious Dialogue for the Society of Jesus. Michel engages the thought of Nursi in an appreciative manner, emphasizing harmonies and areas of convergence. In comparing the perspectives of Nursi with various aspects of Catholic thought, Michel generally leaves points of disagreement in the

---

12. Second Vatican Council, *Dogmatic Constitution on the Church* # 16, 861.

13. Second Vatican Council, *Declaration on the Church's Relation to Non-Christian Religions* # 3, 969.

14. See Fitzgerald and Borelli, *Interfaith Dialogue*, 85–159.

15. Lefebure, "The Resurrection of the Dead," 99–110; Lefebure, "Faith, Reason, and Science in the Modern World," 78–90.

16. Lefebure, "Wisdom, Prophets, and the Guidance of Humanity."

background, fostering an atmosphere of harmony by focusing on shared values and concerns. Irfan A. Omar has interpreted Michel as building a "Community of Witness" together with Muslims, and this phrase serves as a fitting introduction to Michel's engagement with Nursi.[17]

Michel surveys a wide range of Nursi's views on revelation, tolerance, Muslim-Christian dialogue, modernity, violence, peace, and cooperation.[18] Michel begins by noting the importance of dialogue both for Nursi and for Catholic leaders, pointing out that Nursi viewed the Qur'an itself as "a dialogue with no imitation."[19] Michel notes the parallel between Nursi's view and that of Pope Paul VI, who in his encyclical *Ecclesiam Suam* described human history as "a dialogue of salvation" begun by God with humans: "God himself took the initiative in the dialogue of salvation. 'God has first loved us.' We, therefore, must be the first to ask for a dialogue with men, without waiting to be summoned to it by others."[20] As the context for his own engagement with Nursi, Michel praises both Nursi and Paul VI for challenging Muslims and Christians to respectful dialogue rooted in their understandings of divine revelation.[21]

To clarify the basis for Muslim-Christian dialogue in divine revelation, Michel compares Said Nursi's view of the prophets with an influential Catholic perspective.[22] To represent "the Christian understanding," Michel follows closely Karl Rahner's discussion of "Prophetism," which sets forth a number of characteristics of genuine prophets.[23] According to this view, prophets bring a new message, though Michel cautions, "*New* doesn't necessarily mean *different* from what the earlier prophets taught."[24] Producing their own credentials, prophets are unique, religious revolutionaries who criticize the society of their day in the name of God, bringing a transformative message meant for others. For both Rahner and Michel, the prophet is different from other religious leaders: "What he brings is a new revelation which he received from God."[25] According to Rahner and Michel, prophets criticize religion and society in light of the divine message and influence events, organizing religious and social changes in a way that institutionalizes the message.

Turning to Nursi as a spokesperson for Islam, Michel notes that Nursi made a distinction between two main currents of huhumankind's intellectual history: prophethood and religion on the one hand, and philosophy on the other. When the two currents cooperate, there is prosperity and harmony; however, when they conflict, there is "disorder, war, confusion and moral degradation."[26] According to Nursi, philosophy, which includes modern science, can come to a limited knowledge of God; but it fails to understand human weakness and the distance

---

17. Omar, "Building a 'Community of Witness,'" 2.

18. Michel, *Said Nursi's Views on Muslim-Christian Understanding*, 7–42.

19. Nursi, *The Rays*, 161; quoted by Michel, *Said Nursi's Views on Muslim-Christian Understanding*, 9.

20. Paul VI, *Ecclesiam Suam*, #72, quoted by Michel, *Said Nursi's Views on Muslim-Christian Understanding*, 12.

21. Michel, *Said Nursi's Views on Muslim-Christian Understanding*, 12.

22. Michel, *Insights from the Risale-i Nur*, 207–17.

23. Rahner, "Prophetism," 1286–89; cited by Michel, "Prophets," 1.

24. Michel, *Insights*, 208.

25. Ibid., 210.

26. Ibid., 212.

between humans and God. Michel notes that Nursi believes the prophetic tradition is needed to teach humans their true situation before God, both individually and socially, and in relation to the entire natural world.

Michel remarks on the implications of Nursi's perspective for ecology: "A religious approach to nature recognizes the unity of creation and that all that exists in nature is a blessing from God to be used by people with moderation and gratitude."[27] Michel also appreciates Nursi's emphasis on the prophets' speaking to the heart. While philosophy may arrive at monotheism as an intellectual concept, Michel accepts Nursi's insistence that the human heart must grasp the divine unity, beauty, and perfection; this is possible, according to Michel and Nursi, only through prophetic revelation.[28] Michel further concurs with Nursi in seeing the prophets as revealing the mystery of life "as a gift flowing from the eternal life of God."[29] For Michel as for Nursi, "If it were not for the prophets, the cosmos would act as a veil to conceal God's reality and His beautiful names and qualities. However, through the Prophets, the veil is lifted and the cosmos itself is revealed to be God's masterpiece of creative art, a path by which humans can be guided to praise and proclaim the magnificence of the Creator."[30] Throughout this discussion Michel stresses the areas in which Nursi's and Rahner's views on prophets converge; while Michel notes that there are differences between Muslim and Christian perspectives on prophets, he does not focus on them in this article.

Behind Michel's silence regarding the differences between Islamic and Christian theology lies a strategic decision inspired by Nursi. Accepting Nursi's invitation to Muslim-Christian cooperation in the face of the violence and disbelief of modern culture, Michel also embraces Nursi's recommendation not to focus on differences for the sake of a common mission:

His point, with which I agree, is that concentrating obsessively on these differences can blind both Muslims and Christians to the even more important common task which they share, that of offering the modern world a vision of human life and society in which God is central and God's will is the norm of moral values.[31]

Michel is particularly interested in dialogue with Nursi concerning how to live out the implications of revelation in a world torn by violent conflicts. The central hope of this engagement appears in the title of one of Michel's essays: "Is a God-Centered Life an Antidote to a Culture of Violence? Some Reflections from the *Risale-i Nur*."[32] Searching the *Risale-i Nur* for an interpretative key to the whole, Michel cites the "Tenth Word," where Nursi grounds his hope for the resurrection on his faith in God. Michel summarizes Nursi's point: "God manifests Himself to those who believe in terms of truth, love, and mercy and they respond to God with faith, worship, and thanksgiving."[33] For Michel, this text

27. Ibid., 213–14.
28. Ibid., 215.
29. Ibid.
30. Ibid., 217.

31. Michel, *Said Nursi's Views on Muslim-Christian Understanding,* 28–29.
32. Michel, "Is a God-Centered Life an Antidote to a Culture of Violence?" 338–49.
33. Ibid., 338–39.

offers "a succinct statement of Nursi's understanding of human existence. As humans, we exist in order to learn the truth of this world and the next from the Word of God, to worship the loving God who is himself eminently worthy of our love, and to thank and praise God continually for the great mercy that God has always shown to us."[34] Michel expresses his own wholehearted concurrence:

> As a Christian student of the *Risale-i Nur*, I find that Said Nursi's vision of the God-centered life is one that resonates with my own understanding of the purpose of human existence. In the most basic Christian catechism we read that men and women were created "to know, love, and serve God, and to be happy with Him in Paradise." Thus, the ideal of the God-centered life is a point of convergence between the two faiths that should unite Muslims and Christians.[35]

This convergence lies at the center of Michel's engagement with Nursi.

Michel defines a culture of violence in terms of two principles shaping this worldview: the expendability of human life and the willingness to use force to impose one's way.[36] In response, Michel cites Nursi's teaching that religious faith "places in the heart and mind a permanent 'prohibitor.' When sinful desires emerge from the soul, it repulses them and declares them forbidden."[37] Michel further singles out one aspect of Nursi's prohibition: "Belief necessitates not humiliating others through violence and despotism and not degrading them."[38] Michel recalls Nursi's reflections on his sufferings in prison, where he strove to observe the Qur'anic teaching: "Those who suppress their anger and forgive people, truly God loves those who do good."[39] Michel notes with appreciation that Nursi hoped that his sufferings could serve as atonement for his sins and benefit his soul, and he rejected the pursuit of vengeance. Michel draws the lesson from Nursi's example: "A God-Centered life serves as an antidote to a culture of violence by putting injustices, oppression, and discouragement in perspective.... Nursi was only able to avoid recourse to anger and resentment by bearing in mind the verse: 'For us God suffices, and He is the Best Disposer of Affairs!'"[40] Michel has also studied Nursi's spirituality in relation to his physical illness, concluding that Nursi "shows his followers how the unhappy condition of illness can be transformed by God's guidance into an opportunity and occasion for spiritual growth and deeper submission to God's will."[41]

Michel notes that Nursi viewed *jihad* of the sword as passé: "In the past Muslims resorted to violence and war, but in Nursi's view, such actions displayed their weakness and distance from the teachings of Islam rather than their strength of faith."[42] Michel compares Nursi with Pope

---

34. Ibid., 339

35. Ibid.

36. Ibid., 340.

37. Nursi, "First Addendum, Second Part," *The Damascus Sermon* quoted by Michel, "Is a God-Centered Life an Antidote," 340.

38. Nursi, "Sixth Word," *Damascus Sermon*; quoted by Michel, "Is a God-Centered Life an Antidote," 340.

39. Qur'an 3:134; quoted by Michel, "Is a God-Centered Life an Antidote," 341.

40. Michel, "Is a God-Centered Life an Antidote," 343; Qur'an 3:173.

41. Michel, "'For You, Illness Is Good Health,' Said Nursi's Spirituality in His Approach to Physical Illness," 188.

42. Michel, "Is a God-Centered Life an Antidote," 345.

John Paul II on "The Ethics of Pardon and Peace: A Dialogue of Ideas between the Thought of Pope John Paul II and the *Risale-i Nur*."[43] Michel observes that John Paul II stressed that peace rests on the two pillars of justice and forgiveness: "Justice is thus a first, indispensable condition for peace.... Justice alone is not sufficient to heal these wounds; we need to exercise forgiveness."[44] Michel finds that both Said Nursi and John Paul II orient their discussions of ethics primarily toward the social sphere: "In the thought of both men, a religiously based ethical system above all must treat questions of right and wrong in society, and only secondarily regards the goodness or evil of acts of private morality. Moreover, both root this primacy of social ethics in the Scriptural teaching of their respective faiths."[45]

Michel finds in the *Risale-i Nur* a practical guide to peace based upon faith in God, the pursuit of justice, and the practice of forgiveness. He sees Nursi as anticipating major themes that John Paul II would also teach: "When I examine the thought of Pope John Paul and that of Said Nursi, I am struck by the many similarities. Both understand peace to be not only a universal human longing, but also a cornerstone of the Message, which God has revealed to humans. It is not only that humans long for peace, but God desires and intends that men live in peace."[46] Thus for Michel, theological engagement with Nursi begins in the dialogue of revelation and culminates in the hope for peace in a world of violence.

## PIM VALKENBERG

Pim (Wilhelmus) Valkenberg, originally from the Netherlands and currently professor of theology at the Catholic University of America in Washington, DC, discusses Said Nursi as part of an ambitious and thoughtful project in comparative theology, *Sharing Lights on the Way to God: Muslim-Christian Dialogue and Theology in the Context of Abrahamic Partnership*.[47] Valkenberg finds the threshold to this discussion in the ancient virtue of hospitality, which includes both friendly manners and receiving the stranger. In this project, Valkenberg looks to Nursi as a "major contemporary guide" for Christians in dialogue with Islam.[48] Valkenberg acknowledges that his choice of Nursi as a guide has been influenced by his Turkish Muslim dialogue partners in the Netherlands and elsewhere who find inspiration in Nursi. Nonetheless, he comments that the reception of Nursi's work has been mixed: "Some major conferences, both in Turkey and the United States, help expand his fame among scholars of religion. In most countries in Western Europe, however, his name is not very well known nor is he numbered among the great revivers of Islam in the twentieth century."[49]

Valkenberg situates his discussion of Nursi within the framework of comparative theology as proposed by

---

43. Michel, "The Ethics of Pardon and Peace," 37–47; this essay also appears in Michel, *Said Nursi's Views on Muslim-Christian Understanding*, 58–78, and again in Michel, *A Christian View of Islam*, 108–19.

44. Michel, "The Ethics of Pardon and Peace," 38.

45. Ibid., 39.

46. Ibid., 47.

47. Valkenberg, *Sharing Lights on the Way to God*.

48. Ibid., xvii.

49. Ibid., 274.

Francis X. Clooney.⁵⁰ Valkenberg explains: "Comparative theology is not just about comparing texts, but about comparing multilayered traditions that surround these texts, so to say, with a texture of interpretations."⁵¹ Valkenberg recognizes that classic Christian and Muslim theological texts make claims on their readers: "You, reader, you have to reframe your life if you want to be a true reader in this tradition."⁵² In making comparisons, Valkenberg finds that there are multiple levels of interpretation within and between the traditions involved; and there are many possible outcomes, including that "a Christian interpretation of a Muslim text may contribute not only to a rereading of the Christian tradition enriched with Muslim ideas but also to the dialogue between Christians and Muslims on the ideas embodied in the text and their practical consequences."⁵³

In light of this method, Valkenberg locates Nursi's texts within the long Islamic tradition of interpreting the Qur'an: "The *Risale-i Nur* is a body of texts by Said Nursi that presents itself as a commentary on the Qur'an, but it is of course only a minor part of the rich tradition of *tafsīr*. It may be seen as a particular Anatolian Muslim subtradition from the first half of the twentieth century which may be connected to the Qur'an as its source through some intermediate texts that function as theological and spiritual interpretations."⁵⁴ Valkenberg acknowledges that his own theological heritage has been shaped by his doctoral dissertation on Thomas Aquinas' view of "theology as *sacra doctrina* in which the theologian receives instruction of faith from Christ and other teachers and passes this instruction on to his pupils. *Sacra doctrina* equals *sacra Scriptura* because the theologian is by nature a reader and interpreter of Scripture."⁵⁵ This self-understanding of the Christian theologian bears a strong resemblance to Said Nursi's own role as interpreter of the Qur'an.

After proposing a comparative theological reading of Thomas Aquinas and Abu Hamid Muhammad al-Ghazali, Valkenberg briefly surveys Muhyi al-din ibn al-'Arabi and Maulana Jalal al-din Rumi, before turning to Nursi.⁵⁶ Valkenberg notes Nursi's deep respect for al-Ghazali as well as the influence of Ibn 'Arabi upon Nursi.

While Valkenberg respects Nursi deeply, he is willing to pose critical questions to Nursi and his legacy in a way that Michel does not. In reviewing the major moments of Nursi's life, Valkenberg gives particular attention to the Damascus Sermon of spring 1911 and to Nursi's later comments on this text. Valkenberg comments on the exalted tone of Nursi's estimation of the Damascus Sermon, as of the entire *Risale-i Nur*: "Such words are not particularly unpretentious, and they are often repeated in the *Risale-i Nur* itself: they contain the most powerful medicine for all the problems of the Muslim world."⁵⁷ Valkenberg defends Nursi from the potential suspicion of arrogance "since the healing power comes from the Qur'an as the source from which

50. Valkenberg cites Francis X. Clooney, *Theology after Vedanta*.
51. Valkenberg, *Sharing Lights on the Way to God*, 208.
52. Ibid., 209.
53. Ibid.
54. Ibid., 209–10.
55. Ibid., 213–14.
56. Ibid., 213–69.
57. Ibid., 275.

the *Risale-i Nur* flows."⁵⁸ Nonetheless, Valkenberg finds something troubling here: "Yet the rhetoric of eminence applied by Said Nursi has a dangerous side, since some of his followers tend to see the *Risale* as a 'holy text' with special status in the Nurculuk movement."⁵⁹ One effect of this is "a new literalism whereby Nursi's texts become 'semisacred.'"⁶⁰

Valkenberg quotes Nursi's claim in the Damascus Sermon that "the future shall be Islam's and Islam's alone."⁶¹ Valkenberg comments, "It is typical of the old Said that he looks to the political arena for indications of other powers willing to embrace Islam."⁶² Valkenberg also quotes Nursi's prediction that "true Christianity, stripping off superstition and corrupted belief, will be transformed into Islam; following the Qur'an, it will unite with Islam."⁶³ Valkenberg responds: "A Christian reader of this text will probably feel some ambiguity.... There is, of course, a trace of condescension in his remark that Christianity may unite with Islam and be transformed into Islam if it sheds superstition and corruption. This remark may even be seen as a not so subtle form of *da'wa*: Christians may join the true religion if they purify their own religion."⁶⁴

Valkenberg notes that Thomas Michel had stressed the positive aspect of the Damascus Sermon in that Nursi distinguished between true Christianity and the problematic modern West and did not denounce them both. Valkenberg, however, adds that Michel "does not mention the unmistakable inequality in the role of Muslims and Christians. Said Nursi wants to reverse the political and economic situation of 1911, when the Ottoman Empire was weakening and the European powers were gaining strength."⁶⁵ Valkenberg notes that in the *Risale-i Nur*, Nursi hoped that Christianity would "in effect be transformed into a sort of Islam. Following the Qur'an, the collective personality of Christianity will be in the rank of follower, and Islam, in that of leader. True religion will become a mighty force as a result of its joining it. Although defeated before the atheistic current while separate, Christianity and Islam will have the capability to defeat and rout it as a result of their union."⁶⁶

In dialogue with Muslims, Valkenberg has found Nursi's expectation to be very influential: "For many followers of Said Nursi, this idea of a future cooperation between Christians and Muslims against the forces of secularism is the main motive for engagement in interreligious dialogue with Christians."⁶⁷ Valkenberg observes that Nursi further develops this hope in the "Fifth Flash," to which Valkenberg again expresses a response of ambivalence: "Again, this will sound a bit ambiguous for many Christians; they will feel subordinated to another religion that is purer and more powerful and they will have the idea that their Savior is sub-

---

58. Ibid.
59. Ibid.
60. Ibid.; Valkenberg is citing Yavuz, "Nur Study Circles (*Dershanes*), 297.
61. Nursi, *The Damascus Sermon*, 27; quoted by Valkenberg, *Sharing*, 276.
62. Valkenberg, *Sharing*, 276.
63. Nursi, *Damascus Sermon*, 36; quoted by Valkenberg, *Sharing*, 276.
64. Ibid.

65. Ibid. Valkenberg cites Michel, *Reflections on Said Nursi's Views on Muslim-Christian Understanding*, 20–32.
66. Nursi, *Letters*, 78; quoted by Valkenberg, *Sharing*, 277.
67. Valkenberg, *Sharing*, 277.

ordinated to a Prophet with a different message as well."⁶⁸ Valkenberg views the Muslim perspectives toward Christianity in the broader context of relations among the Abrahamic religions. Christians long lived in a subordinate situation in the Ottoman Empire and experienced from Muslims "the same sense of superiority that they [Christians] have demonstrated toward the Jews. And if the condition to purify their religion may be applied to Islam as well as to Christianity, there is no reason why Muslims and Christians cannot cooperate, as long as the fight against materialism is seen as a spiritual and not a military war."⁶⁹ Thus Valkenberg takes Nursi's sense of the superiority of Islam over Christians as a stimulus for Christians to reflect critically on their own traditional sense of superiority over Jews. Valkenberg insists that dialogue between Muslims and Christians include Jews as well.⁷⁰

In discussing *Signs of Miraculousness,* Nursi's commentary on the Qur'an from the period of the "Old Said," Valkenberg compares Nursi's search for meanings in the word order of the Qur'an to traditional Jewish and Christian searches for deeper meaning in the words of the Jewish and Christian scriptures. Valkenberg comments, "Although most modern exegetes hold this genre in contempt, mainly because it is often used in anti-modern strategies culminating in the claim that 'the Bible is right anyway,' the idea of hidden meanings in the word order and numerical value of the Bible resurfaces in the popularity of certain strands in Cabalist literature."⁷¹ Valkenberg compares Nursi's interpretation of the *Surat al-Fatiha,* the first chapter of the Qur'an, to traditional, medieval Christian modes of interpretation. Commenting on the *Surat al-Fatiha,* Nursi sets forth four fundamental aims of the Qur'an: the oneness of God (*tawḥīd*), prophecy, resurrection, and justice.⁷²

Valkenberg follows Lucinda Allen Mosher in emphasizing that Nursi ended this commentary at Qur'an 2:32: "Glory be unto You, we have no knowledge save that which You have taught us; indeed, You are All-Knowing, All-Wise."⁷³ Valkenberg takes this verse as expressing the fundamental presupposition of Nursi's spirituality and of the *Risale-i Nur*: all knowledge comes from God alone. Nursi repeatedly acknowledges the power of God either in compelling him or hindering him in his writing.

Turning to the *Risale-i Nur,* Valkenberg notes the complex structure of the work: "Although the four printed volumes coincide roughly with successive periods in Said Nursi's life, several parts have been moved to other volumes because of thematic relationships."⁷⁴ Valkenberg finds the key to the structure of the *Risale-i Nur* in the four fundamental aims that Nursi finds in the Qur'an: the oneness of God, prophecy, resurrection, and justice. According to Valkenberg, the first parts of the *Risale-i Nur* examine the relation between the oneness of God and resurrection, specifically "the idea that the

---

68. Ibid.
69. Ibid.
70. Ibid., xv, 55–80.
71. Valkenberg, *Sharing,* 279.
72. Nursi, *Signs of Miraculousness,*19; Valkenberg, *Sharing,* 279.
73. Valkenberg, *Sharing,* 281; Mosher, "The Marrow of Worship and the Moral Vision," 181–97.
74. Valkenberg, *Sharing,* 282.

universe in its transitory status refers to its Maker, and therefore refers to the possibility of resurrection. This is certainly the case in Word X which is, according to Şükran Vahide the first part of the *Risale-i Nur* in the historical order."[75] The early sections of the *Risale-i Nur* are often in the form of parables.

Valkenberg notes that in *The Words* Nursi makes a number of sharp contrasts, first of all between the foolish and the trustworthy, and then three corresponding contrasts: "the instinctual soul and the heart; the students of philosophy and the students of the Qur'an; and the people of unbelief and the Community of Islam."[76] Observing that some commentators have seen Nursi as viewing Western science positively but Western philosophy negatively, Valkenberg responds by contextualizing Nursi's relationship to Western philosophy: "It might be better simply to concede that Nursi, due to the way in which European philosophy was used during the Turkish process of secularization, could not develop a sense for the contribution of non-religious philosophical insights. In fact, Nursi uses philosophy in his reflections all the time. But in his view it had to be subordinate to his major goal of explaining the Qur'an."[77]

Regarding the shift from the "Old Said" to the "New Said," Valkenberg interprets the transformation of Nursi's context and concerns as fitting a broader pattern of persons changing "from an 'activist' discourse, oriented to changing the structures of society, to a more 'quietist' discourse, oriented to changing the minds of people, beginning with a small group of dedicated followers."[78] Nursi interpreted his conditions of exile and imprisonment in terms of the "school of Joseph," referring to the Qur'an's description of Joseph languishing in prison for years (Q 12:42). In his situation of exile and imprisonment, Nursi turned to prayer and found an experience of God's presence illumining his life and giving renewed courage and hope. Valkenberg compares Nursi's description of his experience to Blaise Pascal.[79]

Valkenberg cites Yvonne Yazbeck Haddad's analysis of Nursi's experience of moving from estrangement (*ghurba*) to companionship (*uns*) as being rooted in three Islamic virtues: "faith in God (*iman*), trust in God (*tawakkul*) and finally patience (*ṣabr*)."[80] Valkenberg goes on to compare Nursi's experience of comfort in absolute trust in God to that of the Catholic mystic Teresa of Avila: "this form of trust, found or rather received through the hardness of exile is often connected with *ṣabr*, a virtue that connotes endurance rather than patience."[81] Valkenberg cites Jesus' teaching in the Sermon on the Mount as the ground for Christian trust in God (Matt 6:31–33).

Valkenberg uses the three virtues mentioned by Haddad to structure his engagement with the *Risale-i Nur*. He correlates the Islamic virtue of faith with the oneness of God, which is the first aim of the Qur'an in Nursi's interpretation. He sees the virtue of trust as "the connection between the more speculative virtue of *tawḥīd* and the very practical virtue of

---

75. Ibid., 283.
76. Ibid., 284.
77. Ibid., 285.
78. Ibid.
79. Ibid., 286.
80. Valkenberg, *Sharing*, 287; Haddad, "Ghurba as Paradigm for Muslim Life," 309.
81. Valkenberg, *Sharing*, 287.

ṣabr."[82] In the situation of exile, trust in God is crucial, and Valkenberg compares Nursi's trust in God to the prayer of the Catholic hymn, *Te Deum*: "O Lord, let Thy mercy lighten upon us as our trust is in Thee. O Lord, in Thee have I trusted; let me never be confounded."[83] Valkenberg notes that Nursi's views on patience, endurance, and trusting in God as the one who alone suffices are extremely close to the sixteenth-century Carmelite mystic Teresa of Avila, who prayed in language almost identical to Nursi:

> Let nothing upset you,
> let nothing startle you.
> All things pass;
> God does not change.
> Patience wins
> all it seeks.
> Whoever has God
> lacks nothing;
> God alone is enough.[84]

Valkenberg finds more difficulty with Nursi's discussion of prophecy and miracles, especially as set forth in the "Nineteenth Letter," a treatise that discusses the miracles of Prophet Muhammad: "I must confess, however, that I had great difficulty reading this treatise because of my modern Western theological bias that does not set great store in miracles in the way Nursi did. Yet comparative theologians are to pay particular attention to these differences, since critical reflection on these differences may enable us to learn the most."[85] Valkenberg observes that Muslims traditionally stressed the miraculousness of the Qur'an more than any miracles of Prophet Muhammad, but Nursi himself "reports no less than three hundred miracles by the Prophet, all founded on sound *asanid* (chains of authorities) and testified to by many people."[86]

Valkenberg comments that outsiders will generally have difficulty accepting the authenticity of these claims; but he adds, "Like all forms of reasoning about miracles, it is a form of circular argumentation based on faith for those who accept this faith, which does not matter as long as it is recognized as such."[87] Nursi himself acknowledged that the miracles of Prophet Muhammad did not convince everyone: "But his miracles never occurred in such an obvious fashion as would have compelled everyone to believe, whether willingly or unwillingly."[88] For Nursi, miracles are not so obvious as to take away human free will; humans must freely decide to accept or reject miracles. Here Valkenberg can resonate with Nursi's perspective: "This is an important remark that brings Nursi's understanding of miracles closer to the tradition of reasoning to which I adhere."[89]

The question of the credibility of miracles leads Valkenberg to the issue of historical criticism in scriptural interpretation. He notes one of the major differences between many Christians and Muslims: "One of the major problems in most forms of theological dialogue between Christians and Muslims is that Western Christians generally accept this modern rational approach to their

---

82. Ibid., 290.

83. Ibid., 291.

84. Ibid., 304; the translation of the poem is from Vogt, *The Complete Poetry of St. Teresa of Avila*, 32–33.

85. Valkenberg, *Sharing*, 297–98.

86. Ibid., 298.

87. Ibid.

88. Nursi, *Letters*, 122; quoted by Valkenberg, *Sharing*, 298.

89. Valkenberg, *Sharing*, 298.

Scriptures, while most Muslims do not. It would be counterproductive, therefore, if I would use this critical approach in judging Nursi's texts on the miracles of Muhammad, although it obviously influences my reading of these texts."[90] Valkenberg offers a nuanced reflection, citing the virtue of *pia interpretatio* ("benign interpretation") taught by Nicholas of Cusa: "If we meet people of faith, we should presume that differences are important but that understanding them is always possible if we try. We should therefore be cautious in our interpretation of what is not immediately clear to us and proceed by questioning the meaning of these differences rather than by asserting them."[91]

Valkenberg then poses the question why Nursi values the miracles of Muhammad so highly when most of the Islamic tradition had not done so. He speculates that some Muslims emphasized the miracles of Muhammad in response to Jewish and Christian challenges that cited the miracles of Moses and Jesus: "In the course of history the miracles of the Prophet [Muhammad] were used more and more as an apologetic weapon and this determines their use in Said Nursi as well."[92] Valkenberg cautions Catholics not to reject Muslim claims for the miracles of Muhammad before they have reflected on the place of miracles in Catholic life: "Only if I can understand why Fatima, Lourdes, Medjugorge, and even the contested appearances of Our Lady of All Peoples in Amsterdam are so important to many Roman Catholics can I begin to understand why the miracles of Muhammad are so important to Said Nursi and his followers."[93] Thus what is most puzzling and problematic in Nursi's theology becomes for Valkenberg a challenge to probe more deeply into the dynamics of related aspects of Catholic life.

Valkenberg suggests that the usual dynamic equivalence that is posited between Christ and the Qur'an may not apply in the case of Nursi: "In Said Nursi's works the Qur'an and the Prophet seem to be standing on the same level. In 'the Supreme Sign', for instance, Nursi speaks about the Prophet as 'the Pride of the World and the Glory of the Sons of Adam, through the majesty of the sovereignty of his Qur'an.'"[94]

In a more recent essay on Nursi's interpretation of the *Surah al-Fatiha*, Valkenberg recalls the four main themes of the Qur'an that Nursi finds in this short text and poses the question of whether Christians and Muslims together can say this prayer in common.[95] While he understands the reasons that have led some to see this as a possibility, he cautions: "However, the history of interpretation of the final words of the *fatiha* prayer makes it difficult to come to a common word since the 'straight path' of Islam has often been contrasted to the Jews as those who incurred God's wrath and the Christians as those who went astray."[96]

Having posed the challenge, Valkenberg turns to Nursi for guidance. According to Valkenberg, Nursi understands "the straight path" as "justice which is a mixture of three virtues: wisdom,

90. Ibid., 299.
91. Ibid.
92. Ibid., 300.
93. Ibid.
94. Ibid.; quoting Nursi, *Rays*, 156.
95. Valkenberg, "Said Nursi's Commentary," 124–33.
96. Valkenberg, "Said Nursi's Commentary," 130.

chastity, and courage."⁹⁷ Interpreting justice in terms of "the middle way" between extremes, Valkenberg suggests that those who incur God's wrath are those who sin by deficiency and the ones going astray are those who sin by excess. Nursi, according to Valkenberg, "does not make a distinction between good religions and bad religions, but between good human beings who keep to moderation and balance, and evil human beings who commit injustice by abandoning the rules and seeking pleasure and pride."⁹⁸ Above all, Valkenberg recommends that Muslims and Christians attend to Nursi's view of the interrelated levels of community implied in the phrase, "You alone do we worship." Concerning the antecedent of the pronoun in "we worship," Nursi specifies three groups: "all of us members of man the microcosm, and us monotheists, and us beings, seek help and assistance from You for all our needs and aims, the most important of which is worship."⁹⁹ In a later letter, Nursi described a vision he had in the Bayezid Mosque in Istanbul that encompassed all Muslims in the praying community, and then a further vision that reached three even wider circles, including "the vast congregation of believers and those who affirm Divine Unity on the face of the earth" and "a congregation consisting of all beings . . . occupied with the benedictions and glorifications particular to its group and species."¹⁰⁰ From Nursi's description of his vision, Valkenberg draws the cautious conclusion that Nursi

. . . allows for the possibility that Muslims could worship together with other believers who truly follow the tradition of Abraham being "true in faith" (*hanif*, Qur'an 3:67), and who share the intention of *Tawhid* (worshipping the One True God). On the other hand I may be overstating my case here since Said Nursi does not explicitly indicate his intention to describe an "Abrahamic community" here.¹⁰¹

Valkenberg has done much to advance Roman Catholic engagement with Nursi both by acknowledging the many points of convergence and also by frankly discussing many points on which there is disagreement. Valkenberg does not claim to resolve all the issues raised by his discussion, but he is very astute in naming the various challenges facing Catholic theological engagement with Nursi.

## ANDREAS RENZ

Andreas Renz of the Catholic Theology Faculty of Ludwig-Maximilian University in Munich has offered a very thoughtful assessment and critique of Said Nursi, including a comparison of Nursi's perspectives with those of Joseph Ratzinger, who became Pope Benedict XVI.¹⁰² While aware of the many points of convergence that we have already seen noted by Michel and Valkenberg, Renz poses a number of critical questions to Nursi. Renz first investigates how Nursi saw Christianity and Christians, and then reflects on what significance Nursi has for Muslim-Christian dialogue today.

97. Ibid.
98. Ibid.
99. Nursi, *Signs of Miraculousness,* 28; Valkenberg, "Said Nursi's Commentary," 131.
100. Nursi, *Letters,* 461; Valkenberg, "Said Nursi's Commentary," 132.

101. Valkenberg, "Said Nursi's Commentary," 132.
102. Renz, "Said Nursi und das Christentum," 105–12.

Renz observes that while there is relatively little in Nursi's writings regarding the relationship to Christianity, there is much reflection concerning the difficulties of European modernity. Like Michel and Valkenberg, Renz notes that Nursi distinguishes "true Christianity" from the sickness of European modernity and that he hopes for an alliance with true Christianity against atheism. Renz comments on the similarity between Nursi's negative assessment of modern Western culture and the views of many Catholics both of Nursi's time and the present, including Cardinal Joseph Ratzinger/Pope Benedict XVI. Renz sees Nursi and Pope Benedict as kindred spirits in their analysis of cultural problems, even though their respective religious solutions differ.

After reviewing the same texts that Michel and Valkenberg had discussed, Renz poses a number of questions to Nursi, asking whether he proposes a pessimistic view of culture that does not recognize the valuable and necessary developments and the emancipatory impulses of modern culture. Renz challenges the language of "good" and "bad" Europe or of "true" and "false" Christianity as implying a dualistic worldview shaped by stereotypical projections.[103]

While Renz acknowledges that Nursi lived through difficult times, he challenges the ascription of a "dubious past" to Europe and of a "brilliant future" to Islam" as apologetic or naive.[104] Renz also accuses Nursi of idealizing Islamic history and of demonizing European Christian history. Renz charges that Nursi compares the ideal of Islam with the ambiguous realities of Christian history.[105]

Renz also has reservations about Nursi's proposed alliance with Christians against those who do not believe in God. Renz notes that the Second Vatican Council did not seek alliances against other groups, such as nonbelievers, but rather appealed to all humans of good will, including atheists who seek peace and justice. Renz also questions Nursi's call for an alliance with Christians until their common enemy is defeated; Renz asks what will happen after such a putative victory. He points out that Nursi predicted in the Damascus Sermon that the future would belong to Islam alone, expecting that Europe and America would one day be Islamic and that Christians would accept Islam. Renz acknowledges that Nursi defended the rights of Christians in the Ottoman Empire, but he nonetheless worries about the danger of religious hopes becoming the basis for political programs of domination.

Regarding the relation between faith and reason, Renz compares Nursi with Joseph Ratzinger. He notes that both figures strongly oppose modern Western philosophy when it rejects classical metaphysics for a positivism oriented to the natural sciences alone, leading to atheism. Renz notes that Nursi believes the order of the universe "proves" the existence of God, suggesting that this anticipates current questionable theories of intelligent design. He himself accepts the criticisms of the proofs for the existence of God as rendering human freedom and the act of faith meaningless. Renz sees the proofs as arguments for the credibility and reasonableness of faith in God, but

---

103. Ibid., 106–7.
104. Ibid., 107.

105. Ibid.

not as mathematical-scientific proofs. He worries that Nursi's trust in revelation as the only criterion for truth leads to a pure fideism that has fatal consequences for interreligious dialogue because it destroys any common basis for argument. Renz suggests that the question of the relationship between faith and reason demands further discussion and clarification in Muslim-Christian dialogue.[106]

In a more positive vein, Renz finds similarities between the Catholic sacramental view of the world and Nursi's view of creation, and between the Catholic view of the human person as the image of God and Nursi's view of humans as partners with God and vicegerents of the earth.[107] Like Michel, Renz also notes that Nursi applies the obligation to love even to one's enemies and thus is very similar to Jesus' teaching.

After posing many critical questions to Nursi, Renz notes that Nursi must be interpreted in the context of his time, and that a creative, critical, and constructive development of his thought is needed to enrich Muslim-Christian discussions.[108] Renz closes his discussion with aspects of Nursi's thought that offer a bridge to Christian perspectives. He notes that for Nursi, Islamic faith must be a personal conviction and religious experience. He praises Nursi for seeking a spiritual renewal of society without seeking to force change through violence. Renz believes that during a time of tremendous threats to human dignity, Nursi's greatest achievement was to find a path beyond the alternatives of a backward-looking religious fundamentalism or a godless contemporary ideology.

Renz praises another achievement of Nursi in his development of a theocentric and quasi-sacramental worldview, which resonates with Christian faith. Renz closes by listing a number of virtues that Nursi proposes, virtues that challenge Christians, Muslims, and indeed, all people of good will: hope, sincerity, love, unity, recognition of human dignity, and care.[109] Beyond all the differences and difficulties in Muslim-Catholic relations, for Renz, as for Michel and Valkenberg, the faith in God and the virtues that Nursi proclaimed and lived offer a basis for theological engagement and respectful reflection.

## CONCLUDING REFLECTIONS

Nursi's legacy stands as a contribution and challenge to Catholic understanding of Muslims and Islam. As both Michel, Valkenberg, and Renz have ably demonstrated, there are many points of agreement between Nursi and the Catholic tradition. Catholics can admire Nursi's heroic witness to the Islamic faith even at great personal cost. Valkenberg and Renz have rightly noted a number of important areas where Catholics differ from Nursi.

As we have seen, Nursi invited Christians to form an alliance with Muslims against a perceived common enemy, viz., aggressive atheism. To the degree that atheistic movements engage in aggression against religion, Catholics can welcome this invitation to mutual support in a difficult situation. During the lifetime of Nursi, many Catholics would have agreed that atheists were to be seen

---

106. Ibid., 108–9.
107. Ibid., 110.
108. Ibid., 111.

109. Ibid.

as enemies. As Renz notes, the current attitude of the Catholic community toward atheists, however, does not see them in this way. Following the example of Pope John XXIII, the Second Vatican Council reached out to non–believers, seeking to work together on issues of common concern. The *Pastoral Constitution on the Church in the Modern World* (commonly known by the opening Latin words *Gaudium et Spes,* "Joy and Hope") noted that the idea of God that atheists reject may bear "no resemblance to the God of the gospel."[110] More recently, Pope Benedict XVI called for respectful dialogue with non-believers through his initiative known as the "Courtyard of the Gentiles," which invites all persons, especially those without religious faith, to come to a conversation concerning the common good.[111] Thus Catholics will be wary of Nursi's invitation to view Muslims as allies in a confrontation against atheists who are construed as alleged enemies.

In particular, Pope Francis has urged Catholics to cooperate with all persons of good will in fostering more responsible concern for the earth, and he has stressed the importance of interreligious relations in supporting this concern. I will close this essay by noting some points of convergence between Pope Francis and Nursi in this area. In his 2015 encyclical *Laudato Si': On Care for Our Common Home*, Francis rejects a purely instrumental view of nature:

When nature is viewed solely as a source of profit and gain, this has serious consequences for society. This vision of "might is right" has engendered immense inequality, injustice and acts of violence against the majority of humanity, since resources end up in the hands of the first comer or the most powerful: the winner takes all. Completely at odds with this model are the ideals of harmony, justice, fraternity and peace as proposed by Jesus (#82).[112]

Francis rejects a radically anthropocentric view of creation as leading up to humans: "The ultimate purpose of other creatures is not to be found in us. Rather, all creatures are moving forward with us and through us towards a common point of arrival, which is God, in that transcendent fullness where the risen Christ embraces and illumines all things" (#83). At times his language becomes poetic, echoing Francis of Assisi: "The entire material universe speaks of God's love, his boundless affection for us. Soil, water, mountains: everything is, as it were, a caress of God" (#84).

Like Francis of Assisi and Pope Francis, Nursi also believed that humans can in principle know God as creator from the goodness and beauty of creation.[113] Nursi argued: "For since the origins, roots, and sources of things result in their existences with perfect order and extreme art, they show that they are ordered in accordance with a notebook of the principles of Divine knowledge."[114] Nursi affirmed, "Everything becomes a mirror yielding knowledge of God. As Sa'di Shirazi said: '*to the conscious gaze*

---

110. *Pastoral Constitution on the Church in the Modern World*, #19, 1079.

111. Pope Benedict XVI, "Dialogue of Foundation," http://www.cultura.va/content/cultura/en/dipartimenti/ateismo-e-non-credenza/discorso-di-fondazione-di-benedetto-xvi.html, accessed January 16, 2016.

112. Pope Francis, *Laudato Si'*, 60.

113. Nursi, *Rays*, 130–71.

114. Nursi, *Letters*, 55.

*each leaf is a book telling of Divine knowledge.*' In everything a window opens up onto knowledge of God."[115] For Nursi, as for Francis of Assisi and Pope Francis, the entire universe is a book that reveals the power and wisdom of God to those who know how to read it.[116] The image of the universe as a book that reveals the power and wisdom of God resonates deeply with the Catholic tradition.

In another point of convergence with Pope Francis, Nursi believed that the pursuits of modern science can be a way of developing the knowledge of the names that was given to Adam, but he also warned that science can be a new form of self-assertion and idolatry. Salih Yücel and Selma Sivri have explored the implications of Nursi's worldview for care for the environment, noting that "he said that nature should be protected for spiritual reasons as well as for materialistic reasons. He believed that if humans understood the spiritual significance of the environment as an art of the Creator, they would protect it to a greater degree."[117]

Pope Francis warns that there is no guarantee that humans will use their tremendous power over nature wisely, and so Francis warns that "our immense technological development has not been accompanied by a development in human responsibility, values and conscience. Each age tends to have only a meager awareness of its own limitations. It is possible that we do not grasp the gravity of the challenges now before us" (#105). Like Nursi, Pope Francis cautions that technological development does not answer all human problems; indeed, it promotes a dangerous, one-dimensional paradigm based on manipulation and control: "this paradigm exalts the concept of a subject who, using logical and rational procedures, progressively approaches and gains control over an external object. This subject makes every effort to establish the scientific and experimental method, which in itself is already a technique of possession, mastery and transformation" (#106).

Nursi lived before the threat of ecological catastrophe was fully apparent, but his theology strongly rejected the manipulation of nature by modern science and ardently supported a holistic approach to nature as a responsibility entrusted to humans by God. Yücel and Sivri comment on Nursi's view of the responsibility humans have as vicegerents of creation: "This responsibility of humans as vicegerents include[s] using the Earth's resources without wasting, safeguarding environmental balance, and acting while acknowledging that every creation has its purpose in being and should be treated accordingly."[118]

For both Pope Francis and Nursi, if science is employed as a weapon of power and domination, as an instrument of conquest, then it is not fully rational because it is based on an underlying rejection of its origin and goal, which is God. If, however, reason surrenders itself in service of the infinite divine mystery that surrounds it, then it becomes a form of love and can greatly enhance human life and give glory to God. In a time of acute ecological threat, the theology of Nursi regarding human responsibility for creation converges powerfully with the Catholic

---

115. Ibid., 389.
116. Vahide, "The Book of the Universe," 466–83.
117. Yücel and Sivri, "Said Nursi's Approach to the Environment," 96.
118. Ibid., 83.

tradition in supporting care for our common home.

## BIBLIOGRAPHY

Anawati, George. "Louis Massignon et le dialogue islamo-chrétien." In *Louis Massignon et le dialogue des cultures*, 276. Paris: Cerf, 1996.

Baker, Rob, and Henry Gray, eds. *Merton and Sufism: The Untold Story: A Complete Compendium*. Louisville, KY: Fons Vitae, 1999.

Benedict XVI, Pope. "Dialogue of Foundation." Online: http://www.cultura.va/content/cultura/en/dipartimenti/ateismo-e-non-credenza/discorso-di-fondazione-di-benedetto-xvi.html. Accessed January 16, 2016.

Clooney, Francis X. *Theology after Vedanta: An Experiment in Comparative Theology*. Albany, NY: State University of New York Press, 1993.

*Decrees of the Ecumenical Councils*. Volume 2. *Trent to Vatican II*. Edited by Norman P. Tanner. Washington, DC: Georgetown University Press, 1990.

Fitzgerald, Michael L., and John Borelli. *Interfaith Dialogue: A Catholic View*. Maryknoll, NY: Orbis, 2006.

Francis, Pope. *Laudato Si': On Care for Our Common Home*. San Francisco: Ignatius, 2015.

*Globalization, Ethics and Islam: The Case of Bediüzzaman Said Nursi*. Edited by Ian Markham and İbrahim Özdemir. Aldershot, UK: Ashgate, 2005.

Gude, Mary Louise. *Louis Massignon: The Crucible of Compassion*. Notre Dame, IN: University of Notre Dame Press, 1996.

Haddad, Yvonne Yazbeck. "Ghurba as Paradigm for Muslim Life: A Risale-i Nur Worldview." *The Muslim World* 89 (1999) 297–313.

Lefebure, Leo D. "Faith, Reason, and Science in the Modern World: The Contributions of Karl Rahner and Said Nursi." In *The Risale-i Nur: Knowledge, Faith, Morality and the Future of Huhumankind*, 78–90. Istanbul: Istanbul Ofset Basım Yayın San, 2010.

———. "The Resurrection of the Dead: Said Nursi and Jürgen Moltmann." In *Theodicy and Justice in Modern Islamic Thought: The Case of Said Nursi*, edited by İbrahim M. Abu-Rabi`, 99–110. Farnham, UK: Ashgate, 2010.

———. "Wisdom, Prophets, and the Guidance of Humanity: Pope John XXIII and Bediüzzaman Said Nursi." Yet unpublished article.

*Louis Massignon et ses contemporains*. Edited by Jacques Keryell. Paris: Editions Karthala, 1997.

Markham, Ian, and Suendam Birinci Pirim. *An Introduction to Said Nursi: Life, Thought and Writings*. Farnham, UK: Ashgate, 2011.

Massignon, Louis. *The Passion of Al-Hallaj: Mystic and Martyr of Islam*. Abridged ed. Translated and edited by Herbert Mason. Bollingen Series XCVIII. Princeton: Princeton University Press, 1994.

Michel, Thomas F. *A Christian View of Islam: Essays on Dialogue*. Edited by Irfan A. Omar. Maryknoll, NY: Orbis, 2010.

———. "The Ethics of Pardon and Peace: A Dialogue of Ideas between the Thought of Pope John Paul II and the *Risale-i Nur*." In *Globalization, Ethics and Islam: The Case of Bediüzzaman Said Nursi*, edited by Ian Markham and İbrahim Özdemir, 37–47. Aldershot, UK: Ashgate, 2005; this essay also appears in Thomas Michel, *Said Nursi's Views on Muslim-Christian Understanding*, 58–78, and again in Thomas F. Michel, *A Christian View of Islam: Essays on Dialogue*, 108–19.

———. "'For You, Illness Is Good Health': Said Nursi's Spirituality in His Approach to Physical Illness." In *Spiritual Dimensions of Bediüzzaman Said Nursi's Risale-i Nur*, edited by İbrahim M. Abu-Rabi`, 175–89. Albany, NY: State University of New York Press, 2008.

———. "God's Justice in Relation to Natural Disasters." In *Theodicy and Justice in*

*Modern Islamic Thought: The Case of Said Nursi*, edited by İbrahim M. Abu-Rabi`, 219–26. Farnham, UK: Ashgate, 2010.

———. *Insights from the Risale-i Nur: Said Nursi's Advice for Modern Readers.* Clifton, NJ: Tughra, 2013.

———. "Is A God-centered Life an Antidote to a Culture of Violence? Some Reflections from the *Risale-i Nur.*" In *The Risale-i Nur: Knowledge, Faith, Morality and the Future of Humankind*, 338–49. Istanbul: Istanbul Ofset Basım Yayın San, 2010.

———. *Said Nursi's Views on Muslim-Christian Understanding: Eight Papers.* Edited by Şükran Vahide. Istanbul: Söz Basım Yayın, 2005.

Mosher, Lucinda Allen. "The Marrow of Worship and the Moral Vision: Said Nursi and Supplication." In *Islam at the Crossroads: On the Life and Thought of Bediüzzaman Said Nursi*, edited by İbrahim M. Abu-Rabi`, 181–97. Albany, NY: State University of New York Press, 2003.

Nursi, Bediüzzaman Said. *The Damascus Sermon.* Translated by Şükran Vahide. 2nd rev. and exp. ed. Istanbul: Reyhan Offset, 2002.

———. *The Flashes Collection.* Vol. 3. The Risale-i Nur Collection. Translated by Şükran Vahide. Istanbul: Reyhan Ofset, 2000.

———. *Letters 1928–1932.* Vol. 2. The Risale-i Nur Collection. Translated by Şükran Vahide. 2nd and rev. ed. Istanbul: Sözler Nesriyat, 1997.

———. *The Rays Collection.* Vol. 4. The Risale-i Nur Collection. Translated by Şükran Vahide. Istanbul: Reyhan Ofset, 2002.

———. *Signs of Miraculousness: The Inimitability of the Qur'an's Conciseness.* Translated by Şükran Vahide. Istanbul: Sözler, 2004.

Omar, Irfan A. "Building a 'Community of Witness': Father Thomas Michel, S.J., on Islam and Christian-Muslim Relations." In Thomas F. Michel, *A Christian View of Islam: Essays on Dialogue*, edited by Irfan A. Omar, 1–6. Maryknoll, NY: Orbis, 2010.

Rahner, Karl. "Prophetism." In *Encyclopedia of Theology: The Concise Sacramentum Mundi*, 1286–89. New York: Crossroad, 1986.

Renz, Andreas. "Said Nursi und das Christentum." *CIBEDO-Beiträge* 3 (2013) 105–12.

Turner, Colin and Hasan Horkuc. *Said Nursi.* Makers of Islamic Civilization. London: I.B. Tauris, 2009.

Vahide, Şükran. *Bediüzzaman Said Nursi: The Author of the Risale-i Nur.* Istanbul: Istanbul Ofset Basım, 1992.

———. *Islam in Modern Turkey: An Intellectual Biography of Bediüzzaman Said Nursi.* Edited by İbrahim M. Abu-Rabi`. Albany, NY: State University of New York Press, 2005.

———. "An Outline of Bediüzzaman Said Nursi's Views on Christianity and the West." In *Globalization, Ethics and Islam: The Case of Bediüzzaman Said Nursi*, edited by Ian Markham and İbrahim Özdemir, 109–20. Aldershot, UK: Ashgate, 2005.

Valkenberg, Wilhelmus. "Said Nursi's Commentary on *Surah Al-Fatiha*: Its Role in Dialogue and Mutual Understanding between Christians and Muslims." In *The Risale-i Nur: Knowledge, Faith, Morality and the Future of Humankind*, 124–33. Istanbul: Istanbul Ofset Basım Yayın San, 2010.

———. *Sharing Lights on the Way to God: Muslim-Christian Dialogue and Theology in the Context of the Abrahamic Partnership.* Currents of Encounter 26. Amsterdam: Editions Rodopi BV, 2006.

Vogt, Eric W. *The Complete Poetry of St. Teresa of Avila: A Bilingual Edition.* New Orleans: University Press of the South, 1996.

Weld, Meryem. *Islam, the West, and the Risale-i Nur.* Istanbul: Sözler, 2004.

Yavuz, M. Hakan. "*Nur* Study Circles (*Dershanes*) and the Formation of New Religious Consciousness in Turkey." In

*Islam at the Crossroads: On the Life and Thought of Bediüzzaman Said Nursi*, edited by İbrahim M. Abu-Rabi`, 297–316. Albany, NY: State University of New York Press, 2002.

Yücel, Salih and Selma Sivri. "Said Nursi's Approach to the Environment: A Spiritual View of the Book of Universe." *Insights* 1.4 (2009) 77–96.

# Section Four

# Nursi and Politics

# 22

# Said Nursi's Positive Action as a Method of Serving Belief and Peace

AHMET YILDIZ

## INTRODUCTION: WHAT POSITIVE ACTION (*MÜSBET HAREKET*) IS

THE *RISALE-I NUR*, THE most important Qur'anic commentary in republican Turkey, reconstructed Islamic thought by synthesizing miscellaneous Islamic traditions of thought to surpass the challenge of materialism emanating from the positivistic conception of modern science and society. The *Risale* preached a new way of living Islam as the epitome of *insaniyet-i kübra* (the greatest humanity). It posits its method of service (*hizmet*) to Islam as "positive action" (*müsbet hareket*), which means the patient and silent struggle to strengthen the essentials of Islamic belief (*iman*) by peaceful means, non-involvement in politics, and prioritizing religious zeal based on the principles of sincerity and brotherhood rather than a result-oriented course of action.[1] The unique function of the *Risale-i Nur* in the renewal of belief (*tajdīd*) and revitalization (*iḥya*) of Islam inspired and compelled this method owing to the objective constraints imposed upon Muslim

---

1. The term "positive action" is used in miscellaneous occasions in the *Risale-i Nur* by Said Nursi. To illustrate: "In our sacred service, we always act positively." Nursi, *Letters*, 491; "Our duty is to behave positively." Nursi, *Emirdağ Supplement II*, 1912; "Those who are at each other's throats cannot act positively." Nursi, *Letters*, 317; "To act positively, that is, out of love for one's own outlook, avoiding enmity for other outlooks, not criticizing them, interfering in their beliefs and sciences, or in any way concerning oneself with them." Nursi, *Flashes*, 203; "For the sake of acting positively, refraining from behaving negatively and not interfering with the Divine Discretion, I have responded ill-treatment against me with patience and compliance for thirty years." Nursi, *Emirdağ Supplement* II, 1912; "We will act positively in the interior with our utmost power to protect public order." Ibid., 1912.

societies, and to some extent the whole world, through the global modernization process fashioned after what is "Western." Nursi's communicative approach delegitimizes, and in some cases, de-emphasizes the material, power-driven attempts to serve Islam which espouse result-centered, violent, or political methods.[2] The communicative and affirmative nature of positive action is justified by many verses of the Qur'an and traditions of the Prophet. Nursi mentions some of them in his *Risale-i Nur*.[3]

Said Nursi's renowned concept of positive action is a multifaceted concept beyond the scope of the present article. This simple, but complex concept will be treated here through a brief description of its essential components, with particular attention to the form of opposition it prescribes against oppression: attaining basic rights and liberties under non-Islamic despotic and/or secularist regimes prevailing in the Muslim World via a unique practice of seemingly "passive" activism characterized by a "politics of non-politics."

The positive action principle and practice must be understood in the context of the Kemalist radical reforms aimed at secularizing an overwhelmingly Muslim society and polity. In the face of one-party tyranny, a man like Nursi, who had accepted no humiliation whatsoever in his lifetime until then, kept his mood quiet, did not react negatively and preached the strategy of positive action,[4] the components of which he defined as follows: positive action, or one may say "positive *jihad*," requires Muslims in their utterances and deeds:

- To act solely in accordance with the consent of God;[5]
- To engage in faith service only and to content oneself with it;

---

2. In the autobiography of Said Nursi under the heading "About What Ustad Talked with His Visitors," we read the following paragraph: "He used to explain that the only aim of the *Risale-i Nur* service was to strengthen faith (*iman*) which has secured the nation and the land from the perils of irreligion and communism; that the indispensable duty both on individual and societal level was to save and strengthen the faith; that the most important cause of the time was to hold on faith (*iman*); that since the *Risale-i Nur* strictly dwelled upon this cause, the enemies of the nation and the land, the covert holders of irreligion, resorted under many pretexts to provocations, but by calling attention to the fact that 'we are bounded to act positively,' he heralded that the Nur would defeat the enemies of the religion; that the impact of acting positively was like that of an atom bomb; that *Risale-i Nur* has no relationship with politics; that the mainstay of our way was sincerity; that there can no cause other than the Divine assent; and that the grace and mercy of God would protect *Risale-i Nur* through complying with sincerity and positive action . . . ." See Nursi, *Tarihçe-i Hayat*, 2188.

3. To illustrate, following verses from the Qur'an are helpful: "So if they dispute with thee, say: 'I have submitted my whole self to God and so have those who follow me.' And say to the People of the Book and to those who are unlearned: 'Do ye (also) submit yourselves?' If they do, they are in right guidance, but if they turn back, thy duty is to convey the Message; and in God's sight are (all) His servants" (Q 3:20); "Say: 'Shall I seek for (my) Lord other than God, when He is the Cherisher of all things (that exist)? Every soul draws the meed of its acts on none but itself: no bearer of burdens can bear the burden of another. Your return in the end is towards God. He will tell you the truth of the things wherein ye disputed" (Q 6:164); "The Believers are but a single Brotherhood: so make peace and reconciliation between your two (contending) brothers; and fear God, that ye may receive Mercy" (Q 49:10); "God is never unjust in the least degree: If there is any good (done), He doubleth it, and giveth from His own self a great reward" (Q 4:40).

4. Alavi, *Seeds of Change*, 158–62.

5. Nursi, "The Twenty-First Flash," *Flashes*, 213.

- Not to interfere with divine determination, and hence posing themselves as pseudo-gods, the best engineer of what has happened and/or been created;

- To never violate public order and security, which may generate violation of the rights of other human beings, be it Muslim or non-Muslim, and creatures;

- To keep the state of steadfastness and gratitude to God, in every instance of life;[6]

- To avoid violence and politicization based on political partiality (partisanship), i.e., positionally determined biased behaviors;

- Not to forge a one-to-one correspondence between religious and political affiliation because this means to equate the realm of speculative *(nazariyat)* with the realm of indispensable *(zaruriyat)*;

- To delicately decline from politicizing Islam through presenting the club of politics together with the light, i.e., the spiritual *jihad*, and hence not to decrease the impact of conveyance of Islam, i.e., *tebliğ*, directed towards the people of *da'wat* (calling);

- To resort to prayer, both in words and deeds, instead of prioritizing the results of human acts;

- To adopt the principle of "the best stratagem is to be without stratagem" as their motto;

- To embrace the understanding of spiritual *jihad*;

- To refrain from all sorts of behaviors and attitudes that may yield to oppression, cruelty, and the violation of the rights of others;

- To entertain the love of their schools and ways only, and abstain from the description of their identity through deficiencies and mistakes of others;

- To keep the respect for truth above everything;

- Last but not the least, positive action is an individual, social and non-political way of behavior based on the pillars of enthusiasm, patience, gratitude, sincerity, and brotherhood.[7]

Positive action is a faith-based strategy developed against the domination of secularism via oppressive means in the realm of Islam *(dar–al Islam)*, specifically in post-1908 Ottoman Turkey and the Kemalist Republic. It does not encompass everyday politics as a legitimate base and excludes any political end for its course of action. This does not mean the rejection of politics as a legitimate field of Muslim involvement, however. In the evolution of his lifetime, Said Nursi showed us three faces of positive action, involving individual, social and political realms, and putting to the fore any of them in accordance with Islamic expediency. Below I will try to briefly articulate the main components of the conception of positive action.

## POLITICS OF NON-POLITICS BASED ON NONVIOLENCE

Said Nursi's understanding of politics is based on the consideration that politics

---

6. Nursi, *The Emirdağ Supplement II*, 1912.

7. For a summary of these principles laid down in Said Nursi's last lesson to his students, see Alavi, *Seeds of Change*, 162–63.

has secondary importance to faith service, inspired by the motto "the best stratagem is to be without stratagem." It embraces no hidden agenda, and considers to be trusted by others in sociopolitical terms an essential asset. Thus he explains his withdrawal from politics during the New Said period of his life (the years of the single-party era) by pointing out the disappointment caused by his involvement in politics during the period of the Second Constitution in the Ottoman Empire, a period he would later call "the Old Said." His political involvement in this period led him to conclude that political practice is full of lies, and amenable to hijacking by foreign influences.

During the one-party era, he equated involvement in politics, understood as positionally determined political partisanship, with some sort of satanic evil. To him, there was no sense in taking a pro-government position given that he was neither a bureaucrat nor deputy. Taking the side of the opposition, on the other hand, might take two forms: with ideas or with force. Engaging in politics via ideas was pointless because all questions were crystal clear, and there was no space for democratic politics. Dealing with oppositional politics via the use of force, on the other hand, might lead to committing many sins for the sake of obtaining a doubtful goal. This conception of justice that leaves no room for violating the rights of the innocent led Said Nursi to withdraw from oppositional politics either through ideas or the use of force.[8]

The politicizing of Islam is something that Said Nursi avoids most. He prescribed to the principle that "the best stratagem is to be without stratagem," an overt manifestation of his rejecting of any sense of holding a hidden agenda, i.e., *takiyye*. Consequently, he gives utmost importance to openness, transparency, and trustworthiness.[9]

In this article, I prefer the term "peaceful" in characterizing Nursi's method of opposition against the despotic rule of the modernist-secularist government because I contend that it differs from the term "civil" in its view of the use of coercion through violent and/or nonviolent means, as well as in its "goals." Positive action involves *non-acceptance*, *non-practice*, *non-participation*, and *non-cooperation* of/with the unjust and oppressive rule imposed upon Muslim believers by the despotic rulers.[10] The key concept against oppression is patience. In this sense, it can be said that it is the Muslim variant of passive resistance, though devoid of any political means and goals. Although it is ostensibly passive, it has proven to be the most active and successful strategy of disobedience in the long run, given the re-entrance of Islam into public life in present-day Turkey.

What is excluded from positive action is as important as what it embodies. Positive action excludes the following courses of action in a conclusive way:

- Involvement in politics under Islamic banners (civil disobedience is political by nature);

---

8. Nursi, "The Sixteenth Letter," *The Letters*, 84–85.

9. He replies to the accusations levelled against advising his students to be cautious by referring to the need to avoid miscommunication and trigger the biased perception of the ruling regime. See Nursi, "The Sixteenth Flash, The Fourth Curious Question," *The Flashes*, 145.

10. Nursi, *Kastamonu Supplement*, 1675.

- The use of violence in opposition to despotic rules prevailing in the Muslim World; (*satyāgraha*-based understanding of civil disobedience categorically rejects the use of violence in any case of sociopolitical life);
- Attesting actual existence to causality as the working principle of nature and history, and behaving as such.

Said Nursi treats political parties independent of their positions in the political spectrum, be it governmental or oppositional, and sees them as organized forms of political struggle due to the fact that the target group of the faith movement covers adherents of all political parties except for aggressive atheists. He categorically rejects the physical *jihad* in the Muslim realm (*dar-al Islam*) against other Muslims, however indifferent to Islam they might be. Instead, he preaches the spiritual/positive *jihad*, *jihad* with words and deeds instead of coercive or violent means. Unlike satyāgraha-based understanding of civil disobedience, however, positive action does not disdain the role of violence against aggression targeting the Muslim society from outside, and yields a thoroughly legitimate place to material *jihad* as a form of legitimate self-defense. A line of caution by Said Nursi, however, limits material *jihad* directed only to aggressor non-Muslims. Differently, the basic pattern of relation between Muslims and "civilized" non-Muslims is persuasion and dialogue, not compulsion.[11]

Thus, setting himself against the secularist political stance of Kemalism that oppressed Islam, being denied the recognition of basic rights and liberties in de facto terms, and arbitrarily imprisoned and held back in exile for a period of twenty-eight years, Nursi insistently avoided from any violent form of opposition against Kemalist one-party rule, did not express any interest in daily politics, and carefully protected himself against deliberate provocations by the government. His method of opposition to all this was positive action strategically structured by positive activism that centered on the active service of belief.

## PROTECTION OF PUBLIC ORDER THROUGH OBSERVING ABSOLUTE JUSTICE (*ADALET-I MAHZA*)

The positive action approach considers sinking a boat in which there are nine murderers and one innocent soul as a cruelty, and places the right to life in the matrix of absolute justice. Before justice, the right of one is equal to a thousand; there can be no difference. Right is right; it cannot be differentiated in accordance with its size. This understanding delimits the implementation of the principle of absolute necessity in the suspension of fundamental human rights. Nursi rejects the understanding that restricts the implementation of basic human rights upon the considerations that there is a mandatory state, like famine, drought, flood or war; he is against to do so by unilateral action without the consent of the concerned. In Said Nursi's own words,

> Yes, there is a power in our way, but this is for maintaining public order. According to the principle of "No bearer of burdens can bear the

---

11. Nursi, "Yedinci Cinayet"(Seventh Killing), *Divan-ı Harb-i Örfi*, (*Apology in the Marshal Court*), 1922; Nursi, *The Damascus Sermon*, 85.

burdens of another" (Qur'an 6:164), the brother, the family, or children of a criminal cannot be held responsible for him. It is because of this that throughout my life I have endeavored with all my strength to maintain public order. This power may not be employed internally, but only against external aggression. Our duty in accordance with the above verse, is to assist the maintenance of internal order and security with all our strength. It is for this reason that within the Islamic World there have been very few civil wars damaging public order.... The most important condition of the *jihad* of the word is not interfering in God's concerns; that is: "Our duty is to serve; its results are Almighty God's concern. We are charged with carrying out our duty, and are obliged to do so.[12]

## PATIENCE AGAINST OPPRESSION

Among points addressed by Said Nursi in his court defenses and letters to his followers are the rule of law, freedom of thought and expression, freedom of association, the confidentiality of private life, freedom of dissemination of thought, freedom of religion and conscience (this right includes that laïcité be viewed as a principle of neutrality, the protection of the language of religions, the individual right to worship, maintenance of the mother tongue, non-imposition of a certain sect), freedom of travel and settlement, the right to petition, the individuality of crimes and punishment, putting into judgment not thoughts but actions, the definition of citizenship in terms of both rights and obligations, not to take religious education under state monopoly, treating plurality of ideas and opinions as a corollary of human existence, and the right to dissent.

"The Six Questions" from his book *Letters* (*Mektubat*) is a manifesto of this position. Nursi remained patient in spite of continuous exiles and persecutions, and followed his proactive agenda instead of reacting to deliberate provocations by "deep elements" within the government. He lit a candle instead of swearing at darkness. That's why, for example, he criticized the notorious Shaikh Said incident of 1925 and declined to curse the public prosecutor that insistently levelled unsubstantiated claims against him during the Afyon trial.[13]

Thus, thanks to his positive action approach, Nursi showed patience in the face of cruelties committed against him and was able to preserve the legality and legitimacy of his moral ground. This was so despite the arbitrary and oppressive treatment inflicted upon him.[14]

## ENDEAVOR-BASED COURSE OF ACTION INSTEAD OF RESULT-ORIENTED ACTIVISM

Nursi's positive action is centered upon the notion of sincerity (*ikhlās*) and encourages religious communities and associations, as well as individuals, to align themselves with their principles and acts, motivated by the love of their observances and methods, instead of using the mistakes and insufficiencies of

---

12. Nursi, *Jihad of the Word and Positive Action*, 2–3.

13. Nursi, *Emirdağ Supplement II*, 1914–15.

14. For an account provided by Said Nursi for his endurance of crude humiliations, see Nursi, 'The Sixteenth Letter, Third Point," *Letters*, 86–7.

others as a pretext for action/(re)action. This is the first, most important condition to preserve sincerity. In the last lesson he delivered to his students, Nursi's main emphasis was to act in accordance with the principle of positive action. The interpretation of *jihad* as spiritual, both among Muslims and between Muslims and non-Muslims, with the exception of self–defense against non-Muslim aggressors, and the representation of Islam through the means of persuasive argumentation comprise the moral ground of positive action.[15] As a natural corollary of this, drawing upon the privity of crimes and punishments, all sorts of acts that may lead to the violation of others' rights and public order are considered to be in conflict with the principle of positive action.

The concept of positive action recommends that in all acts and deeds, Muslim believers must be oriented toward good will and endeavors, not to the results thereof. The duty of human beings, therefore, is to be constantly endeavoring to attain the assent of God in their lifetime as much as they are able. The end result is determined by God . Muslims must avoid being result-oriented instead of effort-oriented, a kind of prayer (*dua*) in a *de facto* sense. This would secure the inner world of Muslims, and turns them into people, feeling secure and being trustworthy.

Nursi declared that "The Nur students belong only and exclusively to the movement of faith and Islam."[16] Accordingly, freedom before humanity leads to submission before God. In other words, those who resign from their will before God cannot accept the position of slavery to people, because, human beings are created free, but they still need to be the servants of God (*abdallah*).[17]

## WHY POSITIVE ACTION: SAID NURSI'S ANALYSIS OF MODERNITY/SOCIOPOLITICAL CHANGE IN THE MUSLIM WORLD

In response to a question posed to him by his students during the early 1930s while he was in exile in Barla, a mountainous village near the city of Isparta, Nursi draws a very striking picture of the nature of and consequences brought about by modernity in the Muslim World. In this analysis, the sociopolitical process of change in the Muslim World is described as a swamp, and religious Muslims are depicted as having the ability to rescue themselves from this swamp. The mobilization of spiritual reserves for the rescue of those who are in search of truth, meaning and means of salvation deserves a priority. The target group is defined as the bewildered majority that must be rightly guided not via the club of politics, but through the light of faith. This necessitates the avoidance of politics because it requires taking sides either with the government or the opposition, and hence "otherization" of Muslims with differing political opinions. While faith belonging is indispensable (*zaruriyat*), political affiliation is, in comparative terms, a

---

15. See Qur'an, 16:125: "Invite (all) to the Way of thy Lord with wisdom and beautiful preaching; and argue with them in ways that are best and most gracious: for thy Lord knoweth best, who have strayed from His Path, and who received guidance."

16. Nursi, *Tarihçe-i Hayat*, 2143.
17. Nursi, *Damascus Sermon*, 79.

negligible belonging of theoretical speculation (*nazariyat*). This involves a hierarchical stratification in a time of crisis in Muslim ontological, epistemological and moral confidence. Politics is just one manifestation of knowledge at the level of practice that must be circled upon by the formerly said forms of knowledge.

Against this background, Nursi argues that the crisis inflicted by Western modernity upon the Muslim mind from the ontological, epistemological and moral perspectives must be met with a reconstruction of these fields through the lens of Qur'anic understanding based on the Beautiful Names of God (*asmā al-ḥusnā*) that would enlighten humanity of our age. Thus he wrote the *Risale-i Nur*, which, by uniquely combining the theoretical (scientific) and aesthetical (Sufi) dimensions of knowledge in the same verbal text showed a safe way demonstrating that

- The universe is a solid Qur'an, and the Qur'an is a reader for the universe;
- The human self (*ana*) does not have a real existence; it has a nominal existence, and as such, a means of measurement in comprehending the Beautiful Names and attributes of God;
- Human beings can be free by being the servants of God (*abdallah*) only;
- Causality, the essence of modern way of thinking, is valid just in appearance; all things and events have two sides: the apparent (*mulk*) and the real (*melekut*). Qadar, the divine determining, is the real cause, not vice versa;
- What is worthwhile is not the face of things that look at exclusively to the world we live in, i.e., *dunya*;
- Every being testifies to the Creator with ninety-nine signs, while testifying of oneself only in one sign;
- In the same event where humanity behaves unjustly, the divine determining (*qadar*) predestines justice;
- As a corollary of this, huhumankind is obliged in all instances of life either to be steadfast or thankful to God;
- The duty of Muslims is to convey and transmit the commands of God to the people, not to coerce them; humanity is positioned to demand, but the endowment of what they want is up to the discretion of the divine will;

Another basic text to facilitate our understanding of positive action and the reasons for its adoption as the main form of service to Islam is the "Second Curious Question" of the "Sixteenth Flash" in Nursi's book *Flashes*:

> The greatest danger facing the people of Islam at this time is their hearts being corrupted and belief harmed through the misguidance that arises from science and [materialist] philosophy. The sole solution for this is light; it is to show the light so that their hearts can be reformed and their belief, saved. If one acts with the club of politics and prevails over them, the unbelievers descend to the degree of dissemblers. And dissemblers are worse than unbelievers. That is to say, the club cannot heal the heart at this time, for then unbelief enters the heart and is concealed, and is transformed into dissembling. And at this time, a powerless person like myself cannot

employ both of them—the club and the light. For this reason, I am compelled to embrace the light with all my strength, and cannot consider the club of politics whatever form it is in. Whatever physical *jihad* demands, we are not charged with that duty at the moment. Yes, in accordance with a person's way, a club is necessary to form a barrier against the assaults of the unbelievers or apostates. But we only have two hands. Even if we had a hundred hands, they would be sufficient only for the light. We do not have any other hands with which to hold the club![18]

We may draw the conclusion from this passage that prioritization for Muslims in terms of the capabilities they have is of prime importance. Because of the attacks of the materialist paradigm of modern science and philosophy, Muslims are in a state of emergency to keep their faith and morality by way of persuasive argumentation. Politics, which involves coercive means, is not an appropriate channel to secure this because it cannot heal unbelief; on the contrary, it may establish it in clandestine form more firmly. The passage does not exclude the possibility of politics as a barrier against the assaults of militant unbelievers or apostates, however. Thus the physical jihad is restricted tightly. As a corollary of all this, positive action provides a solid base for universal peace with its two basic propositions:

## The Spiritual Jihad (*cihad-ı manevi*)

According to Said Nursi,

> The time for enmity and hostility has finished. Two World Wars have shown how evil, destructive, and what an awesome wrong is enmity. It has become clear that there is no benefit in it at all. In which case, on condition they are not aggressive, do not let the evils of our enemies attract your enmity. Hell and Divine punishment are enough for them.[19]

This observation regarding the practice of Islamic injunctions qualifies the Muslim individual as the final judge of his obligations towards God, and ascribes spiritual sanctions against the violations of those injunctions by adherents of non-Islamic beliefs to be implemented in the hereafter. The objective Islamic justification for pluralism in Muslim societies may be grounded on this observation. The compliance of Islam requires free will, and is sanctified not by any worldly authority. Islam is a global source of peace and pluralism volunteered by its adherents through "good deeds."

When he described "the sword of the Islamic unity" in 1909 in the Marshal Court, Nursi declared:

> Its swords are the firm reasoning. For winning over the civilized is through persuasion, not compulsion. To search out for the truth is through love. Enmity was against savageness and bigotry. Its objective is to exalt the word of God. Ninety-nine percent of the *sharia* too consists of matters of morality, worship, the Hereafter and virtue; it relates to politics only in one percent. Let's leave that part to our rulers.[20]

The way of exalting the word of God in modern times is positive action within Muslim lands, and among Muslims and

---

18. Nursi, "The Sixteenth Flash," *Flashes*, 142–44.

19. Nursi, "The Fifth Word," *The Damascus Sermon*, 51.

20. Nursi, *Divan-ı Harb-i Örfi*, 1922.

non-Muslims within globally defined boundaries.

## ALLIANCE WITH CHRISTIANS

Said Nursi suggests that Muslims should unite "not only with their fellow-believers, but also with the truly pious Christians."[21] We can apply this to all other Abrahamic religions as well. The point of unity is to be able to go beyond tolerance and pave the way for genuine interest in and admiration for each other's religious traditions. Putting oneself in another's shoes in religious terms would make genuine and sincere communication possible and contribute to the formation of an emphatic cognition of one another.

Against this background, the question remains why Nursi, who sacrificed all his life for the happiness in this world and the hereafter of not only Muslims but all humanity, and all creatures, even when this resulted in the trampling on his honor, and enjoyed no worldly pleasures, was exposed to such discriminatory and inhumane treatment by the strictly secularist rule of the one-party era prevailing in Turkey during the first half of the twentieth century, and yet did not resort to daily politics or the means of violent opposition.[22]

Following the so-called Shaikh Said Rebellion of 1925, in which he refused to take part, he was taken from Van province and brought to first Burdur and later to Barla, a mountainous village of Isparta.[23] This life in exile continued until 1953, and sporadically and unofficially, until his death in 1960. His whole life in

---

21. "Both this astonishing time, our way, and our sacred service require from us that let alone Muslims from other ways or *tariqas*, with people holding faith (*iman*) even when they belong to groups who have gone astray, and with people who recognize God and attest to the truth of the Hereafter, even if they be Christian, we should not enter into dispute over the points of divergence between us." See Nursi, *Kastamonu Supplement*, 1667.

22. Nursi, *Emirdağ Supplement II*, 1864. Said Nursi explains why he remained patient instead of protesting the insults of an ordinary gendarme or warden during the whole single-party era in Turkey as follows: "If *sharia* permitted to commit suicide for a man like me who resisted against the Commander-in-Chief of the Russian Army, challenged the execution threat of the British commander of the invasion forces in Istanbul and kept his honour and defied against the extreme anger of the First President of Turkey in the Bureau of the Assembly in the presence of some fifty deputies, there would be no doubt that committing suicide would have pleased him one hundred times more than life against having been forced to tolerate the insults of an ordinary gendarme or warden, and their tortures, betrayals and defamations." Ibid.

23. The fact that Nursi refused the proposal of Mustafa Kemal Pasha, which stipulated for Nursi to be appointed the general preacher to the South-East, membership of the panel of the Diyanet, and to be elected as a member of the Parliament, points to Nursi's spiritual transformation from what he calls "the old Said" to "the new Said." In his own words: "The new Said wanted to work for the next World and cannot work with you, but he will not interfere with you either." Vahide's interpretation of the main reason for Nursi's stance is as follows: "Nursi had perceived the course that would be taken and understood that he could not work alongside the leaders.... In a later work, he wrote: 'So I was compelled to leave those most important posts. Saying that nothing can be gained from working with or responding to those people, I abandoned the world and politics and social life, and spent all of my time on the way of saving belief.' Nursi had also understood that it would be followers of the Qur'an that would combat the leaders, and that these leaders would be defeated not in the realm of politics but with the "immaterial sword" of the Qur'an's miraculousness. So he refused to work together with the new leaders and left Ankara for Van, where he withdrew into a life of solitude." Vahide, *Islam in Modern Turkey*, 171–72.

exile was characterized by his exclusion from the rights of citizenship, namely, arbitrary imprisonment, being poisoned more than twenty times, deliberate humiliation, revoking of his rights of travel, communication, writing, interacting with people, worshipping, and his right to dress as he pleased.

In the courts of Eskişehir, Denizli and Afyon, he was continuously accused of forming political associations, misusing religious feelings in a way that broke the public order, using religion for political and other interests, opposing the regime and disliking the president Mustafa Kemal and his innovations, establishing a Sufi brotherhood, advocating Kurdish nationalism, developing religious interpretations of the contestable issues regarding women, hence arguing for *hijab* and their inheritance right according to *sharia*. He was sentenced to eleven months in prison in the Eskişehir Court by discretion, acquitted in the Denizli Court of 1943, and kept in Afyon prison for twenty months for unjustified claims, finally being acquitted in 1956. He went on continuously to compile the *Risale-i Nur* during all this time of exile, jail, illnesses, and arbitrary treatments by officials. When he was on trial in the court of Denizli, however, he consoled his brothers as follows: "Don't worry! These Lights, [i.e., the *Risale-i Nur*] will shine in the future."[24] This is a clear manifestation of his enthusiasm even in the worst conditions that led to the conception of positive action. His basic motivation was his endless submission to God. From the vantage point of positive action, Nursi clarifies his position vis-à-vis the Kemalist government as follows: "It is neither our duty to reject the regime nor have we the necessary power for this. Yet, we don't accept, follow or request the regime. Rejection is something, non–acceptance is another thing, non–following (practice) is thoroughly another thing."[25] In accordance with this position, Said Nursi never yielded to oppression, didn't lend legitimacy to the oppressor and didn't see it as a legitimate agency of recourse for his basic rights by declaring that "to apply for the recognition of his rights to those who see the unjust as the just is defiance (disrespect) against the Just One."[26]

Accordingly, Nursi's conception of opposition is reflected in his emphasis on the freedom of expression and association. He rejects the use of violence and political partisanship as the vehicles of social and political change, and puts the instrumentalization of Islam in this context outside the scope of positive action.[27] Positive action, which is self-defined and proactive rather than reactive and other-defined can be achieved only by those who treat one another with empathy and compassion. In Nursi's words, "Those who are at each others throat cannot act positively."[28] As a result, Muslim believers approach one another's' deficiencies and mistakes not as opponents but with a compassionate feeling of removing them.

---

24. Nursi, "The Thirteenth Ray," *Rays*, 273.

25. Nursi, *Kastamonu Supplement*, 1675.

26. Nursi, "The Thirteenth Letter," *Letters*, 69.

27. Nursi, "Rü'yada Bir Hitabe" (An Address in Dream), *Sünuhat*, 2050.

28. Nursi, "The Twenty-Second Letter, The Fifth Aspect," *Letters*, 317.

## CONCLUSION: POSITIVE ACTION TODAY

Unlike many groups and individuals who mistakenly aimed to further the cause of Islam by negative means, Said Nursi preached the positive action principle, and accordingly, the Nur students followed this principle. Thanks to this, the one–party oppression could not eliminate Said Nursi despite its heavy demonization efforts, and its provocations proved futile. Under the relatively liberal atmosphere of the Democrat Party governments, the open publication of the *Risale-i Nur* became possible after it had been cleared by the Afyon Court in 1956. Said Nursi encouraged the Democrat Party to lift non-democratic bans on Islamic life. Nevertheless, Nursi and the Nur students were mocked and exposed to various forms of harassment, which made it difficult for them to make use of basic rights and liberties even in a relatively more democratic polity.

The essential means of the positive course of action devised by Said Nursi in the struggle against aggressive atheism and irreligion are the nonmaterial *jihad*. By adopting the "current of belief" and endeavoring proactively for its spread without focusing on the end-results were to work also for public order and tranquility.[29] The key to success in spiritual terms was to be patient against mistreatments and oppression.[30] What worried Said Nursi was not his personal sufferings, but the attacks inflicted upon the Muslim World.[31]

His point of departure was to save the belief pillars of the polity, the end result of which was public security that protected the innocent. Accordingly, due to the crimes, sins or mistakes committed by someone, the people related to him cannot be held responsible. The material power may be used outside the Muslim realm and against foreign aggression and attacks. Muslim believers are not obliged to secure the domination of Islamic teachings all around the world, but commissioned with the conveyance of the divine message in the best manner. This difference between *jihad* inside, i.e., in the Muslim World and *jihad* outside, i.e., against aggressor non–Muslims, in other words spiritual and material *jihad*, is basic to the conception of positive action. Since the problem is defined to be spiritual, the solution too has to be spiritual. Politics may assume importance to the extent it relates to the betterment of faith service. Any action that may lead to the spread of injustices is deemed inappropriate even if

---

29. Vahide, *Islam in Modern Turkey*, 323–24.

30. Said Nursi summarized his position regarding positive action in his last lesson to the Nur students as follows: "We are obliged to be patient and grateful against all difficulties in the positive service to the faith, which yields the protection of the public order and security. For instance, by taking myself as an example, since the beginning, I have not surrendered to domination and disgrace. This has become definite in many instances in my life. For example, not to stand up before the Russian commander in the first World war, and not to attach importance to the questions addressed to me in the Marshal Court while I was under the threat of death penalty clearly demonstrate that I have not yielded to domination. On the other hand, for the sake of the truth of acting positively and keeping away from behaving negatively in order not to defy the Divine Discretion, I have responded to mistreatments inflicted on me with patience and compliance for thirty years. Like the Prophet Cercis (peace be upon him) and those who suffered so much in the battles of Badr and Uhud, I showed steadfastness and compliance..." Nursi, *Emirdağ Supplement II*, 1912.

31. Nursi, *Tarihçe-i Hayat*, 2137.

this is rising against injustice.[32] Protection of peace and tranquility and thus public order is a *sine qua non* of the principle of the positive action. Nursi stated, "I am ready to sacrifice my life, even if I had one thousand lives, honor and dignity for the peace of this nation and the worldly tranquility and otherworldly happiness of especially innocent children, helpless people, the aged, the sick and the poor."[33]

## BIBLIOGRAPHY

Alavi, Mohammed Asım. *Seeds of Change, Thrilling Leadership Lessons from the Life of Bediüzzaman Said Nursi*. Istanbul: Vakıf, 2013.

Nursi, Bediüzzaman Said. *The Damascus Sermon*. Translated by Şükran Vahide. Istanbul: Sözler, 2012.

———. *Divan-ı Harb-i Örfi* (Apology in the Marshal Court). "Yedinci Cinayet" (Seventh Killing). *Risale-i Nur Külliyatı*. Vol. 2. Istanbul: Nesil, 1996.

———. *Emirdağ Supplement I-II*. *Risale-i Nur Külliyatı*. Vol. 2. Istanbul: Nesil, 1996.

———. *Flashes*. Translated by Şükran Vahide. Istanbul: Sözler, 2011.

———. *Jihad of the Word and Positive Action*. Istanbul: Sözler, n.d

———. *Kastamonu Supplement*. *Risale-i Nur Külliyatı*. Vol. 2. Istanbul: Nesil, 1996.

———. *Letters*. Translated by Şükran Vahide. Istanbul: Sözler, 2010.

———. *Rays*. Translated by Şükran Vahide. Istanbul: Sözler, 2006.

———. *Sünuhat*. "Rü'yada Bir Hitabe" (An Address in Dream). *Risale-i Nur Külliyatı*. Vol. 2. Istanbul: Nesil, 1996.

———. *Tarihçe-i Hayat*. *Risale-i Nur Külliyatı*. Vol. 2. Istanbul: Nesil, 1996.

Qur'an. Translated by A. Yusuf Ali. Beirut: Al Rajhi, 1983.

Vahide, Şükran. *Islam in Modern Turkey: An Intellectual Biography of Bediüzzaman Said Nursi*. Albany, NY: State University of New York Press, 2005.

---

32. Nursi, *Emirdağ Supplement II*, 1912–13.
33. Nursi, *Emirdağ Supplement I*, 1687.

# 23

# Religious Struggle in Modern Turkey
## Said Nursi's Interpretation of *Jihad*

### ŞÜKRAN VAHIDE

## INTRODUCTION

THE DIFFERENCES IN SAID Nursi's interpretation of *jihad* between the two main periods of his life, reflecting differences between the two major periods of Turkish history with which they coincided—the final decades of the Ottoman Empire and first thirty-five years of the republic. Though the differences appear to be greater than the similarities, there are in fact essential continuities. These concern his view that endeavors to uphold the Word of God (*i'lâ-yı kelimetullah*), an objective related to *jihad*,[1] should be directed primarily towards internal problems of Muslim society rather than externally towards the unbelievers. This meant a struggle for progress and civilization in the earlier period, and a moral and intellectual "*jihad* of the word" against the "moral and spiritual destruction" of materialistic philosophies in the later. In both periods, he endorsed the view that armed *jihad* was permissible only in the face of external aggression. On the one hand, this reflected a trend that had arisen in the face of the inability of Muslim powers to withstand European colonial expansionism, and on the other hand, it was recognition of the demands of modernity. This chapter will trace Nursi's interpretation of *jihad* in the two periods, and will attempt to relate it to contemporary conditions, while pointing out aspects of difference and continuity. In order to contextualize these ideas, this will be preceded by a few remarks on interpretations of *jihad* in Islamic history and in modern scholarship, and its meaning and purpose as depicted in the Qur'an.

---

1. Yurdagür, "İ'lâ-yı Kelimetullah," 62–63.

## Interpretations of *Jihad* in Islamic History

The prevailing view of *jihad* interprets it as military action for either defensive purposes or, more usually, offensive purposes for "the expansion of Islam"[2] against unbelievers to secure their conversion or, in the case of the People of the Book, their submission and payment of the poll-tax (*jizya*).[3] Recent studies,[4] however, suggest that this view should be moderated by calling attention to the following facts.

First, there are the multiple meanings implied by the term *jihad* and derivatives of its root *jahada*—meaning to strive, strain, or exert oneself to the utmost—in the Qur'an and *hadith* and in the early period of Islam. Frequently qualified in the Qur'an by the phrases "in God's way" (Q 9:19, 2:218, 8:74, etc.) and "with your selves and your property" (Q 61:11, 9:20, 88, etc.), *jihad* signifies strenuous endeavor of any kind to further God's cause.[5] More specifically, the Qur'an enjoins the Muslim community collectively and individually to strive by "commanding good and forbidding evil" to establish "a ... just moral-social order" on the earth, and it introduced the concept of *jihad* to realize this.[6] Armed combat is one means of this. Although prominence is given *jihad* in this latter sense in the many *hadiths* on the subject in the canonical collections, a number signify its broader meanings.[7]

Second, by the third/ninth century, influenced by works of Islamic law, the meaning of *jihad* as warfare came to eclipse its use for other forms of exertion in God's way.[8] Furthermore, debate on the apparently conflicting significations of the term in the Qur'an[9] led to the emergence of divergent interpretations that in the course of time were formulated as legal rulings and included in the corpora of the various schools of Islamic law. The abrogation of earlier pacific verses of the Qur'an enjoining *jihad* by later offensive ones was a point of dispute.[10] Detailed discussion is beyond the scope of this chapter; however, there are some relevant facts: It was a minority of scholars who considered disbelief to be sufficient justification for war; the majority believed that it was aggression and unprovoked attacks on the part of the unbelievers that

---

2. Tyan, "D*jihād*," 538-40.

3. Peters, *Jihad in Classical*, 4.

4. For example, Abdel Haleem, "Qur'anic '*jihad*,'" 147-66; Afsaruddin, "Competing Perspectives," 15-31; Afsaruddin, "Views of Jihad," 165-69; Heck, "'Jihad' Revisited," 95-128; Ahmet Özel, "Cihad," 527-31.

5. Abdel Haleem, "Qur'anic '*jihad*,'" 147-48.

6. Rahman, *Major Themes*, 62-63; Heck, "Jihad Revisited," 122-23.

7. For example, Cânan, *Kütüb-i Sitte*, 5:18-19: "The [true] *mujāhid* is one who struggles (*jāhada*) with his own self" (*Tirmidhī*, Faḍā'il al-Jihād, 2); ibid., 5:19-20: "[Any small act] in God's way morning or noon is better than the world and all it contains" (*Bukhārī*, Jihād, 5, 6, 73; Riqāq, 2, 51; *Muslim*, 'Imāra, 112-15; *Tirmidhī*, Faḍā'il al-Jihād, 17; etc.); ibid., 7:67-68: "Wage jihad against the polytheists with your property, lives, and tongues!" (*Abū Dā'ūd*, Jihād, 8; *Nasā'ī*, Jihād, 1); ibid., 17:538: "The best jihad is to say the truth [stand up for right and truth] in the face of an unjust ruler" (Related from Abū Umāma).

8. Afsaruddin, "Competing Perspectives," 22-23.

9. These are fourfold, corresponding to various stages of the Qur'an's revelation and the Prophet's mission. See, Tyan, "D*jihād*," 538.

10. Tyan, "D*jihād*," 538; Afsaruddin, "Competing Perspectives," 22-23.

legitimized conflict;[11] forcible conversion was also found unacceptable.[12]

The rulings on *jihad* were formulated during the first two centuries of Islam, the period of its rapid expansion, in the course of which the idea of the "domain of Islam" (*dār al-Islām*) and the "domain of war" (*dār al-ḥarb*) found currency.[13] According to this idea, armed *jihad* for the purpose of establishing "the rule of God" against those lands outside Islamic jurisdiction was held to be obligatory. Nevertheless, changing conditions within the extensive Islamic world made such a bipartite division progressively irrelevant and inapplicable.[14] By the fourth/tenth century and halt of Islam's expansion, *jihad* was no longer held to be obligatory by all scholars unless Islamic lands faced outside aggression.[15]

Although with effect from the late eighteenth century European colonialist incursions into Muslim territories were resisted in many cases by *jihad* movements that were finally unsuccessful due to their inability to withstand the superior invading forces,[16] with the establishment of colonial rule over large swathes of the Islamic world and resultant impracticability of repulsing it by force of arms, by the late nineteenth century, Islamic scholars of modernist persuasion advanced new interpretations. In India, Sayyid Ahmad Khan (1817-98) opposed *jihad* against British colonial rule on the grounds that Muslims were not oppressed in the practice of their religion. In Egypt, Muhammad 'Abduh (1849-1905) defended the notion of peaceful coexistence among states, Islamic and non-Islamic, while endorsing the legitimacy of meeting outside aggression—hence colonial occupation—with force.[17] This, however, was not entirely an innovation in *jihad* theory; it has been asserted that the idea of international relations being based on peace rather than on war and of the theoretical equality of states has a place in Islamic, and notably Hanafi, theories of *jihad*, but that the conditions obtaining in the Middle Ages did not allow for its development.[18]

## THE OLD SAID'S INTERPRETATION AND PRACTICE OF *JIHAD*

In many ways—such as his style and his attempt to supply practical solutions for the grave problems facing the Ottoman Empire in its final decades and his native Kurdistan within the empire, and his wish to engage the ordinary people in the realization of those solutions as a form of *jihad*, Said Nursi was original. Yet investigation of his ideas on *jihad* in this period shows that, with his framing his solutions within the concepts of science, progress, and civilization, to a large extent he had internalized the discourse of nineteenth-century modernity, and that along with the majority of Ottoman intellectuals and

11. Özel, "Cihad," 528-30.
12. Khadduri, "Ṣulḥ," 845-46.
13. See, Heck, "Jihad Revisited," 106-8.
14. Watt, *Islamic Political Thought*, 91-92.
15. Khadduri, "Ṣulḥ," 845-46.
16. See, Peters, *Islam and Colonialism*, 39-104.

17. Peters, *Jihad in Classical*, 6, 59, 112, 124-27; Peters, *Islam and Colonialism*, 110-30; Peters, "Jihad: An Introduction," 324.

18. Özel, "Cihad," 530. The author here does not offer any specific sources to support this claim, but is perhaps referring to the eminent Hanafi jurist Muhammad al-Shaybani (d. 189/805); see Heck, "Jihad Revisited," 109-13, esp. 111; Peters, "Jihad: An Introduction," 324.

*'ulema*[19] he believed these values to be intrinsic to Islam and their adoption to be the sole hope for the empire's salvation.

For Nursi the true enemies of the Ottomans and Islamic world were "the internal foes" that were "the enemies of progress." These he epitomized as "ignorance, poverty, and internal conflict," against which it was a religious duty to wage *jihad*. This struggle took precedence over all else. The Europeans were subjugating them with the weapons of science and industry; they therefore should wage *jihad* with the same weapons on their three internal enemies. External *jihad* should be referred to the proofs of the *shari'a*, "for the civilized are to be conquered through persuasion."[20] At this time, external *jihad* should be through love and good will, not through intimidation,[21] and by Muslims showing, through their fine morals and their progress, that Islam is lovable and elevated. Nursi even suggests that since the Europeans had impelled them down the road of material progress and civilization, the Ottomans should look on them as friends and assistants, not enemies.[22]

Of the three weapons Nursi most frequently cited besides science and industry to combat the enemies of progress, namely "the swords of education, human striving and labor, and unity,"[23] education was clearly the most crucial and was the question on which he expended his greatest efforts during this early period of his life, especially for his native region, himself engaging in what may be called a scholarly *jihad*.

The heart of the comprehensive educational reforms Nursi strove to introduce into the area was the combined teaching of modern science and the traditional Islamic sciences.[24] He himself had mastered most of the mathematical and physical sciences through his own efforts when in his early twenties, a move that was unheard of in the east at the time, where the *'ulema* lacked all knowledge of modern science and looked on it as unbelief. Because of the *'ulema's* influence over the ordinary people, Nursi sought ways of introducing them and their students to science in a way that would allay their fears. Hence the educational establishment he strove to found and sought official backing for, even going as far as Istanbul and the Sultan's court, he wanted to be known by the familiar name of *medrese*.[25] The *Medresetü'z-Zehrâ*, as he called it, after the famous university of al-Azhar in Cairo, was to embody his proposals for reform and was to act as a model for other schools. He also set out some of his ideas for updating Qur'anic exegesis, one of the basic *medrese* sciences, in a work addressing the *'ulema* called *Muhâkemat*, in which he sought to demonstrate the truth of scientific facts and their relevance to exegesis, and that there could be no conflict between science and revealed knowledge.[26]

Nursi's proposed reforms, which aimed to bring about the democratization

---

19. See, Kara, *İslamcıların Siyasî Görüşleri*, 24, 39–45; Hanioğlu, *A Brief History*, 205.
20. Nursi, "Hakikat," 3.
21. Molla Said-i Kürdî, "Musâhebe," 284.
22. Nursi, "Lemeân-ı Hakikat," 4.
23. Nursi, "Fihriste-i Makasıdı," 3.

24. For an outline of Nursi's ideas on *medrese* reform see, Vahide, *Islam in Modern Turkey*, 42–47, 48.
25. Molla Said-i Meşhur, "Kürdler Neye Muhtaçtır?" 2.
26. Nursi, *Muhâkemat*, 8, 14–15, 25–26, 27, 49–66.

and diversification of *medrese* education, were also designed to assist in realizing the other two "weapons" that he considered essential for pursuing the struggle for progress: the production of enterprising, industrious individuals, and also social harmony and unity, the absence of all of which had been clearly exploited by Europe.[27] The following is a brief description of how he envisaged achieving these goals.

The production of industrious individuals, which is the weapon against the enemies of progress Nursi succinctly calls "*sa'y* (effort, striving)," as well as the crucial weapon of "unity," may both be examined within the context of his ideas concerning social development, at the heart of which lay his belief in the principles of "Islamic" constitutionalism (*meşrûta-i meşrû'a*) and "the freedom prescribed by the *sharia* (*hürriyet-i şer'iyye*). He was a fervent supporter of constitutional government after the reinstatement of the constitution in July, 1908, after thirty-three years of Sultan Abdülhamid's absolutist rule, and urged that the government be founded on the *sharia*; he also proposed the introduction of its democratic principles in many areas of life, not least in education, as mentioned above.

Nursi's first concern was that the ordinary people were properly informed about the alien concepts of freedom and constitutionalism, and that they understood their individual responsibility to participate in their application. In Istanbul and in the east, therefore, he energetically employed every means at his disposal to enlighten people, and primarily his fellow Kurds, who were among the most deprived "elements" of the empire.[28]

In order to establish constitutionalism, which Nursi held to be synonymous with civilization, the people would have to strive to acquire science and to progress so as to combat the three enemies of ignorance, poverty, and enmity, and also transcend the divisions of the traditionally segmented society and develop an awareness of nationhood.[29] The chief obstacle to these necessary steps, the all-pervasive harms of which Nursi never tired of inveighing against, was despotism. Despotism was the source of backwardness, abasement, and division, and had been greatly reinforced by the absolutism of the former era. In Nursi's view, a correct understanding of freedom and constitutionalism would allow the tribesmen of the east to overcome these hurdles. First, they should release themselves from the domination of the tribal chiefs and *shaykhs* and from subservience to them, for the leaders represented attributes and principles that were the antithesis of constitutionalism; they were embodied despotism, and despotism was "oppression . . . arbitrariness . . . compulsion and force . . . the basis of tyranny . . . the annihilator of humanity," while constitutionalism was "truth, reason, knowledge, the law, and public opinion." As such, some tribal chiefs and "phoney shaykhs" had aggrandized themselves and degraded their followers. They had mounted their backs, stifled their abilities, and extinguished their enterprise and enthusiasm for work.[30] They had also

---

27. Nursi, "Lemeân-ı Hakikat," 4.

28. Vahide, *Islam in Modern Turkey*, 60–61.

29. *Bediüzzaman'ın Münâzaratı*, 22–23, 121–24.

30. Ibid., 27–31.

dried up the pool of the nation's material and moral resources by causing division, due to tribalism and factionalism, and "cut the [binding] rope of [the sense of] nationhood."³¹

What now fell to the people was to develop a consciousness of their nationhood by generating mutual attraction "like particles" and to unite and combine within Islam. Gaining a true understanding of freedom, they had to transcend narrow tribal and group interests and unite.³²

Constitutionalism had delivered the free will from "tyranny and domination" so the people were obliged, with religious and national zeal, to demonstrate their existence through unity. The realization of freedom was therefore a moral struggle. Since the sovereignty of the nation had been guaranteed, "everyone [was] a commander in his own world and [was] therefore obliged to wage the greater *jihad* [in it, with the lower self] and [was] charged with . . . reviving the Prophet's *Sunna*."³³ Nursi was hopeful that the egotism and widespread desire for domination that had caused conflict and disorder in the past would "in the prosperous future palace of civilization" be transformed into ideas and creativity, personal initiative, and liberty.³⁴

Moral *jihad* was also the basis of wider Islamic unity and the progress and development of the Islamic world, not politics. The salvation of the Islamic world was dependent on moral renewal and individual Muslims regaining an awareness of their membership of the Islamic "nation."³⁵

Progress and the building of "true" civilization, in which the weapons of education, striving/work, and unity were to play a crucial role against those things that prevented their attainment, were Nursi's goals in this period. This struggle was the essential *jihad* of this age, hence Nursi constantly emphasized that "upholding the word of God" was contingent on material progress and achieving civilization.³⁶ This was not a struggle against European civilization; its "evils," however, had to be avoided, since in his view they had come to preponderate in the West, and moreover since the nineteenth century, had been foolishly adopted by the Ottomans in preference to its useful aspects like science and technology. Religion had even been given as the bribe. However, Nursi argued that for the people of the Ottoman lands, progress was dependent on religion.³⁷ Also citing such arguments as Islam's compatibility with reason and modern human's search for truth, he predicted that such a civilizational struggle would result in Islam's prevailing over the future.³⁸

---

31. Ibid., 114–16.

32. [Nursi], *İki Mekteb*, 55. Nursi actually uses the term *nation* (*millet*) in three senses: to refer to the component groups of the multi-ethnic, multi-religious empire; to the Ottoman "nation" itself, which all its component groups formed; and to the wider Islamic "nation" or *umma*. He was urging consciousness of, and unity within, all three. See also, Vahide, *Islam in Modern Turkey*, 58, 60.

33. Nursi, "Yaşasın Şeriat-ı Ahmediye," 2; Eng. tr., Nursi, *Damascus Sermon*, 75–76.

34. [Nursi], *İki Mekteb*, 57–58.

35. Nursi, *al-Khuṭba al-Shāmiyya*, 49–50; Eng. tr., *Damascus Sermon*, 54–55.

36. See, for example, Molla Said, "Musâhebe," 284; Nursi, "Reddü'l-Evhâm," 4; "Lemeân-ı Hakikat," 3.

37. Nursi, "Yaşasın Şeriat-ı Ahmediye," 2; Eng. tr., Nursi, *Damascus Sermon*, 75.

38. Nursi, *al-Khuṭba al-Shāmiyya*, 42–46; Eng. tr., Nursi, *Damascus Sermon*, 28–43.

In conclusion, it should be recalled that Nursi was not opposed to armed *jihad*, for upon the Ottomans joining the Central Powers in the early stages of the Great War, he enrolled in the army as a regimental mufti and was sent to the Caucasian front at Erzurum. He fought against the invading Russian forces and was later detailed to raise a militia force, which he then led in numerous actions, being finally awarded a war medal. But he did not lay aside his pen while fighting this defensive *jihad*; he continued to compose his Qur'anic commentary, *Ishārāt al-i'jāz*, on the front under the Russian shelling, demonstrating the primary importance he attached to scholarly and civilizational *jihad*.

Following the Ottoman defeat in 1918 and foreign occupation of Istanbul, Nursi both combated the occupying forces with his pen, and, as a member of the Darü'l-Hikmeti'l-İslâmiye, participated in the scholarly and practical struggle to uphold the interests of Islam.[39] He supported the War of Independence in Anatolia, which in April 1920 was declared a *jihad*, and published a rebuttal of the Istanbul *fatwa* that declared the national forces to be rebels. He engaged in these struggles till mid-1920, when he completely withdrew from social life and underwent the mental and spiritual transformation that resulted in the emergence of the New Said.

## THE NEW SAID'S JIHAD

Nursi's vision of an Islamic modernity and the building or rebuilding of Islamic civilization was incompatible with the objectives of Mustafa Kemal and his followers, who gained control of the Ankara government, and having abolished the sultanate (November 1, 1922) and caliphate (March 3, 1924), set their sights on building a modern Western-style nation-state on what remained of the Ottoman Empire. In consequence, although Nursi had moved to Ankara at the request of the new leaders, he refused their offers of various posts in the nascent regime, and, withdrawing from social and political life, departed for his native east. According to his biography, he had understood that the irreligious trends he had perceived in the new capital would not be effectively combated through political struggle, but with "the immaterial sword" of the Qur'an's inimitablity.[40] It was from a life of seclusion in Van that Nursi was arrested in either 1925 or 1926, along with many hundreds of others, and sent into exile in Western Anatolia.

Nursi did not adopt a confrontational stance towards the new regime and its government; banished to a remote village, he started to compose short pieces proving the basic beliefs of Islam for the local people, that aimed to preserve their faith and cultural identity in the face of the radical changes being wrought by the reforms. In the face of Mustafa Kemal's evident aim of eliminating, through a series of draconian measures,[41] all outward

---

39. For Nursi's activities during this period, see, Vahide, *Islam in Modern Turkey*, chapters 7 and 8.

40. Collective, *Risale-i Nur Müellifi* (hereafter, *Tarihçe*), 131–32. It should be noted that Nursi was not opposed to the abolition of the sultanate and caliphate but believed that their functions should be performed collectively by the (religiously observant) National Assembly. See, *Tarihçe*, 125–27; Vahide, *Islam in Modern Turkey*, 169–71.

41. For the reforms, see, Zürcher, *Turkey*, 180–81, 189–90; Tunçay, *Türkiye*

signs of Islam, and raising Turkey to the level of modern civilization and making it part of the West, Nursi remained entirely detached and engaged in no active or overt political activity of any sort.

Although the educated elite came to identify with Westernism[42] and embraced the Turkish nationalism and scientism that replaced Islam as the ideological basis of the state, the efforts to inculcate Kemalism[43] as the official ideology were largely ineffective when it came to the rural population,[44] which formed 80 percent or so of the total. Notwithstanding this limited success during the twenty-five years of single-party rule, the people did not remain unaffected by the secularizing reforms. Moreover, under force of circumstance religious leaders and networks in Anatolia such as Said Nursi and the movement he initiated adapted their mode of operation to both the onward march of modernity and the adverse conditions, acting also as a modernizing force.[45] Both factors, that is, the ongoing social change, and the adaptation of the underground dissemination of religious ideas ensured the survival and even revitalization of Islam, and its revival in later decades.[46]

## Jihad of the Word and Its Weapons

In a key passage[47] composed probably in 1945, Nursi explains the form *jihad* should take in a modern secular state such as the new Turkey and holds up the *Risale-i Nur* (hereafter, *Risale*), the collective name of the works written during his exile, as an exemplary protagonist in this struggle of ideas and persuasion. To put his exposition in historical perspective, he precedes it, as an explication of allusive meanings of the verse "Let there be no compulsion in religion" and those following it (Q 2:265–7), by a paragraph in which he interprets as attempts "to extinguish the light of the world of Islam" two events in recent history that led directly to the demise of the Ottoman Empire: the 1877–78 Russo-Ottoman War and the peace treaties marking the end of World War I. Although this appears to be a purely political appreciation, from the wording, that is, "the light of the world of Islam," and from his conception of the struggle as it becomes clear in the course of this chapter, Nursi's concern was in fact with the corruption by outside forces of the intellectual underpinning of Islam and the consequences of this for the mass of believers. This is borne out by many passages in the *Risale* that state either explicitly or by inference that "the philosophers of Europe" have for a thousand years conspired to attack the Qur'an and "shake the pillars of belief," and that the purpose of the *Risale* is to mend the

*Cumhuriyeti'nde*, 155–86, 228–35.

42. Hanioğlu, *Atatürk*, 203, 222.

43. For the six principles of Kemalism, see, Jung and Piccoli, *Turkey*, 75–78; Zürcher, *Turkey*, 189–90.

44. Karaömerlioğlu, "The People's Houses," 69, 84; Hanioğlu, *Atatürk*, 207.

45. Mardin, *Religion and Social Change*, 23–27, 36–39, 221–22.

46. See, Brockett, "Collective Action," 60–61; Hanioğlu, *Atatürk*, 224. Although both these authors note the causal relation between these developments and the later emergence of a "Turkish-Islam," it should be pointed out that this was subsequent to Said Nursi's death in 1960; he himself always encouraged identification and non-political unity with the wider Muslim community (*umma*) and was opposed to the Turkification of Islam in any sense (See, Vahide, *Islam in Modern Turkey*, 22, 23, 67–68, 325–26; 208–10).

47. Nursi, *Rays*, 289–91.

accumulated harms they have caused.[48] His citing the principles of secularism as he understood it, that is, the separation of worldly and religious matters and freedom of conscience, when explaining the rationale behind the *jihad* of the word in the passage below, is an example of the line of argument he used to reply to government accusations that his religious activities infringed the Kemalist principle of secularism;[49] he argued that being concerned solely with questions of religious belief, his writings could in no way be construed as contravening the principle:[50]

> By [the matters of] religion being separated from [those of] this world on that date [1350: if according to the Hijri calendar, 1931–32; if according to the Rumi, 1934], freedom of conscience, which is opposed to force and compulsion in religion and to religious struggle and armed *jihad* for religion, [was accepted as] a fundamental rule and political principle by governments, and [this] state became a secular republic. In view of this, [*jihad*] will be a non–physical religious *jihad* (*mânevî bir cihad-ı dinî*) with the sword of certain affirmative belief (*iman-ı tahkikî*) . . . a great hero in the contest of this *jihad* of the word . . . is the *Risale-i Nur*, which bears

48. See, Nursi, *Rays*, 188, 200; Nursi, *Emirdağ Lahikası* (hereafter, *Emirdağ*), 1:74, 104.

49. "[For] the Kemalists . . . religion was seen as a hindrance to progress. . . . Their secularism meant not so much the separation of church and state as the subjugation and integration of religion into the state bureaucracy." Zürcher, *Turkey*, 243–44.

50. Nursi maintained: "freedom of conscience governs everywhere in this age of freedom," (*Letters*, 493) and, "secular (laic) means to be impartial . . . [so] the government should not interfere with the religiously-minded and pious, the same as it does not interfere with the irreligious and dissipated." *Rays*, 386; also, ibid., 305; *Tarihçe*, 195, 205.

the name of light, for its immaterial sword has solved hundreds of the mysteries of religion, leaving no need for physical swords. . . . It is due to this mighty mystery that the *Risale-i Nur* students do not interfere in the politics and political currents of the world and their material struggles, nor attach importance to them, nor condescend to [any involvement with] them. . . . They feel not anger at their enemies but pity and compassion. They try to reform them, in the hope they will be saved.[51]

Before investigating the two weapons mentioned here and their place in the *jihad* of the word, and then further reasons for Nursi's eschewal of political struggle, it may be recalled that the decisive event marking the transition of the Old to the New Said had been his acceptance of the supremacy of divine revelation over reason and decision to take the Qur'an as his "sole guide." This was in distinction to the former period, when, according to his own admission, he accepted certain philosophical and scientific principles in order to contest European philosophy with its own weapons and defend Islam.[52] Henceforth, Nursi directed all his efforts towards developing a method of expounding the Qur'an relevant to current needs that was itself derived from the Qur'an. Philosophy[53] became the opponent, the intrusive other, and the foil for many of his arguments.

51. Nursi, *Rays*, 290.

52. Nursi, *Letters*, 505–6.

53. The term philosophy is generally used in a derogatory sense in the *Risale* to refer to positivism, scientism, or materialistic philosophies of European origin that became increasingly popular in the late Ottoman Empire and were influential in the early Republic. It represents the primacy of reason and rejection of divine revelation.

Thus, the sides of the contest as seen by Nursi emerge, as well as the two chief weapons with which to conduct it: the *Risale* itself and the type of active belief it aimed to gain for believers.

Arguably, although framed differently, Nursi recognized the secularization of the state; his *jihad* of the later period was the continuation of his earlier endeavors to advance education and expedite progress in that it was in many ways a campaign of education.[54] A description of the chief elements of the method[55] he developed will illustrate what he meant by the two weapons and how he envisaged their function.

Nursi described the "way" of the New Said as "reality" (*hakikat*) in distinction to the Sufi way (*tarikat*), and also "the law (*şeriat*)."[56] His use of the term is somewhat ambiguous; he appears to mean the universe or world as it is in reality together with its empirically verifiable face, for it has three aspects or faces.[57] The type of reflective thought on its visible face that forms the basis of this way is characterized by its being practiced with a view to comprehending "*manâ-yı harfî*": that is, the significative meaning of things. By this is meant pondering over or "reading" the beings and processes of the natural world for the meanings they express, as directed by the Qur'an. Materialistic science and philosophy however see only their "nominal meaning" (*manâ-yı ismî*) since they assume that phenomena signify themselves alone and point to no metaphysical truths beyond themselves.[58] The reading of beings from the significative viewpoint comprises a type of deductive reasoning in the form of proofs (*burhân*).[59] Beings are observed and seen to comprise numerous evidences of the acts, names, and attributes of their Maker. Basing his arguments on these evidences, Nursi adduces proofs of all the main tenets of belief and at the same time discloses many cosmic truths. His purpose is also to demonstrate the mutually interpretative function of the two "books" of the Qur'an and the universe; just as the universe gains meaning and is understood through the Qur'an, so with its verses about natural phenomena the Qur'an interprets and expounds the book of the universe.

The physical world is thus Nursi's chief focus, but he presents it in such a way that while proving religious truths, he can refute the concepts underlying the positivistic science and materialistic philosophies that were being propagated at the time: chance, coincidence, nature, and causation. He accorded science an important role in both these functions. Moreover, his desire to claim back science from the hands of the European materialists, who had used it to deny and discredit religion, and from their latter-day followers in Turkey, led him to attempt to legitimize and sacralize it, and use it in

54. This is corroborated by the fact that by the 1940s Nursi was equating the work of the *Risale* with that of the *Medresetü'z-Zehrâ*, the university-level *medrese* he had striven to found in Eastern Anatolia in the early part of his life, of which it was its "cradle." See Nursi, *Kastamonu Lahikası* (hereafter, *Kastamonu*), 79. The *Medrese* was realized in the *Risale* and its students, the leading ones of whom he called "the pillars of the *Medresetü'z-Zehrâ*": *Emirdağ*, 2:109, etc.

55. For a wider discussion of Nursi's method in the *Risale*, see, Vahide, "Bediüzzaman Said Nursi's Approach to Religious Renewal," 58–62.

56. Nursi, *Words*, 491.

57. Ibid., 653–54.

58. For *manâ-yı harfî* and *manâ-yı ismî*, see, Nursi, *Mesnevî-yi Nûriye*. Tr. Nursi, 51; Nursi, *Flashes*, 155–56.

59. Nursi, *Mesnevî-i Nûriye*. Tr. Badıllı, 236.

the service of the Qur'an. Thus, Nursi's conception of the universe is informed by modern science, and his use among many others of such metaphors as "clock," "machine," and "factory" to describe it with its regular motion and change has a distinctly Newtonian ring, yet his purpose, in addition to being educative, is to disprove the efficacy of the natural laws and causes of the mechanistic Newtonian model and their external existence and to prove that they are merely veils to the power and other attributes of their Creator.[60] What he intends to show is that when considered from the significative viewpoint described above, science, which discovers the universal laws and configurations of causes, "make[s] known the Glorious Creator of the universe together with His names."[61] Or to put it another way, "the physical sciences become knowledge of God."[62] Interpreting the verse, "And He taught Adam the names, all of them" (Q 2:21), he suggests that each of the sciences ultimately proceeds from and rests on one of the Divine Names, and that by mentioning the miracles of the prophets, the Qur'an is urging humanity to progress and to strive to achieve the highest moral and material attainments.[63]

From the method of Qur'anic interpretation that Nursi used in the *Risale*, it appears that, while decking out his students with the sword of certain, affirmative belief and providing them with the intellectual equipment to counter the pervasive influences of materialistic philosophy, he intended to fill the gap left by the now-abolished *medreses* in particular and, in respect of spirituality, the Sufi lodges (*tekke*). Thus, in his proofs and expositions he included the gist of the sciences of logic, theology (*ilm-i kelâm*), doctrine (*akide*) and the principles of religion (*usûl-u dîn*), as well as Qur'anic exegesis (*tefsir*). He insisted that this was the way of scholarship (*ilm*) not that of Sufism, which due to its ascetic practices and "perceiving the truths of belief from behind veils," had been defeated by scientistic philosophies.[64] Nevertheless, he was at pains to point out that belief or faith (*imân*) was not attained through intellectual knowledge alone; such human inner faculties as the heart, inner heart, spirit, and emotions should "receive their share." This was the way of the Qur'an, which opened up a way leading to God in everything, in distinction to that of the formal scholars of religion on the one hand, and of the Sufis on the other.[65]

A final feature of Nursi's method in the *Risale* to be mentioned here is his wide use of allegorical comparisons (*temsil*). These he often uses to illustrate the superiority in various fields of the Qur'an and belief over philosophy and misguidance, and to depict some fundamental differences between "true" Islamic civilization and Western civilization.[66] More-

---

60. Nursi, *Flashes*, 243–45. This is taken from his "Treatise on Nature," which proves the divine existence and unity by disproving three of the main assumptions of materialist philosophy: "Causes create this," "It forms itself (spontaneous generation)," and "It is natural. Nature creates it." For the whole treatise, see *Flashes*, 232–53.

61. Nursi, *Rays*, 228.

62. Nursi, *Mesnevî-i Nûriye*. Tr. Badıllı, 86.

63. Nursi, *Words*, 260–73, especially, 269–73.

64. Nursi, *Emirdağ*, 1:91.

65. Nursi, *Letters*, 381–82; *Emirdağ*, 1:65.

66. See, for example, Nursi, *Words*, 143–46, 420–24, 661–68. He says, in fact, that all the *Words* from the First to the Twenty-Fifth, "prove . . . the Qur'an's inimitability and superiority in the face of [modern] civilization." See *Words*, 420.

over, according to Nursi, inspired by the Qur'an, by bringing the loftiest and most profound truths close to the understanding, these comparisons induce conscious affirmative belief in the truths of Islam that remains unshaken by "the misguidance of science."[67] It was also by virtue of the comparisons that he was able to claim that with "the immaterial sword" of the *Risale* he had solved "hundreds of the mysteries of religion," as mentioned in the quote above. Although the significance of this may not be immediately apparent, he attaches such importance to the solving of these "mysteries"—which include such questions as God's existence and unity, the resurrection of the dead, the immortality of human spirit and life of the hereafter, divine determining or predestination and human will, and the wisdom in the transformations of minute particles[68]—because they had hitherto been deemed unsolvable by reason and therefore opposed to it, and had therefore been made a pretext for attacks by the materialists, and had formed an obstacle to acceptance of religious truth. Now that irrefutable proofs of the major truths of belief had been put forward in the *Risale* in a manner accessible to all classes of people, the enemies of religion could no longer prevail,[69] so "no need [remained] for physical swords."[70]

## The Practical Struggle and Formation of the Nur Community

Nursi's *jihad* of the word unfolded over the twenty-three years or so the *Risale* was composed (1926–49) and received a considerable boost when conditions eased with the coming to power of the Democrat Party in 1950. He was alone when sent to his place of exile in the remote village of Barla in 1927; yet in the eight years he remained there the numbers of his students secretly writing out and disseminating his treatises swelled to hundreds, and by 1950, numbered tens of thousands, having spread throughout the country. It was Nursi's students who, under his direction and knit into a community, conducted the *jihad* of the word with the weapons described above.

Conditions were indeed testing for both Nursi and his students, and progressively worsened over the period. The ban on both the publishing of religious materials, and (after December 1928) the use of the Ottoman script, along with the absence of printing presses, made the writing and distribution of Nursi's writings difficult and dangerous. The students suffered the constant threat of gendarme raids, arrest, detention, and mistreatment. Economic conditions also deteriorated over the period. Few of the students were people of means, writing materials were hard to come by, and devoting time to the *Risale* meant neglecting their own livelihoods. Nursi formed close relations with his students and a constant underground flow of letters passed between them. He constantly encouraged them to strengthen their resolve in the "struggle" (*mücâhede*) to spread the truths of belief,

67. Nursi, *Letters*, 434–35.

68. Nursi himself compiled a collection of some of the pieces from the *Risale-i Nur* explicating such mysteries entitled: *Tılsımlar Mecmûası* (The Mysteries Collection).

69. Nursi, *Kastamonu*, 209.

70. Nursi, *Rays*, 290.

stressing its importance,[71] especially when numbers of them suffered three terms of imprisonment together with him.

Nursi had begun to emphasize union as a necessary condition for the *jihad* of the word even before the scattered students had been brought together for the first time in Eskişehir Prison in 1934.[72] For he considered the formation of a community and the "collective personality" it gives rise to essential to the sort of religious struggle he foresaw. In view of the general tendency in modern life for people to form associations, he wanted the students of the *Risale* to form a collective personality as the most effective way of carrying out their work and also combating the collective personalities of the forces of misguidance and unbelief. Such a body might prevail where an individual would be defeated. He therefore impressed on the students the necessity of cultivating the moral qualities required to develop such a collective consciousness, the chief of which were sincerity (*ihlas*) and the renunciation of egotism. To engage in the moral struggle and possess oneself of these virtues was "the essence of the *Risale-i Nur*'s way,"[73] and its strength, and was the reason for its successes.

## Positive Action and *Jihad* of the Word

A notable characteristic of Nursi's *jihad* was its strict avoidance of political involvement. However, his many letters enjoining his students to refrain from evincing any interest even in worldly or current affairs, mostly written between 1936 and 1945 during the most repressive years of single-party rule,[74] should be considered together with his more active stance after the partial easing of conditions following the coming to power of the Democrat Party in May, 1950. This is examined in a later section. Nursi gives many reasons for his stand towards politics, but the main reason is related to the *Risale*'s chief function of saving and strengthening of belief:[75] the preservation of sincerity. Sincerity required that the Nur students worked for the cause of religious belief alone, in expectation of nothing except God's pleasure.[76]

Nursi considered any sort of political involvement to be incompatible with this altruistic single-mindedness, not least because it gives rise to rivalry and partisanship, and a person willy-nilly exploits everything for his political ideals. The resulting clashes and wrangling between the political currents make it difficult to preserve sincerity and not to exploit religion. Even the religiously-minded become hostile to each other and assist in the divisive stratagems of their joint enemies, "kill[ing] themselves with their hands."[77]

---

71. See, for example, Nursi, *Flashes*, 222; *Emirdağ*, 1:82; *Kastamonu*, 83.

72. Nursi, *Flashes*, 209.

73. Nursi, *Rays*, 327. Also, *Kastamonu*, 122, 143; *Emirdağ*, 2:76.

74. For the totalitarian tendencies of the Republican People's Party after 1930 and its elimination of all forms of civil society, see, Zürcher, *Young Turk Legacy*, 253–57, 290–92. See also, Zürcher, *Turkey*, 200–201, 244.

75. Nursi, *Emirdağ*, 1:62, 67.

76. Nursi, *Kastamonu*, 246, 263; *Emirdağ*, 1:39; 2:242.

77. Nursi, *Kastamonu*, 246. Also, *Emirdağ*, 1:39, 56, 272. Nursi's witnessing extreme partisanship among *'ulema* holding opposing political views in the period immediately after the First World War was the reason he withdrew

Also, if those serving the Qur'an are seen to be involved in politics, it causes the people they are addressing to doubt their sincerity; giving a false idea of political propaganda, it degrades its truths in their eyes.[78] Moreover, having been misled by science and philosophy, people need to be shown the truth so their belief may be saved; brandishing "the club of politics" merely scares them off. Confused seekers after truth are found in all the currents, so the one offering it has to remain above politics and free of bias.[79]

Another reason Nursi gives for not "interfering in world politics" is that they exert a fascination over a person and prevent him performing his essential duties. They cause heedlessness and corrupt hearts, and by drawing the person to one side or the other, make him a participant in their crimes.[80]

A further reason, which Nursi reiterates on numerous occasions, is that political involvement, and especially the extreme partisanship it gives rise to, is opposed to "compassion, truth, right, and conscience, which are the fundamental way of the *Risale-i Nur*," for it often leads to the collective punishment of the innocent families and dependents of some guilty opponent, which is totally opposed to justice.[81] Basing this principle on the verse, "No bearer of burdens can bear the burden of another" (Q 6:164, etc.), which he interprets as "No one is answerable for another's error or crime, even if a relative's," he applies it to various situations, including international politics and war, frequently drawing comparisons between Islamic and modern civilization that are unfavorable to the latter.[82] To support his argument, he extends it to legal rulings on *jihad*, according to which external aggression may be met with force because innocents, that is, the dependents of the unbelievers, outside "the sphere of Islam" (*Islam dairesi*), are treated as booty and may be taken into captivity. Within territories under Islamic rule, however, the rights of innocents are protected, even if they are dependents of people with no religion, so they may not be subjected to force. In other words, civil disorder, which inevitably leads to the violation of the rights of innocents, is unjust and should be avoided at all costs.[83]

Nursi attached the greatest importance to this question, emphasizing that in line with this ruling, external and internal *jihad* at the present time are "completely different." Force may not be employed internally; internal action has to be "positive (*müsbet*) and moral and spiritual (*mânevî*) in accordance with the true meaning of sincerity" since the damage [caused ultimately by materialist philosophies] is moral and spiritual. As a key component and prerequisite of *jihad* of the word, therefore, positive action requires that the Nur students act "positively with all [their] strength only to maintain public order."[84]

completely from all forms of political activity, refraining even from reading the newspapers for twenty-five years. See *Emirdağ*, 1:272.

78. Nursi, *Letters*, 82; *Rays*, 371–72; *Kastamonu*, 240.

79. Nursi, *Letters*, 69–70; *Flashes*, 143–44.

80. Nursi, *Emirdağ*, 56–57; *Kastamonu*, 122–23.

81. Nursi, *Emirdağ*, 1:39, 279; 2:241; *Rays*, 372; *Kastamonu*, 240.

82. Nursi, *Rays*, 316–17; *Emirdağ*, 2:98–99. For a discussion of this principle, see, Vahide, *Islam in Modern Turkey*, 327–28.

83. Nursi, *Emirdağ*, 1:39–40, 279; 2:241.

84. Ibid., 2:241–42. This is taken from a second key text expounding *jihad* of the word

## Section Four: Nursi and Politics

Examination of Nursi's letters reveals the reasons for his insistence on positive action, and also its various dimensions. Firstly, were the provocations the Nur students were subject to in their work disseminating his writings, which ranged from objections and verbal attacks from the followers of other paths and teachers, to cabals within the regime either provoking incidents in order to incriminate the students, or else raising suspicions about them with the government and judiciary in order to have them indicted. In all these cases, Nursi impressed on the students the need to be circumspect, and to meet personal attacks with patience and a conciliatory attitude, so as to disallow their involvement in any public disturbances.[85]

The second reason for Nursi's insistence on positive action was the danger of anarchy and the dissolution of society that he perceived to be the inevitable results of the general deterioration in moral standards resulting from the Westernizing social reforms and distancing from Islamic behavioral norms. In the face of this ongoing process, which he predicted would have dire consequences for the coming generations, Nursi considered it the secondary duty of the *Risale* and its students, after the saving of religious belief, "to save this country and nation from the threat of anarchy."[86] His fears were increased by the rapid spread of communism after 1945. Faced with its overwhelming presence pressing down from the north and its "moral and spiritual destruction," he declared that the *Risale* acted and would act as "a Qur'anic barrier" withstanding the flood and countering the schemes of its adherents to destabilize the country and create anarchy. This happened in several ways: Nursi adopted a more assertive stance "in the world of the printed media" by stepping up the publication of the *Risale* and having some parts of it printed in the "new" letters.[87] In addition, he sought to impress on the authorities that the only way to halt the infiltration of atheistic currents and their moral destruction was to reintroduce "the truths of the Qur'an in place of the secular education and Western life-style" (*terbiye-i medeniye*) introduced during the single-party era, by which he presumably meant a religiously-based education and morality such as that given by the *Risale*.[88] In this connection he endeavored to inculcate in his students the Qur'anic virtue of *takva* (Ar. *taqwā*)—variously translated as piety, God-consciousness, or fear of God—as the chief means of protection against the socially corrupting influences. The cultivation of *takva* was "their principal duty" and the *Risale's* successes in instilling the virtue demonstrated its effectiveness as a "repairer" of the corruption.[89]

This was one of Nursi's main lines of defense in the court cases brought against him. Far from causing disturbances, the *Risale* and its students could be deemed "moral police," since they preserved

---

and positive action: Nursi's final address to his students before his death (Istanbul, January 1, 1960). For English translation, see the pamphlet, *Nursi's Interpretation of Jihad*, 2–10.

85. Nursi, *Emirdağ*, 1:102-3, 125; *Kastamonu*, 196, 242; *Letters*, 481–82.

86. Nursi, *Emirdağ*, 1:21–22.

87. Ibid., 102. Until 1946 or '47 when the first duplicating machines were bought, all parts of the *Risale* were copied out by hand in the Ottoman (Arabic) script. Around that date a few collections were reproduced in the Latin alphabet for the first time. See, Vahide, *Islam in Modern Turkey*, 275–76.

88. Nursi, *Emirdağ*, 1:218; also, 102, 128.

89. Nursi, *Kastamonu*, 148–49; Eng. tr.: "On Taqwa," *A Guide For Youth*, 93–94.

public order and prevented anarchy by strengthening the vital principles of "respect, compassion, refraining from what is prohibited, security, and the giving up of lawlessness and obedience to authority." The *Risale* had made one hundred thousand people into useful members of the nation and country, so the authorities should understand their need for it, rather than trying to suppress it.[90]

## The Expansion of the *Jihad* of the Word in the 1950s

After the Democrat Party (DP) came to power in the general elections of May 1950, it adopted a tough anticommunist stand and relaxed some of the Republican People's Party's (RPP) strictly secularist measures. The DP's more liberal interpretation of secularism won for it the support of Said Nursi and provided the Nur movement with opportunities to expand its *jihad* of the word. There were three main areas in which Nursi directed this expansion: the first was in efforts to further their cause in official quarters and to inform members of the government about its importance for the country; the second were his moves towards re-establishing links among Muslims worldwide; the third was the greatly increased publication of the *Risale* and the growth of the movement.

One of the first moves Nursi made after a general amnesty was declared by the new government in July, 1950 was to send copies of the *Risale* to the head of the directorate of religious affairs[91] and to request that he have the ban on it lifted and all confiscated copies returned, and even for the directorate to publish it.[92] In other words, Nursi was seeking official acceptance of the work and the ideas it represented.

From Nursi's communications with members of the government and officialdom that are included in the second volume of *Emirdağ Lahikası*, it is seen that he wanted to impress on them that adherence to the essential teachings of the Qur'an and regaining the support of the Islamic world were the sole ways of saving the country from the various threats to which it was exposed and of securing its security and prosperity.[93] In a number of open letters to Menderes, the prime minister, Nursi explained the function that certain ethical principles taken from the Qur'an and *hadith* could perform in righting many social ills associated with the previous regime, such as factionalism, racism, bribery, and corruption; these principles could also aid in re-establishing true justice and unity, a sense of Islamic nationhood, as well as security and public order,[94] so Nursi believed these principles might be made basic to government policy-making.

The reforging of links with the Islamic world and Muslims worldwide was another matter to which Nursi gave prime

---

90. Nursi, *Rays*, 372; *Kastamonu*, 145, 241; *Emirdağ*, 1:77, 78, 279-80.

91. Ahmed Hamdi Akseki (1887-1951) was "an old *medrese* friend" of Nursi (*Emirdağ*, 2:10).

He was head of the directorate from 1947 to 1951, when he was looked on positively in some Islamic circles as an administrator who intended to reinvigorate Turkey's religious institutions. He had opposed the closure of the *medrese*s in 1924 and supported efforts as head of the directorate to reintroduce institutions of religious education based on the earlier reformed *medrese* models. See, Bein, *Ottoman Ulema*, 75, 145-51.

92. Nursi, *Emirdağ*, 2:6-7, 10-11.

93. Ibid., 16-17, 24-25, 70-72, 176, 222-25.

94. Ibid., 81-84, 172-75.

importance, expending efforts to have the *Risale* translated into Arabic and sending copies to many different places.[95] As a step towards this rapprochement, and towards general peace and reconciliation, he applauded Turkey's signing the Baghdad Pact in 1955, and wrote a letter of congratulation to the president and prime minister.[96] In the letter, Nursi explained the two solutions he had found to what he considered was the gravest problem facing the area: racism and its exploitation by "covert atheists." While the first of his solutions was the *Risale*, which was already strengthening "the brotherhood of belief" in the Islamic world and beyond, the second was his eastern university, the *Medrese*tü'z-Zehrâ, which since his youth he had striven to found as a springboard for progress and also as a means of combating divisive nationalism and bringing together Muslims from all over the eastern Islamic world. In this connection, he urged the president, who had recently announced his intention to build a university in Eastern Anatolia, to give the religious sciences predominance in the institution, which would yield enormous benefits for the country, since the destruction caused by outside forces could be halted only by moral and non-material means, not by material or physical ones.

In addition to supporting a political alliance with the West, Nursi advocated cooperation on a personal level with pious Christians in the struggle against aggressive atheism. Moreover, he perceived an awakening among humanity and a search for truth, and looked forward to the establishment, through acceptance and application of the principles of revealed religion, and specifically of the Qur'an, of "true" civilization, which would bring peace, justice, and prosperity to the majority of huhumankind.[97]

The Nur movement's *jihad* of the word was considerably strengthened after the *Risale* was finally cleared of all legal impediments in 1956 and was for the first time printed on a large scale on modern presses in the Latin alphabet. This made it immediately accessible to the younger generations and greatly expanded its readership. The re-emergence of an Islamist press also acquainted large sections of the population with the movement's struggles, while Nursi's visits to Istanbul in 1952 and 1953 made it possible for many people to meet him in person. The freer conditions also allowed the opening all over the country of Nur *medrese*s or *dershane*s;[98] that is, houses where the Nur students would meet to read the *Risale*, which is the movement's central activity.[99] Thus the students, who had hitherto been concentrated in a few centers in Anatolia, began to coalesce into a cohesive movement. Nursi himself, by keeping with him a small number of young students in order to train them, was preparing its future leaders for when he would no longer be there to direct the movement's activities.

## CONCLUSION

Said Nursi's interpretation of *jihad* reflected a trend, originating with nineteenth-century Muslim reformists though with

---

95. See, Vahide, *Islam*, 307, 316, 323.

96. Nursi, *Emirdağ*, 2:222–25; Vahide, *Islam in Modern Turkey*, 324–26.

97. See, Vahide, "An Outline," 114–18.

98. Nursi, *Emirdağ*, 2:103–4, 109, 231.

99. For the Nur movement, see: Karabaşoğlu, "Text and Community," 263–96; Yavuz, "Nur Study Circles," 297–316; Yavuz, *Islamic Political Identity*, 151–78.

precedents in early Islam, that viewed *jihad* in its broadest sense, as struggle by any non-violent means in God's way to establish "a just . . . moral-social order" on the earth and the supremacy of God's Word, but in a world where peace among nations was the prevailing norm. Later, he even proposed cooperation with adherents of other faiths who pursued similar aims. He diagnosed the most serious obstacles to the achievement of this goal as being various internal problems associated in the earlier period with backwardness; that is, the failure to keep abreast of the civilizational advances of the West, which were seen as resulting primarily from advances in science and technology; and in the later period, with the influx of scientism and materialist philosophies generally. In his view, this was essentially a modern manifestation of an assault by what he called "philosophy" on the knowledge of Islam based on pure revelation that had been continuing "for a thousand years" and had vitiated Islamic thought, ultimately rendering the Muslim masses incapable of offering a genuinely Islamic response to the challenges of modernity.

Nursi's *jihad* in both periods was above all one of education and religious renewal. But it was with the writings of the New Said that he produced his "weapons": first, the *Risale-i Nur*, with its proofs of "the truths of belief" supported by logic and reasoned argument, and based on a view of the physical world that was informed by modern science yet refuted nature and causation, the bases of the scientism that underpinned the Kemalist ideology; and second, the conscious belief and intellectual certainty he intended for it to induce. He considered such a *jihad* of the word with its concomitant positive action to be the form of religious struggle most pertinent to the conditions prevailing in the twentieth century, when Westernization and secular forms of government had become *de facto* realities almost everywhere.

Throughout his life, Nursi strove to demonstrate that Islam and progress were not mutually contradictory, as was assumed by those who looked to the scientism and philosophies of Europe, but that the building of true civilization and the salvation of humanity were dependent on renewed and revitalized religion; Nursi's *jihad* of the word with its various components was directed towards realizing this.

## BIBLIOGRAPHY

Abdel Haleem, M. A. S. "Qur'anic '*jihad*': A Linguistic and Contextual Analysis." *JQS* 12 (2010) 147–66.

Afsaruddin, Asma. "Competing Perspectives on *Jihad* and 'Martyrdom' in Early Islamic Sources." In *Witnesses to Faith? Martyrdom in Christianity and Islam*, edited by Brian Wicker, 15–31. Aldershot, UK: Ashgate, 2006.

———. "Views of Jihad Throughout History." *Religion Compass* 1.1 (2007) 165–69.

Bein, Amit. *Ottoman Ulema, Turkish Republic: Agents of Change and Guardians of Tradition*. Stanford: Stanford University Press, 2011.

Brockett, Gavin D. "Collective Action and the Turkish Revolution: Towards a Framework for the Social History of the Atatürk Era, 1923–38." In *Turkey Before and After Atatürk. Internal and External Affairs*, edited by Sylvia Kedourie, 44–66. London: Cass, 1999.

Cânan, İbrahim, trans. and ed. *Hadis Külliyatı: Kütüb-i Sitte. Muhtasarı ve Şerhi*. 18 vols. Ankara: Akçağ, 1988–94.

Collective. *Risale-i Nur Müellifi Bediüzzaman Said Nursî: Hayatı, Mesleki, Tercüme-i Hâli*. Istanbul: Sözler, 1976.

Hanioğlu, M. Şükrü. *Atatürk: An Intellectual Biography*. Princeton: Princeton University Press, 2011.

———. *A Brief History of the Late Ottoman Empire*. Princeton: Princeton University Press, 2008.

Heck, Paul L. "'Jihad' Revisited." *The Journal of Religious Ethics* 32.1 (2004) 95–128.

Jung, Dietrich, and Wolfango Piccoli. *Turkey at the Crossroads. Ottoman Legacies and the Greater Middle East*. London: Zed, 2001.

Kara, İsmail. *İslamcıların Siyasî Görüşleri I. Hilafet ve Meşrutiyet*. Istanbul: Dergâh, 2001.

Karabaşoğlu, Metin. "Text and Community: An Analysis of the Risale-i Nur Movement." In *Islam at the Crossroads: On the Life and Thought of Bediüzzaman Said Nursi*, edited by İbrahim Abu-Rabi', 263–96. Albany, NY: State University of New York Press, 2003.

Karaömerlioğlu, M. Asım. "The People's Houses and the Cult of the Peasantry." In *Turkey Before and After Atatürk: Internal and External Affairs,* edited by Sylvia Kedourie, 67–91. London: Cass, 1999.

Khadduri, M. "Şulḥ." In *EI*² 9:845–46.

Mardin, Şerif. *Religion and Social Change in Modern Turkey. The Case of Bediüzzaman Said Nursi*. Albany, NY: State University of New York Press, 1989.

*The Meaning of the Holy Qur'an*. Translated by 'Abdullah Yusuf 'Ali. New rev. ed. Brentwood, TN: Amana, 1993.

Nursî, Bediüzzaman Said. Ottoman Turkish and Arabic texts published under various names. The names are alphabetized according to transcription, then the works:

———. Badī'uzzamān. *al-Khuṭba al-Shāmiyya* [1329/1911], bound in *Sunūhat*. Istanbul: Evkâf al-Islāmiye Matbaası, 1338/1336 [1920].

———. Bediüzzaman. *Azametli Bahtsız bir Kıta'nın, Şanlı Tali'siz bir Devletin, Değerli Sahibsiz bir Kavmin Reçetesi veyâhud Bediüzzaman'ın Münâzaratı*. Kostantıniye: Matbaa-yı Ebuzziyâ, 1329 [1913].

———. Bediüzzaman. "Hakikat." *Volkan* 70 (19 Safar 1327/26 Şubat 1324/7 March 1909).

———. *İki Mekteb-i Musibetin Şehadetnamesi veya Divan-ı Harb-i Örfî ve Said-i Kürdî*. 2nd printing. Istanbul: Artin Asaduriyan ve Mahdumları Matbaası, 1328 [1912].

———. Bediüzzaman. "Lemeân-ı Hakikat ve İzale-i Şübühat." *Volkan* 102 (21 Rebi'ülevvel 1327/30 Mart 1325/12 April 1909).

———. Bediüzzaman, "Reddü'l-Evhâm." *Volkan* 90 (9 Rebi'ülevvel 1327/18 Mart 135/31 March 1909).

———. Bediüzzaman, "Yaşasın Şeriat-ı Ahmediye," *Volkan* 77 (26 Safar 1327/5 Mart 1325/18 March 1909).

———. Molla Said-i Kürdî, "Musâhebe: Nutk-ı Sâbıkın Neticesi," *Kürd Teavün ve Terakki Gazetesi* 6 (17 Zilhicce 1326/ 27 Kânunıevvel 1324/[10 January 1909]). In *Kürd Teavün ve Terakki Gazetesi 1908–9*, edited by M. Emîn Bozarslan, 284. Uppsala: Deng, 1998.

———. Bediüzzaman-ı Kürdî Saîd. "Bediüzzaman-ı Kürdî'nin Fihriste-i Makâsıdı ve Efkârının Programıdır." *Volkan* 84 (3 Rebiülevvel 1327/ 12 Mart 1325/25 March 1909).

———. Molla Said-i Meşhur, "Kürdler Neye Muhtaçtır?" *Şark ve Kürdistan* 1 (25 Şevval 1326/Teşrin-i Sâni 1324/19 December 1908), 2.

Nursi, Bediüzzaman Said. Turkish texts published in Latin script:

———. *Âsâr-ı Bedi'iye*. Istanbul: Envar, 2009.

———. *Emirdağ Lahikası*. 2 vols. in 1. Istanbul: Envar, 1992.

———. *Kastamonu Lahikası*. Istanbul: Envar, 1994.

———. *Mesnevî-i Nûriye*. Translated by Abdülkadir Badıllı. Istanbul: n.p., 1998.

———. *Mesnevi-i Nûriye*. Translated by Abdülmecid Nursi. Istanbul: Envar, 1994.

———. *Muhâkemat*. Istanbul: Sözler, 1977.

———. *Tılsımlar Mecmûası.* Istanbul: Tenvir, 1988.

Nursi, Bediüzzaman Said. English translations of Nursi texts:

———. *Bediüzzaman Said Nursi's Interpretation of Jihad in the Modern Age: Jihad of the Word and Positive Action.* Translated by Şükran Vahide. Istanbul: Sözler, n. d.

———. *The Damascus Sermon.* Translated by Şükran Vahide. Istanbul: Sözler Publications, 2004.

———. *The Flashes Collection.* Translated by Şükran Vahide et al. Istanbul: Sözler, 2011.

———. *A Guide For Youth.* Translated by Şükran Vahide. Istanbul: Sözler, 2007.

———. *Letters 1928-1932.* Translated by Şükran Vahide et al. Istanbul: Sözler, 2010.

———. *The Rays Collection.* Translated by Şükran Vahide et al. Istanbul: Sözler, 2013.

———. *The Words.* Translated by Şükran Vahide et al. Istanbul: Sözler, 2008.

Özel, Ahmet. "Cihad." In *Türkiye Diyanet Vakfı Islam Ansiklopedisi* 7:527-31. Istanbul: Diyanet Vakfı, 1993.

Peters, Rudolph. *Islam and Colonialism: The Doctrine of Jihad in Modern History.* The Hague: Mouton, 1979.

———. "Jihad: An Introduction." In *The Legacy of Jihad: Islamic Holy War and the Fate of Non-Muslims*, edited by Andrew G. Bostom, 320-25. New York: Prometheus, 2008.

———. *Jihad in Classical and Modern Islam.* Princeton: Wiener, 2005.

Rahman, Fazlur. *Major Themes of the Qur'an.* 2nd ed. Minneapolis: Bibliotheca Islamica, 1994.

Tunçay, Mete. *Türkiye Cumhuriyeti'nde Tek Parti Yönetimi'nin Kurulması 1923-1931.* Istanbul: Tarih Vakfı, 2005.

Tyan, E. "Djihād." In *EI*² 2:538-40.

Vahide, Şükran. "Bediüzzaman Said Nursi's Approach to Religious Renewal and Its Impact on Aspects of Contemporary Turkish Society." In *The Blackwell Companion to Contemporary Islamic Thought*, edited by İbrahim Abu-Rabi', 55-74. Oxford: Blackwell, 2006.

———. *Islam in Modern Turkey. An Intellectual Biography of Bediüzzaman Said Nursi.* Edited by İbrahim Abu-Rabi'. Albany, NY: State University of New York Press, 2005.

———. "An Outline of Bediüzzaman Said Nursi's Views on Christianity and the West." In *Globalization, Ethics, and Islam: The Case of Bediüzzaman Said Nursi*, edited by Ian Markham and İbrahim Özdemir, 109-18. Aldershot, NY: Ashgate, 2005.

Watt, W. Montgomery. *Islamic Political Thought.* Edinburgh: Edinburgh University Press, 2007.

Yavuz, M. Hakan. *Islamic Political Identity in Turkey.* Oxford: Oxford University Press, 2003.

———. "Nur Study Circles (*Dershanes*) and the Formation of New Religious Consciousness in Turkey." In *Islam at the Crossroads: On the Life and Thought of Bediüzzaman Said Nursi*, edited by İbrahim Abu-Rabi', 297-316. Albany, NY: State University of New York Press, 2003.

Yurdagür, Metin. "İ'lâ-yı Kelimetullah." In *Türkiye Diyanet Vakfı Islam Ansiklopedisi*, vol. 22:62-63. Istanbul: Diyanet Vakfı, 2000.

Zürcher, Erik J. *Turkey: A Modern History.* London: I. B. Tauris, 1998.

———. *The Young Turk Legacy and Nation Building.* London: I. B. Tauris, 2010.

# 24

# The Nation State and Nationalism in the Thought of Said Nursi

## Elmira Akhmetova

Said Nursi lived during the time when, on the one hand, the idea of nationalism had become one of the principal ideologies in the modern world and begun successfully spreading across Muslim lands, through Europe's growing imperial reach, as an alternative to the traditional *ummah* identity. This consequently led to the establishment of the Turkish Republic in 1923 as the first nation state in the Muslim world. On the other hand, the ghastly events of two World Wars once more demonstrated how devastating the consequences of the ideology of nationalism could be. Nursi's ideas on nationalism and the *ummah* identity, therefore, comprise one of the main aspects of his sociopolitical thought. Before discussing Nursi's interpretation of nationalism, it is worth recalling one or two points about the concept generally.

The term nationalism (*nationalismus*) was coined by a German philosopher Johann Gottfried Herder (1744–1803) in the late 1770s. Since then, the concept of nationalism, underlying motives behind its appearance, and its influence on sociopolitical spheres of the modern world, particularly the Muslim world, were interpreted differently.[1] In Western scholarship, the idea of nationalism has been seen as a distinguishing mark of modern times since the Middle Ages and an inevitable stage in political ideological development.

It consequently was applauded for enabling Muslim nations from an "insignificant corner" to enter the age of "social progress" and "middle-class capitalism." For instance, Hans Kohn, a Hungarian-born journalist, who became "the father" of later writers on the development of

---

1. On widely accepted definitions of nationalism, see Carter, *Russian Nationalism*, 3–5; Kausar, *Islam and Nationalism*, 34–43; Kedourie, *Nationalism,*; Kohn, *Nationalism and Imperialism*; and Smith, *Theories of Nationalism*.

nationalism in the Muslim world, initiated a theory that Muslim countries were going through a secularization process similar to that in Europe.² He noticed that

> Just as in Eastern Europe the nations without a history had been roused in the nineteenth century to self-consciousness and the endeavor to play an active part in history, so now the peoples of the Orient were roused from a period of medieval feudalism and religion to one instinct with the watchwords of nationalism and middle-class capitalism.³

On the basis of his observations, Hans Kohn formed a "universal sociological theory" in the study of social change which he saw as signifying the transition from medieval to modern forms of organization: "Religious groupings lose power when confronted with the consciousness of a common nationality and speech."⁴

However, the British academic and intellectual historian Elie Kedourie, who wrote several very influential works on the development of nationalism both in Europe and in regions outside the European-Christian cultural area, challenged the idea of considering nationalism as a universal phenomenon. As he said, "Far from being a universal phenomenon, nationalism is a product of European thought in the last 150 years."⁵ The Iranian Muslim scholar Ali Muhammad Naqawi also defined nationalism as "a creed, a school and a pseudo-religion which the West created to fill an ideological vacuum" existing in Europe; hence it was offered to local populations "as a new religion and a new god which was welcomed by thirsty devotees."⁶

Said Nursi's ideas on the issue of nationalism were comprehensively described in his *Mektûbat* ("Letters") under the "Third Topic" of the "Twenty-Sixth Letter," which, in his own words, was written "in the tongue of the Old Said . . . who was involved in the social life of Islam," with the intention of serving the Qur'an and forming a shield against the unjust attacks against it.⁷ He accepted the fact that a most powerful and widespread wave of nationalistic sentiments had greatly advanced in his time.⁸ But he, unlike the above mentioned well-known scholars, did not define nationalism as a genuine product of the modern European thought or as a power enabling Muslim nations from an insignificant corner to enter the age of social progress and middle-class capitalism, but provided the actual framework for dealing with that ideology on the basis of Islam and other revealed religions. Accordingly, this chapter studies the thought of Nursi on the modern ideology of nationalism and its divisive influence on the *ummah* identity of Muslims.

## NATIONALISM AS A GENERAL CONCEPT

To grasp the thought of Said Nursi on the ideology of nationalism and its product, the nation state, at least four important details should be taken into consideration.

---

2. See al-Ahsan, *Ummah or Nation*, 31.
3. Kohn, *Nationalism and Imperialism*, 18.
4. Ibid., 229.
5. Kedourie, *Nationalism and Imperialism*, 68.
6. Naqawi, *Islam and Nationalism*, 17–18. For further definitions of nationalism by Muslim scholars, see also Akhmetova, *Ideas of Muslim Unity*.
7. Nursi, *Letters*, 379.
8. Ibid., 380.

Firstly, the words "nation" (*millet*) and "nationhood" (*milliyet*) in the writings of Said Nursi were used in accordance with their Arabic meanings to denote a religion and membership of it—as synonyms for the word *ummah*. The Western ideology of nationalism (*fikr-i milliyet*), on the other hand, was applied by Nursi synonymously with racism (*fikr-i unsuriyet*).

Secondly, Nursi was among the rare Muslim scholars who divided sentiments of nationalism (*milliyetçilik*) into two, i.e., the "positive" and "negative" types or levels.[9] In *Sünuhat* (published in 1919), for instance, Nursi stated that the "awakening of nationalism is either positive, in which case it is aroused through compassion for one's fellow men, and is the cause of mutual recognition and assistance; or it is negative, in which case, being aroused by racialist ambitions, it is the cause of antipathy and mutual hostility. And this Islam rejects."[10]

Accordingly, having sentiments of belonging to a certain group for Nursi was a natural phenomenon, and it "arises from an inner need of social life and is the cause of mutual assistance and solidarity; it ensures a beneficial strength; it is a means for further strengthening Islamic brotherhood."[11] However, if these natural sentiments begin demanding the superior loyalty to nation over religion, or claim for superiority of a certain nation over other nations, it moves to its non-natural level, the negative level of nationalism or racism.

Thirdly, Nursi asserted that negative nationalism was not exclusively a recent phenomenon, but in the forms of tribalism or racism had existed throughout human history. It was Islam that abrogated nationalism and tribalism of the pre-Islamic Arabia and replaced such divisive tendencies with a holy, positive Islamic fervor.[12] Nursi supported his view by the *hadith* of Prophet Muhammad who said that in Islam, there is no difference between an Abyssinian slave and a leader of the Quraish, once they have accepted Islam.[13]

Lastly, the stance of Said Nursi towards the negative level of nationalism is perspicuous and firm. He equalized it with racism and strongly condemned it as an artificial conception that destroys harmony in society, resulting in inequity and injustice. He identified the ideology, which considers a particular race to be superior or gives priority to race over religion, as "inauspicious, and harmful; it is nourished by devouring others, persists through hostility to others, and is aware of what it is doing. It is the case of enmity and disturbance."[14] Let us elaborate this view of Nursi in the following pages.

## NATIONALISM AS A SOURCE OF INJUSTICE

The main harm caused by nationalism and racism, according to Nursi, was discrimination and injustice emanating

---

9. Musa Jarullah, a Muslim Tatar scholar of Russia, also differentiated two types or levels of national sentiments. See Akhmetova, "Musa Jarullah Bigiev (1875–1949)," 49–71.

10. Nursi, *Sünuhat*, quoted in Ahmed Davutoğlu, "Bediüzzaman and the Politics of the Islamic World in the 20th Century," Nursi Studies, http://www.nursistudies.com/englishh/data/95e/ahmeddavutoglu95e.htm, accessed 7 May, 2006.

11. Nursi, *Letters*, 381.

12. Haddad, "Ghurbah as Paradigm for Muslim Life," 244.

13. Buḫārī, *Aḥkām*, 4.

14. Nursi, *Letters*, 380.

from these ideologies. In his *Letters*, Nursi affirmed that the principles of racism and nationalism do not follow justice and right; they are tyranny. A ruler of racialist leanings, said Nursi, prefers those of the same race, and cannot act justly. Therefore, "the bonds of nationalism may not be set up in place of the bonds of religion; if they are, there will be no justice; right will disappear."[15]

To demonstrate the harmfulness of negative nationalism and racism, Nursi offered examples from history and contemporary events. According to Nursi, negative nationalism had caused an untold harm in the history of Muslims during Umayyad rule. Due to their combining some ideas of nationalism with their politics, the Umayyads vexed the world of Islam, and, in addition, drew many calamities on themselves.[16] By planting their state on tribalism and putting the bonds of nationalism before those of Islam, as Nursi pointed out, they caused harm in two respects. Firstly, they offended the other nations and frightened them off. Secondly, since the principles of racism and nationalism do not follow justice and right, they imposed tyranny toward other races.[17]

Looking at the political events of his time, Said Nursi contended that the ideas of nationalism and racism disturbed harmony in European society and caused the growth of injustice, enmity and racial discriminations among nations, which eventually led to the overwhelming World War I in Europe.[18]

By analyzing the basic foundations and values of Western civilization, Nursi noticed that in modern Western political system the main principle for relations between peoples and communities was nationalism and racism, which considered a particular race to be superior, or gave priority to race over religion. In "The Twenty-Fifth Word," Nursi stated that,

> By reason of its philosophy, present-day civilization accepts "force" as the point of support in the life of society. It takes as its aim "benefits," and considers the principle of its life to be "conflict." It considers the bond between communities to be "racism and negative nationalism." While its aim is to provide "amusements" for gratifying the appetites of the soul and increasing man's needs. However, the mark of force is aggression.[19]

Said Nursi further emphasized that a system in which the bond between masses was based on negative nationalism or racism could not establish equality and justice within its society:

> And since the benefits are insufficient to meet all needs, their mark is that everyone tussles and jostles over them. The mark of conflict is contention, and the mark of racism, aggression, since it thrives on devouring others. Thus, it is because of these principles of civilization that despite all its virtues, it has provided a sort of superficial happiness for only twenty per cent of humankind and cast eighty per cent into distress and poverty.[20]

Accordingly, negative nationalism and racism for Nursi were one of the main reasons that social, political, and economic

---

15. Ibid., 76.
16. Ibid., 380–81.
17. Ibid., 75–76.
18. Ibid., 381.

19. Nursi, *The Words*, 420.
20. Ibid.

injustice prevailed in the modern world. He believed that injustice and inequality inevitably lead to disunity, enmity, and antagonism among different groups of the society. Discord and antagonism, in its turn, lead to weakness and, consequently, to the collapse of civilizations. Therefore he asserted that "the mark of negative nationalism and racism is ghastly clashes, disastrous collisions, and their result, annihilation."[21]

This strong statement of Said Nursi was made in his *Lemeāt* (Gleams), a collection of writings in free verse on various subjects published in 1921, when he was a member of the *daru'l–hikmeti'l–islamiye*, an embryonic academy of higher Islamic studies.[22] By that time the ideology of nationalism had became a greatly advanced political and social force in Turkey, as well as in the rest of the Muslim world. The position of the institution of the caliphate, which was considered to be a symbol of the unity of worldwide Muslims, on the other hand, was rapidly weakening due to internal as well as external circumstances. Firstly, following the Committee for Union and Progress (CUP) Revolution in 1908, the caliphate gradually lost its political power and had been converted into a puppet of the Turkish government. Then on November 1, 1922, at the prompting of Mustafa Kemal, the Grand National Assembly voted to abolish the sultanate, but retain a shadow-caliphate with spiritual powers only. Accordingly, the caliph was to become a mere spiritual head, "a kind of Islamic Pope," as was called by Elie Kedourie.[23] Two years later, in 1923, a Turkish Republic was founded as a "territorial nation-state based on the Turkish nation in Turkey."[24]

Lastly, the institution of the caliphate was abolished on March 3, 1924, after being held for four hundred and seven years by the Osmanli house. It was blamed by Mustafa Kemal for ruining the Turkish people, as they had spent themselves in vain for an ideal which was not in their national interest, and was impossible in itself.[25] How did Said Nursi view these radical changes in the political system of the Muslim world and the strengthening of the national identity instead of the Islamic one? In order to grasp the matter entirely, perhaps, it is required to observe the stance of Nursi towards sociopolitical changes in Turkey, starting with the revolution of 1908 until his death in 1960.

## FROM THE CALIPHATE TO NATION STATE

The institution of the caliphate as Said Nursi understood it was not stagnant, but a progressive political system, with a great potential for changes and reforms to adjust to the demands and achievements of the time. It was awareness of an urgent need for large-scale reforms in Eastern Anatolia that brought Said Nursi to Istanbul in November 1907. However, after the direct interaction with the "seat of the caliphate," he realized that not only his native land, but the entire caliphate was in a state of serious disease, which could only be cured through radical changes.

---

21. Nursi, *The Words*, 745.

22. On the affiliation of Nursi to the *daru'l-hikmeti'l-islamiye*, see Vahide, *Islam in Modern Turkey*, 136–41.

23. Kedourie, *Politics in the Middle East*, 98 and 293.

24. Lewis, *The Emergence of Modern Turkey*, 352.

25. Atatürk, *Nutuk*, quoted in Hourani, *Arabic Thought in the Liberal Age*, 184.

He later stated accordingly: "I arrived in Istanbul and saw that the hatred, which persons nourished against one another made them all into well-dressed savages. I understood that the reason for the disease was this hypocrisy. They called me crazy. But I saw this bitter truth: I saw and understood that Islam was behind, far behind the civilization of our times."[26]

Therefore, Nursi considered that the institution of the caliphate, in order to become efficient and competitive with other contemporary political powers, should undergo radical structural reforms. He consequently applauded the Young Turk Revolution on July 3, 1908, and estimated its reforms to be the beginning of a new prosperous era for the nation, which had been suffering from the diseases of despotism and backwardness for a long time. Nursi affirmed that a new constitution and democracy would provide "this oppressed nation" with a "progress a thousand times further than in former times." Nursi accordingly offered his full support for the new government and the restoration of the constitution of 1876, and, as he later himself mentioned in *Divan-ı Harb-i Örfî*, "worked with all his strength to make freedom and constitutionalism serve the *sharia*."[27] On the third day of the insurrection, Nursi delivered his renowned welcoming speech entitled *Address to Freedom*, the first of his public speeches explaining the meaning of constitutionalism and how it should be regarded. Nursi gave the same address a second time in Freedom Square in Salonica, the center where the preparations for a coup against the despotism of the sultan Abdulhamid were the most intensive, in the presence of thousands of politicians, members and supporters of the Committee of Union and Progress.

Nursi strongly believed that the constitutional government, through returning back to the true teachings of Islam and applying the *sharia* as the fundamental source for its policies, would help the Ottoman nation, as well as the entire Muslim world, to progress. He explained, "Since the illustrious *sharia* has come from the pre-eternal word of God, it will go to post-eternity." For him, it was dynamic. It adapted and expanded in relation to human's development. It comprised equality, justice, and true freedom with all its relations and requirements. The first period of Islamic history was proof of this. Therefore, Nursi claimed that the present unfortunate condition resulted from four causes: failure to observe the *sharia*; arbitrary and erroneous interpretations of it; bigotry on the part of certain "ignorant externalist scholars"; and "abandoning through ill-fortune and bad choice, the virtues of Europe, which are difficult to acquire, and imitating like parrots or children the sins and evils of civilization, which are agreeable to man's base appetites."[28]

Later in his work entitled *Sünuhat* (published in 1919–20), Nursi suggested that the most important renewal of the institution of the caliphate would be through consultation and the development of a collective personality, which

---

26. On the activities of Nursi in Istanbul during his trip in 1907 and the reaction of the government towards his proposal for educational reforms, see, Vahide, *Islam in Modern Turkey*, 33–51.

27. Nursi, *Divan-ı Harb-i Örfî* in Said Nursi, *Asar-ı Bedi'iye* (n.p., n.d.), 70.

28. Vahide, *Islam in Modern Turkey*, 52–56. On the approach of Nursi towards the restoration of the constitutional system, see Akhmetova, "Hürriyet İçinde Birliğe Çağırdı," 10–12.

would become dominant. As Ahmed Davutoğlu noted, the view that the mechanism of consultation and collective personality, (which took its strength from this mechanism) should be the sources of authority was an original contribution of Nursi to the efforts to reorder the institution of the caliphate in the first quarter of the twentieth century, and secure Islamic Unity.[29]

This view of Nursi, Davutoğlu noted, had introduced new dimensions to the principles of *fiqh*. The tendency towards more anonymous and abstract concepts like the corporate spirit or collective personality in place of the individuality of *ijtihād*, and of allegiance (*bai'ah*), which legitimated the caliphate, may be seen as a new and original effort to establish a tie between Islamic institutions and the concepts of state and sovereignty, which became increasingly anonymous and abstract in the nineteenth century:

> We are not in the old times now. Formerly, a single individual ruled. And the ruler's *mufti* could also be a single individual who corrected and modified his ideas. The present, however, is the time of the social collectivity. And the ruler is an unemotional, stern collective personality, which is somewhat deaf and emerges from the spirit of the collectivity. Councils represent that spirit. The *mufti* of such a ruler should be of similar kind to it, and a collective personality born of an elevated learned council. Then it may make its voice heard, and drive points related to religion down the Straight Path. For an individual is merely like a mosquito before collective personality of the community, even if he is a genius. Through its ineffectiveness, this important position exposes the very source of Islam's life to danger. We may even say that the present weakness of religion, indifference towards the marks of Islam, and anarchy in *ijtihad* resulted from the weakness and ineffectiveness of the office of the *sheikh al-islam* [the highest religious authority]. For one person outside may preserve his opinion before a *sheikh al-islam*'s office which is based on individuality, but the pronouncements of a *sheikh al-islam* relying on a council such as that can make him give up his *ijtihad*, even if he is the most brilliant genius, or it can limit it to him. For sure, all those qualified can interpret the law (*ijtihad*), but such *ijtihad* becomes a guiding principle only when it meets with the confirmation of a sort of consensus or of the masses. A *sheikh al-islam* such as that would reflect this in meaning. In the Illustrious *shari'a*, consensus and the opinion of the majority is always the means of *fatwa*'s (rulings); so too, at the present time in the face of the anarchy of opinions, there is definite need for such an arbiter.[30]

Accordingly, Nursi believed that the modern age is the "mass" age or age of the community or social group. Communities give rise to "collective personalities" or "spirits." In his *Kastanomu Lahikası*, Nursi stated that, "The present is not the time for egoism and the personality for those who follow the path of reality; it is the time of community. A collective personality emerging from the community rules, and may survive. To have a large pool, the ice blocks of the ego and personality have to be cast into the pool and dissolved." While in the past, the age of individuality, persons of great stature like 'Abd al-Qadir Jilani, Imam Ghazali,

---

29. See Davutoğlu, "Bediüzzaman and the Politics of the Islamic World in the 20th Century."

30. Nursi, *Sünuhat*, quoted in ibid.

and Shaykh Ahmad Sirhindi had been sent to guide the Muslim community in accordance with divine wisdom, the unprecedented difficulties and conditions of modern times, as Nursi believed, demanded that a collective personality undertake such duties.[31]

Furthermore, government or authority, in this complex modern age, can only function adequately by means of "collective personalities" of this sort. He said thus with regards to the caliphate:

> The present is the time of community. The collective personality of a community, which is its spirit, is firmer and more capable of executing the ordinances of the *shari'a*. The person of the caliph can only undertake his duties through relying on [such a collective personality]. If a collective personality, the spirit of a community, is righteous, it is more brilliant and perfect [than that of an individual]. But if it is bad, it is exceedingly bad. Both the goodness and badness of an individual are limited, but those of a community are unlimited.[32]

When the Grand National Assembly voted to abolish the sultanate on November 1, 1922, Said Nursi was in Ankara and, on November 9, 1922, he was given an official "welcoming" in the assembly. As Şükran Vahide observed, Nursi accepted the principle of the nation's sovereignty and, accordingly, was not opposed to the abolishment of the sultanate. However, this consent of Nursi was on condition that the representative body was governed by and reflected Islamic perspectives; it should also in some capacity represent the caliphate.[33]

Nursi strongly believed that the Grand National Assembly, in order to represent the caliphate, has to fulfill its religious obligations and see that they are fulfilled by the nation, and answer the nation's religious needs. If it does not do these things, out of need the nation will compel it to "give meaning" to the "name" of the caliphate, which in effect it had undertaken, and will also invest the assembly with the power to carry out the caliphate's functions. However, Nursi said, if due to its members' negligence and laxity in performing their religious obligations the assembly does not have the ability to do this, it will give rise to discord and disunion, which is contrary to the verse, "And hold fast all together to the rope of God" (Q 3:103).[34]

Even after the establishment of the Turkish Republic, based on nationalism and secularism and, subsequently, abolishment of the caliphate in 1924, Nursi still clung to the view that the key to the survival of Islam in the modern age was held by the Turks. As İbrahim Abu-Rabi' pointed out, Nursi did not concede defeat to Turkey in its Islamic duties. To concede defeat would have been, and is still, an abdication of the Islamic responsibilities of modern Turkey.[35]

---

31. Quoted in Vahide, *Islam in Modern Turkey*, 244.

32. Quoted in Ibid., 170–71.

33. Ibid., 168–71.

34. Ibid., 170.

35. For instance, in his *Emirdağ Lahikası*, written in 1944, twenty years after the abolishment of the caliphate, Nursi said that staying put in Turkey to preserve Islam is the answer to the corruption of the times and to the stratagems of detractors. "If I were to possess a thousand souls, were inflicted with a thousand illnesses, and were to undergo lots of difficulties and injuries, I would still decide to remain here [in Turkey] to serve this *ummah* in maintaining its belief." See,

Later on in his *Flashes Collection*, Nursi stated that the collapse of the Ottoman empire and the death of the caliphate's rule saddened him to the utmost degree.³⁶ He was grieved at the passing of the sovereignty of the caliphate and noted that the abolition of the Empire and Caliphate was wrong and an oversight.³⁷ Yet the new political circumstances in the Muslim world and the reality of the absence of the institution since 1924 compelled Nursi to be realistic. If before the abolition of the caliphate he sought to reform the existing institution, the works of Nursi written after 1924 do not touch the issue of reviving the caliphate at all, as during the New Said period of his scholarly life he was mostly concentrating on the unity of Muslims. With a number of Islamic countries gaining their independence from the colonial powers in the late 1940s and the 1950s and new states being formed, he foresaw the Islamic countries as a federation, the United Islamic States.³⁸ Moreover, in his letters to the Democrat Parliament, Nursi repeatedly emphasized that Islamic unity of a nonpolitical nature would be a source for strength of Turkey.³⁹

Accordingly, the traditional Muslim political institution of the caliphate in the thought of Nursi was a progressive establishment. Although its foundations and objectives were decisively established during the time of Prophet Muhammad and the righteous caliphs and do not require any revision, its structure adjusts to the demands and achievements of the time. Presently, the caliphate, Nursi believed, could positively benefit from political advantages of the age, such as the parliamentary system or the structure of federal states. Therefore, he applauded the majority of structural changes in the governing system, with the condition that it fulfill the basic laws of Islam. Those who are holding the position of the leadership, Nursi assumed, should fulfill their obligations determined by the sources of the Islamic political system and never neglect the responsibilities entrusted to them by the *ummah*.

Following the victory of Turkey in the War of Independence in 1922, Nursi came to Ankara and mixed with the deputies with the sincere intention of encouraging those in power to set up a form of government based on the Qur'an and the *shari'a*.⁴⁰ However, he found that atheistic ideas were being propagated. He described it like this: "When I went to Ankara in 1922, the morale of the people of belief was extremely high as a result of the victory of the army of Islam over the Greeks. But I saw that an abominable current of atheism was treacherously trying to subvert, poison, and destroy their minds. 'Oh God!' I said. 'This monster is going to harm the pillars of belief.'" Consequently, Nursi wrote a treatise in Arabic disproving atheism. However, as the scholar pointed out, "those who knew Arabic were few and those who considered it seriously were rare." As a result, the treatise did not have "the effect it should have done and sadly, that current of atheism both swelled and gained strength."⁴¹

---

Abu-Rabi', "How to Read Said Nursi's *Risale-i Nur*," 62.

36. See, Nursi, *The Flashes Collection*, 293.
37. Nursi, *The Rays Collection*, 427.
38. See, Vahide, *Islam in Modern Turkey*, 307.
39. See, Ibid., 325.
40. Ibid., 169.
41. Nursi, *Flashes*, 233.

However, another strong poison for him, which was destroying not only minds, but also harmony and justice in society among Muslims as well as non-Muslims, was nationalism. Therefore Nursi insisted on the Turkish government that "the bonds of nationalism may not be set up in place of the bonds of religion; if they are, there will be no justice; right will disappear."[42] The next point of this chapter views the thought of Nursi on the question of the identity of Muslims, particularly after the establishment of the Turkish nation-state.

## NATIONALISM OR ISLAMIC NATIONHOOD

The establishment of the Turkish Republic in 1923 and its ultra-secular policies resulted in radical changes in the identity consciousness of the local population. Within a short period, peoples of the Turkish Republic, who thought of themselves simply as Muslims for centuries, began to be identified by their ethnic differences and as members of the common Turkish nation. Said Nursi, by witnessing this divisive influence of the nationalistic currents on the religious identity of Muslims, on the one hand tried to establish harmony and hierarchy between these two identities; and on the other, applauded national identities that served the ideal of Islam, considering them to be parts of a unifying Islamic identity.[43] The answer of Said Nursi to a question about religious zeal and national zeal asked of him during Sultan Reşhad's Rumelia tour in 1911 summarizes very succinctly his attitude towards the issue:

> With us Muslims, religion and nationhood are united, although there is a theoretical, apparent and incidental difference between them. Indeed, religion is the life and spirit of the nation. When they are seen as different and separate from each other, religious zeal includes both the common people and upper classes. Whereas national zeal is peculiar to one person out of a hundred, that is, to a person who is ready to sacrifice his personal benefits for the nation. Since this is the case, religious zeal must be the basis with regard to the rights of all the people, while national zeal must serve it and be its fortress.[44]

He further continued:

> Religious zeal and Islamic nationhood have completely fused in the Turks and Arabs, and may not now be separated. Islamic zeal is a luminous chain which is most strong and secure and is not born of this world. It is a support that is most firm and certain, and will not fail. It is an unassailable fortress that cannot be razed.[45]

Nursi condemned his contemporary Muslims for adapting a European ideology of nationalism as a foundation for a political system and a principle for relations between peoples, and warned them about damaging outcomes of the spreading of nationalistic sentiments in the Muslim world. He said that "the cunning European tyrants in particular awaken this [nationalism] among Muslims in negative fashion, so that they may divide them and devour them."[46]

---

42. Nursi, *Letters*, 76.

43. See, Davutoğlu, "Bediüzzaman and the Politics of the Islamic World in the 20th Century."

44. Nursi, *The Damascus Sermon*, 50.

45. Ibid., 50–51.

46. Nursi, *Letters*, 380.

Thus Nursi suggested that in the present Muslim world, when the peoples and tribes of Islam are most in need of one another, and each is more oppressed and more poverty-stricken than the other, crushed as they are beneath European domination, to regard one another as strangers, due to the idea of nationalism, and to consider one another to be enemies is such a calamity that it cannot be described. According to Nursi, the only solution, which empowers all Muslim nations, including Turks, with eternal and extensive success, justice, equality and concord, was Islam, rather than alien ideas of nationalism or racism. He declared,

> O my Turkish brother! You watch out in particular! Your nationhood has fused with Islam and may not be separated from it. If you do separate them, you will be finished! All your glorious deeds of the past are recorded in the book of Islam's deeds. Since these glorious deeds cannot be effaced from the face of the earth by any power, don't you efface them from your heart due to the evil suggestions and devices of Satan![47]

Consequently, Said Nursi openly opposed the concept that ethnic nationalism was the source of a superior identity. According to him, the power inherent in the idea of nationalism could only be used in a positive fashion to serve Islamic identity, which has to be superior. Nursi's statement refers to the positive type of nationalism only, which should be the "citadel and armour" of Islamic identity; but "it must not take the place of it."[48]

However, the attitude of Said Nursi towards the subject of negative nationalism is perspicuous and firm. He strongly affirmed that positive, sacred Islamic nationhood does not need any ideas of negative nationalism and racism. Nursi declared that: "Eternal and permanent Islamic nationalism cannot be bound onto temporary unstable racism and drafted onto it."[49] Therefore, he repeatedly criticized the government of Turkey for abandoning the eternal and permanent Islamic nationhood for their imitation of Western nationalist ideology, which forced Muslims to adopt a national identity. Nursi repeatedly insisted that the only nationhood of Muslims is the one, Islamic nationhood; and Muslims, in order to withstand the European domination and divisive influence of negative nationalist movements, should be united around this common nationhood. Following the proclamation of the Constitution in 1908, he said:

> Since in constitutionalism sovereignty belongs to the nation, the nation's existence has to be demonstrated, and our nation is only Islam. For the strongest bond of Arab, Turk, Kurd, Albanian, Circassian, and Laz, and their firmest nationhood, is nothing other than Islam. The foundations of an array of states are being laid, due to negligence and strife incited through the revival of the partisanship and tribalism of the Age of Ignorance, which died one thousand three hundred years ago. We have seen this.[50]

In his famous sermon delivered at the historic Umayyad mosque of Damascus in 1911, Nursi again called upon Muslim nations to be united around

47. Ibid., 381–82.
48. Ibid.
49. Nursi, *Letters*, 513.
50. Nursi, *The Damascus Sermon*, quoted in Davutoğlu, "Bediüzzaman and the Politics of the Islamic World."

their religious identity. This sermon was delivered at an extremely crucial time for Muslims and prospects of Arab-Turkish relations. The unity of Muslims was heavily threatened by the prevailing dissatisfaction of Arabs with the CUP (Committee of Union and Progress) government because of its centralization policies, securing all privileged positions in officialdom exclusively for Turks, and its anti-Islamic spirit.

Compounding this disunity was the negative role of an anti-Turkish bias in the Arab press.[51] Said Nursi strongly believed that the crucial situation that had arisen in the Middle East was the outcome of the European advocacy of nationalistic ideas among Muslims in a negative fashion. In his sermon, which was delivered to a gathering of close to ten thousand people, including one hundred scholars,[52] he emphasized "the unifying power of Islamic nationhood in the face of the seeds of enmity that were being attempted to be sown between the Turks and Arabs."[53] He said,

> Lawful freedom and lawful constitution have demonstrated the sovereignty of our true nationhood. And the foundation and spirit of our true nationhood is Islam. And in so far as they have carried the standard of the Ottoman caliphate and Turkish army in the name of that nationhood, the two true brothers of Arab and Turks, who are like the shell and citadel of the nationhood of Islam, are the sentries of that sacred citadel.[54]

Consequently, he inferred,

> Thus, through the bond of this sacred nationhood, all the people of Islam are like a single tribe. Like the members of a tribe, the groups of Islam are bound and connected to one another through Islamic brotherhood. They assist one another morally and, if necessary, materially. It is as if all the groups of Islam are bound to each other with a luminous chain.[55]

The attitude of Nursi during the Said Revolt in 1925 once more demonstrated that he considered all Muslims, who belonged to different ethnic groups such as Arab, Berber, Turk, or Kurd, as one united nation. The leader of the revolt, Sheikh Said of Palu, tried to gain Nursi's support and sent a letter to him, requesting that he join the uprising, saying that if he did so they would be "victorious." Nursi replied as follows: "The struggle you are embarking on will cause brother to kill brother and will be fruitless. For the Kurds and Turks are brothers. The Turkish nation has acted as the standard-bearer of Islam for centuries. It has produced millions of saints and given millions of martyrs. The sword may not be drawn against the sons of Islam's heroic defenders, and I shall not draw mine!"[56]

These words of Said Nursi perfectly exemplify that, even after the abolition of the institution of caliphate in 1924 and colonization of almost all Muslim lands by European powers, he persisted in considering all Muslim ethnic groups as members of the common united nationhood, Islam. He put forth an effort to maintain this unity of Muslim nations around the common *ummah* identity by

---

51. See, Vahide, *Islam in Modern Turkey*, 94–95.

52. See, Nursi, *The Damascus Sermon*, 7.

53. Davutoğlu, "Bediüzzaman and the Politics of the Islamic World."

54. Nursi, *The Damascus Sermon*, 41.

55. Ibid.

56. Vahide, *Islam in Modern Turkey*, 182.

words as well as deeds. This position of Nursi did not change until the end of his life.

When the Baghdad Pact was signed in February 1955 between Turkey and Iraq, and was subsequently joined by Pakistan, Iran and Britain, Nursi sent a letter of congratulation to the prime minister of Turkey, Adnan Menderes, and the president, Celal Bayar. In this letter, Said Nursi explained that the greatest danger for the country lied in racism. It had caused harm to the Muslim peoples in the past, and currently there were again signs that it was being exploited by "covert atheists" with the aim of destroying Islamic brotherhood and preventing the Muslim nations from re-unification. The true nationality or nationhood of both Turks and Arabs, he felt, was Islam; their "Arabness" and "Turkishness" had fused with Islam. The new alliance (The Baghdad Pact), as Nursi pointed out, would repulse the danger of racism, and besides gaining for the Turkish nation "four hundred million brothers," it would also gain for them the "friendship of eight hundred million Christians."[57]

Consequently, we can suppose that the religious identity for Said Nursi was the uniting force of the entire Muslim *ummah* in the face of divisive influences of negative nationalism and racism advocated by some European powers. He considered Islamic nationhood to be the basic bond which unites different ethnic groups, societies, and classes, and establishes social harmony. If negative nationalism and racism were the source of inequity, injustice, and enmity among communities, Islamic nationhood was competent to create equality, justice and harmony, not within various ethnic Muslim nations only, but also with other religious groups, especially the Christians.

## BIBLIOGRAPHY

Abu-Rabiʾ, İbrahim, ed. *Islam at the Crossroads: On the Life and Thought of Bediüzzaman Said Nursi*. Albany, NY: State University of New York Press, 2003.

Akhmetova, Elmira. "Hürriyet İçinde Birliğe Çağırdı." *Yeni Asya*, March 23, 2008, 10–12.

———. *Ideas of Muslim Unity at the Age of Nationalism: A Comparative Study of the Concept of Ummah in the Writings of Musa Jarullah and Said Nursi*. Saarbrücken, Germany: Lambert, 2009.

———. "Musa Jarullah Bigiev (1875–1949): Political Thought of a Tatar Muslim Scholar," *Intellectual Discourse* 16.1 (2008) 49–71.

Al-Ahsan, Abdullah. *Ummah or Nation? Identity Crisis in Contemporary Muslim Society*. Markfield, UK: The Islamic Foundation, 1992.

Carter, Stephen K. *Russian Nationalism: Yesterday, Today, Tomorrow*. London: Pinter, 1990.

Davutoğlu, Ahmet. "Bediüzzaman and the Politics of the Islamic World in the 20th Century." *Nursi Studies* Online: http://www.nursistudies.com/englishh/data/95e/ahmeddavutoglu95e.htm. Accessed 7 May, 2006.

Haddad, Yvonne Yazbeck. "Ghurbah as Paradigm for Muslim Life: A Risale-i Nur Worldview." In *Islam at the Crossroads: On the Life and Thought of Bediüzzaman Said Nursi*, edited by İbrahim Abu-Rabiʾ, 237–54. Albany, NY: State University of New York Press, 2003.

Hourani, Albert. *Arabic Thought in the Liberal Age 1798–1939*. Cambridge: Cambridge University Press, 1983.

Kausar, Zeenath. *Islam and Nationalism: An Analysis of the Views of Azad, Iqbal and Maududi*. Malaysia: A.S. Noordeen, 1994.

---

57. Ibid., 325.

Kedourie, Elie. *Nationalism.* 4th ed. Oxford: Blackwell, 1993.

———. *Politics in the Middle East.* Oxford: Oxford University Press, 1992.

Kohn, Hans. *Nationalism and Imperialism in the Hither East.* New York: Fertig, 1969.

Lewis, Bernard. *The Emergence of Modern Turkey.* 2nd ed. London: Oxford University Press, 1968.

Naqawi, Ali Muhammad. *Islam and Nationalism.* Translated by Alaedin Pazargadi. Iran: Islamic Propagation Organization, 1984.

Nursi, Said. *The Damascus Sermon.* 2nd ed. Translated by Şükran Vahide. Istanbul: Sözler, 2002.

———. "Divan-ı Harb-i Örfi." In Said Nursi, *Asar-ı Bedi'iye*, n.p., n.d.

———. *The Flashes Collection.* Translated by Şükran Vahide. Istanbul: Sözler, 2004.

———. *Letters: 1928–1932.* Translated by Şükran Vahide. Istanbul: Sözler, 2001

———. *The Rays Collection.* Translated by Şükran Vahide. Istanbul: Sözler, 2002.

———. *The Words: On the Nature and Purposes of Man, Life, and All Things.* Translated by Şükran Vahide. Istanbul: Sözler, 2004.

Smith, Anthony D. *Theories of Nationalism.* 2nd ed. London: Duckworth, 1983.

Vahide, Şükran. *Islam in Modern Turkey: An Intellectual Biography of Bediüzzaman Said Nursi.* Albany, NY: State University of New York Press, 2005.

# 25

# The Future of Nursi Studies

## Ian S. Markham

It is worth pausing and reflecting on the progress that has been made in Nursi studies since the early 1990s. It was always true that Said Nursi had a significant profile in Turkey. He was the primary advocate for a thoughtful, engaged Islam during the Atatürk period. However, in the broader Middle East and in the English-speaking world, Said Nursi was virtually unknown.

In 2017, the scene is now very different. It is a commonplace to see Said Nursi described as a leading Islamic theologian. His reputation and achievement are widely recognized by specialists in Islamic Studies. The sociological impact of the Nur movement in Turkey has been widely acknowledged. Books have appeared on Said Nursi in English, Arabic, and other languages. The progress has been remarkable.

This collection of essays reflects the energy of Nursi Studies. Twenty years ago, such a volume would have been impossible. So in the concluding article in this volume, let us think about the future: where does Nursi Studies go next? To answer that question, this chapter will set out (a) the distinctive achievement of Said Nursi on which Nursi Studies needs to build, (b) the primary characteristics of Nursi Studies work so far, and (c) the links between Nursi Studies and interfaith dialogue more broadly.

## THE DISTINCTIVE ACHIEVEMENT OF SAID NURSI

Perhaps the best way of understanding Said Nursi is to see him as an inspiration for Islamic renewal. He is living through a turbulent time in Turkish history. As a perceptive reader of his age, he can see the implications of the dramatic change as the Ottoman Empire disintegrates and the secularism of Atatürk emerges. The task is to remind Muslims of the rationality, power, and elegance of the Qur'an. He wants a recovery of the basic Islamic practices of prayer and fasting. It is a renewal movement, where the focus is not on politics but on prayer. It is the relationship with God that matters most.

Although such an emphasis is commonplace in Islam (especially in the Sufi tradition), the way this theme of renewal combines with a deep respect for tradition and a commitment to rationality is impressive and distinctive. Said Nursi saw the practices of Islam as an appropriate response to the extraordinary beauty of the universe (the book of the universe); the evidence for God is so overwhelming it makes perfect sense to live aware of the reality of God. In fact, it is overwhelmingly unwise (almost stupid) to do otherwise.

However, there are other features that make Nursi important. One theme that has been central to my writing about Said Nursi is his location within a tradition and a commitment to living with pluralism *as an act of faithfulness* to that tradition. So much interfaith activity is "liberal" (i.e., heavily influenced by the Enlightenment and skeptical about the key themes of the faith). Said Nursi is committed to dialogue because he is a traditional Muslim; he believes this is what the Qur'an requires of him.

Linked to this, we find in Said Nursi a commitment to building alliances. He sees the trends of atheism, materialism, and secularism and acknowledges that faith traditions need to work together against these trends. The wisdom here is considerable. Instead of old-fashioned competition, he wants an alliance where God and faith are defended.

## PRIMARY CHARACTERISTICS OF NURSI STUDIES

Three themes have characterized Nursi Studies so far. The first is exposition; the second is comparison; and the third is application.

On the first, the finest book so far is Colin Turner's definitive exposition of Nursi's thought called *The Qur'an Revealed*. Although, in my judgment, there is a slight propensity in his description to reduce the commitment to rationality and treat Nursi as more fideistic, this text remains the finest description of Nursi's worldview. It will be a pioneering classic for decades to come.

On the second, Nursi has been compared to Immanuel Kant, Paul Tillich, Meister Eckhart, Bertrand Russell, John Hick, and even Jacques Derrida. This has been a good way for Christian theologians, in particular, to find a route into Nursi. The various conversations have been illuminating.

On the third, we have had the application of Nursi to the issues of anthropology, environment, theodicy, globalization, and multiculturalism. This has been a good strategy. The application strategy has been a way to illustrate the relevance of the work of Said Nursi. So, for example, given the world is worried about globalization, this exercise is a means by which we can learn from Nursi about how to handle the challenge of globalization.

So we have understood Nursi; we have compared Nursi; and we have applied Nursi. There are several areas which have not been developed. Allow me to highlight two: the first is the task of location and the second is developing the Nursi tradition.

In the English speaking literature, there is very little that locates Said Nursi. This is partly because the work of Nursi does not cite authorities or sources in an explicit way. So the task of locating Said Nursi would take some work. But what precisely are the Islamic trajectories which are being developed by Nursi? Who are the people who are either implicitly or explicitly influencing the work of Nursi? This exercise has real value, especially for other Muslims. Once Nursi is placed in a wider stream of Islamic thought, it would help adherents of other Islamic streams to locate and understand Nursi. By connecting Nursi (primarily, I assume with classical Islamic thinkers), other streams that come from those thinkers would recognize the sibling similarity.

The second task is developing the tradition. When one takes the Anglican tradition within Christianity, one is not necessarily always explicitly developing the thought of Richard Hooker (probably the intellectual founder of the Anglican tradition, 1554–1600). Instead, the spirit of Hooker creates a certain approach to theological and ethical questions that has then become part of the DNA of Anglicanism. So Hooker saw Anglicanism as a disposition, deeply grounded in civic life, tending to avoid the extremes of Rome and Geneva, and constantly applying the Christian tradition to the ever changing nature of the present. This has become the Anglican tradition.

This is rich area for development. What exactly are the characteristics of the DNA of the Nursi approach to Islamic theology and ethics? Applying Nursi to new problems that Nursi could never have conceived requires the emergence of a methodological tradition. Genetically modified foods are not explicitly addressed by Said Nursi; however, a tradition of enquiry should have the resources to provide a method that can think through an appropriate attitude to Genetically Modified Foods.

Linked to this is the tricky question of whether you can be a Nursian and disagree with an aspect of Nursi's thought? So could you be in the tradition of Said Nursi and develop a different approach to gender issues than Nursi had? Given that Said Nursi himself was more than happy to recognize an "Old Said" and a "New Said," I think the DNA of the Nursian tradition should be self-critical. I think the emergence of a real internal conversation about this or that aspect of Nursi's thought would be very interesting.

## NURSI STUDIES AND THE FUTURE OF INTERFAITH DIALOGUE

The primary reason why I am so pleased to be involved in the emerging discipline of Nursi Studies is because it is the future of interfaith dialogue. Relationships between all faith groups are fragile. It would be good to see Nursi studies start to work more explicitly in interfaith. For example, work that explores the encounter between Said Nursi and Abraham Joshua Heschel would be a fabulous Islamic-Jewish conversation. The two thinkers lived at a similar time; they are both extremely influential in their traditions. And the same approach could be taken with every other religious tradition.

Elsewhere I have written at length on my frustration with interfaith dialogue. The triumph of Kantian skepticism dominates the scene; the focus is on opaque experience and ethics; and the propensity to criticize anyone who believes in a tradition and insist that such affirmations are incompatible with a commitment to pluralism is so unhelpful.[1] We need real Muslims in conversation with real Christians, Jews, Buddhists, and Hindus. And let us add Mormons and secularists to the list. We need men and women who believe that they are in a tradition which is true but do not think that such a belief makes it impossible or inappropriate to be in conversation with someone in a different tradition.

## CONCLUSION

This book is ending with an invitation to see the end as a beginning. The achievements of the Nur community are amazing. As Turkey has opened up, so the Nur community has taken full advantage. Nursi is now being read.

This is a good foundation on which to build. The challenge now is to go deeper (and this is where the suggestions for locating Nursi in his intellectual Islamic trajectory) and to bring this depth into further and more explicit conversation with other faith traditions.

Naturally the work of expounding, comparing, and applying the thought of Nursi should continue. The suggestion in this chapter is that this can be accompanied with a widening of the circle in respect to location and interfaith conversation. I am excited to be a small part of the creation of a new discipline within the academy. Nursi Studies is still a child, but it is growing. And it is growing in a healthy and very beautiful way.

## BIBLIOGRAPHY

Markham, Ian S. *Engaging with Bediüzzaman Said Nursi: A Model for Interfaith Dialogue*. Farnham, UK: Ashgate 2009.

---

1. See for example, Markham, *Engaging with Bediüzzaman Said Nursi*.

# Index

Chapters written by author are in bold.

Abdel, Haleem, 64, 67, 88, 103, 204, 393, 409
Abdullah, Muhammad Salim, 325, 331, 332, 337
Abdurrahman, 24, 25, 26, 38, 104, 173
Abu-Rabi', Ibrahim M, 21, 22, 148, 149, 157, 158, 159, 160, 375, 410, 411, 420
Açıkgenç, Alparslan viii, xiii, **243-63**
Afsaruddin, Asma, 393, 409
afterlife, 87-91, 93, 95-99, 101, 103
Ahmad, Feroz, 288, 291, 303
Akbulut, Duran, 329, 332, 337
Akgün, Mehmet, 5, 19
Akhmetova, Elmira viii, xiii, **412-25**
Akiba, Jun, 4, 19
Akkach, Samer, 55, 67
Akyol, Mustafa, 185, 191, 195, 203
Al-'Ajlūnī, Ismā'īl ibn Muḥammad, 252, 262
Al-Ahsan, Abdullah, 413, 424
Al-Alousi, Husam Muhi Eldin, 70, 76, 80, 86
Al-Baghawi, H. Bin Mas'ud, 314, 321
Alatas, Seyed Hussein viii, xiii, 6, **223-242**
Alavi, Mohammed Asım, 380, 381, 391
Albayrak, Sadık, 24, 28, 38
alcohol, 28, 216
Algar, Hamid, 24, 38, 86, 334, 336, 337,
Alkan, Mehmet, 4, 19
Altıntaş, Hayrani, 9, 19
Anawati, George, 356, 374
animals, 56-57, 66, 82, 89, 107-8, 119, 127, 164, 166, 182, 185, 190, 198, 201, 208, 210, 213-14, 259, 268-69, 272, 308, 312
Arai, Masami, 291, 303
Asfaruddin, Asma, 206, 218
Ash›arites, 70, 73-75
Atasoy, İhsan, 185, 190, 191
Atatürk, Mustafa Kemal xi, 29, 31, 41, 194, 350, 416

Aydın, Hayrettin, 329, 332, 338

Badıllı, Abdülkadir, 24, 27, 31, 32, 35, 36, 37, 38, 214, 294, 295, 401, 402, 410
Bakar, Osman, 77, 86
Baker, Rob, 356, 374
Baktiar, Laleh, 47, 158
Barbe, Abbe E, 9, 19
Barber, Bernard, 244, 262
Barbour, Ian G, 12, 19
beauty, 41, 51-52, 55, 60-62, 67, 71, 89, 94-95, 98, 102-3, 106-14, 116, 118-19, 121, 130, 137, 143, 149, 151, 166, 199, 210, 227, 312, 360, 372, 427
Bein, Amit, 10, 14, 15, 16, 17, 19, 409
Benedict XVI, Pope, 370, 372, 374
Bensaid, Benaouda viii, xiii, **305-22**
Bergson, Henri, 9
Berkes, Niyazi, 28, 38, 193, 203, 289, 303
Bertrand, Alexis, 9, 20
Bertrand, Russell, 78, 86, 427
Birgeoğlu, Osman, 333, 334, 338
book of creation, 55, 70
Borelli, John, 358, 374
Bourdel, 10
Bozarslan, M. Emîn, 38, 39, 410
Bozkurt, Mahmut, 38
Brockett, Gavin D, 399, 409
Brown, A.C. Jonathan, 203
Bruinessen, Martin Van, 38
Büchner, Ludwig, 5, 6, 20
Al-Bukhari, 249, 252, 262,
Bulut, Mehmet Ali, 286, 303
Burçak, Berrak, 5, 20
Burrell, David, 159, 211, 218

Çalışkan, Koray, 286, 303

## Index

Çalışlar, Oral, 286, 303
Cânan, İbrahim, 393, 409
Carter, Stephen K, 412, 424
Çelik, Hüseyin, 290, 303
Çengel, Yunus viii, xiii, **264–86**
Cevdet Paşa, Ahmed, 5, 6, 7, 10, 20
Cevdet, Abdullah, 5, 10, 12, 20, 289, 303
Chadwick, Owen, 12, 20
Chittick, William C, 149, 158, 160, 206, 207, 218
Chittister, Joan D, 146, 159
Christians and Christianity iv, xi-xiii, xiv, 3, 46, 175, 215, 228, 237, 240, 340–54, 357–58, 360–61, 363–65, 367–71, 375, 388, 408–9, 411, 424, 428
Cilacı, Osman, 159
civilization xiii, 6–8, 10, 12–13, 29, 37, 46, 162, 171, 194, 204, 208, 223–24, 226, 228–32, 238–42, 244, 248, 259, 268, 287, 300, 302, 330, 342–43, 346, 356, 375, 392, 394, 396–99, 402, 405, 408–9, 415–17
Clooney, Francis x, 363, 374
Cole, Jeffrey, 323, 338
Collins, Randall, 7, 20, 245, 263
Committee of Union and Progress, 291, 303, 417, 423
Comte, Auguste, 6, 7, 8, 9, 20, 21, 276
Corbin, Henry, 74, 75, 76, 86
cosmos, 34, 53–61, 63–64, 66–67, 81, 94, 96–97, 99, 110, 179, 184, 186, 210, 253, 294, 341, 360
creation out of nothing, 69–71, 73, 76

Al-Daghamin, Ziyad Khalil Muhammad, 52, 67
Al-Darimi, Abu Muhammad Abdullah ibn Abd al-rahman ibn Fadhl ibn Bahran ibn Abd al-Samad al-Tamini, 263
Davison, Andrew, 7, 22
Davutoğlu, Ahmet, 414, 418, 421–24
death, 55, 58, 87, 92, 97, 99–100, 103, 106, 107, 111–12, 118–19, 122, 130, 137, 141, 144, 147, 150, 170, 199–200, 210, 229, 232, 254, 314–15
dershane, 37, 43, 298, 302, 304, 364, 375, 408, 411
Descartes, Rene, 9, 20, 81
Al-Dhahabi, Muhammad ibn Ahmad ibn 'Uthman ibn Qayyum 'Abu 'Abd Allah Shams ad-Din, 253, 263
Diener, Paul W, 161, 167, 176
Doğan, Atila, 5, 20
Dostoevsky, Fyodor, 231–32, 240, 241
Dummet, Michael, 80, 81, 86

Durkheim, Emile, 7, 9, 12, 20, 22, 228, 232, 241

Eickelman, Dale, 16, 20, 335
Einstein, Albert, 267, 269, 273, 274, 281, 284
Engineer, Asghar Ali, 205, 206, 218
Enlightenment, 12, 228, 231, 268, 427
environmental ethics, 168, 190
Erdem, Rahmi, 254, 263
Ergun, Mustafa, 11, 20
ethics, 161–70, 178–94, 218, 362
Europe, 4–12, 25, 44, 172, 192–95, 203, 205, 224, 228–32, 237–40, 265, 276, 288–92, 322–39, 343–46, 354, 362, 364, 366, 370, 392–401, 409, 412–24
Evered, Emine, 288, 303
evil, 17–18, 64, 105–27, 135–45, 170, 172, 182–83, 199, 227, 240, 305–9, 314, 317, 320, 347–48, 352, 362, 369, 382, 387, 393, 422

Fareed, Muneer Goolam, 165, 176
Feindt-Riggers, Nils, 326, 333, 338
Feyerabend, Paul, 80, 86
Findley, Carter Vaughn, 4, 20, 195, 203, 288, 303
Fitzgerald, Michael L, 358
Fındıkoğlu, Ziyaeddin Fahri, 9, 20
food, 43, 47, 56–57, 125, 166, 200, 274, 320, 428
Fortna, Benjamin C., 4, 20
Francis, Pope, 372, 373, 374
Frank, Richard M, 74, 78, 86, 132, 133, 145, 238, 242, 323, 328, 338, 369
Fraşeri, Şemseddin Sami, 6, 20
free will, 115, 121–27, 129–45, 182, 282, 364, 387, 397
Freuler, Léo, 6, 20
friendship, 319, 340, 342, 349, 354, 424
Fuad, Beşir, 5, 7, 8, 12, 20
Fuller, Steve, 263

Galilei, Galileo, 266, 269, 284, 346
Al-Ghazali, Abü Hâmid, 11, 17, 55, 68, 70, 74, 75, 77, 78, 83, 86, 94, 142, 145, 148, 152, 156, 159, 165, 211, 218, 299, 329, 363, 418
Giere, Ronald N, 263
Gilani, Abdul-Qâdir, 147, 159, 165, 254, 299
Gjertsen, Derek, 263
Göçek, Fatma Müge, 4, 20
God
  concept of, 393, 427
  divine names of (beautiful names of), 54, 55, 58, 63, 69, 85–86, 89, 90–96, 98–99, 102–3, 106–9, 112, 114–23, 126–27,

## Index

151–59, 169, 179, 182–84, 206, 258, 312, 360, 386, 402
Goffman, Daniel, 303
Gray, Henry, 356, 374
Gregory, Frederick, 6, 20
Gregory, Frederick, 6, 20
Grenz, Stanley J., 301, 302, 303
Grice, Herbert P., 52, 53, 67
Gude, Mary Louise, 357, 374
Gür, Metin, 326, 338
Gutierrez, Gustavo, 225, 242

Haddad, Y. Yvonne, 171, 176, 366, 374, 414, 424
Hadith xi, 16, 37, 89–90, 103–4, 130–31, 141, 164, 196, 249, 314, 393, 407, 414
Haeckel, Ernst, 5, 6, 20
hakkı, Kılıçzade İ, 8, 9, 16
Hamid Algar, 24, 38, 86, 334, 336, 337
Hanioğlu, M. Şükrü, 5, 6, 8, 10, 20, 29, 32, 38, 289, 303, 395, 399, 410
Hanson, Hamza Yusuf, 24, 38, 176
Heck, Paul L, 393, 394, 410
Heimbach, Marfa, 326, 332, 338
Heisenberg, Werner, 8, 12, 20
hermeneutics, 51–68, 70–71, 206
Heyd, Uriel, 288, 291, 303
Hilālī, Taqī al-Dīn, 313, 321
Al-Hindi, 'Ali ibn 'Abd al-malik Husam al-Dīn al-Muttaqi, 249, 263
Hodgson, Marshall G. S., 192, 194, 195, 196, 203
honesty, 172, 176, 186, 302
Hörküç, Hasan, 179, 188, 191, 194, 204, 330, 356, 375
Hourani, Albert, 145, 303, 416, 424
Hüttermann, Jörg, 331, 338

Ibn Hanbal, Ahmad, 249, 261, 263
Ibn Khaldun, 233, 236–39, 242
Ibn Rushd, 55, 68, 70, 71, 76–78, 80, 81, 83, 85, 86, 236, 242
Al-Idrisi, xi
İhsanoğlu, Ekmeleddin, 4, 5, 20
İleri, Tevfik, 294
illness, 111–12, 114–17, 122, 127, 223, 228, 240, 274, 310, 361, 374, 389, 419
Infeld, Leopold, 284
Al-'Iraqi, 314, 321
İrem, Nazim, 9, 21
Isaacson, Walter, 269, 284
İshak Effendi, Başhoca, 5, 20, 21
Islamic law, 5, 11, 64, 194, 316, 393
İsmail Hakkı, Kılıçzade, 8, 21

Istanbul, 4–6, 17, 26–28, 30, 37, 42, 45, 147, 289, 291, 294, 327–30, 333, 336–37, 354, 395–96, 398, 408

Jacob, Xavier, 11, 21
James, William, 129, 145, 266
Jihad, 62, 64, 205–6, 234, 361, 383–85, 387, 390, 392–411
  jihad of the word, 35–36, 38, 380–81, 383–85
  moral jihad, 35–36
Jung, Dietrich, 399, 410
Al-Juwaynï, 'Abdalmalik ibn "Abdallāh, 133, 134, 145

Kademoğlu, Ahmet Eren, 152, 159
Kaplan, Yusuf, 287, 303
Karabaşoğlu, Metin, 304, 408, 410
Karaömerlioğlu, M. Asim, 399, 410
Kausar, Zeenath, 412, 424
Kaya, Faris ix, 42, 43, 191, 204, 329, 335, 337, 338
Kaymakcan, Recep, 185, 191
Kedourie, Elie, 409, 410, 412, 413, 416, 425
Kemalism, 31, 34, 383, 399
Khadduri, M, 204, 394, 410
Kirkinci, Mehmet, 196, 197, 204, 328
Kirmizi, Abdullhamit, 25, 38
Koçak, Cemil, 31, 35, 38
Kodaman, Byram, 4, 20
Kohn, Hans, 412, 413, 425
Kurzman, Charles, 6, 21, 288, 303
Kuşpınar, Bilal xiiii, 158, 159

Laçiner, Sedat, 286, 303
Laudan, Larry, 263
Laughlin, R.B, 267, 284
Leaman, Oliver, 15, 21, 224, 242, 335
Lefebure, Leo D viii, xiv, **356-75**
Lemmen, Thomas, 332, 333, 338
Lewis, Bernard, 5, 21, 238, 242, 289, 303, 416, 425
Lewis, Franklin D, 238, 242
Longino, Helen E, 263
Louth, Andrew, 149, 150, 159

MacFarlane, Charles, 4, 6, 22
Madigan, Daniel, 66, 67
madrasas, 10–11, 44
Mardin, Şerif, 5, 8, 13, 14, 18, 21, 24, 25, 39, 45, 148, 159, 289, 303, 334, 335, 399, 410
Marinis, Marco de, 53, 67
Markham, Ian **xi-xii,** 162, 167, 170, 176, 191, 304, 335, 356, 374, 375, 411, **426-29**
Massignon, Louis, 356, 357, 374

# Index

materialist philosophy, 5–6, 8–14, 17, 36, 38, 44, 60, 90, 212, 229, 239, 266, 283, 343, 345, 348, 373, 386–87, 392, 400–403, 409
Mattson, Ingrid, 62, 68, 201, 202, 204
Mawdudi, Sayyid Abul A'la, 176, 234
McCarthy, Justin, 352, 355
Medina, 61, 197, 298
Meriç, Ümit xv, 6, 7, 21, 22
Mermer, Yamina vii, xiv, 17, 21, **51–86**, 113, 117, 127, 138, 145, 337
Merton, Robert K, 244,
Michel, Thomas viii, xiv, 113, 127, 187, 191, 228, 230, 232, 242, 331, 335, 338, **340–56**, 358, 359, 360, 361, 362, 363, 364, 369, 370, 371, 374, 375
modernization, 3–6, 9–10, 12, 15, 19, 233
Moleschott, Jacob, 6
morality, 7, 161–76, 178–91, 200–201, 232–33, 236–37, 240–41, 274, 307, 387, 406
Mosher, Lucinda Allen vii, xiv, **146–60**, 336, 365, 375
Motadel, David, 323, 338
Muhammad – the Prophet, 61, 67, 71–72, 89, 101, 131, 162–64, 169–70, 184, 194, 198, 200–201, 203, 206–7, 211, 213, 215, 306, 313, 344, 346–48, 353, 358, 367–68, 414, 420
Müller, Max, 12, 21
Murata, Sachiko, 149, 160
mysticism, 149–50

Al-Naysaburi, 321
Naqawi, Ali Muhammad, 413, 425
NASA, National Aeronautics and Space Administration, 268, 284
Neusner, Jacob, 218
New Said, 23, 28–31, 90–92, 146–47, 149, 151, 156, 366, 382, 388, 398, 400–401, 409, 420, 428

Old Said, 16–17, 23, 90–91, 94, 147, 173, 199, 254, 364–66, 382, 388, 394, 413, 428
Olson, Robert, 30, 40
Omar, Irfan, 359, 374, 375
Ortaylı, İlber, 4, 21
Ottoman Empire, 3–22, 24–25, 27, 35, 41, 146, 172–73, 175, 193, 195–96, 203, 223, 226, 228, 240, 288–90, 303, 327, 351, 364–65, 370, 381–82, 392, 394–95, 398–99, 403, 417, 423, 426
Özcan, Mustafa, 286, 304
Özdemir, Ibrahim, 230, 231, 242, 335, 374, 375, 411
Özel, Ahmet, 393, 394, 411

Özervarlı, M. Saİt vii, xv, **3–23**, 223, 224, 226, 242

Padwick, Constance E, 160
pain, 97, 111, 115, 117–18, 210, 309–11, 320–21
Parla, Taha, 7, 22
Peirce, Charles S, 53, 68, 130, 145
performance theory, 53–55
Peters, Rudolph, 393, 394, 411
Piccoli, Wolfango, 399, 410
Pirim, Harun viii, xiii, **178–92**
Pirim, Sudendam Birinci, **178–92**, 335, 356, 374
Pohl, Reinhard, 331, 338
Poincaré, Henri, 9
politics, 32, 34, 38, 146, 173, 179, 187, 193–94, 229, 233, 318, 330, 379, 380, 381–83, 385–90, 397, 400, 405, 415, 427
positivism, 5–6, 9, 264–85, 289, 370
prison, 27, 32, 33–36, 41–42, 84, 138, 146–47, 156, 173, 195–97, 199, 216, 294–95, 297, 306–19, 361, 366, 389, 402

Qur'an, 13–14, 18–20, 24–28, 51–67, 70–76, 80–86, 88–90, 130, 149–51, 156–57, 162–67, 181, 184–91, 196–99, 201, 206–9, 234, 249, 251–57, 296, 314, 316–20, 365–67, 386, 401–3
Qutb, Sayyid, 170, 177, 234

Rahman, Fazlur, 358, 393, 411
Rahner, Karl, 358, 359, 360, 374, 375
Al-Razi, Fakhr al-Din Muhammad xi, 14, 57, 62, 67, 72, 86, 99, 103, 104, 114, 128, 329
Reed, Fred A vii, xiv, **41–51**, 156, 160
Renz, Andreas, 369, 370, 371, 372, 375
resurrection, 52, 58, 70, 82–83, 87–103, 148, 170, 184, 209, 236, 358, 360, 365–66, 403
revelation, 13, 23, 38, 53, 56, 60–62, 73, 76, 80, 85, 89, 123, 147, 150, 252–61, 265–66, 282, 341–42, 359–62, 371, 400, 409
Rheinberger, Hans-Jörg, 245, 263
Rizal, José, 235, 239–40, 242
Robinet, Jean-Francois, 7, 22

Şahiner, Necmeddin, 24, 28, 37, 40, 173, 177
Şahinöz, Cemil, 323, 324, 327, 328, 329, 330, 331, 332, 338
Sarıkaya, Yaşar, 11, 22, 289, 290, 304
Sarıtoprak, Zeki, 336, 342, 351, 355
Satan, 16, 60, 111, 122–27, 137, 187, 227, 252, 313, 315, 382, 422
Sayılgan, Salİh vii, viii, xv, **161–77**, **192–204**, 302, 304, 338

434

# Index

Sayılgan, Zeynab, **205-22, 286-305, 322-40**
Schimmel, Annemarie, 162, 177, 207, 219
Schwarz, M, 131, 132, 145, 338
science, 4-8, 12-13, 16-22, 26, 56, 63-64, 78-80, 90, 129-30, 195, 226, 228, 231, 233, 239, 241, 245-48, 252-53, 255-61, 265-66, 272-73, 275-76, 279-90, 292-94, 359, 373-74, 395-97
secularism, 11, 32-33, 37, 295, 322, 364, 381, 400, 407, 419, 426-27
Sells, Michael, 65, 68, 331
Şen, Faruk, 329, 332, 338
Al-Shafi'i, Muhammad ibn Idris, 204
Al-Shatibi, Abu Ishaq Îbrahim Ibn Musa, 72, 86
Shepard, William E, 234, 242
Şİmşek, Cüneyt vii, xv, **87-128**
Sivri, Selma, 373, 376
Smith, Anthony D, 412, 425
Smith, Christian, 225, 242
Smith, William Cantwell, 67, 68, 71, 86
sociology, 7, 243-63, 275, 280
Somel, Selçuk akşin, 4, 22, 288, 289, 304
Sonn, Tamara, 193, 204
Sorokin, Pitirim A, 244, 263
soul, 56, 83, 108, 116-18, 123, 125-27, 144, 149, 163, 168-70, 175, 187, 227, 307, 312-15, 348, 361, 366, 383
Sovik, Margrete, 331, 338
spirituality, 13, 99-100, 192-204, 231, 315, 341, 361, 365, 402
Steinbach, Udo, 326, 333, 338
Stoljar, Daniel, 267, 285
Sunna, 14, 100, 162-65, 167, 175, 192-204, 213, 217-18, 234, 397

Al-Taftazānī, Sa'd al-Din, 99, 100, 104, 133, 134, 140, 145
Tanzimat, 4, 25, 288-90
tawhid, 52, 66, 72, 82, 85, 87, 101, 117, 130, 132-33, 135, 137, 140, 154, 169, 288, 300, 302, 365-66
tefsir, 13-14, 402
Tevfik, Baha, 5, 20
Tevfik, Riza, 7, 9, 20, 22
Tevfik, Samli Hâfiz, 92
Thielmann, Jörn, 323, 338
Al-Tirmizī, Abū 'Isa Muḥammad ibn 'Isá al-Sulamī al-Ḍarīr al-Būghī, 263
Toderini, Giambattista, 4, 22
Tremblay, Rodrigue, 188, 191
Tritton, A.S., 132, 145

truth, 45, 56, 60-61, 81, 89, 93-94, 101, 126, 172, 186-87, 253-57, 265-66, 275-76, 301, 348-49, 353, 403-6, 408-9, 417
Tunaya, Tarik Zafer, 28, 40
Tunç, Mustafa Şekib, 9, 19, 22
Tunçay, Mete, 31, 36, 40, 398, 411
Turner, Colin, 179, 191, 194, 204, 330, 337, 356, 375, 427
Tyan, E., 393, 411

Ülken, Hilmi Ziya, 5, 7, 9, 22
Underhill, Evelyn, 149, 150, 160
usury, 188
Utermann, Claudia, 331, 338

Vahide, Şükran xv, 15, 19, 22, **23-41**, 52, 54, 55, 59, 60, 68, 86, 92, 93, 104, 125, 128, 145, 146, 147, 148, 149, 150, 151, 152, 154, 156, 159, 160, 163, 164, 174, 176, 177, 179, 187, 191, 193, 204, 218, 141, 142, 248, 254, 263, 284, 285, 289, 290, 291, 292, 293, 294, 295, 304, 306, 321, 334, 335, 337, 345, 351, 354-57, 366, 373, 375, 388, **392-412**, 416, 417, 419, 420, 423, 425
Vakkasoğlu, Vehbi, 213, 215, 216, 219
Valkenberg, Wilhelmus, 358, 362-71, 375
Van, 17, 25-27, 30, 43-45, 151, 166-67, 193, 213, 254, 286, 290-91, 295, 342, 388, 398
Vogt, Eric W, 367, 375
Voll, John 0, 8, 9, 15, 22, 301, 304

Waardenburg, Jacques, 9, 10, 22
Wasti, Syed Tanvir, 7, 22
Watt, Montogomery, 132, 145, 394, 411
Weld, Meryem, 357, 375
Wenscik, A.J., 131, 145
Whitley, Richard, 263
World War I – the Great War, 27-28, 41, 91, 147, 166, 215, 351, 357, 398-99, 415
Wunn, Ina, 323, 326, 331, 332, 338

Yalçınkaya, m. alper, 5, 22
Yavuz, Hakan, 298, 302, 304, 327, 331, 335, 338, 339, 364, 375, 408, 411
Yazıcıoğlu, Isra vii, xv, **51-69**, 75, **129-46**
Yildiz, Ahmet viii, xiii, xv, 287, 288, 289, 304, 331, **379-91**
Young Turks, 8, 10, 15
Yücel, Salih, 373, 376
Yurdagür, Metin, 392, 411

Zürcher, Erik J, 27, 30, 31, 32, 34, 37, 40, 196, 204, 398, 399, 400, 404, 411

www.ingramcontent.com/pod-product-compliance
Lightning Source LLC
Chambersburg PA
CBHW080532300426
44111CB00017B/2694